McNae's Essential Law for Journalists

McNae's

ESSENTIAL LAW FOR JOURNALISTS

Twenty-eighth edition

Siân Harrison Gill Phillips Charlie Moloney

OXFORD
UNIVERSITY PRESS

OXFORD
UNIVERSITY PRESS

Great Clarendon Street, Oxford, OX2 6DP,
United Kingdom

Oxford University Press is a department of the University of Oxford.
It furthers the University's objective of excellence in research, scholarship,
and education by publishing worldwide. Oxford is a registered trade mark of
Oxford University Press in the UK and in certain other countries.

Twenty-fifth Edition 2020
Twenty-sixth Edition 2022
Twenty-seventh Edition 2024

Published in the United States of America by Oxford University Press
546 Fifth Avenue, New York, NY 10036, United States of America

British Library Cataloguing in Publication Data
Data available

Library of Congress Control Number: 2026936893

ISBN 9780198985839

Printed in the UK by Bell & Bain Ltd., Glasgow

The manufacturer's authorized representative in the EU for product safety is
Oxford University Press España S.A. of Parque Empresarial San Fernando de Henares,
Avenida de Castilla, 2 – 28830 Madrid (www.oup.es/en or product.safety@oup.com).
OUP España S.A. also acts as importer into Spain of products made by the manufacturer.

FSC
www.fsc.org
MIX
Paper | Supporting
responsible forestry
FSC® C007785

Dedicated to all the court reporters on the front line of open justice, including Sam who has won important battles and gives me strength and inspiration.

Siân Harrison

To all freelance journalists and small news outlets—you are the life blood of press freedom.

Gill Phillips

To Nicole, to Tadisa, and to all the hacks working in the trenches.

Charlie Moloney

Preface

Freedom of speech has been pushed to the forefront of the news agenda in the UK in recent times. As this book went into production, *BBC* Director General Tim Davie and Chief Executive of News Deborah Turness had both recently resigned following a controversy over editorial mistakes aired in a 2024 Panorama documentary about US President Donald Trump, who commenced a $1–5 billion lawsuit against the BBC as a result. This is only the most recent of a number of political attacks by the US President on the media. Trump has regularly used a variety of insults when speaking about outlets that give him unfavourable coverage. He has called the press 'fake news,' 'the enemy of the people,' 'dishonest,' 'corrupt,' 'low life reporters,' 'bad people,' 'human scum,' and 'some of the worst human beings you'll ever meet'. He recently sued the New York Times, Penguin Books and two reporters for US $15 billion (£11.3 billion), accusing them of spreading 'false and defamatory' content about him. These are just some of the latest examples of the way law is increasingly being used to suppress public interest journalism. The so-called 'dictator's handbook' moves ever closer to these shores.

In September 2025, Reform party leader Nigel Farage told a US congressional committee hearing into whether European laws 'threaten Americans' right to speak freely in the US', that the UK was like North Korea. He urged US politicians and businesses to tell the British government, 'you've simply got this wrong' on freedom of speech rules. Farage cited the cases of writer Graham Linehan (arrested and detained by armed police at Heathrow airport under the Public Order Act over three posts on X; he was never charged) and Lucy Connolly, a woman who was jailed for inciting racial hatred in a tweet during the Southport riots, which followed the murders of three young girls. Farage spoke about what he called 'the really awful authoritarian situation that the UK has sunk into'.

However, press freedom in the UK, while it still faces problems, some of which we discuss below, may not be quite as bad as Farage made out. In 2026, the UK was ranked 18 (up two places from 2025) out of 180 countries in the Reporters without Borders Annual Freedom of the Press Index. (North Korea was ranked 179th in the same Index and was described as 'one of the worlds' most authoritarian regimes' which 'tightly controls information and strictly prohibits independent journalism'.) RSF said: 'Alarming attacks on Iranian journalists exiled in the UK, lawsuits aimed at gagging journalists, widespread job cuts, and low public trust in media all mark the UK press freedom landscape.' They went on to say that: 'Despite government assurances that media freedom is a priority, a restrictive political climate has impacted press freedom in recent years. Unlawful police surveillance of journalists, lacklustre political support for British journalists detained abroad and the questioning of several journalists entering the country under counter-terrorism legislation are worrying trends in a country where journalists have generally been able to operate freely.

The long overdue release of Julian Assange in 2024 was a welcome development, though the chilling effect of the five years he spent in a British jail remains.'

As mentioned already, the brutal murders of three young girls—Bebe King, Elsie Dot Stancombe, and Alice Da Silva Aguiar—at a dance class in Southport in July 2024 triggered the worst mass outbreak of violent disorder since the 2011 London riots. This case, shocking in its own right, also highlighted some disturbing trends in the modern media environment. While the mainstream, professional media reported developments in the case in compliance with our contempt laws and restrictions around identifying juveniles—given the suspect was aged just 17—the ever-evolving and unregulated 'new media', which dominates social media platforms, saw an opportunity to step into the resulting information vacuum. A false claim that the suspect was an asylum seeker who had arrived in the UK by small boat in 2023 spread freely online, alongside incorrect reports about his name and religion. By 3pm on the day after the murders, a false name that had been shared online had received over 30,000 mentions on X from 18,000 unique accounts. The broadcast regulator, Ofcom, concluded in a report following the riots that there was 'a clear connection' between online activity and violent disorder seen on UK streets. This case posed profound questions about how the laws of contempt of court operate in the modern media environment. It was suggested that the disorder was an indirect result of contempt of court laws, which were often used to justify the withholding of details about the case. So great was the controversy that the Law Commission decided to substantially address the issue in its consultation paper on contempt laws. They concluded that the publication of certain suspect details—such as their name, age, nationality, and ethnicity—is generally unlikely to meet the conduct threshold under the Contempt of Court 1981. Police forces have increasingly begun releasing this (except for actual names) sort of information to the press after a major incident at an early stage and have updated their media guidance to reflect this. Examples include forces taking the hitherto unusual step of releasing information about the ethnicity and nationality of a man charged with crashing a car into crowds at the Liverpool Football Club victory parade in May 2025, and a man who was arrested on suspicion of stabbing 11 people on a train in Huntingdon in November of the same year. The media, in turn, is increasingly seeing its role in this context as both pushing officialdom—which moved away from being transparent with journalists following the Leveson Inquiry—for greater levels of information while simultaneously fact-checking, verifying and often debunking the ever-increasing volumes of dis- and misinformation which are being shared online.

Journalists are themselves at risk of being hoodwinked by misinformation, as generative artificial intelligence (AI) becomes increasingly persuasive. In October 2025, a reporter for *The Times* published a ChatGPT-generated response to an interview question by a man purporting to be the former mayor of New York. Just weeks earlier, the paper had referenced an AI-generated case study on a fake royal household employee. While inaccuracies will usually pose a regulatory issue, a reporter mistakenly relying on fake AI material could conceivably face legal issues, such as libel, in the future. A reporter believing they had obtained an official court document that would usually be protected by privilege and quoting from it on that basis, only to later discover it was a ChatGPT generated fake, is one such hypothetical example. AI is also posing unique copyright challenges, as it scrapes material from media outlets' websites, and difficulties for reporters as it affects job prospects. But, nevertheless, it is increasingly used for research and transcription purposes, some reporters are now described as 'AI-assisted', and it may also provide some novel opportunities, such as AI-generated courtroom sketches.

The justice system has entered a new period of turbulence. At the time of writing, the backlog in the crown courts—which already stood at around 34,000 cases in 2019 due to funding cuts and was made worse by the Covid-19 pandemic—had surged to nearly 80,000 cases, resulting in trials being listed into 2029. A crisis in prisons saw prisoners released earlier to free up places. Some judges refused to extend custody time limits for people accused of serious crimes, concluding that the lack of resources in the justice system did not constitute a good reason to keep them on remand. Against this backdrop, the Government proposed radical reforms to the justice system based on recommendations by Sir Brian Leveson, a former Lord Justice of Appeal. These reforms included removing the right of people to choose a trial by a jury if accused of 'either-way' offences—less serious crimes which attract sentences of up to three years—and removing juries for complex fraud cases. The Government went a step further than Sir Brian's recommendation of a new court (the Crown Court Bench Division) where people would be tried by a judge and two magistrates, by proposing such defendants would be tried by a judge alone. These proposals attracted significant criticism from lawyers, former judges and politicians, including complaints that such measures would not help to reduce the backlog. Other proposals included expanding the sentencing powers of magistrates. It remains to be seen what changes will eventually be implemented, but the important principle of open justice will have to be factored into any new legislation.

The courts themselves have entered a new era of transparency in some respects, as new rules in family courts allowing greater opportunities for reporting were rolled out in 2025. Cameras in Crown courts to record sentencing remarks were hailed as a success for improved transparency, and plans were mooted to increase the use of cameras to livestream proceedings from other courts. A Transparency and Open Justice Board was established in April 2024, to lead and coordinate the promotion of transparency and open justice across courts and tribunals. However, around half of all criminal cases are now dealt with by way of the Single Justice Procedure, which involves a single magistrate reviewing documents behind closed doors. The *London Standard's* court reporter Tristan Kirk has used provisions which allow journalists to access information about SJP cases to chronicle the way the secretive process has been used to punish people for minor crimes, often without any regard for their mitigation. He revealed that in August 2025 a teenage waitress had been convicted for failing to insure a car she was gifted as a surprise 18th birthday present, before she'd even been given the keys by her family. Tristan warned in January 2025 that a justice system which is mired in crisis, and beset by delays and backlogs, has 'opened the door to secret justice'. His campaigning journalism prompted a Government consultation.

Elsewhere, coroners' courts are facing similar backlogs and 2025 saw more inquests concluded in writing, under power granted to coroners in 2022. This has posed challenges for journalists, who have had to apply to coroners for the outcomes of hearings which they were previously entitled to attend by right. It appears possible that a coroner could now hold an inquest entirely in secret, if the unique circumstances of the case—such as, for example, one touching on family court proceedings and child safeguarding—meant they could justify refusing to disclose the record of inquest and their ruling. More broadly, a decline in the number of dedicated court reporters nationally appears to have led to more instances of erroneous decisions being made to either exclude journalists from hearings or to impose invalid restrictions on their ability to report.

Investigative journalism continues to be hampered by the economic realities of litigation and the continued rise of Strategic Lawsuits Against Public Participation (SLAPPs). The ruinous costs of complex legal cases going all the way to trial was demonstrated following *The Guardian*'s High Court victory in August 2025 against the actor Noel Clarke, who sued the paper over an investigation which accused him of being a sexual predator. *The Guardian*, which defended its investigations on the basis the allegations made against Clarke were true and in the public interest, claimed its costs in the case were 'significantly in excess of £6 million', despite its win in court. The solicitors' regulator has increasingly taken action over SLAPPs, and a number of solicitors have found themselves being taken to disciplinary tribunals over allegations that they improperly attempted to stifle publications about their clients with the threat of litigation. So far, none of the cases taken to the tribunal have succeeded. The threat remains for journalists who can be outflanked by large corporations with deep pockets, and the staying power of 'new media' organisations and individuals—which generally have fewer resources and less experience battling lawfare than traditional media—may be profoundly tested as it inevitably comes into contact with these legal realities in England and Wales.

Acknowledgements

As authors we thank Joanne Forbes, chief executive of the National Council for the Training of Journalists (NCTJ) and the whole NCTJ team for their continued support for *McNae's* and work to champion open justice and court reporting. We are also very grateful for the support of our fellow members of the NCTJ's Media Law Examinations Board and other trainers and lecturers who value this comprehensive resource as a vital tool in the education of journalists. Special thanks to Kelly Lewars and Helen Swann at Oxford University Press for ensuring the safe passage of this edition through the production process.

We also thank the Judicial College for permitting use of diagram material, the Regulatory Funding Company for permitting reproduction of the Editors' Code of Practice, Ofcom for allowing us to cite extracts from its Broadcasting Code, Impress for permission to use extracts from its Standards Code, rulings and guidance, and Ipso for permission to quote from its rulings and guidance; and the *Western Telegraph* for allowing us to quote from its notes of a judge's comments.

We have benefited from assistance and advice from journalists and lawyers who have directly shared their expertise with us, or via social media or blogs. We are extremely grateful to you all the work you do, and for your dedication and continued support of *McNae's*. If we have made any errors, they are our own.

We continue to be grateful to Gill's former employer, Guardian News and Media, and to City St George's London where she is a visiting lecturer; and to Charlie's various employers, but particularly News Associates, for their continuing support.

The main body of the text of this edition was completed in December 2025. The book's website carries updates, on **www.mcnaes.com**.

We welcome comments from readers about this edition and its website.

Siân Harrison, Freelance Journalist and Media Consultant, external examiner for Cardiff University School of Journalism, Media and Culture, member of HMCTS Media Working Group.
Email: sianharrison@gmail.com

Gillian Phillips, Freelance editorial legal consultant, Visiting Lecturer, Department of Journalism, City St George's, University of London.
Email: gill.phillips@btinternet.com

Charlie Moloney, Media Law Commentator, Trainer and Journalist, member of HMCTS Media Working Group.
Email: charlie@charliemoloney.com

This book bears the name of its first author, the late Leonard McNae, who was Editor of the Press Association's Special Reporting Service.

Late News

For a detailed discussion of the latest updates to media law since this edition was written, see the Late News on **www.mcnaes.com**. The Late News considers:

- In March 2026, the first statutory SLAPP case saw a barrister's £8million libel claim against tax expert Dan Neidle thrown out and declared abusive litigation. Mrs Justice Collins Rice said the valuation of the claim was oppressive and declared the claim a strategic lawsuit against public participation as per the Economic Crime and Corporate Transparency Act 2023.
- In the same month, Martin Shipton, associate editor for Nation.Cymru, revealed police forced entry into his house in Cardiff, and served him with a search warrant under the National Security Act 2023. Shipton, who was not arrested, said he had not done anything wrong but believed it was related to his friendship with a man who had been detained on suspicion of spying for China.
- Also in March 2026, a new national Policing and Media Charter aimed at improving communication between policing and professional journalists was launched. Calls for greater co-operation between police and the media came after the Nicola Bulley inquiry highlighted concerns about the breakdown in trust between journalists and police communications teams during major investigations.
- In April 2026, Mr Justice Fordham ruled that an anonymity order protecting the identity of a 24-year-old student, linked to the largest money laundering operation in Singapore's history, should be lifted. She was a respondent to an application by the National Crime Agency for an unexplained wealth order against her. The woman argued her reputation and career aspirations, which include the ambition of working in the banking sector, would be devastated if she was named.
- In the same month, Cynthia Nkiruka Tooley MBE's applications for a *Norwich Pharmacal* order which would disclose of the identity of a person who supplied a video recording and related information to the Times was dismissed. Mrs Justice Steyn said she was not persuaded the interests of justice was so pressing as to require the strong protection against disclosure of journalistic sources to be overridden.
- And financier Crispin Odey discontinued a £79million libel claim against the Financial Times (FT), over articles which alleged sexual assault and harassment by him. Notifying the FT of the discontinuance, Odey indicated his acceptance that, considering the FT's extensive disclosure, its section 4 public interest defence was likely to succeed. But he maintained that the allegations against him are untrue.
- Also in April 2026, parliamentary scrutiny of the Courts and Tribunals Bill was continuing. An amendment to the Bill that would have introduced these specialist courts at every Crown Court in England and Wales to fast-track rape cases was rejected at the committee stage. The Bar Council of England & Wales continued to oppose curbs on the right to trial by jury.

Summary Contents

Contents

McNae's at a glance

McNae's Essential Law for Journalists contains a range of features to help you find the information you need quickly—in class and on the job. This short guide outlines these features and how they can help you.

Glossary terms are highlighted in the text and defined in the glossary at the back of the book and on **www.mcnaes.com**. →glossar

Chapter summaries introduce each chapter and outline the content—and why it matters to a journalist.

Cross-references point out related information in other chapters, helping you navigate key areas and understand the full picture.

Case studies appear throughout the text to provide context and examples of how the law and ethical codes have been applied to real-life situations.

'Remember' features offer advice from the authors on applying media law and ethical codes on the job, and reminders about relevant content elsewhere in the book.

'Remember your rights' features offer advice from the authors on asserting your rights.

The **website** that accompanies this book, **www.mcnaes.com**, contains regular updates from the authors, as well as self-test resources, writing tips, website links, additional chapters and information on a range of key topics.

Each chapter features a **recap** of the essential points—ideal for revision and as an at-a-glance reminder.

A list of **useful websites** is included at the end of each chapter to help students and journalists find information quickly. You can also find these in the online 'additional material' for each chapter.

www.mcnaes.com

McNae's Essential Law for Journalists is accompanied by a free-to-use website—**www.mcnaes.com**—that features extra resources for both students and journalists. Find your unique access code on the inside front cover.

Updates

Whether you are studying or a working journalist, keep your knowledge up-to-date at **www.mcnaes.com** with regular updates from the authors on key changes affecting media law and ethics.

Self-test questions

Test your media law know-how and get instant feedback with chapter-related questions—ideal preparation for exams or to refresh your knowledge.

Online-only chapters

Access exclusive online-only chapters at **www.mcnaes.com** for the following topics:

- Chapter 36 Other UK jurisdictions
- Chapter 37 The Freedom of Information Act 2000
- Chapter 38 Other information rights and access to meetings
- Chapter 39 Boundaries to expression—hate and obscenity
- Chapter 40 Terrorism and the effect of counter-terrorism law
- Chapter 41 Strategic lawsuits against public participation

Glossary

The glossary is available as flashcards for ready-made exam preparation.

Additional chapters

Find updated, supplemental, and additional detail and resources for each chapter in the additional chapter material available online.

Part 1

The landscape of law, ethics and regulation

1

Introduction

Chapter summary

The UK media enjoy freedoms which are the envy of journalists in oppressed societies. Nevertheless, the UK has more laws affecting journalism than some other democracies, so a sound, thorough knowledge of legal matters is especially important for UK journalists, particularly in their role as 'watchdogs' acting on the public's behalf. This chapter explains how the UK's laws are made and how the European Convention on Human Rights helps safeguard freedom of expression. It also looks at what journalism is and outlines the distinction between criminal and civil law, and between solicitors and barristers.

1.1 Free but with restrictions

Free speech is suddenly at the top of the news agenda. In September 2025, the leader of Reform, Nigel Farage spoke to a US congressional committee hearing into whether European laws 'threaten Americans' right to speak freely in the US'. Farage compared the UK to North Korea. Citing the cases of Father Ted writer Graham Linehan (who was arrested at Heathrow Airport in early September 2025 by five armed police officers on suspicion of inciting violence in relation to his posts on X; no further action resulted) and Lucy Connolly who was jailed after pleading guilty to stirring up racial hatred for an online rant about migrants on the day of the July 2024 knife attacks in Southport (two girls died at the scene and a third girl died the following day, six children and two adults were injured) which sparked widespread unrest. Farage spoke about what he called 'the really awful authoritarian situation that the UK has sunk into'. Although the UK has a free press in comparison to the censorship which stifles liberty in many other nations, the description must be qualified because of the many and growing restrictions on what can be published. This book covers the increasing number of laws affecting journalism in the United Kingdom.

The importance of freedom of expression, and of the journalist's position as a watchdog ensuring a properly informed public in a democratic society, have been stressed by both the UK courts and the European Court of Human Rights in Strasbourg.

In 2000, a senior law lord, Lord Bingham said in a case in the House of Lords, predecessor of the Supreme Court:

for more on this case, see 22.7.2.3

> “In a modern, developed society it is only a small minority of citizens who can participate directly in the discussions and decisions which shape the public life of that society. . . . But the majority cannot participate in the public life of their society in these ways if they are not alerted to and informed about matters which call or may call for consideration and action. It is very largely through the media, including of course the press, that they will be so alerted and informed. The proper functioning of a modern participatory democracy requires that the media be free, active, professional and enquiring (*McCartan Turkington Breen v Times Newspapers Ltd* [2001] 2 AC 277).”

It is the journalist's job to help safeguard freedom of expression and a free media, by reporting accurately and ensuring that people are properly informed about what is being done in their name by those who claim to govern them. It is also the job of journalists to safeguard the principle of an independent judiciary by reporting what is going on in the courts, which apply laws intended to safeguard the interests of all.

For more information about who is a journalist, see 1.4 below and the **additional material** for ch. 1 on **www.mcnaes.com**.

To do all this, journalists must know the law: where it comes from, what it says, and what it lets them do—or stops them doing.

The UK has a vibrant and wide-ranging media—newspapers, magazines, radio and television stations, and the ever-growing internet, with the myriad text and audiovisual sites it offers—as well as the offerings of freelance journalists and community bloggers. The law applies to all of them. Many are also subject to regulatory systems. This book explains how reporting restrictions, defamation and privacy laws limit what may be published both online and offline—and the financial consequences of mistakes or recklessness in journalism. But it also emphasises the freedoms to publish and investigate. Only by knowing what is and is not possible, and what may or may not be done, can journalists, broadcasters, website operators and those who work with them keep the freedoms and variety of platforms they have now, campaign for greater freedom and ensure that their work is not discredited or curtailed by some foolish but expensive error. It is also the case that because they hold the rich and powerful to account and shine a spotlight on sometimes unpalatable truths, journalists find themselves under physical attack and subject to abuse.

see Useful Websites at the end of this chapter for the MLA guidance and the Safety Toolkit

Several resources to support journalists concerning their safety and resilience are included as part of the UK Government's National Action Plan for the Safety of

Journalists. These include specific guidance on online harassment published by the Media Lawyers Association (MLA) in 2025, 'A legal guide to combatting online harassment and abuse against journalists', and an online 'Safety Toolkit' launched by the National Union of Journalists (NUJ) and the Society of Editors which hosts a suite of tools and resources for journalists.

chs. 2 and 3 focus on regulatory codes

In addition to observing the law, observing ethical codes—in particular those used by regulators—should be an integral part of how journalists operate, to produce respected, fair journalism, and preserve freedoms. Failure to respect these codes risks the creation of punitive laws aimed at curbing malpractices and limiting everyone's freedoms.

1.2 Sources of law

→glossary

The main sources of the law are the common law, precedent and **statute**.

1.2.1 Common law

When England's legal system began to take shape in the Middle Ages, royal judges were appointed to administer the 'law and custom of the realm'. This developed local laws into the **common law**—that is, law applying nationwide.

→glossary

1.2.2 Precedent

As judges applied the common law to the cases before them, lawyers recorded their decisions. This process continues. Records of leading cases give the facts considered by a court and the reasons for its decision. The UK has a hierarchy of courts, so a decision made by a lower court can be challenged by appeal to a higher court. The decisions made by the higher courts—precedents, often referred to as 'case law'—are binding on all lower courts, thus shaping their future rulings. Precedents evolve and develop the common law.

→glossary

Figure 1.1 is a diagram of the hierarchy of the courts in England and Wales. The nature and role of these courts is explained further in later chapters.

see 1.5 Divisions of the law for an explanation of criminal and civil law

A **Supreme Court** judgment binds all other UK courts, apart from—in most respects—Scottish criminal courts. But the Supreme Court can overrule its own previous decisions, which otherwise can only be overturned or reversed by legislation.

Below the Supreme Court, in the civil sphere the Court of Appeal's decisions bind the High Court and the lower courts and many tribunals, and High Court decisions bind all lower courts. In the criminal sphere, the Court of Appeal's decisions bind the Crown Court and the Magistrates Court.

ch. 9 and ch. 13 explain the roles of the Court of Appeal and High Court

The court systems of Northern Ireland and Scotland are outlined in online ch. 36 on **www.mcnaes.com**.

Figure 1.1 Hierarchy of the courts

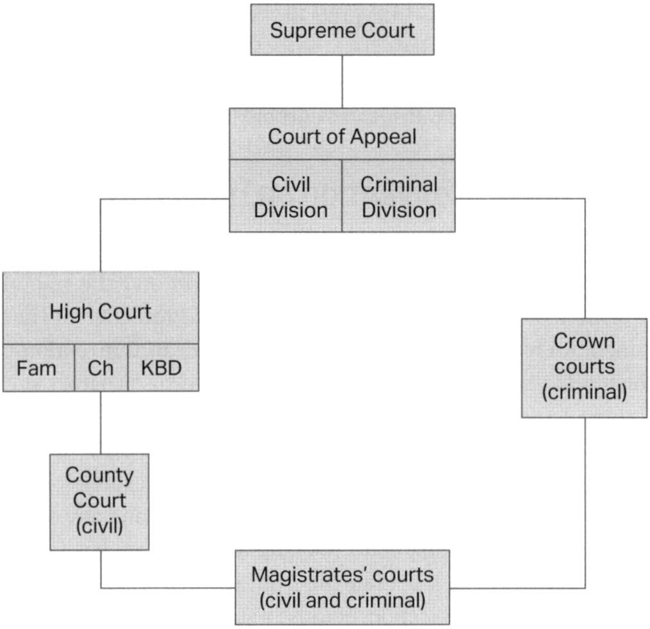

Fam = Family (civil); Ch = Chancery (civil); KBD = King's Bench Division (civil and criminal)—see chs. 9, 13 and 14 for these High Court roles

1.2.3 Statutes and statutory instruments

Common—or case—law can be modified or replaced by statutes—Acts of Parliament, which are primary legislation. UK governments have made increasing use of secondary legislation known as **statutory instruments**. Parliament frequently uses Acts to enshrine broad principles in legislation, but delegates the detailed framing of the new law to the departmental Minister concerned, who sets its detail out in statutory instruments in the form of regulations or rules. Statutory instruments must be approved by Parliament. How part of a statute or statutory instrument should be interpreted—as regards its effect in a particular situation—may be disputed in a court case. The ruling of a higher court on the interpretation will set a precedent. →glossary

1.2.4 European Union law and Brexit

Until 31 January 2020 the UK was part of the European Union, and so was also subject to laws made by the EU through its Council and its Parliament.

While the UK has retained—as part of its national laws—much EU-derived law, over time, these retained laws will likely either diverge from the EU originals, because of amendment by Parliament and interpretation by UK courts, or be completely replaced by new UK law.

The European Court of Justice (ECJ), based in Luxembourg, which is the overriding court for EU member states—interprets EU laws for the national courts of member states. In general, the withdrawal from the EU removed the UK from the ECJ's jurisdiction, other than in the resolution of cases underway before that date. The ECJ is not to be confused with the European Court of Human Rights.

1.3 The European Convention on Human Rights

After the Second World War, Western European nations created the Council of Europe to promote individual freedom, political liberty and the rule of law. The Council's work led to the European Convention for the Protection of Human Rights and Fundamental Freedoms—usually called the European Convention on Human Rights—which sets out rights which must be protected by signatory states, and to the foundation of the European Court of Human Rights (ECtHR), which sits in Strasbourg. The rights the Convention guarantees include the right to respect for privacy and family life, in Article 8, and the right to freedom of expression, in Article 10. Forty-six states are currently signatories of the Convention, and any of their citizens can take a case to the Strasbourg court to argue that the state has failed to protect them from, or to sufficiently compensate them for, a breach of a Convention right. The Convention has very wide application, because a state will be ruled to have breached a right if its legal system fails to stop or to offer an adequate remedy for a violation of an individual's rights, whether the violation was by a private body (such as a business, which could, for example, be a bank or media organisation) or by another individual, or by a state agency (such as a Government department, a local council or a police force).

ch. 15 covers open justice and access to court information

ch. 27 covers the balancing exercise that courts undertake when deciding in any particular case involving the media whether Article 8 rights or Article 10 rights should prevail

1.3.1 The Human Rights Act 1998

The Human Rights Act 1998 came into force on 2 October 2000, putting the Convention directly into UK law and greatly increasing its influence on UK courts. Individuals can require any UK court to consider their rights under the Convention in the context of any case.

The Act requires any UK court determining a question in connection with a Convention right to take account of the ECtHR's decisions, says new UK legislation must be compatible with Convention rights, and says old and new legislation must be construed so far as possible to conform with them.

It is unlawful for UK public authorities to act in a manner incompatible with the Convention.

1.3.2 Convention rights

Adopting the Convention directly into UK law has required judges systematically to consider Convention rights. For journalists, the most important part of the Convention is Article 10, which gives everyone 'the right to freedom of expression', which includes the 'freedom to hold opinions and to receive and impart information and ideas without interference by public authority.' Article 10 makes clear that restrictions on this right must be 'prescribed by law', pursue a legitimate aim, and be necessary and **proportionate**. A court is one type of 'public authority'. The Government, its departments, councils and other official agencies such as the police are also 'public authorities'.

→glossary

Journalists wanting to exercise their Article 10 right to publish information sometimes find themselves facing a legal claim under Article 8—the right to respect for privacy and family life—such as when someone applies to the High Court for an **injunction** to stop media publication of material about an aspect of their personal life, or asks the High Court to order the publisher to pay them damages for intrusion into privacy if the material has been published. The journalists will usually argue that the public's Article 10 right to receive information should also be considered. Another important part of the Convention is Article 6, which creates a right to a 'public hearing'. This can be useful for a journalist who is trying to challenge a court reporting restriction.

→glossary

Extracts from European Convention on Human Rights

Article 8: Right to respect for private and family life

“1) Everyone has the right to respect for his private and family life, his home and his correspondence.

2) There shall be no interference by a public authority with the exercise of this right except such as is in accordance with the law and is necessary in a democratic society in the interests of national security, public safety or the economic well-being of the country, for the prevention of disorder or crime, for the protection of health or morals, or for the protection of the rights and freedoms of others.

Article 10: Freedom of expression

1) Everyone has the right to freedom of expression. This right shall include freedom to hold opinions and to receive and impart information and ideas without interference by public authority and regardless of frontiers:

   This Article shall not prevent States from requiring the licensing of broadcasting, television or cinema enterprises.

2) The exercise of these freedoms, since it carries with it duties and responsibilities, may be subject to such formalities, conditions, restrictions or penalties as are prescribed by law and are necessary in a democratic society, in the interests of national security, territorial integrity or public safety, for the prevention of disorder or crime, for the protection of health or morals, for the protection of the reputation or rights of others, for preventing the disclosure of information received in confidence, or for maintaining the authority and impartiality of the judiciary.”

1.3.3 Other convention rights

In some cases relevant to the media, Article 2 (the right to life) and Article 3 (the prohibition of torture and inhuman or degrading treatment or punishment) are cited by parties arguing that material should not be published—for example, if it is argued that someone's name and/or address should not be published to protect them from violent criminals or vigilantes. For examples of such case law, see 16.11; see too re Article 6 (public hearings) 15.5.

1.4 What is journalism?

Traditionally journalism was a commercial profession where journalists were employed by commercial media organisations. Traditional journalism originated at a time when information was scarce and the provision of it was highly valued, but with the advent of the internet and the rise of the influence of social media as a form of direct contact with the public, competition for the provision of news and information now comes from many new forms and sources, including blogs, user-generated comments and citizen journalists. This has created significant financial pressures on traditional news outlets—particularly in independent local journalism—raising concerns about an increasingly unequal playing field, where tech firms and social media dominate the advertising space but appear to have been allowed to escape with minimal legal liability for what they 'publish' and usually do not belong to any of the regulatory bodies. This already fragile ecospace now has to contend with generative artificial intelligence, from the likes of ChatGPT—which raises a number of practical and ethical implications for journalists.

Journalism, by its very nature, requires gathering, collating, curating and publishing information, some of which may be sensitive. Indeed, in respect of matters of public interest, a good deal of this information may be sensitive and otherwise confidential. This can raise issues around confidentiality, privacy and data protection (see Part 4) as well as source protection (see ch. 33).

1.5 Divisions of the law

There are two main divisions of law—criminal and civil.

Criminal law deals with offences which harm the whole community and thus are considered to be offences against the sovereign. A Crown court case in which John Smith is accused of an offence is listed as *R v Smith*. 'R' stands for Rex (the King) or Regina (the Queen), depending on the monarch at the time, and 'v' for 'versus'. A lawyer talking about this case would generally refer to it as 'The King (or the Queen) *and* Smith' (italics added).

Civil law concerns disputes between individuals and organisations, and includes →glossary the redress of **torts**—that is, wrongs suffered—as well as contractual disputes. Medical negligence, defamation and breach of copyright are all torts. Civil courts also resolve what are essentially private disputes between couples such as divorce actions; as well as disputes over wills and commercial matters; and consider challenges to decisions by public bodies including the Government (known as judicial review).

A case in which Mary Brown sues John Smith will be known in writing as *Brown v Smith*. Lawyers will speak of the case as 'Brown *and* Smith'.

In practice, the two divisions overlap: many acts or omissions are criminal offences for which an individual may be prosecuted and punished as well as civil 'wrongs' for which the injured party may recover compensation—for example, a motorist in a road accident may be prosecuted for dangerous driving and sued by someone who was injured in the crash. Harassment can be both a civil wrong and a criminal offence.

Civil and criminal law cases have different terminologies. In criminal courts a defendant is prosecuted, pleads guilty or not guilty, is acquitted or convicted and, if convicted, is sentenced—for example, fined or jailed. In civil courts a **claimant** sues a defendant or respondent, who admits or denies liability, is found to be either liable or not liable and, if liable, is ordered to pay damages. It is important that journalists use the correct terminology depending on which type of case they are reporting. →glossary

Chs. 5–9 cover the criminal justice system, a huge source of news for journalists. Chs. 13 and 14 explain the civil courts, which have newsworthy cases. Other chapters cover civil laws, such as privacy and copyright, which journalists can be accused of infringing.

1.6 The legal profession

Lawyers are either solicitors or barristers.

By tradition and practice, solicitors deal directly with the client—a defendant in a criminal case or someone seeking advice or representation in a civil case. Solicitors advise, prepare the client's case and take advice, when necessary, from a barrister specialising in a particular area of the law. Solicitors may represent their clients in court, and solicitor-advocates may appear in the higher courts.

Barristers are known, singly or collectively, as 'counsel'. A barrister wears a wig and gown in the higher courts, the Crown courts and the County Court, but not in magistrates' courts. Barristers who have been practising for at least 10 years may apply to the Lord Chancellor for appointment as a King's (or Queen's) Counsel and, if successful, use the letters KC (or QC) after their names. Barristers also provide advocacy in the courts. They are generally self-employed.

1.7 High offices in law

The constitutional position in the UK and other democracies is that the nation's 'executive' (the Government) is separate from the judiciary (the judges), to help ensure that the judiciary is independent of political influence and that the Government is subject to the rule of law, just as other organisations and citizens are.

The head of the judiciary is the Lord or Lady Chief Justice.

The UK Government is advised on law by the Attorney General, which is a political role with holders attending Cabinet meetings. The Attorney General also has a prosecution role—they approve the instigation of, and may personally conduct, prosecutions in certain important cases. These include, as ch. 19 explains, proceedings against media organisations for contempt of court.

Recap of major points

- The media are the eyes and ears of the general public, and a free media is an essential element in maintaining parliamentary democracy.
- The European Convention on Human Rights has codified fundamental freedoms, including that of freedom of expression.
- Sources of UK law include custom, precedent, statutes and statutory instruments, and European Union regulations.
- The two main divisions of the law are criminal law and civil law, and journalists need to use correctly the legal terms appropriate for the type of court case they are reporting.

Useful Websites

UK Parliament, 'How are laws made?', www.parliament.uk

European Court of Human Rights, www.echr.coe.int

The 'Official Texts' link leads to the Convention:

Courts and Tribunals Judiciary, www.judiciary.uk

Information on judges and the courts system:

The Law Society, 'Becoming a solicitor', www.lawsociety.org.uk

The Bar Council, 'About barristers', www.barcouncil.org.uk

Attorney General's Office, www.gov.uk

Media Lawyers Association, 'Combatting Online Harassment and Abuse: A Legal Guide for Journalists in England and Wales', medialawyersassociation.org

National Union of Journalists & Society of Editors, 'Journalists Safety Toolkit', www.journalists-safety.tools

Online resources

Visit the online resources at **www.mcnaes.com** to test your knowledge of this chapter with **self-test questions** and a **flashcard glossary**, and to read **updates** about law and regulatory matters affecting journalism, as well as **additional material** to further your learning.

2

Press regulation

Chapter summary

Outside of the law, ethics play an important role in journalism. Many countries have codes of ethics that they expect their press to abide by. These are not laws but are guides that encourage those who engage in journalism to adopt certain minimum standards and to take responsibility for the information they provide, regardless of medium. In some instances, these codes are looked after and enforced by watchdog bodies.

Rather than resort to legal action, people aggrieved by what has been published about them, or by how journalists have treated them, may want a watchdog body to intervene in or adjudicate on their complaint. For most of the UK's newspapers and magazines, and their websites, this watchdog is the Independent Press Standards Organisation (Ipso), which uses the **Editors' Code of Practice** to adjudicate on complaints. A number of smaller publishers are members of Impress, the regulator recognised by the Press Recognition Panel, which has its own, different Code. Some newspapers and websites are not members of either organisation and self-regulate. This chapter introduces editorial codes and outlines the IPSO and Impress Codes.

→glossary

2.1 Introduction

There are no state controls in the UK on who can own or run newspapers, magazines, their online versions or any kind of news website—publications defined by the term 'the press'. Anyone with the resources can launch a new publication. These liberties help keep the UK's media relatively free from state influence. Newspapers, magazines and websites are free to be partisan about societal and political issues. Editors may use leader columns, news stories and features to campaign on any issue, from environmental law to local hospital closures. They and their journalists may also publish, subject to the restraints of defamation and other laws, their own fierce criticisms of those in the news, or anyone else. The lack of any requirement for these media sectors to be impartial contrasts with the position of the broadcasting industry, as the next chapter explains.

2.1.1 Fragmentation of press regulation

In 2011, the Press Complaints Commission (PCC)—a regulator the press industry created in 1991 to keep the threat of statutory regulation at bay—was much criticised because it failed to realise or investigate the extent of phone-hacking by journalists at the *News of the World*. After revelations about phone hacking, Lord Justice Leveson was appointed to chair a public inquiry into 'the culture, practices and ethics' of the UK press. The publication of the Leveson Report in 2012 led most of the UK's major newspaper and magazine groups, including high-circulation national newspapers and most of the regional and local press, to establish and fund—and be bound by the decisions of—a new regulator, the Independent Press Standards Organisation (Ipso). It replaced the PCC in 2014 with the intention of being a stronger, more credible regulator than the old Press Complaints Commission.

ch. 34 outlines the phone-hacking scandal

In adjudications Ipso considers whether there has been a breach of the Editors' Code of Practice. The Code, which is discussed in detail in this and other chapters, is reviewed by the Editors' Code of Practice Committee—the Code Committee—which is part of the Ipso system. The committee consists mainly of editors, with lay members independent of the press.

see Appendix 1 for the full Editors' Code

Another result of the Leveson Report was that Parliament approved a system of press regulation set out in a Royal Charter—law created by Government Ministers—in 2012.

Some people have criticised the Charter's 'recognition' requirement—under which a Press Recognition Panel must periodically review the work of any regulator in that system—as being a step towards statutory regulation of the press and as amounting to political interference in UK press freedoms.

The UK's only other press regulator, Impress—covered later in this chapter, and which has its own code of ethics—chose to be in the Charter system. Supporters of Impress argue that it implements Leveson's recommendations better than Ipso does.

> For more background about Ipso, Impress and the Charter model of regulation, see the **additional material** for ch. 2 on **www.mcnaes.com**.

The separate existence of Ipso and Impress is not the only reason why UK press regulation is fragmented. Three national newspapers—the *Financial Times, The Guardian, The Observer*—as well as the website-only *Independent* and the *Evening Standard* in London are owned by groups which have so far decided against joining either Ipso or Impress. Each of these groups has its own system—not linked to the Charter model—for handling complaints against their newspapers and websites. Despite being outside the Ipso system, they expect their editors and journalists to comply with their equivalents of the Ipso Editors' Code of Practice. Thus, the vast majority of UK press journalists are expected to know and comply with a set of ethics. For many individual journalists who work for commercial organisations, this is a contractual requirement.

2.1.2 Editors' Code principles

The 31-year continuity in the Code's use under the PCC and then under Ipso means that there is now a searchable set of adjudications interpreting and applying the Code—from which common ethical principles and approaches may be derived—available on its website. This provides valuable guidance for journalists about ethical standards, on which this book draws. Ipso also publishes what is known as the Editors' Codebook, which is available online and acts as a handbook that sets the Code in context and highlights best practice and key adjudications on each clause of the Code. Finally, Ipso provides separate guidance on a number of sensitive issues (such as covering suicide, transgender issues, religion, and court reporting), which can be helpful when reporting on these challenging areas.

see Useful Websites at the end of this chapter for the Code and its history

Ipso's complaints committee makes its adjudications. This book cites adjudications by case name and date of their issue.

2.2 The Independent Press Standards Organisation

Ipso's detractors argue that it is not compliant with the recommendations of the Leveson inquiry, is not independent and is operationally weak and ineffective. Ipso has commissioned two external reviews of its operations. The second of these, in 2023, was broadly positive. In respect of Ipso's governance and structure, the report noted that although Ipso does not conform to the Leveson recommendation for recognition by an independent panel, it does follow Leveson's recommendations in most other significant respects. However, it points out that the way in which Ipso is funded—via a levy on each member publication, based on a formula involving readership and financial turnover—is not transparent and gives rise to concerns about how independent from the industry Ipso really is. The report also expresses concern over the speed with which complaints are dealt with. As well as dealing with individual complaints, Ipso can mount a 'standards investigation' against a particular title, where there appear to have been serious and systematic breaches of the Code, but no such investigation has ever been conducted.

Ipso offers a 24-hour emergency harassment helpline, which is available for people concerned about press intrusion. In an appropriate case, Ipso will contact newspapers and magazine publishers to make them aware of concerns that the Editors' Code may be breached, which it does by sending what is known as a privacy notice. These notices are only advisory and do not have legal powers, but they do put editors on notice and can be effective at dealing with concerns of this nature. Ipso also runs—as recommended by Leveson—a separate arbitration scheme under which it is compulsory for its national newspaper members to offer arbitration to complainants seeking financial redress (damages) because of what was published or other journalistic activity. (Some Ipso members—including regional and local newspapers—do not offer arbitration and Ipso cannot compel them to do so.) This scheme is a low-cost way of resolving legal disputes without going to court. It enables complainants—by paying a maximum £100 fee—to bring claims that would otherwise have to be brought in the courts, for defamation, harassment, intrusion into privacy, and breach of data protection, without having the (much greater) expense of going to court. Ipso does not allow both a Code complaint and arbitration to proceed at the same time, although it is possible to make a complaint first and then go to arbitration. Take-up of the arbitration scheme has been low.

> Ipso's website gives more detail about its arbitration scheme (which can award damages of up to £60,000), its governing board and how it is funded by member publishers. See Useful Websites at the end of this chapter.

> For general explanation of laws on harassment, defamation, intrusion into privacy, and breach of data protection—see this book's chs. 4, 20–23, 27, and 28.

Under the Ipso system a person or organisation aggrieved by what has been published or how journalists have behaved should complain first to the relevant editor to see if their complaint can be resolved internally. A complainant who remains dissatisfied should then contact Ipso. They will be asked to state which part or parts of the Editors' Code have in their view been breached. Ipso offers a free process involving guidance, mediation and, if the complaint remains unresolved, an adjudication. Ipso's complaints committee decides to what extent it needs to make an adjudication. Ipso says a complaint must normally be made within four months of the publication of the complained-of material or of the date of the alleged misconduct by journalists, but that it may be able to take a complaint about an online article up to 12 months after publication.

This chapter concentrates on Ipso's complaints process, which is free for complainants but does not offer financial redress to those whose complaints it upholds. As Ipso's complaints process is free to use, and all media organisations signed up with Ipso are contractually obliged to cooperate with it, this—rather than arbitration—will generally be the route used by most complainants.

✱ Remember

Ipso has the contractual power to fine any member publication—newspaper, magazine or website—up to £1 million for a particularly serious and systemic breach of the Code. But this is a financial penalty on the publisher, not compensation for any complainant. By the time this book went to press, Ipso had not used this power.

2.2.1 Compliance procedures

Ipso member publications must have effective internal complaints procedures and be able to demonstrate to Ipso—for example, in annual reports—the ethical training they give their journalists and show how they handle complaints, which, ideally, should be resolved without the need for Ipso's involvement.

2.3 The Ipso complaints process

Ipso may rule that a complaint was not justified or that, even if it was, an editor's response, such as a private or published apology or an offer to publish a correction, was enough to resolve the issue. It might negotiate a resolution to a problem. It might also intervene before anything is published—for example, by way of a privacy notice in cases in which people want the press to leave them alone. But if Ipso proceeds to a formal adjudication, it requires an editor to publish any adverse adjudication, which it also publishes on its website.

This public acknowledgement that the Code was breached is the redress for those whose complaints are upheld. Ipso, because of its contractual powers to impose financial penalties, can also specify where—for example, which page in a newspaper—a member organisation should publish an adverse adjudication, to ensure suitable prominence.

Ipso also publishes adjudications which do not uphold a complaint, because adjudications illustrate how it interprets the Code.

In its annual report for 2024 Ipso reported that it had received 6655 complaints and enquiries. The vast majority did not raise any potential breach of the Code, were not followed up by complainants, or were about matters outside Ipso's remit. The remaining 307 were taken forward for investigation. The committee upheld 43 of these complaints by deciding that one or more of the Code's clauses had been breached. 134 complaints were resolved directly with the publisher and 31 via Ipso mediation.

see Useful Websites at the end of this chapter for Ipso's Annual Reports

2.4 The scope of the Editors' Code

see Appendix 1 for the full Editors' Code

The Editors' Code has 16 clauses. These set out ethical standards on a range of issues including accuracy, privacy, children's welfare, preventing harassment and intrusion into grief or shock, and banning the use of excessive detail in coverage of suicides, as well as governing how journalists make inquiries at hospitals and their use of undercover tactics involving secret filming, subterfuge or misrepresentation.

In this book some of the Code's clauses are explained in relevant chapters—for example, ch. 4 has a focus on avoiding unjustified intrusion in news-gathering, and so features clause 2 on privacy, clause 3 on harassment, clause 4 on intrusion into grief or shock, clause 6 on children's welfare, clause 8 on hospitals and institutions, and part of clause 9 on relatives of crime suspects and defendants. Other clauses, such as the moral obligation to protect confidential sources of information, are dealt with in other chapters at appropriate points. This book's index entry for the Editors' Code lists pages featuring each clause.

This chapter deals with the other clauses of wide application and clauses governing comparatively rare practices or specialist work in journalism.

see Useful Websites at the end of this chapter for the Codebook and Ipso site

The Code does not deal with issues of taste and decency—for example, if someone complains that an article caused offence—as the industry's position has been that, as these are subjective matters, rulings on them could compromise freedom of expression. Ipso's position reflects this (for example, its adjudication in *Various v The Times*, 11 August 2021, a complaint not upheld).

If someone complains to Ipso that what a reader has posted on a member publisher's website commenting on an article has breached the Code, Ipso will regard the complaint as within its remit if the posting (such as a comment) has been subject to editorial control—that is, if it was moderated (checked) by that publication before it became visible online, or if it remained visible after a complaint was made to that publication about it.

- Note that, for convenience, all references to the Code in this book adopt the clause numbering used in the latest version, which took effect from 1 January 2025. The main change made in 2025 was to Clause 6 (Children) to clarify who can consent to provide information about a child's welfare. The change came after an Ipso ruling (*A woman v South Wales Argus:* ipso.co.uk/rulings/21023-23/.) that the wording of the existing clause was unclear as to whether a father quoted in the story was 'a custodial parent or similarly responsible adult', as required by the Code. The term 'custodial parent' was removed and replaced with a requirement of consent by 'an adult with legal parental responsibility or similarly responsible adult'. In this chapter and ch. 4, a reference to a complaint made to Ipso will say 'not upheld' if the adjudication outcome may not otherwise be made clear.

✱ Remember

Breaching the Editors' Code is not a criminal offence or a civil tort. However, observing its requirements is ethical conduct and can also help journalists avoid legal problems. A number of laws—such as the Human Rights Act and the UK GDPR—now specifically refer to editorial codes. For more legal context, see the section on audit trails below and 2.6.

2.4.1 Public interest exceptions in the Editors' Code

Some clauses or subclauses in the Code are marked with an asterisk, which indicates that breaches of these parts—for example, if a journalist uses deception or intrudes into someone's privacy—can be justified if an editor can demonstrate that what was done was 'in the public interest'.

The Code says the public interest includes, but is not confined to:

- detecting or exposing crime, or the threat of crime, or serious impropriety;
- protecting public health or safety;
- protecting the public from being misled by an action or statement of an individual or organisation;
- disclosing a person or organisation's failure or likely failure to comply with any obligation to which they are subject;
- disclosing a miscarriage of justice;
- raising or contributing to a matter of public debate, including serious cases of impropriety, unethical conduct or incompetence concerning the public;
- disclosing concealment, or likely concealment, of any of the above.

The term 'in the public interest' denotes that the journalism has particularly high potential to be beneficial to society. But the Code also says: 'There is a public interest in freedom of expression itself.' It stresses the need to protect young people, adding: 'An exceptional public interest would need to be demonstrated to over-ride the normally paramount interests of children under 16.'

The Code says editors seeking to rely on public interest exceptions 'will need to demonstrate that they reasonably believed publication—or journalistic activity taken with a view to publication—would both serve, and be proportionate to, the public interest and explain how they reached that decision at the time'. Best practice, therefore, is to maintain a pre-publication document trail which records why using an investigative method, or publishing information or material which would normally breach the Code (e.g. because it was private or personal), was considered to be justified in the public interest. The phrase 'at the time' shows that Ipso normally expects this process to be undertaken before material is published. See 2.6 below for more detail on audit trails and their importance in pre-publication journalistic and editorial processes.

✱ Remember

Being able to prove such reasonable belief by producing an 'audit trail', including about decisions made quickly in a busy newsroom, is important for ethical and legal reasons. This need to be able to evidence 'reasonable belief' before publication is explained in more detail at 2.6.

2.4.2 Accuracy and opportunity to reply

Clause 1 of the Code says: 'The Press must take care not to publish inaccurate, misleading or distorted information or images, including headlines not supported by the text.'

It also says that the press 'while free to editorialise and campaign, must distinguish clearly between comment, conjecture and fact'.

((•)) see Useful Websites at the end of this chapter for Ipso's 'third party' policy

Most complaints to Ipso allege inaccuracy. Clause 1 is not subject to the public interest exceptions—there is no public interest in inaccuracy. This is the only clause for which Ipso will routinely accept 'third party' complaints, because it accepts that publishing a significant inaccuracy on a general point of fact could affect many people in that media organisation's readership/audience.

Publications which led to Ipso adjudicating that clause 1 was breached have included:

- An *express.co.uk* article which reported that Liverpool player James Milner had been booed when playing in a football game, despite Mr Milner not having played and not being booed. The article had been 'written in advance of the game' and had been published by mistake (*Walters v express.co.uk*, 30 April 2020).

- A *mirror.co.uk* article reported that the seaside town of Skipsea in North Yorkshire was 'rat infested' and a 'ghost town'. The complainant said this was not true, and that the photos used in the article were at least ten years old. During Ipso's investigation, the publication offered to remove the article. It also published a standalone correction. This successfully resolved the complaint, so the Complaints Committee did not rule as to whether there had been any breach of the Code (*Illingworth v mirror.co.uk*, 25 July 2023).

Ipso does not require that press coverage of controversies or disputes between people or organisations should meet a legal standard of proof about who is right or wrong. The emphasis in clause 1 is that 'care' must be taken to avoid publication of inaccurate or misleading information. For example, presenting 'speculation' as fact rather than as conjecture breaches the clause (*Metropolitan Police v Mail Online*, 23 August 2021)

In the **additional material** for this chapter on **www.mcnaes.com** there is a guide to what Ipso regards as sufficient 'care' in accuracy, based on its adjudications, including about checking facts, as well as further case studies.

Remember

Publishing unproven allegations against an individual or an organisation could also lead to the publisher being sued for defamation. Such a person may decide not to complain to Ipso, or may not be satisfied with its adjudication, and decide to sue. Chapters 20–23 cover defamation law.

see Useful Websites at the end of this chapter for the Codebook

2.4.2.1 Corrections and apologies

Clause 1 says 'a significant inaccuracy, misleading statement or distortion' must be corrected 'promptly and with due prominence', and, where appropriate, with a published apology, and that in cases involving Ipso due prominence should be as it stipulates.

The Editors' Codebook says that if a correction is offered promptly, a significant inaccuracy will not be a breach of the Code. It gives advice on what 'due prominence' is. Ipso has no power to compel publication of apologies. However, a failure to offer one when appropriate can lead to a complaint being upheld. Ipso has said that an apology is 'required' when an error has been 'personal to' and has the potential to be 'seriously damaging to' the complainant (*McIntosh v The Herald (Glasgow)*, 8 June 2015). Ipso does have the power to require a newspaper to inform its readers of any adverse findings, including on its front page and website.

for the danger in defamation law of the wording and publishing of apologies, see 22.8.2

If the significant inaccuracy was published on a social media platform, such as Twitter, the correction must be published there (*The Family of Sue Woods v liverpoolecho.co.uk*, 2 June 2021).

The Code's clauses 2, 3, 4, 6, and 8, covering the privacy, intrusion and the welfare of children are explained in ch. 4. Clause 7, covering children in sexual offence cases, is explained in 11.7.

2.4.3 **Coverage of suicides**

Research has found that news of suicides may prompt others to take their own lives in the same way. To minimise this risk, clause 5 of the Code says reports of suicides should avoid giving 'excessive detail' about the method used.

See 17.11 on coverage of inquest cases of suicide. However, the clause applies to any coverage of suicide. Clauses 7, 9 and 11 on reporting the courts are covered in other chapters—see Editors' Code in the Index.

2.4.4 **Deception (subterfuge and misrepresentation)**

Clause 10 of the Code says:

> “i) The press must not seek to obtain or publish material acquired by using hidden cameras or clandestine listening devices; or by intercepting private or mobile telephone calls, messages or emails; or by the unauthorised removal of documents or photographs; or by accessing digitally-held information without consent.
>
> ii) Engaging in misrepresentation or subterfuge, including by agents or intermediaries, can generally be justified only in the public interest and then only when the material cannot be obtained by other means.”

This clause makes clear that journalists should normally be open when seeking information or comment by declaring from the outset to anyone unfamiliar with them that they are journalists and the purpose of the inquiries. It also means that normally covert photography or covert filming, or eavesdropping by using 'bugs', or audio-recording by hidden ('clandestine') microphones will breach the Code.

see also 2.4.4.2, Recording interviews and phone calls

But Clause 10 is subject to the public interest exceptions, as discussed earlier. If an editor can demonstrate to Ipso's satisfaction that they reasonably believed that undercover tactics were justified by a sufficient public interest, a journalist's lies about who they are, or use of other subterfuge or hidden cameras or microphones, will not be adjudged to have breached the Code.

Such methods are common in investigative journalism. The Code also requires that it was reasonable for the editor to believe that an open approach ('other means') would not work. As mentioned earlier, editors are expected to be able to demonstrate that they had these discussions *before* they published.

Irrespective of the Code, using cameras or microphones which are hidden could breach the civil law of privacy or data protection law, as chs. 27 and 28 explain, and 'hacking' into phone or email systems secretly to gain information (interception) or into other people's computers will normally be a crime—see ch. 34. But 'public interest' justifications may exist too for journalistic activity which would otherwise breach these laws.

> See the **additional material** for this chapter on **www.mcnaes.com** for a case study in which Ipso cleared the *Mail on Sunday* of a complaint that it had breached clause 10 by using subterfuge for an article it published. What clause 10 says about use of subterfuge is explained earlier in this chapter.

2.4.4.1 'Fishing expeditions'

The Code does not permit subterfuge or misrepresentation—including using hidden cameras or recording devices—or infringement of privacy in 'fishing expeditions'. A 'fishing expedition' is an investigation launched without sufficient prima facie grounds to justify it. For example, investigating an institution or business chosen at random, with no ground to suspect it of wrongdoing, would be a 'fishing expedition'.

> See the **additional material** for ch. 2 on **www.mcnaes.com** for a case study in which Ipso's predecessor, the PCC, ruled that the *Daily Telegraph* had breached clause 10 by conducting a fishing expedition.

2.4.4.2 Recording interviews and phone calls

for context, see 34.11, Recording phone calls

Journalists, particularly those involved in investigations, may record their own telephone calls—for example, when they are interviewing the target of their inquiries—or record a face-to-face encounter. The recording might be needed as proof if the subject sues for defamation over what is published, claiming to have been misquoted or not approached. In the UK it is not a crime for a person making or receiving a phone call to record it, even if the other person is unaware of this and the journalist does not tell them. This is not 'interception'. It is not a crime either to record an interview covertly.

Ipso has ruled several times that a journalist recording a face-to-face interview conducted openly (that is, the journalist makes clear the purpose of the interview, and that what is said may be published), is not deploying subterfuge or misrepresentation, or using a clandestine listening device, even if the other person is not aware that they are being recorded. So such recording does not engage clause 10 and so does not require a public interest justification. Ipso regards such recording merely as an alternative means of or supplement to note-taking (for example, *A woman v The Sun*, 15 February 2019). Ipso has also ruled that a journalist did not breach the code by recording a phone interview. The person who was interviewed complained she was unaware she was being recorded. But Ipso said that the recording enabled the newspaper to demonstrate its compliance with the Code's accuracy requirement in clause 1 (*Goemans v Ely Standard*, 17 January 2022).

But a journalist who fails to declare in a phone call or visit that they are a journalist may breach the Code's ban on subterfuge and misrepresentation, unless one of the Code's public interest exceptions applies and the editor is able to demonstrate that before going ahead the public interest had been considered, and that it was reasonable to conclude there was no other way of obtaining the information. The editor would also have to consider whether publishing material from the recording would breach the Code as regards privacy. The Code's protection of privacy is covered in ch. 4.

2.4.5 **Discriminatory material**

((•)) see Useful Websites at the end of this chapter for guidance on reporting mental illness

Clause 12 of the Code says the press must avoid prejudicial or pejorative reference to an individual's race, colour, religion, sex, gender identity or sexual orientation, or to any physical or mental illness or disability, and that details of an individual's race, colour, religion, gender identity, sexual orientation, physical or mental illness or disability must be avoided unless genuinely relevant to the story.

Ipso accepts that including a person's biographical details, including nationality, in an article would not generally breach the terms of this clause (*Yates v Mail Online*, 15 June 2015, clause 12, not upheld) but has said that a prejudicial or pejorative reference to an individual's race or colour could be made by reference to nationality (*Miller v Mail Online*, 25 April 2017, not upheld).

> ((•)) See Useful Websites at the end of this chapter for an Ipso blog on the scope of clause 12, Ipso's guidance on reporting on Muslims and Islam, and its guidance on researching and reporting stories about transgender people. The guidance includes adjudication case studies.

Clause 12 only applies to material which identifies an individual, so does not cover general reference to groups or categories of people, such as migrants or ethnic groups, even if pejorative—a limitation which has proved controversial, although Ipso can consider under clause 1 (accuracy). In June 2023, Ipso upheld two representative complaints that a Jeremy Clarkson opinion column in *The Sun* in December 2022 was sexist towards the Duchess of Sussex. Ipso described some of the comments about her as 'pejorative and prejudicial'. The article prompted some 25,000 complaints but Ipso only investigated two complaints by representative groups claiming to be directly affected by the article. The ruling is the first time a complaint to Ipso about discrimination relating to someone's sex has been upheld. Ipso said that while the comments individually might not represent a breach of the code, when 'read as a whole' they amounted to a breach of clause 12.

((•)) see Useful Websites for the Financial Journalism Best Practice Note

2.4.6 **Financial journalism**

Clause 13 of the Code seeks to prevent journalists from making personal profit by anticipating movements in share prices on the basis of information leaked to them by business contacts. It says journalists 'must not use for their own profit financial information they receive in advance of its general publication, nor should they pass such information to others'. It also bans journalists from dealing in shares or securities about which they have recently written, or intend to write, as what they publish might affect market prices and it would be unethical for them to take financial advantage of this power. It says journalists must not write about shares or securities in which they or close relatives have a significant financial interest without disclosing it to their editor or financial editor.

Clause 14 of the Editors' Code on protection of sources is covered in ch. 33

This clause, as well as Ipso's existence as regulator to police the Code, and the Financial Journalism Best Practice Note issued by the Editors' Code of Practice

Committee, some of which specifies mandatory practice, led in 2016 to UK journalists being legally exempted from the similar provisions of the European Union's Regulatory Technical Standards of the Market Abuse Regulation.

2.4.7 Payments to witnesses in criminal trials

Media organisations covering high-profile stories may pay people, including the victims of notorious crimes, for the exclusive right to publish their accounts of events. Those accounts would be more than the evidence they could give in court, which would not have exclusive value. The accounts could, for example, include descriptions not limited by the rules of evidence. Clause 15 of the Code aims to prevent these chequebook journalism deals from interfering with the process of justice by influencing the evidence of witnesses or undermining their credibility in the eyes of a jury. A risk of contempt of court can arise from such a deal, or from a reporter interviewing anyone due to testify in a trial.

for context on the contempt risk, see 19.4.6

The first part of clause 15 says: 'No payment or offer of payment to a witness– or any person who may reasonably be expected to be called as a witness–should be made in any case once proceedings are active as defined by the Contempt of Court Act 1981.' The ban applies until a case ceases to be active or the suspect pleads guilty or there is a verdict.

The second part says that:

> "Where proceedings are not yet active but are likely and foreseeable, editors must not make or offer payment to any person who may reasonably be expected to be called as a witness, unless the information concerned ought demonstrably to be published in the public interest and there is an over-riding need to make or promise payment for this to be done; and all reasonable steps have been taken to ensure no financial dealings influence the evidence those witnesses give. In no circumstances should such payment be conditional on the outcome of a trial."

It says a payment or an offer of payment made to a person later cited to testify in proceedings must be disclosed to the prosecution and defence.

2.4.8 Payments to criminals

Clause 16 (i) of the Code says: 'Payment or offers of payment for stories, pictures or information, which seek to exploit a particular crime or to glorify or glamorise crime in general, must not be made directly or via agents to convicted or confessed criminals or to their associates–who may include family, friends and colleagues.' This recognises that people, particularly crime victims, are likely to condemn a deal under which criminals or those close to them profit from tales of wrongdoing. Clause 16 (ii) recognises that payment to a criminal may be justified by the Code's public interest exceptions–see this book's Appendix 1.

2.5 Impress and its Code

In October 2016 the Press Recognition Panel (PRP), formed in 2014 under the Royal Charter model of press regulation, 'recognised' as a regulator the Independent Monitor for the Press, known as Impress. The Board of the PRP has completed three Cyclical Reviews of Impress, the latest being completed in April 2025. Impress is required to demonstrate every three years that it continues to meet the 29 Charter criteria for independent press self-regulation, established by Parliament in the Royal Charter on Self-Regulation of the Press. Impress has successfully demonstrated to the PRP Board that it remains committed to maintaining high editorial standards, protecting its members' freedom of expression, enabling investigative journalism in the public interest, and upholding robust protections for the public.

Impress has its own 'standards code', the scope of which is wider in some places in terms of specified detail of ethical provision than the Editors' Code. For example, Impress's Code requires general disclosure of journalists' conflicts of interest. But much of the content of its code is based on the same broadly accepted ethical principles as Ipso's Editors' Code, and it too has 'public interest' exceptions and indicatively lists the types of story which would be in the public interest to pursue, such as preventing crime or putting the record straight when someone has misled the public 'on a matter of public importance'.

for context, see 2.1.1, Fragmentation of press regulation

Impress has issued guidance on how its Code should be interpreted and, like Ipso, does not charge to handle complaints.

At the time of this book going to press, Impress—which publishes online its adjudications on complaints against its members—was regulating over 120 publishers and over 200 publications, who pay it membership fees. Many of these publishers were hyperlocal or small local publishers. No major press group has joined Impress. It also has an arbitration scheme, which has been used on three occasions to date, all involving defamation claims, in two of which small amounts of damages were awarded to the complainants.

The Impress Code is more explicit about audit trails than the Ipso Editors' Code. It says that before undertaking an action which needs 'public interest' justification—whether the action is publication of an item or a method of news-gathering—the publisher should, where practicable, make a contemporaneous note, which establishes why they believe that:

i) the action is in the public interest;

ii) they could not have achieved the same result using measures that are compliant with the Code;

iii) the action is likely to achieve the desired outcome; and

iv) any likely harm caused by the action does not outweigh the public interest in the action.

Impress's guidance to its members says that maintaining a contemporaneous note is not a strict requirement, but is good practice: 'Such an audit trail may, for instance, identify who gave permission for the action taken, and what discussion there was of the justification for it. This assists journalists in accurately recording the public interest rationale for behaviour that may be contrary to the Code. It also encourages journalists to think carefully *at the time* about why and whether a given action is justified in the public interest.'

It warns publishers against going on 'fishing expeditions', and adds that 'contemporaneous' means that a note should be made as soon as is physically practicable, and that it may take the form of a private note, diary entry or an email to a colleague or editor. 'It may be a brief paragraph, or longer, depending on the circumstances. The date on which the note was made should be clear . . . A failure to make a contemporaneous note will make it harder for a publisher to substantiate any public interest justification in response to an alleged breach of the Code.'

for 'fishing expeditions', see 2.4.4.1

See Useful Websites at the end of this chapter for Impress's Code, guidance and annual reports. Some parts of the Impress Code are covered in other chapters—see Index.

2.6 The importance of 'audit' trails, including in legal cases

As said earlier, the Editors' Code of Practice, used by Ipso, and the Impress Standards Code have public interest exceptions to their normal rules. The Ofcom Broadcasting Code, explained in the next chapter, also has such exceptions.

Where reliance is placed on the 'public interest' exception, each of these regulators expects a media organisation to be able to demonstrate, in the event of a complaint that the relevant code was breached, that 'a reasonable belief' was held on behalf of the organisation before it published that a public interest exception applied.

The regulator will consider what evidence there was to establish a reasonable belief that a 'public interest' matter needed to be probed, and/or consider whether what was published could be reasonably believed to serve the public interest.

Best practice is for the organisation to keep a documentary record–referred to as an 'audit trail'–to help demonstrate that the belief was reasonable, including recording how and what decisions were made about adoption of method(s) (such as a journalist going undercover, and to what extent) and/or what should be published–for example, about a person's private life. It is important that the documented trail should record, as early as possible in an investigation, any information considered relevant to support the 'reasonable belief' that it was in the public interest for example for their journalists to probe deeper by using deception or intruding into someone's privacy. Based on the public interest examples in the Code, this could be evidence that the person concerned was or could be committing a crime, or be guilty of serious impropriety, or be misleading the public or putting people's health or safety at risk etc. An editor will also need to be able to demonstrate that there was careful consideration as the investigation continued, and that the methods to be used would be proportionate and necessary.

Being able to demonstrate adherence to a regulatory code before publication is a relevant issue if the organisation is sued for alleged misuse of private information, or sued or prosecuted for alleged breach of data protection law—see also 27.9 and 28.2.6. It is also relevant if a media organisation is considering running a public interest defence under s 4 Defamation Act 2013.

see ch. 23 on the s 4 defence

Case study

In 2020, a High Court judge ordered *MailOnline* to pay £83,000 damages to Alaedeen Sicri for breach of his privacy because it identified him as having been arrested by police in a terrorism investigation following the Manchester Arena bombing. It soon transpired Mr Sicri was completely innocent of any involvement in terrorism, and he was never charged with any offence. He successfully claimed damages from the *MailOnline* because its reporting of the arrest identified him. The judge was critical of the journalists and editors responsible for the arrest report. He said they had no documentation to show the court why, at the time it was published, they had a 'reasonable belief' under the Editors' Code that identifying Mr Sicri to the world at large as the man arrested would be in the public interest, when the police had not done that. The judge said that the journalists involved in the decision to name Mr Sicri were 'driven by competitive considerations, or herd instinct' and did not weigh up his rights before publication.

for more context on the *Sicri* case, see 5.11.2

Being able to prove from an audit trail the existence of 'reasonable belief' about a public interest justification could also be important for media organisations seeking to rely on the public interest defence in defamation law, explained in ch. 23. In 2021 in the *Lachaux* case, explained in more detail in that chapter, Mr Justice Nicklin said of the reference to audit trails in the Impress Code: 'As an explanation of the importance of contemporaneous documents, it can hardly be bettered.'

See the **additional material** for ch. 2 on **www.mcnaes.com** for more information about the facts of *Lachaux*.

These two cases show that judges—when deciding the outcome of privacy and defamation actions in which a media organisation presents a 'public interest' defence—are increasingly likely to focus on what was in the mind of the individual reporter or feature writer, as well as in the minds of news editors or higher executives, concerning pre-publication decisions about what could justifiably be published. There is similar wording around 'reasonable belief', as well as an express reference to regulatory codes, in the UK GDPR and it will also be expected in that context that editors and journalists are able to produce evidence to show they considered the public interest before publishing personal information about individuals (see ch. 28 for more on the GDPR).

2.7 The European context

The importance of following editorial codes is also reflected in some of the cases of the European Court of Human Rights, which talks about 'good faith' journalism. Article 10 of the European Convention on Human Rights is a qualified right—not absolute—and those seeking Article 10 protections are expected to uphold certain rights and duties. See, for example, the cases of *Stoll v Switzerland* (2007) and *Bedat v Switzerland* (2016), detailed in the **additional material** for this chapter.

Recap of major points

- The Ipso Editors' Code sets standards for journalists working for the UK's largest publishers of newspapers, magazines and websites.
- It has clauses to uphold accuracy and to protect people's privacy.
- It permits undercover reporting, but only if justified by a 'public interest' factor.
- Ipso adjudicates on complaints against editors and journalists in its member press groups, and publishes adverse and some other adjudications.
- Impress, a 'recognised' but smaller regulator, has its own code, and it too publishes adjudications.

Useful Websites

Independent Press Standards Organisation (Ipso), www.ipso.co.uk

- Ipso Annual Reports
- Editors' Code of Practice
- Ipso blog on third party complaints
- Ipso blog on scope of clause 12
- Ipso guidance on reporting of Muslims and Islam
- Ipso guidance on sex and gender identity
- Ipso guidance on researching and reporting stories involving transgender individuals

Editors' Code of Practice, www.editorscode.org.uk

- The Editors' Codebook
- History of Editors' Code
- PCC guidance on the reporting of mental health issues
- Financial Journalism Best Practice Note

Impress, www.impressorg.com

- Impress Standards Code and guidance
- Impress annual reports

Online resources

Visit the online resources at **www.mcnaes.com** to test your knowledge of this chapter with **self-test questions** and a **flashcard glossary**, and to read **updates** about law and regulatory matters affecting journalism, as well as **additional material** to further your learning.

3

Broadcast regulation

Chapter summary

→glossary Television and radio journalism in the UK is regulated by **statute** (the two key pieces of legislation are the Broadcasting Act 1996 and the Communications Act 2003) through an independent regulator, the Office of Communications (Ofcom). Ofcom's Broadcasting Code says broadcast organisations must be impartial when covering politics and societal issues, must be accurate in news, treat people fairly, respect privacy, and avoid causing harm and offence. Ofcom can impose substantial fines for breaches of the Code. The BBC is also required to be impartial and ethical, and is subject to the Code.

3.1 Introduction

In the UK commercial broadcasters—those funded by subscription or advertising revenue—are regulated to ensure their owners are law-abiding, and all broadcasters are regulated about programmes, including journalism. While newspaper, magazine and online-only publishers are not subject to statutory regulation, and so are free to be politically partisan, the statutory regulation of broadcasters means their programmes must be impartial in overall coverage of politics and public policy issues, although they are free to cover such matters in depth. The regulatory system also requires broadcasters to observe 'due accuracy' in news, and other ethical norms in general. These standards are set out in the Broadcasting Code, drawn up by the regulator, Ofcom—the Office of Communications. It has statutory power to levy substantial fines on any broadcaster, and can revoke the licence of a commercial broadcaster, for serious breach of the Code.

3.2 Why regulate broadcasters?

Historically, broadcast media have been seen as having particular potential to influence, offend or harm their audiences. As television and radio could air material instantaneously, historically they were regarded as having greater potential to provoke immediate public disorder or violence. Television was also seen as having greater potential—because moving images and sound can often portray intimate or harrowing experiences more vividly than photographs or text—to intrude into the privacy of those being filmed.

Politicians also decided that broadcasting must be regulated by statute because, for decades, transmission was only possible on analogue wavelengths. These are relatively scarce, so that was another factor in the emergence of a consensus among legislators that a regulator was needed to vet who could own commercial broadcast organisations; to specify requirements for quality in programmes and diversity in output; and to impose and enforce an impartiality requirement.

These justifications for regulating broadcast media have lost much force as technological advances mean that there has been a convergence of different types of media such that newspapers, magazines and other publishers can 'webcast' audio-visual material on websites, so the power of moving images and sound is no longer exclusive to TV and radio. Digital transmission also allows many more channels, giving the public greater freedom of choice, while social media have become the favoured means of communicating for many.

There is also an argument that the statutory regulation of broadcast journalism is a societally beneficial counterbalance to the self-regulated, partisan journalism of newspaper, magazine and website-only publishers, although it could also be said that statutory regulation means broadcast journalism tends, in its mainstream and routine forms, to be more cautious and so have less impact than newspaper journalism.

3.3 Ofcom—its role and sanctions

Commercial broadcasters must be licensed by Ofcom, which began operating in 2003 and replaced previous regulators. It is structurally independent of the Government, although the Secretary of State for Digital, Culture, Media and Sport appoints its chair and non-executive main board members. Ofcom's budget for 2025/26 is projected to be £226.8 million, an increase from the £204.7 million budget for 2024/25. This is primarily due to new responsibilities under the Online Safety Act and other new duties. Its budget is provided mainly by licence fees paid by broadcasters and through other charges it imposes. Its range of duties also includes regulating phone services. Ofcom also has duties under the Media Act 2024, which oversaw the biggest change to the public service media framework in two decades. It made changes to Ofcom's existing responsibilities as the UK's regulator of broadcast media—including around the regulatory framework for commercial radio and on demand programme services as well as on the UK's public service broadcasters ('PSB') around delivery. These are beyond the scope of this book. The Communications Act 2003 makes Ofcom responsible for ensuring the existence of a wide range of TV and radio services of high quality and wide appeal, and for maintaining plurality in broadcasting. When considering applications for national, regional or local broadcast licences, it examines the proposed programming and whether the applicant is 'fit and proper'. Ofcom monitors whether broadcasters comply with the conditions of their licences—for example, by meeting a public service obligation to provide news. Licences are granted for set periods—such as 12 years—and can be renewed.

The 2003 Act and the Broadcasting Act 1996 require Ofcom to draw up standards for programme content. These are detailed in the **Ofcom Broadcasting Code**. Anyone aggrieved by a programme's content or by how they were treated when it was made can—as long as the programme has been broadcast—complain to Ofcom, which assesses complaints against the standards set in the Code.

→glossary

for more detail, see 3.5, The BBC

Online content, even on websites run by broadcasters, is not subject to Ofcom regulation, as that content is not defined in the relevant UK law as 'broadcast' material. There is an exception: the law was amended to enable Ofcom to regulate the BBC's UK 'on demand' programme services, including BBC iPlayer.

If Ofcom upholds a complaint, it can direct that a programme should not be repeated, or order the broadcaster to air a correction or a statement of Ofcom's findings. It can impose a fine if it considers a breach of the Code to be serious or reckless.

Ofcom can shorten, suspend or, in the worst cases, revoke the licences of broadcasters which consistently breach the Code.

Case study

Following the invasion of Ukraine by Russia on 24 February 2022, on 18 March 2022, Ofcom revoked the licences of Russia Today (RT) (the global news and current affairs channel largely produced in Russia and funded by the Russian Federation) to broadcast in the UK with immediate effect. Ofcom did not consider RT's licensee fit and proper to hold a UK broadcast licence. The decision was taken in the context of 29 ongoing investigations by Ofcom into the due impartiality of RT's news and current affairs coverage of Russia's invasion of Ukraine, RT's compliance history and laws introduced in Russia which effectively criminalised independent journalism which departed from the Russian state's own news narrative. RT had previously, unsuccessfully, challenged a fine of £200,000 for repeated failures of impartiality. Ofcom concluded that it appeared impossible for RT to comply with the Broadcasting Code and that it could not be satisfied that RT could be a responsible broadcaster in the relevant circumstances (*Ofcom press release*, 18 March 2022; *Sanction decision*, 18 March 2022; *Broadcast Bulletin*, 18 July 2022).

---

see the additional material for this chapter on www.mcnaes.com for a further Ofcom ruling on 'fit and proper person'

Ofcom cannot shorten, suspend or revoke the licences of the BBC, S4C or Channel 4—they are public service broadcasters. But it can fine the BBC or S4C up to £250,000 for a Code breach. For other broadcasters, the maximum fine is £250,000 or 5 per cent of the broadcaster's qualifying revenue.

3.4 The scope of the Broadcasting Code

The Broadcasting Code's most recent version took effect in June 2023, but the Code is constantly updated online. It has rules on protecting under-18s (section 1); avoiding harm and offence (section 2); covering crime, disorder, hatred, and abuse (section 3); covering religion (section 4); due impartiality and due accuracy, and undue prominence of views and opinions (section 5); covering elections and referendums (section 6); fairness (section 7); protecting privacy (section 8); commercial references in television programming (section 9); and commercial communications in radio programming (section 10). Ofcom publishes Guidance to accompany each section of the Code, which is regularly updated.

The Code covers all broadcast output, not just journalism. Most descriptions in this chapter do not include where the Code has been adapted to cover the BBC's 'on demand' services. But see Useful Websites at the end of this chapter for the Code's full text.

3.4.1 Protecting under-18s

Section 1 of the Code says: 'Material that might seriously impair the physical, mental or moral development of people under 18 must not be broadcast' (rule 1.1). Broadcasters must take all reasonable steps to protect those under 18 (rule 1.2), it says, adding: 'Children must also be protected by appropriate scheduling from material that is unsuitable for them' (rule 1.3). 'Children' in this rule are those under 15.

3.4.2 The TV watershed

Rule 1.4 says television broadcasters must observe the 9pm 'watershed' marking the transition for free-to-air TV channels between the times of day—from 5.30am to 9pm—when children are most likely to be watching and later slots for which the audience is assumed to be more adult. (For premium subscription film services the watershed is at 8pm.)

Material unsuitable for children must not, in general, be broadcast pre-watershed (there are restrictions for example on showing the use of illegal drugs, solvent abuse and the misuse of alcohol as well as on the coverage of sexual and other offences), and the transition to post-watershed material must not be unduly abrupt (rule 1.6). For pre-watershed broadcasts clear information should, if appropriate, be given about content which may distress some children (rule 1.7)—for example, news anchors can warn if footage about to be shown portrays violence.

The section says that violence or its after-effects must be 'appropriately limited' in pre-watershed broadcasts and be justified by context. It also limits the pre-watershed televising of offensive language and portrayal or discussion of sexual behaviour and nudity.

3.4.3 Times when children are likely to be listening to radio

The term 'watershed' is not used for radio. But the Code says radio broadcasters must have particular regard to what is aired 'when children are particularly likely to be listening' (rule 1.5). Rules on content involving violence, offensive language, sexual material, and so on apply to radio at such times—for example, the school run and breakfast time.

3.4.4 Duty of care for children involved in programmes

see Useful Websites at the end of this chapter for Ofcom guidance

The Broadcasting Code's rule 1.28 says broadcasters must take 'due care' over 'the welfare and the dignity' of children under 18 who take part or are involved in programmes, irrespective of any consent they, their parents or guardians give. Ofcom guidance says that 'due' means the level of care must be 'appropriate to the particular circumstances'. Rule 1.29 says that such children must not be caused unjustified distress or anxiety by involvement in programmes or by broadcast of them.

Other elements of the Code's protection of children are dealt with elsewhere in this chapter or book.

See 3.4.10.1, Informed consent, about children; 4.11, Protecting children's welfare and privacy; 5.14, People aged under 18 in investigations, on children involved in 'pre-trial investigations' into crime, and 11.7.2, Ofcom code's protection of children involved in sexual offence cases.

3.4.5 Harm and offence

Section 2 of the Broadcasting Code says in rule 2.1 that 'generally accepted standards' must be applied to the content of television and radio broadcasts, so to provide adequate protection for the public from the inclusion of harmful and/or offensive material. Material which might cause offence includes: offensive language, violence, sex, sexual violence, humiliation, distress, violation of human dignity; discriminatory treatment or language; and treatment of people who appear to be put at risk of significant harm as a result of their taking part in a programme.

Material which might cause offence must be justified by context, and appropriate information should be broadcast where it would help avoid or minimise offence (rule 2.3)—for example, a warning that news footage shows people distressed and badly injured after a terrorist attack.

The definition of 'context' in section 2 includes the programme's editorial content, the time of the broadcast, and the likely size and composition of the potential audience.

The Code says demonstrations of exorcism, the occult, the paranormal, divination or related practices which purport to be real (as opposed to entertainment) must be treated with due objectivity, and if they are for entertainment, this must be made clear (rules 2.6 and 2.7). There is also a general rule (2.2) that factual programmes or items or portrayals of factual matter must not materially mislead the audience (though accuracy in news output is regulated under the Code's section 5: see 3.4.9, due impartiality and due accuracy). Two further recent Ofcom rulings on 'harm and offence' can be found in the additional materials for this chapter.

Case study

In 2023, Ofcom found the Mark Steyn programme on GB News, which made serious claims about the Covid-19 vaccine, was in breach of rule 2.1 of the Code. The claims were made in an interview with a guest, Dr Naomi Wolf, and included that the vaccine rollout amounted to a pre-meditated crime—'mass murder'—and was comparable to the actions of 'doctors in pre-Nazi Germany'. Ofcom was concerned that she was presented as a figure of authority, with particular knowledge and expertise which would have had the potential to impact on viewers' decisions about their health and were therefore potentially harmful. As this breach followed another breach (of rule 2.2, from March 2023), Ofcom requested GB News Ltd to attend a meeting to discuss its compliance approach (*Ofcom Broadcast Bulletin*, Issue 473, 9 May 2023).

In October 2025, the BBC was found to have been 'materially misleading', in breach of rule 2.2, by failing to disclose that the narrator of the documentary 'Gaza: How to Survive a Warzone' was the son of a Hamas official. Ofcom ordered the BBC to broadcast a prime-time statement about its conclusions. It is the first time the BBC has received a sanction from Ofcom and been ordered to make an on-air apology since 2009. Ofcom said: 'This failing had the potential to erode the significantly high levels of trust that audiences would have placed in a BBC factual programme about the Israel-Gaza war.'

3.4.6 Imitation of harmful behaviour

Programmes should not include material which, taking the context into account, condones or glamorises violent, dangerous or seriously anti-social behaviour and is likely to encourage others—particularly children—to copy it (rule 2.4, and see rules 1.12 and 1.13). Methods of suicide and self-harm must not be included in programmes except where justified editorially and by context, to avoid people imitating them (rule 2.5).

For the rationale of rule 2.5, see in this book 2.4.3; Coverage of suicides, about similar content in the Editors' Code of Practice, and see 17.11, Ethical considerations when covering deaths.

3.4.6.1 Photosensitive epilepsy

Broadcasters must take precautions to maintain a low level of risk to viewers who have photosensitive epilepsy (rule 2.12), who can be affected by broadcasts of flashing lights, including news footage of photographers using flash equipment. Where the broadcast of flashing lights and/or patterns is felt to be editorially justified, a warning must be given at the start of the broadcast.

3.4.7 Crime, disorder, hatred, and abuse

Section 3 of the Code says material likely to encourage or incite the commission of crime or lead to disorder must not be included in television or radio services (rule 3.1). The rule includes 'hate speech which is likely to encourage criminal activity or lead to disorder'. Recent decisions suggest Ofcom adopts a wider definition of hate speech than just incitement to hatred to include stereotypical portrayals. In a decision published in October 2024 against Samaa BCR (a community radio service broadcasting predominantly in Urdu), Ofcom held that statements in the broadcast of a pre-recorded 38 minute speech by the leader of a religious organisation in Pakistan amounted to antisemitic hate speech and derogatory and abusive treatment of Jewish people in breach of Rules 3.2, 3.3 and 2.3. It imposed a fine of £3,500 (*Ofcom Broadcast and On Demand Bulletin*, Issue 508, 21 October 2024).

Section 3 also includes a ban on material 'promoting or encouraging engagement in terrorism'. The Broadcasting Code uses the UK law's definition of terrorism, which is explained on **www.mcnaes.com** in the online ch. 40: 'Terrorism and the effect of counter-terrorism law'.

Rules 3.2 and 3.3 say that material containing 'hate speech' (even if not likely to encourage crime or disorder) or abusive or derogatory treatment of individuals, groups, religions or communities, must not be included in programmes except where justified by the context. The code defines 'hate speech' as 'all forms of expression which spread, incite, promote or justify hatred based on intolerance on the grounds of disability, ethnicity, gender, sex, gender reassignment, nationality, race, religion or belief, or sexual orientation, colour, genetic features, language, political or other opinion, membership of a national minority, birth or age'. The section makes clear it does not ban broadcasters interviewing people with extreme or challenging views in news and current affairs coverage, 'which is clearly in the public interest', but warns against any programme setting out to influence the audience on a subject or theme, or giving 'an uncritical platform for an authoritative figure to advocate criminal activity or disorder'.

> In 2017 Ofcom fined the Ariana International satellite channel £200,000 for broadcasting a murderous terrorist's hate speech, and in 2020 fined Club TV Limited, concerning its Peace TV Urdu international satellite channel, £200,000 for broadcasting material relating to the Islamic punishment by death of magicians and those who practise magic—see the **additional material** for this chapter on **www.mcnaes.com**.

Section 3 also says that descriptions of criminal techniques with detail which could enable the commission of crime must not be broadcast unless editorially justified (rule 3.4).

Rule 3.8 says broadcasters must use their best endeavours not to broadcast material which could endanger lives or prejudice the success of attempts to deal with a hijack or kidnapping.

* Remember

Police dealing with kidnaps may ask news media to observe a news 'blackout' to help preserve the victim's life. Also, coverage of an anti-terrorist or hostage recovery operation should not include broadcasts of live material which might alert the perpetrators to the activity of armed police or special forces who are, for example, approaching the building where the terrorists are.

3.4.7.1 Payments to criminals and witnesses

Section 3 forbids making any payment or promise of payment, directly or indirectly, to 'convicted or confessed criminals' for a programme contribution by those individuals relating to their crimes unless doing so is in the public interest (rule 3.5).

It also forbids making or offering a payment to a witness, or anyone who might reasonably be expected to be called as a witness, in an 'active' criminal case, and—unless a public interest exception applies—the ban applies too when it is 'likely or foreseeable' that the case will become 'active', as regards anyone who might reasonably be expected to be a witness (rules 3.6 and 3.7). The full wording of these rules is, in essence, identical to such rules in the Editors' Code—see 2.4.7, 2.4.8 and 19.3.3 in this book for context and why these rules exist.

for context, see 3.4.11, Public interest exceptions in the Broadcasting Code

3.4.8 Religion

Section 4 of the Broadcasting Code says that the views and beliefs of those belonging to a particular religion or religious denomination must not be subject to abusive treatment. Rule 4.7 says religious programmes containing claims that a living person (or group) has special powers or abilities must treat such claims with due objectivity, and must not be broadcast when significant numbers of children may be expected to be watching or listening.

3.4.9 Due impartiality and due accuracy

Section 5 of the Code sets out impartiality and accuracy requirements for broadcasters.

Rule 5.1 says: 'News, in whatever form, must be reported with due accuracy and presented with due impartiality.' Here, the term 'due' is key and means 'adequate or appropriate to the subject and nature of the programme'. Ofcom guidance on section 5 says more about this definition—see Useful Websites at the end of this chapter.

3.4.9.1 How impartiality must be achieved

The Code says impartiality means not favouring one side over another. It adds: 'So "due impartiality" does not mean an equal division of time has to be given to every view, or that every argument and every facet of every argument has to be represented. The approach to due impartiality may vary according to the nature of the subject, the type of programme and channel, the likely expectation of the audience as to content, and the extent to which the content and approach is signalled to the audience.'

Ofcom guidance says rule 5.1 is potentially applicable to any topic included in news programming, and that broadcasters 'should take care before making any unequivocal interpretations or statements about contentious issues'. But the guidance says there is no requirement on broadcasters to provide an alternative viewpoint in all news stories or all issues in the news, and that due impartiality might be achieved through broadcasting different viewpoints on a particular issue on successive days.

There are special impartiality requirements for news and other programmes which deal with 'matters of political or industrial controversy and matters relating to current public policy'. Owners of broadcast organisations may not use them to project their own views on such matters. The Code offers a general definition of such matters in Rule 5.4.

Rules 5.5–5.12 require the providers of television programme services, teletext services, national radio, and national digital sound programme services to preserve due impartiality on such matters in all their output (not just in news). This may be achieved over a series of programmes 'taken as a whole' rather than in a single programme. Under the Code, any personal interest of a reporter or presenter which would call the due impartiality of the programme into question must be made clear to the audience (rule 5.8). 'Views and facts must not be misrepresented' (rule 5.12).

The Code seeks to ensure the presentation of a diversity of opinion in respect of major political and industrial controversy and major matters of current public policy. It says in rule 5.12 that 'an appropriately wide range of significant views must be included and given due weight in each programme or in clearly linked and timely programmes'. Two further recent Ofcom rulings on impartiality can be found in the additional materials for this chapter.

Case study

In September 2023, Ofcom ruled that episodes of 'Saturday Morning with Esther and Phil' (Esther McVey and Philip Davies were at the time both sitting Conservative MPs) which aired on GB News were in breach of impartiality rules 5.11 and 5.12. Ofcom considered that rule 5.3 (which states that politicians should not be 'used as a newsreader, interviewer or reporter in any news programmes unless, exceptionally, it is editorially justified, and the individual's political allegiance is made clear to the audience') did not apply. One of the programmes featured a pre-recorded interview between the two presenters and the then-Chancellor of the Exchequer, Jeremy Hunt MP, together with studio discussion and analysis from guest panellists, a live interview via video link with two business owners and some viewers' comments. Ofcom did not consider that the analysis or views expressed by the panellists and the two presenters, nor the interview, contained statements which amounted to views that could be considered an 'appropriately wide range of significant views' as required under the Code. Accordingly, Ofcom found GB News to be in breach of the impartiality rules. In March 2024, Ofcom again found GB News to be in breach of its impartiality rules over its use of Sir Jacob Rees-Mogg in two episodes of '*Jacob Rees-Mogg's State of the Nation*', in May and June 2023.

However, in February 2025, the Ofcom decisions about Jacob Rees Mogg were quashed by a High Court judge, after GB news successfully applied for a judicial review. Ofcom later rescinded the previous rulings of due impartiality breaches it had made against GB News about the episodes of 'Saturday Morning with Esther and Phil'. The judge in the judicial review proceedings determined that Ofcom were misapplying Rule 5.3 of the Code, because the prohibition on politicians as newsreaders applied to news programmes, and the Rees-Mogg programme had been 'instantly and intuitively recognisable as a current affairs programme'. Ofcom and GB News agreed during the proceedings that there had been 'no issue of content partiality'. As a result of the ruling, Ofcom also discontinued investigations into six other broadcasts that involved politicians, including on Talk TV and LBC.

In May 2025, following the court ruling, Ofcom opened a consultation on 'Politicians presenting news'. As a result of the consultation, Ofcom decide not to change the rule (it decided that there was sufficient protection for audiences through the existing combination of rules 5.1 and 5.3) but instead, with effect from 20 October 2025, it updated its guidance concerning politicians presenting news shows. The updated guidance broadens the definition of a politician, expanding it to include members of the House of Lords, for example. The revised guidance explains the interaction between due accuracy and due impartiality in news (rule 5.1), and the rule which prevents politicians from presenting news programmes (5.3). The update also makes clear that, if an MP presented news in a non-news show, their status 'would likely be a relevant factor' in considering whether 'due impartiality was preserved in the programme as a whole.' The new guidance also signposts that where politicians present news in news programmes, Rule 5.3 applies. There is no Ofcom rule that prevents a politician from presenting or appearing in a non-news programme, including current affairs programmes, providing they aren't standing in an election taking place, or about to take place, and that the programme otherwise complies with the Broadcasting Code.

3.4.9.2 Impartiality in 'personal view' and 'authored' programmes

Rule 5.9 says: 'Presenters and reporters (with the exception of news presenters and reporters in news programmes), presenters of "personal view" or "authored" programmes or items, and chairs of discussion programmes may express their own views on matters of political or industrial controversy or matters relating to current public policy. However, alternative viewpoints must be adequately represented either in the programme or in a series of programmes taken as a whole. Additionally, presenters must not use the advantage of regular appearances to promote their views in a way which compromises the requirement for due impartiality. Presenter phone-ins must encourage and must not exclude alternative views.'

'Personal view' programmes are defined as those presenting a particular view or perspective. The Code says these could involve a person who is a member of a lobby group and is campaigning on a subject expressing highly partial views, or 'the considered "authored" opinion of a journalist, commentator or academic, with expertise or a specialism in an area which enables them to express opinions which are not necessarily mainstream'. The Code says a personal view or authored programme or item must be clearly signalled as such at the outset.

3.4.9.3 Undue prominence of views and opinions

Rule 5.13, which applies to local radio services and local digital sound programme services, including those at community level (but excluding any BBC services), says their broadcasters 'should not give undue prominence to the views and opinions of particular persons or bodies on matters of political or industrial controversy and matters relating to current public policy' in programming when 'taken as a whole', by which it means programming 'dealing with the same or related issues within an appropriate period'. It defines 'undue prominence of views and opinions' as a significant imbalance of views.

> Section 6 of the Code sets out specific requirements for broadcasters to maintain impartiality during election and referendum periods—see ch. 31.

3.4.9.4 Accuracy considerations

The Code's requirement in rule 5.1 is for 'due' accuracy in news, the term 'due' is key. Ofcom guidance on section 5 explains that this means 'adequate or appropriate to the programme's subject and nature'. Where a matter is of particular public interest, the requirement to present that matter with due accuracy will be correspondingly higher. See the additional material for this section for a case study about the omission of information and accuracy.

The Code says significant mistakes in news should normally be acknowledged and corrected on air quickly (rule 5.2).

Case study

Ofcom ruled that Sky News was in breach of accuracy rule 5.1 on 10 September 2022 when, during news coverage of the death of Queen Elizabeth II, presenters inaccurately described images shown of peaceful protests held in London relating to the death of Chris Kaba (a 24-year-old man who had been shot dead by the police in South London on 5 September 2022) as a crowd going to pay tribute to the Queen. However, as Sky News (and the individual presenters) broadcast subsequent clarifications, Ofcom considered that the matter had been resolved. Ofcom also considered whether there had been a breach of rule 5.2 as to the acknowledgement and correction of significant mistakes. Ofcom considered that it was appropriate to seek senior editorial sign-off for any correction and that in the circumstances there was no breach of rule 5.2 (*Ofcom Broadcast Bulletin*, Issue 468, 20 February 2023).

✱ Remember

A journalist who, to produce a dramatic effect, edits footage or an audio-recording in a way which, when it is broadcast, misrepresents a sequence of events will breach the Code, as will a broadcaster which airs a reconstruction of a news event and fails to make clear to the audience that it is not the real event.

Case study

The highest regulatory fine imposed for unethical broadcast journalism is £2 million. This was paid by Central Independent Television, part of the ITV network, after a 1998 ruling by a predecessor of Ofcom, the Independent Television Commission, that scenes in *The Connection*—a documentary which claimed to show a new heroin-smuggling route from Columbia to the UK—were fabricated. The ITC said this was 'a wholesale breach' of the trust viewers placed in programme-makers.

3.4.10 Fairness

Section 7 of the Code sets out general principles on fairness. Rule 7.1 says: 'Broadcasters must avoid unjust or unfair treatment of individuals or organisations in programmes.' The section details 'Practices to be followed'. In the Code, a failure to follow a practice can mean a rule is broken. As will be indicated, section 7 has some cross-referenced overlaps with section 8 (which is about privacy). Practice 7.2 says broadcasters and programme-makers should be fair in dealings with potential contributors to programmes unless, exceptionally, doing otherwise is justified.

3.4.10.1 Informed consent

Practice 7.3 says people or organisations who agree to take part in programmes should do so on the basis of 'informed consent'. The practice says that a person invited to contribute to a programme should—unless the subject matter is trivial or their participation minor—normally be told:

- its nature and purpose, and what it is about, and be given a clear explanation of why they have been asked to contribute, and when and where it is likely to be first broadcast;
- the kind of contribution they are expected to make—live, pre-recorded, interview, discussion, edited, unedited, etc;
- the areas of questioning and, wherever possible, the nature of other likely contributions;
- if there are any significant changes to the programme as it develops which might reasonably affect their original consent, and which might cause material unfairness.

Practice 7.3 lists other information which the person should be told for it to be likely that their consent is 'informed' (for example, see later in this chapter about welfare of contributors).

for 'public interest' see 3.4.11

Ofcom guidance on section 7 says there may be times when it is unnecessary to follow some or all of the 'informed consent' measures—'for instance, in the production of a news item where there will likely be a public interest justification for not doing so'.

If a contributor is under 16, a parent's or guardian's consent should normally be obtained, and those under 16 should not be asked for views on matters likely to be beyond their capacity to answer properly without such consent (practice 7.4).

See the **additional material** for ch. 3 on **www.mcnaes.com** for a case study on 'informed consent'.

3.4.10.2 Honouring guarantees including of confidentiality and anonymity

The Code says: 'Guarantees given to contributors, for example relating to the content of a programme, confidentiality or anonymity, should normally be honoured' (practice 7.7).

See ch. 33 for context about this ethical obligation, and cases in which journalists kept secret the identities of their sources.

3.4.10.3 Getting facts right and airing the other side of the story

Practice 7.6 says that when a programme is edited, contributions should be represented fairly. Care should be taken to ensure that any reuse of material does not result in unfairness (Practice 7.8). Practice 7.9 says that before broadcasting a factual programme, including programmes examining past events, broadcasters should take reasonable care to satisfy themselves that material facts have not been presented, disregarded or omitted in a way that is unfair to an individual or organisation; and that anyone whose omission could be unfair to an individual or organisation has been offered an opportunity to contribute. Practice 7.11 says that if a programme alleges wrongdoing or incompetence or makes other significant allegations, those concerned should normally be given an appropriate and timely opportunity to respond. The guidance explains that for this purpose, sufficient information concerning the arguments and evidence to be included in the programme needs to be given. Where a person approached to contribute to a programme chooses to make no comment or refuses to appear, the broadcast should make this clear—and give that person's explanation if it would be unfair not to do so (practice 7.12).

3.4.10.4 Welfare of contributors

In 2021, a new element was added to the list of 'informed consent' measures in practice 7.3, saying that normally contributors to programmes should be 'informed about potential risks arising from their participation in the programme which may affect their welfare (insofar as these can be reasonably anticipated at the time) and any steps the broadcaster and/or programme maker intends to take to mitigate these'. At the same time, practice 7.15 was added to the Code. It says that broadcasters should take due care over the welfare of a contributor who might be at risk of significant harm as a result of taking part in a programme, except where the subject matter is trivial or their participation minor.

These additions to the Code were the consequence of consultations which Ofcom held after receiving 'a steady rise in complaints about the mental health and wellbeing of programme participants'. Much of the concern was for people taking part in reality TV programmes, such as *Celebrity Big Brother, Loose Women* and *Love Island*. The importance of conducting such a review was underlined following the death in 2019 of Steve Dymond, a participant in (and therefore a 'contributor' to) *The Jeremy Kyle Show* in which participants were questioned about problems in their lives. Practice 7.15 says that a contributor might be regarded as being at risk of significant harm as a result of taking part in a programme for reasons including (but not limited to) the following:

- they are considered a vulnerable person (for the Code's categorisation of 'vulnerable', see 4.12 of this book);
- they are not used to being in the public eye;
- the programme involves being filmed in an artificial or constructed environment;
- the programme is likely to attract a high level of press, media and social media interest;
- key editorial elements of the programme include potential confrontation, conflict or emotionally challenging situations; or
- the programme requires them to discuss, reveal or engage with sensitive, life changing or private aspects of their lives.

Practice 7.15 says that broadcasters should conduct a risk assessment to identify any risk of significant harm to the contributor, unless it is justified in the public interest not to do so; and that the level of care due to the contributor will be proportionate to the level of risk associated with their participation in the programme. Ofcom guidance to section 7 includes an example of a 'risk matrix'—a checklist of levels of risks and considerations and measures.

Ofcom's section 7 guidance says that it recognises 'that there may be occasions when it is unnecessary or impractical to inform the contributor of potential risks, for instance in the production of many news and current affairs programmes and other programmes where it is warranted in the public interest not to do so'. But Ofcom has not excluded news and current affairs programmes from the terms of the additional 'informed consent' measure in 7.3 and the obligation in 7.15 to carry out risk assessments, though it accepts that the risk to a person arising from appearing in a news programme is likely to be 'very low' (Ofcom statement 18 December 2020—see Useful Websites). Its guidance says that consideration should be given to carrying out a risk assessment 'at an early stage to identify potential

for the Ofcom guidance, see Useful Websites at the end of this chapter risks and to consider what steps can be taken to mitigate them' and that it may be helpful to record in writing, where risks have been identified, what was discussed with the contributor about them.

3.4.11 Public interest exceptions in the Broadcasting Code

Sections 7 and 8 of the Code recognise that on occasion, programme-makers may be justified in breaching some of its normal provisions. It uses the term '**warranted**' to indicate when there must be a public interest or some other exceptional justification to do that. In those parts, the Code says that the broadcaster should be able to demonstrate (to Ofcom) why in the particular circumstances of the case, what was done was warranted and why (section 8) the public interest outweighs the right to privacy.

→glossary

In section 8 (privacy), but applying too for section 7, the Code says that examples of public interest include:

- revealing or detecting crime;
- protecting public health or safety;
- exposing misleading claims made by individuals or organisations; or
- disclosing incompetence that affects the public.

> There is a similar exception for section 3 of the Code on Crime (see 3.4.7 above). There are similar public interest exceptions in the Editors' Code—see 2.4.1 in this book. They signify the types of journalism which are considered to be of particularly high value to society.

3.4.12 Deception and misrepresentation

The Broadcasting Code says in practice 7.14 that:

> "Broadcasters or programme makers should not normally obtain or seek information, audio, pictures or an agreement to contribute through misrepresentation or deception."

But it adds that it may be warranted to use material gained by such tactics if it is in the public interest *and* the material cannot reasonably be obtained by other means. For example, a journalist who lies about the nature of a programme in order to trick a criminal into taking part (so the criminal has not given 'informed consent' to participation) will not breach the Code if the programme-makers can establish that the trickery would help expose sufficiently serious offences. Similarly, giving a false reason to an organisation when seeking consent to film its activities will not be a breach if the programme-makers can establish that this would be in the public interest, such as exposing incompetence affecting the public.

The public interest can justify journalists misrepresenting themselves—for example, by posing as members of another profession or an uninformed citizen—or intrusion into the privacy of a person who has not given any consent to be filmed or recorded (see too what the next chapter says about intrusion). But if a complaint is made, Ofcom will consider whether what was done for or included in the broadcast was **proportionate** (not excessive) and whether there was any other way the material could reasonably have been obtained. →glossary

3.4.13 Secret filming and recording—deception and privacy

Both sections 7 and 8 of the Code are relevant to secret filming. The Code says in practice 7.14 that 'surreptitious'—secret or undercover—filming or recording is a type of deception. Under the Code, material gained in this way should not normally be broadcast unless the person filmed or recorded gives informed consent for broadcast. Surreptitious filming or recording includes using long lenses or recording devices, or leaving an unattended camera or recording device on private property without the full and informed consent of the occupiers or their agent, and may also include the recording of a telephone conversation without the knowledge of the other party or deliberately continuing a recording when the other party thinks it has ended (practice 8.13 and see also the guidance to section 7).

But practice 7.14 says it may be warranted to use, without consent, material gained surreptitiously if this is in the public interest and the material cannot reasonably be obtained by other means. Practice 7.14 says that if an individual or organisation filmed or recorded surreptitiously is not identifiable in the programme their consent for the material to be broadcast will not be required.

Surreptitious filming or recording can violate privacy—for example, by recording private conversations without consent—even if the person is not identified, or the conversations included, in what is broadcast. Section 8 of the Code says any infringement of privacy in programmes, or in connection with obtaining material included in programmes, must be with the consent of the person and/or organisation or be otherwise warranted (rule 8.1 and practice 8.5), and the means of obtaining material must be 'proportionate in all the circumstances' (practice 8.9).

Practices 8.13 and 8.14 say surreptitious filming or recording should only be used and broadcast when warranted and that normally it will only be warranted if:

- there is **prima facie** evidence of a story in the public interest; and →glossary
- there are reasonable grounds to suspect that further material evidence could be obtained; and
- it is necessary to the credibility and authenticity of the programme.

The requirement for prima facie evidence is to prevent 'fishing expeditions'. Secret filming should not be used just to add 'colour' to a programme.

for explanation of 'fishing expeditions', see 2.4.4.1

Ofcom will deem a failure by programme-makers to observe the 'practices to be followed' in section 8 as breaching the Code if it leads to an unwarranted infringement of privacy.

> See the ch. 3 **additional material** for a case study in which Ofcom considered whether there had been a breach of privacy by the BBC when it broadcast secretly recorded footage of staff from a juvenile offenders centre restraining an individual.

Ofcom guidance says broadcasters should take care not to infringe the privacy of bystanders who might inadvertently be caught in a covert filming or recording—for example, it might be necessary to obscure the identities of those filmed or recorded incidentally.

3.4.13.1 Recording phone calls

Practice 8.12 of the Code says broadcasters can record telephone calls if they have, from the outset of the call, identified themselves and explained to the other person the call's purpose, and that it is being recorded for possible broadcast (if that is the case) unless it is warranted not to identify themselves or give such explanation. This means that failing to tell the person that the call is being recorded for broadcast, failing to explain its purpose or broadcasting a recording of it without the person's consent can be justified if the journalism is 'in the public interest'.

Recording a phone call without the other person's knowledge is likely to amount to a surreptitious recording, and therefore—if the intention is to broadcast it—practices 7.14 and 8.13 apply. But Ofcom guidance on section 8 says it is acceptable for journalists to record their own calls for note-taking purposes. However, if at a later stage, such a call is to be used in a broadcast, and the possibility of this was not explained to the other party at the time, the broadcaster must obtain consent, unless it is warranted not to do so.

> ((•)) See Useful Websites at the end of this chapter for Ofcom guidance, and see 2.4.4.2, Recording interviews and phone calls, on how it is not a crime to record one's own calls.

3.4.14 Privacy in general and 'doorstepping'

Section 8 of the Code includes general provisions for protecting people's privacy in relation to journalists openly filming or audio-recording. These are explained in ch. 4, which also explains the Code's use of the term 'legitimate expectation of privacy' and its restrictions on 'doorstepping'.

3.4.15 Financial journalism

Appendix 1 of the Code sets out 'binding guidance' on how journalists working for commercial broadcasters must operate to comply with legislation on investment recommendations.

3.4.16 Other parts of the Broadcasting Code

Section 9 regulates commercial references in television programming and section 10 regulates commercial communications in radio programming. These rules seek to ensure there is a distinction between editorial and advertising content, and set out specific principles of editorial independence as regards television—for example, news and current affairs programmes on television must not be sponsored (rule 9.15).

3.5 The BBC

The BBC is the biggest broadcasting organisation in the world. Its TV services include eight pan-UK TV channels, a service for Scotland and programming for Northern Ireland, Wales and English regions. It has 10 national radio stations and more than 40 regional and local radio stations, and its website.

The legal basis for the BBC's independent existence is its Royal Charter, which is renewed every 10 years, and the accompanying Agreement. These make the BBC's programmes, including its UK 'on demand' services funded by the licence fee (e.g. BBC iPlayer), subject to Ofcom regulation under the Broadcasting Code. Anyone dissatisfied with the BBC's response to a complaint can complain to Ofcom, but the complaint should first be made to the BBC. Ofcom does not regulate the BBC's World Service.

((•)) see Useful Websites at the end of this chapter for the BBC's complaints process

'On demand' services can be accessed by people at times they choose, so the Broadcasting Code requires the BBC to put in place in them measures which provide a safeguard for children in their audiences. The measures must be 'equivalent' to that achieved by scheduling of transmission times—for context, see 3.4.2 and 3.4.3 in this chapter.

Ofcom does not regulate the BBC's other online content, which include its news webpages. So, if an online news item is justifiably complained about, Ofcom cannot sanction the BBC. But if such a complainant is unhappy with the BBC's response, Ofcom can investigate and publish its 'independent opinion' as to whether the relevant content meets the BBC's Editorial Guidelines. The BBC's Editorial Guidelines set out in detail standards for its journalism, covering areas such as accuracy, impartiality, harm and offence, fairness and privacy. The Guidelines are supplemented by detailed policy guidance notes.

In March 2023 Ofcom published a new Operating Licence for the BBC, which came into effect on 1 April 2023 and which comprehensively regulates the BBC's online services, requiring the BBC to make important content available for online audiences and to make that content easily discoverable. It also imposes transparency as a core obligation. In September 2023, after controversy over the use of social media to express personal views by high-profile BBC presenters, in particular by the sports broadcaster Gary Lineker, the BBC published new guidance as to the use of social media, including by presenters of stipulated flagship programmes outside news and current affairs. This guidance allows such presenters, who the BBC says have a particular responsibility to balance commitments to both freedom of expression and impartiality because of their profile, to express opinions on issues that matter to them, including issues that may be the subject of political and public debate. The guidance, which emphasises the need for respect and civility in public discourse, says that while a programme is on air, and for a two-week window before

see Useful Websites at the end of this chapter for the Guidelines

and after the series, presenters on flagship shows must not endorse or attack a political party, nor criticise the character of individual politicians in the UK, or comment on any issue of political debate during an election period, or take up an official role for a campaigning group. Breach of the guidance may lead to disciplinary action for employees, including possible termination of employment or contracts in serious circumstances.

Recap of major points

- Broadcast journalism is regulated by the Office of Communications (Ofcom).
- Broadcast organisations must comply with the Broadcasting Code, which requires them to avoid causing harm and offence, to be fair, and to protect people's privacy.
- Ofcom can fine broadcasters for the worst transgressions of the Code and can close a commercial broadcaster which persistently or recklessly flouts it.
- There must be 'due accuracy' and 'due impartiality' in all broadcast news.

Useful Websites

Ofcom, www.ofcom.org.uk

- 'What is Ofcom?'
- The Ofcom Broadcasting Code
- 'Statement: Protecting participants in TV and radio programmes'—Ofcom's statement of 18 December 2020 about additional Code content to protect programme participants
- Consultation on proposed amendment to Rule 5.3 of the Ofcom Broadcasting Code
- 'Procedures for handling complaints relating to BBC online material'

BBC, www.bbc.com

- 'About the BBC'
- 'Editorial Guidelines'—BBC Editorial Values and Standards
- 'Guidance: Secret Recording'

BBC, 'Contact the BBC: Complaints', www.bbc.co.uk

Online resources

Visit the online resources at **www.mcnaes.com** to test your knowledge of this chapter with **self-test questions** and a **flashcard glossary**, and to read **updates** about law and regulatory matters affecting journalism, as well as **additional material** to further your learning.

4

Journalism avoiding unjustified intrusion

Chapter summary

Intruding into the private lives of people or onto people's property or into confidential business affairs, can be both a matter of law and regulation. The legal aspects will be dealt with later in the book, but as far as regulation is concerned, journalists should avoid unnecessary intrusion into people's lives, but know when it can be justified. This chapter shows how regulators' adjudications on complaints about intrusion provide guidance covering a far wider range of situations than is dealt with in privacy and confidentiality case law. Ch. 26 covers the law of confidence and ch. 27 covers privacy law. Ch. 34 covers other criminal offences. Few people can afford to go to court if they feel their privacy is breached. Many complain to regulators about journalists taking photos, filming and audio-recording, and about what is published. A journalist could be accused of harassment, which is unethical and could also be a crime (see 4.6). Publishing photographs or footage supplied by the public, or material from social media sites can be unethical. This chapter also shows how the codes seek to minimise intrusion into grief and have particular rules for when children are interviewed, filmed or photographed by journalists.

4.1 Introduction—the codes and intrusion

People may suffer intrusion if they are photographed, filmed or audio-recorded without their knowledge or consent, even if in a public space. Or the intrusion may be from the simple act of obtaining their information as well as the publication of such material, or other intrinsically private information—for example, someone's medical records, or what an ex-partner betrays of an individual's confidential conversations or sex life. Much of this is covered by the ethical codes, but it also overlaps with people's legal rights. See Part 4 of this book for how the laws of confidentiality, privacy and copyright can affect a journalist.

The codes used by the UK media regulators—the Independent Press Standards Organisation (Ipso), Impress and Ofcom—introduced in chs. 2 and 3—are not law but

see 27.5 on how courts assess a reasonable expectation of privacy

may be referred to by judges in court cases. Where privacy is concerned, the press codes use the criterion of a 'reasonable expectation of privacy' as a starting point for the regulator to assess complaints that intrusion occurred because of what a media organisation did. Ofcom's Broadcasting Code uses the term 'legitimate expectation', but this means the same.

If the regulator decides the complainant, in the relevant circumstances, did have that expectation of privacy, intrusion will breach the relevant code, unless the media organisation can demonstrate that it has a sufficiently strong **public interest** justification for publishing what it did.

→glossa

see 2.6 on the importance of audit trails

The 'public interest' justification signifies that the story being pursued is of a particularly high value to society.

4.1.1 Public interest exceptions in the codes

The public interest exceptions in the Editors' Code and Broadcasting Code are outlined in chs. 2 and 3. The exceptions can, for example, allow use of intrusive methods to expose crime or negligence imperilling people's safety, or expose that the public has been misled by an organisation or individual, such as a politician, or when a media organisation aims to publish material to contribute to a general debate about an important issue. The Impress Code has similar provision. There are differences in how each code defines the exceptions and when they can apply.

See 2.4.1, Public interest exceptions in the Editors' Code; 2.5, Impress and its Code; and 3.4.11, Public interest exceptions in the Broadcasting Code.

* Remember

All three codes make clear that if people complain that a media organisation has unjustifiably published private information about them, the regulator will take into account any extent to which it was already in the public domain. For example, a celebrity may have previously chosen to publicise information about their private life, to gain publicity, which may reduce or nullify the likelihood of a complaint being upheld about publication of similar material. Remember too that breach of privacy is not the only kind of intrusion covered by the codes, as this chapter explains.

Ofcom will only adjudicate if the material is broadcast—see 3.3

4.1.2 Justifiable intrusion is proportionate

Even when a media organisation can successfully argue that a public interest factor justified some intrusion, a media regulator will consider the degree of harm or distress which the act(s) of gathering the material and/or its publication has caused to the person who brought the case.

→glossary

Regulators say the media must adopt a '**proportionate**' approach to the intrusion, if any intrusion is justifiable. There may be a strong public interest in capturing and showing something of the situation, or revealing part of what was said, but not everything. A face in the image captured may need to be pixelated before publication, to prevent violation of privacy, and it may be that only some of the private information in a document or someone's conversation should be published.

✱ Remember

As regards use of cameras and microphones, this chapter mainly considers what the regulators' codes and adjudications say about journalists working openly. What codes say about covert (undercover) photography, filming or recording is covered in chs. 2 and 3. But even when journalists work openly, it is possible that people—for example, in crowds or in the chaos after an accident—might be unaware that their images or voices are being captured.

4.1.3 Adjudications cited in this chapter and its additional material

When this book went to press, Impress—the youngest of the regulators—had only adjudicated on a few complaints about intrusion into privacy, and/or harassment (with none upheld). As a consequence this chapter refers only to adjudications by Ofcom and Ipso. These adjudications (rulings) can be read online. The **additional material** for this chapter on **www.mcnaes.com** has relevant case studies, including of adjudications alluded to in this chapter, and includes a 'Checklist on Intrusion'.

For the Editors' Code in full, see this book's Appendix 1. See Useful Websites at the end of this chapter for full text of the other codes, and regulators' webpages, where adjudications can be found.

4.2 The codes' general protection of privacy

for how a code can figure in a privacy lawsuit, see 27.9

Breaching the codes is not necessarily to breach privacy law, but complying with the codes is ethical and helps reduce the likelihood of a privacy lawsuit, or of such a claim succeeding.

Clause 2 (Privacy) of the Editors' Code, used by Ipso, states:

> "i) Everyone is entitled to respect for their private and family life, home, physical and mental health, and correspondence, including digital communications.
>
> ii) Editors will be expected to justify intrusions into any individual's private life without consent. In considering an individual's reasonable expectation of privacy, account will be taken of the complainant's own public disclosures of information and the extent to which the material complained about is already in the public domain or will become so.
>
> iii) It is unacceptable to photograph individuals, without their consent, in public or private places where there is a reasonable expectation of privacy."

Note that subclause i) draws on the wording of Article 8 (see 4.1). References to photography in the Editors' Code include filming.

Case study

Ipso has ruled that a media organisation breached clause 2 by revealing, without justification under the code, that a man was a refugee. Ipso said: 'In general, an individual's immigration status is personal, sensitive information which relates to the individual's private and family life' (*A man v Thurrock.nub.news*, 17 February 2021).

The Impress Code clause 7 begins: 'Except where justified by the public interest, publishers must respect people's reasonable expectation of privacy'. It lists factors likely to determine whether the expectation is reasonable—for example, whether the information relates to family or health matters.

for the term 'practice', see 3.4.10

→glossary

Rule 8.1 of the Broadcasting Code says: 'Any infringement of privacy in programmes, or in connection with obtaining material included in programmes, must be warranted.' Practice 8.3 says: 'When people are caught up in events which are covered by the news they still have a right to privacy in both the making and the broadcast of a programme, unless it is warranted to infringe it.' The rule applies too to programmes which revisit events. The term '**warranted**' in the Broadcasting Code includes reference to public interest exceptions, and a 'practice' is guidance to uphold a rule.

4.3 Public and private places

Ipso has repeatedly ruled that normally photographing a person in a public space, such as a public highway, does not breach clause 2 of the Editors' Code. Usually there is no reasonable expectation of privacy there and so publication of such photos does not breach the clause when this does not reveal anything private about the individual. For example, Ipso has ruled that a man was in a public place, and did not have a reasonable expectation of privacy, when he was seated inside a coffee shop near a large window, clearly visible to passers-by, and when the photo taken of him there from outside did not show him engaging in any private activity (*Luck v The Mail on Sunday*, 23 May 2019). However, see also 4.7, Coverage of accidents, major incidents, suffering, distress and deaths.

see too 4.11 on families in public places

The Impress Code's guidance says that people may have a reasonable expectation of privacy in a public place 'when they are engaging in an activity that is part of their private or family life'.

Ofcom says that normally filming and recording someone in a public place does not breach the Broadcasting Code. But section 8 of this Code says:

> Legitimate expectations of privacy will vary according to the place and nature of the information, activity or condition in question, the extent to which it is in the public domain (if at all) and whether the individual concerned is already in the public eye.

> There may be circumstances where people can reasonably expect privacy even in a public place. Some activities and conditions may be of such a private nature that filming or recording, even in a public place, could involve an infringement of privacy. People under investigation or in the public eye, and their immediate family and friends, retain the right to a private life, although private behaviour can raise issues of legitimate public interest. ”

The Broadcasting Code adds in practice 8.4: 'Broadcasters should ensure that words, images or actions filmed or recorded in, or broadcast from, a public place, are not so private that prior consent is required before broadcast from the individual or organisation concerned, unless broadcasting without their consent is warranted.'

see Useful Websites at the end of this chapter for Ofcom guidance

Ofcom guidance says: 'Some activities and conditions may be of such a private nature that filming, even in a public place where there was normally no reasonable expectation of privacy, could involve an infringement of privacy. For example, a child in state of undress, someone with disfiguring medical condition or CCTV footage of suicide attempt.'

Ofcom guidance says property which is privately owned but readily accessible to the public, such as a railway station or shop, can be a public place.

Case study

Mr and Mrs R complained to Ofcom about a five-second clip in a Channel 4 documentary, *When Cruises Go Wrong*, in a segment on problems arising from excessive consumption of alcohol. It showed Mrs R and another woman seemingly involved in an altercation. Mr R appeared to be attempting to break it up by putting himself between them. Mrs R's face was not visible, while his was visible briefly and his voice could be heard. Mrs R complained that they did not consent to this clip of mobile phone footage being shown. She said her husband had been trying to stop two 'extremely drunk' women from 'attacking' her. Channel 4 argued that the couple did not have a legitimate expectation of privacy because they were in a public place, on a busy cruise ship, and members of the public witnessed the event (and one had filmed it). Ofcom agreed it was a public place, but said that being involved in a physical altercation or intervening to protect your spouse was a sensitive situation. Therefore, Ofcom ruled that the couple had a 'legitimate expectation of privacy', even though it was a 'limited' expectation because of the circumstances, and that the broadcast of the footage amounted to an interference with their privacy. However, it ruled that the interference was warranted in the public interest, because the footage showed how cruise ships can struggle to deal with fights and physical altercations in the absence of the police. Ofcom said it took into account that the footage was very brief, that the programme did not name the couple or reveal anything of a particularly personal or confidential nature about them and that Mrs R was not readily identifiable except possibly to a very limited number of people who had identified Mr R from the footage because they knew him (*Ofcom Broadcast Bulletin*, issue 414, 9 November 2020).

For Ofcom adjudications on coverage of arrests of people in public places, see the **additional material** for this chapter on **www.mcnaes.com**. For legal context about the privacy implications of arrests and covering incidents in public places, see 5.11.3 and ch. 27, including 27.5 on the *Peck* case, which involved broadcast of CCTV footage of a suicide attempt, and ch. 35 on the legal right to photograph and film in public streets.

4.3.1 'Long lens' photos

for use of cameras on drones, see 4.3.5

Unless the camera is hidden, use of a 'long' (telephoto) lens does not fall under clause 10 of the Editors' Code, a clause explained in 2.4.4. But a long lens can mean people are unaware of being photographed.

Case study

In 2022, Downton Abbey star Lily James complained about *MailOnline*'s use of photographs of her having dinner with two other individuals, away from the front of a restaurant. She said that the set of photographs had been taken and published in breach of Clause 2. She said she had intentionally sat in a corner towards the back of the restaurant so that she was not readily visible to other diners, away from public view; therefore, she said, she had a reasonable expectation of privacy. The paper said she must have been visible from the street, otherwise the photographer—who was an agency photographer, rather than a member of the public—would not have been able to photograph her from there, as he had shot the photographs from a public street and through the windows of the restaurant. Ipso accepted she 'was not engaged in "public-facing" work and there was no suggestion that she was engaged in a public activity.' The photograph had been taken surreptitiously from outside the restaurant and with the aid of a 200mm camera-lens. Taking these factors into account, the Committee considered that James had a reasonable expectation of privacy. The Committee then considered whether the public interest in publishing the photographs was sufficient to outweigh her reasonable expectation of privacy. The Mail said there was a public interest as the pictures appeared to show James meeting others inside a restaurant, in contravention of the Covid-19 regulations in force at the time, which allowed only for meetings between people from different households for the purposes of business. James said it was a 'working dinner'. The Committee accepted that, in certain circumstances, there may be a public interest in reporting on breaches of Covid regulations. However, it did not consider that the public interest had been satisfactorily established in this case where, prior to publication, James's position that the meeting complied with the rules in place at the time had been made known and had not been challenged. (02643-21 *James v Mail Online*, 4 May 2022)

See too the Prince Harry case study in the **additional material** for ch. 4 on **www.mcnaes.com**.

4.3.2 **Crowds**

Ipso and Ofcom will not adjudicate against images of people in crowds being published if what is shown is innocuous or in the public interest. But a regulator may make an adverse adjudication if there was an intrusive focus on an individual—for example, if they were identifiably shown as having fallen ill in the crowd. Note, however, there may also be personal data issues under the Data Protection Act arising in these cases (see ch. 28).

see too 4.11.1, Children in crowds and at public occasions

4.3.3 **Addresses**

this chapter's use of 'not upheld' is explained in 2.4

Ipso says that in general disclosing someone's home address does not breach clause 2 of the Editors' Code, but may in special circumstances—for example, a person with a 'high public profile' may face security problems if their address is published and is not already in the public domain (*Beckham v Mail Online*, issued 6 June 2017, not upheld).

Practice 8.2 of the Broadcasting Code says information disclosing the location of a person's home or family should not be revealed without permission, unless this is warranted. Ofcom adjudications show this does not mean that shots of a person's home filmed from the public street cannot be broadcast, because the image alone does not reveal to many people where the home is, but that the street name should not be broadcast unless relevant, that the property's street number should be blurred if in shot, and other particularly distinguishing characteristics of the property should not be shown.

4.3.4 **People at home and the home's interior**

Publishing images of people in their homes, or of the home's interior, without their consent is likely to breach any of the codes unless a public interest exception applies. Ofcom has on several occasions ruled that footage in the Channel 5 series *Can't Pay? We'll Take It Away!*—showing High Court Enforcement Officers legally entering homes to seize possessions in lieu of debts—intruded too far into the privacy of families (see, for example, *Ofcom Broadcast Bulletin*, issue 367, 3 December 2018). Ipso rulings show that if a photograph is taken from a public street, showing the exterior of someone's home or a person who is visible—for example, standing in a driveway—to any passer-by on the street, taking and publishing it will not breach clause 2 of the Editors' Code if the person is not engaged in private activity (for example, see *Yates v Lyynnews.co.uk*, 4 December 2020; *Abbasi v Manchester Evening News*, 28 October 2021). But publication of a photo of someone in a back garden which could not be seen from a public place will breach clause 2 unless a justification applies under the code (for example, see *A man v Thurrock.nub,news*, cited earlier, upheld).

✱ Remember

Ipso has said that a journalist venturing onto private property could be an intrusive breach of clause 2 (*Beckham v Mail Online*, cited earlier). For trespass laws, see 35.3.

For regulators' adjudications on people being filmed or photographed after opening their home's door, see this chapter's **additional material** on **www.mcnaes.com**. Legal and regulatory issues arising from journalists accompanying police in operations to arrest people in or to search their properties are covered in the **additional material** for ch. 5.

4.3.5 Using drones to get images

for the BBC guidance, see Useful Websites at the end of this chapter

Using a drone to get images may well mean that people on the ground do not realise they are 'on camera'. It can create a high risk of intrusion.

BBC Editorial Guidelines on privacy say: 'Drones should not normally be used to identify individuals without their consent, or capture close-up images of areas such as private homes, private gardens or private areas of offices without the consent of the owner, unless they can be seen from a public vantage point or there is a public interest that outweighs any legitimate expectations of privacy.'

4.4 Doorstepping

Section 8 of the Broadcasting Code defines 'doorstepping' as 'the filming or recording of an interview or attempted interview with someone, or announcing that a call is being filmed or recorded for broadcast purposes, without any prior warning'.

Doorstepping is an ambush technique which can be used against someone unlikely to agree to an interview—for example, a crook being investigated or a politician in a scandal, when they open the door at their home or workplace, or answer their phone.

Practice 8.11 of the Code says: 'Doorstepping for factual programmes should not take place unless a request for an interview has been refused or it has not been possible to request an interview, or there is good reason to believe that an investigation will be frustrated if the subject is approached openly, and it is warranted to doorstep.' In 2017 Ofcom ruled that the BBC consumer affairs programme *X-Ray* did not breach the Code by 'doorstepping' a car dealer on his showroom's forecourt about complaints by car purchasers. Ofcom said there was a public interest justification (*Ofcom Broadcast Bulletin*, issue 330, 5 June 2017).

Practice 8.11 adds that broadcasters may normally, without prior warning, interview, film or record people 'in the news' when they are in public places. It also makes clear that vox-pops (short surveys sampling the views of random members of the public) are not considered 'doorstepping'.

4.5 The codes' protection against harassment

Clause 3 (Harassment) of the Editors' Code says:

> “i) Journalists must not engage in intimidation, harassment or persistent pursuit.
>
> ii) They must not persist in questioning, telephoning, pursuing or photographing individuals once asked to desist; nor remain on property when asked to leave and must not follow them. If requested, they must identify themselves and whom they represent.
>
> iii) Editors must ensure these principles are observed by those working for them and take care not to use non-compliant material from other sources.
>
> For a case on the application of clause 3 against a media publisher, see the *James v MailOnline* case referred to earlier.”

The Broadcasting Code's practice 8.7 says: 'If an individual or organisation's privacy is being infringed, and they ask that the filming, recording or live broadcast be stopped, the broadcaster should do so, unless it is warranted to continue.'

Under the codes, a journalist should normally respect a person's refusal to answer questions or their request to stop photographing, filming or recording them. But the public interest exceptions may mean that a journalist could, for example, be justified in further attempts to question a fraudster about a fraud or a politician about involvement in a scandal, including pursuing them for a short while with such questions, or photographing or filming them as they walk away.

The Impress Code clause 5, on harassment, says publishers must ensure that journalists do not engage in intimidation. There is no public interest exception to clause 5. Impress guidance includes that sending a person repeated and unsolicited emails can be harassment.

4.6 Law against harassment

Irrespective of what the codes say, paparazzi who hound people could be prosecuted or sued under the Protection from Harassment Act 1997, which created criminal offences and civil remedies.

The 1997 Act—created to deal with obsessive stalkers rather than journalists—says harassment can include causing alarm or distress and is 'a course of conduct', which means the conduct must have occurred at least twice. It also contains specific stalking offences—following, watching or spying on someone could be stalking if alarm or distress is caused. For a case on the application of the Act against a media publisher see *Sube v NGN and others* [2020] EWHC 1125: only an exceptional case, involving nothing short of a conscious or negligent abuse of media freedom, will justify a finding of harassment.

See the **additional material** for ch. 4 on **www.mcnaes.com** for case studies on harassment law, including whether publishing articles can be harassment. One case concerns a warning given controversially by police to a reporter after he sought comment from a convicted fraudster about a website scam she was running. She had complained he was 'harassing' her.

4.7 Coverage of accidents, major incidents, suffering, distress, and deaths

Accidents and major incidents are newsworthy. Photographs and footage help the public understand what has happened. Such events may occur in public places, but there are sensitivities in covering them, and a number of clauses in the codes may need to be considered (for example, privacy, harassment, intrusion into grief, children and hospitals) before publishing information or images of such incidents. The Kerslake Report on the Manchester Arena attack on 22 May 2017 found that 'the behaviour of some of the media covering the Manchester attack fell well short of the [relevant code] standards'. Ipso has issued special guidance on the reporting of major incidents.

Case study

In 2015 Ipso ruled that the *Derby Telegraph* breached three clauses of the Editors' Code because a member of its staff took a photo of two 11-year-old girls—one of them injured—following a traffic accident outside a school, which was published online. It showed the injured girl lying on the pavement, with her face pixelated, a girl next to her, who was identifiable, and two passers-by. The newspaper did not know the girls were sisters and therefore that publishing the image was likely to identify both. The girls' mother complained that the photo depicted a distressing incident for her daughters, and was taken when everyone involved was in shock and emergency services had yet to arrive. Publication of the photo added to the family's distress and, as it related to her daughters' welfare, it should not have been used without her consent, she said, adding that she was also concerned that the newspaper had not pixelated the face of her uninjured daughter. The newspaper had not been able to contact the family as the injured girl's name had not been released. After hearing of the complaint, the newspaper immediately removed the image from its website. Ipso said the injured girl had, in the circumstances, including her age, a reasonable expectation of privacy. Photographing her breached clause 2 of the Code and publishing the photo, which had risked notifying friends and relatives of the accident, breached clause 4 (intrusion into shock) and clause 6 (children) because it was done without parental consent. The *Telegraph* suggested that the accident was of public interest, because of previously expressed concerns about the area's road safety.

But Ipso said the *Telegraph* had not explained how publishing the photo contributed to that public interest and that no 'exceptional' public interest—it had to be exceptional because children were involved—appeared to exist (*A woman v Derby Telegraph*, adjudication issued 13 February 2015). Clauses 4 and 6 are explained later in this chapter.

for more on 'exceptional public interest', see 4.11

Ipso says that a person in a public place receiving medical treatment or experiencing an emergency may have a reasonable expectation of privacy (*McDonald v Evening Telegraph (Dundee)*, 9 August 2019, not upheld). But pixelating the person's face in a published image will help ensure there is no breach of the Editors' Code.

Practice 8.16 of the Broadcasting Code, on covering of suffering and distress, says: 'Broadcasters should not take or broadcast footage or audio of people caught up in emergencies, victims of accidents or those suffering a personal tragedy, even in a public place, where that results in an infringement of privacy, unless it is warranted or the people concerned have given consent.'

* Remember

To some extent, Ipso and Ofcom will allow exceptions to their normal privacy rules in respect of coverage of major incidents such as terrorist bombings because of the very strong public interest in showing what has happened, including the distress in people's faces, even if they have not consented to being photographed or filmed.

See 'Coverage of major incidents' in the **additional material** for ch. 4 on **www.mcnaes.com**.

4.7.1 Prohibitions on intrusion into grief or shock

Clause 4 (Intrusion into grief or shock) of the Editors' Code says:

> "In cases involving personal grief or shock, enquiries and approaches must be made with sympathy and discretion and publication handled sensitively. These provisions should not restrict the right to report legal proceedings."

see too 4.15 on needing to be sensitive

see Useful Websites at the end of this chapter for this Ipso guidance

Ipso guidance on reporting deaths and inquests says journalists must also use sensitivity when choosing pictures or videos, and says if there is a complaint it will consider whether graphic information was published or asked about. Its guidance on reporting major incidents says checks should be made on whether photos and footage show injured people identifiably or a dead person.

The Ipso guidance also warns that clause 4 is breached if a media organisation breaks news of a death to the deceased's family either directly by a journalist seeking comment or by publishing some detail about the death. This could happen, for example, if a photo of a fatal road accident scene shows a vehicle's registration number,

ch. 17 covers inquests

or some other unique characteristic. For a recent example, see the recent Ipso ruling 01761-24 *The family of John Chapman v The Sun*.

The same principle applies to incidents in which someone is or could be badly hurt, because for relatives to hear or realise this from media coverage would be intrusion into shock (a point Ipso made in its ruling in the *Derby Telegraph* case, cited earlier, in which a published photo identified the accident victim). Even if a photo does not show a face, what the person is wearing may mean relatives will realise who it portrays. The 'public interest exceptions' in the Editors' Code do not apply to clause 4 and so cannot justify such intrusion.

Practice 8.18 of the Broadcasting Code says broadcasters should take care not to reveal the identity of a person who has died, or of a victim of an accident or violent crime, unless and until it is clear that the next of kin have been informed or unless it is warranted.

Broadcast of images or descriptions in coverage of major incidents or any crime could, depending on the context, breach the Broadcasting Code's section 8 (privacy) or prohibitions explained in this book in 3.4.5, Harm and offence.

Case study

In May 2024, Ipso ruled that an *Aberdeenlive.news* article which reported on the open court case of a man who had pleaded guilty to the rape and assault of a woman not previously known to him, while not in breach of clause 2 (privacy) or 11 (identification of a victim of sexual assault), had breached clause 4. The article described the rape and assault and included details of the attack, as well as the complainant's reactions during it. The Committee made clear that the publication was entitled to publish the article: it emphasised that journalists' right to report on court proceedings is an essential part of open justice and is also in the public interest. However, it concluded in the context of the crime and article, the inclusion of the extremely personal information about the complainant's reaction to the attack amounted to an unnecessary level of detail which intruded into her grief and shock. (22051-23 *A woman v Aberdeenlive.news*)

4.7.2 Funerals and the bereaved

Ofcom guidance says that at funerals, programme-makers should respect requests to withdraw. Ipso guidance is that the wishes of the family should be taken into account, where they are known or can reasonably be inferred. It notes a funeral procession may happen in public view but says that care should be taken with photographs of people in states of extreme distress.

see too 4.12, Vulnerable people

The Broadcasting Code, section 8, warns broadcasters that the bereaved may need special consideration as a 'vulnerable person' who may not be able to give informed consent to be featured in a programme.

See also the **additional material** for ch. 4 on **www.mcnaes.com** about covering traumatic past events.

4.8 Privacy in hospital and institutions

Clause 8 of the Editors' Code says journalists must identify themselves and obtain permission from a responsible executive of hospitals or similar institutions before entering non-public areas to pursue inquiries. This reflects that all patients have a reasonable expectation of privacy during their treatment, and that some may not be well enough to make the best decision if approached for an interview. The Code allows this clause to be overridden if there is a sufficient public interest for a journalist to go into a non-public area—see the **additional material** case studies on **www.mcnaes.com**. The Impress Code guidance says people in hospitals, private clinics and residential homes may reasonably expect a high level of privacy, and that journalists should 'take great care' when conducting inquiries there, but that these can be justified if in the public interest.

The Broadcasting Code practice 8.8 says:

> "When filming or recording in institutions, organisations or other agencies, permission should be obtained from the relevant authority or management, unless it is warranted to film or record without permission. Individual consent of employees or others whose appearance is incidental or where they are essentially anonymous members of the general public will not normally be required. However, in potentially sensitive places such as ambulances, hospitals, schools, prisons or police stations, separate consent should normally be obtained before filming or recording and for broadcast from those in sensitive situations (unless not obtaining consent is warranted). If the individual will not be identifiable in the programme then separate consent for broadcast will not be required."

'informed consent' is explained in 3.4.10.1

Broadcasters may need to ask the people filmed or recorded to sign consent forms so that, should there be a complaint, there is proof of their informed consent.

By 'separate consent', the Broadcasting Code means there needs to be a two-stage consent—for example, consent must normally be obtained before filming/recording begins, and then further consent must be obtained from those individuals for the broadcasting of footage or audio which identifies them. It would be warranted to record or film and broadcast such material without their consent if the public interest justifies that, such as when showing retrospectively how in a police station, officers dealt with an individual later convicted of the crime being investigated.

4.9 Health information generally

Information about an individual's health, such as an illness or condition, is normally private. It is also considered to be special category data under data protection laws (see ch. 28). If that information leaks out—even when relayed by a friend or relative with good motive—publishing it without the individual's consent (or in the case of a child, parental consent, see later) would almost certainly breach each code's provision about privacy, unless a sufficiently strong public interest justification applied.

The Editors' Codebook warns that early speculation about whether a woman is pregnant, or accurately reporting a pregnancy before the normal 12-week ultrasound scan confirms it, can be intrusive.

The Codebook is introduced in 2.4, and see Useful Websites at the end of this chapter. See also the *Soames v The Sunday Times* case study in the **additional material** for ch. 4. Publication of medical or therapy details without the individual's consent could breach confidentiality, privacy or data protection law—see 26.2, 27.9 and 28.2.6.

4.10 Relationships and communications

for context, see 4.1.2, Justifiable intrusion is proportionate

Ipso, Impress and Ofcom are likely to adjudicate that publishing intimate details of a person's relationships, such as their sex life, or content from their private communications, without their consent breaches the relevant code's privacy provision, unless there is a public interest justification, when the 'proportionality' principle could still mean that little detail should be published.

Clause 2 of the Editors' Code specifically protects the privacy of correspondence, including digital communications.

Case study

In 2017 Ipso ruled that the *Daily Star Sunday* breached clause 2 by publishing the content of phone texts a woman alleged were sent to her by an 'England ace' celebrity (apparently the woman revealed the private texts to the newspaper—they were not 'hacked'). But Ipso ruled that the paper's coverage of her account of the alleged relationship—in which she said where they kissed, when they first had sex, and that he misled her by not telling her he was still in another relationship—did not otherwise breach clause 2. Ipso said the detail given was 'limited' and she had a right to freedom of expression—a right enshrined in the Code—to tell her story (*A man v Daily Star Sunday*, 21 June 2017).

for privacy law context regarding relationships, see 27.3.4

Clause 10 of the Editors' Code specifically bans the 'interception' of private and mobile phone calls, messages and emails. That clause too is covered by the Code's public interest exceptions. But a journalist who 'hacks' phone calls, messages or emails risks being prosecuted for a criminal offence, as the Impress Code guidance warns.

for context on recording calls, see 2.4.4.2

Ch. 34 outlines the law against hacking and the 'phone-hacking' scandal in which people's private voicemail messages were illegally accessed ('intercepted') by or on behalf of journalists seeking stories. But recording your own phone calls is not 'hacking'.

4.11 Protecting children's welfare and privacy

The Editors' Code, clause 6 (Children), says:

" i) All pupils should be free to complete their time at school without unnecessary intrusion.

ii) They must not be approached or photographed at school without permission of the school authorities.

iii) Children under 16 must not be interviewed or photographed on issues involving their own or another child's welfare unless a custodial parent or similarly responsible adult consents.

iv) Children under 16 must not be paid for material involving their welfare, nor parents or guardians for material about their children or wards, unless it is clearly in the child's interest.

v) Editors must not use the fame, notoriety or position of a parent or guardian as sole justification for publishing details of a child's private life. "

Clause 6 means that the school's permission is normally needed for a journalist to approach, photograph or film a pupil of any age on school premises.

The clause is subject to the Code's public interest exceptions. But the Code warns: 'An exceptional public interest would need to be demonstrated to override the normally paramount interests of a child under 16.'

Clause 6 i) can be breached if what is published has an adverse effect on the child's time at school, even if the subject matter is not about the school. Ipso ruled that a newspaper's publication of an account of a woman's disputed allegations of domestic abuse, made against her husband, represented an unnecessary intrusion into their children's time at school because the family was identifiable from details published (*A man v Isle of Wight County Press*, 10 June 2021).

The Editors' Code may not be breached by a photo or footage which has a focus on a child in a public place, but the definition of 'welfare' in clause 6 is wide. Ipso adjudications make clear that publishing images in which children are identifiable concerns their welfare if they are shown in a way or circumstance which may cause them distress, embarrassment, humiliation or have another adverse effect on them, and that in such circumstances consent is normally needed from an adult with legal parental responsibility or a similarly responsible adult to obtain the image and to publish it. Ipso also publishes separate guidance on reporting on children (see Useful websites below).

Case study

In 2001 the PCC upheld a complaint by author J.K. Rowling that *OK!* magazine breached clauses 2 and 6 by using 'long lens' photos of her eight-year-old daughter on a public beach wearing a swimsuit. The PCC said she was vulnerable to comments from her peers and that J.K. Rowling's solicitors had stated the girl was embarrassed by attention as a result of the photographs.

See the *Derby Telegraph* case earlier in this chapter for another example of breach of clause 6.

Some celebrities ask Ipso to record that they do not want their children's faces shown in media coverage. The Editors' Codebook says that editors should determine the position in any particular case.

Under clause 6, consent from an adult with legal parental responsibility or a similarly responsible adult is needed before interviewing any child about a matter which concerns their welfare—for example, health or family life—as the child might say something they could regret after publication. The interview itself could distress the child. Asking a child questions by email or via social media would be an interview. Ipso has warned that the term 'interview' includes a media organisation's publication of a statement a child under 16 has posted online, even if it has not contacted the child. So consent from an adult with legal parental responsibility will normally be needed to report or reproduce an online post, even though the child has already published it, if the child's welfare could be affected.

for privacy law context, see the *Weller* case in 27.3.1.1

Impress Code clauses 3.1 and 3.2 have provision to protect children's welfare, including about when they can be photographed. Its guidance on privacy says a family may have a reasonable expectation of privacy in a public place, for example when on a shopping expedition.

The Broadcasting Code has protection for children's welfare in section 8, on privacy. This too is subject to public interest exceptions. Practice 8.20 says: 'Broadcasters should pay particular attention to the privacy of people under 16. They do not lose their rights to privacy because, for example, of the fame or notoriety of their parents or because of events in their schools.'

Practice 8.21 says:

> “Where a programme features an individual under 16 or a vulnerable person in a way that infringes privacy, consent must be obtained from:
>
> - a parent, guardian or other person of eighteen or over in loco parentis; and
> - wherever possible, the individual concerned;
> - unless the subject matter is trivial or uncontroversial and the participation minor, or it is warranted to proceed without consent.”

Practice 8.22 says that persons under 16 and vulnerable people should not be questioned about private matters without the consent of a parent, guardian or other person of 18 or over in loco parentis (in the case of persons under 16), or a person with primary responsibility for their care (in the case of a vulnerable person), unless it is warranted to proceed without consent.

This Code, like the Editors' Code, states that normally broadcasters must get a school's permission before filming pupils—see practice 8.8, cited earlier in this chapter at 4.8. The Broadcasting Code includes other general protection for under-18s involved in programmes, covered in this book's 3.4.4 and 3.4.10.1.

4.11.1 Children in crowds and at public occasions

Publishing innocuous photos or footage of crowds does not normally intrude into the lives of children shown in them at random. A regulator will probably accept a parent's consent for a child being a spectator or participator at an event which is likely to be photographed or televised by the media as implied consent for the child to appear in coverage. A code could be breached if there is a particular focus on a child and it could be foreseen that publishing the image could affect their welfare. For example, the Impress Code clause 3.1 does not apply to use of images of children in 'general scenes'—such as street fairs or protests—unless there is a 'detriment' to their well-being or safety.

> The **additional material** for ch. 4 on **www.mcnaes.com** has other case studies of adjudications concerning children. For protection in codes for children in crime investigations, see 5.14.

4.12 Vulnerable people

The Broadcasting Code's practices 8.21 and 8.22, cited earlier, give a 'vulnerable person' the same protection as a child under 16. It says those vulnerable may include those (over 16) with learning difficulties or mental health problems, the bereaved, people with brain damage or forms of dementia, people who have been traumatised or people who are sick or terminally ill.

4.13 Relatives and friends of those accused or convicted of crime

Clause 9 i) of the Editors' Code says: 'Relatives or friends of persons convicted or accused of crime should not generally be identified without their consent, unless they are genuinely relevant to the story.' It has public interest exceptions.

Ipso has ruled that a defendant's children, if mentioned in court proceedings, are 'genuinely relevant' and that a person who attends court in support of a defendant is too—see the **additional material** for ch. 4 for cases.

4.14 User-generated content

Pictures and footage supplied by readers and viewers, including from mobile phones, often feature in media coverage, particularly of major events such as the aftermath of terrorist atrocities. Journalists handling this 'user-generated content' (UGC) should realise it might breach the privacy of those depicted, or intrude into grief or shock. Also, some UGC pictures published have turned out to be faked or supplied in breach of someone else's **copyright**.

ch. 29 covers copyright law

→glossary

4.15 Material from social media sites

Journalists routinely search social media sites, including Facebook, Instagram and Twitter, for pictures or footage of people in the news, or for news. Publishing this material may breach copyright (see ch. 29). Publishing it might also be an intrusion into privacy, particularly if the person portrayed did not know they were being photographed or filmed, or did not know that the material was on the social media site. If there is a complaint, Ipso will decide whether the person had a reasonable expectation of privacy in relation to the material. For example, who uploaded it to the internet? Was the material hidden behind privacy settings on the social media site? If it was, Ipso will ask how the media organisation obtained it. Ipso will consider too if it showed information intrinsically private, such as medical information or private activities.

((•)) see Useful Websites at the end of this chapter for this Ipso guidance

In guidance issued on use of social media material, Ipso suggests that journalists should take screenshots of the material to be published, showing the dates and any privacy settings, if possible; keep contemporaneous notes of any discussion around the public interest in publishing information, where relevant; and pixelate or remove any individuals who might feature in the photo to be published but are not relevant to the story. The notes would be needed for the 'audit trails'.

for context on audit trails, see 2.4.1

The Impress Code guidance also says privacy settings should be respected unless a public interest exception applies.

Case study

In 2017 a woman complained that a *MailOnline* article about a controversy in which she was involved had featured, without her consent, a photo of her in a Halloween costume. Ipso said clause 2 of the Editors' Code was not breached because the photo was not private information. It noted that before the complained-of article appeared the woman had placed the photo in the public domain by posting it on her Twitter account, which had some 36,000 followers, so she did not have 'a reasonable expectation of privacy' in respect of the photo (*Bryan v Mail Online*, 5 October 2017).

In some circumstances, even if the person in the image is the one who placed it in the public domain, journalists must consider whether it is ethical to use it in the context of a news story projected to a different, and probably much bigger, audience. For example, the grieving family of a teenager who has died might be even more distressed if media reports include a social media image showing the young person apparently drunk at a gathering, which Ipso might consider to be an insensitive use of the photo—a breach of clause 4 of the Editors' Code.

see 4.7.1 for clause 4

Ipso's position is that publishing an innocuous image, obtained from a publicly accessible page on a social media website, of someone who died in a shocking event or who is a crime victim does not breach the Code provided that the manner of publication is sensitive to people's grief or shock—for example, see *Cross v Airdrie and Coatbridge Advertiser*, 12 February 2015, not upheld.

Ipso has also ruled that the Editors' Code is not normally breached by a media organisation quoting comments or messages—such as tributes to someone who has died—which people make on publicly accessible pages of social media sites (*Hodder v Dorset Echo*, 16 April 2015, not upheld) but, as explained earlier, caution is needed before quoting children's postings.

For further case studies about media publication of social media or user-generated content, see the **additional material** for ch. 4 on **www.mcnaes.com**.

Recap of major points

- Media regulators and civil courts use the criterion of 'a reasonable expectation of privacy' when deciding whether the media have intruded into a person's private life.
- Intrusion into privacy can be ethical and lawful if there is a public interest justification but editors need to be able to demonstrate that before publishing they considered the public interest, and balanced the competing privacy and freedom of expression rights.
- The regulators' codes require journalists to have parental consent for photographing, filming or recording a child if their welfare or privacy is involved.
- Journalists should not intrude into shock or grief—for example, when publishing images of accident scenes, photographing funerals or publishing photos from social media sites.
- Journalists must take care when deciding whether to publish pictures or footage supplied by the public or copied from social media sites, as publication may breach privacy and/or copyright.

Useful Websites

Independent Press Standards Organisation (IPSO), www.ipso.co.uk

- Editors' Code of Practice
- Guidance on deaths and inquests
- Major incidents guidance
- Information about Ipso's 'harassment' phone line for people to ask for its help
- Guidance on use of social media material
- Guidance on reporting of children

Editors' Code of Practice, The Editors' Codebook, www.editorscode.org.uk

Impress Standards Code and guidance, www.impressorg.com

Press Complaints Commission, Cases archive, www.pcc.org.uk

Archive of Press Complaints Commission adjudications

Ofcom Broadcasting Code, www.ofcom.org.uk

BBC, Editorial Guidelines, 'Section 7: Privacy', www.bbc.co.uk

BBC Editorial Guidelines on privacy, including about filming in public and private places, filming children and vulnerable people, 'doorstepping', use of social media material and drones

Online resources

Visit the online resources at **www.mcnaes.com** to test your knowledge of this chapter with **self-test questions** and a **flashcard glossary**, and to read **updates** about law and regulatory matters affecting journalism, as well as **additional material** to further your learning.

Part 2

Crime, courts and tribunals

5

Crime—media coverage prior to any court case

Chapter summary

This chapter explains how police investigations are driven by the standard of proof needed to convict someone of a crime. Reporters should understand police powers to arrest and detain. There is a strong public interest in media reporting of crime and police investigations, but journalists must be wary of contempt of court law, made 'active' when a suspect is arrested and in other circumstances. There are legal risks in publishing the identities of suspects before they are charged.

5.1 Standard of proof in criminal law

Those accused of crime enjoy 'the presumption of innocence'. This legal principle means that those charged with crimes are not required to prove themselves innocent—the prosecution must prove guilt 'beyond reasonable doubt', the standard of proof required for a court to convict the accused. Police and other agencies which investigate crime need clear evidence to meet this standard.

The principle also means that the role of a Crown court jury is to reach a verdict on each charge solely by considering the evidence presented in the trial, and not by being influenced by media reports or social media. This is why laws explained in this book restrict what can be published about a criminal case which has potential to or has become a jury trial.

5.2 Arrests

Under the Police and Criminal Evidence Act 1984 a police officer can arrest a person who has committed, is committing or is about to commit an offence (however minor), or anyone of whom there are reasonable grounds for suspicion. But the officer must have reasonable grounds for believing the arrest is necessary to achieve one of the purposes specified in the Act—for example, to allow 'prompt and effective investigation' of a crime, or to stop a person from obstructing the highway. Police may use 'reasonable force' to make an arrest. An arrest automatically makes the case 'active' under the Contempt of Court Act 1981, limiting what can be published about it. At the time of writing this book, the Law Commission had recommended moving the point at which a case becomes 'active' to the point a person is charged with an offence—see www.mcnaes.com for updates.

✱ Remember

The 1981 Act, explained in ch. 19, safeguards the fairness of trials, which is why it restricts what can be published about an active case. That chapter sets out what types of material, if published about an active case, can amount to a contempt of court, for which a media organisation can be heavily fined.

5.3 Police questioning of suspects

An arrested person is usually taken to a police station. A suspect who goes there voluntarily may be arrested there. Journalists should check whether the suspect is helping police voluntarily or is under arrest—if the case has become 'active' contempt law affects what can be published.

5.3.1 Limits to detention by police, prior to any charge

The law says no one should normally be held under arrest for more than 24 hours—they must be released if they have not been charged within that period. The time limit runs from the time of arrest or from when the suspect arrived at the police station, depending on circumstances. A police superintendent can authorise a further 12 hours' detention of someone suspected of an **indictable offence**. Police can then ask a magistrates' court to authorise the person's detention for another 36 hours. If a further application is made, the court cannot extend this detention beyond a maximum total of 96 hours. However, people suspected of terrorism can be detained for 14 days without charge.

→glossary

ch. 35 explains that photojournalists covering tense incidents may be threatened with arrest

5.3.2 False imprisonment

An arrested person who later sues the police for damages, alleging unlawful arrest or 'false imprisonment', must prove that the police grounds for detaining them were unreasonable.

5.4 The Crown Prosecution Service

Most prosecutions are the responsibility of the Crown Prosecution Service (CPS), a Government department, spread across 14 areas serving the 43 police forces in England and Wales. The head of the CPS is the Director of Public Prosecutions.

The CPS is independent of police, but has a duty to direct them in investigations, except into the most minor crimes. It decides, in all major cases involving police investigation, whether a suspect should be prosecuted and, if so, on what charge(s).

see Useful Websites at the end of this chapter for the CPS site

- A charge is a formal accusation, giving the alleged offender basic details of the alleged crime, including, for example, the date and place, and the name and section of the statute which defines the crime, if it is not a common law crime. For an alleged theft, the charge gives detail of the property allegedly stolen, its value, and the owner's name. For an alleged offence against a person, including violence or a sexual offence, the charge includes the name of the alleged victim. A charge means the case will be prosecuted and go to court.

Usually a suspect is charged at a police station. A suspect should be given the charge in written form, but may already have been charged orally before the document was ready. A charge makes a case 'active' under the Contempt of Court Act 1981 if it is not active already because of an arrest.

→glossary
→glossary

If a person is released on **police bail** or '**released under investigation**', the case remains 'active' as officers want more time to complete investigations. A suspect on police bail must return to a police station on a specified date, when they may be charged or released without charge. The case only ceases to be 'active' if an arrested person is released without charge and is not on bail or under investigation. Police should tell the media whether a suspect who has not been charged remains on police bail or is 'released under investigation', because journalists need to know—to comply with contempt law—if the case is 'active'.

Under the Police, Crime, Sentencing and Courts Act 2022, the duration of police bail is limited initially to three months, but a police inspector or more senior officer can authorise it to be extended for a further three months if no decision has been taken on whether the suspect should be charged, provided certain conditions are met and the person on bail is given the chance to make legal representations. A police superintendent or higher-ranking officer may further extend bail for another three months after the end of the initial six-month period. Any further extension has to be approved by magistrates.

For more context, see 19.4.3, When do criminal proceedings cease to be active? and 5.10, Police guidelines on naming of suspects and victims.

When considering whether a suspect should be prosecuted, CPS lawyers assess whether there is 'a realistic prospect of conviction'. If the case passes that test, they consider whether it is in the public interest to prosecute. In almost all serious cases, consideration of the public interest leads to a decision to prosecute.

5.5 Limits to detention by police, after any charge

Once someone is charged, police must stop questioning them, except in limited circumstances. The person, if under arrest, must by law be taken before a magistrates' court on the day they are charged or on the following day, except Sundays, Christmas Day or Good Friday. Alternatively, after being charged the person may be released on police bail to attend court on a specified date.

In all major cases lawyers employed by the CPS conduct the prosecution in court, although police have power to prosecute in some cases.

5.6 Other prosecution agencies in the public sector

Various other governmental agencies investigate and prosecute offences—for example, local authorities may investigate and prosecute landlords for breach of tenants' rights, the Health and Safety Executive prosecutes breaches of health and safety regulations, and the Serious Fraud Office, a Government department, investigates and prosecutes serious and complex fraud.

5.7 Laying or presenting of information; summonses; service of written charge

The decision whether to prosecute may be taken quickly—for example, soon after an arrest—or it could be taken after several weeks or months if time is needed to gather evidence. A prosecution can begin with a charge. It can also begin by 'laying' or 'presenting'—either term is used—'information' before a magistrate. In this procedure an allegation that a crime has been committed is made orally or in writing to a magistrate who will, without full consideration of evidence at that stage, issue a summons to be served on the alleged perpetrator.

- A summons is a formal document, issued by a magistrates' court, setting out one or more allegations in similar detail to a charge. It requires attendance at court on a specified date to respond to the allegation(s).

The issue of a summons makes the case 'active' under the Contempt of Court Act 1981, as ch. 19 explains.

For public prosecutors—including the CPS—laying or presenting 'information' has been replaced with 'written charge and requisition' in which the prosecuting agency serves (usually by post) such documents on the accused. Requisition is formal notification of the date the accused must appear at the magistrates' court. Summonses and requisitions are used routinely for minor offences not resolved by a 'fixed penalty'. The 'single justice procedure' (SJP) involves service of 'written charge and notice'. Any type of service of a written charge makes a case 'active' under the 1981 Act.

for context, see 7.7 on 'fixed penalty' and 7.8 on SJP

5.8 Arrest warrants

A Magistrates' court can issue an arrest warrant if sworn, written information is laid before them that a person has committed an indictable offence, or any **summary offence** punishable by imprisonment, or in relation to any offence if the suspect's current address is not sufficiently established for a requisition or summons to be served.

→glossary

- An arrest warrant is a formal document in which a magistrate empowers any police officer to arrest a suspect, wherever they are in England or Wales, to be taken to the magistrates' court.

for types of offence, see 6.1, Categories of criminal offences

Police have wide powers to arrest nationally without a warrant but one may be needed—for example, if the suspect has gone abroad and the UK authorities need to request that nation to extradite the suspect to the UK.

The issue of an arrest warrant makes the case 'active' under the 1981 Act if it has not already become active because of the issue of a summons or service of a written charge.

5.9 Private prosecutions

the Attorney General's role is explained in 1.7, High offices in law

Any citizen can, by laying information before a magistrate, start a prosecution, seeking to prove that an accused individual has committed a specified crime. Police and the CPS might have been aware of the allegation but concluded there was no or insufficient evidence. Allowing any citizen to start a 'private prosecution' is seen as a fundamental right to counterbalance any inertia or partiality by police or other official agencies. However, a private prosecution may quickly become unsustainable for lack of evidence. The CPS can take over a 'private prosecution' and withdraw the case. The Attorney General can stop private prosecutions. A government consultation on reform for private prosecutions took place in 2025, but no legislation had been proposed by the time this book went to print.

The Royal Society for the Prevention of Cruelty to Animals conducts private prosecutions for cruelty to or neglect of animals.

5.10 Police guidelines on naming of suspects and victims

Guidance issued to police by the College of Policing, which sets standards for police forces, says they should not normally reveal to the media the identity of a person suspected of a crime or who has been arrested. The rationale is to avoid a risk of unfair damage to the person's reputation, because they may not be charged with any offence. The guidance says that releasing the person's name is justified for 'a legitimate policing purpose', such as preventing or detecting crime, avoiding a threat to life, or warning the public about a 'wanted' person.

The College guidance says that police can (even if not releasing the name) release an arrested person's age and gender, and the name of the town or city where they live, the nature, date and general location of the alleged offence, the date of the arrest, whether they are in custody or have been released on police bail, and the subsequent bail date, or if they were released without bail or with no further action being taken. But the College adds that some of this limited detail—such as exact age, or the town—should not be released if that would have the effect of confirming identity. Updated guidance, which was out for consultation when this book went to print, says police should confirm the nationality and/or ethnicity of the defendant in high-profile or sensitive investigations or operations. The updated guidance says forces should consider whether there is a policing purpose for doing so, a related impact on public safety (such as rising community tensions), misinformation and a significant level of media or social media interest. This measure was introduced following the murders of three young girls in Southport in 2024, which sparked riots in towns and cities across England and

Northern Ireland. Police later gave details about the killer, Axel Rudakubana's nationality and religion in an effort to counter inflammatory misinformation about his origins on social media.

The College guidance says that, after an adult is charged or summonsed, police should release their name (unless there is an exceptional and legitimate policing purpose for not doing so or reporting restrictions apply), and that the named person's date of birth, address, details of charge, and date of court appearance should also be released, as well as their occupation if relevant to the crime. It also says that the identities of people dealt with by cautions, speeding fines and other fixed penalties—out-of-court disposals—should not be released.

((•)) see Useful Websites at the end of this chapter for the College guidance and the updated version

The guidance says a crime victim's name will not normally be released unless they consent and no reporting restriction applies.

5.11 Legal risks in media identification of crime suspects

The media may discover that someone is being investigated by police or another agency—for example, that the person is under arrest. A media report which includes the suspect's name, or other detail identifying them in this context, could create legal problems for the publisher.

5.11.1 Defamation risk in reporting a suspect's identity

Identifying a person as being under police or any official investigation may allow that individual to successfully sue the publisher for defamation and receive damages if the investigation does not lead to a charge. Publishing a statement that someone is under investigation, even when this is factually correct, can create an inference that they are guilty, if not carefully worded. Chs. 20 and 21 explain defamation dangers, including 20.2.3, Inferences.

As regards defamation law, the media can safely publish the name of a person under investigation or arrest if the name is officially supplied for publication by a spokesperson for a governmental agency—for example, the police, CPS or a local council—because the report will be protected by qualified **privilege** if that defence's requirements are met—see 22.7.2.5.

→glossary

Case study

In 2011 Bristol landlord Christopher Jefferies won 'very substantial' settlements in libel actions against eight national newspapers for articles published after one of his tenants, landscape architect Joanna Yeates, was found dead. Police arrested Mr Jefferies, but later released him. The newspapers published grave falsehoods about him and gave the impression he was guilty. Another man was later charged with murdering Joanna and subsequently convicted (*Media Lawyer*, 29 July 2011). What was published about Mr Jefferies also led to two newspapers being convicted of contempt of court—for detail, see 19.5.2.

5.11.2 Risk in privacy law of reporting a suspect's identity

As already outlined, in most cases the police do not, unless the person is charged, tell the media who is or was suspected of committing a crime—for example, someone who has been questioned and/or arrested and/or whose premises have been searched.

The Court of Appeal ruled in 2020 in the case of *ZXC v Bloomberg* that a person who has 'simply come under suspicion' by any 'organ of the state', such as the police or any other law enforcement body, has in general a 'reasonable expectation of privacy' in relation to that fact, unless they are charged. This development of privacy law—upheld by the Supreme Court, see later—means that a media organisation which discovers a suspect's identity and publishes that they are being investigated by such an agency could face a legal claim from that person for misuse of private information if the person is not subsequently charged.

for detail of privacy law, see ch. 27

Case study

On 22 May 2017 Salman Abedi detonated an explosive device in Manchester Arena at the end of a concert by singer Ariana Grande, murdering 22 people, including children, and injuring more than 800 as well as killing himself. Greater Manchester Police (GMP) feared he had been aided by terrorist plotters and arrested 15 suspects in various places. Aladeen Sicri, 23, a Libyan who came to the UK to study and trained as a pilot, became the 16th person to be arrested, on 29 May at his home in Shoreham-by-Sea, West Sussex. Within minutes of his arrest, GMP issued a press release stating that 'a 23-year-old man' had been arrested in Shoreham 'in connection with the Manchester Arena attack' and 'on suspicion' of terrorism offences. Complying with College of Policing guidelines, the release did not identify Mr Sicri. Soon afterwards *MailOnline* engaged freelance journalists to make inquiries in Shoreham and later that day published Mr Sicri's name and two photos of him as being the arrested man. Five days later he was released without charge because he had no connection with the bombing. He was arrested simply because Abedi, who was a stranger to him and whose family was from Libya, had contacted him seeking to exchange some Libyan currency, a business service advertised by Mr Sicri. But Mr Sicri had for commercial reasons declined to transact an exchange. *MailOnline* did not report that Mr Sicri had been released. Its report of his arrest remained online until February 2018 and was only taken down after his lawyers sent a letter of claim to *MailOnline*. Mr Sicri sued *MailOnline* for damages for breach of confidence and misuse of private information, because it had identified him in the reporting of his arrest. During the High Court trial of his claim in 2020, it was agreed the case could be decided by reference to privacy law. Mr Sicri gave evidence of his distress at finding on his release that his name, address and Facebook photograph were published globally in reports of the arrest. He said he had feared for his safety, suffered the impact of hostile social media messages, and had been prescribed an anti-depressant.

The negative publicity about his arrest led to him losing his job. *MailOnline* argued Mr Sicri did not have a reasonable expectation of privacy in relation to his arrest, because it had been part of 'a lengthy and highly visible police operation around his home'—over a 48-hour period officers could be seen entering, searching and leaving his flat. It also argued that, if he did have such an expectation, his Article 8 privacy rights were overridden by *MailOnline*'s Article 10 rights in its 'watchdog' role, because the public 'is entitled to know' who has been arrested in the course of an investigation into a very serious terrorist incident; because his identity had been obtained by 'lawful journalistic inquiries'; and because 'there is a legitimate public interest in transparency in police investigations into such incidents and proper public concern in seeing that the police are making progress'. But Mr Justice Warby ruled that Mr Sicri did have a reasonable expectation that his identity as an arrested 'suspect' would not be revealed and said the context of the Arena bombing investigation meant that *MailOnline*'s resultant intrusion into his privacy 'was of an especially grave nature'. Mr Sicri had not behaved 'in such a way as to bring suspicion upon himself', the judge said. He said too that the arrest itself was in a private place, and went almost unnoticed locally, adding that *MailOnline*'s identification of Mr Sicri as a suspect was not capable of making any contribution to any public debate about the Manchester bombing, or the police investigation: 'This is not a case about scrutiny of the merits of official action'. Mr Justice Warby was critical that Marianna Partasides, *MailOnline*'s UK News Editor, and other staff journalists involved in its reporting of Mr Sicri's arrest were 'ignorant' of the College of Policing guidance. He awarded £83,000 damages to Mr Sicri (*Sicri v Associated Newspapers Ltd* [2020] EWHC 3541 (QB)).

see 1.3 for context on Articles 8 and 10

For other significant aspects of the *Sicri* case, see 2.6, 27.8 and 27.9. See the **additional material** for this chapter on **www.mcnaes.com** for a case study about how in 2018 the entertainer Sir Cliff Richard was awarded £210,000 in damages, and was later paid £2 million towards his legal costs and financial losses after he won an action against the BBC for misuse of private information and breach of data protection law, in relation to the corporation's reporting on his home being searched by police investigating an allegation that he had committed a sexual assault. Sir Cliff said the allegation was false and was never arrested or charged with any offence. For context on data protection law concerning people involved in criminal investigations, including crime victims, see 28.2.6.

for a privacy case arising from a mentally ill man's arrest, see 27.5 on 'reasonable expectation of privacy'

5.11.3 When there is no or a reduced 'expectation' of privacy

In the *ZXC* case, a man sued financial news organisation Bloomberg for misuse of private information because it revealed he was under investigation by a UK law enforcement agency. The High Court ruled for him and awarded him £25,000 damages. It ordered that his identity as a suspect in the case cannot be revealed. Bloomberg appealed to the Court of Appeal and subsequently to the Supreme Court, but both courts upheld the High Court's decision (*ZXC v Bloomberg LP* [2020] EWCA Civ 611; *Bloomberg LP v ZXC* [2022] UKSC 5).

The High Court, Court of Appeal and Supreme Court recognised in *ZXC* that the media's Article 10 rights in its watchdog role may in some circumstances override a suspect's privacy rights. The Court of Appeal said that may be the case, for example, when a media organisation 'highlights any perceived deficiencies or unwarrantable delays in the police investigation', or if leaked documents suggested that the investigators had been 'subjected to improper political pressure not to pursue certain people or lines of inquiry'. However, this remains hypothetical as, by the time of writing, there had been no court decision in which a media organisation's Article 10 rights have overridden a suspect's privacy rights under Article 8. The media have consequently become reluctant to identify suspects who have been arrested, even when they are prominent public figures (including politicians).

The Court of Appeal also said that in some circumstances a suspect under investigation by a state enforcement agency may have a reduced or no expectation of privacy as regards that fact, because of 'the public nature of the activity' under consideration, such as rioting or electoral fraud, or when an armed bank-robber is arrested after having held people hostage in a televised three-day siege.

From what the Court of Appeal and Supreme Court indicated in *ZXC*, it remains the case that an adult who obviously commits a crime in a public place and is arrested there shortly afterwards is, unless mentally incapacitated or mentally ill, unlikely to be able to use privacy or data protection law to sue successfully a media organisation which publishes identifying images of these events to report the arrest.

Similarly, publishing identifying images of a person being arrested when participating in public protest will not in general breach such law (and the public nature of such protests implies they consent to some such publication).

5.11.4 Assessing the risk

Media organisations reporting high-profile investigations by an enforcement agency such as the police, especially if a celebrity or public figure is a suspect, may choose—because of the fierce competition to break news—to publish the suspect's name before it is known if they will be charged and without any qualified privilege. They might assess that the person is unlikely to sue for defamation or breach of privacy or data protection law, because the person may not wish to alienate the media or stir up more publicity. Or the media might assess that there is little risk in their reports naming the person because a police leak or other information suggests a charge is sure to follow. Those assessments may be wrong—and if they are, legal proceedings for defamation and/or misuse of private information may follow. But if the person *is* charged, they will appear in court proceedings which can be reported, or will already have been identified by an official police statement about the charge(s), and so will no longer have any right of privacy or rights under data protection law in respect of the fact of that they are under police investigation. A defamation action over pre-charge publicity also becomes less likely as any damage it caused to the person's reputation will usually be outweighed by, or indistinguishable from, damage caused by reports of the police statement or of the court case, which—as ch. 22 shows—the media can safely publish with privilege.

5.12 Automatic statutory anonymity for victims of some crimes

Statutory reporting restrictions which are automatically in force mean that it is normally illegal for anyone to publish any detail which identifies or is likely to identify a victim or alleged victim of a sexual, trafficking, female genital mutilation or forced marriage offence—see ch. 11, which also covers the anonymity provision for such people in the media's regulatory codes.

* Remember

Developments in the civil law of privacy and data protection law mean that in some circumstances a media organisation could be successfully sued for damages by a victim/alleged victim of crime whose identity was published without their consent, if a court ruled—for example—that the victim/alleged victim suffered distress because a police officer unofficially 'leaked' the person's identity to the media: see too 27.12.

5.13 Accused teachers given automatic anonymity

Section 141F of the Education Act 2002 normally and automatically makes it illegal to publish material identifying a teacher in respect of any allegation that they have or may have committed an offence against a pupil at their school—for example, a physical assault or sexual abuse—unless they are charged with the offence.

For more detail of this anonymity law, including about circumstances in which it ceases to apply, see the **additional material** for this chapter on **www.mcnaes.com**.

5.14 People aged under 18 in investigations

Codes used by media regulators provide specific safeguards against reports identifying children and young persons as being under investigation for an alleged crime (of any type), or as being a witness or the victim/alleged victim of any crime.

Part of clause 9 (Reporting of crime) of the Editors' Code of Practice says: 'Particular regard should be paid to the potentially vulnerable position of children under the age of 18 who witness, or are victims of, crime. This should not restrict the right to report legal proceedings.'

chs. 2 and 3 introduce the codes

As explained in ch. 10, when a defendant aged under 18 appears at a youth court, law automatically bans publication of their identity and the identity of any witness, or victim/alleged victim, under 18, as regards them being 'concerned' in the case; or if the case is in a magistrates' or Crown court, it decides whether to make an order granting such anonymity to any such person aged under 18.

Clause 9 also says:

> "Editors should generally avoid naming children under the age of 18 after arrest for a criminal offence but before they appear in a youth court unless they can show that the individual's name is already in the public domain, or that the individual (or, if they are under 16, a custodial parent or similarly responsible adult) has given their consent. This does not restrict the right to name juveniles who appear in a Crown court, or whose anonymity is lifted."

Another part of clause 9 relevant to the ethics of who should be identified in crime reporting is covered in this book at 4.13. The Code's public interest exceptions apply.

The Broadcasting Code says in rule 1.9:

> "When covering any pre-trial investigation into an alleged criminal offence in the UK, broadcasters should pay particular regard to the potentially vulnerable position of any person who is not yet adult who is involved as a witness or victim, before broadcasting their name, address, identity of school or other educational establishment, place of work, or any still or moving picture of them. Particular justification is also required for the broadcast of such material relating to the identity of any person who is not yet adult who is involved in the defence as a defendant or potential defendant."

Revealing the identity of a child under 16, as being a person involved in a police investigation, could breach rule 3.2 of the Impress Code.

→glossary

As already mentioned, victims or alleged victims (whatever their age) of some types of crime have **automatic anonymity** in law from the time an allegation is made as in ch. 11.

See the **additional material** for ch. 5 on **www.mcnaes.com** for law banning the disclosure of identities of police informants, including 'investigation anonymity orders', and for legal and ethical considerations when journalists accompany police 'raids' to make an arrest or search properties. For examples of how the regulator Ofcom has adjudicated on TV coverage of arrests in public places, see the **additional material** for ch. 4.

Recap of major points

- Covering crime stories presents contempt of court dangers for the media, because an arrest, an oral charge, service of a written charge, or the issue of a summons or an arrest warrant makes a case 'active' under the Contempt of Court Act 1981.
- There could be a libel risk if a suggestion is published, prior to any charge, that a suspect may be guilty of a crime, if what is published identifies the suspect.
- Revealing that a person is under police investigation could lead to an action for misuse of private information and/or breach of data protection law.
- Teachers accused of an offence against a pupil normally have anonymity in law unless they are charged.
- Police should normally release the name of a person charged.
- Codes used by media regulators have provision to protect children and young persons from publicity if they are involved in a police investigation into crime.

Useful Websites

Crown Prosecution Service, www.cps.gov.uk

The Code for Crown Prosecutors, www.cps.gov.uk

College of Policing 'Media relations' guidelines, www.college.police.uk

Online resources

Visit the online resources at **www.mcnaes.com** to test your knowledge of this chapter with **self-test questions** and a **flashcard glossary**, and to read **updates** about law and regulatory matters affecting journalism, as well as **additional material** to further your learning.

6

Crimes—categories and definition

Chapter summary

All criminal cases begin in magistrates' courts. The most serious, such as murder, rape or robbery, progress to a Crown court. Journalists must know the different categories of crimes to understand when reporting restrictions affect what can be published in court stories, and the legal definitions of some crimes to avoid libel problems when referring to offences. At the time of writing, the Government was considering, and proposing to legislate for within months, a radical and controversial overhaul of the criminal justice system. This would include the creation of an intermediate court (the Crown Court Bench Division, where cases would be heard by either a judge alone or a judge and two lay magistrates instead of a jury) and jury trials would no longer be available for certain crimes—see this book's Late News for more detail and www.mcnaes.com for updates.

6.1 Categories of criminal offences

Criminal charges are grouped into three categories: indictable-only, either-way and summary.

→glossary
→glossary
(1) **Indictable-only** offences are the most serious crimes, punishable by the longest prison terms—for example, murder, rape, **robbery**. Such cases are processed initially by a magistrates' court, but cannot be dealt with there, as magistrates have limited sentencing powers (see 7.6.1). So indictable-only cases progress quickly to a Crown court, as explained in ch. 8. The term 'indictable-only' derives from 'the **indictment**', the document used at a Crown court to record the charge(s).
→glossary

→glossary
(2) **Either-way offences** include **theft**, sexual assault and assault causing grievous bodily harm. These charges can be dealt with either at a Crown court or by magistrates, hence the term 'either-way'. For this category, magistrates may—after hearing an outline of a case—decide that it is so serious that only a

Crown court can deal with it. As ch. 8 explains, even if magistrates decide they can deal with the case, the defendant can exercise the right to choose trial by jury at Crown court. Either-way offences are regarded as being less serious than indictable-only offences, but nevertheless include distressing, harmful crimes.

(3) **Summary offences** are comparatively minor offences such as common assault, drunkenness and speeding offences. Summary charges are dealt with in magistrates' courts, except in some cases in which a defendant faces both summary and either-way or indictable-only charges arising from the same event, in which instance a Crown court may deal with all of them. People charged only with a summary offence have no right to a jury trial. 'Summary proceedings' means 'proceedings in a magistrates' court', with the term 'summary' indicating the relative speed of the process.

→glossary

ch. 9 explains Crown courts

✱ Remember

Confusingly, indictable-only and either-way charges are sometimes referred to collectively as 'indictable' charges, because they both share the possibility of jury trial at Crown court. But, as stated earlier, magistrates can decide to deal with an either-way case in their summary proceedings—that is, as if it were a summary offence.

6.2 Defining criminality

There are two elements in most crimes:

- an act which is potentially criminal—which lawyers call the *actus reus*; and
- a guilty mind—the *mens rea*, which means that the act was carried out, or planned or attempted, with guilty intention—that the perpetrator knew they were acting, or intended to act, unlawfully.

Generally, the prosecution must prove both elements. In the crime of murder, the *actus reus* is that of unlawfully killing someone, and the *mens rea* is that the act was done with intent to kill or cause grievous bodily harm. If there is no such intent, a killing may be a lesser crime—for example, manslaughter.

6.2.1 Strict liability

Some offences are of **strict liability**. Strict liability, when it applies in law, removes or limits the defences to the charge. Strict liability means that a motorist who exceeds the speed limit commits an offence even if they did not realise how fast they were driving. A motorist who drives with too much alcohol in their blood commits an offence even if they did not intend to breach the alcohol limit. Strict liability can be seen as a practical, societal solution to deter dangerous or anti-social conduct for which, in many cases, it would be impossible to prove that *mens rea*—a guilty mind—existed.

→glossary

see 19.4, Contempt of Court Act 1981—strict liability

Journalists must understand this concept, not least because some criminal offences arising from publishing material are strict liability offences, meaning it is not a defence to say 'Sorry, I didn't intend to . . .'—for example, publishing material which breaches the Contempt of Court Act 1981.

6.3 Definitions of crimes

chs. 20 and 21 explain defamation

A victim of theft may tell friends they have been 'robbed'. A journalist who makes this colloquial error when reporting a court case will seem foolish and—worse—the error could lead to a defamation action.

Reporting that a defendant who is guilty of a minor theft was guilty of robbery suggests to the public that they committed a much worse crime, as robbery—which involves violence or threatened violence—is generally regarded as worse than theft.

The crime definitions in the following list are simplified. For fuller definitions, see the Crown Prosecution Service's Prosecution Guidance section, listed at the end of this chapter under Useful Websites, or *Blackstone's Criminal Practice*.

6.3.1 Crimes against people

Murder The unlawful killing of a human being with the intention of killing or causing grievous bodily harm. An adult convicted of murder must be sentenced to life imprisonment. Indictable-only.

Manslaughter Killing by an unlawful act likely to cause bodily harm but without the intention to kill or cause grievous bodily harm. Manslaughter can be a charge in its own right. A jury in a murder trial might in some circumstances find the defendant not guilty of murder but convict them of manslaughter as an alternative. Indictable-only.

Corporate manslaughter An organisation such as a company, a police force or a Government department can be convicted of this offence if the way in which its activities were managed or organised caused someone's death and amounted to a gross breach of a duty of care the organisation owed to the deceased. Indictable-only.

Infanticide The killing of an infant under 12 months old by its mother, when her mind is disturbed as a result of the birth. Indictable-only.

→glossary

Assault; common assault; battery; assault by beating The way these offences evolved in **case law** led their definitions to overlap. These charges are likely to be used in cases in which no, or only transient or trifling, bodily injury is allegedly caused. 'Assault' and 'common assault' can mean an unlawful infliction of force/violence, or a hostile act—for example, a threatening gesture—which puts another person in fear of immediate violence. Journalists should not assume that an assault charge necessarily alleges that a physical attack occurred. Either type of act must be proved as intentional or reckless. A push can be a common assault. Battery can also be expressed as a charge of 'assault by beating'. They are summary charges, unless the assault is alleged to have been aggravated by hostility towards the alleged victim's race or religion, when they are either-way. There is also an either-way charge of assaulting an emergency worker during their work.

Assault occasioning actual bodily harm (ABH) An assault—that is, a threat and/or attack, see earlier—which caused more than transient and trifling harm. The harm could be psychiatric illness. Either-way.

Wounding or inflicting grievous body harm (GBH) These charges are in section 20 of the Offences against the Person Act 1861. It must be proved that the defendant intended or foresaw causing some harm and—depending on which charge the prosecution sees as accurately describing the injury—that the harm caused was a wound or grievous (that is, serious) harm which was not, or not only, a wound. Either charge, in full form, includes the term 'malicious'—for example, 'malicious wounding'. A 'wound' is the slicing through or breaking of skin and can be a mere cut. However, a wounding charge tends to be used only if the wound is serious. A GBH charge tends to be used, for example, if the harm includes broken bone, or led to substantial loss of blood and/or extended medical treatment, and/or permanent disfigurement, and/or permanent disability. These charges are either-way.

Wounding 'with intent'/inflicting grievous body harm 'with intent' Under section 18 of the 1861 Act, the wounding or GBH is deemed to have been 'with intent' if there is intent to cause GBH or to resist 'lawful apprehension'. Such a charge is indictable-only. It carries a maximum penalty of life imprisonment.

Rape Indictable-only. See definitions of sexual offences in ch. 11, which also explains that victims of these offences must have anonymity in media reports.

6.3.2 Crimes against property or involving gain

Theft Dishonest appropriation of property belonging to another with the intention of permanently depriving the other of it (Theft Act 1968). Either-way. The act of theft is stealing. Do not refer to this offence as robbery.

Robbery Theft by force (that is, violence), or by threat of force. Indictable-only.

Handling Dishonestly receiving goods, knowing or believing them to be stolen, or dishonestly helping in the retention, removal, disposal or sale of such goods. Either-way.

Burglary Entering a building as a trespasser and then:

- stealing or attempting to steal from it; or
- inflicting or attempting to inflict grievous bodily harm to anyone in it; or
- making trespassing entry to a building with:
  - intent to steal; or
  - intent to inflict GBH; or
  - intent to do unlawful damage.

Generally, burglary is an either-way charge, but in some circumstances it is indictable-only.

Aggravated burglary Burglary while armed with a firearm, imitation firearm, or any other weapon or explosive. Indictable-only.

Fraud Under the Fraud Act 2006, there are now general offences of fraud, defined as conduct 'with a view to gain or with intent to cause loss or expose to a risk of loss' involving either:

- dishonestly making a false representation (for example, using a credit card dishonestly or using a false identity to open a bank account); or
- dishonestly failing to disclose information when under a legal duty to disclose (for example, failure when applying for health insurance to disclose a heart condition);
- dishonestly abusing a position (for example, an employee swindling money from their employer).

The Act also includes a fraud offence of obtaining services dishonestly. These statutory fraud offences are either-way, but if deemed to be of sufficient 'seriousness or complexity', they are treated procedurally as indictable-only (as explained in 8.3.1.3, Two types of either-way case are simply 'sent'). Conspiracy to defraud is indictable-only.

Blackmail Making an unwarranted demand with menaces with a view to gain. This offence could be a threat to disclose embarrassing secrets or photos involving the victim unless money is paid, or another type of extortion such as a threat to contaminate goods on a supermarket company's shelves unless money is paid. Indictable-only.

Taking a vehicle without authority Sometimes referred to as 'taking without owner's consent' (TWOC). It can cover conduct known as 'twocking' or 'joy-riding' in which offenders abandon a car after using it. This offence does not involve an intention to deprive the owner permanently of the vehicle and so should not be described as theft. Summary.

Aggravated vehicle taking When a vehicle has been taken (as above) and someone is injured, or the vehicle or other property is damaged because of how it was driven. Either-way.

6.3.3 Motoring crimes

Driving under the influence of drink or drugs Driving a motor vehicle when the ability to do so is thus impaired. Summary.

Driving with excess alcohol When alcohol in the driver's body exceeds the prescribed limits—80 milligrams of alcohol in 100 millilitres of blood; 35 microgrammes of alcohol in 100 millilitres of breath; or 107 milligrams of alcohol in 100 millilitres of urine. Summary.

Causing death by careless driving when under the influence of drink or drugs The driver is unfit to drive as a result of drink or drugs, or has consumed excess alcohol or failed to provide a specimen. Indictable-only.

✻ Remember

It may not be fair or accurate (and therefore could be a libel problem) to describe a driver with more than the prescribed limit of alcohol as 'drunk'. They may only be marginally over the limit. It is safe to use the term 'drunk' if it is expressed in evidence or if—in the case of a convicted defendant—the evidence clearly supports this.

6.3.4 Other noteworthy crimes

Perjury Knowingly giving false evidence after taking an oath as a witness to tell the truth in court (including in a tribunal which a court), or in an **affidavit**. Indictable-only. →glossary

Perverting the course of justice Concealing evidence or giving false information to police. Indictable-only.

Wasting police time A lesser offence, committed by a person knowingly making a false report that a crime has been committed or falsely claiming to have information material to an investigation. Summary.

Recap of major points

- There are three main categories of criminal offences:
  - indictable-only, which can only be dealt with by a Crown court
  - either-way, dealt with by a Crown court or a magistrates' court—see ch. 8
  - summary—almost all such cases are dealt with by magistrates.
- If an offence is of 'strict liability', the defendant can be convicted even if they had no clear 'intention' to do wrong.
- A media organisation which fails to report an offence or charge accurately might be successfully sued for libel by the defendant.

Useful Websites

Crown Prosecution Service, 'Prosecution guidance', www.cps.gov.uk

Online resources

Visit the online resources at **www.mcnaes.com** to test your knowledge of this chapter with **self-test questions** and a **flashcard glossary**, and to read **updates** about law and regulatory matters affecting journalism, as well as **additional material** to further your learning.

7

Magistrates' courts—summary cases

Chapter summary

Magistrates' courts deal with more than 90 per cent of all criminal cases and send the rest—the most serious—to Crown courts. Hearings in which magistrates try or sentence defendants are called 'summary proceedings'. They deal with offences such as burglaries, sexual assault and dangerous driving. Magistrates can jail some convicted defendants but only for a maximum of one year. This chapter also explains bail and details the automatic reporting restrictions on what the media can publish from pre-trial hearings at magistrates' courts. Youth courts, which deal with defendants aged under 18 when they are charged, are covered in ch. 10.

7.1 Who are magistrates?

The role of magistrates originated in the twelfth century. They still use the ancient title of 'justice of the peace'. Most are volunteers and part-time—that is, lay magistrates. There are about 14,600 lay magistrates, who are trained and paid expenses, sitting in around 150 magistrates' courts in England and Wales.

At least two lay magistrates must 'sit' to try a criminal case. A trial in a magistrates' court is known as a **summary trial**, reflecting the fact that magistrates dispense quick and relatively informal justice whereas the higher courts, handling more serious and complex cases, have slower processes.

→glossary

One magistrate is sufficient for some court duties. When a court hearing has more than one magistrate, one acts as chair and announces decisions. Lay magistrates are advised on law by a justices' clerk or one of their staff of legal advisers, who sits in front of the magistrates in court. Ushers assist in the courtroom.

See the **additional material** for ch. 7 on **www.mcnaes.com**, 'More about magistrates'.

7.1.1 District judges

About 150 professional district judges (and more than 100 deputy district judges) who must have at least five years' experience as a lawyer or legal executive, also sit in magistrates' courts. Most are in city districts with high caseloads. A district judge can preside in cases on their own (a clerk or legal adviser is there too). But for convenience, this book refers to 'magistrates' (plural) sitting in court, because two or three lay magistrates sit in many hearings.

for context, see 6.1, Categories of criminal offences, and 7.6, Sentencing by magistrates

7.2 The taking of pleas

Defendants facing summary charges are asked, usually during their first appearance in the magistrates' court, how they plead. Pleading guilty to a charge means they are convicted of it. Sentencing usually takes place at a later date, to enable preparation of a 'pre-sentence report'. A contested case will in most instances be adjourned for summary trial. When it is first adjourned, the magistrates must decide, unless the charge is a minor one, whether to grant **bail**.

→glossary

Defendants who deny **either-way** charges can choose jury trial at the Crown court or ask magistrates to try them. Magistrates might decide in the **allocation (mode of trial)** procedure, which is outlined in the next chapter, that the case is too serious for them to deal with.

→glossary
→glossary

A defendant under arrest or previously denied bail might appear at a pre-trial hearing via a 'live link' from a police station or prison in a 'hybrid' hearing. Some types of hearing can be 'virtual'.

for context on live links, hybrid and virtual hearings, see 15.14

7.3 Bail

Bail is the system by which a court grants a defendant their liberty until the next hearing.

The court can impose conditions—for example, that the defendant should; live at a particular address, surrender their passport, report to a police station once a week, not contact someone who is a witness.

Failing to 'surrender to bail' (i.e. failure to turn up to the next hearing) is a criminal offence which will probably result in the court issuing an arrest warrant.

The Bail Act 1976 has a general rule that a defendant must be granted bail unless:

- the court is satisfied there are substantial grounds for believing that if bail is granted, the defendant
  - will abscond, or
  - commit another offence, or
  - obstruct the course of justice (for example, by interfering with witnesses), or
  - will, or will be likely to, cause mental or physical injury to an associated person or cause them to fear such injury;
- the court decides the defendant should be kept in prison for their own protection (for instance, if the alleged crime has so angered the community that a mob may attack them);

→glossary

- the defendant is alleged to have committed an **indictable offence** when they were on bail granted in an earlier case;
- the defendant is already serving a jail sentence;
- there is insufficient information to decide on bail.

A court must give reasons for refusing bail. A defendant charged with murder can only be given bail by a Crown court judge.

7.3.1 Evidence and previous convictions aired

When deciding on bail, the court is told of the defendant's relevant previous conviction(s) and some details of prosecution evidence about the charge(s) faced. A defence lawyer arguing for bail may outline defence evidence.

7.3.2 Surety

→glossary

In some cases, a court will insist that the defendant has a **surety** before bail is granted. A surety is someone such as a relative or friend of the defendant who guarantees that the defendant will 'surrender' to bail—that is, appear at court as required—and agrees to forfeit a sum of money, fixed by the court, if they abscond. If the defendant does abscond, a surety who fails to pay the sum can be jailed.

7.3.3 Appeals

Defendants refused bail by magistrates can apply to a Crown court judge for bail. When the alleged offence is imprisonable, the prosecution can appeal to a Crown court judge to challenge a grant of bail by magistrates.

7.4 Reporting restrictions for pre-trial hearings

When a charge is heading for a summary trial, because the defendant has pleaded 'not guilty', magistrates may hold at least one pre-trial hearing to consider and decide any dispute between prosecution and defence on admissibility of evidence or other questions of law, and/or to decide on bail.

→glossary

Section 8C of the Magistrates' Courts Act 1980 imposes **automatic** restrictions limiting contemporaneous reporting of these pre-trial hearings. These restrictions are intended to prevent the risk of prejudice should a case originally due to be tried by magistrates end up being tried by a Crown court jury. Parliament anticipated that, because of changes to integrate the courts' system, a case—even if a magistrates' court prepares to try it—might end up being tried at a Crown court with a 'related' either-way or indictable-only case. A magistrates' court might also initially agree in the allocation procedure to try an either-way case but later in a pre-trial hearing decide that a Crown court should try it because the alleged offence is more serious than it first appeared.

The type of material aired in a pre-trial hearing which could, if published contemporaneously by the media, subsequently prejudice a jury's verdict at Crown court—such as a defendant's previous convictions—is outlined in 8.2.1, Types of prejudicial matter.

7.4.1 The scope of the section 8C reporting restrictions

The section 8C restrictions automatically apply to reports of pre-trial hearings at magistrates' courts in cases due for summary trial.

They temporarily ban publication of reports of:

- any ruling by magistrates on admissibility of evidence or on any other question of law relating to the case, and of any order to discharge or vary such a ruling, which is made in the pre-trial hearing;
- 'proceedings on applications' for such rulings and for such orders—which means the ban prevents the reporting of the legal argument and discussion in the pre-trial hearing about whether such a ruling or order should be made.

The Act defines a pre-trial hearing as one relating to a charge due to be tried by magistrates to which the defendant has pleaded not guilty and which takes place before magistrates start hearing prosecution evidence at the trial. So section 8C could cover a defendant's first appearance at court, as well as any other pre-trial hearing, but does not prevent contemporaneous reporting of the plea.

While the restrictions are in force, only seven categories of information can be reported from such pre-trial proceedings. These are (in simplified form):

- the names of the court and magistrates;
- the names, ages, home addresses, and occupations of the defendant(s) and witnesses;
- the charge(s) in full or summarised;
- the names of solicitors and barristers in the proceedings;
- if the case is adjourned, the date and place to which it is adjourned;
- any arrangements as to bail;
- whether **legal aid** was authorised. →glossary

It is also safe to publish that reporting restrictions are in force—this is not prejudicial. The effect of the restrictions is to ban publication of any reference to evidence, except as it is encapsulated in the wording of the charge(s), or to other potentially prejudicial matter aired in the hearing—again, 8.2.1 explains what such matter is. 'Publication' includes in any speech, writing, programme or other communication in whatever form which is addressed to the public at large or any section of the public.

As regards 'arrangements as to bail', it will be safe to report, unless the court orders otherwise, whether bail was granted, and, if it was granted, any bail conditions and surety arrangement. But if bail is refused, the report should not in most instances include that the prosecution opposed bail, and in particular, why it was opposed, or the reasons magistrates gave for refusing it, as this could be prejudicial. However, it would be safe to report that someone was remanded in custody for their own protection.

for context, see 8.2.4, Describing the court-room scene, and 8.2.5, Background material

The explicit ban in section 8C on publishing pre-trial argument, rulings and orders about admissibility of evidence and other questions of law reinforces the limiting of reports to the seven categories, which has the same banning effect.

A report of a pre-trial hearing can safely include bland descriptions of the court scene and neutral background information.

7.4.1.1 The defendant's current and past addresses

Home addresses which can be published include any current one, and any past address from 'any relevant time'—that is, a time when events giving rise to the charge(s) in the case occurred.

A report which refers to a defendant's former address or includes a photo or footage of it should make clear that they no longer live there. Failing to do so could cause the current occupants to sue for libel because the report will link them to the court case.

7.4.2 When do the section 8C restrictions cease to apply?

The court can lift the section 8C reporting restrictions, wholly or in part, to allow the media to publish contemporaneously fuller reports of these pre-trial applications and of any ruling or order made in them. If a defendant objects, the court can lift the restrictions only if satisfied that doing so is in the interests of justice. Section 8C says that if a defendant makes such objection, the proceedings relating to it (that is, the objection, and argument, and discussion in court about whether the restrictions should be lifted) cannot be reported until the case is 'disposed of', even if restrictions are lifted earlier in other respects. However, the fact that an order to lift the restrictions was made, or not made, *can* be reported at the time of that order.

The section 8C restrictions automatically lapse when the case is 'disposed of', which happens when all defendants in the case are acquitted or convicted of all charges in the case, or the court dismisses the case, or the prosecution decides not to proceed with it.

So, at the end of the trial, a media organisation could publish a report of evidence ruled inadmissible some weeks or months previously in a pre-trial hearing, or of any ruling or order made in it.

for context, see 19.9.3, Court reporting—the section 4 defence, and 22.5, Absolute privilege

7.4.2.1 If published 'as soon as practicable'

A report published 'as soon as practicable' after the relevant reporting restrictions are lifted or expire will be regarded as a contemporaneous report and so enjoy the protection of section 4 of the Contempt of Court Act and absolute privilege in defamation law if the report is fair and accurate, and other requirements of those defences are met.

7.4.3 Liability for breach of the section 8C restrictions

Those who can be prosecuted for breach of the section 8C restrictions are the same as for breach of section 49 of the Children and Young Persons Act 1933, and include a publication's proprietor and editor. See 10.3.4, Breach of section 49 anonymity—liability and defences.

The penalty for breach is a fine unlimited by statute.

7.5 Procedure in summary trials

Though reporting restrictions cover pre-trial hearings, what is said in a trial at a magistrates' court can usually be reported fully as it occurs. No restrictions under the 1980 Act apply, but they could apply under other law, explained in chs. 10–12. Again, to be legally safe the reporting must be fair and accurate.

The usual summary trial procedure is as follows.

- The prosecutor makes an opening speech, describing the alleged crime.
- Witnesses testify, after swearing an oath or affirming that their evidence is true.
- Prosecution witnesses are called first. Each is asked questions by the prosecutor to elicit their **evidence-in-chief** (that is, evidence given during questioning by the side which called them). The defence can cross-examine them. The prosecution may then re-examine them.

→glossary

- Normally, to ensure witnesses tell of events in their own words, lawyers are not allowed to put leading questions to them when they give evidence-in-chief.

for context, see 5.1, Standard of proof in criminal law

- When prosecution evidence ends, the defence may submit, for any or all charges faced, that there is no case to answer—for example, that the prosecution cannot meet the standard of proof required.
- If the magistrates agree with this submission, they dismiss the relevant charge(s). Otherwise, or if no such submission is made, the trial continues.
- Defence witnesses are called. These may include the defendant, though they cannot be compelled to testify.
- Defence witnesses are questioned to elicit their evidence-in-chief. They can be cross-examined by the prosecutor and then re-examined by the defence.
- When the court has heard all witnesses, the prosecution and the defence may address the court in a closing speech, arguing how facts and law should be interpreted. Each side can address the court twice in total, in opening or closing speeches. The defence has the right to make the final speech.
- If the magistrates feel a charge is not proved, they acquit the defendant.
- If they find the defendant guilty on any charge, they are convicted of it, and the magistrates sentence the defendant, or adjourn to sentence at a later date.

! Remember your rights

There are court rules and case law on what case material journalists can see to help them report a trial, and a national protocol on what prosecution material can be released to them to help coverage of cases—see ch. 15 on open justice.

for context, see 5.1 on the presumption of innocence

7.5.1 'Bad character'

As a general rule, prosecutors in trials cannot refer to a defendant's previous 'bad character' because—to comply with the principle of the presumption of innocence—the focus is on evidence for the charge(s) being tried, not any past crime.

But evidence of previous offences and other reprehensible behaviour can be introduced to correct a false impression given by the defendant, or as evidence that they follow a distinctive method when committing offences of the kind with which they are charged, or if the defendant's evidence has attacked another person's character.

for context, see 15.16 on what must be stated aloud in court

7.6 Sentencing by magistrates

→glossary

At sentencing hearings for an admitted offence, the prosecution should tell the court details of the crime. If there is dispute about the facts of an admitted offence, the magistrates must accept the defence version unless the prosecution proves its version in a **Newton hearing**. Otherwise, defendants who admit an offence and those convicted at trial are sentenced in the same way, as follows.

The court will consider any statement from the victim or the victim's family about the crime's impact. Before sentence is passed, the defendant's lawyer can make a speech in mitigation, citing any extenuating circumstances while asking for leniency. A defendant may ask for other offences to be 'taken into consideration'. Offences to be 'taken into consideration', which should not be confused with previous convictions, are crimes which the defendant admits although they have not been charged with them.

see Useful Websites at the end of this chapter for the Government's guide to probation

The defendant brings these to the court's attention to be sentenced for them as well as for the charged offence(s). By admitting uncharged crimes—for example, burglaries—the defendant removes the possibility of being prosecuted for them in future, giving the opportunity of a fresh start.

Magistrates may also consider a 'pre-sentence report' about the defendant's background, prepared by a probation officer. A defendant being sentenced may appear in court via a video link from a prison if they have been denied bail or jailed because of an earlier conviction.

7.6.1 Jail sentences

Magistrates can jail a defendant for up to six months for a summary offence and, since November 2024, 12 months for a single either-way offence. Where magistrates are sentencing for more than one offence and decide to pass consecutive jail terms, they can impose a maximum of 12 months in total:

- Consecutive sentences are two or more jail terms ordered by the court to run one after the other, imposed when the defendant is convicted of more than one crime. For example—if a sentence of six months is made consecutive to one of three months, the overall sentence is nine months.
- **Concurrent sentences** are those where the defendant is sentenced overall for only the length of the longest sentence imposed. In the example just given, this would be six months. →glossary
- A defendant given a suspended sentence does not have go to jail unless they commit a further offence or breach a requirement of the suspended sentence—for example, to do unpaid community work—during the period for which the sentence is suspended. So, a jail term of six months can be suspended for two years. If the defendant commits no other offence in that time and does not breach any requirement, the suspended sentence lapses.

* Remember

A report which inaccurately portrays a suspended sentence as an immediate jail term could create a defamation risk, as an offender may complain this infers that the crime was worse than it was. For context on the need for accuracy in court reporting see 22.5, and 22.7 on the requirements of defamation defences.

7.6.2 Committal for sentence

Magistrates dealing with a defendant who has pleaded guilty to or been convicted of an either-way offence in a summary trial can, in most instances, send the case to the Crown court for a judge to sentence if they consider that their own limited sentencing powers are insufficient to meet the seriousness of the offence. This is called '**committal for sentence**'. A Crown court judge can impose longer jail terms. →glossary

7.6.3 Fines

Some offences can be punished by a fine but not by a jail sentence, though failure to pay the fine could lead to such a sentence. For years the maximum fine which magistrates could impose was £5,000, although most fines were much lower. But there is now a wide range of offences, such as health and safety breaches by employers, for which there is no maximum fine.

7.6.4 Other types of sentence

- *A community order, sometimes referred to as a 'community sentence'* or '*community punishment*'—The court orders a defendant to obey one or more →glossary

requirements, at least one of which (for an adult defendant) should normally be deemed by the court to be punitive, which could include:
- unpaid work in the community under a probation officer's direction, now branded 'community payback';
- a curfew, with a requirement that the offender wears an electronic 'tag' to monitor whether they obey it;
- a fine; and one or more non-punitive elements, for example a requirement to attend treatment for drug or alcohol dependency.

Any breaches of a community order can result in further punishment, such as additional hours of unpaid work or, in the most serious cases, a custodial sentence.

((•)) see Useful Websites at the end of this chapter for more detail on sentencing, including on community orders

- *A conditional discharge*—This means that the court has not immediately imposed or specified punishment, but states that if the offender commits any other offence within a period specified by the court, such as a year, they are liable to be punished for the first offence as well as for the subsequent conviction.
- *An absolute discharge*—This means that the court feels that no punishment, other than the fact of the conviction, is necessary.

As well as imposing a sentence a court can order an offender to pay compensation to a crime victim.

7.6.5 Binding over, restraining and protection orders

Since the fourteenth century, courts have had power to 'bind over' a person 'to keep the peace'. This can be used to resolve, without trial, minor allegations of assault, threatening behaviour or public disorder, in that the prosecution may drop a charge if the defendant agrees to be 'bound over'. A binding over can also follow a conviction. A witness too can be bound over, if, for example, they seem to have been involved in a fracas.

When binding over, the court specifies an amount which the person must pay if they breach the peace—for example, by violent or threatening conduct—within a specified period.

A court may impose a restraining order on a defendant, even one acquitted at trial, to protect another person—for example, an ex-partner—from harassment. The order may ban the defendant from any contact with that person. Police forces also have powers to apply to magistrates—even before a conviction or acquittal—for bespoke orders against a defendant to protect those at risk of domestic abuse or stalking.

All the above orders are preventative, civil law measures, not punishments, and they are *not* equivalent to a conviction and should not be reported as such.

7.6.6 Section 70 committal

Magistrates can make an order under section 70 of the Proceeds of Crime Act 2002 committing the case of a convicted offender to a Crown court hearing to assess what money or property they have gained from crime and, if necessary, to make a confiscation order. No automatic reporting restrictions apply to the committal hearing or the Crown court hearing, as such proceedings are considered by a judge rather than a jury. Note that magistrates also deal with applications made by police forces under the Act for court orders which can freeze the assets held by individuals or companies. Again, these are civil proceedings and the decision to grant a freezing or forfeiture order should not be reported as though it is a criminal conviction.

7.7 Many cases dealt with by post or online

For 'fixed penalty' offences a defendant need not appear at court if, having received written notice of the charge, they return a form admitting guilt and pay the fine. For such traffic offences—including speeding and driving without insurance—pleas can be made online, and many such cases are dealt with in the 'single justice procedure'.

7.8 Single justice procedure

Law created in 2015 allows a single magistrate—either a lay one or a district judge—to deal with some types of case in private. Around 65 per cent of all cases in the magistrates' courts are now dealt with via this 'single justice procedure' (SJP), detailed in sections 16A–16F and other amended sections of the Magistrates' Courts Act 1980.

The procedure is conducted entirely 'on the papers'—that is, solely by the magistrate considering the case documents—in private and in the absence of the defendant, who must have either pleaded guilty or failed to respond to a request for a plea. The magistrate does not hear any oral evidence or submissions. A defendant can request a hearing in open court, if they do so that is dealt with as a new case and not part of the SJP.

The procedure can take place only if all these conditions are met:

- the alleged offence is summary and not punishable by imprisonment;
- the defendant was 18 or older at the time of the alleged offence;
- the defendant sends by post or online a plea of guilty or has not responded to the 'written charge and notice'—which asks for a plea—served on them by the relevant prosecuting agency and;
- the defendant or their representative has not objected before the hearing to the procedure being used.

If no plea is indicated or the defendant has not responded to the 'written charge and notice' the magistrate decides in the SJP whether guilt is proved. A legal adviser (a court official) must be present, but a prosecutor does not have to be. This type of trial—because it involves a district judge or only one lay magistrate, and only documents—is called 'trial by single justice on the papers'.

A defendant whose case is dealt with in the SJP might not know the date or venue of the private hearing, because cases can be quickly switched from one courthouse to another if the first is too busy. The magistrate can decide that the case should be dealt with in open court if they consider it is 'not appropriate' to deal with the case in the SJP, and if so, the defendant must be summonsed to appear in open court.

Also, if a magistrate in the SJP proposes to use section 34 or 35 of the Road Traffic Offenders Act 1988 to ban the defendant from driving for any period—for example, for speeding—a defendant who wishes to make representations to oppose or limit the ban must do so in open court.

The Government has consulted on possible reforms to the SJP in recent years, after it came under renewed scrutiny following concerns raised in the media, most notably by the *London Evening Standard's* Court reporter Tristan Kirk, about defendants' circumstances not being properly considered before penalties were imposed on them, and a ruling which concluded it had been used incorrectly to prosecute rail fare evasions. No proposals had been issued at the time this book went to press—check www.mcnaes.com for updates.

! Remember your rights

Journalists may feel the single justice procedure, introduced to save costs, breaches the fundamental principle of open justice. Chapter 15 covers open justice matters including in 15.17, Getting information about and from 'single justice procedure' cases, the rights journalists have to discover the outcome and some detail of any SJP case.

7.9 New online procedures

Legislation introduced in the Judicial Review and Courts Act 2022 amended the Magistrates' Courts Act 1980 to create, as an alternative to the SJP, an 'automatic online conviction and penalty' procedure for certain summary cases concerning non-imprisonable offences which have 'no identifiable individual victim', such as speeding. This will enable defendants who wish to plead guilty to choose to have their entire case dealt with online, and to accept a penalty thereby determined automatically by a computerised system (e.g. a standard fine and/or 'points' added to their driving licence). At the time this book went to press, the pertinent parts of the Act were not yet in force (they are due to be implemented when parliamentary time allows), so it was unclear how the open justice principle can be maintained to enable the media to quickly report evidence and mitigation in such cases). See **www.mcnaes.com** for updates.

7.10 Appeal routes from magistrates' courts

The defence or prosecution may contest a ruling on law by a magistrates' court by appealing to the High Court through the 'case stated' procedure. In other types of challenge, the defence (or the media, if challenging a reporting restriction) can ask the High Court for a **judicial review**. → glossary

A defendant appealing against a conviction by a magistrates' court, or the severity of the sentence imposed, appeals to a Crown court.

for context, see 9.12, The Crown court as an appeal court, and 9.13, The High Court

Recap of major points

- Trials and sentencing at magistrates' courts are known as summary proceedings.
- Automatic reporting restrictions under section 8C of the Magistrates' Courts Act 1980 limit what the media can report from pre-trial hearings.
- Many trials at a magistrates' court can be reported fully and contemporaneously, though under the 'single justice procedure' many cases are now dealt with in private if the alleged offence cannot lead to a prison sentence.

Useful Websites

Magistrates' Association, www.magistrates-association.org.uk

Government guide to probation, www.gov.uk

Sentencing Council, 'Types of sentence', www.sentencingcouncil.org.uk

Online resources

Visit the online resources at **www.mcnaes.com** to test your knowledge of this chapter with **self-test questions** and a **flashcard glossary**, and to read **updates** about law and regulatory matters affecting journalism, as well as **additional material** to further your learning.

8

Magistrates' courts—the most serious criminal cases

Chapter summary

Adults charged with the most serious crimes—such as murder and robbery—make their first court appearance in a magistrates' court, usually having been held since arrest in police cells. Journalists may be on the court's press bench. But automatic reporting restrictions are in force in these preliminary hearings, to safeguard the defendant's right to fair trial by jury, because the case is bound for the Crown court. It is illegal for the media to breach the restrictions, but some newsworthy facts can be reported immediately from the magistrates' court. The restrictions also apply in preliminary hearings for either-way charges, such as sexual assault. Magistrates try some either-way cases. Youth courts, which deal with defendants aged under 18 when they are charged, are covered in ch. 10.

8.1 Processing of indictable-only and either-way charges

→glossary

Defendants charged with the most serious crimes cannot be tried by magistrates. These cases are, as ch. 6 explains, **indictable-only**. They have an initial phase in the magistrates' court, where decisions on case management may be made, but are quickly 'sent for trial' to a Crown court where, if the defendant denies the offence, a jury trial will take place.

A hearing at which a defendant on an indictable-only charge appears in a magistrates' court is therefore only a preliminary hearing, known as a 'sending' hearing. But it will be newsworthy if the alleged crime is already notorious. Usually a 'sending' hearing is the defendant's first—and only—appearance before magistrates.

bail is explained in 7.3

For most indictable-only cases, magistrates can decide in the sending hearing whether the defendant should be released on bail. But only a Crown court judge can decide on bail if the charge is murder (when bail is exceptional).

8.1.1 'Sending' of either-way cases

Some **either-way** cases are sent to the Crown court for trial if in the '**allocation**' procedure—explained later in this chapter—magistrates do not offer the defendant the option of **summary trial** or if the defendant wants trial by jury. An allocation hearing is a preliminary hearing which, if it determines that the either-way case is going to Crown court, is normally followed immediately by the sending hearing.

→glossary

→glossary

* Remember

Most decisions in a magistrates' courtroom are made by two or three lay magistrates but can be made by a district judge (who is a professional magistrate) sitting alone, as explained in 7.1. For convenience, this chapter refers only to 'magistrates' making decisions.

8.2 Section 52A automatic reporting restrictions

Automatic reporting restrictions, set out in in section 52A of the Crime and Disorder Act 1998, tightly limit what the media can publish contemporaneously from a **preliminary hearing** in a magistrates' courtroom concerning any indictable-only case, or an either-way case which retains potential for trial. The scope of the restrictions is set out in the next section. They restrict media reports of 'allocation' and 'sending' hearings from disclosing information which could create a risk of prejudice to jury trials—and cover *any* hearing of such cases at the magistrates' courts which occurs before 'allocation' or 'sending'.

→glossary

The concern is that people reading or listening to a news report of a preliminary hearing might include some who will later be called to be jurors in that case when it is tried at Crown court. Justice demands that jurors try the case only on the evidence presented at the trial and should not be influenced by what they remember from pre-trial coverage, so the law in section 52A limits what that coverage can be.

the jury system is explained in ch. 9

8.2.1 Types of prejudicial matter

The section 52A restrictions are designed to prevent publication from preliminary hearings of:

- any reference to evidence in the case, apart from what is encapsulated in the wording of the charge(s);
- a defendant's previous conviction(s);
- any other material with potential to create prejudice.

Evidence Some evidence might be referred to in detail in an allocation or sending hearing—for example, magistrates may need to hear it to assess the risk of a defendant reoffending if given bail or, in an either-way case, to assess whether they should be offered the option of summary trial (and, if that offer is made, for them to reach a decision on indication of sentence, see later). However, some evidence mentioned by the prosecution or defence at such a preliminary hearing might not figure in the trial. When the case reaches the Crown court a judge might rule, before the trial itself, that some evidence is inadmissible—for example, evidence that a defendant confessed to police that they committed the crime will be ruled inadmissible if the judge accepts that the confession was made under duress. Therefore, reports of a preliminary hearing at a magistrates' court should not refer to evidence. Otherwise a juror might recall, from such reports, inadmissible evidence. The law assumes that one juror would tell the others. That might mean the jury wrongly convicts a defendant.

Previous convictions Generally, because of the 'presumption of innocence', a Crown court jury is not told if a defendant has previous conviction(s). But a defendant's criminal record may have been referred to months earlier in a sending hearing—for example, to help magistrates decide on bail. In an either-way case, magistrates will be told in the allocation procedure whether the defendant has a criminal record, for them to decide whether to offer summary trial and to make bail decisions. If a media report of an allocation or sending hearing was allowed to disclose what was said in it about a defendant's criminal record, jurors who recalled or were told of the report could remember that the defendant had that record, and that knowledge could prejudice them against the defendant when deciding a verdict.

presumption of innocence is explained in 5.1

Other potentially prejudicial material This could include suggestions by the prosecution in an allocation or 'sending' hearing that a defendant is guilty of more offences than the crime alleged in the charge(s). For example, in a rape case police might check other unsolved rapes if they suspect that the defendant is a serial rapist, and magistrates might hear of those inquiries from a prosecutor opposing bail. The inquiries might come to nothing, but allowing media reports of the sending hearing to air those suspicions could lead to a juror remembering them, and so could influence jurors against the defendant. It could also be prejudicial to report from an allocation hearing that an indication of sentence was given in an either-way case—for example, if a jury realised that this could mean the defendant at that preliminary stage was considering pleading guilty—see later.

8.2.2 The scope of the section 52A restrictions

The section 52A restrictions list categories of information from preliminary hearings at a magistrates' court which can be published, and so to a large extent implicitly define what cannot be published.

The list of what can be published is expressed here in simplified format:

- the name of the court and the magistrates' names;
- the accused's name, age, home address and occupation;
- the charge(s) in full or summarised—which typically includes the name of the victim(s);
- in the case of an accused charged with a 'serious or complex' fraud, any 'relevant business information'—see later;

- the names of **counsel** and solicitors engaged in the proceedings; →glossary
- if proceedings are adjourned, the date and place to which they are adjourned;
- 'arrangements as to bail'—whether bail was granted, and if it was, any conditions and **surety** arrangement; →glossary
- if bail is refused, the usual approach is that media organisations do *not* report that the prosecution opposed bail, and in particular should not report why it was opposed, or the magistrates' reasons for refusing bail, as such information might be prejudicial—but it would be safe to report that someone was remanded in custody for their own protection;
- whether **legal aid** was authorised to pay for the defendant(s) to be represented by a lawyer. →glossary

Home addresses can include any current one, and past addresses from 'any relevant time'—that is, a time when events giving rise to the charge(s) in the case occurred. To avoid defamation, care is needed in references to former addresses—as explained in 7.4.1.1.

Section 52A says that if the case in the preliminary hearing is 'serious or complex' fraud, a report of the hearing can include 'relevant business information'. This business information is the same as that which can be reported from Crown court hearings dealing with applications for such fraud charges to be dismissed—see 9.4.3.

for 'serious or complex' fraud, see also 8.3.1.3

The scope in section 52A for reporting the place to which the case has been adjourned permits, on any logical interpretation, saying that a case has been 'sent for trial' to the relevant Crown court.

The fact that reporting restrictions are in force can be reported. Section 52A does not specify this, but it cannot be prejudicial to publish this fact. Any argument or discussion in court about whether the section 52A reporting restrictions should be lifted should not be reported contemporaneously even if the court decides to lift them—see 8.2.7.1.

8.2.3 Reporting denials of guilt and choice of jury trial

When reporting preliminary hearings covered by section 52A media organisations routinely publish:

- *basic protestations of innocence* made by the defendant from the dock or through a solicitor—in an indictable-only case no formal plea is taken at the magistrates' court, but it may be made clear there that the charge is denied; and defendants are asked to give a non-binding indication of how they will plead;
- *that a defendant, in an either-way case, has chosen trial by jury*. Although publication of even basic protestations of innocence and choice of jury trial is beyond what strict application of section 52A would permit, the media are safe in reporting these facts, because:
- it seems only fair to the defendant to quote their denial of guilt—if made in relation to the only charge faced or to all charges—and choice of jury trial, which too indicates denial of the charge(s);

- publishing such matter cannot be prejudicial—a jury, obviously, will know if a charge is denied, but it would not be safe to include, without legal advice, any allegation which the defendant makes in a denial voiced in a preliminary hearing—for example, against the police.

The media should be wary, when the restrictions apply, of reporting anything suggesting a defendant will enter, at Crown court, a mixture of pleas—for example, quotes suggesting they are likely to admit one charge but deny another. There may be no such admission, or the jury may not be told of it. If any juror can recall the suggestion from a report, this might prejudice the jury against the defendant.

✱ Remember

The Government is considering radical proposals to remove the option of a jury trial for certain offences—see Late News for details and check **www.mcnaes.com** for updates.

8.2.4 Describing the courtroom scene

The media routinely report, even when section 52A restrictions apply, scene-setting information: that the hearing lasted 10 minutes; what the defendant wore; that they 'spoke only to confirm their name and address'; that guards stood on either side of them. Such bland material will not cause prejudice.

8.2.5 Background material

Media organisations publishing reports of preliminary hearings usually add some background material about the defendant and/or the alleged crime if it has already been in the news. Background material, from sources other than the court hearing, is not itself a report of those proceedings and so does not contravene section 52A. But the Contempt of Court Act 1981 would cover such material, so nothing should be published which creates a substantial risk of serious prejudice or impediment—see ch. 19. Mingling background material into a court report without sufficient care could create such a risk—for example, potential jurors who see/hear the report could draw wrong inferences about what the evidence is.

An option for the media, when they want to report on an alleged crime committed, say, in the previous 24 hours, but for which the alleged perpetrator has already appeared in court in a preliminary hearing, is to publish items segregated by page design or separate narrative. Each item could have its own headline/introduction—a story on the alleged incident, conforming to contempt law, not citing material from the court hearing, and, segregated, a separate report solely of the preliminary hearing, conforming to the section 52A restrictions.

8.2.6 Liability for breach of the section 52A restrictions

Section 52B of the 1998 Act says 'any proprietor, editor or publisher' of a newspaper or periodical can be prosecuted if it breaches the section 52A restrictions. If the breach is published in any other type of written report—for example, on a website not linked to a newspaper—'the person who publishes it' can be prosecuted.

In the case of a TV or radio programme, 'the body corporate which provides the service' and any person 'having functions in relation to the programme corresponding to those of an editor of a newspaper' can be prosecuted. The penalty is a fine unlimited by statute.

Case study

In 2013 *The Sun* newspaper was fined £3,350 after it admitted breaching the section 52A restrictions in its report of the hearing in which Oldham magistrates' court sent the case of Andrew Partington, charged with manslaughter and criminal damage, to Manchester Crown court for trial. The report—including its headline 'Gas pipe's cut, boom . . . you bitch'—quoted evidence from texts, described as the crux of the prosecution case, in which Partington threatened his girlfriend. Fining *The Sun*, District Judge Jonathan Taaffe said at Manchester magistrates' court that this was 'shoddy' journalism. He endorsed the view that it went way beyond what was permitted, and that its content and tone created a substantial risk of prejudice. At Crown court Partington, 28, of Buckley Street, Oldham, was jailed for 10 years after admitting causing the gas blast which destroyed houses and killed a neighbour's child (Judiciary of England and Wales press release, *The Independent* and BBC online news, 5 April 2013).

see Useful Websites at the end of this chapter

Remember

If a breach of the section 52A restrictions occurs after a trial has begun and is serious enough—because of what is published—to cause the trial to be aborted, a media organisation might also become liable for huge costs under section 93 of the Courts Act 2003 which can punish 'serious misconduct'. For detail of this law in the 2003 Act, see 19.13 in this book.

8.2.7 When do the section 52A restrictions cease to apply?

The restrictions cease to apply in three sets of circumstances.

8.2.7.1 A magistrates' court can lift the restrictions

Magistrates' courts have a discretionary power to lift the restrictions, wholly or in part, including at the request of a defendant. If a defendant objects, the restrictions may only be lifted if the magistrates decide that doing so is in the interests of justice. A defendant might want restrictions lifted so their solicitor can publicise an appeal for witnesses through a full media report of the hearing—for example, the defence solicitor might be seeking witnesses to help corroborate the defendant's **alibi**: 'My client was at the funfair, not the crime scene. Did anyone see him at the fair?'

→glossary

Section 52A says that if any defendant (whether a sole defendant or a co-accused) makes such objection, the proceedings relating to it (that is, the objection, and argument and discussion in court about whether the restrictions should be lifted) cannot be reported, even if the restrictions are lifted in other respects, until it is clear there will be no trial in the case or until the 'conclusion' of all trials in the case—see next sections. However, the fact that an order to lift the restrictions was made, or not made, *can* be reported at the time of that order.

It can be construed from case law that if a magistrates' court decides, after a request from one defendant, to lift the section 52A restrictions, they are lifted in respect of all defendants in the case—even if any objected (*Leeds Justices, ex p Sykes* [1983] 1 WLR 132).

For an example of a report of a hearing in which the restrictions were lifted, see *Express and Star* report in Useful Websites at the end of this chapter.

8.2.7.2 The restrictions lapse if it becomes clear there will be no trial

The section 52A restrictions automatically cease to apply to a report of an allocation hearing if the sole defendant, or all the defendants in the case, plead guilty to each either-way charge faced (and there are no indictable-only charges in the case). This means there will be no trial and no 'sending' of the case to Crown court.

8.2.7.3 The restrictions lapse after the last trial ends or if the case does not proceed

The section 52A restrictions on a report of an allocation and/or sending hearing automatically cease to apply 'after conclusion' of the trial of the defendant(s) or—if there is more than one trial—the last trial in the case. This means that if an either-way case is tried summarily, the restrictions cease to apply at the end of that trial if that is the only one in the case.

As regards a case sent to Crown court for trial, they automatically cease to apply if the sole defendant pleads guilty there to the sole charge or all charges, or, if there is more than one defendant, they all plead guilty to each charge they face. The restrictions also automatically finish if in either court all the charges are discontinued or withdrawn, and the court therefore formally acquits the defendant(s). Otherwise, the restrictions cease to apply after delivery of the last verdict in the only or last trial in the case.

✱ Remember

The section 52A restrictions affect only what can be reported from allocation and/or sending proceedings, and do not affect the reporting of a trial, wherever it is held.

8.2.7.4 Why the media may want to air material from preliminary hearings

When section 52A restrictions automatically cease to apply to a case, all evidence, discussion and argument aired in its preliminary hearing(s) at a magistrates' court weeks or months earlier can (unless the court imposed another restriction) be fully reported. For example, the media may wish to highlight evidence which, for legal reasons, the jury did not hear, but which might throw more light on the defendant or on how the crime was investigated.

> See the **additional material** for ch. 8 on **www.mcnaes.com** for an example of a newspaper reporting evidence aired at a preliminary hearing months after it occurred.

for context, see 19.9.3, Court reporting—the section 4 defence, and 22.5, Absolute privilege

8.2.7.5 Contempt and defamation considerations

A report of preliminary proceedings published as soon as practicable after the section 52A restrictions are lifted or expire will be regarded as a contemporaneous report and so enjoy the protection of section 4 of the Contempt of Court Act 1981 and absolute privilege in defamation law. To be legally safe the reporting must be fair and accurate.

8.3 Procedure in allocations hearings and whether section 52A applies

To understand whether the section 52A restrictions continue to apply in an either-way case, it is necessary to know how a magistrates' court deals with these cases.

All either-way cases will have at least one preliminary hearing in a magistrates' courtroom. If the defendant indicates that their plea will be 'not guilty', the allocation procedure takes place. Either-way cases include **theft**, burglary and sexual assault charges. A defendant in an either-way case has a right to jury trial, but may choose not to exercise it. Allocation determines whether a defendant whose indication of plea is 'not guilty' will be tried summarily (that is, by magistrates) or by a jury on that charge. So allocation determines the 'venue' of the trial. Figure 8.1 summarises how an either-way case is processed in a courtroom.

→glossary

8.3.1 Plea, allocation and sending procedure in most either-way cases

In most types of either-way case the defendant is asked, usually in its first hearing in the magistrates' court, to indicate how they intend to plead to the charge. This is called the 'plea before venue' procedure.

8.3.1.1 If the defendant indicates an intention to plead guilty

If a defendant indicates an intention to plead guilty, this is usually treated as a formal plea of guilty, convicting them of that offence (unless, exceptionally, the court does not accept the plea—for example, if it has concerns that the defendant does not fully understand what is happening).

If this is the only charge in the case, the section 52A restrictions automatically lapse because of that conviction, as there will be no trial. The magistrates will sentence the defendant at that hearing or a later one. But they may decide, after hearing more detail of the offence and of the defendant's previous conviction(s), that their powers of punishment are insufficient and that the case should be 'committed for sentence' to the Crown court, which means the defendant will be sentenced there.

magistrates' sentencing powers are explained in ch. 7

Figure 8.1 Processing of either-way cases in magistrates' courtrooms

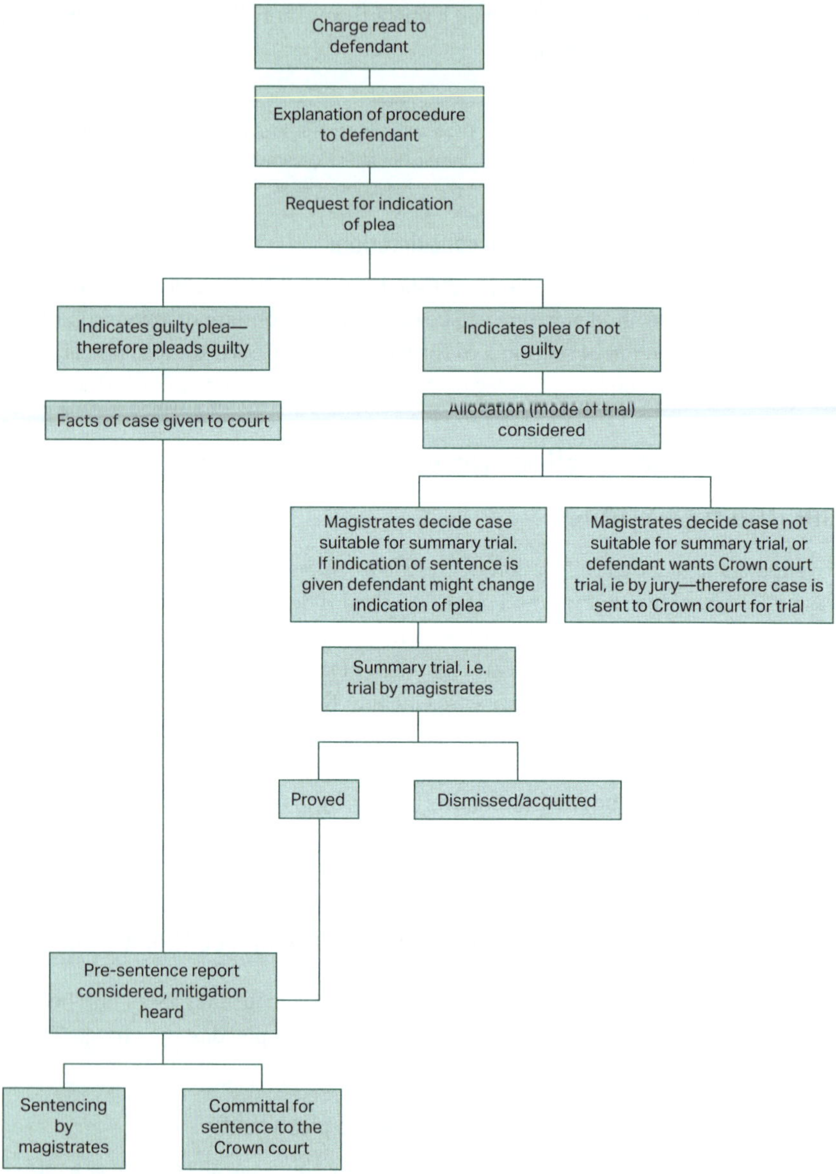

Source: Adapted from a design produced by the Judicial College

8.3.1.2 If the defendant indicates that they will plead not guilty

If the defendant indicates that they will plead not guilty, or does not give an indication of plea, the magistrates will decide in allocation procedure whether they should be offered the option of summary trial. This decision is based primarily on whether the magistrates consider that they have sufficient power to punish the defendant, should they convict them. The maximum sentence which a magistrates' court can impose is 12 months for a single offence (see 7.6.1).

In the allocation procedure, the magistrates are told some detail of the evidence which gave rise to the charge, so they can assess the seriousness of the allegation—for example, the crime's effect on the alleged victim. They are told too whether the defendant has any previous conviction(s), because a defendant with a criminal record may well deserve more severe punishment than a first-time offender. If the magistrates decide the case is too serious for them to try, it is sent to Crown court for a jury trial, and the section 52A restrictions normally continue to apply to reports of the 'allocation' hearing and 'sending' until that trial concludes (as outlined earlier in 8.2.7).

If magistrates agree that they can try the case—that is, they 'accept jurisdiction'—the defendant is then asked if they want a summary or jury trial. Juries are regarded as more likely to acquit, but if the case goes to Crown court, the defendant risks getting a heavier sentence than magistrates can impose if convicted, will probably have to wait longer to be tried, and faces high legal expenses (if not on legal aid).

Section 20 of the Magistrates' Courts Act 1980 means that at this stage of the allocation hearing, the defendant can ask the magistrates for an indication of sentence. If an indication is given, it is on the basis that the defendant will agree to the case being dealt with summarily and, despite the earlier indication of a 'not guilty' plea, will plead guilty; and the magistrates say merely whether the court would impose a jail term for the offence, or a more lenient, non-custodial punishment (which is not specified). The magistrates can choose not to give this broad indication of sentence. But if they give it, and if the defendant does opt to be dealt with summarily and proceeds to plead guilty, and if that is the only charge in the case, the section 52A restrictions cease to apply, because, as explained in 8.3.1.1, the defendant is convicted of the offence. The defendant must normally be sentenced in accordance with the indication given.

If no indication of sentence is requested, or magistrates choose not to give one, or after hearing the indication, the defendant decides to persist with the intention to plead not guilty (for example, because that seems their best hope of avoiding jail), they must then choose between having a summary trial or a jury trial.

If the defendant chooses jury trial, magistrates will send the case to Crown court—see the next chapter for what happens there.

If the defendant chooses to be tried by the magistrates' court, they are asked to enter a formal plea. If they plead not guilty, it will be arranged for the trial to take place there, most likely after an adjournment to permit preparations. Also, other reporting restrictions, under section 8C of the Magistrates' Courts Act 1980, automatically come into force to cover any subsequent pre-trial proceedings which take place before the summary trial. These restrictions, similar in format to those of section 52A (in the 1998 Act), are explained in ch. 7. The section 52A restrictions normally continue to apply to reports of the allocation hearing until the trial concludes (again, see 8.2.7). Again, the section 52A and section 8C restrictions do not affect the reporting of a trial itself.

8.3.1.3 Two types of either-way case are simply 'sent'

The exception to the normal procedures is that two types of either-way case do not have allocation hearings but are simply 'sent' to the Crown court for trial, as if they were indictable-only offences. These are 'serious or complex' fraud cases, or cases in which the alleged offending is sexual or violent *and* a child (possibly the alleged victim) is due to be a witness.

This streamlined procedure indicates that such cases are too serious to be dealt with by magistrates and, as regards the latter category, expedites the sending to minimise the time a child witness has to wait before giving evidence.

Recap of major points

- An indictable-only case will be 'sent for trial' to the Crown court.
- A denied either-way offence can in most instances be tried by magistrates or by a jury. The defendant can choose trial by jury.
- Reporting restrictions in section 52A of the Crime and Disorder Act 1998 automatically apply to media reports of 'allocation' and 'sending' hearings in the magistrates' court.

Useful Websites

***Express and Star*, 'Halesowen murder suspect acted in self-defence, claim', www.expressandstar.com**

Express and Star newspaper report of a preliminary hearing in which reporting restrictions were lifted

***R v News Group Newspapers Limited*, sentencing remarks of District Judge Jonathan Taaffe, www.judiciary.gov.uk**

District Judge Jonathan Taaffe's remarks when fining *The Sun* for breach of the section 52A restrictions in the Andrew Partington case

***The Independent*, 'Sun fined £3,000 for Oldham gas explosion reporting breach', www.independent.co.uk**

The Independent's report of *The Sun* being fined

BBC News, 'Jamie Heaton blast death: Andrew Partington jailed', www.bbc.co.uk

BBC report of Partington being sentenced

Online resources

Visit the online resources at **www.mcnaes.com** to test your knowledge of this chapter with **self-test questions** and a **flashcard glossary**, and to read **updates** about law and regulatory matters affecting journalism, as well as **additional material** to further your learning.

9

Crown courts and appeal courts

Chapter summary

Crown courts deal with the most serious criminal cases, including murder. Their trials lead to the tense moment when the jury announces the verdict, with the press bench full for major cases. This chapter details the work of Crown courts, the jury's role and how reporting restrictions ban the media from publishing full reports of pre-trial hearings. It also outlines the work of the High Court, Court of Appeal and Supreme Court.

9.1 Roles at Crown courts

There are Crown courts at around 80 locations in England and Wales, in administrative regions referred to as 'circuits'. The most famous is the Central Criminal Court in London—known as the Old Bailey.

In Crown court trials:

- juries decide if each charge is proved;
- judges rule on law and sentence convicted defendants.

In exceptionally rare circumstances—for example, if there is a real risk that criminals could intimidate jurors to acquit a defendant—a Crown court trial can proceed with no jury, leaving the judge to decide the verdict(s).

9.1.1 Who are jurors?

A Crown court jury consists of 12 people, aged between 18 and 75, selected randomly from electoral rolls for the local districts and summoned to appear for jury service. Some categories of people, such as anyone jailed in the previous 10 years, are barred from being jurors.

* Remember

The Government is considering restricting the use of jury trial for some offences and creating a new tier of court between Magistrates and Crown—see Late News and check **www.mcnaes.com** for updates.

9.1.1.1 Types of Crown court judge

Three types of judge sit in Crown courts:

- High Court judges—those who can sit in the High Court and Crown courts. They are referred to as, for instance, 'Mr Justice Smith' or 'Mrs Justice Smith', and wear red robes for criminal cases. They sit in Crown courts to try the most serious offences, such as murder, as they are generally the most experienced judges.
- Circuit judges, referred to as 'Judge John Smith' or 'Judge Mary Smith', are lawyers who have held 'rights of audience' (that is, the right to represent clients) for at least seven years, or have been a Recorder (or held other judicial roles on a full-time basis) for at least three years.
- →glossary **Recorders**—part-time judges—are barristers, or solicitors who have held 'rights of audience' at Crown court. Recorders are usually referred to as 'the Recorder, Mr John Smith' or 'the Recorder, Mrs Mary Smith'.

* Remember

Some cities have bestowed the title of 'Honorary Recorder of—' on the senior circuit judge, who also carries out ceremonial duties.

9.1.2 Lawyers at Crown court

→glossary

Prosecutions at Crown court are conducted by barristers. Barristers also usually appear for the defence. Barristers are referred to as '**counsel**'. Solicitors have 'rights of audience' in some circumstances. A court clerk sits in each Crown court in front of the judge, to assist in procedures. Ushers assist in the courtroom.

see the roles of solicitors and barristers explained in 1.6

9.2 Routes to Crown court

A case yet to be tried reaches a Crown court because it has been sent for trial by a magistrates' court or youth court—see 8.1, Processing of indictable-only and either-way charges, and 10.2.4, Some youth court cases go to an adult court—or by a High Court judge by means of a voluntary bill of indictment, a rare legal process explained in the **additional material** for ch. 9 on **www.mcnaes.com**.

A case may also be heard by the Crown court if it has been committed by a magistrates' court for sentence or subject to 'section 70' committal—see in 7.6.2 and 7.6.6. Or if an appeal, see 9.12.

9.3 Arraignment

A defendant whose case is sent to a Crown court for trial is asked to plead guilty or not guilty to each charge on the **indictment**, so formal pleas can be recorded. This process is known as '**arraignment**'. At Crown court charges are referred to as 'counts'. See also 9.5, Reporting the arraignment.

→glossary

→glossary

9.4 Hearings prior to jury involvement—automatic reporting restrictions

for context, see 7.3, Bail

In cases in which a defendant denies guilt, there will be at least one hearing at Crown court before the jury is involved. A defendant might appear at a pre-trial hearing via a video link from prison, if **bail** has been denied previously. **Statutes** impose **automatic** reporting restrictions on what can be published contemporaneously from some of these hearings. The hearings are for the judge to make rulings, some of which may determine what the jury will be told if the case goes to trial, or make bail decisions.

→glossary

→glossary

The reporting restrictions are to prevent publication of information which could prejudice a trial. The principle is that potential jurors should not know what was discussed at hearings before the trial in which they will sit. Potentially prejudicial material which could be discussed at these hearings includes a defendant's previous conviction(s), or evidence ruled inadmissible. For examples of what can cause prejudice if published, see 8.2.1, Types of prejudicial matter, which also explains similar restrictions in section 52A of the Crime and Disorder Act 1998, which apply—for the same reason—to media coverage of **preliminary hearings** in magistrates' courts.

→glossary

9.4.1 The scope of the automatic reporting restrictions

The automatic restrictions limiting media reports of some types of pre-trial hearing at Crown courts are in various statutes, but of the same format. They restrict these reports to seven categories of information:

- the name of the Crown court and judge;
- the names, ages, home addresses and occupations of defendant(s) and witness(es);
- the charge(s), or a summary of it/them;
- the names of solicitors or barristers in the case;
- if proceedings are adjourned, the date and place to which they are adjourned;
- any arrangements as to bail—that is, whether bail was granted, and if it was, any bail conditions and surety arrangement;
- whether **legal aid** was authorised.

→glossary

Witnesses are unlikely to take part in a hearing before trial. But if they do, or are mentioned in court, under these restrictions they can be named in reports, unless other law gives them anonymity.

Chs. 11–12 explain anonymity law, and ch. 10 explains that it may cover children or young persons in Crown court cases.

In cases in which bail is refused, the usual interpretation of the restrictions is that the media should not report if and why the prosecution opposed bail or the reasons the judge gave for refusing it, as such information could be prejudicial.

Home addresses can include any current one, and past addresses from 'any relevant time'—that is, a time when events giving rise to the charge(s) in the case occurred. To avoid defamation risk, care is needed in references to former addresses—as explained in 7.4.1.1.

9.4.2 Which types of hearing?

The types of hearing for which the above format of restrictions apply are:

- ***Unsuccessful applications for a case to be dismissed, prior to arraignment*** A defendant whose case is sent for trial to Crown court may apply to a judge, before arraignment, for it to be dismissed because of insufficient evidence. The reporting restrictions on such hearings are detailed in Schedule 3 to the Crime and Disorder Act 1998.
- ***'Preparatory hearings'*** A Crown court may hold a 'preparatory hearing' in a case involving a serious offence or which will involve a complex or lengthy trial. A preparatory hearing must be held in a terrorism case. The hearings are so the judge can make preparatory rulings, such as on the admissibility of evidence, and discuss with the lawyers how the jury can best be assisted in understanding trial issues. Such a hearing, if held, takes place before the jury is sworn. If the arraignment has not yet taken place, it must happen at the start of the preparatory hearing. The reporting restrictions—again, in the format set out earlier—are in section 11 of the Criminal Justice Act 1987 for preparatory hearings in 'serious or complex fraud' cases, and in section 37 of the Criminal Procedure and Investigations Act 1996 in respect of preparatory hearings in other types of case.

for what 'sworn' means, see 9.6.1

The same restrictions apply, generally under section 37 of the 1996 Act and—for serious or complex fraud cases—under section 11 of the 1987 Act to media reports of any application to a Crown court judge for leave to appeal against rulings made at a 'preparatory hearing' and to any such appeal in a higher court.

9.4.3 'Relevant business information'

Section 11 of the Criminal Justice Act 1987 allows journalists covering an unsuccessful application for a 'serious or complex' fraud case to be dismissed, or covering a preparatory hearing in such a case to include 'relevant business information' in reports of the hearing even when the automatic restrictions are in place. This means the media can include in the report:

- any address used by the defendant for carrying on a business on their own account;
- the name of any such business at any relevant time—that is, when events which gave rise to the charge(s) occurred;
- the name and address of any firm in which they were a partner at any relevant time or by which they were engaged at any such time, and the address of any such firm;
- the name of any company of which they were a director at any relevant time or by which they were otherwise engaged at any such time, and the address of its registered or principal office;
- any working address of the defendant in their capacity as a person engaged by any such company.

'Engaged' means under a contract of service or a contract for services.

9.4.4 What else can be reported?

In addition to the information which the format of restrictions lists as safe to publish, it is safe to include in reports of pre-trial Crown court hearings neutral descriptions of the court scene and non-prejudicial background facts of the type outlined in ch. 8 in relation to preliminary hearings before magistrates—see 8.2.4 and 8.2.5.

9.4.5 'Pre-trial' hearings—automatic reporting restrictions

The Criminal Procedure and Investigations Act 1996 defines a 'pre-trial hearing' as any hearing at a Crown court before a guilty plea is accepted (that is, before it becomes clear there will be no trial), or—in cases which remain contested—all hearings which occur before a jury is sworn or before the beginning of a 'preparatory' hearing. Reporting restrictions in section 41 of the Act automatically ban publication, before the conclusion of all proceedings in the case, of what is said in 'pre-trial hearings', which are:

- proceedings on applications for rulings on the admissibility of evidence or any other question of law;
- proceedings on applications for such a ruling to be varied or discharged.

The ban also covers what is said in any such ruling or order by the judge.

9.4.6 The safest course to obey the restrictions

The law enshrining these various sets of restrictions developed piecemeal. Their definitions of hearings held at Crown court before a trial overlap, and the extent to which the restrictions apply to all types of these hearings is unclear.

see also 9.5, Reporting the arraignment, about charges

A journalist's safest course, to avoid breaching the law in a contemporaneous report of a Crown court hearing held before a jury becomes involved—that is, a contested case—is to include only the categories of information listed under the heading 'The scope of the automatic reporting restrictions', plus in fraud cases 'relevant business information', and non-prejudicial descriptive or background information (see 9.4.4), unless the judge has lifted the relevant restrictions.

9.4.7 When do the automatic reporting restrictions cease to apply?

A Crown court judge can lift the restrictions, wholly or in part, including at the request of a defendant, to allow more detailed contemporaneous media reports of such hearings. If any defendant objects to this, the judge may lift them only if satisfied that doing so is in the interests of justice. The fact that there was such an objection, and argument and discussion in court about whether the restrictions should be lifted, cannot be reported until it is clear there will be no trial in the case or until the 'conclusion' of all trials in the case, even if the restrictions were lifted earlier, by the judge, in other respects. The fact that an order to lift the restrictions was made, or not made, *can* be reported at the time of that order.

The 1998 Act makes clear that its restrictions automatically cease to apply if all charges in the case against each of the defendants are dismissed for lack of evidence—so there will be no trial. Otherwise, they automatically cease to apply 'at the conclusion of the trial of the person charged, or of the last of the persons charged to be tried'. In essence, this wording is also used in the 1987 and 1996 Acts to define the automatic endpoints of their restrictions. From this, it can be safely construed that each of these sets of restrictions automatically ceases to apply at the acquittal or conviction of a sole defendant or, when there are co-accused, of all defendants, in respect of all charges in all trials in the case. If any such charge does not result in a guilty plea, a finding of guilt or an acquittal, or has not been dismissed for lack of evidence, and it is not clear whether it has been withdrawn by the prosecution, the journalist should check with the court whether any such restriction remains in force.

for context, see 19.9, Court reporting—the section 4 defence, and 22.5, Absolute privilege

A report published 'as soon as practicable' after the relevant reporting restrictions are lifted or expire will be regarded as a contemporaneous report and so enjoy the protection of section 4 of the Contempt of Court Act and absolute privilege in defamation law if the report is fair and accurate, and other requirements of those defences are met.

! Remember your rights

These restrictions on the reporting of pre-trial hearings do not prevent the contemporaneous reporting of what is said in any trial in the case. Reporting restrictions under other law may still apply—see chs. 10–12.

For a case study on how in 2014 a judge at Southwark Crown court agreed to lift reporting restrictions covering a pre-trial hearing, see the **additional material** for ch. 9 on **www.mcnaes.com**.

9.4.8 Liability for breach of the automatic reporting restrictions

Liability and penalty for breach of the reporting restrictions under the Acts cited earlier are the same as for breach of restrictions in section 52A of the Crime and Disorder Act—see 8.2.6. If a breach occurs after a trial has begun, and is serious enough—because of what is published—to cause it to be aborted, a media organisation may also become liable for huge costs under section 93 of the Courts Act 2003—see 19.13.

9.4.9 Appeals against rulings by judge—reporting restrictions

The Criminal Justice Act 2003 gives the prosecution the right to appeal to the Court of Appeal against a ruling by a Crown court judge which would terminate all or part of the case—for example, that there is no case to answer, or a ruling on the admissibility of prosecution evidence—no matter what stage the case has reached when the ruling is made. Section 71 of the Act, intended to prevent prejudice to the trial or to any linked trial, automatically bans reporting of any Crown court discussion (which, if the trial has begun, would be in the jury's absence) about such an appeal. It also restricts reports of the Court of Appeal hearing, and of any further appeal made to the Supreme Court, to the seven categories of information listed earlier (see 9.4.1). These restrictions apply, unless lifted earlier, until the conclusion of all trials in the case. Liability and penalty for breach of the reporting restrictions are the same as for breach of restrictions in section 49 of the Youth Justice and Criminal Evidence Act 1999—see 10.3.4.

> In the proceedings featured in the 2014 case study, the Court of Appeal lifted the section 71 restrictions. See the **additional material** for ch. 9 on **www.mcnaes.com**.

9.5 Reporting the arraignment

If, at the arraignment, defendants in a case plead guilty to each charge, they are convicted of each charge, in which case the restrictions detailed earlier in this chapter cease to apply as there will be no trial.

If, at the arraignment, a sole defendant or all defendants deny the charge or charges, the media can safely report those pleas contemporaneously if there will be just one trial in the case.

But if a defendant or co-defendants enter a mixture of guilty and not guilty pleas, or if denied charges are to be dealt with in more than one trial, a judge may—to avoid what they consider a substantial risk of prejudice—make an order under section 4(2) of the Contempt of Court Act 1981 postponing publication of some of that information. A judge could do this, for example, to ban media reports of an arraignment from mentioning, until the trial ends, any charge which has been admitted (if the jury is not to be told about it) or—if the case will involve more than one trial—any charge not due to be dealt with in the first trial. Or the judge could use section 4(2) to ban any reporting of the arraignment, and of the first trial, until any further trial in the case is concluded.

For detail on section 4(2) orders and for considerations to be borne in mind even if a judge does not make such an order, see, 19.10, Section 4(2) orders.

9.6 Procedure in Crown court trials

chs. 10–12 explain these restrictions and anonymity laws

The media can publish full, contemporaneous reports of what the jury is told at a Crown court trial once it has started, but must comply with any discretionary reporting restriction or any automatic anonymity for a victim/alleged victim of a sexual, trafficking, female genital mutilation or forced marriage offence.

* Remember

Until the jury has returned all verdicts, no report of a trial should include—unless the judge says otherwise—any ruling, discussion or argument which takes place in the jury's absence. This is to comply with the law on contempt of court—see 19.10.2. To comply with contempt law and defamation law, reporting of the trial must be fair and accurate—see 19.9, Court reporting—the section 4 defence; 22.5, Absolute privilege; and 22.7, Qualified privilege by statute.

9.6.1 Selection of the jury and the giving of evidence

A Crown court trial is under way when the jury is 'empanelled'—that is, when a group of potential jurors is taken into the courtroom and the court clerk selects 12 at random. These will be 'sworn'—required to swear an oath or make an affirmation that they will try the case according to the evidence.

for the sequence, see 7.5, Procedure in summary trials

Soon after this prosecution counsel 'opens the case' by outlining it. Prosecution witnesses then testify. A Crown court trial usually follows the same sequence used in magistrates' trials as regards the giving of evidence, including cross-examination, and speeches by lawyers.

At Crown court defence counsel may choose to make a speech 'opening' the defence case prior to calling defence witnesses. After all these have been heard, prosecuting counsel in most cases makes a closing speech to the jury, which is followed by the defence's closing speech.

The judge then sums up the case, to remind jurors of evidence and direct them on the law. The judge will, if they decide that evidence is not sufficient to support a charge, direct the jury to bring in a verdict of not guilty on that charge.

→glossary

Otherwise, and to consider any other charge, the jury 'retires' to a jury room to decide the verdict(s). A jury **bailiff** (one of the ushers) escorts jurors to and from the room, and is the only official allowed contact with them in it. The jury will have been directed to elect a foreperson to speak on its behalf.

9.6.2 Majority verdicts

A judge initially asks a jury to reach a unanimous verdict on each charge—that is, a unanimous decision to acquit or convict.

- But if a jury has deliberated the case for at least 2 hours and 10 minutes and has failed to reach a verdict, the judge can recall it to the courtroom to direct it that a majority verdict is acceptable (for each charge). This may mean such a verdict is thereafter delivered quickly, so a journalist covering the case will ideally be aware that a majority direction has been given, to be prepared for a quick return to the courtroom. But in practice, judges usually wait for longer than 2 hours 10 minutes to give the 'majority direction'.
- For a full jury of 12, majority verdicts of the ratios 11–1 or 10–2 are acceptable.
- If a jury is reduced in number for any reason—for example, because one or two jurors have fallen ill during the trial—a majority of 10–1 or 9–1 is allowed. If the jury is reduced to nine jurors, its verdict(s) must be unanimous. If the jury is reduced to fewer than nine, the trial must be abandoned, and the defendant(s) will probably face a fresh trial on the same charge(s), with a new jury.
- If a defendant is convicted by a majority, rather than unanimously, the media should report the fact that it was by a majority decision, as this indicates fairly that one or two people in the jury disagreed with the guilty verdict.

The legal ban on interviewing jurors about verdicts is explained in 12.3, Confidentiality of jury deliberations.

If the verdict is an acquittal, the court asks no questions of the jury about the ratio of the vote—so usually no indication of how many jurors concurred in the verdict is given. But if the foreperson volunteers in court the fact that acquittal was by a majority, it is by convention regarded as unfair to publish this fact, because stating that one or two jurors voted against acquittal could leave a stain on the defendant's character even though they are cleared of the charge.

A jury which cannot reach a verdict by a sufficient majority (or if reduced to nine jurors, unanimously) is known as a 'hung jury'. The prosecution then has to decide if it wants to seek a re-trial.

! Remember your rights

There are court rules on what case material journalists can see to help them report a trial and a national protocol on what prosecution material can be released to them to help coverage of cases. For more detail, see ch. 15.

9.7 Sentencing at Crown court

If a defendant pleads guilty at a Crown court to all charges, the judge will pass sentence, often after an adjournment. First, the judge will hear the prosecution's summary of the facts, and be told if the defendant has previous convictions and of any offences to be **taken into consideration**. The judge will also consider any statement from the victim(s) about the impact of a crime or—for instance, in a homicide case—a statement by bereaved relatives about the crime's effect on them. The judge will also hear **mitigation**.

→glossary
→glossary

Sentencing after a Crown court trial follows a similar pattern, though the judge, having presided at it, will not normally need to hear again detail of the offence(s).

The same sentencing procedure is used for a defendant who, after conviction in a magistrates' court, has been committed for sentence to the Crown court. A defendant may appear at a sentencing hearing via a video link from prison if they have been denied bail or are already serving a jail term.

Crown courts frequently impose jail terms, but have the same range of other sentencing options as magistrates—see 7.6, Sentencing by magistrates.

If no other factors apply—for example, the defendant is not sentenced to life or to an 'extended' sentence—they can expect, if they behave well in prison, to be released 'on licence' halfway through the term imposed by the court, which means that after release they will be monitored by a probation officer and may be returned to prison to serve the remainder of the jail term if a licence condition is broken. Changes introduced in 2024 to ease overcrowding in prisons allow certain prisoners to be released after serving 40 per cent of their sentence in jail, rather than 50 per cent.

9.7.1 Life sentences and extended sentences

Life sentences are imposed for murder and other serious offences. The sentencing judge will state a minimum term of the sentence which the defendant should serve before they can be considered for release, and may pass 'a whole life order', meaning the sentence will actually be for life.

A defendant convicted of a specified sexual, violent or terrorism offence can be categorised as 'dangerous'. In summary, an offender can be categorised as 'dangerous' if the judge considers there is significant risk of them committing further offences which might cause members of the public serious harm. Such offenders could incur a life sentence or receive an 'extended' sentence, meaning they must serve at least two-thirds of their sentence in prison and will be subject to an extended licence period upon their release.

> For information from the Sentencing Council about different types of sentence, see Useful Websites at the end of this chapter.

9.7.2 Parole Board

The Parole Board, which is an independent body, decides whether prisoners who are serving certain types of sentences can be released. It holds panel hearings when making such risk assessments. These were all held in private. But after controversy in 2018 over the Board's decision to release the notorious rapist John Worboys (which was overturned by the High Court) new rules, which came into force in July 2022, now allow anyone, including a media organisation, to request that a panel hearing due to consider a particular defendant's release be held in public. Such a request will be successful if the Board's chair decides that a public hearing would be 'in the interests of justice', but the Board will be able to restrict what information is disclosed.

Convicted murderer, Russell Causley, who killed his wife, Carol Packman, in 1985, became the first prisoner to have a public parole hearing under the new rules. Members of the public and journalists were able to observe his hearing at Lewes prison over a video link. The Board subsequently ruled he should be released, subject to various licence conditions (Government website, 12 December 2022). The Board can also release a summary of its decision, if the request for the summary is not made more than six months after the decision, and if the Board chair does not decide that there are exceptional circumstances justifying refusal of the request.

((•)) for the Rules and the Parole Board's work, see Useful Websites at the end of this chapter

9.8 The Court of Appeal

A defendant wishing to appeal against a Crown court conviction or the severity of the sentence imposed by a Crown court can seek permission to appeal to the Court of Appeal Criminal Division, based in London. Permission to appeal can be granted by the Crown court trial judge or the Court of Appeal itself, or a case may later be referred to the Court by the Criminal Cases Review Commission, which investigates potential miscarriages of justice. Appeals are usually heard by three senior judges who will give either a unanimous or majority ruling. The Attorney General (or Solicitor General) can also refer a sentence to the Court of Appeal if they consider it to be 'unduly lenient', and the Court may decide to increase the sentence.

Figure 1.1 in 1.2.2 shows the hierarchy of the court system

The Court of Appeal may, if it allows an appeal against conviction, quash the conviction. It may decide there must be a re-trial of the case, by another Crown court jury. In that event, the court may impose a reporting restriction under section 4(2) of the Contempt of Court Act 1981—see 19.10. Appeals beyond the Court of Appeal go to the Supreme Court.

9.9 Journalists can visit prisoners

The right of a convicted prisoner to be visited in jail by a journalist investigating whether there has been a miscarriage of justice was upheld in *R v Secretary of State for the Home Department, ex p Simms* [2000] 2 AC 115.

See too the **additional material** for ch. 9 on **www.mcnaes.com**.

9.10 The Supreme Court

In 2009 the Supreme Court replaced the appellate committee of the House of Lords (also known as the Law Lords) as the highest court in criminal and civil law. Its judges are referred to as 'Justices of the Supreme Court'. It only hears appeals of high significance, usually no more than 40–50 each year. Appeals are heard by several Justices, with a majority decision being binding. The court sits in the former Middlesex Guildhall. NB: References in other chapters to 'House of Lords' judgments are to those of the appellate committee.

9.11 Re-trials after 'tainted acquittal' or after compelling new evidence emerges—reporting restrictions

Under what is known as the 'double jeopardy rule', the law usually prevents someone acquitted of an offence being tried for it again. But there are two major exceptions.

((•)) see Useful Websites at the end of this chapter for CPS guidance on section 82

- If a Crown court trial convicts a person of interference with or intimidation of a juror, witness or potential witness in an earlier trial in which the same or another defendant has been acquitted, the prosecution can apply to the High Court for an order quashing that acquittal, to allow a re-trial.
- Under the Criminal Justice Act 2003, if 'new and compelling evidence' emerges after a defendant has been acquitted at Crown court of a serious charge as defined by the Act, the prosecution can apply to the Court of Appeal for the acquittal to be quashed and a new trial to be held.

The Court of Appeal, when dealing with applications under the 2003 Act, can make an order under the Act's section 82 imposing reporting restrictions which make it an offence to publish anything which would create a substantial risk of prejudice to a re-trial. Such an order can ban the media from reporting the application to quash the acquittal, or anything relating to it—for example, reporting that there are ongoing police investigations about the new evidence. The restrictions can be in force until the end of any re-trial or the matter is dropped. Liability and penalty for breach of the reporting restrictions are the same as for breach of restrictions in section 49 of the Children and Young Persons Act 1933—see 10.3.4.

9.12 The Crown court as an appeal court

Defendants can appeal to a Crown court judge against refusal by magistrates to grant bail.

Defendants can appeal to the Crown court against conviction by magistrates, including in youth courts. In the appeal there is no jury—a judge will sit, normally with two lay magistrates. The Crown court also hears appeals against the severity of sentences imposed by magistrates and may confirm a sentence, substitute a lesser penalty or increase it, but not to more than the highest sentence magistrates could have imposed.

9.13 The High Court

see 13.3, The High Court, for its role in civil law

The High Court King's Bench Division, which deals with both criminal and civil matters, has about 100 judges and sits in major cities.

A defendant convicted by magistrates, or who has appealed unsuccessfully to the Crown court, may appeal to the King's Bench Division on the grounds that a decision was wrong in law. This procedure is known as appeal by way of 'case stated' and no evidence is given verbally to the High Court, which considers a written record of the case. The prosecution can also use this procedure to challenge an acquittal by magistrates. The High Court has wide powers to reverse, affirm or amend magistrates' decisions, including those of youth courts. It can order the case to be re-tried summarily.

9.13.1 Judicial reviews

Part of the High Court's work involves **judicial reviews**, hearings in which it reviews the lawfulness of a decision made or action by a public body, such as a Government department or court. This allows the High Court to consider types of challenge to decisions made by magistrates (that is, challenge other than by the 'case stated' procedure). The media can use the judicial review procedure to challenge discretionary reporting restrictions imposed by magistrates or coroners—as explained in 16.6.3.1, Judicial review by the High Court of reporting restrictions imposed by magistrates or coroners. →glossary

9.14 Courts martial

People in the armed forces are subject to UK law in the courts martial system, even if the alleged offence was committed in another country. These military courts are usually open to the public and media.

For more information on courts martial, see Useful Websites at the end of this chapter and the **additional material** for ch. 9 on **www.mcnaes.com**.

Recap of major points

- Crown courts deal with the most serious criminal cases.
- Crown court judges rule on law and decide on punishment, and in trials juries decide whether each charge is proved.
- Automatic reporting restrictions limit what the media can report from most Crown court hearings held prior to trial.
- A defendant convicted in a Crown court may seek to appeal to the Court of Appeal, and thereafter to the Supreme Court.
- Crown courts hear appeals from magistrates' courts against conviction or sentence.
- The High Court is also an appeal court for certain matters.

Useful Websites

Gov.uk, www.gov.uk

- Guidance on jury service
- Guidance on probation
- Probation Service
- The Parole Board
- The Parole Board Rules 2019 as amended in 2024

Sentencing Council, www.sentencingcouncil.org.uk

The Supreme Court, www.supremecourt.uk

Crown Prosecution Service (CPS), 'Retrial of Serious Offences', www.cps.gov.uk

Crown Prosecution Service guidance on section 82

Courts and Tribunals Judiciary, 'Military', www.judiciary.uk

Courts martial

Online resources

Visit the online resources at **www.mcnaes.com** to test your knowledge of this chapter with **self-test questions** and a **flashcard glossary**, and to read **updates** about law and regulatory matters affecting journalism, as well as **additional material** to further your learning.

10

Children and young persons in court proceedings

Chapter summary

Most defendants aged under 18 are dealt with in youth courts by magistrates. The public cannot attend these courts, but journalists can. Reporting restrictions automatically ban identification of the children and 'young persons' involved as defendants, witnesses or crime victims, to protect their welfare. People aged under 18 are involved in cases in other types of court, criminal and civil—these courts can make an order banning any publication from identifying a specified child or young person in reports of the case. The media may argue against this—for example, if the person aged under 18 has been convicted of serious or persistent crime. Chapter 14 explains anonymity provision for children in Family Court cases.

10.1 The age of criminal responsibility

Children under the age of 10 have not reached 'the age of criminal responsibility,' so cannot be prosecuted for a crime as they are considered too young to distinguish between right and wrong. But they may be placed under the supervision of social workers.

ch. 14 covers interventions by social workers

The distinction between a 'child' (which in criminal law covered in this chapter is a person aged under 14) and a 'young person' (a person aged 14–17) is not important for journalists reporting courts, although some statutes use both terms. In some law, the term 'juvenile' broadly describes anyone under the age of 18, and this term may be used for convenience in court.

10.2 Youth courts

Most children and young persons who are prosecuted are dealt with by youth courts, presided over by magistrates or a district judge. Youth courts are usually in the same building as magistrates' courts (where adult defendants appear) but have smaller courtrooms to make the defendants, and any witnesses aged under 18, feel less nervous than they might be in an adult court.

Magistrates who sit in youth courts receive special training. Procedures there, including trials, are similar to those in adult magistrates' courts, described in chs. 7 and 8.

→glossary A child or young person denied **bail** may be sent to non-secure accommodation run by the local authority, or—if the alleged offending is persistent or serious—to custody, as explained later in this chapter.

10.2.1 Youth courts' powers

Most offences dealt with by youth courts are minor. Because youth courts' sentencing powers are limited, they cannot try extremely serious cases, such as homicide, and must send such cases to a Crown court, in a procedure discussed later. But a youth court has discretion, if it considers its punishment powers sufficient in a particular case, to try other offences—such as rape or **robbery**—which, if the defendant were an adult, could only be tried at Crown court. →glossary

10.2.2 Sentencing

→glossary →glossary A youth court can impose **community punishment**, **absolute discharges** and **conditional discharges**—sentences explained in 7.6.4, other types of sentence—and can fine. A parent must pay this fine if the offender is aged under 16. A youth court can also make a 'youth rehabilitation order', a type of community punishment which can involve several requirements, such as a curfew, unpaid work or a requirement for mental health treatment.

Many young offenders who admit a first offence are merely made subject to an order which means they must cooperate with a referral to a youth offender panel of trained youth workers. This seeks to get the offender to address their offending behaviour and repair harm it caused. An offender who fails to cooperate can be given a more severe punishment.

In serious cases, youth courts can make 'detention and training orders' of between four months and two years. Normally this means that the offender spends half the period in custody with training and the other half being supervised in the community.

The court may make 'a parenting order' requiring, for example, a parent to attend counselling and guidance sessions.

10.2.3 Custody

A child or young person refused bail by a youth court, or sentenced to detention and training, can be held on **remand** or, for that sentence, in a secure children's home, a secure training centre or a young offenders' institution. A Court must consider the interests and welfare of a child before remanding them in custody. →glossary

10.2.4 Some youth court cases go to an adult court

A few cases involving defendants under 18 are—after beginning in a youth court—then dealt with in a magistrates' or Crown court, where most defendants are adults. The particular reporting restrictions which may apply to such cases at the youth court stage are explained shortly.

A child or young person charged with a homicide offence, such as murder, or one of a range of firearms offences, cannot be tried or sentenced by a youth court because of the seriousness of the charge. There are other categories of charge—for example, of serious or complex fraud—which can only be dealt with at a Crown court. Such defendants initially appear in a youth court for decisions on bail and procedure before their cases are sent to a Crown court.

The law on youth court defendants allows some crimes to be classified as 'grave'—those for which an adult offender could be jailed for 14 years or more (apart from the homicide and firearms offences referred to earlier) and some sexual offences. In such cases the youth court considers whether its maximum power of punishment—a two-year detention and training order—would be sufficient if the defendant were to be convicted. This is allocation procedure, similar to that for **either-way** charges in an adult magistrates' court, but a youth court defendant cannot insist on being tried by a jury. If the youth court considers its sentencing power insufficient, the case is sent to a Crown court for trial if the offence is denied, or sent there by **committal for sentence** if guilt is admitted.

→glossary

→glossary

There may be an allocation procedure in the youth court in other circumstances; it will also send a case for Crown court trial if it considers that the defendant would, if convicted, be classed as a 'dangerous offender' for sentencing—see 9.7.1.

allocation procedure is explained in 8.3

Cases in which a person aged under 18 is co-accused with an adult may be sent to the Crown court or to a magistrates' court for a joint trial (which is economic, and prevents witnesses having to testify there and in the youth court). A youth court can transfer a case to the magistrates' court if a defendant turns 18 after the proceedings begin, or decide to continue to deal with it.

A youth court which convicts a defendant of a serious crime can also consider at this stage whether they should be classed as a 'dangerous offender'. If the answer is 'yes', it will commit them to Crown court for a judge there to decide the sentence.

10.2.5 Pre-trial reporting restrictions

The **automatic** reporting restrictions of section 52A of the Crime and Disorder Act 1998 apply to any hearing in a youth court where the case must be sent to the Crown court, and—unless guilt is admitted for the sole charge or all charges by the defendant formally indicating the intention to plead guilty—to allocation hearings, and to any type of sending or transfer hearing for a case in which there remains potential for a trial, wherever that trial may be.

→glossary

See 8.2, Section 52A automatic reporting restrictions, which explains them in relation to cases in the (adult) magistrates' courts—but they apply identically in respect of such pre-trial (preliminary) hearings at youth courts.

10.2.5.1 Section 8C restrictions

Pre-trial hearings of a case to be tried by a youth court are covered by the automatic reporting restrictions in section 8C of the Magistrates' Courts Act 1980—see 7.4.

✻ Remember

Other reporting restrictions, preventing identification of persons aged under 18 concerned in the proceedings, normally apply automatically to coverage of youth court cases, as this chapter will explain. So, for some hearings, section 52A of the 1998 Act or section 8C of the 1980 Act *and* anonymity will apply.

! Remember your rights

The reporting restrictions in section 52A of the 1998 Act or section 8C of the 1980 Act do not affect the reporting of a trial at a youth, magistrates' or Crown court; or of a youth court hearing which decides whether to or does commit for sentence after a conviction. These restrictions only apply to reports of pre-trial hearings.

10.2.6 Admission to youth courts

For why open justice is important, see 15.1.1. For the Press Card, see 15.9.

Parliament has decided that the public should not be allowed inside youth courts, to avoid children and young persons suffering adverse contemporaneous publicity from their involvement in the proceedings, whether they are defendants facing allegations or convicted of immature law-breaking, or witnesses or victims/alleged victims of the crime.

See Useful Websites at the end of this chapter for the HMCTS guidance and Bench Book.

- But journalists are allowed into youth courts to cover cases—section 47 of the Children and Young Persons Act 1933 gives 'bona fide representatives of newspapers or news agencies' the right to attend. Reporters may need to cite section 47 to be allowed into court, and can direct court staff to general guidance issued for them by His Majesty's Courts and Tribunals Service (HMCTS), which refers to this right. The guidance also says that a journalist wanting to attend a youth court must be able to show on request a UK Press Card. The Youth Court Bench Book published by the Judicial College, which is other official guidance, says: 'Fair and accurate reports of proceedings, even where individuals are not identified, should be encouraged where appropriate as they can help promote public confidence.'

There can be exceptions to the ban on the public attending a youth court—for example, an adult or child who is the victim of the crime may be allowed to see an offender being sentenced.

10.3 Section 49 automatic restrictions on identifying persons aged under 18

Parliament decided to shield all children and young persons 'concerned in the proceedings' in youth court cases—defendants, victims/alleged victims, witnesses—from publicity by banning the media from identifying them in any publication referring to their cases while they are under the age of 18. This automatic anonymity is bestowed by section 49 of the Children and Young Persons Act 1933.

Section 49 says (here summarised):

- no matter relating to any child or young person concerned in proceedings shall, while they are under the age of 18, be included in any publication if it is likely to lead members of the public to identify them as someone concerned in the proceedings.

It also says that the following matters in particular should not be included if likely to identify the person:

- their name;
- their address;
- the identity of any school or other educational establishment they attend;
- the identity of any place of work; and
- any still or moving picture of them ('picture' includes 'a likeness however produced')

The definition of witness includes any person called, or proposed to be called, to give evidence in the proceedings. The definition of 'concerned in the proceedings' includes a child or young person 'in respect of whom the proceedings are taken', which means that section 49 anonymity applies to a person aged under 18 who is the victim/alleged victim in the case even if they are not a witness—for example, because they are too young to give evidence.

But a victim/alleged victim who is dead *can* be identified by the media, because a dead person is not 'concerned in the proceedings'—see 16.12.3.6 for more detail.

Section 49 says 'publication' includes 'any speech, writing, relevant programme or other communication in whatever form, which is addressed to the public at large or any section of the public'.

10.3.1 No detail likely to identify should be published

The section 49 restrictions mean that media reports of youth court cases should not include any detail which could identify a child or young person concerned in the proceedings. Describing a defendant as 'a 14-year-old Bristol boy' would not identify him because Bristol is large. But naming a small village as that defendant's home community could well identify him to people who know he lives there. Reporting a defendant's nickname or an unusual physical characteristic might identify them to some people. Reporting that a defendant is the 12-year-old twin son of a policeman will identify him to anyone who knows of such twins. The test is always whether, as a result of the report, any members of the public could realise who the child or young person is. Adults who figure in youth court cases as witnesses or are mentioned in evidence can be identified, as long as this does not identify a child or young person concerned in the proceedings (or breach any reporting restriction imposed by the court in respect of the adult). But a journalist may need to leave a name and detail identifying an adult out of a report to avoid identifying such a child or young person—for example, a father who gives evidence about his son, the defendant, cannot be identified. For more about the care needed to exclude identifying detail, see 10.8, Jigsaw identification, and the **additional material** for ch. 10 on **www.mcnaes.com**.

Case study

In 2003 a district judge fined the *Plymouth Evening Herald* £1,500 for publishing a photograph of a 15-year-old boy convicted at a youth court of stabbing a fellow pupil. The district judge said evidence by friends and relatives that they had recognised the boy, even though his face was pixelated, meant that the paper had breached section 49 (*Media Lawyer*, 4 March 2004).

see too 10.3.4, Breach of section 49 anonymity—liability and defences

Remember

Section 49 does not only apply to reports of youth court cases. It applies to any published material referring to a child or young person as being concerned in a youth court case. For a publisher to be convicted of breaching section 49, it does not have to be proved that identification of the child or young person to the public definitely occurred, but that it was likely to occur because of what was published.

Section 49 is not a blanket ban on identifying the child or young person's school, in that it may be possible for a report to identify the school if it is large, without being likely to identify them. But journalists should err on the side of caution, and the safest course is to ask the court for specific permission to identify the school if this is 'in the public interest'—see 10.3.5. The court might give permission, for example, to let the media highlight a problem of drug-dealing at a particular school, because—as will be explained—the 1933 Act allows the court to disapply section 49 'to any specified extent'.

10.3.2 When does the section 49 anonymity begin?

Section 49 refers to court proceedings. Therefore, strictly speaking, its anonymity provision does not take effect until the first hearing begins in the youth court. Journalists may decide, to avoid the risk of defamation or breach of privacy law—see 5.10—not to identify someone aged under 18 being investigated by police even though section 49 applies only if and when the case reaches a youth court hearing. Another consideration is that clause 9 of the Editors' Code or rule 1.9 of the Broadcasting Code may be breached if a child or young person being investigated by police is identified in reporting—see 5.14 (in this book).

10.3.3 Anonymity retained for appeal and youth rehabilitation order hearings

Section 49 anonymity also applies to reports of Crown court hearings of appeals from the youth court against conviction or severity of sentence, and to reports of High Court hearings of appeals from the youth court (or from the Crown court appeal hearings) by way of 'case stated' (that is, an appeal about how law should be interpreted), and to reports of appeal hearings in higher courts, should either type of appeal go higher, so the anonymity travels up with the appeal.

see 9.12, The Crown court as an appeal court, and 9.13, The High Court

The anonymity also applies to reports of proceedings in a magistrates' court for breach, revocation or amendment of youth rehabilitation orders if the court announces that section 49 applies, and to reports of the hearings in higher courts of appeals from such proceedings, including by 'case stated'.

The section 49 restrictions do *not* apply to reports of the Crown court proceedings involving a defendant aged under 18 sent there for trial or committed there for sentence. But the Crown court may make an order giving them anonymity under section 45 of the Youth Justice and Criminal Evidence Act 1999, as explained later.

10.3.4 Breach of section 49 anonymity—liability and defences

Publishing material likely to identify a child or young person who should have section 49 anonymity is a criminal offence. Section 49 says that those who can be prosecuted for such breach of anonymity are the newspaper or periodical's proprietor (usually a company), the editor and the publisher, or in the case of a programme, any 'body corporate' (such as a company) providing the programme service and any person whose functions in relation to the programme correspond to those of an editor of a newspaper, or as regards any other form of publication, any person publishing it. If a body corporate is convicted of a breach, an 'officer' of it (for example, the director or manager of a company) can be convicted of the offence if it can be proved that officer consented to or connived with the breach, or that it was attributable to any neglect on that person's part.

see too 10.9 on liability for readers' postings which breach anonymity provision

The punishment on conviction is a fine unlimited by statute.

It is a defence for someone accused of breaching section 49 to prove that at the time of the alleged breach they were not aware, and neither suspected nor had reason to suspect, that the publication included material 'likely to identify' the child or young person.

10.3.5 When section 49 anonymity ceases to apply

see 10.6, Injunctions to provide longer anonymity

Section 49 anonymity automatically expires when the person whose identity it protected—whether a defendant, witness or victim/alleged victim—reaches the age of 18. The 1933 Act was amended to make this clear, following *R (on the application of JC & RT) v Central Criminal Court* [2014] EWCA Civ 1777. Anonymity could be extended beyond the age of 18 by a High Court injunction but that would be exceptional.

Section 49 allows a youth court to revoke the anonymity—that is, before the person turns 18—to allow the media to identify them 'to any specified extent' for any of the following three reasons:

(1) *To avoid injustice*—This power is rarely exercised. A youth court could use it to allow a media report of a preliminary hearing to identify a defendant whose lawyer says they want publicity to help trace witnesses to prove an **alibi**—'My client John Doe was at the funfair that night, not the crime scene. Did anyone see him at the funfair?' The court might also do so to quash rumours suggesting that the victim was in fact the defendant.

→glossary

(2) *To help trace a child or young person unlawfully at large*—A youth court can lift section 49 anonymity, if asked to do so by or on behalf of the Director of Public Prosecutions, to help to trace a person aged under 18 who is 'unlawfully at large' after being charged with or convicted of a violent or sexual or terrorism offence, or any offence for which a person aged 21 or more could be jailed for 14 years or more. This would let the media name and publish a photograph of a youth court defendant who has failed to answer bail or who escaped from secure accommodation and may be a threat to public safety.

(3) *In the public interest*—A youth court can lift the anonymity of a defendant it convicts of any offence if satisfied that doing so is 'in the public interest'—for example, if the court felt that it would benefit the community to let the media identify a defendant who had committed a notorious crime or was a persistent offender.

Before taking this decision, it must give the prosecution and defence the opportunity to argue for or against lifting the anonymity.

> See 16.13 for the 'public interest' grounds the media can cite to argue in a youth court for a convicted defendant's anonymity to be removed.

* Remember

A court can only lift section 49 anonymity 'in the public interest' in respect of a convicted defendant. Remember too that though section 49 anonymity expires when the person whose identity it protected turns 18, a youth court can under another statute give lifetime anonymity—as regards reporting of or reference to a case—to a child, young person or adult who is a witness or victim/alleged victim in it, as this chapter explains shortly.

! Remember your rights

HMCTS guidance to court staff is that accredited journalists can be given some information about youth court cases they do not attend—see 15.15.6.

10.4 Sections 45 and 45A anonymity for children and young persons in adult criminal courts

As explained earlier in this chapter, a child or young person may be 'concerned in the proceedings' of a (adult) magistrates' court or the Crown court as a defendant; or as a witness and/or as the victim/alleged victim in the case.

There is no automatic ban on identifying anyone under 18 as being 'concerned in the proceedings' of an adult criminal court—magistrates', Crown or higher court. But these courts have a discretionary power in section 45 of the Youth Justice and Criminal Evidence Act 1999 to ban any publication from identifying a specified person as being concerned in the proceedings, while they remain under the age of 18.

While usually Crown court judges exercise their discretion and grant anonymity to every defendant under the age of 18 as a matter of routine, they might decide not to if there is a good reason. On 1 August 2024, Judge Andrew Menary KC, sitting at Liverpool Crown Court, decided not to impose a section 45 order to prevent the press from naming 17-year-old Axel Rudakubana, who had murdered three young girls in Southport, sparking riots in towns and cities in England and Northern Ireland. The judge said releasing Rudakubana's identity would help to 'dispel misinformation', particularly online, and noted the defendant was due to turn 18 in less than one week, at which point the anonymity would automatically expire.

Section 45A of the 1999 Act permits these courts and youth courts, in particular circumstances, to bestow anonymity for a witness or victim/alleged victim aged under 18 for that person's lifetime, as will now be explained.

10.4.1 Section 45 orders give anonymity to the age of 18

A section 45 order should specify the individual it covers. Its scope normally is that (here summarised):

- no matter relating to that child or young person shall be included in any publication while they are under the age of 18 if it is likely to lead members of the public to identify them as a person concerned in the proceedings.

Section 45 says that the following matters in particular should not be included if likely to identify the person:

- their name;
- their address;
- the identity of any school or other educational establishment they attend;
- the identity of any place of work; and
- any still or moving picture of them ('picture' includes 'a likeness however produced').

A section 45 anonymity order can be made in respect of a defendant, witness or victim/alleged victim The definition of witness includes any person called, or proposed to be called, to give evidence in the proceedings.

If a section 45 order is made, any detail in the charge(s) or evidence which would be likely to identify the person cannot be reported. That could mean that an adult defendant or adult witness in the case also cannot be identified.

see also 10.8.1, Cases of abuse within a family

For example, if a father is charged with assaulting his child, whose identity is protected by a section 45 order, the relationship cannot be included in any report naming the father as the defendant, as this would identify the child. Even mentioning the child's age in such reports could inadvertently reveal a familial relationship and so unlawfully identify the child.

The types of detail which could breach section 45 anonymity are the same as those which could breach the automatic anonymity provided in respect of youth court cases under section 49 of the Children and Young Persons Act 1933, see earlier. Media organisations must guard against 'jigsaw identification'—see 10.8.

✻ Remember

A section 45 order can apply to a child or young person 'in respect of whom the proceedings are taken'. It therefore can be used to prevent a media report of a truancy case from identifying a child whose parent is prosecuted in the adult magistrates' court for failing to ensure the child attends school. The effect would be that the report could not identify the parent either and should not identify the school if there is any likelihood of this identifying the child.

Case study

In 2020 two BBC TV news bulletins named two youths accused of murder, despite a section 45 order banning publication of their identities. Judge Ian Pringle QC said during a preliminary hearing of their case at Oxford Crown court that it was a 'clear breach' of the reporting restriction. The youths, aged 15 and 17, were charged with murdering Robin Williamson, 43, in Oxford's Wood Farm district. Their names, ages and whereabouts were broadcast in bulletins which reported an earlier preliminary hearing. The judge referred the breach to the chief prosecutor to decide whether the BBC should be prosecuted. Barrister Ben Gallop, for the BBC, told the judge that staff at BBC *South Today* would receive 'refresher training for court reporting'. The BBC's legal director Nick Wilcox and BBC *South Today* editor Richard Spalding were in court as Mr Gallop made his apology to the judge (*Oxford Mail*, 5 August 2020; *Press Gazette* 10 August 2020).

10.4.1.1 When section 45 anonymity ceases to apply

Anonymity under a section 45 order automatically expires when the person whose identity it protected turns 18. The Court of Appeal has said the section makes that clear (*R (on the application of JC & RT) v Central Criminal Court* [2014] EWCA Civ 1777).

Exceptionally, anonymity could be extended beyond the age of 18 by a High Court injunction—see 10.6.

A criminal court can revoke a section 45 order, so removing the anonymity provision for the relevant person before they reach the age of 18, or relax (that is, limit) the order's scope, by making an 'excepting direction' (another type of order).

> Media organisations sometimes argue in court for section 45 orders to be lifted so—for example—reports can identify a defendant convicted of serious crime. See 16.12 for detail about a court's power to revoke such an order, and for case law which the media can cite to challenge the provision or continuation of section 45 anonymity.

10.4.1.2 The 2015 changes

Section 45 of the 1999 Act was brought into force on 13 April 2015. In the criminal courts it replaced—as the discretionary power to provide anonymity for a person aged under 18—section 39 of the Children and Young Persons Act 1933. Use of section 39 is now restricted to non-criminal proceedings, as explained later in this chapter.

10.4.1.3 Invalid anonymity orders

- A court, to pay proper heed to the principle of open justice, should not make a section 45 order under the 1999 Act or a section 39 order under the 1933 Act without considering whether this is necessary. It should consider for each child or young person whether there is a good reason for such anonymity.
- These sections can only provide anonymity for a living person, not one who is dead—for example, a murder victim aged under 18.
- A court cannot use either type of order to specifically give anonymity to an adult.

> See 16.12 for guidance and case law on media challenges to section 45 or section 39 orders which are invalid or unnecessary.

10.4.2 Section 45A orders provide lifetime anonymity for a witness or victim/alleged victim aged under 18

Youth, magistrates' and Crown courts and higher courts can—if certain conditions apply—make an order under section 45A of the 1999 Act in respect of a witness, or victim/alleged victim, aged under 18. The normal form of the order is that:

- no matter relating to that person shall, during their lifetime, be included in any publication if it is likely to lead members of the public to identify that person as being concerned in the proceedings.

The Act makes clear that this lifetime anonymity cannot be given to a defendant, even if they are also a witness. Otherwise, the definition of 'witness' is the same as for section 45 orders.

The scope of this anonymity (for example, what the Act specifies as information which should not be published if likely to identify the person) is the same as that provided by a section 45 order, see earlier—except that a section 45A order means the anonymity does *not* expire when the person reaches 18.

A condition which has to be met for the court to make a section 45A order is that the court is satisfied that:

- the quality of any evidence given by the person, or the level of cooperation given by the person to any party to the proceedings in connection with that party's preparation of its case, is likely to be diminished by reason of fear or distress on the part of the person in connection with being identified by members of the public as being concerned in the proceedings.

The 1999 Act says that when deciding whether to grant the anonymity, the court must take into account: the person's view about such anonymity, the nature and circumstances of the alleged offence(s) being tried; the person's age, social and cultural background and ethnic origins; their domestic and employment circumstances, religious beliefs or political opinions; and any behaviour towards the person on the part of the defendant, or the defendant's family or associates, or anyone else likely to be a defendant or witness in the proceedings.

Section 50 of the Act says that a person protected by section 45A anonymity provision can waive it by giving written consent to be identified. There is no requirement for a court to approve this consent, which can be given direct to a journalist. But the consent is not valid unless the person who gives it has reached the age of 18. Also, the consent will be invalid if it was obtained by interfering with the person's 'peace or comfort'. See too 11.6.4.1, Good practice in wording consent.

As explained in 12.8 of this book, under section 46 of the 1999 Act, a criminal court can make the same type of anonymity order in respect of an adult witness. See too 16.14.2 for grounds on which a section 45A or 46 order can be opposed.

10.4.3 Breach of section 45 or 45A anonymity—liability and defences

for liability for readers' postings which breach anonymity provision, see 10.9

The law about who can be prosecuted for breaching anonymity under a section 45 or 45A order under the 1999 Act is the same as for breaching section 49 anonymity under the Children and Young Persons Act 1933, and the definition of 'publication' is the same in both Acts. See earlier in this chapter. The punishment is the same too for those convicted of breach—a fine unlimited by statute.

Section 50 of the 1999 Act says it is a defence to a charge of breaching section 45 or 45A anonymity for the publisher to prove that they were not aware, and neither suspected nor had reason to suspect, that the publication included the matter or report in question; or in the case of section 45A, to prove that there was valid written consent for identification.

10.5 Section 39 reporting restrictions in civil proceedings and coroners' courts

People aged under 18 who are 'concerned' in civil law proceedings—for example, in the High Court or County Court as **claimants**, defendants or witnesses, or in a coroner's court as a witness—*can* be identified in the media as being involved in the case unless the court specifically forbids it.

→glossary

A court which 'in relation' to such proceedings wants to ban the identification of such a child or young person in what is published can make an order under section 39 of the Children and Young Persons' Act 1933.

ch. 13 explains civil courts and ch. 17 explains coroners' courts

The scope of a section 39 order is normally that no publication referring to the case shall include:

- any particulars 'calculated' (that is, likely) to lead to the identification of the child or young person as being concerned in the proceedings, and the order could specifically ban publication of;
  - their name;
  - their address;
  - their school;
  - a picture of or including the child or young person.

The wording of section 39, which has not been fully standardised with that of the reporting restrictions explained earlier, means that unless the court decides otherwise, the order may well ban identification of the child or young person's school in any publication referring to the case, irrespective of whether identifying the school is likely to identify that individual. The order may also ban publication of a picture of or including that individual, irrespective of whether it is likely to identify them.

As with section 49 anonymity in respect of youth court cases—see 10.3.1—a journalist must take care not to breach a section 39 order made by a civil or coroner's court by including too much detail about any child or young person it protects.

Section 39 says 'any person' who includes in a publication material which breaches the anonymity is liable for the breach. The definition of 'publication' is the same as in section 49 of the Act, see earlier. The maximum penalty for breaching section 39 anonymity is a fine unlimited by statute.

For an example of illegal identification of a child's or young person's school, see the *Newcastle Journal* case study in the **additional material** for ch. 10 on **www.mcnaes.com**.

10.5.1 When section 39 anonymity ceases to apply

In 2014 the Court of Appeal, upholding previous case law, ruled that section 39 anonymity automatically expires when the person reaches the age of 18 (*R (on the application of JC & RT) v Central Criminal Court* [2014] EWCA Civ 1777).

See 16.12, Challenging court orders giving a child or young person anonymity, and its subsections for guidance and law on how the media can challenge section 39 orders which are invalid or unnecessary.

10.6 Injunctions to provide longer anonymity

As has been explained, the automatic anonymity under section 49 of the 1933 Act in respect of youth court cases, or anonymity provided by an order made under section 45 of the 1999 Act or section 39 of the 1933 Act expires when the person reaches the age of 18.

The High Court has in rare circumstances made orders providing anonymity beyond the age of 18 for a person convicted as a child or young person of a serious crime. Such an order—that is, an injunction—draws directly on powers derived from the European Convention on Human Rights. Civil courts also have a specific power in the Civil Procedure Rules (CPR) to order that the identity of a witness or party in a civil case should not be disclosed.

For more detail on such injunctions, see 12.10. See too the summary of the *R v Aziz* case in 16.12.1.1, in which the Court of Appeal made clear such injunctions are exceptional.

10.7 Anti-social behaviour injunctions and criminal behaviour orders

See the **additional material** for ch. 10 on **www.mcnaes.com** for how law detailed in this chapter may give anonymity to a child or young person in reports of a court hearing concerned with an application for an anti-social behaviour injunction (ASBI) or a criminal behaviour order (CBO), or concerned with an alleged or admitted breach of an ASBI or CBO.

10.8 Jigsaw identification

'Jigsaw identification' describes the effect when someone to whom the law has given anonymity is nevertheless identifiable to the public because of a combination of published details. It can occur when two or more media organisations cover the same case. Each may publish a report which in itself preserves the anonymity. But jigsaw identification will occur if someone who reads, views or hears the reports of more than one organisation can, by combining the different detail in each, recognise the person who should be anonymous.

Sexual offences law is explained in ch. 11. Other law giving anonymity is explained in chs. 12, 13, 14, 17, and 18.

Jigsaw identification can also occur through publication of too much detail in either a single report or series of reports by the same organisation.

The examples given below relate to anonymity provision, described in this chapter, for children or young persons. But jigsaw identification can also destroy anonymity bestowed by other laws, such as anonymity automatically provided for victims and alleged victims of sexual offences, or by a regulatory code.

Example 1 A defendant in a youth court, who has anonymity under section 49 of the Children and Young Persons Act 1933, admits causing criminal damage to a sports car owned by local millionaire John Doe. One local paper reports: 'A 15-year-old boy vandalised a sports car owned by London tycoon John Doe, costing him £5,000 in repairs.' Another local paper reports: 'A 15-year-old boy vandalised his rich neighbour's sports car, causing £5,000 damage.' Each report is accurate. Neither paper names the boy, and the second paper does not name Doe. But anyone reading both will know the boy is Doe's neighbour, which will identify the boy locally.

Example 2 A witness granted anonymity by an order under section 45 order of the Youth Justice and Criminal Evidence Act 1999, testifies at Crown court in a murder trial. A local radio station describes her as 'a 16-year-old who works as a shop assistant in London.' Another radio station does not mention her job but describes her routine as 'commuting each morning to work in Charing Cross'. A newspaper reports that she lives in Islington. Each report is accurate, but this or further accumulation of detail could lead those who know her, and who listen to both stations and read that newspaper, to realise that she is or could be the witness.

10.8.1 Cases of abuse within a family

There is a particular danger of jigsaw identification in reporting court cases concerning violence or sexual abuse against a child or young person by a relative or family 'friend'. In such cases, when the charge is of physical but not sexual abuse, it is standard practice for magistrates and/or the Crown court judge to make a section 45 order. In cases where the charge is of sexual abuse, the victim/alleged victim has automatic anonymity under other law—see ch. 11—so a section 45 order is not necessary.

When covering such abuse cases in courts, a media organisation has two options (for convenience the term 'child' in (a) and (b) includes 'young person'—that is, someone under the age of 18):

(a) *The report can name the adult defendant*—but if the defendant is a relative, the report must not include any detail of their relationship to the child, to protect the child's anonymity. This can severely restrict what is published—for example, about how the defendant had opportunity to abuse the child, or even the child's age. In 2005 in the Court of Appcal, Lord Justice Maurice Kay, alluding to a case in which a father was convicted of conspiracy to rape a child and of distributing indecent photographs of her said: 'Offences of the kind established in this case are frequently committed by fathers and step-fathers . . . If the offender is named and the victim is described as "an 11-year old schoolgirl", in circumstances in which the offender has an 11-year old daughter, it is at least arguable that the composite picture presented embraces "particulars calculated (likely) to lead to the identification" of the victim' (*R v Teesside Crown Court, ex p Gazette Media Company Ltd and others* [2005] All ER (D) 367 (Jul)).

(b) *The report does not identify the adult defendant in any way*, which means it can therefore refer to the familial or household relationship between the defendant and child, can definitely refer to the child's age and can include greater detail of evidence, while preserving the child's anonymity.

An editor's instinct is usually that it is in the public interest to name people charged with crime—and particularly those convicted of it—as a deterrent and so that a community can be wary of that individual. This is achieved by the approach in (a), if it is possible to construct a meaningful report without revealing the family relationship or identifying the child in any other way. But another editor may feel that the public interest is best served by the approach in (b), which can make clear that the alleged abuse was, for example, by a relative. Approach (b) preserves the child's anonymity and allows publication of more evidential material than (a) does, and so enables more questions to be publicly raised about why the community, social services or the police remained unaware of the abuse within the household.

Jigsaw identification may occur if two media organisations covering the case adopt different approaches. If one follows policy (a), naming the adult defendant but obscuring his relationship to the child victim, and the other follows approach (b), not identifying the defendant but reporting, for example, that he was the child's father, anyone reading both reports will be able to identify the child even though neither report names them. To avoid jigsaw identification of the child, all the newsrooms involved need to agree on and adopt the same approach.

10.9 Liability for readers' postings

It is possible that a reader will post directly onto a media organisation's website a comment or assertion which illegally identifies a child or young person who should have anonymity because of a reporting restriction covered in this chapter.

The general principle in law is that if the website operator has not moderated (that is, not checked) the posting's content before it became visible there, the operator will *not* be held liable legally for the breach of the anonymity provision, provided that the operator had no prior knowledge that the unlawful material would be posted, and deleted it, or disabled public access to it, 'expeditiously' after being given notice of or otherwise becoming aware its unlawful nature. This is known as the 'notice and take down' (NTD) procedure. For more detail of the extent of protection from liability which this procedure offers, see ch. 30.

10.10 Code anonymity provision for children or young persons involved in court cases

chs. 2 and 3 introduce the regulators and codes

Any breach by a media organisation of anonymity provided by law for a child or young person involved in a court case would also breach the relevant regulator's code, in that a person whose identity is protected by law has in that respect 'a reasonable expectation of privacy'. See 4.2, The codes' general protection of privacy.

The Impress code rule 6.2 says specifically that publishers must not directly or indirectly identify persons under the age of 18 who are or have been involved in criminal proceedings, except as permitted by law.

For what regulatory codes say about anonymity in sexual offences cases, see 11.7.

* Remember

If a media organisation, by breaching a reporting restriction which the law automatically or court imposes, illegally identifies a person in what is published, it may have to pay damages to the person in civil law for that breach of their privacy—see 27.12.1—as well as pay a large fine for the breach offence.

Recap of major points

- Most children or young persons charged with a crime are dealt with by youth courts. The public cannot attend these courts, but journalists can.
- Section 49 of the Children and Young Persons Act 1933 bans media reports from identifying anyone aged under 18 as being involved in a youth court case, whether as defendant, witness or crime victim/alleged victim.
- Section 49 anonymity can be lifted, in the case of a convicted defendant, to allow the media to identify them in the public interest—for example, after persistent offending.
- There is no automatic anonymity for a child or young person involved in adult court proceedings. But an adult court can make an order under section 45 of the Youth Justice and Criminal Evidence Act 1999 to give them anonymity.
- There is no automatic anonymity for a child or young person involved in civil proceedings or inquests at coroners' courts. But these courts can make an order under section 39 of the Children and Young Persons Act 1933 to give them anonymity.

Useful Websites

Gov.uk, 'Young people and the law', www.gov.uk

Government guidance on the youth justice system

Gov.uk, 'HMCTS staff guidance on supporting media access to courts and tribunals', www.gov.uk

Youth Court Bench Book [changed link], sentencingcouncil.org.uk

Judicial College guidance, *Reporting Restrictions in the Criminal Courts*, www.judiciary.uk

5th edition as issued in July 2023 by the Judicial College, Media Lawyers Association, News Media Association and Society of Editors

Judicial College guidance, Child Defendants in the Crown Court, June 2025, www.judiciary.uk

Youth Justice Legal Centre, Resources (including legal updates), yjlc.uk

Online resources

Visit the online resources at **www.mcnaes.com** to test your knowledge of this chapter with **self-test questions** and a **flashcard glossary**, and to read **updates** about law and regulatory matters affecting journalism, as well as **additional material** to further your learning.

11

Anonymity for victims and alleged victims of sexual, and other, offences

Chapter summary

Law gives victims and alleged victims of sexual offences, including rape, lifetime anonymity in any reports of these crimes and of any subsequent prosecutions. This includes victims/alleged victims of imaged-based sexual offences such as 'cyber-flashing' and sexually-explicit 'deepfake' images. Several media organisations have been fined for publishing material which breached this anonymity and so caused considerable distress to those identified. Laws also give anonymity to victims/alleged victims of human trafficking for sexual and non-sexual exploitation, including slavery or forced labour; and to victims/alleged victims of female genital mutilation or forced marriage offences. As this chapter explains, the anonymity may be removed in some circumstances, allowing the media to identify the individual, but journalists should consider the ethics of doing so.

11.1 Introduction—automatic, lifelong anonymity

It is illegal in almost all circumstances to publish any detail or image which identifies or is likely to identify a person in their lifetime as being a victim or alleged victim of a sexual offence, or of a human trafficking offence or of a female genital mutilation (FGM) or forced marriage offence.

As this chapter explains, this anonymity provision is automatic and lifelong. It applies from the time an allegation is made that such an offence has occurred, whether made by the alleged victim or anyone else—for example, when someone tells any other person they have been raped; or when a parent complains to police, or to a journalist, that a child has been sexually abused; or a teacher is told by a teenager that her parents are coercing her to marry. The anonymity normally remains in place regardless of whether the allegation is later withdrawn, or the police are told, or an alleged offender is prosecuted, or anyone is convicted.

An organisation or person who publishes such illegal material can be prosecuted, and is liable to pay a fine unlimited by statute—see 11.5.

11.1.1 The wide application of the anonymity

The anonymity applies to any story which features a victim or alleged victim of a sexual offence (including image-based abuse), a human trafficking offence, a female genital mutilation (FGM) or forced marriage offence. This includes court reports on such cases. Publication in any form—including any blog or social media post—which is likely to reveal the identity of such a victim/alleged victim is illegal. Publishing a picture of a property where a sexual offence was said to have taken place, or as having been used by human traffickers, could identify a victim/alleged victim who lived or was known to have stayed there.

Case study

In 2016 the Telegraph Media Group was fined £80,000—the highest fine yet imposed for breach of any statutory reporting restriction—because the *Daily Telegraph* published a photo which could have identified a teenager as a victim of sexual offences. It was published with a report of the conviction at Bradford Crown court of Adam Johnson, the former England and Sunderland football player, on a charge that he had sexual activity with the girl, aged 15. He had admitted 'grooming' her and one lesser charge of sexual activity. The photo was copied from a Facebook page image which, in its original form, showed Johnson with the girl. The *Telegraph* is understood to have 'significantly modified' the image before publication to disguise her identity. But, after being charged under the Sexual Offences (Amendment) Act 1992, the *Telegraph* accepted at Westminster magistrates' court that publication of the modified version was likely to identify her, although there was no evidence that this had happened because of that publication. As well as being fined, the *Telegraph* was ordered to pay £1,473 in prosecution costs, and £10,000 in compensation to the girl. *The Sun's* former editor previously also had to pay £1,000 in compensation to the victim after social media users recognised her from a photograph published in the newspaper, despite it having been heavily obscured and the article containing a warning about the risk of prosecution for anyone identifying the girl online (*Media Lawyer*, 10 October 2016, *Press Gazette*, 8 March 2016). See the **additional material** for ch.11 on www.mcnaes.com for more details of *The Sun* case.

for civil courts see ch. 13 and for courts martial see 9.14

The anonymity applies to reports of any type of legal proceedings, including courts martial and civil cases. So a rape or trafficking victim who sues the alleged perpetrator in a civil court must normally remain anonymous in reports of that litigation. The anonymity also applies to reports of a court being asked to make or making an order to protect someone from FGM or a forced marriage, as explained later in this chapter. Similarly, anyone who claims at an employment tribunal that they were the victim of a sexual or a trafficking offence must be anonymised in reports of the case.

ch. 18 explains employment tribunals

A journalist needs to realise from the nature of the allegation being related that the anonymity applies. It protects any person who says—for example, when being interviewed for a biographical feature—that they were at some time a victim of any such offence.

11.1.2 Anonymity applies even if the 'target' offence was not committed

The anonymity also applies to anyone who is or has been alleged to be the victim of any attempt or conspiracy to commit one of the relevant offences—for example, a woman who fought off a man's attempt to rape her; a man who escaped from a gang planning to traffic him; a young girl whose parents tried to arrange for her to go abroad for FGM; or a woman tricked into travelling abroad in an attempt to forcibly marry her. Such attempts or conspiracies are themselves offences, even if the 'target' offence—the rape, trafficking, FGM or forced marriage—did not occur.

11.1.3 Jigsaw identification

Jigsaw identification—identification caused by a combination of published detail—must be avoided. For example, suppose a newspaper reporting a rape trial describes the alleged victim as 'a mother of three' who lives and works locally, a TV station describes her as 'a nurse', and a radio station describes her as 'a woman in her 30s' who works nights. This combination of detail could identify her to colleagues and acquaintances—see also 10.8, Jigsaw identification. Another example: reporting that a rape victim is a student at a specific university is unlikely to identify them, however giving further detail, such as that the victim is a 25-year-old music student, is likely to do so.

A report will break the law if it includes any detail 'likely to lead members of the public to identify that person as the person against whom the offence is alleged to have been committed'.

* Remember

Prosecutors alleging that a media organisation or person has published material breaching the anonymity law outlined in this chapter need only prove that what was published was *likely* to identify a victim, not that it actually did so.

Case study

In 2017 *Pembrokeshire Herald* editor Thomas Sinclair was convicted of breaching the 1992 Act because of a report of a court case published in the sister paper, the *Ceredigion Herald*. Llanelli magistrates' court heard that the report named a man convicted of voyeurism, gave his age and occupation, and detailed his 'familial links' to the victim. The Crown Prosecution Service did not argue that the victim was identified to the public, but that the report made her identification likely. District judge David Parsons was told that the trainee journalist who wrote the report was sent to the voyeurism case without training, supervision or support. The judge ruled that Sinclair, as editor, had breached the 1992 Act, which he denied. He was fined £1,500 and ordered to pay £1,500 compensation, £500 costs and a £150 surcharge. He said that since the offence he had arranged for better training for the paper's court reporters. Sinclair lost an appeal against the conviction (*Western Telegraph*, 12 May 2017 and 22 January 2018).

For details of other cases in which media organisations were fined for breach of the 1992 Act, see the **additional material** for ch. 11 on **www.mcnaes.com**.

11.1.4 When the person can be identified

The statutory anonymity does not apply in some circumstances—most notably when a person aged 16 or older gives written consent to be identified as such a victim/alleged victim—see 11.6. But when such a person can be legally identified, journalists should consider if the anonymity provision in media regulators' codes of conduct continues to apply—see 11.7.

Remember

A media organisation which illegally identifies such a person will breach the relevant code of conduct as well as the law.

11.1.5 A publisher could be sued under privacy law

Media organisations should realise that if they publish material which discloses that a person is the victim/alleged victim of an offence in respect of which they are provided with anonymity by UK statute, and the person did not consent to that identification, they could successfully sue the publisher in civil law for damages for breach of privacy. A person may be able to do this even if they do not have statutory anonymity—for example, because the offence was committed/allegedly committed abroad and the perpetrator/alleged perpetrator cannot by law be prosecuted in the UK. See later explanations on UK 'jurisdiction'. For context on privacy law, see 27.12.1.

11.1.5.1 Postings by readers which breach anonymity

A media organisation which discovers that a reader has posted on its website material identifying a person who should have anonymity under statutes covered in this chapter is protected from liability, provided that it did not have knowledge that such material was due to be posted, did not moderate (check) the posting before it appeared, and deleted the material expeditiously after it was notified of or otherwise became aware of the unlawful content. For context, see 11.7.1.4 and ch. 30.

11.2 Lifelong anonymity for victims/alleged victims of sexual and human trafficking offences

Section 1 of the Sexual Offences (Amendment) Act 1992 says that after an allegation of a sexual or human trafficking offence is made:

- no matter relating to that victim/alleged victim shall, during their lifetime, be included in any publication if it is likely to lead members of the public to identify them as the victim/alleged victim of the offence.

It says the ban includes, in particular, if likely to identify that person:

- their name;
- their address;
- the identity of any school or other educational establishment they attend;
- the identity of any place of work;
- any still or moving picture of them ('picture' includes 'a likeness however produced').

Section 6 of the Act defines publication as any speech, writing, relevant programme or other communication in whatever form addressed to the public at large or to any section of the public.

The Act uses the term 'complainant' to refer to a victim/alleged victim.

11.2.1 Sexual offences for which victims/alleged victims have anonymity

The 1992 Act applies the anonymity for victims and alleged victims of virtually all offences with a sexual element. It applies in respect of all offences referred to in this section, unless otherwise stated.

The most serious are **indictable-only**, with a maximum sentence of life imprisonment. These include (with offences definitions being simplified for brevity): →glossary

- *rape*—penetration of vagina, anus, or mouth without consent, by penis. If the victim is aged under 13, any such conduct is defined as rape even if the victim says there was no compulsion, because the victim is so young (Note that while legally a person without a penis cannot commit rape, a female may be guilty of rape if they assist a male perpetrator in an attack);

- *assault by penetration*—of vagina or anus, without consent and otherwise than by penis—for example, by finger or object;
- *causing or inciting a child under 13 to engage in sexual activity*;
- *causing or inciting a person who has 'a mental disorder impeding choice' to engage in sexual activity* in which the activity caused or incited involves penetration.

→glossary Some sexual crimes are **either-way** charges. For some of these, an offender can be sentenced to a jail term of up to 14 years. Either-way charges include:

- *sexual assault*—intentional sexual touching, without consent;
- *administering a substance with intent to engage a person in sexual activity*—for example, spiking someone's drink with a drug, with a sexual motive;
- *trespass with intent to commit a sexual offence*;
- *sexual activity with a child; causing or inciting sexual activity with a child*—that is, someone aged under 16. These offences are either-way if the child is at least 13 years old and indictable-only if the child is under 13;
- *engaging in sexual activity in the presence of a child; causing a child to watch a sexual act*—these are crimes if done for the perpetrator's sexual gratification;
- *arranging or facilitating commission of a sexual offence against a child*—anywhere in the world;
- *sexual communication with a child*—an offence if by an adult;
- *meeting or arranging to meet a child following sexual grooming*—for example, an adult contacting a child over the internet—the child has anonymity even if no meeting takes place;
- *sexual activity by an adult with a child family member* (note that it is incorrect to describe such an offence as incest, because incest is a consensual relationship);
- *taking an indecent photograph of a child; paying for the sexual services of a child; causing, inciting, arranging or facilitating the sexual exploitation of a child or controlling a child for this purpose*;
- *abuse of a position of trust, through sexual activity with someone aged under 18*—so, for example, a male teacher having consensual sex with a 17-year-old girl who is not a school pupil is not committing a crime as she is over 16, the age of sexual consent, but if she is a pupil at the school where he works, the sexual relationship is criminal abuse of his position of trust as a teacher;
- *sexual activity by a care worker*—for example, in a hospital—if it involved such activity with a person in their care who has a mental disorder but did not involve penetration (which would be indictable-only);
- *causing or inciting or controlling prostitution for gain*—the anonymity covers a person who is or has allegedly been a 'controlled' prostitute, in respect of this victimhood;
- *exposure* (colloquially called 'flashing') of genitals with the intent to cause alarm or distress;

- *voyeurism*—observing for sexual gratification someone else or people doing something private (for example, taking a shower, or having sex), knowing they did not consent to being observed, because, for example, a hidden camera was used. A specific offence of breastfeeding voyeurism exists;

  '*upskirting*'—an additional type of voyeurism which prohibits the taking of a photograph under a person's clothing, without their consent, with the intention of viewing their genitals or buttocks, or underwear covering these, for the purpose of sexual gratification; or to cause humiliation, distress or alarm—for example, what the perpetrator claims is a prank. The Government has introduced legislation to broaden voyeurism law so it applies to other types of behaviour, such as 'down-blousing', in the Crime and Policing Act 2026.

The Online Safety Act 2023 and Data Use and Access Act 2025 amended the Sexual Offences Act 2003 to add various 'image-based' sexual offences, which also attract anonymity. These include:

- *sending photographs or film of genitals*—commonly referred to as 'cyber flashing';
- *sharing or threatening to share intimate photograph or film*—An offence is committed where an image or film is distributed (or a threat to do so is made) which shows, or appears to show a person in an intimate state without their consent. This includes so-called 'deepfake' images and expanded on previous 'revenge porn' legislation introduced in 2015;
- *creating or requesting the creation of purported intimate images*—this includes deepfake images created by Artificial Intelligence.

Buggery is no longer illegal between consenting adults, but is an offence if perpetrated on someone aged under 16—who is a victim and therefore has anonymity.

The anonymity does not apply to two adult relatives who are charged with consensual, illegal sexual activity with each other—which would have been charged as 'incest' under the old law—but if only one of them is charged, the other retains anonymity. It does not apply to an adult charged with intentionally engaging in sexual activity in a public lavatory. It also does not apply in cases involving a person accused of sexual activity with an animal.

11.2.2 Older definitions of offences

A sexual offence which allegedly occurred before 1 May 2004 will be charged according to older definitions, but anonymity applies. One such older offence is 'indecent assault'. For other sexual offence definitions, see the Crown Prosecution Service guidance listed at the end of this chapter under Useful Websites.

✱ Remember

The anonymity applies whenever there has been or is alleged to have been an attempt or conspiracy or any type of encouragement or assistance to commit a 'target' sexual offence—see 11.1.2.

11.2.3 Preserving anonymity in cases of sexual abuse of children within a family or household

Media organisations covering a case involving actual or alleged sexual abuse of a child by an adult in the same family or household should—to maintain the child's anonymity by avoiding 'jigsaw identification'—liaise about whether their reports (a) name the adult defendant, but omit any detail of any relationship to the child and of the location of the offending, or (b) do not identify the adult defendant by any detail, an approach which enables the report to state that the abuse was familial or within a household. For more context about the need for media organisations to avoid jigsaw identification, see 10.8.1.

If a report of a court case identifies the defendant, and the charges are of sexual abuse of a child, the journalist should take care that references to the frequency or period of the alleged or actual abuse do not inadvertently make identification of the child likely, because such detail could reveal that they were in the defendant's family or household. In such a case, including the child's specific age in years could breach the anonymity if the report identifies the defendant.

11.2.4 Court orders purporting to give a defendant anonymity under the 1992 Act

The media may decide, particularly when covering a court case involving alleged sexual abuse within a family, that the only way to preserve anonymity for the alleged victim(s) is not to publish anything identifying the adult defendant. But occasionally magistrates' courts and Crown court judges have sought to make that choice for the media by passing an order, purportedly under the Sexual Offences (Amendment) Act 1992, stating that the adult defendant should not be identified. There is no power in the Act to make such an order. It should be challenged, because it is invalid—see 16.15.

> A court hearing an application for a sexual harm prevention order, a sexual risk order, a slavery and trafficking prevention or risk order may use section 11 of the Contempt of Court Act 1981 to give anonymity in reports of the hearing to the person against whom the order is sought. For context, see the **additional material** for ch. 16 on **www.mcnaes.com**. Any victim or alleged victim of such crime who is referred to in the hearing, or in any hearing about actual or alleged breach of the order, normally has anonymity under the 1992 Act.

11.2.5 Sexual offences committed or allegedly committed abroad

The anonymity under the 1992 Act applies too in respect of victims/alleged victims of sexual offences actually or allegedly committed abroad by a UK national or someone habitually resident in the UK, if UK law allows the person to be prosecuted in the UK for that offence/alleged offence. Since 29 June 2021 almost all sexual offences fall into that category, because the Domestic Abuse Act 2021 amended the Sexual Offences Act 2003 to extend the jurisdiction of the UK courts to deal with such overseas offences/alleged offences in which the victim/alleged victim is an adult. Earlier law had already extended that jurisdiction in respect of sexual offences in which a child is the victim/alleged victim.

Schedule 2 of the 2003 Act lists the sexual offences for which a UK national/resident can be prosecuted in the UK for what was done/allegedly done abroad.

However, as has already been indicated in this chapter, a media organisation which discloses that someone was a victim/alleged victim of a sexual offence, wherever it occurred/allegedly occurred, and irrespective of whether the UK criminal courts have jurisdiction, risks being sued by that person for damages under the UK's civil law of privacy, and could have breached a regulatory code, unless the person had given valid consent to that disclosure.

11.2.6 **Trafficking offences for which victims/alleged victims have anonymity**

The Modern Slavery Act 2015 was created to clarify and consolidate the law on slavery, forced labour and human trafficking, and to increase the penalties for such offences—which for some offences is a life sentence.

The 2015 Act amended section 1 of the Sexual Offences (Amendment) Act 1992 so that the lifelong automatic anonymity given to victims/alleged victims of sexual offences now also covers victims/alleged victims of 'human trafficking for exploitation' offences in section 2 of the 2015 Act. These—defined in section 3 of the 2015 Act—are (summarised):

- arranging or facilitating the travel of another person with a view to that person being exploited
  - by being held in slavery or servitude, or
  - being required to perform forced or compulsory labour, or
  - because something is done to or in respect of the person which involves or would involve the commission of an offence listed in Part 1 of the Sexual Offences Act 2003, or in section 1(1)(a) of the Protection of Children Act 1978 (indecent photographs of children), or
  - by being encouraged, required or expected to donate or sell an organ from their body, or
  - when the person is a child, or is mentally or physically ill or disabled, or has a family relationship, by being subject to force, threats or deception designed to induce them to provide any kind of service, or to provide or enable someone else to obtain benefits of any kind, in circumstances when an adult who was not ill or disabled or did not have that family relationship would be likely to refuse to be thus exploited.

Sexual offences listed earlier in this chapter are in Part 1 of the 2003 Act, so the trafficking could include travel being arranged to control people for prostitution or to sexually exploit children, and the anonymity would apply even if, as events turned out, such a victim of the trafficking did not suffer any sexual offence—because, for example, police intervened.

Journalists should know that, for there to be a trafficking offence, there must be the element of 'arranging or facilitating of travel'. This covers arranged or actual travel within the UK, another country or from one country to another, or merely recruiting someone for such travel for such exploitation. If the person is also the victim/alleged victim of a sexual offence, it is clear that anonymity applies. But otherwise journalists—for example, when interviewing someone complaining of exploitation—need to understand how such 'trafficking' offences are defined, as anonymity applies in the case of a claim of forced labour and other non-sexual forms of exploitation.

The anonymity will cover, for example, a 'trafficked' woman forced to work as a household maid, or 'trafficked' immigrants or mentally vulnerable people being compelled to work by threats of violence.

The anonymity applies for anyone for whom such a destiny of exploitation was planned, as regards a report of the plan—see 11.1.2.

If a journalist knows or suspects anonymity may apply, yet the victim/alleged victim is willing to be identified in an account of such an ordeal or plan, the best course is to obtain their written consent to be identified—see 11.6.4.

The anonymity applies wherever the actual or alleged trafficking offence took place if the perpetrator/alleged perpetrator is a UK national as defined by the Modern Slavery Act. If the perpetrator/alleged perpetrator is not a UK national but any part of the actual or alleged arranging or facilitating of travel took place in the UK or the actual or arranged travel consists of arrival in or entry into, departure from, or travel within, the UK, the anonymity applies (because that person can be prosecuted in the UK).

See the **additional material** for ch. 11 on **www.mcnaes.com** for a case study of how freelance journalist Michelle Rawlins took care to preserve the anonymity of a victim of modern slavery in a *Guardian* feature.

11.3 Lifetime anonymity for victims/alleged victims of female genital mutilation offences

Schedule 1 of the Female Genital Mutilation Act 2003 makes it an offence to publish anything likely to lead members of the public to identify someone as a victim/alleged victim of a female genital mutilation (FGM) offence in that person's lifetime. For details about who can be prosecuted for breach of this anonymity, see 11.5.

This automatic ban has the same scope—for example, as regards detail which the law says in particular should not be published—as the anonymity provision for the victims/alleged victims of sexual and trafficking offences covered earlier.

FGM is prevalent in many countries around the world, including parts of Africa, Asia and the Middle East—for example Somalia, Bangladesh and Yemen. There is evidence that it is inflicted on girls and young women from ethnic communities in the UK which share that culture—for example, the FGM could be inflicted when they visit relatives abroad.

FGM is usually arranged by the victim's parents or another adult relative, so a report which can identify a defendant without identifying the victim may well be rare. FGM has been illegal in the UK since 1985, but by late 2023 there had been only two successful prosecutions.

In some circumstances such a victim/alleged victim can be identified—see 11.6.

for reports of those FGM prosecutions, see Useful Websites at the end of this chapter

11.3.1 FGM offences for which victims/alleged victims have anonymity

It is an offence for any person in England or Wales (regardless of their nationality or residence status) to inflict FGM, or to assist a person to carry out FGM on herself. It is also an offence to provide assistance from the UK to a non-UK national or resident to carry out FGM outside the UK on a UK national or permanent UK resident. It is also an offence for a UK national or permanent UK resident to perform FGM abroad, assist a person to perform FGM on herself outside the UK, or to assist from outside the UK a non-UK national or resident to carry out FGM outside the UK on a UK national or permanent UK resident.

The anonymity arising from any such actual or alleged offence applies for any woman or girl who suffered FGM or who was the intended victim. Assisting is aiding, abetting, counselling or procuring. The anonymity also applies for the victim/alleged victim of an actual or alleged attempt, or actual or alleged conspiracy or encouragement, to commit an FGM offence—see 11.1.2 for context.

It also applies when a UK national or resident is accused of failing to protect a girl aged under 16 from the risk of FGM—a failure for which a parent could be prosecuted—and in cases such as the prosecution of a healthcare or social care professional or teacher for failing to tell police of an apparent case of FGM.

See Useful Websites at the end of this chapter for more on FGM offences.

11.3.2 FGM protection orders

The anonymity means that normally any report of an application to the Family Court for an 'FGM protection order' or that such an order was made, or that it was actually or allegedly breached should not contain detail likely to identify the girl or woman it is meant to protect. Such orders can, for example, ban parents from arranging for a girl to leave the UK if it is feared she would suffer FGM abroad. If such an order is sought or made in a hearing which also involves child protection proceedings under the Children Act 1989, the anonymity provision under that Act would also apply.

For Children Act anonymity, see ch. 14.

11.4 Lifetime anonymity for victims/alleged victims of forced marriage offences

Schedule 6A of the Anti-social Behaviour, Crime and Policing Act 2014 makes it a criminal offence to publish anything likely to lead members of the public to identify someone as a victim/alleged victim of a forced marriage offence in their lifetime.

This automatic ban has the same scope—for example, as regards detail which the law says in particular should not be published—as the anonymity provision for the victims/alleged victims of sexual, trafficking and FGM offences covered earlier.

UK victims of forced marriage offences are often girls or women from communities with a South Asian cultural heritage, who may have been tricked by a relative into travelling abroad for the marriage to take place, but forced marriage is not limited to these communities. For details about who can be prosecuted for breach of the anonymity, see 11.5.

11.4.1 Forced marriage offences for which victims/alleged victims have anonymity

Under the Marriage and Civil Partnership (Minimum Age) Act 2022, Parliament raised the legal age of marriage and civil partnership (in England and Wales only) from 16 to 18, including for non-legally binding religious and cultural forms of marriage. The new law makes it an offence to carry out any conduct for the purpose of causing a child to enter into a marriage before their 18th birthday. This law applies, for example, if at the relevant time the perpetrator or the child or both were in England or Wales, or at least one of them was habitually resident in England or Wales (which means there can be prosecution in the UK even if the offence is committed abroad).

The offence occurs whether or not the 'conduct' is violent, threatening, coercive or deceptive, or leads to a 'marriage'. The new law was enacted by amendment to the Anti-Social Behaviour, Crime and Policing Act 2014 and, consequently, the 2014 Act's Schedule 6A means it is normally illegal to publish any detail likely to identify a person in their lifetime as a victim/alleged victim of the 'conduct' offence, whether or not there has been a prosecution. See too what is said after 11.6.4.1 about this law.

Under section 121(3) a person commits a forced marriage offence if they practise any form of deception with the intention of causing another person to leave the UK, and intend the other person to be subjected to conduct outside the UK that is a forced marriage offence under section 121(1), or would be such an offence if the victim were in England or Wales.

A person only commits the offence if, at the relevant time, the perpetrator or victim or both were in England or Wales, or if neither were but at least one of them was either habitually resident in England and Wales or a UK national (which means there can be prosecution in the UK of such an offence committed abroad).

The aim of this law is to protect a person from any plan or plot to force them to marry. An offence under the Act can be committed even if there was no such marriage, regardless of where it was intended to happen, or if the marriage was forced on someone who lacked the mental capacity to consent. 'Marriage' under the Act is any religious or civil ceremony of marriage, and the ceremony does not have to be legally binding. Note that an arranged marriage—in which families take the lead in selecting a marriage partner but the couple have the free will and choice to accept or decline the arrangement—is not a forced marriage.

Forced marriages are usually organised and planned by the victim's parents or other adult relatives, so reports which can identify a defendant charged with an offence will be rare because of the danger of breaching the victim's/alleged victim's anonymity.

For when it is legal to publish the identity of such a victim/alleged victim, see 11.6.

11.4.2 Forced marriage protection orders

The anonymity provisions mean that normally any report of an application to the Family Court for a 'forced marriage protection order', or of the making of such an order, or that it was actually or allegedly breached, should not contain any detail likely to identify the individual for whom the protection was sought. If such an order is sought or made in a hearing which also involves child protection proceedings under the Children Act 1989, anonymity provision under that Act would also apply.

For Children Act anonymity, see ch. 14.

See Useful Websites at the end of this chapter for more information on such orders and forced marriage offences.

11.5 Breach of the anonymity—liability and defences

The law about who can be prosecuted for breaching anonymity under the 1992, 2003 or 2014 Acts is the same as for breaching section 49 anonymity under the Children and Young Persons Act 1933—see 10.3.4 in this book.

They include the editor of the newspaper or magazine, whoever has that editor role in respect of the relevant programme, and the owner of such a media organisation—for example, a company. For any other form of publication, it is any person publishing it. The punishment for those convicted of breach is a fine unlimited by statute.

For all cases, it is a defence for a person accused of breaching the anonymity:

- to show that they were not aware, and neither suspected nor had reason to suspect, that what was published contained matter likely to identify such a victim/alleged victim; or
- to show that the victim/alleged victim gave valid, written consent to be identified, as explained later in this chapter.

Case study

In January 2019, BBC Asian Network head of news Arif Ansari, was acquitted of breaching the 1992 Act after a trial at Sheffield Magistrates' Court. One of his senior reporters had repeated the name of a grooming gang victim during a radio broadcast, wrongly believing the victim's name he heard in court was a pseudonym. Arif said it did not occur to him the reporter might make that mistake, because not naming victims of sexual offences was 'as basic as it gets'. District Judge Naomi Redhouse said she could not be sure Arif had reason to suspect the report would have breached the Act but remarked 'there may be lessons in this case for the training of court reporters'. (*BBC News,* 18 January 2019).

11.6 When the anonymity ceases to apply

The anonymity automatically banning people from being identified as the victims/alleged victims of offences covered in this chapter does not apply to dead people—for example, a murdered rape victim—and in some circumstances will not apply for a lifetime.

((•)) See online ch. 36 on Other UK Jurisdictions for detail of law in Northern Ireland which preserves anonymity for 25 years after the death of a victim or alleged victim.

11.6.1 By court order—to avoid substantial prejudice to a defence

A criminal court due to try someone for a sexual, trafficking, FGM or forced marriage offence can remove an alleged victim's anonymity if it is satisfied that otherwise the accused person's defence at the trial would be 'substantially prejudiced'—see section 3(1) of the 1992 Act (as regards sexual or trafficking offences); paragraph 1 of Schedule 1 of the 2003 Act (FGM offences); and paragraph 1 of Schedule 6A of the 2014 Act (forced marriage offences).

This law allows lawyers for a defendant seeking to lift an alleged victim's anonymity to argue that publicity identifying that person would induce witnesses to come forward to help the defence. For example, if this is an **alibi** defence, allowing the media to identify the alleged victim of a sexual offence could jog people's memories about that person's whereabouts at the time of the alleged crime (were they really where it is alleged to have been committed?) or about who was with or following the alleged victim at that time and place (for example, was it someone who did not resemble the defendant?). But courts are rarely asked to lift anonymity on this ground.

→glossary

If the alleged sexual or trafficking offence is indictable-only, a magistrates' court does not have power to waive the anonymity.

11.6.2 By court order—to lift 'a substantial and unreasonable' restriction on reporting

Under the 1992 Act, the judge or a magistrate at a trial of a sexual or trafficking offence can lift the alleged victim's anonymity if satisfied that it would impose a substantial and unreasonable restriction on the reporting of proceedings, at the trial, *and* that is in the public interest to remove or relax the restriction.

Cases in which the media have asked courts to lift anonymity on this ground are extremely rare. An example is *R v Hutchinson* detailed in the **additional material** for ch. 11 on **www.mcnaes.com**, when the law now in section 3(2) and (3) of the 1992 Act was detailed in an earlier statute.

Section 3 of the 1992 Act says the court cannot remove the anonymity 'by reason only of the outcome of the trial'—meaning that a victim/alleged victim cannot be identified simply because the defendant was acquitted. Again, if the alleged offence is indictable-only, a magistrates' court does not have power to lift the anonymity.

Paragraph 1 of Schedule 1 of the 2003 Act, on FGM offences, and paragraph 1 of Schedule 6A of the 2014 Act, on forced marriage offences, say that in *any* criminal proceedings a court can remove the anonymity of a victim/alleged victim, if that court is satisfied that the anonymity would impose a substantial and unreasonable restriction on the reporting of the court proceedings, *and* it is in the public interest to remove or relax the restriction.

11.6.3 If a person faces a criminal charge that a false claim of victimhood was made as regards a sexual or trafficking offence

People alleged to have falsely claimed to police that they have been victims of an offence may be charged with wasting police time, or perjury, or perverting the course of justice.

definitions of these offences are given in 6.3.4

- A person appearing in court on such a charge—for example, perjury—in relation to what is said to be a false allegation of a sexual or trafficking offence can be identified in reports of those proceedings as someone who has claimed to have been the victim of that offence.

This is because section 1(4) of the 1992 Act says that a victim or alleged victim of a sexual or trafficking offence can be identified in articles which consist 'only of a report of criminal proceedings other than' proceedings for the actual or alleged sexual or trafficking offence which entitled them to anonymity.

Thus, it would also be permissible to identify in a report of a court case a woman charged with assaulting a man, even though she had told the court that she was retaliating because he had raped her—however, it would also be important to check that those proceedings had not at any earlier time included a charge in which she was allegedly the victim of a sexual offence. A journalist covering such a case would still need to consider whether it would be ethical to identify her in the circumstances of the case.

See the **additional material** for ch. 11 on **www.mcnaes.com**, 'Newspaper breached anonymity after the rape charge was dropped'. In 2017 the Court of Appeal removed any doubt that criminal proceedings in which a rape or sexual assault complainant is accused of perjury or wasting police time fall into the category of 'other' proceedings. See the *Beale* case study in the **additional material**.

11.6.4 The victim/alleged victim can give written consent to be identified

The media may identify someone as being the victim/alleged victim of a sexual, trafficking, FGM or forced marriage offence if the person consents.

But:

- the consent must be in writing;
- the person waiving their anonymity must be aged 16 or older; and
- the consent will not be valid if it is proved that anyone 'interfered unreasonably with the peace and comfort' of that person with the intention of obtaining it—this wording guards against anyone being pressured into giving consent.

Parents of victims/alleged victims under 16 cannot consent on their behalf.

A court's permission is not needed for this consent to be given. Understandably, most victims do not seek to relinquish anonymity. But many victims of sexual offences have given such consent. For example, a victim of rape may feel that letting the media identify them sends a powerful signal to other rape victims that they can find the courage to seek justice, and that there is no stigma in being a victim. Some victims of trafficking, or of FGM or forced marriage offences may feel the same.

Efforts should be made to secure a waiver, but when one publisher has, having obtained valid written consent, published material identifying the person as such a victim/alleged victim, other publishers may take the view it safe to identify them, even if they did not get written consent, as they could consider the risk of a complaint will be low—see the **additional material** for this chapter on **www.mcnaes.com** for more detail, and for a case in which television presenter Holly Willoughby waived her right to anonymity at the outset of the trial of a man who plotted her kidnap, rape and murder.

11.6.4.1 Good practice in wording consent

Whenever a person protected by statutory anonymity is willing to waive it, it is good practice to ask the individual to state explicitly in the written waiver that they have not been subjected to any interference with their peace or comfort. This helps remind them to think deeply about waiving anonymity, and to protect the journalists and publications in law if the individual later complains about being identified.

> As regards the 'conduct' offence created in the Marriage and Civil Partnership (Minimum Age) Act 2022 (see 11.4.1) it will be legal to identify the victim/alleged victim if the court makes an order on either ground set out in 11.6.1 and 11.6.2, or if a victim/alleged victim who is 16 or older gives written consent and there has been no unreasonable interference with their peace or comfort to gain that consent.

11.7 Provision for anonymity in regulatory codes

As explained in chs. 2 and 3, there are regulatory systems governing the ethics of UK journalists, with three regulators.

Any breach by a media organisation of anonymity provided by law for a person would also breach the relevant code, in that a person whose identity is protected by law has a 'reasonable expectation of privacy' in that respect. For the codes' general protection of privacy, see 4.2. But each code also contains specific provisions for coverage of actual or alleged sexual offences. Some of these provisions go further than the law in providing anonymity.

11.7.1 Editors' Code of Practice clauses on sexual offence cases

The combined effect of clause 7 'Children in sex cases' and clause 11 'Victims of sexual assault' of the Editors' Code of Practice, used by the Independent Press

Standards Organisation (Ipso), is to ban media organisations which are Ipso members, or any others which adhere to the Code, from identifying any victim or alleged victim of a sexual offence unless the law permits identification. So, breach of anonymity provided by the 1992 Act—for example, by publication of too much detail from a court case—would lead to Ipso ruling that the Code was breached too, if it received a complaint from that person or one made on their behalf.

Even if the law allows identification of any victim or alleged victim, clauses 7 and 11 of the Code mean that anonymity should be preserved in coverage of the case, on an ethical basis, unless an exception stated in the relevant clause applies.

For the Editors' Code, see this book's Appendix 1. For Ipso adjudications on breach of the anonymity, see the **additional material** for ch. 11 on **www.mcnaes.com**.

11.7.1.1 'Children in sex cases'

Clause 7 ('Children in sex cases') says: 'The press must not, even if legally free to do so, identify children under 16 who are victims or witnesses in cases involving sex offences.' It adds that:

- the word 'incest' must not be used where a child victim might be identified;
- the child must not be identified in any press report of a case, but the adult may be;
- care must be taken that nothing in the report implies the relationship between the accused and the child.

The clause applies whatever the context or legal forum in which a sexual offence is alleged.

Clause 7 is subject to the Code's public interest exceptions, which means Ipso accepts there may be 'exceptional' circumstances in which the press may identify a child who is a witness, victim or alleged victim in a sex case (if the law permits this).

for the Codebook, see Useful Websites at the end of this chapter

The Editors' Codebook, produced to aid interpretation of the Code, says that clause 7 also means that *defendants* aged under 16 accused of sexual offences should not be identified in coverage of their case, unless the court permits identification but that, if it does, there could be a public interest in reports identifying such a child convicted of a sexual offence. As explained in ch. 10, defendants aged under 18 may have automatic anonymity in law or have had anonymity bestowed by a court (but no defendant has it under the 1992 Act).

see too 4.11 on interviewing, photographing and filming children

The Codebook also notes that girls who become mothers after conceiving under the age of 16, who may in law be victims of a sexual offence even if no prosecution takes place, sometimes put their motherhood into the public domain. But the Codebook points out—in this context—that no-one under 16 can in law give valid consent to be identified as a victim of a sexual offence, and that parents cannot give this consent on their behalf.

11.7.1.2 'Adequate justification'

The Code's clause 11 says: 'The press must not identify or publish material likely to lead to the identification of a victim of sexual assault unless there is adequate justification and they are legally free to do so.'

This covers all victims or alleged victims of sexual offences, whatever their age, and whatever the context or legal forum in which the allegation arises, and—as is the case with clause 7—wherever in the world the offence allegedly took place. But the particular, overriding provision in clause 7 as regards the identification of those under 16 means that clause 11's term 'adequate justification' applies to editorial decisions on the identification of those aged 16 or older. An example of 'adequate justification' is when such an adult wants to be identified, and has given valid, written consent so their identification is legal.

Clause 11 is not formally subject to the Code's public interest exceptions, but the term 'adequate justification' embraces public interest considerations.

> See case studies concerning 'adequate justification' in the **additional material** for ch. 11 on **www.mcnaes.com**.

11.7.1.3 Clause 11 also warns against identification during news-gathering

In 2017 Ipso received a complaint that what a journalist said, did and displayed on his phone when visiting a property in a bid to find and interview sexual offence victims during a court case, and in a phone call to their parents, led to the parents and a third party being able to identify them as the victims. Ipso upheld the complaint, ruling there was a breach of clause 2, covering privacy, but said that it was unclear whether clause 11 applied in such circumstances (*Warwickshire Police v Daily Mail*, issued 14 December 2017). This led in 2019 to clause 11 being extended to say: 'Journalists are entitled to make enquiries but must take care and exercise discretion to avoid the unjustified disclosure of the identity of a victim of sexual assault.' This means the clause now covers news-gathering activity as well as published information.

see 4.2 for detail of clause 2

11.7.1.4 Ipso guidance, including about readers' postings

see too 11.1.5.1, Postings by readers which breach anonymity

Ipso has produced guidance on reporting of sexual offences which warns editors that publishing coverage of sexual offences on social media, or other online sites under their control, creates risk that readers may post material identifying a victim/alleged victim. For this Ipso guidance, see Useful Websites at the end of this chapter.

11.7.2 Ofcom code's protection of children involved in sexual offence cases

Rule 1.8 of the Ofcom Broadcasting Code says broadcasters should 'be particularly careful not to provide clues' which may lead to the identification of children when by law they should have anonymity 'as a victim, witness, defendant or other perpetrator in the case of sexual offences featured in criminal, civil or family court proceedings'.

This rule warns against jigsaw identification and that inadvertent use of the term 'incest' may identify such a child.

11.7.3 Impress code's protection of victims/alleged victims of sexual offences

Impress guidance on rule 6.2 of its Standards Code is that publishers must not identify children under 18 who are victims or witnesses in cases involving sexual offences, regardless of whether the court or a responsible adult allows publication.

Its clause 6.3 says: 'Publishers must preserve the anonymity of victims of sexual offences, except as permitted by law or with the express consent of the person'. Impress guidance makes clear the clause covers alleged victims, and warns against jigsaw identification. It says publishers should not commission journalists to interview such people's neighbours because of the risk of identification.

((•)) See Useful Websites at the end of this chapter for the Broadcast and Impress codes, and Impress guidance. For jigsaw identification, see 11.1.3.

Recap of major points

- It is illegal for the media to identify the victims/alleged victims of sexual offences—including rape and sexual assault—in reports of these crimes or of court cases which follow.
- The same anonymity applies for the victims/alleged victims of offences of 'human trafficking for exploitation' and, under other law, for the victims/alleged victims of female genital mutilation offences and forced marriage offences.
- A court can remove the anonymity in certain circumstances, but this rarely happens.
- There is a danger of 'jigsaw identification', particularly when several media organisations are covering a case of alleged sex abuse within a family.
- A victim/alleged victim who is aged 16 or over can waive the anonymity by giving a media organisation written consent to being identified.

((•)) Useful Websites

www.legislation.gov.uk

- Sexual Offences (Amendment) Act 1992
- Sexual Offences Act 2003
- Modern Slavery Act 2015

- Explanatory Notes to the Modern Slavery Act 2015
- Female Genital Mutilation Act 2003
- Anti-social Behaviour, Crime and Policing Act 2014, including law banning forced marriages
- Online Safety Act 2023

Crown Prosecution Service, www.cps.gov.uk

- Crown Prosecution Service guidance on sexual offences
- Crown Prosecution Service guidance on FGM offences
- 'Woman convicted of aiding FGM of young girl abroad in legal first'—CPS press release about first UK case to involve FGM committed abroad

www.gov.uk

- Female genital mutilation resource pack, published by the Home Office
- Government information about 'FGM protection orders'
- Government information about 'forced marriage protection orders'

***The Guardian*, 'Mother jailed for 11 years in first British FGM conviction', www.theguardian.com**

The Guardian's report of the UK's first successful prosecution for an FGM offence

BBC News, 'Forced marriage: Leeds parents jailed over Bangladesh wedding', www.bbc.co.uk

The Editors' Codebook, www.editorscode.org.uk

Provides detailed advice on clauses 7 and 11 of the Editors' Code

Independent Press Standards Organisation (IPSO), 'Sexual offences guidance', www.ipso.co.uk

Ofcom, 'The Ofcom Broadcasting Code', www.ofcom.org.uk

Impress, www.impressorg.com

- Impress Standards Code and guidance

Online resources

Visit the online resources at **www.mcnaes.com** to test your knowledge of this chapter with **self-test questions** and a **flashcard glossary**, and to read **updates** about law and regulatory matters affecting journalism, as well as **additional material** to further your learning.

12

Court reporting—other restrictions

Chapter summary

Earlier chapters have shown that reporting crime and courts is not a job for an untrained amateur. Reporting restrictions may dictate what can be published and breaching them is an offence. This chapter details more restrictions, including the bans on using cameras and audio-recording devices in any court, and on recording a sound or image from a court's transmission of its proceedings. Revealing how individual jurors voted in verdicts is also illegal. Reporting what a court has heard in private can be punished as contempt of court. The chapter also outlines how courts can stop the media identifying some adult witnesses and blackmail victims, or postpone reporting of a case. Chapter 15 covers journalists' rights to uphold open justice and be notified of orders made by a court to impose a reporting restriction. But journalists are expected to make checks, and to know that some restrictions apply permanently, with no need for the court to make an order. Chapter 16 shows how to challenge a reporting restriction as invalid or unnecessary. Chapter 22 deals with defamation dangers in court reporting.

12.1 Bans on photography, filming, recording, and unauthorised transmission

Photography and filming in courtrooms, courthouses and their 'precincts' is banned by law, with some limited exceptions explained later. It is normally illegal to make an audio-recording of a court hearing. It is illegal without a court's authority to capture any sound or image from an official transmission of its proceedings. Publication of any such illegally gained material is an offence too. The bans also apply in respect of tribunals which are courts.

ch. 18 covers tribunals

These laws protect the administration of justice in particular cases and more generally. A witness's testimony could be disrupted if they become distressed because someone in a court's public gallery is photographing or recording them. This could prevent a just outcome to the case. Similarly, a juror or defendant who becomes anxious about being filmed in such locations may be unable to focus on the court's proceedings.

The authority of and public confidence in our courts could be undermined if sounds or images of witnesses, defendants, claimants or jurors—created by such illegal use of a mobile phone to make a video in a courtroom, for example—were reproduced on social media in a manner ridiculing them or the proceedings. That prospect could deter people called as witnesses or summonsed as jurors in future cases from attending court, or deter claimants from seeking justice.

12.1.1 **Ban on photography, filming and sketching in courts and precincts**

Section 41 of the Criminal Justice Act 1925, covering all courts, makes it illegal to:

- take or try to take any photograph of,
- or make or try to make any portrait or sketch with a view to publication of:
  - 'any person, being a judge of the court or a juror or a witness in or a party to any proceedings before the court' while such a person is in the courtroom, or in the building where the court is held, or in that building's precincts;
  - such a person entering or leaving any such building or its precincts.

It is also illegal to publish such a photo, portrait or sketch or any reproduction of it.

Case law has established that section 41 also bans filming of these categories of people in those locations, and publication of any such footage (for example, *HM Attorney General v Yaxley-Lennon* [2019] EWHC 1791 (QB)).

ch. 17 covers coroners' courts

Section 41 says 'a judge' includes any 'registrar, magistrate, justice and coroner'. The term 'party' would include any defendant or claimant.

Breach of section 41 can be punished with a fine of up to £1,000.

12.1.1.1 **Precincts, and 'entering or leaving'**

The Act does not define 'precincts', which causes practical difficulties. The term includes any café, rooms, foyers or corridors within the courthouse building. But it is unclear to what extent it includes areas immediately outside. If unsure, check with the particular court.

In the *Yaxley-Lennon* case (see 12.1.3), the High Court said: 'We would be inclined to give the term "precincts" a flexible but purposive interpretation, regarding it as intended to allow a zone of relative calm around the perimeter of a court building, within which the protected categories of participant could be confident that their progress to and from the court building for the purposes of the relevant litigation would not be disrupted or intruded upon by the capture or publication of images.'

Journalists standing on the public pavement frequently photograph or film judges, defendants, witnesses, claimants, and lawyers entering or leaving court buildings.

While this practice has become customary, it would seem to breach the section 41 ban on showing them 'entering or leaving'. It is rare for a court to object, but jurors should not be photographed or filmed entering or leaving, as it may be a contempt of court to do so.

✱ Remember

His Majesty's Courts and Tribunals Service guidance to criminal court staff says that defendants should not be allowed to use a side entrance to a court building unless police or a judge advise staff on security grounds to permit this. See Useful Websites at the end of this chapter for this guidance.

12.1.2 Artists' sketches of court cases

The media publish artists' sketches of scenes in court, including the face of the defendant, to illustrate newsworthy cases. To comply with section 41, these artists visit the court's public gallery or press bench before sketching the scene from memory elsewhere outside the courtroom, such as a court's press room. Note, an AI-generated image of a defendant or courtroom scene is unlikely to breach section 41 if it is created outside of the courtroom or court building.

12.1.3 Photography, filming or portrait-making could be a contempt of court

Use of a camera or sketching or making a 'portrait' in a courtroom, a courthouse or its precincts and/or publication of such an image or the footage could be ruled to be a contempt of court in common law. This is a graver offence than breach of the 1925 Act—see additional material for more detail.

for context, see 19.3, on contempt in common law

A contempt will be ruled to have occurred if, for example, the photography or filming, or even a threatened use of a camera, interfered or created a real risk of interference with the administration of justice—for example, if taking a photograph of a juror, witness or defendant and/or its publication on social media was done to intimidate that person. It could be ruled too that a contempt occurred because publication of such a photo or footage (whatever the motive of the person who did this) created a real risk that other people would be reluctant to be a witness or juror in any future case, a consequence which would be 'interference'. Also, publication could breach the Contempt of Court Act 1981, which is explained in ch. 19. A person ruled to have committed a contempt could be fined a sum unlimited by statute and/or be jailed for up to two years.

Members of the public have been jailed for using mobile phones to take photos or film in a courtroom. Notices there warn such activity is banned.

In 2019 the Right-wing extremist and self-styled 'journalist' Stephen Yaxley-Lennon—also known as Tommy Robinson—was jailed for nine months by the High Court for committing three offences of contempt of court. These arose from incidents in the precincts of the courthouse of Leeds Crown court, in which using a video camera he confronted defendants arriving to attend their trial. In one of its rulings, the High Court said that he had committed a contempt in common law, indicating this was because his actions were 'molestation' of the defendants. For more details, see 19.5.2.

A media photographer's conduct could be ruled to be molestation, and therefore a contempt, even if the activity is some distance from the courthouse. Case law suggests that running after a defendant for a short while in order to photograph them would not usually be seen as molestation (*R v Runting* [1989] Crim LR 282). But stalking a defendant or witness further, or jostling them, could be contempt.

12.1.4 Ban on audio-recording in court

It is illegal to use any audio recording device, including a mobile phone's recording facility, in a court without its permission.

The ban is in section 9 of the Contempt of Court Act 1981, which makes it a contempt:

- to use in court, or bring into court for use, any tape recorder or other instrument for recording sound, except with the permission of the court;
- to publish a recording of legal proceedings made by means of any such instrument, or any recording derived directly or indirectly from it, by playing it in the hearing of the public or any section of the public, or to dispose of it or any recording so derived, with a view to such publication.

If a court does give permission to record, it is a breach of section 9 to use the recording in contravention of any condition(s) specified by the court.

The penalty for breaching section 9 is a jail term of up to two years and/or a fine unlimited by statute. The general purpose of the ban is, as outlined earlier, to ensure that the administration of justice is not undermined.

- One particular purpose is to stop secret recordings being made in the public gallery by, for example, a defendant's criminal associates, who could use them to intimidate a prosecution witness.
- Another purpose is to stop dishonest witnesses colluding in false corroboration. For example, a witness could listen to a recording of another's evidence and repeat the same information in their own evidence, but claim to have recalled it independently.

Case study

In 2019 a judge sentenced *Mail on Sunday* writer Marcia Angella Johnson, 59, to a jail term of seven days, suspended for 12 months, and fined her £500 because a month earlier in the public gallery at Southwark Crown court she used her mobile phone to record a hearing, as a method of note-taking for feature material. She was confronted by police and an usher who suspected she was recording. She admitted being in contempt of court by making those recordings. Her lawyer said she made them because she was concerned that if she used shorthand or made written notes, she would not be able to keep up. Sentencing her, Mr Justice Edis said her offence, though at the lower end of the scale, was aggravated by the fact she was an experienced professional journalist who knew 'perfectly well' about the rule against recording (*Media Lawyer*, 23 October 2019).

12.1.4.1 Permission to audio-record

A court has discretion to allow audio-recording, including by a journalist, for note-taking. Rule 6.9 of the Criminal Procedure Rules (CrimPR) says anyone who wants permission to record in a criminal court must apply as soon as reasonably practicable, notify the parties in the case, and anyone else the court specifies, that permission is being sought, and explain why recording should be allowed.

Criminal Practice Direction 2.5 says that relevant factors in the court's decision on whether to grant permission may include 'the existence of any reasonable need' on the part of the applicant for the recording to be made. The Direction also says the court should always consider whether to impose conditions regarding the use of any recording made, and that the 'identity and role of the applicant . . . and the nature of the subject matter of the proceedings' may be relevant to this. Rule 39.9(2) of the Civil Procedure Rules, which apply to civil courts, recognises that recording can be permitted.

The 1981 Act does not give a court power to authorise publication of the recording (*R (Spurrier) v Secretary of State for Transport* [2019] EWHC 528 (Admin)).

Shortly before this book went to press, the Law Commission made a number of recommendations regarding reform of the 1981 Act, including provisions that would enable accredited journalists to record proceedings without having to ask permission—see www.mcnaes.com for updates.

((•)) For context on criminal and civil court rules and Practice Directions, see 15.11. For links to these rules, see Useful Websites at the end of this chapter. On note-taking in courts, see 15.10.

12.1.5 Jury visits to the scene of crime or death

If a judge or coroner decides that jurors should visit an outside location such as a crime or accident scene to help them understand evidence, the press are generally entitled to attend, but the risk of committing a contempt means that the visit should not be filmed, photographed, sketched or recorded without the court's permission. The judge or coroner may allow such activity if the images created are not of the court in session there, but impose conditions—for example, that no juror or witness or the defendant is shown in what is published. The visit means the court has moved temporarily to that location.

coroners' courts are covered in ch. 17

12.1.6 The bans apply in the courtroom's annexe

For cases of 'high interest' to the media, likely to fill the press bench in the courtroom, a court can arrange for other journalists to be in an annexe, or 'overspill court'—for example, another room in the courthouse—to see a 'live-stream' audiovisual transmission of the proceedings, or hear an audio one. In these circumstances, the annexe is an extension of the courtroom (*R (Spurrier) v Secretary of State for Transport*, cited earlier), so the bans on photography, filming, portrait-making, sketching and audio-recording, and on publication of such material, apply in respect of that location too.

12.1.7 Some transmission and broadcasting allowed

ch. 9 explains the Court of Appeal's and Supreme Court's roles

Provisions in other statutes mean the Supreme Court and Court of Appeal can allow transmission of their courtroom proceedings to the public, 'live' or recorded (for example, online or in TV news bulletins). Their proceedings, being concerned with points of law, are unlikely to involve witnesses in person and do not have jurors, and what is filmed for these transmissions, using installed cameras, is in the court's control. The **additional material** for ch. 12 on **www.mcnaes.com** explains those provisions.

Law made in 2020 allows TV companies, when arrangements are authorised in advance, to film senior judges sentencing defendants at Crown court—that is, the sentencing remarks made by the judge presiding in the case—and to broadcast this footage. This law does not permit anyone else in the court to be filmed, nor any other part of proceedings. For more detail, see the **additional material** for this chapter on **www.mcnaes.com**.

12.1.8 Bans on recording or transmitting images and sounds from a court's transmission

for context on 'special measures', see 12.13

Courts have powers in some circumstances to allow participants, such as witnesses, to take part in a courtroom hearing from a remote location—for example, as a 'special measure'.

A telephone or other electronic system provides a 'live link' which enables such participants to see and/or hear a transmission of what is happening in the physical courtroom, and for their participation to be transmitted back to screens or a speaker system there. This mixed use of the courtroom and remote participation is known as a **hybrid hearing**. →glossary

Courts can also conduct some types of hearings wholly as audiovisual ('video') or audio proceedings, using online or telephone conference facilities. These hearings are known as remote or **virtual hearings**, because each participant is using a 'live link' or phone, and so none are communicating within a physical courtroom or are in the same place as the judge(s) or magistrates. For context, see 15.14. →glossary

The Police, Crime, Sentencing and Courts Act 2022 amended section 85A of the Courts Act 2003 so that courts (including most tribunals) can now allow an audio or video live stream of any proceedings (whether 'virtual', 'hybrid' or 'in-person') to be transmitted so members of the public and journalists can see and/or hear it. The transmission can be to 'designated' premises (which could be a room in a courthouse) where the public and journalists can attend, or online to individuals who have identified themselves to the court, who can observe the hearing using a home or work computer, or a phone. The legislation also permits the court to record the transmission.

for context on section 85A, see 15.14.3

However, the legislation also amends section 85B of the 2003 Act, which makes it an offence for anyone to make or try to make an unauthorised recording or an unauthorised transmission of any image or sound which is in the court's transmission of its proceedings. Here, 'recording' means a recording on any medium of a single image (so a 'recording' could be a screengrab from the transmission, or a photograph of a face as shown in it—for example, that of a judge, defendant, witness or lawyer) or of a moving image or any sound. For the offence to be committed, the image or sound recorded does not have to be of a person. So, a journalist observing the transmission in the 'designated' premises, or anywhere else, must not photograph, film or audio-record any of it, or publish any such unauthorised 'recording' supplied by anyone else (because publication would be unauthorised transmission). It is a defence for someone charged with this offence to prove that, at the time of the actual or attempted unauthorised recording/transmission, they were not in designated live-streaming premises, and did not know, and could not reasonably have known, that the image or sound was being transmitted in court proceedings.

It is a separate offence for anyone to make or try to make an unauthorised recording/transmission of any image of or sound of a person taking part in, watching or listening to a court's authorised transmission as an observer. Therefore, for example, journalists should not photograph, film or audio-record another person watching or listening to the live transmission, whether in the 'designated' premises or elsewhere, even for footage which does not show the transmission or include sound from it, and should not publish such material. They should also not photograph, film or audio-record, for example, a witness, party or lawyer during the hearing, nor publish such material. It is a defence for a person charged with this offence to prove that, at the relevant time, they were not in designated live-streaming premises, and did not know and could not reasonably have known that the image or sound was of someone watching or listening to the transmission. The 2003 Act makes clear that it is irrelevant whether the person who made or tried to make an unauthorised recording/transmission intended it to be seen or heard by any other person—so it is illegal, for example, for a journalist to record the authorised transmission for note-taking purposes, unless the court gives permission.

Anyone who commits one of these offences can be fined up to £1,000. But such a breach could instead be dealt with as a contempt of court, which would mean a harsher penalty—see what is outlined earlier about contempt. An individual cannot be both convicted of an offence and punished for contempt in respect of the same conduct.

NB: The bans in section 85B do not apply in respect of the Supreme Court's proceedings.

for context on this law, see 15.14.3

Case study

On 17 November 2020, staff working for BBC *South East* committed contempt of court in common law by recording a court's transmission of its virtual hearing and broadcasting images from the recording. The hearing was a judicial review in the High Court brought by environmental campaigner Sarah Finch, challenging Surrey county council's planning approval for fracking operations at Horse Hill. The court authorised provision of electronic 'links' for media representatives to see and hear a live transmission of the hearing from the Microsoft Teams facility being used to conduct the case online. The BBC *South East* reporter assigned to cover the story knew she would be unable to observe the transmission live, because she had to film interviews and shoot footage at Horse Hill. So, at her request, BBC technicians based at its Tunbridge Wells newsroom recorded the transmission, using a provided link. That recording was an offence under section 85B of the Courts Act 2003. Further such offences were committed in the transmission of the recording among BBC staff, and in its editing, and because the reporter included a six-second, 'scene-setting' clip from the recorded footage—showing the judge, solicitors, counsel, and other participants in the Teams 'gallery' setting—in her report on the court case; and because this was broadcast in two regional news bulletins. The High Court initiated proceedings against the BBC for contempt of court, because of all this illegality. The BBC apologised and admitted the contempt. In a February 2021 ruling, Lady Justice Andrews and Mr Justice Warby said it 'beggared belief' that the team of experienced journalists involved had not considered the propriety of recording and broadcasting footage of the court's transmission. The judges accepted there was no intention to break the law, but said that what happened was contempt, beyond the summary offences in the 2003 Act, and that illegal photography 'will in general interfere with the proper administration of justice through the very fact that it defies the criminal law relating to the administration of justice'. They said that images of individuals involved in the court hearing were recorded and broadcast without those people's knowledge or consent. Fining the BBC £28,000, the judges said that factors adding to the seriousness of its contempt included 'the assumption of an unfettered right to take and deal with images and sounds generated by legal proceedings', that multiple offences occurred, and that the footage was broadcast to a large audience (*R on the application of Sarah Finch v Surrey County Council* [2021] EWHC 170 (QB)).

for context on common law contempt, see 19.3

12.2 'Live, text-based communications' can be used to report from court

The normal rule is that mobile phones must be turned off or switched to silent mode in court. Journalists who make or receive calls on mobile phones during court hearings could be punished for contempt because it is disruptive and so could interfere with the administration of justice.

But since 2011 accredited journalists and legal commentators attending courts have been allowed to report cases by using a mobile phone or laptop to post online, text or email without having to ask the court's permission. This was first allowed in 2011 when the Lord Chief Justice issued practice guidance giving a general permission for reporting of cases from all types of court by using 'live, text-based communications'. This permission, as regards criminal proceedings, is set out in Criminal Practice Direction 2.4.

see 15.9 on accreditation

The Direction and the 2011 guidance say:

- the devices must be silent and unobtrusive;
- a court can decide 'at any time' to forbid all use of such devices—for example, if there is concern that a witness due to testify could be coached or briefed on what to say by reference to online posts of earlier evidence (for example, if the concern is that particular witnesses will try to collude to give matching evidence), or that a witness giving evidence feels under pressure because of such 'live' textual reporting from the courtroom of what is said.

This general permission to use such devices for communicating information from a court applies only for 'journalistic purposes' and does not extend to non-accredited student journalists, or members of the public, who can ask the court for permission. Such devices, if silent, can normally be used in court by anyone for note-taking, with no need to ask for permission—see 15.10.

The Supreme Court has a policy allowing the use of live text-based communications from court (including for members of the public) on mobile phones. Laptops are not permitted in the courtroom. For certain types of case, or where restrictions are in place, live text-based communications are not allowed.

see Useful Websites at the end of this chapter for the Rules, Directions and Supreme Court policy

12.3 Confidentiality of jury deliberations

It is illegal to breach the confidentiality of a jury's deliberations, whether the jury was empanelled for a Crown court trial, an inquest or a civil trial. Juries arrive at their verdicts in secret discussions, in rooms guarded against intrusion. The secrecy helps jurors to be frank in discussions, without fear of facing a public backlash for an unpopular decision, or retribution from a party in the case, such as a defendant they convict. For the role of juries in criminal trials, civil cases and inquests, see chs. 9, 13 and 17.

Section 20D of the Juries Act 1974, which applies to Crown courts, the High Court and the County Court, makes it a criminal offence for a person intentionally to obtain, solicit or disclose (for example, by publication) any detail of:

- statements made,
- opinions expressed,
- arguments advanced, or
- votes cast

by jurors during their deliberations.

A juror who discloses such detail, other than to the court, would in almost all circumstances breach this law, as would a journalist if they asked a juror to disclose such detail. The ban can be breached even if what is published does not identify an individual juror or even the particular trial. The penalty for breaching this law is a jail term of up to two years and/or a fine unlimited by statute.

Exceptions in the Act's section 20E mean that, if as part of the public proceedings of the trial, anyone refers to such detail for the purpose of enabling the jury to arrive at their verdict or in connection with the delivery of that verdict, or the judge refers to such detail for the purposes of dealing with the case, what is said can be reported, unless the judge forbids this.

After the trial, the media is safe to publish a juror's general impressions of the experience of jury service, provided the individual is willing to volunteer these and is not asked about and does not refer to statements made, opinions expressed, arguments advanced or votes cast during the deliberations. A juror could be interviewed, for example, on whether they felt that evidence was clearly presented.

Journalistic investigations of alleged miscarriages of justice such as a controversial murder conviction sometimes prompt jurors to contact journalists months or years after a case to say that, in the light of new evidence which has emerged, they are no longer certain of the accused's guilt. The safest course is to seek legal advice before conducting or publishing such an interview.

The Times newspaper was fined £15,000 in 2009 for publishing material ruled to have breached the confidentiality of a jury's deliberations—see the case study in the **additional material** for ch. 12 on **www.mcnaes.com**.

12.4 Contempt risk in identifying or approaching jurors

see 19.3, for a general explanation of common law contempt

A media organisation which identifies a juror against their wishes, even after that trial, could be accused of common law contempt.

The disclosure could be ruled to have interfered with the judicial process by putting the juror at risk of harm from someone unhappy with a verdict or potentially deterring others from jury service. A reporter deemed to have harassed a juror for an interview, or by photographing a juror, might be ruled to have committed a contempt, as such harassment could discourage people from jury service.

A juror discharged during a case for late attendance or being drunk may well be named in open court and could be punished by the judge. In the absence of any court order to the contrary, the media can safely identify them, if named, and say how they were dealt with.

See online ch. 36 on Other UK Jurisdictions for detail of the statutory ban on identifying jurors in Northern Ireland.

12.5 Section 11 orders—blackmail, secrets and personal safety

A court can ban the media from reporting a person's name, or other information, in coverage of a case.

Section 11 of the Contempt of Court Act 1981 says (here summarised):

- A court can ban the publication of a name or other matter in connection with the proceedings as long as it has first allowed that information to be withheld from the public.

Section 11 orders are not used routinely, but typical uses are as follows.

To protect the identity of victims/alleged victims of blackmail involving a secret Someone who is the target of blackmail involving a threat to reveal a shameful secret, or something else that person wishes to hide, will be less likely to report the threat to police or give evidence if it is likely that their identity will be given in open court, and so could be reported by the media, because that would expose that person in connection with the secret. In blackmail cases, the victim/alleged victim is usually referred to in open court simply by a letter, for example, 'Mr X'. Normally the court makes a section 11 order to ban anyone from publishing the person's identity in coverage of or reference to that case, bearing in mind that journalists or others may somehow discover who the person is. This also protects the administration of justice as a continuing process, because the anonymity granted in a particular case encourages other blackmail victims to come forward in future cases.

for the legal definition of blackmail, see 6.3.2

To protect commercially sensitive information or secret processes For example, a company may sue another for damages over breach of confidence about valuable research data. The court may hear evidence about the data in private to preserve its confidentiality—if it does not stay confidential, the case would be pointless. 'In private' means that journalists and the public are excluded. A section 11 order will normally be made to ban reports of the case from publishing leaks of the evidence.

To protect national security, state secrets For example, a defendant prosecuted under the Official Secrets Act 1911 might be accused of betraying UK military secrets to a foreign power—evidence of which the court will probably hear in private to protect the material's secrecy. A section 11 order could be used to ban publication of such evidence, in case it was leaked from the private proceedings. Such an order could also ban publication of the identities of intelligence officers who testify, if the court has ordered that their names should not be mentioned in open court, as identification would end their usefulness as undercover agents and put them at risk.

ch. 32 explains official secrets law

To protect a person from the risk of harm A court might be persuaded to ban publication of a witness's name and address, or the address of a defendant—for example, a sexual offender—to prevent an attack on that person by criminals or vigilantes, or some other harm. But the media may choose to oppose such an order on the grounds that it is unnecessary—see 16.11, Anonymity, addresses—and risk of harm?

12.5.1 Two-stage process

A section 11 order is the second step in a two-stage process. The court first has to make an order (based on its common law powers or a court rule) that a name or other information should not be aired in its public proceedings. Only then can it impose a section 11 order. If the name or information then slips out by mistake in a public session—for example, in what a witness or lawyer says—or if the media discover it by other means, the order makes it illegal to publish it in any context which connects it to the case. Section 11 orders remain in force indefinitely, or until revoked.

for context, see 10.8, Jigsaw identification

When a section 11 order is in force to ban publication of a person's identity, journalists must guard against 'jigsaw identification'.

Breaching a section 11 order is an offence of contempt of court punishable by a jail term of up to two years and/or an unlimited fine. But section 11 only bans the reporting of the name or matter 'in connection with the proceedings'.

See the **additional material** for this chapter on **www.mcnaes.com** for how the BBC got a section 11 order lifted to be able to report on the National Crime Agency's seizure of a businessman's assets.

ch. 30 covers liability for readers' postings which breach anonymity provision

✱ Remember

Court staff should take steps to alert journalists that the court has made an order restricting reporting. But journalists must check if any such order has been made. Ch. 15 covers this and rules which mean journalists should be notified of applications for reporting restrictions.

12.6 Ban on reporting a court's private hearing

Courts sit in private, with the public and media excluded, for some cases, including those concerning state secrets, and cases about whether mentally ill people should be confined in hospital. The media is **automatically** banned from publishing what is said in some categories of cases heard by a court in private.

→glossary

This is because section 12 of the Administration of Justice Act 1960 makes it a contempt of court to publish, without the court's permission, a report of proceedings it has heard in private which:

→glossary

- relate to the exercise of the **inherent jurisdiction** of the High Court with respect to children;
- fall under the Children Act 1989 or the Adoption and Children Act 2002, or otherwise relate wholly or mainly to the maintenance or upbringing of a child;
- fall under the Mental Capacity Act 2005, or under any provision of the Mental Health Act 1983 authorising an application or reference to be made to the First-tier Tribunal, to the Mental Health Review Tribunal for Wales or to the County Court;

- involve national security;
- involve a secret process, discovery or invention;
- are those, of any kind, where the court expressly bans publication of all or specified information relating to the private hearing.

ch. 14 explains children cases in family courts and ch. 18 covers mental health tribunals

A reporter may be told what has happened in a private hearing by one of the parties. But section 12 automatically prohibits publication of anything heard by a court sitting in private for cases in the particular categories listed, to protect the welfare and privacy of children and the mentally ill or incapacitated, and to safeguard state or commercial secrets. However, open reporting provisions have been introduced in family courts which mean section 12 can be disapplied, which mean journalists can report on what they see and hear subject to restrictions—see ch. 14 for details. The Law Commission has also recommended reform of section 12, see www.mcnaes.com for updates.

A breach of section 12 is punishable by a jail term of up to two years and/or a fine unlimited by statute.

for context, see 18.6.1, Ban on reporting the private proceedings of some types of tribunal cases

- Any document 'prepared for use' in a court's private hearing is deemed to be part of those proceedings. If a case falls into the section 12 categories, the court will normally regard media publication of information or quotations from such a document, such as a psychiatric reports, as a contempt, even if the people involved in the case are not identified in what is published from the document.

The definition of court in section 12 includes tribunals classed as courts.

12.6.1 **Some detail about a private hearing can be published**

Some material about a private hearing in these types of case can be published. Section 12 makes clear that publishing the text, or a summary, of any order made in such a hearing is not contempt unless the court has specifically prohibited its publication.

In *Re B (A Child)* [2004] EWHC 411 (Fam), Mr Justice Munby said section 12 did not ban publishing a reference to 'the nature of the dispute' being heard in the private hearing. He added that what could be published without breaching section 12 included:

- the names, addresses or photographs of parties and witnesses involved in the private proceedings;
- the date, time or place of hearings in the case; and
- 'anything which has been seen or heard by a person conducting himself lawfully in the public corridor or other public precincts outside the court'.

But he added that the court itself could ban publication of even these details, or that automatic restrictions under other law might apply. For example, if the private hearing involves proceedings under the Children Act 1989 the child must not be identified, as ch. 14 explains.

ch. 19 explains contempt law and ch. 22 explains privilege

If the court hearing in private does not fall into the categories listed in section 12 of the 1960 Act, a media organisation may be able to publish an account of it which is safe in law—for example, if guided by a person who was in it. But a media report of

→glossary

a case heard in private is not protected by any statutory **privilege** in relation to defamation law, even when the report is fair and accurate, and will not be protected by section 4 of the Contempt of Court Act 1981 if it creates a substantial risk of serious prejudice or impediment to an 'active' case.

12.7 Other bans on unauthorised publication of case material

Even when reporting a case heard in public, a journalist should exercise care before quoting from a document used in it if the material has not been read out in court.

It is safe to quote from any document the journalist obtains from the court with permission for it to be reported, or from any case document they are able to inspect, or have a copy of, by right under a court rule, subject to obeying any reporting restriction. Also, if the civil case is heard in public, it will be safe to quote from any **skeleton argument** provided to a journalist by lawyers involved unless the court forbids this. In coverage of all types of court case, the media can apply to see case material referred to in public proceedings, to aid reporting. A general right for journalists to gain access to case material, and access rights under the rules for civil and criminal courts are explained in ch. 15.

→glossary

for access to material in Family Court, coroners' court and tribunal cases, see chs. 14, 17 and 18

Any reporting restrictions applying—for example, those protecting the identity of a child or alleged victim of a sexual offence—must be observed when reporting from such documents. The reporting must be fair and accurate to comply with the Contempt of Court Act 1981 and defamation law.

For these requirements for reporting to be fair and accurate, see 19.9, Court reporting—the section 4 defence; 22.5.1, The requirements of absolute privilege; and 22.7.1, The requirements of qualified privilege.

→glossary

If a journalist obtains irregularly a document from one side or the other in a court case, which one party was compelled or had a duty to produce as part of the **disclosure** process and which has not been read out or referred to in open court, the journalist should realise that publishing material from it could be punished as a contempt of court. 'Disclosure' is the pre-trial exchange of evidence and information. Contempt law applies because of the danger that parties who fear that material they provide to the other side might be published, even though it was not used in court, might decide not to cooperate fully with the disclosure process. Also, unauthorised use of material which the prosecution discloses to the defendant in a criminal case is a contempt under sections 17 and 18 of the Criminal Procedure and Investigations Act 1996. Again, publication of material not aired in open court—even if the reporting fairly and accurately reflects the material—is not protected by statutory privilege in defamation law or by section 4 of the Contempt of Court Act 1981, unless publication is sanctioned by a court or its rules.

12.8 Lifetime anonymity for an adult witness in 'fear or distress'

Section 46 of the Youth Justice and Criminal Evidence Act 1999 gives a criminal court (and so a youth court, a magistrates' court or Crown court) a discretionary power to make an order that:

- no matter relating to a witness who is aged 18 or older shall during the person's lifetime be included in any publication if the matter is likely to lead members of the public to identify him/her as being a witness in the proceedings.

However, section 46 says that the order can only be made if the court is satisfied that:

- the quality of the person's evidence, or level of cooperation given by the witness to any party to the proceedings in connection with that party's preparation of its case is likely to be diminished by reason of fear or distress in connection with being identified by members of the public as a witness in the proceedings; and
- granting such anonymity is likely to improve the quality of the witness's evidence or the level of their cooperation.

Therefore such an order cannot be made indiscriminately for each adult witness but only when these 'conditions' apply in respect of an individual witness.

In section 46, the term 'witness' includes anyone proposed to be called as a witness. The aims of this law include giving better protection to adults who fear that the fact that they testify in a case, or are due to do so, will provoke hostility from criminal elements in their communities.

Section 46 says a party in the proceedings—including the defence, though it is usually the prosecution—can ask the court to make the order in respect of the witness. The court may hear this request in private. In the section, the order is called a 'reporting direction'.

In the 1999 Act, 'publication' includes any speech, writing, relevant programme or other communication in whatever form, which is addressed to the public at large or any section of the public, and so includes newspapers, magazines and websites.

12.8.1 The scope of a section 46 order

The wording of section 46 means that the order's normal scope is that no detail which could identify the witness should be included in a report of the case or any published reference to it.

Section 46 says the following matters in particular should not be included if likely to identity the person as being a witness:

- the witness's name;
- their address;
- the identity of any educational establishment attended by the witness;
- the identity of any place of work; and

- any still or moving picture of them ('picture' includes 'a likeness however produced').

If the witness is the alleged victim in the charge(s) being considered in the trial, the effect on reports may well be substantial, and similar to that of the lifetime anonymity automatically given by other law to victims/alleged victims of sexual, trafficking and some other offences, who therefore do not need section 46 anonymity as witnesses. When a section 46 order is made, journalists must avoid jigsaw identification.

The Act says that a section 46 order *cannot* be used to give a defendant anonymity, even though a defendant may choose to be a witness.

For context, see 10.8, Jigsaw identification. Law which provides lifetime anonymity for victims/alleged victims of sexual, trafficking offences and some other offences is explained in ch. 11.

12.8.2 Factors a court must consider

The 1999 Act says that, when deciding whether to grant section 46 anonymity, the court must take into account any views expressed by the witness, the nature and circumstances of the alleged offences(s) in the case, the witness's age, and any behaviour towards the witness on the part of the defendant, or the defendant's family or associates, or anyone else likely to be a defendant or witness in the proceedings; and, as appear to be relevant, the witness's social and cultural background, ethnic origins, domestic and employment circumstances, religious beliefs, or political opinions.

The court must also consider:

- whether it would be in the interests of justice to make the anonymity order; and
- the public interest in avoiding imposing a substantial and unreasonable restriction on the reporting of the proceedings.

See the additional material for this chapter for case studies on the use of section 46 anonymity.

Case study

Judge Andrew Menary lifted anonymity orders made under section 46 of the 1999 Act in respect of four adult complainants injured when a car was driven into a crowd at a victory parade for Liverpool Football Club in May 2025. The judge concluded that continuing anonymity would be contrary to the open justice proposal. Whilst he accepted the complainants were 'sincere in expressing concern and emotional difficulty' at their names being publicised during proceedings, adding that 'emotional upset alone does not meet the threshold' for imposing an order under section 46. He said he had not been provided with any psychiatric or psychological evidence to suggest their ability to give evidence during the trial of a man charged with offences over the incident would be impaired by their identification. He also said anonymising them would 'risk setting a unfortunate pattern' where anonymity becomes the norm for witnesses in criminal cases. The judge added: 'the public interest in open and accurate reporting outweighs the potential distress, anxiety or discomfort to these witnesses.' (*The Guardian*, 3 June 2025)

12.8.3 **Breaches of section 46 orders**

Publishing material which breaches section 46 anonymity incurs the same liability, as regards who can be prosecuted and fined for that offence (editor, publisher, etc.), as breach of section 49 anonymity under the Children and Young Persons Act 1933.

It is a defence for a person accused of breaching section 46 to prove that:

- they were not aware, and neither suspected nor had reason to suspect, that the publication included the matter or report in question; or that
- the witness concerned gave written consent for the material to be published.

There is no requirement for a court to approve this written consent, which can be given directly to a journalist. But the 'written consent' defence will fail if it is proved that the consent was obtained by interfering with the witness's 'peace or comfort'.

The court which imposed the section 46 anonymity, or a higher court, can make 'an excepting direction' to remove the anonymity, or relax it to some extent, if satisfied that it is necessary to do so in the interests of justice; or that the restriction imposes a substantial and unreasonable restriction on reporting the proceedings *and* that it is in the public interest to remove or relax the restriction.

for more on breach of section 49 anonymity, see 10.3.4

for context, see too 11.6.4.1, Good practice in wording consent

Remember

Criminal courts can use section 45A of the 1999 Act to make this type of lifetime anonymity order for a witness or alleged crime victim under the age of 18 if similar 'conditions' apply (they are in fear or distress, etc.), and after considering the same factors and the person's welfare. See 10.4.2 for more detail about section 45A orders. Grounds on which the media can challenge imposition or continuation of a section 45A or 46 order can be found in 16.14.

ch. 30 covers liability for readers' postings which breach anonymity provision

12.9 **Other anonymity orders**

The High Court can ban reports of its proceedings from identifying people concerned in them. For example, it can give such anonymity to children involved in high-profile cases, or individuals seeking privacy injunctions. It also usually gives anonymity to mentally incapacitated adults when protecting their interests in civil cases, and to people challenging immigration decisions. A media organisation or editor responsible for publishing information identifying such people in breach of such an order could be jailed and/or fined for contempt of court. The High Court's

→glossary
→glossary

general power to make such orders include the making of **injunctions** is enabled by its **inherent jurisdiction** and the European Convention on Human Rights, and usually by Article 8 of the Convention, concerning the right to respect for privacy and family life.

for further detail of use of such orders in family law, see 14.10. For their use in privacy cases, see ch. 27

The Civil Procedure Rules apply in civil cases in the County Court and the High Court. Rule 39.2 enables a court to order that the identity of any person shall not be disclosed if it considers non-disclosure necessary to secure the proper administration of justice and in order to protect the interests of that person. For context, see 16.2.2 of this book.

The Court of Appeal has ruled that the High Court, when dealing with applications to approve settlements in personal injury claims brought by children (and adults who lack capacity to litigate) should normally make anonymity orders, though judges should hear representations from a media organisation wishing to argue against such orders being made (*JXMX (by her mother and litigation friend, AXMX) v Dartford and Gravesham NHS Trust, with the Personal Injury Bar Association and the Press Association as interveners* [2015] EWCA Civ 96).

✱ Remember

Mere embarrassment does not justify anonymity for adults in reports of court cases—see 15.6 and 16.10.6.

See the **additional material** for ch. 5 on **www.mcnaes.com** about anonymity for police informants. For information on anonymity for persons subject as suspected terrorists to a 'terrorism prevention and investigation measure', see online ch. 40, 'Terrorism and the effect of counter-terrorism law', on **www.mcnaes.com**.

12.10 Indefinite anonymity for convicted defendants and others

In exceptional instances, the High Court uses injunctions to stop anyone publishing the new identities, including the whereabouts, of people who became notorious because they committed or were associated with horrific crimes (in most such cases, the person committed the crime as a child or young teenager). The aim is to protect them from public hostility, safeguard them from possible vengeance attacks and help rehabilitate them after their release from imprisonment. Publication of detail which breaches an injunction is punishable as a contempt of court. These court orders are based on the protected person's human rights—Article 2 (right to life), Article 3 (right not to be subject to torture or other degrading treatment) and Article 8 (right to respect for privacy and family life) of the European Convention on Human Rights.

For example, in 2001 the High Court granted such indefinite anonymity to Jon Venables and Robert Thompson who in 1993, when they were 11, were convicted of the murder of two-year-old James Bulger in Merseyside; and in 2021 the High Court granted such anonymity to the murderers of vulnerable adult Angela Wrightson, who were aged 13 and 14 when that crime was committed.

for law which may protect website operators if a reader posts material breaching anonymity, see ch. 30

See the **additional material** for ch. 12 on **www.mcnaes.com** for detail of such cases, including those of Mary Bell, Maxine Carr and RXG. See too online ch. 36 on Other UK Jurisdictions for Northern Ireland media law: 'Bans on identifying defendants'.

12.11 Ban on publishing 'indecent' matter

Section 1 of the Judicial Proceedings (Regulation of Reports) Act 1926 prohibits publication in any court report of any 'indecent matter or indecent medical, surgical or physiological details . . . the publication of which is calculated to injure public morals'. In this era, what material could cause such 'injury' is open to debate, and—anyway—it is unlikely that mainstream media organisations would want to publish 'indecent' detail which is particularly explicit.

12.12 Postponement power in the Contempt of Court Act 1981

Section 4(2) of the Contempt of Court Act 1981 gives courts the power to order the postponement of publication of reports of a court case, or any part of it, where doing so appears necessary to avoid a substantial risk of prejudice to the administration of justice in those proceedings, or any other proceedings which are pending or imminent.

This restriction is best understood in the context of contempt law, so is explained in 19.10, Section 4(2) orders. See also 16.7, Challenging section 4(2) postponement orders.

12.13 Postponed reporting of 'special measures' and section 36 orders

A court can make a 'special measure' direction (order) under section 19 of the Youth Justice and Criminal Evidence Act 1999 to help a 'vulnerable' or 'intimidated' witness give evidence. For example, the witness may be allowed to testify from behind a screen or by live video link, or all the reporters but one might be asked to leave court during their testimony. Section 36 of the same Act allows a court to make an order to bar a defendant representing themselves from cross-examining a witness. The Act automatically bans the media from reporting during the trial that a 'special measure' direction or a section 36 order has been proposed or made, and why, because the jury might be improperly influenced if it had such knowledge. Breach of the ban is an offence . . .

For more details about these reporting restrictions, see the **additional material** for ch. 12 on **www.mcnaes.com**.

✱ Remember

Decisions on 'special measures' and cross-examination issues are likely to be taken at pre-trial hearings, or when a jury is out of the court, so other statutes, or contempt law, will probably also be in effect to restrict contemporaneous reporting of what is decided about such measures and issues—see 9.4, Hearings prior to jury involvement—automatic reporting restrictions; 19.10.2, Proceedings in court in the absence of the jury; and 19.10.3, The law is not clear.

12.14 Postponing a report of a 'derogatory assertion'

Sections 38 and 39 of the Sentencing Act 2020 allow a court to make a 'derogatory assertion order' postponing the reporting of an assertion made by or for a defendant during a speech in mitigation when the court is deciding on sentence, or on whether they should be 'committed for sentence', or made in a submission in appeal proceedings concerning a sentence.

› glossary

for context on mitigation, 'committed for sentence', and appeals, see chs. 7, 8 and 9

The court can make the order if it decides there are substantial grounds for believing that the assertion is derogatory of someone's character and is false or irrelevant. Breach of the order is an offence. More detail of this reporting restriction is in the **additional material** for this chapter on **www.mcnaes.com**.

12.15 Sentence review for informants

Section 75 of the Serious Organised Crime and Police Act 2005 and (as regards offenders convicted after 1 December 2020) section 390 of the Sentencing Act 2020 enable a Crown court to impose reporting restrictions prohibiting 'the publication of any matter relating to the proceedings' when reviewing a sentence previously imposed on a defendant who pleaded guilty, and who has given or offered assistance—for example, information about a crime—to a prosecuting or investigating agency, such as the police. For context, see 15.4 and for further detail of this power, and its purpose, see the **additional material** for ch. 15 on **www.mcnaes.com**.

12.16 Extradition hearings

Media coverage of hearings in the UK about whether a person should be extradited to another country—which usually take place in Westminster magistrates' court—are not affected by any automatic reporting restrictions as regards what can be reported from the hearing.

! Remember your rights

For details of the *Guardian News and Media* judgment concerning journalists' rights to see case material when reporting extradition proceedings, see the **additional material** for ch. 15 on **www.mcnaes.com**.

Recap of major points

- It is illegal to take photographs of, film or sketch people in a court or its precincts.
- It is illegal to make an audio-recording of a court hearing without permission.
- It is illegal to record or capture, or publish such reproduction of, any image or sound from a court's official transmission of its proceedings, or of another person watching or listening to the transmission, or of anyone participating remotely in a court hearing.
- Publishing such illegally gained material is also an offence.
- Journalists have a general permission to post online, email or send text from a courtroom when reporting, and to take notes, but other use of mobile phones or devices there could be punished as a contempt of court.
- It is illegal to seek to discover, or to publish, what a jury discussed in deliberating on a verdict, or how an individual juror voted in the verdict.
- Publishing material identifying a juror may be a contempt of court.
- In certain cases it is contempt of court to publish material heard by a court in private.
- An order under section 11 of the Contempt of Court Act 1981 prohibits publication of a name or other matter which has been withheld from the public proceedings of the court—for example, the name of a blackmail victim.
- Section 46 of the Youth Justice and Criminal Evidence Act 1999 allows a court to give an adult witness in a criminal case lifelong anonymity in media reports of it.
- In exceptional cases, the High Court has given convicted offenders indefinite anonymity, so the media cannot reveal their whereabouts after they are released.

Useful Websites

Gov.uk

- HMCTS staff guidance on supporting media access to courts and tribunals: Criminal courts guide

Judicial College, www.judiciary.uk

- 'Reporting Restrictions in the Criminal Courts', 4th edition, as revised in May 2016 by the Judicial College, Media Lawyers Association, News Media Association and Society of Editors
- 'Practice guidance: the use of live text-based forms of communication'—issued in 2011 by Lord Chief Justice

Criminal Procedure Rules 2025, legislation.gov.uk

Supreme Court policy on 'live text-based communications' [https://supremecourt.uk/visit-the-court/plan-your-visit]

Ministry of Justice, Civil Procedure Rules and Practice Directions, www.justice.gov.uk

Online resources

Visit the online resources at **www.mcnaes.com** to test your knowledge of this chapter with **self-test questions** and a **flashcard glossary**, and to read **updates** about law and regulatory matters affecting journalism, as well as **additional material** to further your learning.

13

Civil courts

Chapter summary

Civil courts deal with private disputes and wrongs and are a rich source of news. Some cases involve companies or individuals suing for damages. Some are brought against the state and public bodies—for example, when a patient sues a hospital trust for medical negligence. The County Court deals with most civil litigation. The High Court deals with complex or high-value claims. Few civil cases involve juries. Bankruptcies and company liquidations are civil law matters. Magistrates have some civil law functions.

13.1 Types of civil litigation

Most civil litigation is concerned with:

- breaches of contract, including recovery of debt;
- torts—civil wrongs for which monetary damages can be awarded (including negligence, trespass, defamation, infringement of **copyright**, and misuse of private information); →glossary
- breach of statutory duty;
- proceedings by financial institutions against borrowers;
- possession proceedings by landlords against tenants, usually for failure to pay rent;
- 'Chancery' matters, discussed later;
- insolvency, including bankruptcy and the winding up of companies;
- family law cases, including divorce and disputes between estranged parents over residence arrangements for and contact with their children, and applications by local authorities to take into care children considered at significant risk of violence or neglect.

family law is explained in ch. 14

13.2 The County Court

The County Court deals with most civil cases and sits in more than 100 locations in England and Wales.

13.3 The High Court

The High Court deals with the most complex or serious civil cases and those of highest value. Most High Court cases are dealt with at the Royal Courts of Justice and the Rolls Building in London. Outside London the High Court is divided administratively into 'district registries', which have offices and courtrooms, mostly in cities, and share buildings with the larger County Court centres.

The High Court comprises three divisions:

- the *King's Bench Division* (KBD), within which there are also specialist courts, including the Admiralty Court, the Commercial Court and the Technology and Construction Court;
- the *Chancery Division*, which deals primarily with company work, trusts, estates, insolvency, and intellectual property (the County Court also has limited jurisdiction in this area);
- the *Family Division*—see ch. 14.

ch. 18 explains tribunals. The High Court's role as a criminal court is explained in 9.13.

High Court judges normally sit alone to try cases. The High Court is also an appeal court in civil law. In appeals and for some other functions, two or three judges hear the case, and it is then known as the 'Divisional Court'. A KBD court carrying out certain functions is referred to as the 'Administrative Court'. It handles **judicial review** of the administrative actions of Government departments and other public authorities, and of the decisions of some tribunals.

→glossary

13.4 The Court of Appeal

see Figure 1.1 for the hierarchy of the civil and criminal courts

The Court of Appeal, Civil Division, is (in practice) for most cases the court of final appeal in civil law. It hears appeals from the County Court and the High Court, and certain tribunals. Most cases are heard by three judges, and some by only two. When there are three judges, each may give a judgment but the decision is that of the majority. In a limited number of cases, appeals can be made to the Supreme Court.

13.5 Types of judge in civil courts

Three types of judge preside in the County Court and High Court:

- *District judges*—These are appointed from among practising solicitors and barristers. Their casework includes many fast-track and small claims cases, discussed later, family law disputes and insolvency. They may be referred to in media reports as, for example, 'District Judge John Smith', but are increasingly referred to 'Judge John Smith'. Deputy district judges are part-time appointments.

- *Circuit judges*—Busier County Court centres may have two or more senior judges known as 'circuit judges'; in some regions they travel round a circuit of several towns or cities to hear cases. Circuit judges also sit in Crown courts in criminal cases. Recorders are barristers and solicitors who sit part-time with the jurisdiction of a circuit judge. Retired circuit judges who sit part-time are known as 'deputies'. Circuit judges hear some fast-track and most multi-track trials, discussed later, and may also hear appeals against the decisions of district judges. Appeals from a circuit judge are heard by the Court of Appeal. Circuit judges are referred to as 'Judge John Smith' or 'Judge Mary Smith'. Recorders are referred to as 'Recorder John Smith', although they are increasingly referred to as 'judges' after first mention.
- *High Court judges*—These are more experienced, and so more senior, than circuit judges. They are referred to as, for example, 'Mr Justice Smith' or 'Mrs Justice Smith'. Deputy High Court judges are experienced legal professionals who are appointed to sit part-time in the High Court.

13.6 Legal terms for parties in civil cases

In most civil actions, the party, whether a person or organisation, who initiates the action—for example, claims damages for a **tort**—is called the 'claimant'. The party against whom the action is taken is the 'defendant'. In some actions—for example, bankruptcy and divorce cases—the person making the claim is the petitioner and the other party is the respondent, and in appeals they are the appellant and respondent.

→glossary

ch. 14 explains divorce law

13.7 Media coverage of civil cases

Fair, accurate and contemporaneous reports of what is said in the public proceedings of a court are protected by the section 4 defence of the Contempt of Court Act 1981, if published 'in good faith', see 19.9; and by absolute **privilege** in defamation law, explained in 22.5. In that law, qualified privilege protects non-contemporaneous reports and those based on case documents made available by the court, if that defence's requirements are met. Qualified privilege is explained in 22.6 and 22.7, and see too 15.28.

→glossary

13.7.1 Open justice and case documents

Rule 39(2) of the Civil Procedure Rules says the general rule is that hearings are heard in public but the rules have some exceptions allowing a court to sit in private.

A journalist could argue against a decision to hold a hearing in private, citing the purposes (societal benefits) of open justice. See 15.1.1 which sets out those purposes, and 15.11 and 15.13 for details of these rules.

Civil courts can authorise transmissions of 'virtual' hearings, to enable journalists to report cases, and members of the public to observe them, through electronic links provided by court staff for online, 'remote' access, or because the transmission is live-streamed to a 'designated' room or 'overspill' (usually another courtroom) where journalists and members of the public can see and/or hear it. Courts have also allowed journalists to have online, remote access to 'hybrid' hearings. For context, rules and explanation of 'live links', 'hybrid' and 'virtual', see 15.14.

Judges have power to decide some small claims cases without a hearing.

* Remember

It is a criminal offence to make an unauthorised transmission or 'recording' (such as a photo, footage or audio-recording) of any image or sound in authorised transmissions of court proceedings, or to photograph, film or record a person watching or listening to the transmission or participating by live link. For context, see 12.1. See 13.7.4 for other reporting restrictions.

13.7.2 Online service for money claims

There is an online system for some civil money claims—for example, the sum claimed must be under £100,000—which means they can be resolved completely in writing online with no court hearing, if the case is not defended.

! Remember your rights

Journalists (and members of the public) have some rights to see case material used in all types of civil proceedings, current and concluded, as it might otherwise be impossible to understand cases, particularly trials, meaningfully. For example, evidence is presented in documents and may not be aired orally in a hearing, or the case is being dealt with completely in writing online. The routine rights of access to case material are explained in 15.24. But see too 15.19 for wider rights of access, set out by the Supreme Court in the case known as *Dring*. For detail of advance lists and registers of civil cases, and about how court staff should help journalists, see 15.22 and 15.23.

13.7.3 Settlements

for context, see 13.7.5, Formal offers to settle

A case in which one party sues another may well be settled before trial, usually by one side paying the other a sum of money. The settlement means there will be no court judgment on the facts.

- A media report of a settlement should not suggest that the side paying the money has admitted liability—that is, blame—for the wrong allegedly suffered by the other, unless liability *is* admitted. Wrongly suggesting that a settlement indicates an admission of liability could be defamatory.

For example, a private health clinic might sue for libel if a report wrongly suggests it has admitted liability for medical complications after cosmetic surgery even though it *has* paid out to a claimant to settle the case.

13.7.4 Reporting restrictions and contempt law

Judges in civil cases can impose reporting restrictions. They can use section 39 of the Children and Young Persons Act 1933 to ban the identification, in any report of a particular case, of a person aged under 18 who is a claimant, defendant or witness—see 10.5. They can use section 11 of the Contempt of Court Act 1981 to ban indefinitely a name or other information from being included in reports of a case—see 12.5. They have other powers to ban reports from identifying people, on privacy or other grounds—see 12.9.

The statutory ban on taking photographs of, filming, sketching or making portraits of judges, parties, witnesses and jurors applies in civil courts, their building and precincts. Other prohibitions in law—such as the ban on audio-recording of court proceedings, the ban on seeking information about or disclosure of jury deliberations, and the general protections of jurors and witnesses, and the administration of justice generally, in the common law of contempt of court—also apply to civil cases. For more detail, see chs. 12 and 19. Also, because the Contempt of Court Act 1981 applies to civil cases, once a case is 'active' no extraneous material—for example, comment on it—must be published if that publication creates a substantial risk of serious prejudice or impediment to the course of justice in that case. But as juries are rarely used in civil cases, the Act is considerably less restrictive of pre-trial coverage than it is for criminal cases.

see ch. 11 on automatic anonymity for victims/alleged victims of sexual, trafficking, FGM, and forced marriage offences

> Ch. 19 explains the 1981 Act, particularly in 19.12 as regards civil cases. Ch. 15 explains the open justice principle. Ch. 16 shows how journalists can challenge invalid or overbroad reporting restrictions, including anonymity orders made under section 39 of the 1933 Act or section 11 of the 1981 Act.

13.7.5 Formal offers to settle

The defendant in certain types of civil action—for example, a contract dispute or a defamation case—may make an 'offer to settle' before or during the trial. This is a formal offer of payment of a specified sum to the claimant to settle the case, and must be made in compliance with procedure laid down in court rules. Journalists who discover such an offer has been made should not report it unless and until it is referred to in open court at the end of the proceedings.

Disclosing at any earlier stage that an offer has been made will probably be regarded as contempt of court as it could prejudice the court's decision (see Civil Procedure Rule 36.16). The judge in the case (or jury, if there is one) is not told of the offer before reaching a judgment or verdict. If at the end of the trial the court finds for the claimant, but awards less than the defendant has offered, the claimant will have to pay all of the costs they incurred after the first date on which the offer could have been accepted.

13.8 Starting civil proceedings

Most civil actions in the High Court and County Court are begun by the court issuing a **claim form** prepared by the claimant. It details the claim against the defendant and the remedy or remedies sought. The remedy sought might be an **injunction**—an order compelling the other party to do something or stop doing something—or an order for the defendant to pay a debt or to pay damages. The claim form is served on the defendant.

→glossary
→glossary

The vast majority of money claims—for example, for debts—do not go to trial as the defendant usually does not file any defence, and in these circumstances the claimant simply writes to the court asking for judgment to be entered 'in default'.

If damages are claimed, there might be a hearing to decide the sum. Once a judgment for the claimant is entered in the court's records—which means the defendant has been held 'liable'—the claimant can enforce it, seeking the money from the defendant. The court's enforcement procedures could include **bailiffs** taking the defendant's goods to sell to pay the money owed.

→glossary

13.9 Trials in civil cases

The general rule is that a defendant who wants to dispute a civil claim must file a defence within 14 days of service of the particulars of the claim (which can be served with the claim form) or, if the defendant files 'an acknowledgment of service', 28 days after service of the particulars of claim.

→glossary

A civil trial is confined to issues which the parties set out in their **statements of case** which include the claim form, the 'particulars of claim', the defence to the claim, any counterclaims or reply to the defence and 'further information documents'. As a general rule, the public, including journalists, have the right to see these documents.

the routine right to see such documents is explained in 15.24

Each case is allocated to an appropriate 'track' based on various factors including the value of the claim and its complexity. The three tracks are:

- small claims track;
- fast track;
- multi-track.

While the money value of the claim is not necessarily the most important factor, claims for more than £10,000 but less than £25,000 are generally allocated to the fast track. Claims below these levels are in general allocated to the small claims track, with some exceptions depending on the type of claim.

Cases allocated to the fast track are intended to be heard within 30 weeks and to be concluded in a trial lasting no more than one day.

Many multi-track claims are only a little more complicated than those on the fast track. Courts encourage negotiated (or mediated) settlements.

Most civil cases are resolved without reaching trial.

13.10 Small claims cases

Cases on the small claims track are decided at the County Court by a district judge and intended to be heard within a few months. The procedure is designed to allow litigants to present their own case, without the need for a lawyer. Proceedings are informal. The judge must give reasons for the final decision. A public hearing may be in a courtroom but will usually be in the district judge's 'chambers' (that is, a private room) with access allowed. The judge can deal with the case without a public hearing if satisfied that this is necessary to safeguard the justice process, but should allow a journalist to make representations against the hearing being private—see 13.7.1. As explained earlier, some money claims are now being dealt with completely online.

13.11 Full trials

In fast-track and multi-track claims there is, if necessary, a formal trial, conducted by a judge sitting alone, unless the case is in the few categories in which there may be a jury—see later in the chapter.

Most parties involved in trials at the County Court and the High Court instruct solicitors to prepare their cases. Solicitors either brief **counsel**—instruct a barrister to advise and to argue the case in court—or represent the client themselves in a County Court trial. Solicitor-advocates can appear for their clients in the higher courts without needing to brief a barrister.

→glossary

for context, see 1.6, The legal profession

Where claimants and defendants represent themselves in court, they are referred to as 'litigants in person' and can be assisted by a lay person (often called a 'McKenzie friend').

13.11.1 Full trial procedure

Unless there is a jury, civil trials are now largely based on documents, read beforehand by the judge, with each party disclosing its documents to the other side before trial. The documents are those listed earlier, plus witness statements. Each party may also supply a **skeleton argument** setting out its case. In the trial, witnesses may do no more than confirm that their written statement is true, although usually the judge allows some supplementary questions from that side's lawyer, and there is usually cross-examination by the other party's lawyer.

→glossary

! Remember your rights

Journalists' routine rights to access case material in civil cases are explained in 15.24; for example, they should normally be able to see witness statements during the trial. See too 15.19 and 15.26 for wider access rights established by a Supreme Court judgment, including to skeleton arguments.

The claimant and their witnesses testify first, and are cross-examined by the defendant or their advocate, then the defendant and their witnesses testify and are cross-examined by the claimant or their advocate. Expert evidence may be admitted only with the court's permission. The court may appoint a single expert, who is jointly instructed by the parties.

After all the evidence, the parties or their advocates make their submissions on the evidence and law. Finally, the judge gives their judgment and the reasons for it, including the decision on the amount of damages if these are awarded.

for context, see 5.1, Standard of proof in criminal law

- In civil law, the standard of proof—the criterion used by a judge (or jury—see later) to determine which of any competing pieces of evidence will be accepted as the truth—is that each is to be proved 'on the balance of probabilities'. This means the judge (or jury) decides which version of a disputed event is more likely to be true. This is a lower standard of proof than that needed for criminal convictions.

the rights journalists have to see or be told of judgments are explained in 15.23 and 15.24

A judge may 'reserve'—delay—giving judgment, to have more time to weigh evidence and consider the law. The judge may read the judgment out in court or 'hand it down' (either as a printed copy or on email) at a later date. Court reporters should be provided with copies of written judgments. After the judgment (or, in jury trials, the verdict, explained later in this chapter) there may be argument about costs—an issue on which the judge must make an appropriate order, as it is not simply a question of the loser paying the winner's costs, though the loser can expect to pay a major part of these.

13.11.2 Trials with juries

In civil law, there is a presumption that there will be trial by a jury if the claim involves:

- an allegation of fraud; or
- false imprisonment; or
- malicious prosecution.

The reasons why juries can be used in these categories of case were described in a House of Lords judgment as 'historical rather than logical'. They include the notion that fraud claims particularly concern allegations against someone's honour and that false imprisonment or malicious prosecution cases usually involve allegations against an arm of the state such as the police, and so a jury is needed to give the public confidence that the case has been independently decided as a judge alone might be seen as another arm of the state.

A judge has discretion to allow jury trial in other types of civil case, but such instances are exceptional. As ch. 20 explains, the Defamation Act 2013 removed the presumption of jury trial in defamation cases, but left the court the discretion to call a jury (though this has not yet been used since the Act came into force).

If there is a jury trial, the judge will sum up the case after each side has made final submissions. In some cases the judge might ask the jury for a general verdict, but in more complicated cases the judge will give the jury a series of questions to answer in the verdict. Juries decide the level of damages if the verdict is for the claimant. Juries in civil cases, like those in criminal trials, are selected at random from the electoral roll. A County Court jury consists of eight people and a High Court jury of 12.

13.12 Civil functions of magistrates

The role of magistrates' courts in family law cases—a branch of civil law—is outlined in ch. 14. Magistrates also hear appeals from decisions of local authority committees on licensing public houses, hotels, off-licences, and betting shops.

13.13 Bankruptcy

The civil courts deal with bankruptcy cases, some of which yield news stories of wild extravagance at the expense of creditors or HM Revenue & Customs. The term 'bankruptcy' only applies to people. Companies go into liquidation—see 13.14.

13.14 Company liquidation

Care should be taken, when reporting that a limited company has gone into liquidation, to make the circumstances clear. There are different types of liquidation. Misuse of terms could create a libel problem.

> The **additional material** for this chapter on **www.mcnaes.com** explains bankruptcy procedures; what being bankrupt means; the defamation danger in wrongly stating someone is bankrupt; that court documents in a bankruptcy case can be inspected by a journalist; and the different types of company liquidation.

Recap of major points

- The County Court handles most civil litigation. The High Court deals with the more serious or high-value claims.
- Civil case hearings are mainly conducted by reference to documents. A journalist has rights to see the key documents of cases heard in public.
- Civil courts can impose reporting restrictions. Contempt law applies to media coverage of their cases, but is less restrictive if no jury is involved.
- Journalists must take care before suggesting a person is bankrupt or a company is insolvent, because this could be defamatory if untrue.

Useful Websites

Citizens Advice, 'Law and courts', www.citizensadvice.org.uk

Citizens Advice guides to the legal system, including small claims

Courts and Tribunals Judiciary, www.judiciary.uk

County Court and High Court

Online resources

Visit the online resources at **www.mcnaes.com** to test your knowledge of this chapter with **self-test questions** and a **flashcard glossary**, and to read **updates** about law and regulatory matters affecting journalism, as well as **additional material** to further your learning.

14

Family courts

Chapter summary

Family law is a branch of civil law which includes divorce proceedings and disputes between estranged parents—for example, about contact with a child—and cases brought by local authorities seeking to protect children and vulnerable adults.
A court can order removal of a child from their parents because of suspected abuse or neglect. Previously strict rules on reporting family court cases have been relaxed in recent years, with the aim of increasing transparency to improve public confidence and accountability in the family justice system. Family courts are now generally open to the media, though reporting restrictions apply to protect the identities of those involved in cases, particularly children, and journalists may be excluded from some hearings.

14.1 Introduction

The term 'family cases' covers a range of matters in civil law. They are dealt with in the Family Court, which operates from courthouses throughout England and Wales, including magistrates' courthouses, and in the High Court's Family Division. Whether lay magistrates, a district judge, a circuit judge, and/or a High Court judge preside(s) in a case depends on the type of proceedings, including whether it is an appeal.

see ch. 13 for an overview of the civil court system

14.2 Types of case in family courts

Two categories in family proceedings are 'private' and 'public' law cases.

Private law cases include:

- matrimonial cases—proceedings for divorce, judicial separation or nullity, or to end a civil partnership;
- deciding financial arrangements between estranged or divorced couples;
- disputes between estranged parents about their children—for example, over who children live with or a parent's rights to contact with them, with the courts making 'child arrangement orders' under the Children Act 1989;

for context see ch. 11 on forced marriages and FGM

- applications for court orders—for example, to secure the return of a child abducted by one parent;
- paternity disputes;
- applications in domestic violence cases for 'non-molestation' orders;
- applications to protect someone from a forced marriage or female genital mutilation (FGM).

Public law cases include:

- applications, mainly by local authorities, for court orders allowing social workers to intervene to protect a child they suspect is being neglected or abused. This can include supervision and such orders are made under the Children Act 1989. Courts can also make emergency protection orders allowing police or social workers to remove children or babies from their homes if there is immediate concern for their safety;
- adoptions—a court can sanction adoptions of children who have been removed from their birth parents by a local authority in public law cases. But other adoptions may formalise existing relationships, and so be private law cases.

14.3 Reporting family law cases

The Family Procedure Rules (FPRs), which govern the conduct of cases in the family courts, bar the public from most types of case, but usually allow accredited journalists and legal bloggers—legally qualified observers—to attend (and these courts have discretion to allow other people to attend). Journalists are automatically barred from some hearings, including:

- hearings conducted for the purpose of conciliation or negotiation, such as Financial Dispute Resolution hearings
- applications for adoption, placement and related proceedings
- proceedings for parental orders under the Human Fertilisation and Embryology Act 2008

accreditation is explained in 15.9

A judge may also decide that members of the media should be excluded from a hearing due to the particular circumstances of the case, or following an application by one of the parties to exclude the press.

Family courts are subject to various reporting restrictions designed to protect the identities of those involved, especially children. Anonymity provisions in the Children Act 1989 expressly prohibit the identification of children in proceedings (with limited exceptions). Contempt of court provisions in section 12 of the Administration of Justice Act also apply in family cases, as they are generally held in 'private'. This onerous restriction used to mean express permission was required from a court to allow any reporting, and judges would specify what could be published. But since 2025, following a two-year pilot in select courts, rules are in force across England and Wales which enable journalists—once the court has made a 'Transparency Order'—to report on what they see and hear in court, and in some supporting documents, subject to the restrictions set out in that order. Journalists are also able to speak to parties involved in family proceedings to obtain details of their case (though this information cannot be published). There are other restrictions in place on certain types of case. Therefore, whilst there has been a major shift towards increased transparency, reporting family law cases remains complex and journalists should take great care to understand the rules.

> See Useful Websites at the end of this chapter and the **additional material** for this chapter on **www.mcnaes.com** for more about the rules.

✱ Remember

Ethically, journalists should not normally interview children aged under 16 on matters concerning their welfare without the consent of a parent or responsible adult—for this and related issues, see 4.11, Protecting children's welfare and privacy.

14.4 Anonymity under the Children Act 1989

Section 97 of the Children Act 1989 makes it an offence to publish:

- a name or other material intended or likely to identify a child—anyone under the age of 18—involved in any current case in a court in which any power under the Act has or may be exercised with respect to that or any other child;
- an address, as being that of a child involved in such an ongoing case;
- detail identifying the child's school.

Section 97 anonymity automatically applies to children in unresolved disputes between parents, and cases involving intervention by social workers. It applies to any report of what is said in court or a written judgment, and to any wider feature about a child who is involved in an ongoing case. Clearly, it also means the child's family cannot be identified. Avoid jigsaw identification. In some instances, the media has not been able to identify a local authority criticised in a judgment in child protection cases because of concerns this would identify the local area and so make identification of the family more likely because of other detail in the judgment.

see 10.8, Jigsaw identification

- Breaching section 97 by publishing material intended or likely to identify a child is punishable by a fine of up to £2,500. It is a defence for an accused person to prove that they did not know, and had no reason to suspect, that the published material was intended or likely to identify the child.

for liability for readers' postings which breach anonymity provision, see ch. 30

Remember

A child or family identified in breach of a reporting restriction may be able to sue the publisher successfully in the civil law of privacy, for damages. Because of the risk of a posting by a reader identifying any such person, media organisations should consider preventing readers from posting material underneath reports of family law cases, if the material is not checked before it appears.

14.4.1 Adoptions

Section 97 also bans reports of adoption proceedings—which journalists cannot attend—from identifying the child concerned while they are under the age of 18.

14.4.2 Anonymity can be waived in a child's interests

- Section 97(4) of the Children Act 1989 says a court may waive, to any specified extent, anonymity otherwise automatically bestowed on a child, if their welfare requires it to be waived.

For example, judges have waived the anonymity to allow the media to identify and show pictures of children abducted by a parent or hidden from social workers, in the hope—usually borne out—that the public will help find them.

14.4.3 Anonymity under the 1989 Act ends when the case concludes

for more on injunctions, see 14.10

→glossary

The Court of Appeal ruled that the anonymity provision in section 97 only applies to Children Act proceedings which are ongoing, and therefore this anonymity provision ends when the case ends (*Clayton v Clayton* [2006] EWCA Civ 878). The then-President of the Family Division said that if a court felt that anonymity should continue beyond a case's conclusion to protect a child's welfare or privacy, it should issue an **injunction** to continue it. The High Court or the County Court can thereby order that the anonymity continues until, for example, the child is 18.

Remember

A journalist wanting to identify to any extent a family as having been involved in a case under the 1989 Act—for example, in a story about a mother's battle with social workers or a parent's account of marriage break-up—should be sure that the proceedings have ended and that no order has been made to continue a child's anonymity. Breaching an injunction is a contempt of court, punishable by up to two years jail and/or a fine.

14.4.3.1 Wards of court

Children who are made wards of court by the High Court, or are the subject of proceedings to make them wards, are automatically protected by section 97 anonymity while the case is ongoing. See the **additional material** for this chapter for how a reporter was able to interview a 16-year-old ward who ran away from home.

14.5 Anonymised judgments

The texts of family case judgments published by the court are usually anonymised to prevent a child or adult from being identified. It is a contempt of court to report an anonymised judgment in a way which identifies any protected person. One problem in media coverage of the Family Court is that most of its judgments, while made known to the parties, are not routinely made publicly available by the Court, because the pressure of work on its judges gives them little time to anonymise them (though efforts are ongoing to improve the rate of published judgments).

14.6 Private hearings and contempt risk

Most family court hearings are classed as private, even though journalists can attend and legal bloggers can attend most types of case. However, the media can be excluded if the court considers it is:

- in the interests of any child concerned in, or connected with, the proceedings;
- for the safety or protection of a party, a witness in the proceedings, or a person connected with such a party or witness;
- for the orderly conduct of the proceedings; or
- that justice will otherwise be impeded or prejudiced.

In cases where a judge is considering whether to exclude reporters from court altogether, the FPRs state they should be given the opportunity to make representations and that, in the event the court decides to exclude the media, brief reasons should be given. The rules also state that where an application to exclude the press has been made, the applicant must notify relevant media organisations 'where possible'. See Practice Direction 27B for details of the rules.

Section 12 of the Administration of Justice Act 1960 makes it a contempt of court to publish, without a court's permission, a report of a private hearing if the case falls into certain categories, including those which:

- relate to the exercise of the High Court's **inherent jurisdiction** with respect to children; →glossary
- are under the Children Act 1989 or the Adoption and Children Act 2002, or otherwise relate wholly or mainly to a child's maintenance or upbringing;
- are under the Mental Capacity Act 2005, or any provision of the Mental Health Act 1983 authorising an application or reference to be made to the First-tier Tribunal, the Mental Health Review Tribunal for Wales or the County Court;
- are of any kind where the court expressly bans publication of all or specified information relating to the private hearing.

ch. 18 explains the tribunal system

* Remember

'Private' hearing should not be confused with 'private' law, see 14.2.

for more detail on section 12 of the 1960 Act, and the basic detail which can be reported, see 12.6

But section 12 does allow publication of any order a court makes in private proceedings unless the court specifically bans publication of the order. Also, section 12 does not stop the media making basic reference to a case being heard in private, although anonymity provisions may be in place under the Children Act 1989 or because of a court order, making it illegal for a report to identify the family involved. Section 12 continues to apply after a case is concluded, unlike the anonymity under the 1989 Act.

14.6.1 Rules which 'mitigate' section 12 to allow greater reporting

Section 12 reporting restrictions apply if a family case is heard in private, which most are (see above). However, rules now in force in all family courts in England and Wales (including magistrates' courts) 'mitigate' the effect of section 12, by reversing the presumption that what is said in hearings cannot be reported without the court's express permission, in cases where the court makes a Transparency Order. Such an order will set out what can and cannot be published if a journalist or legal blogger attends a hearing, and will usually be made unless a court has good reason not to. A Transparency Order should also provide that, on request, reporters are entitled to be given copies of, see, and quote from documents—including case outlines, skeleton arguments, summaries and position statements. Reporters attending any hearing must be given a copy of the Transparency Order. Detail of the rules governing Transparency Orders can be found in Practice Direction 12R. They include that a court should consider whether to make a Transparency Order at the outset of a hearing, and give reasons if it declines to do so.

> ((•)) See Useful Websites at the end of this chapter for the Open Reporting Provisions guidance and rules, which contains details of Transparency Orders and links to the FPRs and Practice Directions. It also details a coding system used to help journalists determine what type of case is listed on a court's daily list, as they are heavily restricted to avoid identification of parties.

14.7 Disclosure restrictions

Part 12.73 of the Family Procedure Rules, reflecting section 12 of the 1960 Act, says no information 'relating to' court proceedings concerning children and held in private, whether or not the information is in documents filed with the court, may be communicated to the public, or to anyone other than lawyers, officials or other specified categories of people, without the court's permission. A similar ban applies in adoption cases.

However, new rules mean that a party (such as a parent) is able to communicate details of a case to accredited journalists and legal bloggers. Journalists are not permitted to publish that account, but it may help them to decide whether to attend the case to report what is said in court, for example, or report it retrospectively from a published judgment, subject to reporting restrictions. Details of these rules can be found in Practice Directions 12R and 14G. The ban on disclosure of detail does not stop a parent from telling in general terms how they feel about the court case or the wider experience of, for example, a child being removed from them—though any anonymity applying under the Children Act 1989, or through a court order, must be preserved in any report.

14.8 Other reporting restrictions in family cases

Automatic reporting restrictions under section 2 of the Domestic and Appellate Proceedings (Restriction of Publicity) Act 1968 cover some types of family case—for example, legitimacy, or failure to pay maintenance—in any court hearing such a case or an appeal. For more detail of the 1968 Act restrictions, see the **additional material** for this chapter on **www.mcnaes.com**. Divorce cases, referred to later in this chapter, have their own reporting restrictions.

14.9 Challenging reporting restrictions in family cases

Practice guidance on reporting in the family courts, which deals with media challenges to reporting restrictions, is extremely helpful to journalists. It suggests that generally reporters in courts should be allowed to make representations on lifting or amending reporting restrictions without first having to make a formal written application and pay the associated fee. It also says that media organisations or journalists who seek to challenge or change reporting restrictions should not be ordered to pay costs for making their applications unless they have 'engaged in reprehensible behaviour or . . . taken an unreasonable stance'. See Useful Websites at the end of this chapter for the guidance (The President's Guidance as to Reporting in the Family Courts).

A full explanation of reporting restrictions and journalists' rights to attend family cases is provided in the **additional material** for this chapter on **www.mcnaes.com**, with case studies of successful challenges to reporting restrictions, which enabled journalists to report cases in detail.

14.10 Anti-publicity injunctions in family cases

The High Court has inherent jurisdiction to order that a person must be anonymous in published reports of its proceedings and judgments. It is a contempt of court to breach such an injunction. Injunctions can be issued to protect children and mentally or physically incapacitated adults in family cases, and in other types of case in which the court is ruling on their medical treatment or whether they should be kept alive—for example, injunctions have protected the identities of treating clinicians where there have been fears for their safety. A Supreme Court ruling concluded that while the High Court has jurisdiction to anonymise clinicians, such orders should usually lapse at the end of the proceedings and/or after the child at the centre of the case has died (*Abbasi and another v Newcastle upon Tyne Hospitals NHS Foundation Trust* [2025] UKSC 15).

> See **additional material** for this chapter on **www.mcnaes.com** for the procedure to alert the media to applications for family law injunctions, and for examples of family court injunctions.

14.10.1 News-gathering activity can be banned

An injunction can forbid particular news-gathering activity, such as journalists visiting a community or institution to ask about events related in or to a family court case, if that activity is deemed likely to jeopardise the welfare or privacy (for example, the anonymity) of an adult or child involved in the case, or could lead to such a person feeling harassed.

14.11 Coverage of divorce, nullity, judicial separation, and civil partnership cases

Divorce, judicial separation or nullity cases, or proceedings to end a civil partnership, are usually dealt with by family courts, although some are transferred to the High Court.

Most divorce proceedings are uncontested. Law enacted in April 2022 introduced 'no-fault' divorce and changed terminology in divorce proceedings so that, for any divorces issued after that date, the 'decree nisi'—the first stage of a divorce—is referred to as a 'conditional divorce', and a 'decree absolute'—which dissolves the marriage formally—is called a 'final order'. Pronouncements of the first stage are read out in open court and the second stage is usually completed six weeks after being granted. The new law means a divorce application can only be contested in 'exceptional circumstances'.

Reporting restrictions, as explained in this chapter's **additional material**, apply to divorce, judicial separation and nullity cases, and proceedings to end a civil partnership—whether the report is of a hearing in a contested case or about case documents which are open to inspection. Rules on when such cases can be heard in private are also explained there. Matrimonial cases may involve hearings on financial matters (formerly known as 'ancillary relief' and now as 'financial remedy')—that is, the division of property and other financial arrangements between estranged couples. Again, see the **additional material**.

14.11.1 Inspection of evidence and copy of order/decree

Part 7.10(7) of the FPRs (7.20(8) for divorces issued before April 2022) permits anyone, within a period of 14 days after a conditional order/decree nisi is made, and if it has not been contested, to inspect and make copies of the decree certificate and the evidential statement which rule 7.9(4) (17.19 for pre-April 2022 divorces) requires the petitioner to supply before the order/decree can be made. The reporting restrictions covering divorce proceedings may limit what can be published from the statement. Part 7.35 (7.36 pre-April 2022) allows anyone to obtain from the court a copy of the final order/decree absolute. For more detail, see the **additional material** on **www.mcnaes.com**.

14.12 The Court of Protection

The Court of Protection is a specialist court established by the Mental Capacity Act 2005 to make decisions for people who lack the mental capability to decide for themselves—for example, on financial or welfare matters or medical treatment. It makes decisions for some elderly people suffering from dementia, for example. It used to sit in private, but proceedings are now normally held in open court, with reporting limited by the imposition of restrictions to protect the identities of the individuals and families involved. Its judgments are usually anonymised. It has its own rules. For more detail, see the **additional material** for this chapter on **www.mcnaes.com**, and Useful Websites, at the end of this chapter.

Recap of major points

- Family courts have been difficult to report on as reporting restrictions apply in most cases, and the hearings are classed as private. But new rules currently being trialled in a pilot scheme will increase transparency.
- A child involved in ongoing proceedings under the Children Act 1989 should not be identified in media reports as being involved in the case unless the court authorises this.
- The High Court has wide-ranging powers to protect the welfare of children and others, including anonymity orders, as does the unified Family Court, which has a High Court tier.

Useful Websites

HM Courts & Tribunals Service, 'Jurisdictional guidance to support media access to courts and tribunals—Family courts guide', gov.uk

Courts and Tribunals Judiciary, www.judiciary.uk

- Open Reporting Provisions guidance and rules
- The President's Guidance as to Reporting in the Family Courts
- The Remote Access Family Court (2020)

Gov.uk, Court of Protection

The Open Justice Court of Protection Project, openjusticecourtofprotection.org

Online resources

Visit the online resources at **www.mcnaes.com** to test your knowledge of this chapter with **self-test questions** and a **flashcard glossary**, and to read **updates** about law and regulatory matters affecting journalism, as well as **additional material** to further your learning.

15

Open justice and access to court information

Chapter summary

Open justice is vital to democracy. If justice is done in secret, the public can have no confidence in it, because secrecy may hide injustice. Journalists are the public's eyes and ears in courtrooms, so need to know their rights of admission to courts. This chapter explains them, and refers to statute, case law and court rules which journalists can cite to oppose attempts to exclude them from court hearings. The law does allow courts to sit in private or with restrictions on what can be reported, but any such 'derogation' (departure) from the important principle of open justice should be 'exceptional' and only where 'necessary' to secure the proper administration of justice. This chapter also explains journalists' rights to know about pending court cases, to see case documents when reporting on cases, and to gain information about what happened in a court hearing they were unable to attend or were unaware of. Chapter 16 explains the ways in which a journalist can challenge exclusion from any court, or a reporting restriction. Other chapters refer to admission rights for particular types of court—youth courts in ch. 10, family courts in ch. 14, coroners' courts in ch. 17, and tribunals in ch. 18.

15.1 Open courts—a fundamental rule in common law

In 1913, the House of Lords in *Scott v Scott* [1913] AC 417 affirmed the common law rule that normally courts must administer justice in public. One law lord, Lord Atkinson, said in that case:

> “The hearing of a case in public may be, and often is, no doubt, painful, humiliating, or deterrent both to parties and witnesses, and in many cases, especially those of a criminal nature, the details may be so indecent as to tend to injure public morals, but all this is tolerated and endured, because it is felt that in public trial is to be found, on the whole, the best security for the pure, impartial, and efficient administration of justice, the best means for winning for it public confidence and respect.”

The **additional material** for ch. 15 on **www.mcnaes.com** gives more detail of *Scott v Scott* and other cases about open justice.

15.1.1 Purposes of open justice

The purposes—in essence, the benefits to society—of open justice include (with examples of the many cases in which they have been listed):

- It promotes public confidence in and respect for the administration of justice in all types of proceedings, civil or criminal; deters inappropriate behaviour on the part of the court and others participating in the proceedings; allows the public to scrutinise the process of justice and working of the law; and enables the public to understand how the justice system works and why decisions are taken (*Scott v Scott*; *R v Legal Aid Board, ex p Kaim Todner* [1998] 3 All ER 541; *R (on the application of Guardian News and Media Ltd) v City of Westminster Magistrates' Court* [2012] EWCA Civ 420; *Cape Intermediate Holdings v Dring* [2019] UKSC 38).
- It stimulates informed debate about the criminal justice system (*Re S (FC) (A Child)*).
- It allows the public to scrutinise the processes by which criminal cases are investigated and brought to trial (*Khuja v Times Newspapers and others* [2017] UKSC 49).
- It enables society to judge the quality of justice administered in its name and whether the law needs modification; it enables the exposure of 'matters of public interest worthy of discussion other than the judicial task of doing justice between the parties in the particular case' (*Harman v Secretary of State for the Home Department* [1983] 1 AC 280 (HL), 316).
- It serves as a discipline upon parties who are tempted to make exaggerated or unfounded assertions if they face the possibility of having to answer at trial for what they have chosen publicly to assert (*Malik v Central Criminal Court [2006] EWHC 1539 (Admin)*); it puts pressure on witnesses to tell the truth (Judicial College guidelines, referred to later in 15.6)—the premise is that a lie told in public proceedings is more likely to be exposed than one told in private proceedings.
- It can result in evidence becoming available which would not become available if the proceedings were conducted behind closed doors or with one or more of the parties' or witnesses' identity concealed (*R v Legal Aid Board, ex p Kaim Todner*)—for example, a person who reads a media report of a case may come forward with new evidence. Mr Justice Tugendhat said in the High Court: 'It is not necessary, in order for a newspaper to rely on the principle that reporting may encourage witnesses to come forward, for there to be any evidence in support of such likelihood' (*PNM v Times Newspapers and others* [2013] EWHC 3177 (QB)), which went to the Supreme Court and became known as the *Khuja* case. For more details about this important case, see 16.8.2.

- Publicity about criminal trials, including convictions, and the identities of defendants, is a deterrent to anyone considering committing crime (*R (Y) v Aylesbury Crown Court and others* [2012] EWHC 1140 (Admin)).
- Full, contemporaneous reporting of criminal trials in progress promotes the values of the rule of law (*Re S (FC) (A Child)* [2004] UKHL 47, [2005] 1 AC 593).
- It reduces the likelihood of uninformed, inaccurate comment and rumour about the proceedings, including about what is said in them (*R v Legal Aid Board, ex p Kaim Todner; PNM v Times Newspapers and others*).

Lord Woolf noted in *R v Legal Aid Board, ex p Kaim Todner* that a court which departs from the open justice principle must, because of the benefits which will thereby be lost, have an overriding justification. This chapter and ch. 16 provide grounds on which journalists can challenge a proposal or a court's decision that they should be excluded from a hearing or be restricted in what they can report about it. A challenge will probably involve a journalist making reference to the specifics of that particular case. But the foundation of all such challenges is that general benefits, including those listed above, always flow to society from open justice, and so one or more of these general purposes of open justice should be cited, with case law, as appropriate.

15.2 The media's role in open justice

A journalist's vital role in reporting court cases as trustee for the wider public has been recognised in many judgments. In *R v Felixstowe Justices, ex p Leigh* [1987] QB 582, [1987] 1 All ER 551, Lord Justice Watkins said:

> "The role of the journalist and his importance for the public interest in the administration of justice has been commented upon on many occasions. No-one nowadays surely can doubt that his presence in court for the purpose of reporting proceedings conducted therein is indispensable. Without him [or her], how is the public to be informed of how justice is being administered in our courts?"

15.3 The limited scope of common law exceptions to public hearings

It is generally acknowledged that departing from the open justice principle by excluding journalists and the public from a court hearing, or part of it, is only justified in common law in three sets of circumstances:

- *when their presence would frustrate the process of justice*—for example, when it could affect the willingness of a victim to give evidence, or it is feared that some people would try to disrupt the hearing if allowed into the court's public gallery;
- *when unchecked publicity would defeat the object of the proceedings*—for example,

  - when a case concerns a trade secret, and the presence of the public or reporting of the case could lead to the secret being revealed to commercial rivals or would reveal confidential information which is sought to be protected, or
  - when a case concerns a matter relating to national security which could be damaged if the presence of the public or reporting of the case causes exposure of state or operational secrets, such as detail of how the intelligence services or police covertly investigate spies or terrorists, or
  - when the court is considering granting an order to one party that another party must not make certain information public, and the information in question would be revealed during an open court hearing;
- *when the court is exercising a parental role to protect the legitimate interests of vulnerable people*—mainly:
  - children, for example, in family law cases, or
  - people with mental incapacity or mental illness

  and unchecked publicity could harm the welfare of those involved.

ch. 14 explains family law and incapacity cases

Statutes which allow courts to exclude the public—and in some instances journalists—in specified circumstances cover, to an extent, the same kinds of occasion for which common law justifies exclusion. Common law can be used if no statutory power covers the occasion, but does not give courts a general licence to exclude journalists and/or the public.

Lord Diplock, emphasising that common law departs from the open justice principle only in rare circumstances, said in a 1979 House of Lords judgment that the rule should only be set aside when:

> “... the nature or circumstances of the particular proceeding are such that the application of the general rule in its entirety would frustrate or render impracticable the administration of justice or would damage some other public interest for whose protection Parliament has made some statutory derogation from the rule (*Attorney General v Leveller Magazine Ltd* [1979] AC 440).”

The **additional material** for ch. 15 on **www.mcnaes.com** provides more detail of this case.

15.4 What statutes say about open and private hearings

see 7.8 for 'single justice procedure' and 15.17 for how journalists can probe such cases

Magistrates' cases Section 121 of the Magistrates' Courts Act 1980 says magistrates must sit in open court when trying a case or considering jailing someone, or hearing a civil law complaint, unless other enactment (statute law) permits them to sit in private. There is a very wide exception in the 1980 Act itself—inserted as sections 16A–16F by the Criminal Justice and Courts Act 2015—which is the 'single justice procedure'. In this, a case may be tried in private, in the defendant's absence, and a fine imposed if they are convicted.

Indecency cases Section 37 of the Children and Young Persons Act 1933 gives any court the power to exclude the public—but not journalists—when a witness aged under 18 is giving evidence in any proceedings 'in relation to an offence against, or any conduct contrary to, decency or morality'.

ch. 11 explains anonymity provision for complainants (victims/alleged victims) in sexual offence cases

Sexual history Section 43 of the Youth Justice and Criminal Evidence Act 1999 requires a criminal court to sit in private when hearing an application to introduce evidence or questions about a complainant's sexual history—for example, in a rape case. The court must give in open proceedings its decision on whether such evidence or questions will be allowed.

One journalist can stay Section 25 of the 1999 Act allows a court to make a 'special measures direction' to exclude the public and some journalists when, for example, a witness is due to testify in a sexual offence or domestic abuse case, or one brought under the Modern Slavery Act 2015 involving alleged slavery, servitude, forced or compulsory labour, or human trafficking for exploitation, or when there are reasonable grounds for believing that someone other than the defendant wants to intimidate the witness. But one journalist must be allowed to stay in court. The Law Commission recommended in July 2025 that this measure should be used to routinely exclude the public while a complainant in a sexual offences case is giving their evidence, but said there should be a 'reformed exemption' to allow journalists (more than one) to remain in court. No proposal had been made to implement this recommendation when this book went to press—check **www.mcnaes.com** for updates. Law in the 1999 Act which postpones the reporting of 'special measures' is outlined in 12.13.

Official secrets trials—see 32.5 for this exclusion law.

Sentence review for informants Section 75 of the Serious Organised Crime and Police Act 2005 and (for offenders convicted after 1 December 2020) section 390 of the Sentencing Act 2020 permit a Crown court to exclude the public and press when reviewing a sentence previously imposed on a defendant who pleaded guilty, and who has given or offered assistance—for example, information about a crime—to a prosecuting or investigating agency such as the police. The Court of Appeal and Supreme Court have this exclusion power as regards any appeal proceedings about sentence review.

> The **additional material** for ch. 15 on **www.mcnaes.com** has detail about this power of exclusion, including about circumstances in which a journalist has a strong argument to oppose exclusion from a sentence review. Also, there is explanation of 'closed material procedure' set out in Part 2 of the Justice and Security Act 2013, which allows a court considering a civil claim to hear evidence in private—and without the **claimant** having access to it—if the court accepts that disclosing it would damage national security.

→glossary

This chapter considers later what court rules say about when hearings must be in public or when they can be in private, and about information concerning and from cases which should be made available to the public and/or journalists.

15.5 Article 6 and Article 10

The first part of Article 6 of the European Convention on Human Rights (ECHR) says:

> "In the determination of his civil rights and obligations or of any criminal charge against him, everyone is entitled to a fair and public hearing within a reasonable time by an independent and impartial tribunal established by law. Judgment shall be pronounced publicly but the press and public may be excluded from all or part of the trial in the interest of morals, public order or national security in a democratic society, where the interests of juveniles or the protection of the private life of the parties so require, or to the extent strictly necessary in the opinion of the court in special circumstances where publicity would prejudice the interests of justice."

Article 6 primarily protects the rights of parties in civil litigation and defendants in criminal cases rather than those of the media or wider public. A journalist challenging exclusion from a court hearing, or a reporting restriction should cite Article 10, which safeguards the societal benefits of open justice by protecting freedom of expression- including the right to impart information, and the public's right to receive it. A court considering such a challenge must carry out a 'balancing exercise', based on the facts of the particular case, in which the journalist's and public's rights under Article 10 are weighed against the rights of the party wanting the exclusion or restriction. The common law rule of open justice should also be cited by the journalist—it is independent of Article 6 or 10 rights, is much older, and deeply rooted in case law.

15.6 Is it necessary to exclude or restrict?

It is an established principle that no court should depart from open justice—whether using a common law power, or a statutory power—unless doing so is necessary to achieve the court's objective. The wording of Articles 6 and 10 of the ECHR reflect this. For Article 10's full wording, see 1.3.2.

Journalists opposing being barred from a criminal court hearing or opposing a reporting restriction can direct the court to guidance issued by the Judicial College, *Reporting Restrictions in the Criminal Courts*—see Useful Websites at the end of the chapter. It states: 'The public and the media have the right to attend all court hearings and the media is able to report those proceedings fully and contemporaneously. Any restriction on these usual rules will be exceptional. It must be based on necessity.' The burden of proving a restriction is necessary falls on the party seeking it, so it is not for the press to justify why they wish to report.

15.6.1 Is there 'clear and cogent' evidence that exclusion or restriction is necessary?

A party seeking exclusion or a reporting restriction must establish 'on the basis of clear and cogent evidence' that it is necessary in that particular instance (*R v Central*

Criminal Court, ex parte W, B and C [2001] 1 Cr App R 2). This principle applies in any type of court. The Judicial College guidance, citing *Scott v Scott* and *Global Torch v Apex Global Management Ltd* [2013] EWHC 223 (Ch), says the fact that hearing evidence in open court will cause embarrassment to witnesses or air allegations damaging to an individual's reputation does not justify excluding the press and public, because it does not meet the test for necessity.

Case study

A High Court judge criticised Malvern magistrates' decision to sit **in camera** to hear **mitigation** for a woman who admitted driving with excess alcohol. Her solicitor had asked the court to sit in private because she would refer to embarrassing details of her pending divorce and medical history. The solicitor said the woman had an overwhelming fear of revealing these publicly, and that her emotional state had produced suicidal tendencies. The High Court agreed that magistrates did have power to sit in camera but Lord Justice Watkins said too that in this case their reason for doing so was 'wholly unsustainable and out of accord with [the open justice] principle' (*R v Malvern Justices, ex p Evans* [1988] QB 540, [1988] 1 All ER 371). →glossary →glossary

---

The necessity test means that the duration of any such exclusion or the duration and scope of the restriction, if either measure is justified, must be **proportionate**—it must be limited to what is necessary. →glossary

The necessity test also means that, before deciding whether to exclude a journalist, the court must consider whether using a reporting restriction—for example, an order giving a witness anonymity—would mean exclusion is not necessary. The next chapter gives detail of arguments journalists can make to oppose reporting restrictions which are not necessary or proportionate.

15.6.2 Journalists can sometimes stay when the public is excluded

If the public are lawfully excluded, it does not follow that journalists must necessarily go too. The Court of Appeal recognised this in *R v Crook (Tim)* (1989) 139 NLJ 1633.

For example, disruptive supporters of a defendant may be banned from a court's public gallery, but it would not be necessary to exclude journalists in those circumstances.

15.6.3 Criminal courts cannot sit in private to protect a defendant's business interests

The risk that publicity might severely damage a defendant's business does not justify a criminal court sitting in private (*R v Dover Justices, ex p Dover District Council and Wells* (1991) 156 JP 433).

15.7 The terms—in private, in chambers and in camera

→glossary
- The term **in chambers** refers to occasions when a hearing, usually a preliminary one in the case, is held in the judge's chambers or another room rather than a formal courtroom, and is not in public.

→glossary
- The term **in camera** is used when the public and media are excluded from all or part of the main hearing in a case—such as a criminal trial. The hearing is effectively being held in secret.

→glossary
- The term **in private** is used to cover both the above terms. But a hearing may be held in chambers for administrative convenience, rather than because of a decision or rule that it should be private.

15.7.1 Hearings in chambers are not always private

for bail applications in chambers at Crown court, see 15.12

A hearing may be in chambers—for example, a judge's office—rather than in a courtroom, because of routine administrative convenience. Lord Woolf said in the Court of Appeal in 1998 that members of the public and journalists who ask should be allowed to attend a hearing in chambers if this is practical, if the case is not in a category listed in section 12 of the Administration of Justice Act 1960 (see 15.8), and if the court has made not an order for another reason that the hearing is private (*Hodgson v Imperial Tobacco* [1998] 2 All ER 673, [1998] 1 WLR 1056).

15.8 Contempt and libel issues in reporting of private hearings

If a case being heard in private falls into certain categories—for example, it is about national security or the upbringing of children—it is a contempt of court (and therefore illegal) for anyone, including a journalist, who discovers what has been said in the private hearing to publish without the court's consent such information about the hearing or material from documents prepared for use in the case—see 12.6 for explanation of section 12 of the Administration of Justice Act 1960, including that some basic facts can be reported about such private hearings.

Also, publishing information from a private hearing in any court case:

- is not protected by section 4 of the Contempt of Court Act 1981 if what is published creates a substantial risk of serious prejudice or impediment as regards later stages of that case, or any other 'active' case—see 19.9.

→glossary
- is not protected by statutory **privilege** if someone defamed by what is published sues for libel—see 22.5 about absolute privilege and 22.7 about qualified privilege.

15.9 HMCTS guidance and accredited journalists

His Majesty's Courts and Tribunals Service (HMCTS) has issued guidance to its staff about support to be given to journalists. It makes clear that to qualify for support they should be 'accredited'—a term it uses to help distinguish a genuine journalist from anyone claiming to be one. Court rules allow some types of information from cases to be supplied to accredited journalists but not to members of the public because, for example, the latter may have no knowledge of the law on reporting restrictions.

In this chapter, ch. 14 and ch. 16, any reference to what HMCTS guidance or a court rule or practice direction says about 'journalists' is to accredited journalists. HMCTS, courts and tribunals recognise the UK Press Card Authority accreditation scheme. Court and tribunal staff can check if a person is an accredited journalist by asking to see their UK Press Card. HMCTS tells staff to seek advice from its press office if someone without this card says they are a journalist. See Useful Websites at the end of this chapter for HMCTS guidance, including a Reporters' Charter, and the scheme.

for context on rules and practice directions, see 15.11. Ch. 18 covers the tribunal system.

15.9.1 The press seats

HMCTS general guidance says that journalists 'should be given priority' as regards 'dedicated press seating' in courts and tribunals. The guidance for cases of 'high interest' to the media, likely to fill the press bench, explains how court staff can arrange for other journalists to be in an annexe to see and/or hear an authorised 'live stream' transmission of the courtroom proceedings, and details of arrangements in place for such high-profile cases is often sent to journalists in advance to assist planning. They may also be allowed to attend remotely online, by the court providing an electronic link—see 15.14 for context about 'remote observation'.

✱ Remember

Bans on photography, filming and recording apply in the annexe, and as regards the content of the authorised transmissions—see 12.1.

15.9.2 Student journalists

HMCTS general guidance says that student journalists (who are not accredited) are not entitled to sit in press seats and should sit in the public gallery. It adds that their attendance should be supported 'to encourage greater court reporting'. Student journalists need the court's specific permission to use any device there, such as a laptop or phone, to send 'live text' reports of any case, but journalists have a general permission to do this—see 12.2.

15.10 No need to ask permission to take notes

A High Court ruling has established that the common law permits anyone to take notes in a court's public proceedings without first needing the court's permission, although the court can ban the taking of notes there if there is a particular concern that it could undermine the process of justice in that individual case (*Ewing v Cardiff and Newport Crown Court v DPP* [2016] EWHC 183 (Admin)). Reflecting this, Criminal Practice Direction 2.3 says no permission is needed for anyone to take notes.

see 15.11 on the role of these Directions

The Practice Direction says that court staff can make enquiries where there is reason to suspect that note-taking is for an unlawful purpose (for example, to facilitate improper collusion between witnesses or a breach of reporting restrictions), or may disrupt the proceedings. But it is the court (that is, a judge or magistrates, not a member of court staff) which has power to ban note-taking by a specified individual or individuals, and any ban must be necessary and proportionate.

The HMCTS general guidance to court staff says that when student journalists are in the public gallery at 'sensitive cases', such as those involving organised crime, it would help the court 'to avoid any misunderstanding' if they identify themselves in advance to explain they plan to make notes.

15.11 The role of court rules and practice directions

All court rules are a form of law, created by statutory Instruments.

Procedure for criminal cases in magistrates' courts, Crown courts and the Court of Appeal's Criminal Division is governed by the Criminal Procedure Rules (CrimPR), and Criminal Practice Directions which explain and supplement them. The Civil Procedure Rules (CPR) and their Practice Directions govern procedure in the County Court, the High Court (for most types of its proceedings) and the Court of Appeal's Civil Division. This chapter will explain what these rules and Directions say about public and private hearings; about what advance and basic information must be provided to the public and/or journalists about cases; and about whether other information or copies of case material can be made available to them.

The Magistrates' Courts Rules 1981 govern procedure for civil cases dealt with by magistrates (other than in the Family Court).

> See Useful Websites at the end of this chapter for full versions of all these rules and Directions. The rules of the Family Court and the Court of Protection are referred to in ch. 14. The rules for coroners' courts and tribunals classed as courts are referred to in chs. 17 and 18, respectively.

Particular rules say that if someone is punished for contempt of court—for example, for disobeying a court order—the court must announce this in public proceedings. Those rules are covered in the **additional material** for this chapter on **www.mcnaes.com**.

15.11.1 Rules are subject to the necessity test

Some court rules specify general grounds for when a hearing can be held in private. A journalist facing exclusion from a court should ask what rule is being applied, and should argue that the court's interpretation of it must take full account of the open justice principle and that—whatever the rule's wording—the court must apply the necessity test to consider whether (and to what extent) the particular circumstances justify exclusion—see 15.6. In *Scott v Scott*, Lord Shaw stressed that judges must be vigilant to ensure that the open justice principle is not usurped, saying: 'There is no greater danger of usurpation than that which proceeds little by little, under cover of rules of procedure, and at the instance of judges themselves.'

15.12 Criminal courts—rules about public and private hearings

Criminal Procedure Rule 6.1 deals with access to court, reporting restrictions and permission for audio recording and 6.2 says a court must have regard to the importance of dealing with criminal cases in public and allowing public hearings to be reported.

Rule 3.16 (magistrates' courts) and 3.21 (Crown courts) say that a pre-trial case management hearing must be in public, as a general rule, but all or part of the hearing may be in private if the court so directs.

Rule 24.2 says the general rule is that a trial or sentencing in a magistrates' court must be in public (and that journalists can attend youth courts).

The rules allow courts to conduct some procedures in private—for example, an application to a Crown court judge for bail after magistrates have refused it. But the presumption in law is that a journalist who requests access to such a bail hearing must be allowed to attend unless it is necessary for a valid reason for it to remain private (*Malik v Central Criminal Court* [2006] EWHC 1539 (Admin)).

Rule 3.21 says that where the Crown court determines a pre-trial application in private (for example, about bail) it must announce its decision in public.

Criminal Practice Direction 2.1 says the general principle is that the administration of justice must be done in public, the public and the media have a right to attend all court hearings, and the media is able to report those proceedings fully and contemporaneously.

'special measures' and law which postpones reporting of them are explained in 12.13

15.12.1 There must be notice if journalists might be excluded

Rule 6.6, covering magistrates' and Crown courts, says that if the prosecution or defence wishes to argue that a trial or part of it should be heard in private, that party must apply in writing to the court no less than five business days before the trial is due to begin—though rule 6.3 allows a court to hear an application made orally, or shorten or extend the five-day period. Rule 6.6 says that the court officer—a term explained shortly—must display notice of the application prominently in the courtroom's vicinity and give the media notice of it. The application itself will be heard in a private hearing, unless the court orders otherwise, and if in a Crown court will be heard after the **arraignment** but before the jury is sworn.

ch. 9 explains Crown court procedure

→glossary

Rules 6.2 and 6.4 together say that a court must not exercise a power to sit in private or to restrict reporting unless each party and 'any other person directly affected'—a definition which Criminal Practice Direction 6.3.55 makes clear would include a representative of the media—is present, or has had an opportunity to attend or make representations. Rule 6.4 also says any party which wants to make an application to restrict access to, or reporting of, a hearing must notify 'reporters' (see also 16.2.1.1).

Rule. 6.6 says that if a court orders that a trial will be heard wholly or partly in private, it must not begin until the business day after the application was granted or until any appeal or review of the decision has been concluded (if later), giving the media time to challenge the decision.

For case studies of how reporters challenged exclusion from hearings see the **additional material** for this chapter on **www.mcnaes.com**. For challenge procedure, see ch. 16.

15.13 Civil courts—rules about public and private hearings

In rule 39.2 of the Civil Procedure Rules (CPR), the general rule is that a hearing is to be in public and that the court shall take reasonable steps to ensure that hearings are of an open and public character unless held in private. It says that:

> "a hearing, or any part of it, must be held in private if, and only to the extent that, the court is satisfied of one or more of the matters set out in sub-paragraphs (a) to (g) and that it is necessary to sit in private to secure the proper administration of justice—
>
> (a) publicity would defeat the object of the hearing;
>
> (b) it involves matters relating to national security;
>
> (c) it involves confidential information (including information relating to personal financial matters) and publicity would damage that confidentiality;
>
> (d) a private hearing is necessary to protect the interests of any child or protected party;
>
> (e) it is a hearing of an application made **without notice** [*that is, one party in the case is not yet aware of the proceedings*] and it would be unjust to any respondent for there to be a public hearing;
>
> (f) it involves uncontentious matters arising in the administration of trusts or of a deceased's estate; or
>
> (g) the court for any other reason considers this to be necessary to secure the proper administration of justice."

→glossary

! Remember your rights

Rule 39.2 says any non-party (including journalists) may apply to attend the hearing and make submissions, or apply to set aside or vary the order that it should be private. The rule adds that unless the court otherwise directs, a copy of the court's order that a hearing will be private shall be published on the Judiciary website (www.judiciary.uk).

The CPR also provide that other types of hearing may be held in private. A journalist excluded from a civil court should ask which rule applies, and can politely remind the judge that the fact that a rule indicates a hearing may be held in private does not mean that the press and public should automatically be excluded—see 15.11.1. Parties are expected to consider if a measure short of exclusion can meet their concerns, as will normally be the case (*Ambrosiadou v Coward* [2011] EWCA Civ 409).

for context, see 15.6, Is it necessary to exclude or restrict?

> The **additional material** for ch. 15 on **www.mcnaes.com** provides summaries of civil cases in which media organisations have successfully argued for their rights to attend a court hearing, even when a party asserted this would expose 'confidential' information.

for general information on civil courts, see ch. 13. For law on coverage of private hearings, see 12.6

15.14 Remote hearings and access by journalists

In some circumstances (see below) (*there needs to be a link to the following list?*), courts have powers to allow a person in a place remote from the courtroom to participate in a hearing taking place in it. Their participation is by 'electronic communication'—telephone, or audio or video (audio-visual) 'live link'. For example, in criminal cases it is common for a defendant already in prison custody to participate via a live link from jail when being sentenced.

1. When all the participants in a court case are physically in one room (the courtroom), and therefore there is no use of 'live links', this is referred to as a 'physical' hearing (or a 'face-to-face' or 'in-person' or 'fully attended' hearing).
2. If some participants are in the one room but some attend by telephone or 'live link' (for example, using their home or office computers), the hearing is referred to as 'hybrid' (or 'partly remote'),
3. If all the participants in a hearing are using 'live links' to communicate with each other by telephone or online from different locations, this is referred to as a 'virtual hearing' (or 'fully remote'). They could, for example, be using the HMCTS Cloud Video Platform (CVP).

In this chapter, references to journalists attending a hearing include remote access ('remote observation', see later) unless it is clearly stated that the attendance is at a courtroom or other physical room.

15.14.1 Criminal courts practice direction—open justice in hybrid hearings

Criminal Practice Direction 5.5.2 tells criminal courts that, to uphold the open justice principle, the participation of a person who attends a hybrid hearing by telephone or live link 'must be, as nearly as may be, equally audible and, if applicable, equally visible to the public' as if the person was physically present. This means implicitly that a journalist observing in court must be able to see and/or hear the person clearly.

see 15.11 on the role of these Directions

15.14.2 Civil courts practice direction—open justice in hybrid hearings

Annex 3 to Practice Direction 32, supplementing the Civil Procedure Rules, says that if a civil court uses 'video conferencing'—for example, to take evidence from a witness at a remote location—and does so in a room other than the courtroom, the party arranging the conferencing must ensure that there is sufficient accommodation to enable a reasonable number of members of the public to attend, an instruction which should enable journalists to attend.

15.14.3 'Remote observation' and transmission of court hearings

The Police, Crime, Sentencing and Courts Act 2022 amends section 85A of the Courts Act 2003 to enable a court to permit live transmission of proceedings to be observed by members of the public and journalists. This has increased the circumstances in which criminal courts can use live links for participants and further facilitated open justice through 'remote observation'. Transmission can be either to 'designated live-streaming premises' (which could be a courtroom) or via an electronic link provided to journalists or other individuals by court staff, enabling them to watch proceedings online remotely from, for example, their home or workplace.

Section 85A of the 2003 Act as amended also says a court may direct that a recording of the transmission be made for the purpose of enabling the court to keep a record of the proceedings, but this does not permit journalists to record such hearings—remember there are other rules which prohibit unauthorised recording of online hearings. This section and the rules governing it apply in England, Wales, Scotland, and Northern Ireland.

NB: section 85A does not apply to the Supreme Court. It has its own powers to permit transmissions of its proceedings—see 12.1.7.

The 2022 Act also made provision for the Lord Chancellor to draw up rules regarding transmission, which were introduced in the Remote Observation and Recording (Courts and Tribunals) Regulations 2022 and set out what the court must take into account when allowing (or banning or circumscribing) such transmission.

Regulation 3 says the court must be satisfied, before authorising transmission, that it would be in the interests of justice to do so, and:

- there is the 'capacity and technological capability' to enable such a transmission, and that facilitating remote observation would not create an 'unreasonable administrative burden'.

Regulation 4 sets out the matters the court must take into account when considering whether to authorise a transmission, which are:

- the need for the administration of justice to be, as far as possible, open and transparent;
- the timing of any request or application to the court or tribunal to make a direction, and its impact on the business of the court or tribunal;

- the extent to which the technical, human and other resources necessary to facilitate effective remote observation are or can be made available;
- any limitation imposed by or under any enactment on the persons who are entitled to be present at the proceedings;
- any issues which might arise if persons who are outside the United Kingdom are among those watching or listening to the transmission;
- any impact which the making or withholding of such a direction, or the terms of the direction, might have upon the content or quality of the evidence before the court or the public understanding of the law and the administration of justice;
- the ability of the public, including the media, to observe and scrutinise the proceedings;
- the safety and right to privacy of any person involved with the proceedings.

Regulation 5 says any direction to permit transmission must prohibit anyone 'other than a person entitled to be present at those proceedings' from watching or listening to it and should also require an individual wishing to observe proceedings remotely to demonstrate 'the capacity in which that person is so entitled'. For journalists, this is likely to mean showing a press card. Rule 5(2) says no one can observe proceedings without first giving their name and email address, unless the court dispenses with this requirement. It also says those given access must conduct themselves appropriately and in accordance with any instructions the judge directs to those observing remotely.

Practice Guidance issued by the Lord Chief Justice and Senior President of Tribunals sets out the scope of the remote observation law and expands on the Lord Chancellor's regulations. It also says remote observers must be warned that they must not make a recording of any transmission, and may commit an offence or be in contempt of court if they do. This guidance also says it could be relevant for courts in England and Wales to consider whether any issues might arise from giving access to individuals in another UK jurisdiction, and journalists are routinely asked to provide information as to their location for the duration of a hearing when requesting remote access.

Remote Observation Guidance for criminal courts says there are many advantages of transmission, provided it is properly controlled, including: increased transparency and access to courts, which is in the interests of open justice; greater efficiency for journalists reporting on criminal proceedings, which is in the public interest as it may be expected to 'enhance the quantity and quality' of reporting; and increased access for high-profile cases where courtrooms may not be big enough to accommodate large numbers of journalists and other individuals.

> ((•)) See Useful Websites at the end of this chapter for section 85A of the 2003 Act, the Lord Chancellor's rules, the Practice Guidance, and the Remote Observation Guidance for criminal courts.

Remember

A court's decision to exclude the media from a virtual hearing which cannot validly be 'private' could—if no access is given to the recording—be challenged by a media organisation, citing as appropriate the open justice case law or the relevant rules and practice directions.

For case studies on media organisations challenging exclusion from courtroom hearings, see the **additional material** for ch. 15 online. Ch. 16 explains how procedurally a journalist can in any court oppose or challenge exclusion or a reporting restriction. For law affecting coverage of private hearings—see 12.6.

Remember

It is a criminal offence to make an unauthorised transmission or 'recording' (such as a photo, footage or audio-recording) of any image or sound in authorised transmissions of court proceedings, or to photograph, film or record a person watching or listening to the transmission or participating in a hearing by live link. See 12.1.

15.15 Criminal courts—provision of basic information about cases

see Useful Websites at the end of this chapter for the guidance

The HMCTS guidance for criminal court staff says that even if the contact is from a journalist 'outside of a hearing', staff can provide factual information of what was said or read out in open court, contained within a court document that is open to inspection or placed on a public notice board. HMCTS operates a centralised media enquiries service for journalists wishing to request information for magistrates courts and single justice procedure cases (as well as some civil courts and tribunals), but Crown courts should be contacted directly.

for 'legal adviser' and 'clerk', see 7.1 and 9.1.2

As this chapter will explain, the Criminal Procedure Rules (CrimPR) specify duties which 'the court officer' must fulfil as regards publishing or supplying information about or from cases. The rules say 'the court officer' is 'the appropriate member of the staff of a court'. If an inquiry has to be made to the court's administration office, rather than in a courtroom to the legal adviser or clerk, staff there should know who has these duties.

Remember

See 15.22 onwards for civil court rules on provision of information.

15.15.1 Advance information about criminal cases to be held in public

Rule 5.11 says when a case is due to be held in public, the court officer must publish for no longer than five business days certain information about it, if the information is available and not covered by a reporting restriction, by displaying a notice somewhere prominently in the vicinity of the courtroom due to hear the case, or by other arrangements as the Lord Chancellor directs, including for publication by electronic means. The information which must be published is the date, time and place of the hearing; the identity of the defendant; and such information as it may be practicable to publish concerning the type of hearing, the identity of the prosecutor, the identity of the court, the alleged offence(s), and whether any access or reporting restriction applies. For what rule 5.11 says must be published in advance about cases dealt with in the private 'single justice procedure', see 15.17.1 in this chapter.

15.15.2 Criminal court lists and registers

Under a protocol agreed with the News Media Association and the Society of Editors, and approved by the Lord Chancellor, HMCTS sends (usually by email) to journalists, on request and free of charge, copies of the daily lists of defendants due to appear in magistrates' courts. Home Office Circular no. 80/1989 said the lists should contain each defendant's name, age, address, the charge(s) they face and, where known, their occupation. Under the protocol, copies of these courts' 'registers' are also sent, for publication. These briefly record each day's basic details of convicted defendants, the charge(s) and the outcomes of their cases—for example, a fine—whether the case was dealt with in public proceedings or under the single justice procedure (the SJP is covered later in this chapter). Note that the protocol states the media will agree to destroy data supplied within six months 'or other appropriate longer period, if recommended by their legal advisers or insurers'. The protocol also says details of individual cases for journalistic purposes can be retained. These provisions are to ensure compliance with data protection rules—see chapter 28.

((•)) see Useful Websites at the end of this chapter for the protocol

If the register includes details of defendants aged under 18, check whether they were dealt with by the youth court, in which case they must not be identified in what is published unless the court confirms that the automatic anonymity provision—explained in 10.3—has been lifted in respect of that child or young person.

Crown court lists can be accessed from an internet service, www.courtserve.net/homepage.htm, as well as seen on noticeboards at the courts, but give less information than those supplied to the media for magistrates' courts. For example, in these Crown court lists the defendant's name is shown but not the charge(s). HMCTS guidance to criminal court staff is that in response to media inquiries, Crown court staff 'are encouraged' to provide information 'equivalent' to that included in the lists and registers of magistrates' court cases (and such information must normally be supplied under CrimPR rule 5.8 as regards requests about particular cases, as this chapter will explain).

15.15.2.1 Relevant defamation defences

In defamation law, qualified privilege will protect a fair and accurate media report of court lists and registers, or of any information or material provided by a court or officially by a court officer for publication, if all that defence's requirements are met. But a journalist who attends a hearing of a case should report the details as given in it and not from the list or register. A fair, accurate and contemporaneous report of a court's public proceedings will be protected by absolute privilege.

for privilege, see 22.5, 22.6 and 22.7

15.15.3 Basic details of ongoing and recent criminal cases must normally be supplied under rule 5.8

Under CrimPR rule 5.8 members of the public and journalists can request basic details about a magistrates' or Crown court or Court of Appeal Criminal Division case. Unless the details are not 'readily available' (for example, because of the location or condition of the storage of the information), the court officer must supply the details if the case is ongoing or the verdict was not more than six months ago, and if no reporting restriction prohibits supplying the details.

Rule 5.8(3)(a) says such a request about such an ongoing or recent case may be made orally or in writing, and need not explain why the information is requested. HMCTS guidance to criminal court staff (see earlier) makes clear that the request can be made by phone or email, or by a journalist at court. The rule says that the details can be supplied 'by word of mouth', in writing or by such arrangements as the Lord Chancellor directs. This rule therefore allows reporters to gain basic details about what happened in a court hearing they were unable to attend or were initially unaware of.

These details, set out in rule 5.8(4), are:

- the date of any public hearing in the case, unless the date is a future one and a party in the case has yet to be notified of that date;
- each alleged offence and any plea entered;
- the court's decision at any public hearing about bail or the committal, sending or transfer of the case to another court;
- whether the case is under appeal;
- the outcome of the case;
- the identity of the prosecutor; of the defendant, including the defendant's date of birth; of the 'parties' representatives'—normally lawyers—including their addresses; and the identity of the judge, magistrate(s), or justices' legal adviser by whom a decision at a hearing in public was made.

types of reporting restrictions are explained in chs. 10–12

The court officer must also supply details of any reporting or access restriction ordered by the court.

Rule 5.8(4) does not refer to a defendant's address. But the HMCTS guidance to criminal court staff says that to comply with the rule they should give such detail to the media—see too 15.16.1 for case law about a defendant's address being part of their identity.

There is also case law that magistrates' names must be supplied—see 15.15.5.

> A public register shows if a fine is unpaid—see the **additional material** for this chapter on **www.mcnaes.com**.

> For how to apply for such basic detail about older cases heard in open court, or for other details or for copies of case material, see 15.18 and 15.19. For single justice procedure cases, see too 15.17.

15.15.4 Journalists at court must be shown the charges

Rule 5.8 means that a journalist attending a magistrates' court case must be given the basic details specified, including of the charges, from the charge sheet, and one attending a Crown court case must be given detail of the charge(s) as set out on the **indictment**. →glossary

The HMCTS guidance to criminal court staff reflects rule 5.8 in saying that journalists attending a case who ask for a copy of the charge sheet or indictment should be given it, even if a charge refers to a victim/alleged victim whose identity is protected by a reporting restriction. It remains the publisher's responsibility to find out about the restriction before publication. The guidance adds that a copy of the indictment should be supplied even when it is in draft form, and that court staff can confirm later the version of the charge(s) on which the defendant was **arraigned**. →glossary

If the indictment includes the name of a person who has anonymity in law as an actual or alleged victim of crime, this fact should not stop a journalist being shown it. The anonymity provision in the relevant statutes does not cover indictments (the statutes make that clear).

15.15.5 Magistrates', judges', legal advisers', and lawyer's names must be supplied

As reflected in rule 5.8, case law says a court *must* give the media and public the names of magistrates—also known as 'justices of the peace' (JPs)—dealing with a case. In 1987 in *R v Felixstowe Justices, ex p Leigh*, cited earlier, Lord Justice Watkins said in the High Court: 'There is, in my view, no such person known to the law as the anonymous JP.'

The HMCTS general guidance to court staff is that the media are entitled to full names of magistrates, judges and their legal adviser, reflecting rule 5.8, which says too that the identities of lawyers must be provided.

15.15.5.1 CPS prosecutors are instructed to give their full names

The Crown Prosecution Service's 'Instructions for Prosecuting Advocates', issued to lawyers appearing in court on its behalf says they should give their full name to any media representative who asks for it. See Useful Websites at the end of this chapter.

15.15.6 The rule covers youth court cases

The HMCTS general guidance makes clear that rule 5.8 applies to youth court cases. For example, it says staff asked about a youth court case should supply to a journalist the defendant's name and address (with a reminder that these details cannot normally be published), date of birth, result of the case, and details of any court order made to dispense with the automatic anonymity which normally applies for children and young persons (that is, those aged under 18) concerned in such proceedings. That anonymity provision is explained in 10.3 of this book.

15.15.7 Requests must be specific, may incur a fee, and could be slowly answered

For all the request provisions in rule 5.8, the requester must specify what information is requested and pay 'any fee prescribed'. No fee had been prescribed for journalists when this book went to press. In view of case law on open justice, arguably a journalist could not properly be charged a fee for basic details needed for contemporaneous reporting of a court case. The rule does not specify how quickly the details must be supplied. The HMCTS general guidance reminds court staff that journalists have deadlines.

15.16 What should be aired aloud in criminal cases?

For those cases dealt with in public proceedings at magistrates' and Crown courts, the open justice principle means there are safeguards to help ensure that essential information is aired. The most important are listed here.

15.16.1 A defendant's name and address should be stated in open court

The Home Office said, in Circular no. 78/1967 and a similar circular in 1969, that defendants' names and addresses should be stated orally in magistrates' court hearings. The 1967 Circular said: 'A person's address is as much part of his description as his name. There is, therefore, a strong public interest in facilitating press reports that correctly describe persons involved.'

The High Court ruled in 1988 that a defendant's address should normally be stated in court, with Lord Justice Watkins making clear he considered a defendant's address to be part of their 'identity' (*R v Evesham Justices, ex p McDonagh* [1988] QB 553, [1988] 1 All ER 371).

The Judicial College guidance says: 'Announcement in open court of names and addresses enables the precise identification vital to distinguish a defendant from someone in the locality who bears the same name and avoids inadvertent defamation.'

((•)) See Useful Websites at the end of this chapter for the College guidance. For how court orders banning publication of a defendant's name or address can be challenged, and a case study, see ch. 16.

! Remember your rights

Even if the defendant's address is not referred to in court, it must in most circumstances be supplied by the court officer, see 15.15.3.

15.16.2 What else must be stated aloud in a criminal court?

Under Parts 9 and 24 of the Criminal Procedure Rules, in a magistrates' court hearing the allegation of the offence must be read to the defendant. Charges put to a defendant in arraignment at Crown court must be read or summarised aloud (rule 3.32). As explained earlier, a journalist should be allowed to see or have a copy of the charge sheet (magistrates' court), or the indictment.

In a magistrates' court, each relevant part of the following documents must, unless the court directs (formally decides) otherwise, be read aloud or summarised aloud if any member of the public, including any reporter, is present:

- a witness's written statement which is admitted as evidence in a trial, including evidence from an expert witness (rule 24.5).
- if the defendant has pleaded guilty in writing (and so is not there), the material on which the prosecutor relies to set out the facts of the offence and to provide information relevant to sentence, and any written representations by the defendant (rule 24.14).

Rule 25.12, which applies to Crown court trials, says that each relevant part of a witness's written statement which is admitted as evidence must be read or summarised aloud, unless the court directs otherwise.

Rule 50.15, which applies to extradition hearings, says any written statement by a witness or any relevant part of it must be read aloud or summarised aloud.

15.16.3 A witness's address is not aired unless 'relevant'

((•)) see Useful Websites at the end of this chapter for the CPS guidance

Crown Prosecution Service guidance says prosecution witnesses should not be generally required to disclose their address in open court unless it is necessary (e.g. it was the locus of a burglary). Rule 25.11 (Crown courts) says a witness's address must not be given in public unless it is 'relevant to an issue in the case'.

15.17 Getting information about and from 'single justice procedure' cases

The 'single justice procedure' (SJP) was created in 2015 to save costs. It permits a single magistrate to deal with some types of criminal case in private. For more explanation of the SJP, see 7.8. The rapid expansion of the SJP means each year that most—that is, hundreds of thousands of—summary cases are being sentenced or tried in private, including proceedings for evasion of the TV licence fee, for a wide range of traffic offences and against parents for a child not attending school. In the SJP, the defendant does not need to attend court if the offence is admitted or they did not object to private trial.

As the SJP operates in private, journalists cannot attend to hear what evidence or mitigation the magistrate considers, or scrutinise how they deal with the case—for example, if a celebrity or politician has been caught speeding. As the Magistrates Association and others have pointed out—the SJP is a deep erosion of the open justice principle.

The magistrate can in some circumstances order the SJP proceedings to be converted into an open court hearing to take place at a later date, with the defendant being required to attend—for example, if a ban on driving is proposed or the magistrate considers it 'not appropriate' for the case to continue in the SJP (see section 16C of the Magistrates' Courts Act 1980).

15.17.1 Advance listing of SJP cases and issue of SJP registers

Rule 5.11 of the Criminal Procedure Rules says that when a case is ready to be dealt with under the SJP the court officer must publish 'by such arrangements as the Lord Chancellor directs', including arrangements for publication by electronic means, and for no longer than five business days, the identities of the defendant and prosecutor, the offence(s) alleged, and whether any reporting restriction applies, subject to the information being available to the officer and there being no reporting restriction to prevent publication.

As outlined earlier in this chapter, a protocol says that advance lists of SJP cases, giving basic details, should be sent to local media. But these lists cannot state a definite date when each SJP case is scheduled to be dealt with, and instead indicate the date by which each is due to have been dealt with. This is because SJP cases are not allocated specific hearing dates but each is dealt with when a magistrate has time. Also, casework can be transferred from one court centre to another if the first is too busy.

Basic information about the outcomes of SJP cases—for example, what fine was imposed on the defendant—should be included on the registers of magistrates' court cases sent to local media: see 15.15.2.

15.17.2 Getting information on and case material from SJP cases by use of rule 5.8

SJP cases are subject to the requirement in the Criminal Procedure Rules, see 15.15.3 in this book, that the court officer must supply on request the basic details listed in rule 5.8(4), subject to that rule's conditions.

Under the protocol referred to earlier, a journalist can also, for an SJP case, apply in writing to the court officer for a copy of the prosecution 'statement of facts' or, if there is no statement of facts, a copy/copies of the witness statement(s), and a copy of 'any defence representations in mitigation'. Under rules 5.8(4)(g) and 5.8(5) the court officer must supply the copies (again, if such information is 'readily available', the case is ongoing or the verdict was not more than six months ago and if no reporting restriction bans the supply of the information). The protocol, and the rules, leave open the possibility that, for example, a defendant will object in advance to all or part of representations in mitigation being supplied to a journalist, and that a district judge will then have to decide whether to uphold the objection.

for context on the protocol, see 15.15.2

The protocol adds that media applications (requests) for such copies 'will need to be made with our Courts and Tribunals Service Centre at the following email mailbox: SJSTeamLeaders@justice.gov.uk'; and that the copies should be provided within one working day from the receipt of the request by email, which should 'include [a copy of] the individual's UK Press Card to authenticate the request'. When this book went to press, there was no report of any journalist being asked to pay a fee to make the request, though the rule enables this—see too 15.15.7.

for context on UK Press Cards, see 15.9

The protocol says that any dispute about such a request must be referred to the HMCTS press office.

15.18 Requests for other information or case material about or from criminal cases, including older ones

Rule 5.8(7), when read with other parts of the rule, says that a request for the basic details specified in rule 5.8(4) concerning a case in which the verdict was more than six months ago, or for information about any case which is not 'readily available' to the court officer, or for information other than those basic details (either about an ongoing or recent case or about an older one) must be made in writing, unless the court otherwise permits. Also, the request must explain why the information is requested.

for rule 5.8(4), see 15.15.3 of this chapter

Rule 5.8(7) says the court officer must refer any such request to the court for a decision on whether the information can be supplied. As regards a magistrates' court, the decision is likely to be made by a district judge, and for a Crown court by a judge there. HMCTS guidance to staff says there is a process in place to facilitate court staff referring such requests to a judge and that, in most instances, a decision is made within five working days, depending on the nature of the request and the age and complexity of the case.

This provision in the rules gives journalists opportunity to apply for copies of criminal case material—including photographs and footage used in evidence—even when they have not attended the relevant trial or sentencing, and even if the case was concluded some time ago. The provision also gives journalists opportunity to apply to a court for confirmation that a person was convicted there of an offence more than six months previously—for example, 10 years ago—and for details of it.

A journalist making such an application could cite as appropriate one or more of the purposes (societal benefits) of open justice—see 15.1.1—and, if the application is part of investigative journalism, explain why publication of the information will serve the public interest—for example, why the public should know of someone's past offending.

Case study

In 2021 ITV's West of England crime and investigations reporter Rob Murphy successfully used rule 5.8(7) to obtain basic details of two offences committed by a politician 19 years previously—drink-driving and failing to stop after a road accident in which another vehicle was damaged.

15.18.1 The court must alert others to the request

Rule 5.10 says the court officer must serve any request made under rule 5.8(7) on a party or person 'likely to be affected by it'. For example, it may decide to do this to alert the person who was the defendant, or the prosecutor, in the relevant case that the request has been made.

Under the rule, a party or person who objects to the information being supplied to the requester must give notice of the objection to the court officer and the requester not more than 20 business days after service of the request copy, or within any longer period allowed by the court. The court, after it is satisfied that anyone served with a copy of the request has had a reasonable opportunity to state the grounds of objection, can decide in a public or private hearing, or without a hearing, whether the information should be supplied to the requester. If there is a hearing, the requester and the objector can make representations to the court. Under the rule, at the hearing the court must allow the objector to make further representations in the absence of the requester—this allows, for example, the objector to refer to the requested information without the requester gaining knowledge of it.

Rule 5.10 requires the court to have regard to the following in its decision on the request:

- the open justice principle;
- any reporting restriction;
- rights and obligations under other legislation;
- the importance of any public interest in the withholding of the information, or in its supply only in part or subject to conditions;
- the extent to which the information is otherwise available to the requester.

The rule lists, as examples, the public interest in preventing injustice, protecting others' rights, protecting the confidentiality of a criminal investigation or protecting national security.

A note to the rule lists laws which may affect the court's decision. These include privacy rights, data protection law, Article 10 rights and the Rehabilitation of Offenders Act 1974. The Act offers some protection to people as regards the disclosure of a 'spent' conviction they have, but does not in itself prevent the court or a journalist revealing in the public interest that a conviction exists.

For context, see ch. 24 about the 1974 Act and 27.13 on the privacy 'right to be forgotten'. Ch. 28 outlines data protection law. This chapter has referred to Article 10 rights.

A court's decision on any request made under rule 5.8(7) is subject to case law concerning requests for access to case material and court records, which will now be explained, and a practice direction explained in 15.20.

* Remember

A journalist covering a criminal case contemporaneously can request copies of prosecution case material under a protocol explained in 15.21.

15.19 Case law on journalists' access to case material or records from any court's proceedings

To fully understand and report on a court case, or to investigate issues or a matter raised in it, journalists may wish to see—and quote from or show in reports—material from the case, whether this is **skeleton arguments**, witness statements or other documents or photographs or footage, or cite what court records say about the case. For example, a relevant case document may not have been read out in full in the court's proceedings, or may only have been referred to briefly.

→glossary

In 2019 a Supreme Court judgment made clear that there is a presumption in common law that all types of court should allow non-parties to a case, such as journalists, access to a case document or other case material if:

- it was placed before the court, referred to in its public proceedings and is sought for a 'proper journalistic purpose' to 'advance the open justice principle';
- the open justice benefits of disclosure are not outweighed by any risk of harm it may cause to the effective judicial process or to the legitimate interests of anyone else (for example, national security or personal privacy)—so the court may need to conduct a 'balancing exercise' to decide whether access is granted.

for context on 'balancing exercise', see 1.3.3

The Supreme Court judgment is *Cape Intermediate Holdings Ltd v Dring (for and on behalf of Asbestos Victims Support Groups Forum UK)* [2019] UKSC 38—hereafter referred to as *Dring*. It should be cited by any journalist who asks any type of court to supply copies or allow inspection of case material, or to supply information from its case records.

15.19.1 Advancing the open justice principle

The Supreme Court's judgment in *Dring* said that a person seeking access to case material should explain to the relevant court 'how granting him access will advance the open justice principle'. The meaning of this phrase is clearer in the (apparently synonymous) reference elsewhere in the judgment to advancing 'the purpose' of the open justice principle.

Delivering the judgment, Lady Hale acknowledged there may be several such purposes, saying: 'The principal purposes of the open justice principle are two-fold and there may well be others . . . The first is to enable public scrutiny of the way in which courts decide cases—to hold the judges to account for the decisions they make and to enable the public to have confidence that they are doing their job properly . . . But the second goes beyond the policing of individual courts and judges. It is to enable the public to understand how the justice system works and why decisions are taken.' She added: 'It is difficult, if not impossible, in many cases, especially complicated civil cases, to know what is going on unless you have access to the written material.'

From the *Dring* judgment, it is clear that:

- A journalist applying for access to case material or case information should explain why it is needed for the fullest possible reporting of the case, and state any other 'proper journalistic purpose' which the material or information would serve, and cite as context one or more of the purposes of the open justice principle, as appropriate and as stated in case law, and explain why access will advance the purpose(s)—see too 15.1.1.

The request in *Dring* to see case material—thousands of pages in a range of documents—was made on behalf of a support forum for people suffering from asbestos-related illnesses. But in *Dring* the Supreme Court also allowed the Media Lawyers Association to make arguments to it in support of greater access to case materials for journalists because of their role in upholding open justice.

15.19.2 The purposes of open justice include 'stimulating informed debate' about an issue

A journalist making such an application should also cite the Court of Appeal's judgment in *R (on the application of Guardian News and Media Ltd) v City of Westminster Magistrates' Court*, referred to in 15.1.1, which concerned media access to material from an extradition case and considered the scope of CrimPR rule 5.8(7), and which was endorsed by the Supreme Court in *Dring*.

The Court of Appeal's judgment accepted that *The Guardian* newspaper had a 'serious journalistic purpose' in seeking access to the relevant documents, and accepted too that 'the open justice principle' had purpose beyond the reporting of the particular case, because the judgment said that *The Guardian*—in wanting to report the extradition case fully by means of access to the documents—'wants to be able to refer to them for the purpose of stimulating informed debate about the way in which the justice system deals with suspected international corruption and the system for extradition of British subjects to the USA'.

15.19.3 The open justice principle can be advanced by disclosure of information which may be 'germane' to a 'serious journalistic story'

Open justice case law has developed in recent years to the point where judges may accept that material referred to publicly in a court case should be disclosed to help a journalist pursue 'a serious journalistic story' about a related matter, which is in the public interest.

Case study

This development was clearly demonstrated in 2021 in a High Court ruling by Mr Justice Calver, in which he ordered The Hut Group (THG) company to disclose to a *Guardian* journalist a copy of an internal report written in 2011 about a fraud within THG which led to it dismissing its financial controller James

McCarthy that year for gross misconduct. The report had been referred to in a High Court case which concluded in 2014. Nearly six years later the journalist Simon Goodley used rule 5.4C(2) of the Civil Procedure Rules to apply to the High Court for a copy of the report (this rule is explained later in this chapter at 15.26). He said he wanted to see it to better understand matters referred to in the 2014 case but also 'to obtain further information about this matter that may assist in further journalistic investigation'. His barrister said that Mr Goodley 'seeks to explore whether the contents of the report give rise to other grounds for journalistic inquiry'. In ruling that a copy of the report should be given to Mr Goodley, Mr Justice Calver referred to the Supreme Court's ruling in *Dring*, and said '. . . the open justice principle will . . . typically be advanced by disclosure to a journalist in pursuit of a serious journalistic story of a document referred to in open court which may be germane to that story' (*Goodley v The Hut Group and Nobahar-Cookson and Barclays Private Bank and Trust Ltd* [2021] EWHC 1193 (Comm)).

For more detail of *Dring*, which concerned the scope of rule 5.4C(2), and the *Guardian News and Media* and *Goodley v The Hut Group* judgments, see the **additional material** for this chapter on **www.mcnaes.com**, where there are details of other cases in which journalists have gained access to case material to order to stimulate public debate by deeper coverage.

15.19.4 General principles when a court considers a request for access to case material or records

The Supreme Court decision in *Dring* means the following principles apply when any type of court, including a tribunal, has to make a decision on whether to grant a request made by a 'non-party', such as a journalist, for access to case material (as this chapter explains, in many instances a court is not required to make such a decision, because some court rules give journalists or the public a routine right to inspect or have copies of case material, or be provided with case information). The numbers of relevant paragraphs of the *Dring* judgment are given:

- Non-parties should not seek access to case material unless they can show the court a good reason why this will advance a purpose of the open justice principle (45, 47).
- The court must consider the request if the material was placed before it for the case and has been referred to in the court's public proceedings, even if the material was not read out in court or treated as read out, or not read by the judge during the proceedings (37, 38, 41, 44).
- Apart from when the rules contain a valid prohibition, the extent of any access to case material permitted by the rules is not determinative. The court has inherent power in common law to decide the extent to which access is granted in the particular case, if statute does not forbid access (41).

- The court will consider the potential value of the information in question in advancing the cited purpose(s) of open justice, and, conversely, any risk of harm which its disclosure may cause to the maintenance of an effective judicial process or to the legitimate interests of others (39).
- That the case has been concluded or settled does not of itself prevent journalists or the public getting access to case material, but it is highly desirable that the request for access is made during the trial when the material is still readily available (47).
- People who request access after the proceedings are over might find that the court decides it is impracticable or disproportionate to provide it because the court will probably not have retained the material and the parties might not have done so or the burdens on them of retrieving it might be out of all proportion to benefits to the open justice principle, and, at that stage, the burden on the trial judge in making decisions on access may have become harder to discharge; or the reasons why access should not be granted—for example, to protect someone's privacy, or commercial confidentiality—might be stronger after proceedings end (46, 47).
- Increasing digitisation of case material might ease practical problems in supplying it (47).
- If access is granted, the most practicable way of providing it might be in the form of a clean copy of the trial bundle (the file or files containing all material expected to be referred to in the trial) if one is still available (48). NB: The normal contents of a trial bundle in a civil case are listed in Practice Direction 32 relating to the Civil Procedure Rules.
- Those seeking access will be expected to pay the reasonable cost of granting it (47).

As appropriate, some of the above principles will apply when a court is considering an application for information from its records about a case, rather than for material referred to in the case.

15.19.5 Costs could arise

A journalist attending an ongoing case who wants to see or have a copy of an item of case material (for example, a skeleton argument) should first make an informal request to the party who presented it to the court. If no one objects to it being supplied, there is no need to consider whether to make a formal application to the court.

It is possible, if such a formal application was made and was wholly unsuccessful, that the applicant will be ordered to pay the legal costs (such as lawyers' fees) incurred by a party in opposing access—particularly if the court held a hearing especially to consider an application which was made some time after the relevant court case ended.

In *Goodley v The Hut Group*, cited earlier, Mr Justice Calver said that whenever a contested application arises for a non-party to proceedings to be granted access to documents on the court file or which have been referred to in open court, the default position is that there will need to be an oral hearing of the application. He said that the complexity of 'the balancing exercise' that must be conducted by the court means that such an application will not be suitable to be determined on paper.

It is less likely that costs will be awarded against an unsuccessful applicant if an application for access to case material is made during the proceedings of the relevant case and the court can deal with the matter briefly, because each party's lawyers will be attending court on the day, irrespective of the application. Also, unless an unsuccessful applicant has taken an unreasonable stance in the litigation, it can be argued that an award of substantial costs against them would be a disproportionate interference in her or his Article 10 rights.

Nevertheless, a journalist without the financial backing of a media organisation should exercise caution before making a formal application which, if unsuccessful, could prove costly, just as any party considering opposing such an application should be sure that its ground(s) of opposition is/are clear and cogent—see 15.6.1. If access is granted to case material or information from court records and—for example—photocopying is necessary, the journalist or media organisation who applied for the access will be expected to pay the cost of the copying.

see also 15.25 on fees for copies of civil case documents

! Remember your rights

The HMCTS general guidance to courts and tribunal staff says that they should facilitate journalists using their mobile devices to photograph court documents they are 'entitled to', if this is requested. See Useful Websites at the end of this chapter.

15.19.6 A journalist does not have to attend to get case material

In the *Guardian News and Media* judgment, cited earlier, the Court of Appeal ruled that the newspaper could have access to case material although its reporters were not able, for practical reasons, to attend all the extradition hearings in the underlying case. The Supreme Court emphasised in *Dring* that it adopted that ruling, so the principle that access to case material is not dependent on attendance applies to all courts (see too the EAT ruling in the **additional material** for ch. 18).

*** Remember**

If a journalist obtains a copy of case material by unofficial means—that is, without the court's permission and not through the rules—reporting what the material says might be a contempt of court under law explained in 12.6 and 12.7 of this book. Also, such a report would not be protected by section 4 of the Contempt of Court Act 1981 if publication of the material breaches that Act's section 1, because it would not be a report of court proceedings. The Contempt of Court Act is covered in ch. 19.

for further context on defamation law, see 15.28

A media organisation might also be successfully sued for defamation if it publishes material from an unofficially obtained copy of a document not read out in open court, and not treated by the court as having been read out.

15.20 Practice direction on access to case information or material from criminal proceedings

for the Direction, see Useful Websites at the end of this chapter

Criminal Practice Direction 2.6 covers access to material held by the courts. It says that the basic information detailed in rule 5.8(4) of the Criminal Procedure Rules about recent and ongoing cases, should be given (by the court officer) to a journalist or anyone else seeking it (as explained earlier in this chapter).

The Direction says material should be requested from the person who presents it to the court (e.g. the Crown Prosecution Service) before an application is made to the court. It also states that the same procedure applies to applications for access to information by reporters as to other members of the public, but that there is a 'greater presumption in favour of providing the requested material' if the application is made by an 'accredited' journalist (who can produce a valid press card), or by legal representatives for the media. The term 'documents' includes images in photographic and digital format, including DVD, video, CCTV or any other form.

for context on 'purpose', see 15.19

The Direction says that, where an application is made by a reporter, the 'general principle' is that the court should supply documents and information unless there is a good reason not to, in order to protect the rights and legitimate interests of others, and if the request will not place an undue burden on the court. It also states that judges must not 'exercise an editorial judgment' about 'the adequacy of the material already available to the [media organisation] for its journalistic purpose'. It adds that the recipient is responsible for complying with the Contempt of Court Act 1981, and any and all restrictions on the use of the material.

ch. 19 explains contempt law, and chs. 10–12 cover other reporting restrictions

Direction 2.6.10 sets out considerations for the court regarding the release of various types of material. It says skeleton arguments, written submissions and the court's written decisions are likely to fall into the category of documents which a court treats as having been read aloud in their entirety, even if they were neither read nor summarised aloud, and they should generally be made available on request.

for context of the judgment, see 15.19

It says Victim Personal Statements, pre-sentence reports, medical reports and reports in confiscation proceedings will usually be confidential, even where they have been referred to in open court (although there is no automatic restriction to prevent reporting of passages read to the court).

Sentencing remarks should usually be provided (subject to reporting restrictions) if the judge was reading from a prepared script which was handed out immediately afterwards. Otherwise permission to obtain a transcript should usually be given. The direction also states that transcripts can be obtained for a fee from the relevant transcription service, although these are expensive and there may be some delay in obtaining one.

for context, see 15.27, Transcripts

Direction 2.6.11 says it may be convenient to provide material electronically, if this can be done securely. It also states that journalists are expected to be aware of the limitations on the use to which such material can be put—for example, that legal argument in the absence of the jury must not be reported before the conclusion of the trial.

Direction 2.6 makes clear that material covered by existing protocols should, before an application is made to the court, first be sought in accordance with those protocols from the relevant organisation(s), which would be from:

1. HMCTS, as regards information in lists and registers from magistrates' courts—see 15.15.2;
2. the Crown Prosecution Service (CPS) or police for material covered by the 'Publicity and the Criminal Justice System' protocol, explained next.

✱ Remember

A journalist's application to see case material should cite *Dring* and *Guardian News and Media*—see 15.19.

15.21 The 'Publicity and the Criminal Justice System' protocol

The protocol 'Publicity and the Criminal Justice System' says that material on which the prosecution relied in a trial which *should* normally be released to the media includes:

see Useful Websites at the end of this chapter for the protocol

- maps and photographs, including custody photos of defendants, and diagrams produced in court;
- videos showing crime scenes;
- videos of property seized—for example, weapons, drugs, stolen goods;
- sections of transcripts of interviews which were read to the court;
- videos or photographs showing reconstructions of the crime;
- CCTV footage of the defendant, subject to **copyright** issues.

→glossary

The protocol also says that material which *might* be released following consideration by the CPS, in consultation with the police, victims, witnesses and others directly affected by the case, such as family members, includes:

- CCTV footage showing the defendant and victim, or the victim alone, which the jury and public saw in court;
- video and audio tapes of police interviews with defendants, victims and witnesses;
- victim and witness statements.

The protocol also enables the media to ask the CPS head of strategic communications to become involved in the event of a dispute over disclosure.

When this book went to press, a revised version of the protocol was awaited following a consultation which ended in May 2025—check www.mcnaes.com for updates.

! Remember your rights

Despite the reference to copyright considerations in part of the protocol, fears that the media might infringe copyright by using case material should not stop it being provided for the reporting of a case. See 29.10 on why copyright is not infringed by that usage.

15.22 Advance information about civil cases—registers and listing

The Civil Procedure Rules (CPR) apply to cases in the County Court and High Court—see 15.11.

Rule 5.4 of the CPR says any person who pays the prescribed fee may see a civil court's register of claims—that is, its list of cases due to be dealt with. As such registers are open to public inspection, a fair and accurate report of what they say is safe to publish in defamation law—see 22.7.2.4. This inspection right is of limited value to journalists scouting for newsworthy cases, because although the High Court at the Royal Courts of Justice in London has registers for the King's Bench Division, Chancery Division and the Admiralty and Commercial Court, which deal with many major cases, no other part of the High Court—for example, its district registries (in other cities)—or any County Court venues have them at present (Practice Direction 5A).

Lists of cases being heard at the Royal Courts of Justice, London, and in the County Court can be accessed for no payment via the Courtserve.net site, or via the HMCTS Court and Tribunals Hearing service www.gov.uk, drawing on administrative data. These show hearings listed to take place that day and the next, and in some instances over the next few days—for example, the date on which a judgment is due to be 'handed down'. But they usually have scant detail—for example, the nature of the case is often not stated. These lists have email addresses for journalists to arrange remote access to a hearing—see too 15.14.

((•)) see Useful Websites at the end of this chapter for links to court rules

Rule 66E of the Magistrates' Courts Rules 1981, as amended in 2021, specify what basic details should be published in advance by such courts about their civil cases, such as the identities of the parties. What must be done to publish these details is similar to such obligations which these courts have in respect of their criminal cases—see 15.15.1.

15.23 What help should civil court staff provide?

HMCTS guidance to civil court staff is that journalists who phone or email about a case should—if all parties have acknowledged service or defence or the case is listed or judgment is entered—be given factual information about it such as listing dates, the names of parties, the names of judges, barristers and solicitors, the type of case and—if the hearing was in open court—the result and details of the judgment. But the guidance says that fuller details of the nature of the claim can only be supplied via a request made for the statement of case, under rule 5.4C(1) of the CPR, which is explained later in this chapter.

((•)) see Useful Websites at the end of this chapter for this HMCTS guidance

If magistrates are presiding in a civil case, their name must be supplied—see 15.15.5.

15.24 Routine access under rules to civil case material

The Civil Procedure Rules (CPR) allow non-parties such as journalists routine access to specified types of case documents filed with the court in civil claims lodged after 2 October 2006. This access is important, as civil cases are now largely conducted by reference to documents rather than by oral evidence and submissions. A civil trial may be impossible to report meaningfully if a reporter has not read key documents. Access to documents can prove difficult on a practical level, as there is no centralised system of obtaining them. For certain types of High Court case, some documents are available via an online filing system (efile.cefile-app.com) for a fee. As part of an ongoing drive for increased transparency across the justice system, a two-year pilot scheme to provide access to court documents through this filing system has been introduced in the Commercial Court, which is part of the High Court, under Practice Direction 51ZH. See the additional material for this chapter for further details of this pilot.

See 15.11 for context on the CPR.

15.24.1 Statement of case

Rule 5.4C(1) of the CPR provides that, as a general rule, anyone who pays the prescribed fee can obtain from the court staff a copy of any 'statement of case':

- if the sole defendant has, or all defendants have, filed an acknowledgement of service or a defence; or
- if there is more than one defendant, at least one defendant has filed such an acknowledgement or a defence and the court (that is, a judge) specifically permits provision of the copy; or
- if the claim has been listed for a hearing; or
- if judgment has been entered in the claim (a judgment means part or all of the case is concluded).

This rule also allows anyone to obtain a copy of any judgment, or order, made or given in public.

'Statement of case', which is defined in rule 2.3, means the **claim form**, particulars of claim (if not in the claim form) and defence, and also any additional claim, counterclaim or reply to the defence. For further detail of the nature of these documents, see CPR Parts 16 and 20. 'Further information documents' which the court requires a party to supply under rule 18.1 are also part of a statement of case. The request for the statement of case must be in writing (rule 5.4D).

→glossary

A party or any person identified in a statement of case may ask or have asked the court to restrict or ban access to it. The court (that is, a judge) would hold a hearing if there is any dispute over this—see later about costs.

15.24.2 Witness statements

A statement of case does not include witness statements. But rule 32.13 of the CPR says: 'A witness statement which stands as **evidence-in-chief** is open to inspection during the course of the trial unless the court otherwise directs.' This enables public access during the course of the trial to written evidence relied on in court but not read out. But the court may rule that a witness statement should not be made available because of the interests of justice, the public interest, or the nature of expert medical evidence or confidential information, or because of the need to protect the interests of any child or protected party. Rule 32.13 does not apply to small claims cases.

> The general rights in rules 5.4C(1) and 32.13 for anyone to see and have copies of the specified types of documents means that a person requesting such access does not have to give notice of the request to any party in the case, unless a judge's permission is needed for access. But these rules do not cover some types of sensitive, civil cases—for example concerning orders to restrict the activities and movements of suspected terrorists. For detail on such orders, see **www.mcnaes.com** for the online chapter, **'Terrorism and the effect of counter-terrorism law'**.

15.24.3 Skeleton arguments

Each side in a civil case draws up a skeleton argument—a document outlining the case and summarising the legal arguments.

Senior judges have made clear that parties or their legal representatives should supply journalists with copies of skeleton arguments, unless there is a confidentiality issue or some other valid reason not to (for context, see 15.26).

For example, an updated guide endorsed by the Lord Chief Justice, issued in 2022 for users of the Commercial Court, which is part of the High Court, says (at J7.3):

> "The general rule is that a hearing is to be in public: rule 39.2(1). In consequence, parties and their legal representatives should be prepared to provide a copy of that party's skeleton argument for the hearing, by email, to any law reporter, media reporter or member of the public who requests it. Unless a party has solid grounds for declining to provide a copy, a party should comply with the request voluntarily, without the need for intervention by the Court. Where a skeleton argument contains information which is subject to a confidentiality order or which is to be referred to at a hearing in private, a suitably redacted version of the skeleton argument can be made available."

((•)) for the guide and Practice Direction, see Useful Websites at the end of this chapter

Paragraph 33 of CPR Practice Direction 52C requires parties in a Court of Appeal civil case normally to supply a copy of their skeleton arguments to journalists at the hearing.

15.25 Fees for copies of civil case documents

The fees which a civil court can charge for copying or providing digital copies of several documents provided under rule 5.4C(1) might be high in total (hundreds of pounds) if the case being covered is complex. Under civil and family court fee rules, a court can currently charge a minimum of £11 per document (for either an electronic copy or up to 10 pages of a physical copy).

If during the case's proceedings, the judge agrees that a journalist can be given a copy, the fee rule may not be applied (or be applicable) but the judge may specify a copying charge. A party to the case may agree to supply a copy (for example, digitally) without a copying charge.

15.26 The presumptive right of access to case material or records from a civil court's proceedings

Under rule 5.4C(2) of the CPR, anyone can apply to the court to obtain from 'the records of the court' a copy of any other document filed by a party, or of communication between the court and a party or another person. The application must be made in writing. The court will decide if such access should be granted.

Factors which the court will consider have been set out earlier in this chapter—see 15.19. As explained, the Supreme Court in the *Dring* case made clear that in common law there is a presumptive (default) right of non-parties such as journalists to have access to case material referred to in any court hearing held in public. But a judge might rule against such access being given because of the risk of harm it may cause to the effective judicial process or to the legitimate interests of anyone else.

Rule 5.4C(2) was considered in *Dring*. The Supreme Court said the wording of any court's rules was not—unless there was a valid prohibition in them—the central issue when a court was deciding what access to case material should be given, because the court has a wider, inherent jurisdiction in common law to uphold open justice.

This means a journalist covering a civil court case can apply for access to a wide range of material used or otherwise referred to in the court's public proceedings, such as skeleton arguments, written submissions, chronologies, *dramatis personae* (that is, a list of people featuring in case material)—and can apply for such access and to witness statements after the case has ended, even if the documents are no longer held by the court but have been retained somewhere else—for example, by one or more of the parties.

However, as the Supreme Court made clear, the earlier the application is made the more likely it is to be successful. If a court decides to hold a special hearing to consider an objection to such access, costs could be awarded against the applicant—see 15.19.5.

Again, there is no need for a journalist covering a case to make a formal application to the court if the relevant party is willing to supply the material.

* Remember

Someone applying under rule 5.4C(2) for such access must under rule 5.4D give notice to the relevant party in the case in accordance with Part 23 of the CPR, in case that party objects.

15.26.1 Objections based on 'confidentiality'

The Court of Appeal has ruled that if a party to a civil court case objects to a document being made available for publication, a court will require 'specific reasons' why the party would be damaged by its publication. 'Simple assertions of confidentiality', even if supported by both parties in the case, should not prevail, it said (*Lilly Icos Ltd v Pfizer Ltd* [2002] EWCA Civ 2).

> The **additional material** for ch. 15 on **www.mcnaes.com** has case studies of how the media, including a regional newspaper, have used the CPR to gain copies of case documents, including for investigative journalism, and how judges have interpreted the Rules. It also covers rights of access information and case material from civil proceedings in magistrates' courts. See also the **additional material** for ch. 13 on **www.mcnaes.com** for information about what bankruptcy records can be inspected.

> See ch. 14 in this book for access to documents in Family Court cases and inspection rights for divorce records. See chs. 17 and 18 for access to case material referred to in coroners' courts or tribunals.

15.27 Transcripts

For rules on how transcripts of court hearings may be obtained, see the **additional material** for this chapter on **www.mcnaes.com**.

15.28 Defamation law considerations when reporting from case material or information made accessible under rule or by a court

There is a strong argument that a contemporaneous report of a court hearing which draws on case material, or case information, made available routinely under a rule, or supplied by a court for publication, or supplied by a party in accordance with official guidance for court users, will be protected in its entirety by absolute privilege in defamation law, if all the defence's requirements are met. The defence of qualified privilege will protect such reports, and those solely based on such case material and such case information, if the defence's requirements are met. For either defence to succeed, the reporting must reflect the case fairly overall—for example, if the item of case material was discredited in the proceedings of the relevant case, the report should make that clear.

> For context, see 22.5 and 22.7 on privilege, and see too the **additional material** for ch. 15 on **www.mcnaes.com** as regards *Irfan Qadir v Associated Newspapers Ltd*.

Recap of major points

- A journalist arguing against being excluded from a court represents the wider public's interest in open justice.
- Common law, statute and courts' procedural rules enshrine the open justice principle, but do allow courts to sit in private in some circumstances.
- Staff at criminal and civil courts should give journalists basic details of cases.
- Journalists covering any type of court can apply to see a wide range of case material referred to in court, and the court will rule on such requests. Some information and copies of case material can be obtained routinely under rules, from court staff.
- A protocol enables the media to have access to some types of prosecution material—for example, photos and video footage—to help it report a criminal trial.

Useful Websites

Courts and Tribunals Judiciary, www.judiciary.uk

- Judicial College guidance, *Reporting Restrictions in the Criminal Courts*, 5th edition, as revised in July 2023 by the Judicial College, Media Lawyers Association, News Media Association and Society of Editors
- 'Open Justice—Remote Observation of Hearings—new powers: Practice guidance'
- 'Remote Observation of Hearings in Criminal Courts: Guidance'
- Commercial Court Guides

The UK Press Card Authority, presscards.co.uk

Gov.uk, 'HMCTS staff guidance on supporting media access to courts and tribunals'

- General guidance to staff on supporting media access to courts and tribunals
- Guidance to staff on 'managing high-profile/high-interest trials or hearings'
- 'Protocol on sharing court lists, registers and documents with the media'
- Guidance to criminal court staff on supporting media access
- Guidance to civil court staff on supporting media access
- Reporters' Charter

Ministry of Justice, Procedure rules, www.justice.gov.uk

- Civil Procedure Rules and Practice Directions
- Criminal Procedure Rules and Practice Directions

www.legislation.gov.uk

- Magistrates' Court Rules 1981
- Section 85A of Courts Act 2003 (as amended)
- The Remote Observation and Recording (Courts and Tribunals) Regulations 2022

Crown Prosecution Service (CPS), www.cps.gov.uk

- Instructions for Prosecuting Advocates
- 'Publicity and the Criminal Justice System' protocol agreed by the Crown Prosecution Service, the National Police Chief's Council and media representatives

Online resources

Visit the online resources at **www.mcnaes.com** to test your knowledge of this chapter with **self-test questions** and a **flashcard glossary**, and to read **updates** about law and regulatory matters affecting journalism, as well as **additional material** to further your learning.

16

Challenging in the courts

Chapter summary

Courts often restrict media coverage of cases and journalists must be prepared to challenge invalid or overly broad restrictions—they may be the only people in court arguing for the open justice principle (see ch. 15). This chapter explains the case law and rules journalists can cite when opposing reporting restrictions, and how to make challenges.

16.1 Introduction—why a challenge may be needed

A court may try to restrict reporting of a case when it has no power to do so, or to impose a restriction which is valid but wider than necessary.

A journalist challenging a proposed or existing reporting restriction, or possible exclusion from a court, should remind the court of the general and fundamental rule in **common law** that justice should be open because of the societal benefits this brings, and the media's role in enabling them—see 15.1–15.2—as well as raise specific points, covered in this chapter, about the restrictive power the court is considering using or has used. →glossary

Also, journalists should cite the rights of the media and public to impart and receive information, under Article 10 of the European Convention on Human Rights—see 15.5.

16.1.1 A reporting restriction must be obeyed

Reporting restrictions, even if they are invalid or too broad, must be obeyed unless the court amends or lifts them (*HM Attorney General v Yaxley-Lennon* [2019] EWHC 1791 (QB), at paragraph 49).

((•)) for full versions of the rules and Practice Directions, see Useful Websites at the end of this chapter

16.2 Court rules—the media's right to have notice of restrictions and to challenge

Court rules and Practice Directions—see 15.11—govern court procedures, including those allowing reporting restrictions to be challenged. The rules reflect the established principle in law that the media should be given adequate opportunity to challenge a reporting restriction requested by one or more of the parties in a case.

16.2.1 What rules for criminal courts say about challenge procedure

Together, rules 6.2 and 6.4 of the Criminal Procedure Rules (CrimPR), and Criminal Practice Direction 6.3.55, make clear that a magistrates' or Crown court should not restrict reporting or access to a hearing unless each party and any other person directly affected, including any representative of the media, is present or has had an opportunity to attend or make representations.

16.2.1.1 Notice of applications for restrictions and of opposition to them

Rule 6.4(3) of the CrimPR requires that parties applying for a reporting restriction, or for a court hearing to be held partly or entirely in private must give 'reporters' advance notice. HMCTS facilitates this by court staff maintaining lists of journalists' contact details, to be passed to parties' representatives who need to issue such a notification. Rule 6.5(3) imposes obligations on media organisations to apply 'as soon as reasonably practicable' if they wish to oppose a reporting or access restriction, and to notify the parties—the defence and prosecution—that such representations are to be made and why the restriction is opposed or should be amended. But rule 6.3 gives the courts discretion to hear applications for restrictions, or media representations against them, without notice, and made orally rather than in writing.

Under rule 6.3, anyone wanting more time to make representations (where the court has set a time limit) must explain why.

Case study

In 2018 the then-Lord Chief Justice, Lord Burnett of Maldon warned judges to be cautious about imposing reporting restrictions when the prosecution or defence asks for them shortly before a trial is due to begin. In a Court of Appeal judgment, he said: 'Judges must be on their guard against applications which are advanced at the last minute or without proper consideration of the principles in play ... Although a reporter may be in court ... he or she is unlikely to be in a position instantly to advance considered submissions in response to an application.' He also warned courts to bear in mind before imposing reporting restrictions that the reality is that most local newspapers are unable to justify the cost of applying or appealing for them to be lifted (*R v Sarker* [2018] EWCA Crim 1341).

As this chapter will explain, in *Sarker* the Court of Appeal was considering an order made under section 4(2) of the Contempt of Court Act 1981 by a Crown court judge to postpone reporting of a trial. But the Lord Chief Justice's warning can be cited to oppose a 'last minute' application for reporting restrictions of any type, in any court. However, see the additional material for this chapter for details of a recent case which underlines the importance of the media giving timely notice of an application to lift a reporting restriction, as per rule 6.5(3).

! Remember your rights

Journalists opposing applications for reporting or access restrictions, or continuation of restrictions, should tell the court if they were disadvantaged because no notice was given. This may gain them more time to prepare their argument.

16.2.1.2 A record should be made and the media told

Rule 6.8 of the CrimPR says that if a reporting or access restriction is made or varied or removed, or an order made for a trial to be held in private, the court officer must record the reason for the decision. For details of who the 'court officer' is, see 15.15. The rule adds that notice of the decision should be displayed somewhere prominent in the courtroom's vicinity and communicated to reporters. It remains the responsibility of those reporting on a case to ensure no order is breached by checking if there are reporting restrictions in case of doubt.

16.2.2 What rules for civil courts say about challenge procedure

The Civil Procedure Rules (CPR) cover the County Court, most High Court cases and the Court of Appeal Civil Division. Rule 39.2(3) sets out the criteria which may lead a court to order that a hearing, or any part of it, must be held in private (see 15.13 for details).

Rule 39.2(4) of the CPR enables a court to order that the identity of any person shall not be disclosed if it considers non-disclosure necessary to secure the proper administration of justice and to protect the interests of that person. If such an order is made, it means that the protected person's identity should not be disclosed in the case's public proceedings or in any case information or documents, including the judgment, which the public and journalists can see, or published in any way in connection with the case.

Rule 39.2(5) says that unless and to the extent that the court otherwise directs, when it makes an order to hold a hearing in private or to withhold a person's identity, a copy shall be published on the Judiciary website (www.judiciary.uk). This rule also says that any person who is not a party to the proceedings—for example, a journalist—may apply to attend the hearing and make submissions, or apply to set aside or vary the anonymity order.

for case law on challenging anonymity provision in general and section 11, see 16.8–16.11

✱ Remember

A civil court which makes a non-disclosure order under rule 39.2 may also make an order under section 11 of the Contempt of Court Act 1981 to ban the person's identity from being published in connection with the case, so a challenge to an order made under this rule may also be a challenge to a section 11 order.

See the **additional material** for this chapter online for a case study involving use of redactions to anonymise civil servants, which a High Court judge ruled against.

16.3 HMCTS guidance to staff of all courts

for context on the guidance, see 15.9

His Majesty's Courts and Tribunals Service's (HMCTS) general guidance to its staff in all types of court says that the media should be given advance notification of, and an opportunity to make representations about, an application for reporting restrictions to imposed. It adds that a restriction order should be put in writing as soon as possible and the media should be 'put on notice' about it.

law postponing reporting of 'special measures' is explained in 12.13, and Article 10 is explained in 15.5

16.4 The necessity principle, proportionality and precision

A journalist challenging a proposed or imposed reporting restriction in any type of court may need to remind it that in law the test for a reporting restriction is necessity—see 15.6. A court should only impose a reporting restriction if it is necessary to achieve the desired objective, and its scope should be limited solely to what is required to do that. For example, where a lesser measure exists—such as a 'special measure' allowing a witness to give evidence over a video link—a court should adopt that. The terms of any order should also be **proportionate** to comply with Article 10.

→glossary

16.5 Judicial College guidance for criminal courts

Guidance entitled *Reporting Restrictions in the Criminal Courts*, published by the Judicial College, can be cited usefully in challenges to actual or proposed reporting restrictions or threatened exclusions. The guidance cites case law and the Criminal Procedure Rules. It says, for example, that the necessity for a proposed restriction on access or reporting must be 'convincingly established' by clear and cogent evidence by those seeking it (see its pp. 5, 7 and 18), that courts which have imposed or are considering imposing a restriction on access or reporting should hear media representations as soon as possible, because contemporaneous court reporting is important and news is perishable (pp. 6 and 18), and that the media are well placed to represent the wider public interest in open justice (p. 18).

16.5.1 Precision

The guidance says an order which restricts reporting should be 'clear and precise' in its terms and put in writing as soon as possible, then notified to the media.

((•)) see Useful Websites at the end of this chapter for the guidance

16.6 Methods of challenge

Reporters challenging a proposed or actual reporting restriction or exclusion of the media from a court should raise the issue as soon as possible. They can make oral submissions or submit their legal arguments in writing.

A journalist covering a case in which a reporting or access restriction is proposed or imposed should approach the clerk/legal adviser as the first step to challenging it—for example, if a hearing is under way, by asking an usher to pass a note to the clerk/legal adviser.

- If an order has already been made, the clerk/legal adviser can be asked to:
  - supply it in written form, if this has not already been provided;
  - specify in writing why it was made, if the order does not make this clear;
  - state in writing the statute and section under which it was made, if the order does not state this.

Such a request might prompt the court to reconsider the order, especially if a reporter—or an editor, by letter or email—quotes case law against it.

Journalists opposing a restriction or exclusion should remind the court of their and the public's Convention rights under Article 10, and refer as appropriate to the 'necessity' principle and (if the relevant case is in a criminal court) to the Judicial College guidance.

- Raising a query or challenge in person in court, or by writing to the court, has the advantage that doing so may resolve the matter quickly and cheaply as there may be no need to involve a lawyer.

16.6.1 Costs

Courts do not normally make costs orders against journalists or a media employer when these informal challenges are made, even if they fail. But it is important to make the challenge as early as possible so it can be considered when the court is already due to be dealing with the case. If a special hearing has to be arranged on another date to consider a challenge made by formal application, a costs order is more likely to be made.

16.6.2 If there is concerted opposition to the media's challenge

A journalist whose challenge in a criminal case is being opposed by both the defence and prosecution, or in a civil case by both parties, should remind the court of the warning by Court of Appeal judge Sir Christopher Staughton that '... when both sides agreed that information should be kept from the public, that was when the court had to be most vigilant' (*Ex p P* (1998) *The Times*, 31 March, quoted with approval by Lord Rodger in the Supreme Court case *In Re Guardian News and Media Ltd* [2010] UKSC 1).

16.6.3 Challenges taken to a higher court

If a challenge by a reporter or an editor fails, the court's decision can be challenged by a formal application being made to a higher court.

16.6.3.1 Judicial review by the High Court of restrictions imposed by magistrates or coroners

→glossary

- A journalist or media organisation can apply to the Administrative Court, part of the High Court for **judicial review** of a decision by a magistrates' or coroner's court. This normally involves hiring lawyers and there is a court fee, and, if the challenge fails, the journalist or media organisation may have to meet some or all of the costs of any party which opposed the application. An applicant media organisation may have to bear its own costs even when successful.

16.6.3.2 Crown court restrictions can be challenged at the Court of Appeal

Decisions by Crown court judges to impose reporting restrictions or exclude the media can be challenged under section 159 of the Criminal Justice Act 1988, which gives the media a route of appeal to the Court of Appeal Criminal Division.

((•)) for the Rules, see Useful Websites at the end of this chapter

- The disadvantages are that the appeal may not be considered quickly, so a story might have lost any news value, and will normally involve hiring lawyers, paying court fees and, possibly costs, even if it is successful.

Part 40 of the Criminal Procedure Rules sets out the procedure for such appeals.

16.7 Challenging section 4(2) postponement orders

Section 4(2) of the Contempt of Court Act 1981 empowers any court in any type of case to postpone publication of reports of all or part of those proceedings to 'avoid a substantial risk of prejudice' to later stages of the same proceedings or to other proceedings pending or imminent. See also 19.10, which explains that a court may use this power to postpone reporting of a criminal trial, or several trials, if trials are linked because they arise from the same police investigation.

for context, see 15.1.1 on the benefits of open justice

Postponement orders frequently mean that when the restriction ends the case receives substantially less detailed coverage than it would otherwise have done, especially if the order means that coverage of a sequence of trials has to be compressed into one day's publication on the day the last trial ends. The societal benefits of open justice will have been eroded.

The Lord Chief Justice warned in 2018 in the Court of Appeal's *Sarker* judgment, cited earlier, that even postponing reporting for a short period was likely 'to have a damaging effect on the very important public interest in reporting proceedings in courts', and could mean that the case is not reported at all:

> "In order to publish a postponed report of a trial, the media organisation would have to commit the resources of a journalist attending the trial in the certain knowledge that only a fraction of what would have been published in daily reports will be likely to be published when the order is lifted."

for more detail of *Sarker*, see 16.7.6

16.7.1 Risk of prejudice in sequential cases

Lord Justice Farquharson said in *R v Beck, ex p Daily Telegraph* [1993] 2 All ER 177 that the fact that a defendant expected to face a second **indictment** after a trial of the first did not in itself justify making a section 4(2) order—it depended on all the circumstances, including the nature of the charges, and the timing and location of the second trial. If substantial prejudice to the defendant could be avoided by extending the period between trials, or transferring the case to another court, that course should be followed, he said.

→glossary

16.7.2 The risk of prejudice must be substantial

A section 4(2) order should only be made if the risk of prejudice to current or pending proceedings is substantial.

In 1993 in the Court of Appeal the then-Lord Chief Justice, Lord Taylor, said that a court, in determining whether publication of information from its proceedings would cause a substantial risk of prejudice to a future trial, should credit that trial's jury with the will and ability to abide by the judge's direction to decide the case only on the evidence before it. The court should also bear in mind that the staying power and detail of publicity, even in cases of notoriety, were limited and that the nature of a trial was to focus the jury's minds on the evidence put before them rather than on matters outside the courtroom (*Ex p Telegraph plc and other appeals* [1993] 2 All ER 971).

Risk of prejudice if one defendant is sentenced before others are tried In 2006 the Court of Appeal overturned a section 4(2) order postponing reporting of the sentencing of terrorist Dhiran Barot. The Crown court judge had made the order on the grounds that reports would prejudice the forthcoming trial of other defendants. But lawyers for the media successfully argued that five months would elapse before that jury trial and so the 'fade factor' would mean that contemporaneous reporting of Barot's sentencing would not create a substantial risk of prejudice. Sir Igor Judge said in the Court of Appeal judgment that the right to a fair trial had to be balanced with the hallowed principle of the media's freedom to act as the eyes and ears of the public. Juries had 'passionate and profound belief in, and a commitment to, the right of a Defendant to be given a fair trial', he said, emphasising the capacity of juries to concentrate on the trial evidence (*R v B* [2006] EWCA Crim 2692). For more detail of Sir Igor's remarks in this case, see, 19.7.1 Juries are told to put pre-trial publicity out of their minds.

see 19.7.2 for an explanation of 'fade factor'

Principles for decisions on section 4(2) orders In *R v Sherwood, ex p Telegraph Group* [2001] EWCA Crim 1075, [2001] 1 WLR 1983, the Court of Appeal set out three principles on section 4(2) orders:

> “(1) Unless the perceived risk of prejudice was demonstrated, no order should be made;
>
> (2) The court had to ask whether an order was necessary under the European Convention on Human Rights. Sometimes wider considerations of public policy would come into play to justify refusing to make a section 4(2) order even though there was no other way of eliminating the prejudice anticipated;
>
> (3) Applications for postponement orders should be approached as follows:
>
> (i) Would reporting give rise to a substantial risk of prejudice? If not, that would be the end of the matter;
>
> (ii) if such a risk was perceived to exist, would an order eliminate it? If not, obviously there could be no necessity to impose such a postponement. But even if the judge was satisfied that an order would achieve the objective, they would have to consider whether the risk could satisfactorily be overcome by less restrictive means;
>
> (iii) the judge might still have to ask whether the degree of risk of prejudice contemplated should be regarded as tolerable in the sense of being the lesser of two evils, when compared to the harm which a 4(2) order could cause to the benefits of open justice.”

These *Sherwood* principles were endorsed by the Court of Appeal in 2017 (*R v Beale in the matter of an appeal by News Group Newspapers* [2017] EWCA 1012 (Crim)) and *Sarker* in 2018.

see 16.5.1 for context about why a restrictive order must be precise

16.7.3 A section 4(2) order cannot be indefinite or permanent

A section 4(2) order can only be temporary in effect. It can be challenged as invalid if its wording does not specify the duration of its effect—that is, for how long publication of reports must be postponed.

The Court of Appeal said in 2017 that such an order should refer to its ‘end point’ being a specified date or as being the point at which the particular case will have concluded (*R v Beale*, cited earlier).

16.7.4 The possibility of re-trial does not mean it is ‘pending or imminent’

The mere fact that a defendant has lodged an appeal against a conviction does not mean that re-trial proceedings are ‘pending or imminent’ and so cannot justify use of section 4(2) to postpone the reporting of another case they are involved in (*Beggs v The Scottish Ministers* [2006] CSIH 17).

16.7.5 Section 4(2) cannot be used to protect reputation or safety

Magistrates and Crown court judges have occasionally made section 4(2) orders for a purpose other than avoiding a substantial risk of prejudice to current or future proceedings. Such orders are invalid. For example, a section 4(2) order cannot be used to ban publication of a name or material to encourage a witness to give evidence, or to protect a defendant's or anyone's reputation or general welfare or safety. The Court of Appeal made this clear in *Re Trinity Mirror plc and others* ([2008] QB 770, [2008] EWCA Crim 50) and in *Re Times Newspapers Ltd* ([2007] EWCA Crim 1925).

16.7.6 Section 4(2) orders cannot be made because of concern about social media comments or earlier online reports

In *Sarker*, cited earlier, the Court of Appeal ruled that a court cannot validly make a section 4(2) order because of concerns that jurors might, by their own research or social media comments, be led from contemporaneous online reports of the trial to prejudicial material about the defendant(s) which remains online from earlier reporting of past events. The Court said that media organisations were able, on their website reports of jury trials, to disable any facility which allowed readers to post comments. The Court added that the risk of 'parasitic damage' which might be caused by social media comments should not be exaggerated, but was not a risk of prejudice arising from fair and accurate reporting of trials, and could not justify making a section 4(2) order.

Members of the public who post social media comments which cause a substantial risk of serious prejudice or impediment can be dealt with under section 1 of the 1981 Act—see 19.4 of this book. For more context, see 19.7.5 on readers' postings.

Journalists challenging a section 4(2) order should refer the court to pp. 27–29 of the Judicial College guidance—see Useful Websites at the end of this chapter.

For more context, see the **additional material** for ch. 16 on **www.mcnaes.com**, including 'Section 4(2) orders cannot restrict reports of events outside the court or because of material already in the public domain.' There is also a case study on *Sarker*.

16.8 Anonymity for people involved in court proceedings—Convention rights

Lawyers acting for a defendant in a criminal case, or for a party in a civil case, or arguing in respect of a witness in any type of case, may cite Article 2 (the right to life) and/or Article 3 (the right to freedom from degrading treatment including torture) of the European Convention on Human Rights, when asserting that publication of the person's identity could lead to her or him being killed or harmed—for example, by vigilantes or vengeful criminals, suicide or self-harm. Later, this chapter explains grounds on which a journalist can challenge a reporting restriction proposed or imposed because of an asserted risk of death or harm.

for context, see 1.3 on the Convention

However, an attempt to persuade a court to provide anonymity for a person, or to otherwise restrict reporting, such as by banning publication of the person's home address, may be solely based on Article 8 rights to respect for privacy and family life.

→glossary

In criminal cases the power in common law to make an order (**injunction**), based directly on a Convention right, to restrict reporting rests only with the High Court, or higher courts, but this power may be extended to the Crown court in relation to matters 'incidental to the court' (*Re Trinity Mirror plc and others*, cited earlier). Otherwise, Magistrates' and Crown courts can restrict reporting to the extent specified in **statutes** and should take their wording and case law—including about Convention rights—into account in those decisions, as this chapter explains.

→glossary

16.8.1 Article 8 rights versus Article 10's protection of open justice

When law enables a reporting restriction to be imposed to provide anonymity for a person, or to ban publication of their address or some other detail, the court should—when deciding on whether to impose or continue it—conduct a balancing exercise to see whether the person's Article 8 rights (if those are the rights being claimed), or the media's and public's Article 10 rights should prevail, considering the facts of the particular case—see 27.6 for how courts should weigh these competing rights. In this context, Article 10 protects the public interest by protecting the societal benefits of open justice, which can be cited by the media in the challenge, as appropriate to the particular case—see 15.1.1.

! Remember your rights

The party who wants the restriction must justify it. The media should not be required to prove why the reporting of particular detail from the case would be in the public interest. In the *Rai* case (see 15.1–15.2) Mr Justice Nicklin said:

> "The starting point is that *any* restriction on publication of information from open court proceedings is a significant interference with the Article 10 right that requires justification . . . there is an inherent and significant value in uninhibited reporting of everything that takes place in court proceedings held in public . . . By definition, everything that is disclosed in open court proceedings (and the subsequent reporting of it) is a matter of public interest. (*R (on the application of Babita Rai) v The Crown Court sitting at Winchester, PA Media and the DPP*) [2021] EWHC 339 (Admin))"

The Court of Appeal endorsed this when upholding the High Court's decision in *Rai*. For context, see 16.11.

16.8.2 Public proceedings in criminal cases, reputation, family life, and the Convention

In 2017 the Supreme Court made clear, when upholding the principle of open justice in the *Khuja* case, that a person's general right to respect for privacy and family life enshrined in Article 8 of the Convention does not mean that the media can be banned from identifying them in reports of what was said in public proceedings in a criminal case, if such anonymity in the reports cannot validly be imposed by a statutory power.

Case study

Tariq Khuja, a prominent figure in the Oxford area, was referred to in evidence and by lawyers in public proceedings in the magistrates' court and Crown court as having been a suspect in Operation Bullfinch, a police investigation into the 'grooming' and sexual abuse, including rape and prostitution, of girls aged between 11 and 15. It led to seven men being convicted of such offences in 2013. Mr Khuja was not one of the men charged and—the Supreme Court said—there was no reason to think he ever would be. But it upheld rulings by the High Court and Court of Appeal that he should not be granted anonymity in media reports of the Bullfinch trials. His lawyers argued that his Article 8 rights to respect for privacy and family life meant that he should be granted an anonymity injunction, to protect his reputation and avoid any impact of publicity on his family life. But the Supreme Court ruled that the open justice principle meant he had 'no reasonable expectation of privacy' in respect of what was said about him in public proceedings (and so his Article 8 rights were not engaged). The Court said the 'collateral impact' on reputation of 'disagreeable statements' which might be made about people in any high-profile criminal trial was 'part of the price to be paid for open justice' and for the freedom of the press to report public, judicial proceedings fairly and accurately (*Khuja v Times Newspapers and others* [2017] UKSC 49).

Part of the significance of the Supreme Court ruling in *Khuja* is that it did not grant him anonymity even though—because he was not a defendant or witness—he did not have the chance to clear his name by testifying in the relevant proceedings, and even though the Court accepted that without anonymity there was a 'real risk' that Mr Khuja would suffer reputational damage. It follows there is an even stronger argument that those who *do* have opportunity within criminal or civil cases to reply publicly to allegations made against them—that is, defendants, **claimants** or witnesses—should not on reputational grounds alone be granted anonymity in media reports of such public proceedings. →glossary

Ch. 27 explains Article 8 and 'reasonable expectation of privacy'. There is more detail about *Khuja* in the **additional material** for ch. 16 on **www.mcnaes.com**.

16.8.3 Limit of common law power

In *Khuja* the Supreme Court confirmed that the common law power of courts to sit in private or anonymise case material used in open court has never extended to restricting reporting of what happens (for example, what has already been said) in open court. Any power to do that must be found in legislation—that is, a power specified in statute.

16.9 Names and full details serve open justice best

Journalists arguing against a reporting restriction banning publication of someone's identity can make the general point that this could mean that some evidential details cannot be reported (if they would identify the person) and that in respect of a name alone, the highest court has recognised that such bans make reports of court cases less interesting and so less likely to be command the public's attention; and so the bans reduce the societal benefits of open justice.

for context on such benefits, see 15.1.1

Case law is that only 'rare circumstances' justify a ban preventing reports from identifying an adult defendant in a criminal trial (*R v Marines A, B, C, D & E* [2013] EWCA Crim 2367). Lord Steyn said in a judgment in which the House of Lords upheld the media's right to identify an adult defendant:

> ". . . it is important to bear in mind that from a newspaper's point of view a report of a sensational trial without revealing the identity of the defendant would be a very much disembodied trial. If the newspapers choose not to contest such an injunction, they are less likely to give prominence to reports of the trial. Certainly, readers will be less interested and editors will act accordingly. Informed debate about criminal justice will suffer (*Re S (FC) (A Child)* [2004] UKHL 47, [2005] 1AC 593)."

The same point can be made about reports of proceedings which are not trials.

Case study

In 2010 the Supreme Court dismissed the argument that the Article 8 rights of men suspected of funding terrorism meant that they should have anonymity in reports of court proceedings held in public, concerning orders freezing their assets. The Supreme Court said that members of the public 'are more than capable of drawing the distinction between mere suspicion and sufficient evidence to prove guilt'. Lord Rodger, giving the Court's unanimous judgment, said: 'What's in a name? "A lot", the press would answer. This is because stories about particular individuals are simply much more attractive to readers than stories about unidentified people. It is just human nature.' He added that editors know best how to present material in a way that will interest the readers of their particular publication and so help them to absorb the information. Lord Rodger continued: 'A requirement to report it in some austere, abstract form, devoid of much of its human interest, could well mean that the report would not be read and the information would not be passed on' (*In Re Guardian News and Media Ltd*, cited earlier).

In exceptional circumstances, the High Court has used the Convention in the context of family law to ban media reports from identifying a defendant in a criminal case—see the **additional material** for ch. 14, Family Courts on **www.mcnaes.com**. For law on anonymisation of claimants in privacy civil cases, see ch. 27.

16.10 Challenging orders made under section 11 of the Contempt of Court Act 1981

for context on rule 39.2(4), see 12.9 and 16.2.2 in this book

All courts have power in common law to order that a name or other information should be withheld from the public during proceedings, and civil courts have specific power too under rule 39.2(4) of the Civil Procedure Rules to order that a person's identity should not be disclosed in the proceedings.

A court which uses either power can then make an order under section 11 of the Contempt of Court Act 1981 indefinitely banning publication of the name or matter in connection with the proceedings. The order may well state that no details that could lead to the person being identified can be published, and so may prevent the identity of someone else involved in the case—for example, the person's partner—or other evidential details from being included in reports of it.

for context, see 12.5, Section 11 orders—blackmail, secrets and personal safety

The media generally accept that blackmail victims should have such anonymity, to help them to give evidence.

But—as this chapter explains—journalists have opposed defendants in criminal cases being given such anonymity; and they have also opposed section 11 being used to ban publication of a defendant's address or a witness's identity, in cases in which reasons put forward for such a ban were insufficient or invalid.

16.10.1 'In connection with the proceedings'

A section 11 order only bans publication of a name or matter 'in connection with the proceedings'—that is, a particular court case. It does not stop the media referring to someone by name in other contexts.

16.10.2 Has the name or matter been withheld from the public?

for context, see 15.16.1, A defendant's name and address should be stated in open court

In most circumstances, a section 11 order cannot validly be made if the name or matter has already been mentioned in public proceedings in the case. The High Court made that clear when a media organisation challenged a section 11 order made by magistrates which banned publication of the name and address of a man charged with burglary offences. The High Court ruled in that judicial review that the magistrates had no power to make the order, as the defendant's details had already been given in public—when the clerk routinely checked the information with the defendant in the first hearing (*R v Arundel Justices, ex p Westminster Press* [1985] 2 All ER 390, [1985] 1 WLR 708). See too *Rai*.

The Court of Appeal has said: 'Unless the court deliberately exercises its power to allow a name or other matter to be withheld, section 11 of the 1981 Act is not engaged'

(*Re Trinity Mirror plc and others*, cited earlier). But a court which *has* made a deliberate decision to withhold a name or matter from a case's public proceedings can use a section 11 order to forbid its publication after it is mentioned by mistake (*Re Times Newspapers Ltd*, cited earlier).

For an example of a challenge on this ground, see the Watson Press Agency case study in the **additional material** for ch. 16 on **www.mcnaes.com**.

16.10.3 Section 11 was not enacted to protect the 'comfort and feelings' of defendants

A section 11 order should not be made for the 'comfort and feelings' of a defendant in a criminal case. In 1987 Evesham magistrates agreed that a defendant's address should not be given in court because he feared harassment by his ex-wife, and made a section 11 order banning its publication. But in a judicial review quashing the order, Lord Justice Watkins said 'it is well established practice that, save for a justifiable reason', a defendant's address must be given publicly in court (*R v Evesham Justices, ex p McDonagh* [1988] QB 553, [1988] 1 All ER 371). He said:

> "There are undoubtedly many people who find themselves defending criminal charges who for all manner of reasons would like to keep unrevealed their identity, their home address in particular. Indeed, I go so far as to say that in the vast majority of cases, in magistrates' courts anyway, defendants would like their identity to be unrevealed and would be capable of advancing seemingly plausible reasons why that should be so. But section 11 was not enacted for the comfort and feelings of defendants."

16.10.4 Section 11 anonymity is not to protect a defendant's children

A section 11 order cannot be used in a criminal case to shield a defendant's children from the effects of publicity about a criminal case. The Court of Appeal ruled in 2008 that Croydon Crown court was wrong to use an order to stop the media naming a man who had admitted 20 charges of downloading child pornography from the internet. The judge who made the order justified it by saying the defendant's daughters, aged 6 and 8, who were neither victims nor witnesses in the case, would suffer significant harm if their father were to be identified. The Court of Appeal said the judge was wrong to conclude that the children's privacy rights under Article 8 of the European Convention outweighed those of the media and the public under Article 10 to publicly identify the man. In the Court of Appeal judgment, Sir Igor Judge said 'there is nothing in this case to distinguish the plight of the defendant's children from that of a massive group of children of persons convicted of offences relating to child pornography'. Allowing the defendant anonymity would be 'to the overwhelming disadvantage of public confidence in the criminal justice system' (*Re Trinity Mirror and others*, cited earlier).

For challenging section 11 anonymity for offenders or suspects in hearings on applications for sexual harm prevention orders, sexual risk orders or slavery and trafficking prevention or risk orders, see the **additional material** for this chapter on **www.mcnaes.com**.

16.10.5 Someone else may be wrongly perceived as the defendant

see 16.5 for context

Page 34 of the Judicial College guidance warns courts that banning disclosure of a defendant's address creates the risk of 'inadvertent defamation', in that the public might think, wrongly, that someone entirely unconnected with the criminal case but with the same name is the defendant. A court may need reminding of this.

see Useful Websites at the end of this chapter for this guidance

16.10.6 Anonymity law should not be used to spare people from embarrassment or to protect reputation

A section 11 order made by a Crown court judge giving anonymity to a witness on the grounds that the stress of publicity might cause her to relapse into heroin addiction was criticised in the High Court. Lord Justice Brown said:

> "There must be many occasions when witnesses in criminal cases are faced with embarrassment as a result of facts which are elicited in the course of proceedings and of allegations made which are often without any real substance. It is, however, part of the essential nature of British criminal justice that cases shall be tried in public and reported and this consideration must outweigh the individual interests of particular persons (*R v Central Criminal Court, ex p Crook* (1984) *The Times*, 8 November)."

on embarrassment, see too 15.6, Is it necessary to exclude or restrict?

In *R v Legal Aid Board, ex p Kaim Todner* [1998] 3 All ER 541, Lord Woolf said that, in general, parties and witnesses in civil cases had to accept the embarrassment, damage to their reputation and possible consequential loss which could be inherent in being involved in litigation, and that their protection was that normally a public judgment would refute unfounded allegations.

16.10.7 Section 11 is not to protect a defendant's business interests

A section 11 order cannot be used to protect a defendant's business interests, the High Court ruled in *R v Dover Justices, ex p Dover District Council and Wells* (1991) 156 JP 433.

16.10.8 Anonymity is generally not needed for corporations in blackmail cases

A High Court judge said in 2020 that when a corporation (such as a company) is the alleged victim in a blackmail case, the administration of justice does not generally require it to have anonymity in reports of the proceedings (*R v Wright (Ruling on*

Anonymity) [2020] EW Misc 22 (CCrimC)). For more detail about this case, see the **additional material** for this chapter on **www.mcnaes.com**.

16.11 Anonymity, addresses—and risk of harm?

Lawyers sometimes urge courts to give a defendant or a witness anonymity, or to ban publication of a defendant's address, on the grounds that they are at risk of violence from criminals or vigilantes, or at risk of self-harm or suicide.

The grounds of the application may be that the order is necessary to uphold rights set out in Articles 2 and 3 of the European Convention on Human Rights. As this chapter has explained, these Articles protect the right to life and the right to freedom from degrading treatment (for example, vigilante attacks), respectively.

In 2010 the Supreme Court said that in 'an extreme case' a court has power to ban the media from identifying a witness or 'a party' to a case [such as a defendant], if doing so is necessary to protect that person or their family from risks to their lives or safety which could arise, for example, because of what the person had said about 'some powerful criminal organisation' (*In Re Guardian News and Media Ltd*, cited earlier).

Relevant case law about Articles 2 and 3 says:

- a court asked to give a defendant or witness anonymity, or to ban publication of their address, on safety grounds must be satisfied that the risk to their safety is 'real and immediate'; and
- the risk must have an objective, verifiable basis—be backed by evidence to the court and not be assessed merely on the person's subjective fears.

In the House of Lords in 2007 Lord Carswell referred to this established criterion that there should be 'a real and immediate risk' to the person's safety to justify anonymity. He said that a real risk was one which was objectively verified, and an immediate risk was one which was present and continuing. He added: 'It is in my opinion clear that the criterion is and should be one that is not readily satisfied: in other words, the threshold is high' (*Re Officer L* [2007] UKHL 36).

This test is the same for any type of court, whether the person allegedly at risk is a defendant or witness, whether the anonymity is sought for the proceedings—that the person should not be identified in court—or only in respect of media reports, whether the restriction being sought is to cover any identifying detail or just an address, or whether it is sought under section 11 of the Contempt of Court Act 1981 or other law.

for context on 'clear and co-gent', see 16.5

The Judicial College guidance says on p. 26 that the person seeking a ban on publication of their identity on safety grounds has to provide clear and cogent evidence to show that such publication 'will create or materially increase a risk of death or serious injury'.

Case study

In 2020 at Winchester Crown court, Judge Cutler revoked a section 11 order—imposed by another judge—which had banned publication of the home address of a woman due to be tried for allegedly murdering her baby (she was later acquitted of murder but convicted of infanticide). Her lawyers, when asking for the ban, argued that her address had not been aired in the magistrates' court, and said she had been dismayed and made anxious by the prospect of it being published. But they did not produce evidence that publication of the address would endanger her (if she was released from custody) or her family. Judge Cutler, the Recorder of Winchester, decided after conducting a balancing exercise that there was not sufficient justification to ban publication of her address. His ruling was upheld by the High Court and Court of Appeal (*R (on the application of Babita Rai) v The Crown Court sitting at Winchester, PA Media and the DPP*) [2021] EWHC 339 (Admin) and [2021] EWCA Civ 60; BBC online, 20 May 2021).

for context on 'balancing exercise', see 1.3.3, and for more about *Rai* see 16.11.4

16.11.1 Threats made on social media may not be credible

If publicity about a case has already led to threats of violent retribution against the defendant being posted on social media by members of the public, that in itself is not evidence of a 'real and immediate' risk to the person's safety. The High Court said that 'rhetoric and invective [from social media and online comments] is generally insufficient, without more, to amount to a credible threat of violence' (*RXG v Ministry of Justice and persons unknown* [2019] EWHC 2026 (QB)).

16.11.2 Are the public already aware of the case and the defendant's address?

If the nature of the charge(s) against a defendant and where they live are already known locally, there may be no point in banning publication of their home address if the alleged risk to them comes from that community.

In 2021 a district judge in Ballymena agreed with freelance reporter Tanya Fowles that it was pointless to use section 11 to ban publication of the address of a 53-year-old defendant, because it was already known in his community, where his alleged crime had led to 'high community tensions'.

For more detail of this Ballymena case, see the **additional material** for this chapter on **www.mcnaes.com**. See also online ch. 36 Other UK Jurisdictions for challenges by the same reporter after orders were made preventing the identification of convicted offenders.

16.11.3 Does the nature of a person's job put them at risk of attack?

Lawyers may argue in court that a party should have anonymity or that the media should not publish the party's home address because—it is said—the general nature of their job puts them at risk of attack or harassment.

Case study

In 2021 Mr Justice Nicklin refused to grant such anonymity to 216 people who were or had been employed by Members of Parliament. In that case they were suing the Independent Parliamentary Standards Authority, which paid their wages, because their names, salaries and other basic details of their employment, such as holiday entitlements, were by error published for just over four hours on its website. They claimed that this breached privacy, confidentiality and data protection law, and wanted the High Court to award them damages. Their lawyers argued that because of these claimants' employment by MPs, publication of identifying details in reports of the case could create a safety risk for them or expose them to the risk of other harm. But Mr Justice Nicklin said:

'There might exist a very small number of people whose attitude towards MPs (and those who work for them) is so hostile that they might conceivably be moved to offer some threat of physical violence to them, but this risk is remote. The claimants have not put forward any credible and specific evidence that one or more claimants is at particular risk of any such threat. The civil justice system and the principles of open justice cannot be calibrated upon the risk of irrational actions of a handful of people engaging in what would be likely to amount to criminal behaviour. If it did, most litigation in this country would have to be conducted behind closed doors and under a cloak of almost total anonymity. As a democracy, we put our faith and confidence in our belief that people will abide by the law. We deal with those who do not, not by cowering in the shadows, but by taking action against them as and when required.' (*Various claimants and Independent Parliamentary Standards Authority* [2021] EWHC 2020 (QB))

16.11.3.1 **Police and prison officers**

Lawyers in criminal cases defending police or prison officers have argued that their clients should have anonymity or that the media should not publish their home addresses because—it is said—this would put them at risk of attack or harassment from vengeful criminals.

Case study

Two senior police officers were charged in 2010 with misconduct in public office after alleged improper interference in prosecutions for speeding. They wanted a section 11 order to be made to ban publication of their home addresses. But Aldershot magistrates refused to make one. The officers sought judicial review, arguing that publication would put them at risk because of their past involvement in investigating serious crime. The High Court, refusing to make an order, noted that the Press Association, which with a regional media group had argued against a ban, had shown that anyone could use internet records of electoral registers, at a cost of £4.95, to discover the officers' addresses within five minutes. Any risk to the officers' safety, if it existed, would be from someone who targeted them, who would not be deterred merely because the media had not published the addresses, the Court said, adding that the type of charges the officers faced were unlikely to provoke a vigilante attack (*R (on the application of Harper and Johncox) v Aldershot Magistrates' Court and others* [2010] EWHC 1319 (Admin)).

For case studies of the media opposing anonymity for a police officer and prison officers, see the **additional material** for ch. 16 on **www.mcnaes.com**.

16.11.3.2 Police officers in court after firearm or taser incidents

Police firearms officers involved in fatal shootings while on duty have been given anonymity at inquests (for example, *R (on the application of Officer A and another) v HM Coroner for Inner South London* [2004] All ER (D) 288 (Jun)). But police officers involved in 'tasering' a man who died soon afterwards were not granted anonymity at an inquest. see the **additional material** for this chapter for details.

The Recorder of London decided in October 2023 that a Metropolitan Police firearms officer, Sergeant Martyn Blake, could be identified during his trial for the murder of Chris Kaba—who was shot and killed in a car in south London, in September 2022 (though there was a restriction in place to prohibit publication of his address and image). Following Sgt Blake's acquittal, the Government announced it would introduce a presumption of anonymity for firearms officers who face prosecution where they have discharged their firearm in the line of duty, in the Crime and Policing Bill. This measure was opposed by media organisations who said it would harm open justice. The Bill was still progressing through parliament when this book went to press—see www.mcnaes.com for updates.

16.11.4 Risk of suicide or self-harm

It may be argued on a defendant's behalf that they may be at risk of suicide or self-harm if their address or full identity is published. Even if there is evidence that the defendant has this state of mind, the court should take into account that this is unexceptional in such circumstances, and that medical and/or other measures (such as procedures to monitor a defendant who is in custody) can be taken to avert the risk. Again, it must be proved to the court that the risk is real and immediate for it to be the determinant factor in the decision on whether reporting is restricted.

In the *Rai* case cited earlier, the defendant said in a witness statement produced at the High Court hearing that she was concerned for her family and had been assessed to be at risk of suicide or serious self-harm. But the High Court, in a judgment upheld by the Court of Appeal, pointed out that no psychologist's report had been submitted, and said of her statement: 'Much of the evidence could be advanced, credibly, by any defendant facing a serious criminal charge as a basis for prohibiting publication of their address.' It added that her evidence 'does not come close to demonstrating

the High Court was told in the *Malvern Justices* case that the defendant had suicidal tendencies—see 15.6.1

convincingly an interference with her Article 8 rights of a sufficient weight or seriousness that displaces the Article 10 interest in open justice'. The Court of Appeal summarised her evidence as 'unexceptional'.

16.11.5 Anonymity based on fairness to witnesses who have safety fears

It might be argued in a civil or tribunal case or a public inquiry or an inquest that law should be used to provide anonymity in the proceedings and (consequently) in reports of them, for a witness who fears for their safety even though there is not a 'real or immediate risk' to them. Such arguments are based on the common law ground that the court has 'a duty of fairness' to witnesses to help them give evidence. Case law is that an assertion that the prospect of being identified has caused a witness to suffer ill-health (for example, depression or anxiety) should be tested by the court considering if medical evidence supports this (*Re Officer L*, cited earlier). For the statutory 'fear or distress' criterion as regards anonymity provision for witnesses in reports of criminal cases, see 16.14.2.1.

See also ch. 12 for details of anonymity given to witnesses during the trial of former nurse Lucy Letby for the murder of a number of babies in her care.

16.12 Challenging court orders giving a child or young person anonymity

As explained in ch. 10, courts have specific powers under two statutes to make an order banning publication of any detail likely to identify a child or young person as being concerned in a case. A child or young person is someone aged under 18.

When there are sufficiently strong, open justice reasons, or when such an order has been invalidly made or is over-broad, the media has made successful challenges against such orders being imposed or continued.

16.12.1 Challenging section 45 anonymity

for context on this anonymity power, see 10.4

Section 45 of the Youth Justice and Criminal Evidence Act 1999 gives a criminal court the power to ban publication of anything likely to identify a child or young person as being a defendant or witness or the victim/alleged victim of the crime/alleged crime in the case it is dealing with.

For example, Crown court judges routinely make a section 45 order pre-trial to bestow such anonymity on a defendant aged under 18.

Case law is that the welfare of a defendant aged under 18 is in itself a good reason to make a section 45 order (*Markham and Edwards v R* [2017] EWCA Crim 739—hereafter referred to as *Markham*, see case study below).But section 45(4) enables a court which has made the order to subsequently make an 'excepting direction' (counter-order) to revoke the order completely or vary the scope of its reporting restrictions to any extent the court specifies, if the court is satisfied this is necessary 'in the interests of justice'.

Section 45(5) enables a court to make an 'excepting direction' to revoke or vary the order if the court is satisfied:

> (a) that the effect of the section 45 order is to impose a substantial and unreasonable restriction on the reporting of the proceedings; and
>
> (b) that it is in the public interest to remove or relax that restriction.

Section 45 requires a court considering making such an order or an 'excepting direction' to have regard to the welfare of the child or young person.

Case study

In 2017 the Court of Appeal ruled that the media could name Kim Edwards and Lucas Markham, both 15, who together murdered Edwards' mother and sister. The Court said that preserving their anonymity would impose 'a substantial and unreasonable restriction' on the reporting of the case, and that it was in the public interest to remove that restriction. Markham admitted the murders, while Edwards pleaded guilty to manslaughter by reason of diminished responsibility but denied the two murder charges. An order under section 45 of the Youth Justice and Criminal Evidence Act 1999 granted anonymity to both Edwards and Markham in respect of any publication about the case throughout her trial, but this was lifted after Edwards was found guilty. Lifting the restriction, the judge concluded there was a strong public interest in full and unrestricted reporting of the case, and a high public interest in identifying Edwards and Markham because they were guilty of an exceptionally grave crime. The anonymity remained in place for a further six months because Edwards and Markham appealed against the lifting of the order, but the Court of Appeal upheld the decision to lift the anonymity (*Markham and another v R* [2017] EWCA Crim 739).

See the additional material for this chapter for more detail on the *Markham* case and other examples of such restrictions being lifted.

---

see 16.5 for the guidance

16.12.1.1 Challenges can be made at the conclusion of a case

Section 45 says that no 'excepting direction' shall be made merely because the case before the court has been 'determined in any way' or has been 'abandoned'. But, as the Judicial College guidance points out, the outcome of the case 'may be a very relevant consideration', and challenges to such orders are most commonly made once a defendant under the age of 18 has been convicted.

see also Useful Websites at the end of this chapter for the guidance

In *R v Aziz* [2019] EWCA Crim 1568, the Court of Appeal again had a sustained focus on circumstances justifying revocation of section 45 anonymity.

Case study

Eddie Ratcliffe and Scarlett Jenkinson were found guilty in December 2023 of the murder of 16-year-old Brianna Ghey. They were both 16 at the time of their trial at Manchester Crown Court, and were anonymised throughout by way of an order under section 45 of the Youth Justice and Criminal Evidence Act 1999. But media organisations challenged the order immediately following their conviction, and Mrs Justice Yip agreed it should be lifted. In her ruling, she said Brianna, who was transgender, had a significant social media profile and her killing attracted immediate interest from members of the public—which grew as the details of her brutal murder emerged—and the case was reported widely across the UK and abroad. The judge said full and accurate reporting of the proceedings served an important purpose in assisting public understanding. She also considered it a relevant factor that the widespread public interest in Brianna's killing would not have subsided by the time the reporting restrictions automatically expired when Ratcliffe and Jenkinson turned 18. The judge added: 'The shock generated by Brianna's murder and the circumstances of it has spread well beyond the local community, across the nation and indeed internationally. The public will naturally wish to know the identities of the young people responsible as they seek to understand how children could do something so dreadful. Continuing restrictions inhibits full and informed debate and restricts the full reporting of the case.' Mrs Justice Yip said there was a 'strong public interest' in full and unrestricted reporting of what was plainly an exceptional case, at the conclusion of the proceedings, and that continuing the restriction until they turned 18 would represent a 'substantial and unreasonable restriction on the freedom of the press'. The judge postponed the lifting of the order until she sentenced the pair in February 2024, in part so arrangements could be made to prepare them and their families for the consequences of being identified (*R v X and Y* [2023]).

16.12.1.2 How can section 45 anonymity be challenged as being a substantial restriction?

Any restriction banning reports of a case from identifying a person concerned in it deprives the public of some of the benefits of open justice—see 15.1.1. Beyond making that general point, a media organisation challenging the imposition or continuation of a section 45 order should, bearing in mind what section 45(5) says, illustrate to the court how 'substantial' the restriction is or would be.

The court should be told what significant detail, beyond the name of the child or young person, the anonymity requirement would prevent being reported in that particular case, and how that might reduce the public's understanding of the case and therefore reduce informed debate about it.

In *Markham*, Mr Justice Haddon-Cave—when lifting the section 45 order at the conclusion of the trial—said that if the media were unable to report Markham's and Edwards' identities, reporting of the trial would be deprived of meaning and context because it would be impossible for the public to properly to understand that the murders took place in a closed family context, leaving a vacuum 'which exacerbates the risk of uninformed and inaccurate comment'.

It can be strongly argued in other cases that the restriction is substantial if it would prevent the local community knowing whether a defendant convicted of a grave crime was local or not, or that such a crime took place within it, or knowing of an ongoing crime problem (for example, drug-dealing) which needs to be tackled in a particular location or school, or that it has been tackled, and how.

In such circumstances, a court—even if it does not agree to revoking the section 45 order in its entirety, may relax it—for example, by making it a term of the order that it does not prevent naming of the defendant's school.

If section 45 anonymity imposed for someone aged under 18 would prevent an adult defendant in the case from being identified, that too is a particularly 'substantial' restriction.

for context, see 16.9

16.12.1.3 How can section 45 anonymity be challenged as being an unreasonable restriction?

On what is 'unreasonable', a journalist can—as the media did in *Markham*—argue that a restriction which prevents a serious crime's circumstances being reported places an unreasonable burden on the media.

The journalist can also, as appropriate, cite case law outlined in 16.12.3 to argue that: anonymity should not be bestowed merely because of the age of a defendant, witness or victim/alleged victim; there must be a 'good reason' (such as their welfare) to provide it for that particular child or young person; it might be inappropriate to bestow it for a defendant if previous coverage has already legally identified them; an anonymity order is invalid if made in respect of a child or young person who is dead, or if it specifically seeks to ban identification of an adult defendant.

It can be argued that, because of the fundamental rule that a restriction on open justice should be 'necessary', imposing or continuing section 45 anonymity is unreasonable if it does nothing or little to protect the young person's welfare, because they will shortly reach the age of 18, when the anonymity automatically expires—see 10.4.1.1.

for context, see 15.6, Is it necessary to exclude or restrict?

If the defendant aged under 18 is to serve a long term in prison, this adds weight to this argument because the section 45 anonymity would be too short in its duration to be of help in their rehabilitation in the community—a point accepted by the Court of Appeal in *Markham* and *Aziz*.

In *Aziz*, the trial judge said he was unpersuaded that losing anonymity would have a significant detrimental effect on Aziz's treatment and/or rehabilitation, noting that the section 45 order was due to expire in less than a year, when Aziz turned 18, and that he would remain in custody for years beyond that date.

✱ Remember

The High Court has ruled that Parliament did not see such anonymity's function as being to help the defendant achieve rehabilitation after the age of 18 (*R (on the application of JC & RT) v Central Criminal Court* [2014] EWHC 1041 (QB)). However, rehabilitation was a factor which led to the Court granting lifelong anonymity to a teenager convicted of involvement in a foiled terrorist plot (*RXG*, cited above at 16.11.1).

16.12.1.4 The public interest in lifting or relaxing an anonymity order

Section 52 of the 1999 Act says that, in considering 'the public interest' when deciding whether section 45 anonymity should be revoked or relaxed, the court must have regard in particular, and as relevant, to the interest in the open reporting of crime and matters relating to human health or safety, and in the prevention and exposure of miscarriages of justice.

Particular arguments that can be made in the public interest against section 45 anonymity are:

Deterrence In some instances judges who revoked section 45 anonymity after the defendant was convicted have said that a reason for the revocation is the deterrent effect on others who may be at risk of committing such crime (as stated in *Aziz*, see earlier, and see too 16.12.3.1). The senior courts have recognised that if a report can identify the defendant this enhances its impact—see too 16.9.

The community has a right to know who perpetrated a serious crime, and its full circumstances Senior judges have said—for example, in *Markham*, and in *R v Crown Court at Winchester ex p B*, cited later—that when courts are dealing with serious crimes, the grave nature of the offending means there is a high public interest in identifying the offender.

Case study

In October 2025, Mohammed Umar Khan, 15, was jailed for life with a minimum term of 16 years at Sheffield Crown Court for the murder of 16-year-old Harvey Willgoose, a fellow pupil who he stabbed to death during lunch break at their school. Following a challenge by media organisations, Mrs Justice Ellenbogen lifted a section 45 order which had prevented Khan from being named during his trial. The judge said: 'The public will wish to know the identity of a person who commits such a serious offence, in seeking to understand how it is that a child of that age can do so. Knife crime in general and the circumstances of this particular case are matters of substantial public interest.' She concluded the order imposed a 'substantial and unreasonable restriction' on the reporting of the case and it was in the public interests to remove it. The order had previously been varied to allow the press to name the school throughout the trial *(R v Mohammed Umar Khan* [2025]).

✻ Remember

In *R v X and* Y, Mrs Justice Yip said it is clear from case law there is a strong presumption in favour of open justice and therefore the burden is on the defence to justify reporting restrictions. Again, the law's starting point is that it is in the public interest for all detail from a court case to be reported—see 16.8.1.

16.12.1.5 **In the interests of justice**

As said earlier, the 1999 Act says in section 45(4) that the anonymity order can be revoked if the court is satisfied this is necessary 'in the interests of justice'.

In *Aziz*, the trial judge (in a decision upheld by the Court of Appeal) ruled that the section 45 order should be revoked because the excepting grounds in both sections 45(4) and 45(5) applied.

A journalist opposing the imposition or continuation of a section 45 order can argue that it is usually in the interests of justice for proceedings to be as transparent as possible—see 15.1.1.

Case study

In January 2025, Alkhader Qasem, 17, and Ishaaq Mia, 16, were identified as the murderers of 17-year-old Prince Walker-Ayeni, who was stabbed to death in the street. Mrs Justice Ellenbogen said it was in the public interest to lift a section 45 order following an application by Andrew Bardsley, court reporter for the *Manchester Evening News*, who argued that knife crime is an issue of great concern to the wider public, and that naming the killers would assist in the debate of that serious societal issue. In a ruling made earlier but stayed until sentencing, the judge said the public would wish to know the identities of the killers as well as the context of the killing in order to try and understand how children can commit such serious offences. She was satisfied it was in the interests of justice to lift the restriction, which she considered imposed a 'substantial and unreasonable restriction' on the reporting of the case. She also said that whilst the principal aim of the youth justice system is to prevent offending or reoffending by children, that was not to say the deterrent effect on others was of no relevance or value *(R v Mohammed Umar Khan (Boy A)* [2025]).The Act's wording means that a section 45 order can be revoked 'in the interests of justice' even if the court does not rule under section 45(5) that the effect of the restriction is substantial and unreasonable.

16.12.1.6 **Crown Prosecution Service guidance on anonymity for defendants aged under 18**

see Useful Websites at the end of this chapter for this CPS guidance

CPS guidance to prosecutors accepts that in some cases letting the media identify a convicted (and therefore disgraced and punished) defendant aged under 18 can help deter others from committing crime.

16.12.2 International treaties do not trump case law

Articles 3 and 40 of the United Nations Convention on the Rights of the Child and Rule 8.1 of the United Nations Standard Minimum Rules for the Administration of Juvenile Justice (known as 'the Beijing Rules') have been cited in several cases by lawyers arguing for anonymity to continue for defendants aged under 18. Rule 8.1, for example, says that juvenile defendants' 'right to privacy' should be respected at all stages in order to avoid their being caused harm by 'undue publicity' or by the process of 'labelling' (stigmatisation). Some emphasis is placed on these treaties in the CPS guidance to prosecutors though the point can be made, as the following explanation shows, that emphasis is at variance with the Court of Appeal's approach.

In the *Markham* case—cited earlier in this chapter—lawyers arguing for the defendants to remain anonymous submitted that the Crown court judge who had decided to lift the section 45 order failed to have sufficient regard for these treaties. But the Court of Appeal said such submissions ignored the UK's own well-established law, which took into account the international dimension relating to the protection of children. The Court made clear that citing the two UN treaties did not trump UK case law.

16.12.3 Other case law on anonymity for children and young persons, including about section 39

for context on section 39, see 10.5

Section 39 of the Children and Young Persons Act 1933 is the power used in civil courts to ban in any publication the identification of a person aged under 18 as being concerned in the proceedings as a party and/or witness, although in April 2015 it was replaced in criminal courts by section 45 of the 1999 Act. Coroners can use section 39 to ban reports of inquests from identifying a witness aged under 18.

Case law on section 39 may be relevant in a challenge a journalist needs to make in a civil court or inquest to proposed or imposed anonymity for such a person, and can be cited too in challenges to orders made or proposed in criminal courts under section 45 of the 1999 Act, as the Court of Appeal made clear in *R v H* [2015] EWCA Crim 1579.

16.12.3.1 Principles to decide whether anonymity is justified

Lord Justice Simon Brown in *R v Crown Court at Winchester, ex p B* [2000] 1 Cr App R 11 identified the following seven principles a criminal court should consider when deciding whether to make or revoke an anonymity order as regards a defendant aged under 18:

(1) In deciding whether to impose or lift the reporting restrictions, the court will consider whether there are good reasons for allowing the defendant to be named.

(2) It will give considerable weight to the offender's age and the potential damage to this person of public identification as a criminal before they have the benefit or burden of adulthood.

(3) It must have regard to the defendant's welfare.

(4) The prospect of being named with the accompanying disgrace is a powerful deterrent and naming a defendant in the context of their punishment serves as a deterrent to others. These deterrents are proper objectives for the court.

(5) There is a strong public interest in open justice and in the public knowing as much as possible about what has happened in court, including the identity of those who have committed crime.

(6) The weight to be attributed to different factors may shift at different stages of the proceedings and, in particular, after the defendant has been found, or pleads, guilty and is sentenced. It may then be appropriate to place greater weight on the interest of the public in knowing the identity of those who have committed crimes, particularly serious and detestable crimes.

(7) The fact that an appeal has been made may be a material consideration.

16.12.3.2 **A section 45 or section 39 order cannot be in force if the person has turned 18**

The wording of section 45 of the 1999 Act and section 39 of the 1933 Act makes clear that these orders can only be made to give anonymity to a person aged under 18. Case law has made clear that anonymity provided by either power automatically expires when the person turns 18. So neither type of order can validly be made *after* the defendant reaches the age of 18.

See 10.4.1.1, on when section 45 anonymity ceases to apply, and 10.5.1 on when section 39 anonymity ceases to apply.

16.12.3.3 **There must be a good reason for an anonymity order**

A court should not make an anonymity order in a civil or criminal case automatically because of a witness's or victim's/alleged victim's age, or unthinkingly as a 'blanket' order covering all children and young people concerned in the proceedings, or on the basis of age alone retain section 45 anonymity after a defendant aged under 18 is convicted.

- In 1993 Lord Justice Lloyd pointed out that there should be a 'good reason' for such anonymity orders, because the 1933 Act made a distinction between section 49 anonymity, which automatically under the Act bans the identification of any child or young persons concerned in youth court proceedings, and section 39 anonymity, which is not automatic in other courts—'a distinction which Parliament clearly intended to preserve' (*R v Lee* [1993] 2 All ER 170, [1993] 1 WLR 103). This distinction was preserved in the creation of section 45 of the 1999 Act to replace—in criminal courts—section 39 of the 1933 Act, so the same point can be made about section 45 being used in Crown courts.

16.12.3.4 The identity of the child or young person is already in the public domain

In *R v Cardiff Crown Court, ex p M (A Minor)* (1998) 162 JP 527 (DC) the High Court ruled that if a section 39 order under the 1933 Act was not made when the case was first listed, publicity which has already identified the child or young person might make it inappropriate to make such an order at a later stage. The same reasoning will apply to orders under section 45 of the Youth Justice and Criminal Evidence Act 1999.

It may be significant that a young offender has publicly identified himself as a hardened criminal. But where an offender has been publicly identified due to breaches of an existing order (for example, on social media) courts will not consider this a proper basis to lift a restriction (see *R v X and Y*).

16.12.3.5 Is the child or young person concerned in the proceedings?

Neither a section 39 order nor a section 45 order is valid if the person for whom it is made is not 'concerned in the proceedings'. This means that criminal courts should not use section 45 to give a child or young person anonymity merely because their parent is the defendant, *unless* the child or young person is 'concerned' because they are a witness, or victim/alleged victim of the offence, or is the person 'in respect of whom the proceedings are taken'—for example, in a case of a parent prosecuted for failing to ensure a child attends school. For context, see 10.4.1.

In 2000 Mr Justice Elias said in the High Court:

> “Sadly, in any case where someone is caught up in the criminal process other members of the family who are wholly innocent of wrongdoing will be innocent casualties in the drama. They may suffer in all sorts of ways from the publicity given to another family member. But I do not consider that in the normal case that is a relevant factor or a good reason for granting a direction under section 39 (*Chief Constable of Surrey v JHG and DHG* [2002] EWHC 1129 (Admin), [2002] All ER (D) 308 (May)).”

The fact that such anonymity cannot validly be conferred on children not 'concerned in the proceedings' was also acknowledged in *Re S* [2003] EWCA Civ 963.

* Remember

It may be unethical to name a child in a report of a court case if they were not named in the proceedings. The Editors' Code says that relatives of people convicted or accused of crime should not generally be identified without their consent unless they are 'genuinely relevant' to the story. The Broadcasting Code says that children do not lose their right to privacy because of a parent's notoriety. See 4.11, Protecting children's welfare and privacy and 4.13, Relatives and friends of those accused of or convicted of a crime.

However, sometimes a defendant's children *are* relevant in a court case even when they are not 'concerned in the proceedings'. Moreover, the media—even if they do not intend to publish the name of a child—may have to challenge a section 45 order if its blanket ban on publication of any detail which could identify the child has a 'substantial and unreasonable' effect of preventing reports from identifying the adult defendant; or challenge or a section 39 order which has substantially restrictive effect on the reporting of a civil case or inquest.

Case study

The Court of Appeal in 2013 said that a judge at Swindon Crown court was wrong to impose a section 39 order banning the media from identifying a 15-year-old boy whose father—a former Army officer—was on trial for defrauding taxpayers. The Court said that the boy was not a witness or otherwise 'concerned in the proceedings' (*R v Robert Jolleys, ex p Press Association* [2013] EWCA Crim 1135). He was relevant to the reporting of the case because it was alleged in the trial that his father used the fraud proceeds to pay for all three of his sons to attend a private school.

16.12.3.6 An anonymity order cannot validly be made if the person is dead

Orders should not be made under section 45 of the 1999 Act or section 39 of the 1933 Act to provide anonymity for a child or young person who is dead. The Judicial College guidance says that for such an order to be validly made the person 'must be alive', referring to case law. Instances continue to occur of magistrates and judges needing reminders of this case law. If they are referred to the Judicial College guidance that should stop the imposition or continuation of such anonymity.

see this chapter's additional material for a recent case study

see Useful Websites at the end of this chapter for the guidance

Courts have purported to make such orders, following applications by prosecution or defence lawyers, or by a local authority asserting a 'child protection' role, in criminal cases when a parent is charged with murdering or causing the death of one of their children. It is often argued this is necessary to protect the defendant's other surviving children who are not 'concerned in proceedings' from publicity about the case. But, as explained earlier, neither section 45 or section 39 can be used to protect the welfare of any child or young person not 'concerned' in the case, and—as explained in 16.9—the principle of open justice means that a ban on the identification of an adult defendant (or what amounts to one due to the risk of jigsaw identification) is rarely justifiable.

16.12.3.7 Section 39 and section 45 orders cannot specifically give adults anonymity

The Court of Appeal ruled in 1991 that section 39 orders could not be used to specifically ban the publication of the identity of an adult defendant (*R v Southwark Crown Court, ex p Godwin* [1992] QB 190, [1991] 3 All ER 818), a ruling cited in 2014 by the High Court (*R (on the application of JC & RT) v Central Criminal Court* [2014] EWHC 1041 (QB)). The same reasoning will apply to orders under section 45 of the Youth Justice and Criminal Evidence Act 1999.

Lord Justice Glidewell said in *Godwin*:

> "In our view, section 39 as a matter of law does not empower a court to order in terms that the names of [adult] defendants should not be published... If the inevitable effect of making an order is that it is apparent that some details, including names of [adult] defendants, may not be published because publication would breach the order, that is the practical application of the order; it is not a part of the terms of the order itself."

for context, see 10.8.1, Cases of abuse within a family

In 2005 the Court of Appeal ruled there was no power under section 39 to prohibit identification of adults charged with sexual offences against children. But it warned of the danger of publishing material which might identify the children if the adult's name were published (*R v Teesside Crown Court, ex p Gazette Media Co Ltd* [2005] EWCA Crim 1983).

16.12.3.8 Victim is too young to need anonymity

The Judicial College guidance says of section 45 and section 39 powers: 'Age alone is not sufficient to justify imposing an order as very young children cannot be harmed by publicity of which they will be unaware...'

Courts have accepted that a baby or a toddler who is the victim/alleged victim of a crime does not need anonymity, because by the time they are old enough to be affected by the case's publicity it is likely to have been forgotten.

Case study

In 2013 the High Court upheld a refusal by Lowestoft magistrates' court to grant section 39 anonymity for a three-year-old girl in a case in which her mother, Tess Gandy, aged 35, was convicted of being drunk in a public place while in charge of the child. Gandy had been cautioned previously for a similar offence. Section 39 anonymity would have prevented the media identifying Gandy, a local councillor. The High Court ruled that the child was too young to be directly affected by publicity about her mother's conviction, and that open justice and the Article 10 rights of the media and public should prevail. The Court said it was 'speculative' to argue, as Gandy's lawyer had, that the girl might be distressed because she might read a report of the case online when she was older. It noted that Archant Community Media, which argued that it should be able in the public interest to identify Gandy as the defendant, pointed out that its policy was to remove from its websites reports of convictions after they became 'spent', if removal was requested (*R (on the application of A) v Lowestoft Magistrates' Court, with the Crown Prosecution Service and Archant Community Media Ltd as interested parties* [2013] EWHC 659 (Admin)).

for context, see 24.1, which explains when a conviction becomes 'spent'

16.12.3.9 Which proceedings are covered by an order?

In 1993 Lord Justice Lloyd in the Court of Appeal said the word 'proceedings' in section 39 must mean proceedings in the court making the order and not any proceedings anywhere (*R v Lee*, cited earlier). So, it can be construed that a section 45 order made in a magistrates' court does not apply to reports of the case when it reaches Crown court—but that the Crown court can make a new section 45 order. A journalist should check with the court whether it has or wants to.

16.12.3.10 An order must be clear about whom it protects

The child or young person covered by an anonymity order should be clearly identified in it, so the media can be clear about who it covers (*R v Central Criminal Court, ex p Godwin and Crook*, cited earlier, which concerned a section 39 order). And see 16.5.1, Precision.

16.12.4 Challenges to section 45A lifetime anonymity

As explained in 10.4.2, in April 2015 the Government inserted a new section—section 45A—into the Youth Justice and Criminal Evidence Act 1999, to give criminal courts a discretionary power, in certain circumstances, to ban any publication from identifying a specified child or young person in their lifetime as being concerned in a case as a witness or victim/alleged victim. In the same type of circumstances, section 46 of the same Act empowers a criminal court to grant such lifetime anonymity for an adult witness.

16.12.5 Challenges to anonymity in anti-social behaviour or criminal behaviour cases

There are grounds on which a journalist can argue that, to benefit a community, reports should be allowed to identify persons aged under 18 who are subject to anti-social behaviour injunctions or criminal behaviour orders. For detail, see the **additional material** for ch. 16 on **www.mcnaes.com**.

16.13 Challenges to youth court anonymity

for context, see 10.3.5, When section 49 anonymity ceases to apply

As 10.3 explains, section 49 of the Children and Young Persons Act 1933 gives all children or young persons 'concerned' in youth court proceedings, or in appeals from youth courts, automatic anonymity in media reports of or referring to such cases.

A youth court which convicts a defendant can, by using section 49(4A), lift the anonymity if satisfied that it is 'in the public interest' to do so.

In 1998 the Home Office and Lord Chancellor's Department issued a joint Circular, *Opening up Youth Court Proceedings*, which said that lifting the anonymity would be particularly appropriate in respect of a defendant aged under 18:

- whose offending was persistent or serious; or
- whose offending had had an impact on a number of people; or
- in circumstances when alerting people to their behaviour would help prevent further offending.

It said occasions when it would not be in the best interests of justice to lift section 49 anonymity included:

- when publicity might put the offender or their family at risk of harassment or harm;
- when the offender was particularly young or vulnerable;
- when the offender was contrite and ready to accept responsibility for their actions;
- when public identification of the offender would reveal the identity of a vulnerable victim and lead to unwelcome publicity for that victim.

16.14 Lifetime anonymity under the 1999 Act

Section 46 of the Youth Justice and Criminal Evidence Act 1999 gives a criminal court a discretionary power to ban all publications from including any detail likely to identify an individual aged 18 or older as being or having been a witness in the court's proceedings, with the ban lasting for the individual's lifetime, as explained in 12.8 of this book.

Section 45A gives a criminal court an equivalent anonymising power in respect of a witness or alleged crime victim aged under 18, as explained in 10.4.2.

Applications for a person to have either such anonymity are most likely to be made by the prosecution, but can be made by the defence.

16.14.1 Necessary conditions

Before a court makes a section 45A or 46 order, it must be satisfied that (here summarised):

- the quality of the person's evidence, or level of cooperation given by the person to any party to the proceedings in connection with that party's preparation of its case is likely to be diminished by reason of fear or distress in connection with being identified by members of the public as a witness/alleged victim in the proceedings.

The court must also consider whether it is in the interests of justice to make the order, as well as the public interest in avoiding imposing a substantial and unreasonable restriction on reporting of the case and, as regards section 45A, must consider the welfare of the child or young person.

For what else the court must consider before making either type of order, see 12.8 and 10.4.2. As outlined there, the effect of either type of order may be substantially restrictive on the reporting of the case's evidential detail, because of the requirement to avoid publication of any detail likely to identify the person.

16.14.2 Challenging section 45A or section 46 anonymity

Sections 45A and 46 say that a court can revoke—or relax the scope of—the order if satisfied that it is in the interests of justice to do so; or that its effect is to impose 'a substantial and unreasonable restriction' on the reporting of the case *and* that it is in the public interest to revoke or relax it. Some of what is said earlier in this chapter about grounds of challenge to the imposition or continuation of a section 45 order may be relevant to challenges to a section 45A or section 46 order, including as appropriate some of what is said about the terms 'substantial', 'unreasonable' and 'public interest'.

For example, the 1999 Act applies what its section 52 says about 'the public interest' to what a court must consider in decisions on whether to impose or revoke section 45A or section 46 anonymity.

for section 52 on 'public interest', see 16.12.1.4

However, the fact that a witness or alleged crime victim aged under 18 may be more vulnerable than an adult witness to the effects of publicity should make the media particularly cautious in instigating challenges to section 45A orders.

* Remember

A section 45A or 46 order cannot validly be made specifically to give a defendant anonymity. But the effect of such an order may be to prevent reports of the case from identifying the defendant—for example, if they were in a relationship with the witness or alleged crime victim—and/or from meaningfully conveying to the public the circumstances of the crime/alleged crime. See also 16.1, Why a challenge may be needed, and 16.9 about the open justice norm that an adult defendant should be identified in reports of criminal cases. As with challenges to section 45 anonymity regarding a witness, a journalist challenging section 45A anonymity may not want to publish the name of the young witness or alleged crime victim, but aims to ensure the report can identify the defendant.

A journalist wishing to challenge the imposition or continuation of a section 45A or 46 order should follow the rule 6.5(3) procedure in the Criminal Procedure Rules, explained in this chapter at 16.2.1.1, and—as relevant for the particular case—can make the following arguments.

16.14.2.1 Is there 'fear' or 'distress' and would the quality of evidence really be diminished?

A court's failure to consider procedurally whether the statutory conditions have been met—for example, whether evidence has been submitted about the person being in fear or distress about identification—means the section 45A or 46 order can be challenged as invalid.

Home Office Explanatory Notes to the 1999 Act state: 'Neither "fear" nor "distress" is seen as covering a disinclination to give evidence on account of simple embarrassment.' Because of Criminal Procedure Rule 6.4 and the 'necessity' principle (for both, see earlier in this chapter), the party asking the court for the anonymity must explain why it is needed.

on embarrassment, see too 15.6 and 16.10.6

16.14.2.2 Does the section 45A or 46 order serve much purpose?

The identity of a person for whom a section 45A or section 46 order has been made or proposed will in almost all cases already be known to defendant, and the defendant can therefore tell associates who the person is. In such cases, the only purpose of section 45A or section 46 anonymity would be to shield the person's identity from the rest of the population. A journalist can ask the court why the person's identity has to be protected if the defendant already knows it and can tell others.

16.14.2.3 Is the person due to give evidence?

There have been occasions when a court has made a section 46 order although it was already clear at that point that the person whose identity was thereby protected would not be giving evidence because the defendant had pleaded guilty—so there would not be any trial. If either a section 45A or section 46 order is made at that stage for a witness, it can be challenged on the ground that there is no longer a need to safeguard the quality of the person's evidence or level of cooperation. But if the order is made before the defendant pleaded guilty, it cannot be challenged merely on the ground that the guilty plea means there is no longer a need for it—sections 45A and section 46 say that such an order cannot be revoked or relaxed 'by reason only of the fact that the proceedings have been determined in any way or have been abandoned'.

> See the **additional material** for ch. 16 on **www.mcnaes.com** for case studies on successful challenges by the media to proposed or imposed section 46 anonymity.

16.14.3 Written consent to lift the lifetime anonymity

A person whose identity is protected by a section 46 order can give written consent to be identified in reports of the case—see 12.8.3.

A person whose identity is protected by a section 45A order can, after they reach the age of 18, waive the anonymity by giving written consent. For more detail, see 10.4.2.

16.15 Sexual offence law does not give anonymity to defendants

As ch. 11 explains, the Sexual Offences (Amendment) Act 1992 automatically bans the media from identifying victims and alleged victims of sexual offences. Occasionally magistrates and judges assert that the Act allows them to ban the media from identifying a defendant, insisting that anonymity for a defendant is necessary as an extra precaution to prevent media reports including detail likely to identify a victim/alleged victim. But there is no such power in the Act. The Judicial College guidance states this. The point was also made by the Court of Appeal in *R (on the application of Press Association) v Cambridge Crown Court* [2012] EWCA Crim 2434 and in *R v Jemma Beale* [2017] EWCA Crim 1012.

((•)) see Useful Websites at the end of this chapter for the College guidance

16.16 Challenging a 'derogatory assertion order'

Sections 38 and 39 of the Sentencing Act 2020 allow a court to make an order postponing the reporting of an assertion made by or for a defendant in a speech of mitigation or proceedings to appeal a sentence, if it decides there are substantial grounds for believing the assertion is derogatory of a person's character, and false or irrelevant—see 12.14.

> See the **additional material** for ch. 12 on **www.mcnaes.com** for more details of this reporting restriction and grounds of challenge if it is made invalidly.

Recap of major points

- A challenge to a reporting restriction can be made by a reporter addressing the court or by an editor writing to it. If this fails, the challenge can be taken to a higher court.
- An order under section 4(2) of the Contempt of Court Act to postpone media reporting of a case should only be made to avoid a substantial risk of prejudice to those proceedings or pending or imminent proceedings.
- An order under section 11 of the Contempt of Court Act 1981 should only be made if the relevant name or matter has already been deliberately withheld by the court from its public proceedings.
- A court order bestowing anonymity on safety grounds is only justified if the risk which publicity would create for that person is 'real and immediate', verified by evidence.
- A section 45 or section 39 anonymity order cannot be made in respect of an adult, and cannot be made in respect of a child or a young person who is dead. It can be argued that a baby or toddler is too young to need such anonymity.
- Journalists arguing for a youth court to permit reports of a case to identify a defendant aged under 18 can cite Home Office guidance on this.
- An anonymity order under sections 45A or 46 of the Youth Justice and Criminal Evidence Act 1999 should only be made if the witness or alleged victim is eligible, and if the order is needed to achieve the relevant section's purpose.

Useful Websites

Gov.uk, Criminal Procedure Rules and Practice Directions

Ministry of Justice, CPR—Civil procedure rules and Practice Directions, www.justice.gov.uk

Judicial College, www.judiciary.uk

- *Reporting Restrictions in the Criminal Courts*, 5th edition, as revised in July 2023 by the Judicial College, Media Lawyers Association, News Media Association and Society of Editors

Crown Prosecution Service (CPS), www.cps.gov.uk

- General guidance to prosecutors: on reporting restrictions 'Contempt of Court, Reporting Restrictions and Restrictions on Public Access to Hearings'

Online resources

Visit the online resources at **www.mcnaes.com** to test your knowledge of this chapter with **self-test questions** and a **flashcard glossary**, and to read **updates** about law and regulatory matters affecting journalism, as well as **additional material** to further your learning.

17

Coroners' courts

Chapter summary

Coroners investigate certain types of death to establish the cause. The inquests they hold are court hearings and can be newsworthy. This chapter outlines coroners' duties and explains why some inquests have juries. The Contempt of Court Act 1981 affects what can be reported, and coroners can impose reporting restrictions to give witnesses and children anonymity. Media coverage of inquests must be sensitive to the grief of the bereaved. In another role, coroners' courts decide whether a found object should be classed as historical 'treasure'.

17.1 Overview of the coroner system

A coroner—an office which dates from the twelfth century—is appointed to investigate the causes and circumstances of certain types of death, in some cases holding court hearings to do so. Their other role is to decide whether found historical objects should be classed as 'treasure'. Both types of hearing are called 'inquests'.

Coroners must have practised as a barrister or solicitor, or been a Fellow of the Chartered Institute of Legal Executives for at least five years. While some longer-serving coroners were not lawyers but practised as doctors, the Coroners and Justice Act 2009 says new coroners must be legally qualified.

Coroners serve districts known as 'areas' and are ranked as senior coroner and area coroner. They are often supported by assistant coroners.

17.2 Chief Coroner

The 2009 Act created the national post of Chief Coroner, currently held by Her Honour Judge Alexia Durran, whose duties include providing leadership for coroners, setting national standards for their work, approving coroner appointments (which are made by local authorities) and reporting annually to the Lord Chancellor on how the coronial system is performing.

17.3 Investigations into deaths

Under the 2009 Act a coroner must investigate certain categories of death: those for which they have reason to suspect that:

- the deceased died a violent or unnatural death,
- the cause of death is unknown, or
- the deceased died while in custody or otherwise state detention [which includes people held in police stations, prisons, immigration detention centres and mental hospitals].

'Violent or unnatural' deaths include those caused by crime, accidents, suicide, neglect or lack of care, excessive alcohol, drug abuse or any other form of poisoning. Police and doctors have a duty to report such deaths to the local coroner. Anyone concerned about the circumstances of a death can report it.

→glossary A coroner has the right in **common law** to take possession of a body, to make inquiries.

17.4 Inquests into deaths

Not all investigations require an inquest. There may be no need if, for example, a post-mortem examination shows that someone died of natural causes. But an inquest means a coroner can require witnesses to testify. Inquests help keep communities and institutions vigilant about fatal dangers and reassure the public that suspicious deaths are investigated. Inquest decisions on how people died are included in national statistics such as those for road accidents.

✱ Remember

An inquest is a fact-finding hearing to establish the reason for a death. It does not decide who, if anyone, might be criminally responsible—that is the role of the criminal courts. The civil courts decide if any party must pay damages to a deceased person's family.

A coroner's jurisdiction to hold an inquest arises from the fact that the body is in their area. A coroner must hold an inquest if a body has been brought into their area from abroad and they have reason to suspect the death was violent or unnatural—which is why the deaths of UK service personnel overseas lead to inquests in the UK.

17.4.1 Purposes of inquests into deaths

The purposes of an inquest into a death are to:

- determine who the deceased was;
- determine how, when and where they came by their death; and
- make 'findings' on the particulars about the death which have to be registered according to statute.

Establishing a deceased's identity is usually straightforward, but may require lengthy investigation if, for example, a decomposed body is found. The particulars which have to be communicated to the Registrar of Births, Marriages and Deaths include the deceased's name, the date and place of death, and their gender, age, address and occupation.

17.4.2 Inquests which have juries

In most inquests a coroner sits alone. But juries are called in some, to decide on facts, with the coroner presiding to rule on law and procedure. The practice of having juries in some types of inquests helps safeguard civil liberties and public health—for example, by providing outside scrutiny of police, prisons and workplace safety. The 2009 Act requires an inquest to be held with a jury if the senior coroner has reason to suspect that the death falls into one of these categories:

- the deceased was in custody or otherwise in state detention *and* the death was either violent or unnatural or the cause is unknown;
- the death resulted from an act or omission of a police officer or member of a police force of the armed services in the execution of their duty;
- the death was caused by one of the types of poisoning or disease or accidents, such as a workplace fatality, which by law must be notified to a Government department or inspector.

An inquest into any other type of death may also be held with a jury if the senior coroner thinks there is 'sufficient reason'. An inquest jury, selected randomly from electoral rolls, comprises at least seven and not more than 11 people.

17.5 Rules and Chief Coroner's guidance

The Coroners (Inquests) Rules 2013 govern inquest procedure. They are set out in a **statutory instrument** (SI 2013/1616).

→glossary

A coroner investigating a death by means of an inquest may hold three types of hearing—a 'pre-inquest review hearing' (rule 6), the inquest opening, and the full hearing, also known as a 'final' hearing (which may take place over more than one day and, in complex cases, last for weeks).

((•)) see Useful Websites at the end of this chapter for the Rules

The 'opening' is usually an initial, brief hearing for the coroner formally to ascertain the deceased's identity. The inquest can then be adjourned—there having already been a post-mortem examination and possibly burial or cremation—and is usually resumed after some weeks or months to hear evidence gathered about the circumstances of the death.

In January 2025, the Chief Coroner issued a 'Bench Book' with updated guidance on all aspects of court inquest work for coroners. Chapter 4 touches on documentary inquests and inquests in writing, Chapter 6 touches on remote hearings and Chapter 8 provides guidance on open justice.

17.5.1 Advance information about inquests

see Useful Websites at the end of this chapter

Rule 9 says the date, time and place of the inquest hearing must be 'publicly available' before it starts. The Chief Coroner's guidance says:

- the coroner must, in advance of a 'final' inquest hearing, and where possible seven days before it, publish online the date, time and place of the inquest, the name of the coroner, whether it is a jury inquest, the name and age of the deceased, and date and place of their death.
- Details of openings and pre-inquest review hearings should also be published, and at least one working day's notice of openings should be given. Notice should also be given of inquests in writing but giving a specific date or time for an inquest in writing is not required.

Case study

In 2017 Southwark Coroners' Court agreed to share with the media the recording of the opening of an inquest into the deaths of three terrorists shot dead by police, after media organisations complained they were given no advance notice of the hearing (*Press Gazette*, 27 June 2017). See 17.5.4.4 for more on recordings.

17.5.2 Open justice at inquests

Rule 11 says that generally any pre-inquest hearing and the inquest hearings must be held in public but that:

- a coroner may direct that the public be excluded from a pre-inquest review hearing if they consider it would be in the interests of justice or national security to do so, but the Chief Coroner's guidance states this must not be used 'for mere convenience';
- a coroner who does not have immediate access to a courtroom or other appropriate place in which to open the inquest may open it privately and then at the next hearing held in public announce that it has been opened;
- a coroner can direct that the public (including journalists) should be excluded from all or part of any inquest hearing if they consider that doing so would be in the interests of national security.

as regards exclusion, see too 17.9, Defamation and contempt issues in media coverage

The Chief Coroner's guidance says that any consideration of excluding the public from a hearing or imposing a reporting restriction should, where possible, be addressed at a pre-inquest review hearing. It says too that the media should be given due notice of the issue so they can object there to exclusion or restriction if they wish. If the coroner does direct that the public should be excluded from a hearing, then the outcome of the closed hearing should be announced in open court, giving a summary and brief reasons for any decision.

> See 17.10, Reporting restrictions, about media challenges to them. Arguments for open justice, some of which can be made against exclusion from any court, are listed in 15.1.1, Purposes of open justice.

17.5.2.1 Use of live links, hybrid and virtual hearings for inquests

The Judicial Review and Courts Act 2022 introduced provision for entirely 'virtual' or 'hybrid' inquest hearings, meaning some or all participants can attend remotely, but the coroner must be in the publicly accessible courtroom, as must the jury if there is one. The Police, Crime, Sentencing and Courts Act 2022 enables coroners to authorise, on a case-by-case basis, audio and audiovisual transmissions of inquests hearings (whether 'virtual', 'hybrid' or 'physical') for 'remote observation' by the public and journalists, and for coroners' courts to keep recordings of the transmissions. The Chief Coroner's guidance says that individuals (including members of the press) who want to observe an inquest remotely, do not have a right to do so and will need to explain why it is in the interests of justice to allow them to observe a hearing remotely when there is the option to attend in person.

for context of both 2022 Acts and on 'live links' 'physical', 'hybrid' and 'virtual', see 15.14

It is already the case that coroners can grant journalists access to audio-recordings of inquests, see 17.5.4.4.

✱ Remember

It will continue to be a specific, criminal offence to make an unauthorised transmission (including publication) or 'recording' (such as a photo, footage or audio-recording) of any image or sound in a court's authorised transmission of its proceedings, or to photograph, film or audio-record anyone watching or listening to the transmission or participating in the hearing by live link. Such activity may already be punished as a contempt of court. See 12.1.

17.5.2.2 Inquests in writing and open justice

The Judicial Review and Courts Act 2022 has allowed coroners to conclude certain inquests in writing, without a public hearing. This procedure was introduced to avoid stressful hearings for grieving families and its use has become increasingly prevalent in recent years. For example, in October 2025, the Isle of Wight County Press reported that the Isle of Wight coroner listed 35 inquests in writing in the space of two weeks. While ostensibly only 'non-contentious' inquests should be concluded in writing, journalists have found many newsworthy cases are being dealt with in this way.

A senior coroner can rule in specified circumstances that it is 'unnecessary' for an inquest to have a hearing, including if 'it appears to the coroner that no public interest would be served by a hearing' and if in that case 'no interested person has represented on reasonable grounds that a hearing take place'. Under the 2009 Act, a journalist is not an 'interested person' (see later). However, the Chief Coroner's guidance states that basic information about the inquest in writing should be published before it is conducted, to enable members of the public and press to make representations and/or request copies of documents. It adds that coroners should usually provide the 'Record of Inquest' (see 17.5.4.5) and the ruling—which contains information that attendees would have heard in court –if requested after concluding an inquest in writing. Coroners will need a strong justification for refusing to provide copies of the ruling to the public given the otherwise secretive nature of an inquest in writing. Journalists have found that the level of detail included in coroners' rulings can vary significantly depending on which coroner is concluding the inquest.

Case study

In 2025, the senior coroner for Buckinghamshire concluded an inquest in writing but refused to provide the Record of Inquest and ruling to freelance journalist (and McNae's co-author) Charlie Moloney. The coroner said this was to protect the deceased's family from 'any glare of publicity'. After Charlie sent the coroner a pre-action letter threatening judicial review, the coroner provided the documents, though reserved the right to refuse requests in future. The ruling provided included just over 200 words of detail. (*Law Society Gazette*, 4 March 2025)

17.5.3 'Live, text-based communications'

The Chief Coroner's guidance says journalists and legal commentators attending inquests are permitted to use phones and laptops for 'live, text-based communications'—that is, to post online (including social media), text and email—for the sole purpose of reporting the proceedings, But electronic devices should not be used in a manner that causes a disturbance or distraction in the courtroom, and the coroner retains full discretion to prohibit live, text-based communications from court if such a prohibition facilitates the administration of justice.

For context, including why such a ban could be imposed, see 12.2, Live, text-based communications. See 17.10, Reporting restrictions, for when a journalist can use an audio-recorder for note-taking purposes at an inquest.

17.5.4 The airing of evidence and access to inquest material

Unlike the criminal courts, where the process is accusatorial, adversarial and subject to strict rules on how evidence is given, an inquest is inquisitorial. The coroner can 'lead' witnesses through their evidence.

17.5.4.1 Written evidence

Rule 23 allows a coroner to take written rather than oral evidence from any witness if satisfied that the evidence is unlikely to be disputed, or that it is not possible for the witness to attend, or to do so within a reasonable time, or that there is a 'good and sufficient reason' why they should not attend or for the coroner to believe that the witness will not attend. For example, the coroner may decide that a busy hospital doctor need not testify in person at an inquest into a death.

But the rule says a coroner accepting written evidence must announce at the inquest the nature of the evidence and the witness's full name. Any 'interested person' is entitled to see a copy of any written evidence. Definitions of 'interested persons' are listed in section 47 of the Coroners and Justice Act 2009, and include relatives of the deceased (but not journalists).

Rule 23 adds that: 'A coroner may direct that all or parts only of any written evidence submitted under this rule may be read aloud at the inquest hearing.'

17.5.4.2 Inspection or copying of case material

Coroners generally read written evidence aloud if the witness does not attend in person. But if it is referred to in the inquest, but not read out, a journalist would have a strong argument to be allowed to have access to it, because of the open justice rule in common law, reflected in the decisions of the Supreme Court in *Cape Intermediate Holdings Ltd v Dring (for and on behalf of Asbestos Victims Support Groups Forum UK)* [2019] UKSC 38 (referred to hereafter as *Dring*), and of the Court of Appeal in *R (Guardian News and Media) v City of Westminster Magistrates' Court* [2011] 1 WLR 3253, [2011] EWCA Civ 1188. A journalist applying to see any type of case material referred to or shown at the inquest should cite these decisions, which acknowledge the media's 'watchdog role'.

The Chief Coroner's guidance says that if a 'bona fide' journalist requests access to any document (including witness statements) which have been referred to in the course of proceedings, there is a presumption in favour of disclosure.

The Chief Coroner's guidance also says journalists may be given access to other types of case material referred to or shown in the inquest—for example, voice recordings and images from CCTV and body worn recorded footage; and '**skeleton arguments**' and written legal submissions which have been put before the court on behalf of the interested persons. It says too that the precedent set by the *Guardian News and Media* case means that a coroner should normally accede to a media request for access to such case material, unless there is a compelling reason not to. →glossary

The Chief Coroner's guidance says that—since it is not an offence to photograph an inanimate object in the court precincts—journalists may be permitted to use their mobile devices to photograph court documents to which they are entitled and coroners should generally facilitate this when requested. A coroner may have reason to restrict the use to which the photograph of a document is then put. The use might, for example, be limited to aiding accurate media reporting of the precise text of a long document.

It is incorrect to say the media are 'entitled to disclosure' or that it should take place 'by default'. A coroner can refuse disclosure requests 'for good and justifiable reasons'. In the *Guardian News and Media* case it was described as 'some strong contrary argument' or 'countervailing reasons'. The coroner must make these decisions on a case by case basis, document by document, noting the presumption of disclosure and bearing in mind the important role of the press as 'public watchdog' in a democratic society. It is advisable to make access requests in writing.

The rules permit a coroner to redact a document before disclosure—for example, to avoid prejudice to related criminal proceedings.

see too 17.7, Related criminal proceedings. Prejudice is covered in ch. 19 on contempt of court

Any concern about potential breach of copyright is not a good reason to refuse a journalist access to an inquest document. Copyright law has an exception for court reporting—see 29.10, Copying to report Parliament and the courts.

For context, see 15.2, The media's role in open justice. More detail of the *Dring* and *Guardian News and Media* cases is in 15.19, Case law on journalists' access to case material or records from any court's proceedings.

The **additional material** for this chapter on **www.mcnaes.com** includes a case study of *Buzzfeed*'s successful application to see case material referred to during the 2018 inquest into the death of a Russian businessman.

17.5.4.3 Names

The Chief Coroner's guidance also says that the first and last names of the deceased, of witnesses (unless granted anonymity) and of 'interested persons' will always be given in open court, and therefore to the media.

17.5.4.4 Official recordings of inquest proceedings

The 2013 Rules require coroners to keep an audio-recording of every inquest hearing, including 'pre-inquest reviews'. The Coroners (Investigation) Regulations (SI 2013/1629) allow a copy of such a recording to be provided to anyone considered by the coroner to be 'a proper person to have possession of it'. The Chief Coroner's guidance says coroners have a discretion whether to provide a recording and should decide on a case by case basis. A coroner needs to be satisfied there are reasonable grounds for disclosure, but the presumption of openness for court proceedings 'gives rise to a presumption of disclosure'. A £5 charge can be made for the copy. It would be a contempt of court to broadcast or webcast the official or any unauthorised (illegal) recording, or to play it to any section of the public, as explained in 12.1 of this book.

Case study

In 2022, broadcaster Jamie Bartlett applied to the Senior Coroner for Inner North London for an audio recording of an inquest held at St Pancras Coroner's Court on 16 November 2018. The request was declined on the basis Jamie was not an interested person, but the coroner said given the nature of the inquest—which touched upon the death of a charity founder who had faked having a brain tumour—permission was granted for Jamie and his team to attend the court and listen to the recording. They employed a court stenographer to make a full transcript of what they heard. (BBC, 8 May 2023).

17.5.4.5 'Record of inquest'

The Chief Coroner's guidance says members of the press should be allowed to inspect and copy the completed 'Record of Inquest'—that is, the official document recording the 'findings', the 'determination' and 'conclusion' of an inquest.

see 17.4.1, Purposes of inquests into deaths, on what particulars are in 'findings'

17.6 Determinations and conclusions—formerly 'verdicts'

An inquest produces a 'categorising decision' reached by the coroner (or the jury if there is one) on what caused a death. These decisions, announced at inquests, were traditionally referred to as 'verdicts' but are now referred to as 'conclusions'. It has become the convention to report that a coroner's jury *returns* a conclusion and that a coroner sitting without a jury *records* a conclusion. Some journalists continue to use 'verdict' colloquially, though 'conclusion' is now the official term for the categorising decision.

Conclusions can, as was the case with verdicts, be expressed in 'short-form', comprising one or two words or short phrases including 'natural causes', 'accident', 'road traffic collision', 'misadventure', 'drug-related', 'industrial disease', 'unlawful killing' or 'suicide'. An 'open' conclusion is recorded or returned when an inquest decides there is insufficient evidence for any other conclusion.

17.6.1 Narrative conclusions

Narrative conclusions are simply a number of words that make up a brief factual statement of how the deceased came by their death. They should generally be used where using a short-form conclusion is insufficient to 'record as many of the facts concerning the death as the public interest requires'.

→glossary

The use of such narrative conclusions also fulfils a requirement that a coroner should allow a jury to express a brief conclusion about disputed facts at the centre of the case, so that inquest procedure complies with Article 2 of the European Convention on Human Rights, the right to life, on the principle that a jury must be able to express conclusions in a way which can help avoid similar loss of life. Coroners may also make concluding remarks to focus public attention on lessons to be learnt from a death.

for context, see 1.3, The European Convention on Human Rights

17.6.2 Reports to prevent other deaths

Coroners have a legal duty to produce reports for the Chief Coroner if an inquest has revealed circumstances which could continue to place lives at risk. The reports are published on www.judiciary.uk.

17.7 Related criminal proceedings and public inquiries after deaths

When someone is suspected of crime in connection with a death, an inquest is usually opened, then adjourned until after any criminal proceedings have ended. The inquest may then be resumed if there is sufficient cause. For example, if someone accused of a murder is acquitted, an inquest may subsequently return a conclusion of 'unlawful killing' while not attributing blame.

If a public inquiry is instigated under the Inquiries Act 2005 to consider why a person or people died—for example, in a rail crash or terrorism attack—the Lord Chancellor can direct that any inquest into the death(s) should be adjourned. This happened when a public inquiry was instigated to investigate the terrorist attack at Manchester Arena in 2017 which killed 22 people. In these circumstances, the inquest will not be reopened unless there is an exceptional reason.

The law on public inquiries is outlined in ch. 18 and its **additional material** on **www.mcnaes.com**.

17.8 Review of inquest decisions

There is no direct route of appeal against an inquest decision, but an aggrieved person with sufficient legal interest in the case—for example, a deceased's next of kin—can apply to the High Court for **judicial review**. This could result in that court making an order to quash an inquest's decisions and to order that a fresh inquest should be held.

→glossary

17.9 Defamation and contempt issues in media coverage

→glossary

for context, see 22.5, Absolute privilege, and 22.7, Qualified privilege by statute

Inquests are court proceedings, so the defence of absolute **privilege** will protect from any defamation action a fair, accurate and contemporaneous report of an inquest held in public. Non-contemporaneous reports are protected by qualified privilege if the requirements of that defence are met. The privilege will cover material reported from documents which the coroner has made available to aid coverage, if the relevant defence's requirements are met.

Publication of what is said or material considered in any part of an inquest held in private will not be protected by statutory privilege in defamation law and—if the inquest is being conducted in private on national security grounds—could be deemed a contempt of court as a breach of section 12 of the Administration of Justice Act 1960, as explained in 12.6, Ban on reporting a court's private hearing.

An inquest is covered by the Contempt of Court Act 1981 (the 1981 Act). As explained in ch. 19, it is a contempt to publish material which creates 'a substantial risk of serious prejudice or impediment' to an active case. The Court of Appeal has ruled that an inquest becomes 'active' when it is opened (*Peacock v London Weekend Television* (1986) 150 JP 71). It seems unlikely that media reports—when the inquest is 'active'—which probe the death's circumstances would prejudice a coroner, an experienced professional, in their considerations. But the media should take care, in a case in which a jury is or could be involved, not to publish material which creates a substantial risk of serious prejudice to its deliberations, or material which could breach the Act by affecting a witness's testimony in any inquest, or which could create a risk of impediment by deterring people from offering evidence. For risks of committing common law contempt, see 19.3.

An inquest might occur before a hearing in a criminal court into the same events—for example, an inquest might be opened, then adjourned, because someone is charged with murdering the deceased. The media can safely report that inquest hearing contemporaneously if it is held in public, because the report—provided it is fair, accurate and published in good faith—will be protected by section 4(1) of the Act.

for context, see 19.9, Court reporting—the section 4 defence, and 19.10, Section 4(2) orders

17.10 Reporting restrictions

Coroners can make orders restricting media reports of inquests—for example, to give anonymity to a witness aged under 18, as explained in 10.5.

Coroners also have **inherent jurisdiction** in common law and under Articles 2 and 3 of the European Convention on Human Rights to order that a witness should have anonymity at inquests—for example, to prevent a real and immediate risk to their life (*R (on the application of Officer A) v HM Coroner for Inner South London and others* [2004] EWHC Admin 1592). Article 8 rights—for protection of family life—may also be cited. Police firearms officers have been given anonymity after fatal shootings.

→glossary

the 'real and immediate' criterion is explained in 16.11.1

Powers which coroners can use to restrict reporting include some listed in ch. 12, Court reporting—other restrictions. The Chief Coroner's guidance tells coroners that when possible the media must be given opportunity to argue against a reporting restriction—see too 17.5.2, Open justice at inquests. Ch. 16, Challenging in the courts, lists grounds on which invalid or over-broad restrictions can be challenged by the media and explains the significance in this context of Convention Articles 2, 3, 8, and 10.

> See the **additional material** for this chapter **www.mcnaes.com** for a 2015 case study involving five media organisations which successfully opposed an application by Greater Manchester Police for anonymity for five officers due to give evidence at an inquest into the death of a man who died shortly after being tasered by one of them.

Common law and statutory protections of witnesses and jurors apply to inquest proceedings, such as the automatic ban on photography, filming and audio-recording in courts. Ch. 12 explains these laws. For the common law on note-taking, see 15.10. The Chief Coroner's guidance says that requests by bona fide journalists to make a recording of a hearing 'should be treated sympathetically'. A coroner can permit a journalist to record proceedings but only 'for ensuring accurate media reporting', and the recording must not be used for broadcast or any other purpose.

Part 1A of Schedule 6 to the Coroners and Justice Act 2009 protects the confidentiality of an inquest jury's deliberations. This law is, in essence, the same as law in the Juries Act 1974, which covers other courts—see 12.3, Confidentiality of jury deliberations.

17.10.1 Media challenges to reporting restrictions or lack of access

A media challenge to reporting restrictions imposed by a coroner, or to a decision to exclude the media from an inquest, must—if the coroner refuses to reconsider—be made to the High Court as an application for judicial review—see 16.6.2.1, Judicial review by the High Court of restrictions imposed by magistrates or coroners.

17.11 Ethical considerations when covering deaths

chs. 2 and 3 introduce these codes and the relevant regulators

Some parts of the Editors' Code of Practice, the Broadcasting Code and the Impress Code, which set out ethical standards, are particularly pertinent to help prevent journalists from aggravating the grief of the bereaved. See 4.7.1, Prohibitions on intrusion into grief or shock.

Also, each code warns that coverage of any suicide—for example, in reports of an inquest hearing—must not include excessive detail about the method used. This is to avoid people copying such methods, as research has found that media coverage of suicides can lead to others taking their own lives in the same way.

Clause 5 of the Editors' Code says: 'When reporting suicide, to prevent simulative acts care should be taken to avoid excessive detail of the method used, while taking into account the media's right to report legal proceedings.' The clause is covered by the Code's public interest exceptions.

Rule 2.5 of the Broadcasting Code says that methods of suicide must not be included in programmes except when justified editorially and by context.

Clause 9.1 of the Impress Code says: 'When reporting on suicide or self-harm, publishers must not provide excessive details of the method used or speculate on the motives.' There is no public interest qualification to this clause.

> For what a regulator may regard as excessive detail about suicide methods, see case studies in the **additional material** for ch. 17 on **www.mcnaes.com**. For guidance published by Ipso, Impress and the Samaritans charity on covering suicides, including those which happen at outdoor locations, see Useful Websites at the end of this chapter.

17.12 Treasure inquests

The Treasure Act 1996 empowers coroners' courts to determine whether historical objects found on or buried in the ground should be classed as 'treasure'. Those who find such objects—for example, metal-detectorists—must declare discoveries so that museums can decide if they want the articles. If they do, a reward based on the find's value is paid to the finder and, possibly, the landowner. The Act has various definitions of treasure, including:

- a found object which is not a single coin, is at least 300 years old and contains at least 10 per cent gold or silver, and any other object found with it.

- any object at least 200 years old when found, which is considered to be of outstanding historical, archaeological or cultural importance (regardless of its material composition).

For more detail on treasure inquests, see the **additional material** for ch. 17 on **www.mcnaes.com**. Government guidance is in Useful Websites at the end of this chapter.

Recap of major points

- The purposes of an inquest into a death are primarily to find out who a deceased person was and how they died.
- A coroner can exclude the public and journalists from an inquest on the ground of national security.
- Coroners can impose reporting restrictions.
- Inquests are court hearings and so are covered by the law of contempt of court, which can affect media coverage.
- A treasure inquest decides if a found historical object should be classed as 'treasure', in which case a museum is given the opportunity to acquire it.

Useful Websites

Coroners (Inquests) Rules 2013, www.legislation.gov.uk

- 'When a death is reported to a coroner'—Government guidance on inquests into deaths
- 'Report treasure'—Government guidance on treasure, including definitions

Courts and Tribunals Judiciary, Chief Coroner's Guidance for Coroners on the Bench http://www.judiciary.uk

'Chapter 8: Open Justice'

'Chapter 5: The Inquest Hearing'

The Coroners' Society of England and Wales, www.coronersociety.org.uk

Independent Press Standards Organisation (Ipso), www.ipso.co.uk

- Deaths and inquests guidance
- Reporting suicides guidance
- Samaritans' guidance in Ipso blog on reporting suicides that take place at outdoor locations

Impress, Standards Code and guidance, www.impressorg.com

Samaritans' media guidelines for reporting suicide, www.samaritans.org

Inquest, www.inquest.org.uk

A charity providing advice to the bereaved on contentious deaths

Online resources

Visit the online resources at **www.mcnaes.com** to test your knowledge of this chapter with **self-test questions** and a **flashcard glossary**, and to read **updates** about law and regulatory matters affecting journalism, as well as **additional material** to further your learning.

18

Tribunals and public inquiries

Chapter summary

Tribunals are specialist judicial bodies which decide disputes in particular areas of law. The UK has a wide range of tribunals with a huge annual caseload which can yield news, including human interest stories. For example, tribunals adjudicate in asylum and immigration cases, on rents tenants can be charged, on benefit entitlements and in employment disputes, and on whether a patient in a secure mental health hospital is safe to return to the outside world. Some tribunals are termed a 'commission' or 'panel'. Some regulate professions and decide, for example, whether doctors or lawyers should be banned from practising because of misconduct. A 'public inquiry' is an investigatory process into a matter of public concern.

18.1 Introduction

There is a wide range of tribunals. Most tribunals are official bodies which make decisions determining someone's legal rights.

More than 40 types of these are in the UK's 'administrative justice' system—administered by His Majesty's Courts and Tribunals Service (HMCTS). This system's annual workload can exceed 400,000 cases. Its tribunals are grouped into several categories (chambers)—see Figure 18.1. The majority rule on disputes between an individual, or a private organisation, and a state agency—for example, about tax obligations, benefit entitlements, educational issues or immigration status. Increasingly, to cut costs and for other reasons, they are using 'hybrid' and 'virtual' hearings (see 15.14), in which parties and other witnesses participate from locations remote from the judge/panel members.

Tribunals listed here are among those which may be of particular interest to journalists.

Figure 18.1 Tribunals organisation chart

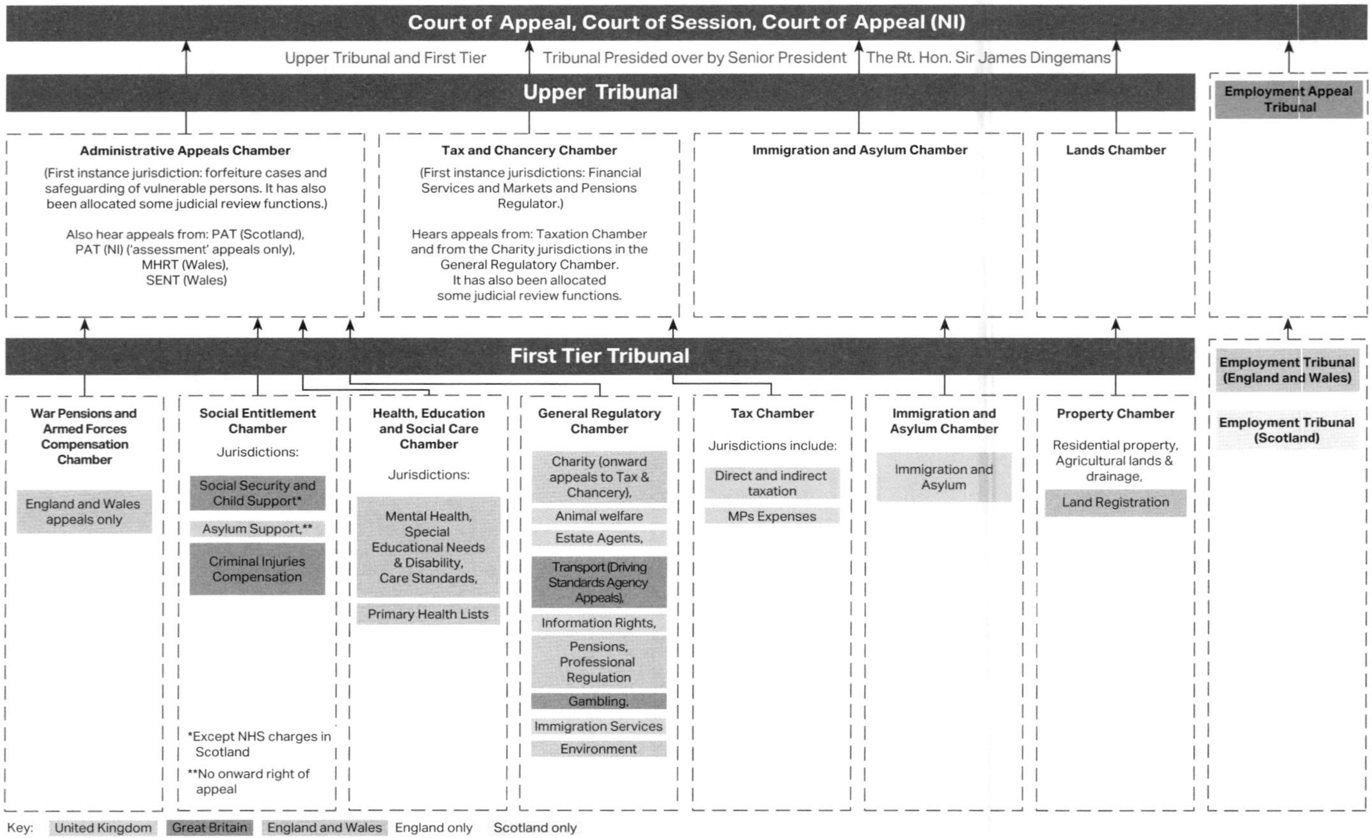

Source: Adapted from the January 2023 chart accessed on judiciary.uk website. © Crown Copyright.

Health, Education and Social Care Chamber of the First-tier Tribunal This hears, for example, appeals from people who have been banned from working for organisations concerned with children and vulnerable adults. It includes the First-tier Tribunal (Mental Health) for England, which hears appeals from patients detained under the Mental Health Act 1983 for release from secure mental hospitals. That tribunal usually sits in private and has a rule that information from and the names of patients in its cases must not normally be made public. Wales has a separate Mental Health Review Tribunal.

Property Chamber (Residential Property) of the First-tier Tribunal This hears, for example, appeals against rent levels fixed by a rent officer for regulated tenancies.

The First-tier Tribunal is a generic tribunal created to merge the administration of most tribunals dealing with appeals against decisions made by state officials. First-tier Tribunal decisions may, in some instances, be appealed to, or be reviewed by, the next tier of the administrative justice system, the Upper Tribunal.

18.2 Tribunals classed as courts

A tribunal is classed as a court if it exercises 'the judicial power of the State'—a definition in section 14 of the Defamation Act 1996 and section 19 of the Contempt of Court Act 1981. Many tribunals do have this power, including all those in the HMCTS system.

One noteworthy tribunal outside of the First-tier/Upper Tribunal structure is the Special Immigration Appeals Commission (SIAC), a court which hears appeals against Home Office decisions to deport, or exclude, people from the UK on national security or public interest grounds, and appeals against decisions to deprive people of UK citizenship.

18.3 Open justice and rules on exclusion

Each tribunal type has its rules. Those which are courts have rules set out in **statutory instruments** covering, for example, when the tribunal can sit in private. For further detail on rules, see the **additional material** for this chapter on **www.mcnaes.com**.

→glossary

for context on remote hearings and use of live links, see 15.14

18.3.1 Journalists' access to case material

As landmark judgments by the Court of Appeal and Supreme Court have made clear, the open justice rule in common law gives journalists a presumptive right of access to case material, including documents, referred to in all types of court, including tribunals—see 15.19. This applies in respect of hearings held in public, even when a journalist did not attend. Access to documents may well be crucial for a journalist to fully understand a tribunal's proceedings. But a tribunal may rule in a particular case that this right of access is outweighed by the risk of harm which such access may cause to the effective judicial process or to the legitimate interests of anyone else—for example, a privacy right.

For a case study of a journalist using this common law right to gain access to a tribunal case document, see the **additional material** for this chapter on **www.mcnaes.com**.

for context on 'accredited' see 15.9 and for employment tribunals, see 18.7

18.3.2 HMCTS guidance and case listings

HMCTS has issued guidance to its staff to support media access to tribunals in the administrative justice system and employment tribunals. For example, it says dates of hearings and (usually) the names of those involved can be released in advance to accredited journalists making inquiries. It shows which tribunals have advance lists of cases and where tribunal decisions are online. See Useful Websites, at the end of this chapter, for the guidance.

18.4 Examples of disciplinary tribunals

The disciplinary tribunals of regulated professions are not part of the administrative justice system but have powers derived from statute. Examples are:

Medical Practitioners Tribunal Service This tribunal of the General Medical Council hears complaints against doctors in its 'fitness to practise' panels. These normally sit in public, but can sit in private—for example, when considering confidential information concerning a doctor's health.

Solicitors Disciplinary Tribunal This must, in general, sit in public to hear allegations of professional misconduct against solicitors. But it can in some circumstances exclude the public from all or any part of a hearing.

For these two tribunals, see Useful Websites at the end of this chapter. For more detail on the disciplinary tribunals or panels for professions—for example, barristers, nurses and police—and case law on which are classed as courts, see the **additional material** for this chapter on **www.mcnaes.com**.

for detail of these defamation defences—see 22.5, Absolute privilege and 22.7, Qualified privilege by statute, and for the Schedule see Appendix 2

18.5 Defamation issues in reporting tribunals

For tribunals classed as 'a court', a fair and accurate media report of proceedings held in public, if published contemporaneously, is protected by absolute privilege under the Defamation Act 1996. A non-contemporaneous report is protected by qualified privilege under Part 1 of the Act's Schedule 1, with no requirement to publish 'explanation or contradiction'.

In the case of any tribunal constituted by or under, or exercising functions under, statutory provision, a media report of its public proceedings will be protected by qualified privilege under paragraph 11 of Part 2 of Schedule 1 to the Defamation Act 1996 if all the requirements of that defence are met. One requirement is that a publisher, if asked by anyone who claims to have been defamed by the report, must publish a reasonable letter or statement of explanation or contradiction from that person. This type of qualified privilege also protects fair and accurate reports of the findings (but not of the proceedings) of the disciplinary committees of certain private associations—for example, in the field of sport, business and learning.

18.6 Automatic restrictions which apply if the tribunal is a court

The Contempt of Court Act 1981 automatically applies in respect of any 'active' case being dealt with by a tribunal which is classed as a court. This means that the media must not publish material which could create 'a substantial risk of serious prejudice or impediment' to such a case. The 1981 Act is explained generally in ch. 19. The Act says a tribunal case is 'active' 'from the time when arrangements for the hearing are made or, if no such arrangements are previously made, from the time the hearing begins', and remains 'active' until 'the proceedings are disposed of or discontinued or withdrawn'.

18.6.1 Ban on reporting the private proceedings of some types of tribunal cases

If a tribunal is classed as a court, what is said in its private hearings or in documents prepared for them is covered by section 12 of the Administration of Justice Act 1960 as regards the types of cases which that law specifies. This means that for those types, which include mental health tribunal hearings, it is normally a contempt of court to report what was said in those hearings or documents, though a tribunal can decide to allow such reporting in a particular case—see 12.6.

for liability for readers' postings which breach anonymity provision, see ch. 30

18.6.2 Reporting restrictions and other restrictions

As mentioned, each type of tribunal has rules—see 18.3. In some circumstances, these enable them to give people anonymity in proceedings and to impose reporting restrictions forbidding their identification.

Taking photographs or filming at a tribunal classed as a court, or in the building or its precincts is illegal, and it is illegal to audio-record such a tribunal's proceedings without permission. These laws are covered in 12.1, and there are similar offences associated with 'hybrid' and 'virtual' hearings (see 15.14 for details on these types of remote hearing).

For more detail of how restrictions may affect the reporting of tribunal cases, see the **additional material** for this chapter on **www.mcnaes.com**.

18.7 Employment tribunals

Employment tribunals, which are a type of court, adjudicate on complaints against employers such as unfair dismissal, or discrimination because of the employee's gender, race or age. They are administered by HMCTS but are not part of the First-tier/Upper Tribunal structure—see Figure 18.1. Appeals challenging tribunal decisions can be made to the Employment Appeal Tribunal (EAT).

The automatic bans on photography, filming and audio-recording apply in respect of employment tribunals and the EAT—see 12.1.

The HMCTS guidance to staff points out that accredited journalists can normally see case documents—see Useful Websites at the end of this chapter, and what 18.3.1 says about the law.

18.7.1 Rules of employment tribunals

Rules governing employment tribunals and the EAT allow them to sit in private for some reasons—for example, national security or to protect a person's privacy. The rules are in the Employment Tribunals (Constitution and Rules of Procedure) Regulations 2013.

((•)) for the 2013 rules, see Useful Websites at the end of this chapter

Rule 50 empowers employment tribunals to make an order 'with a view to preventing or restricting the public disclosure of any aspect of those proceedings' if the tribunal considers it necessary 'in the interests of justice' or in order to protect the rights in the European Convention on Human Rights—including privacy rights—of any person. Rule 50 also gives employment tribunals discretionary power to make temporary anonymity orders in cases involving allegations of sexual misconduct—for example, that a woman was forced to leave her job because her boss sexually harassed her—and in disability cases.

The **additional material** for this chapter on **www.mcnaes.com** gives more detail of employment tribunal and EAT rules, including rights which journalists have to challenge restrictions.

* Remember

The Sexual Offences (Amendment) Act 1992 means that anyone in employment tribunal or EAT proceedings who is, or is alleged to be, a victim of a sexual offence must not be identified in media reports of the case in their lifetime, unless they have given valid written consent for this. This law is explained in ch. 11.

18.8 Public inquiries

Public inquiries can be broadly categorised either as local inquiries, set up routinely in certain circumstances, or those which are set up ad hoc to consider a matter of national concern.

A local inquiry might be held, for example, before planning schemes are approved. Public inquiries initiated ad hoc by Government Ministers have in recent years included the ongoing inquiry into events at the Countess of Chester Hospital following the convictions of former neonatal nurse Lucy Letby for the murder and attempted murder of babies at the hospital, the UK Covid-19 Inquiry to examine the impact of the pandemic, and another examining events around the murders of three young girls in Southport in 2024. These are statutory inquiries held under the Inquiries Act 2005.

> The **additional material** for this chapter on **www.mcnaes.com** sets out the reporting restrictions which can be imposed under the Act, outlines the powers of an inquiry chair to compel production of evidence, including from a journalist, and explains how the Act gives journalists some rights to view an inquiry's documents.

18.8.1 Coverage of public inquiries—defamation law

Reports of the public proceedings of public inquiries held under the 2005 Act have the same privilege as reports of court cases—absolute privilege if contemporaneous and qualified privilege if non-contemporaneous, if the respective requirements of these defences are met. The Defamation Act 1996 also provides qualified privilege for reports of a public inquiry's public proceedings, though such reports of inquiries of the type defined in paragraph 11 in Part 2 of the Act's Schedule 1 enjoy that privilege subject to the additional requirement to publish 'explanation or contradiction' if this is requested.

see Appendix 2 of this book for the Schedule to the 1996 Act

> Again, these defences are explained in 22.5 Absolute privilege, and 22.7, Qualified privilege by statute. The **additional material** for this chapter on **www.mcnaes.com** has more detail of defamation law affecting coverage of public inquiries.

Recap of major points

- Most types of tribunal adjudicate in disputes in specialist areas of law. Some are regulatory tribunals for professions—for example, doctors or lawyers.
- Media reports of the public proceedings of tribunals are protected by qualified privilege and, as regards those classed as courts, by absolute privilege when reports are contemporaneous.
- For any tribunal classed as a court, contempt law applies, as do automatic bans on photography, filming and audio-recording.

- Tribunals can make anonymity orders in some circumstances, and can hold 'virtual' or 'hybrid' hearings.
- When a public inquiry is held under the Inquiries Act 2005, there may be reporting restrictions.

((•)) Useful Websites

www.gov.uk

- HM Courts and Tribunals Service—HMCTS site which has links to First-tier, Upper Tribunal and other tribunal sites
- Tribunal Procedure Committee which draws up rules for the First-tier Tribunal and the Upper Tribunal
- Upper Tribunal procedure rules
- HMCTS general guidance to staff on supporting media access to courts and tribunals
- HCMTS jurisdictional guidance to staff on supporting media access to tribunals
- Employment Tribunal
- Employment tribunal procedure rules

Medical Practitioners Tribunal Service, www.mpts-uk.org

Solicitors Disciplinary Tribunal, solicitorstribunal.org.uk

Inquiries Act 2005, www.legislation.gov.uk

Online resources

Visit the online resources at **www.mcnaes.com** to test your knowledge of this chapter with **self-test questions** and a **flashcard glossary**, and to read **updates** about law and regulatory matters affecting journalism, as well as **additional material** to further your learning.

19

Contempt of court

Chapter summary

The law of contempt of court protects the integrity of the administration of justice, including the fundamental principle that a defendant in a criminal case is presumed innocent unless proved guilty. This law can be used to punish a media organisation which publishes material which interferes with the outcome of a trial. That is a contempt of court, because such material might improperly influence a jury's verdict directly, or indirectly (for example, by influencing a witness's evidence). What is published about a case might have potential to 'impede' the course of justice—for example, by creating a substantial risk that witnesses will refuse to come forward to help the prosecution or defence. Impediment is another type of contempt. Media organisations which have committed contempt have been fined heavily. The law of contempt protects all types of legal proceedings, including those in civil courts. Lawyers and others sometimes use the term 'sub judice', which is a term indicating that a legal action has begun. But this is not the same as the case being active, as we will see below.

19.1 Introduction—what does contempt of court law protect?

The purpose of the law of contempt was described in the case of *Re Yaxley-Lennon* [2018] EWCA Crim 244 (the defendant is also known as Tommy Robinson):

> The law of contempt exists to protect the course of proceedings from interference, to safeguard the fairness and integrity of proceedings and to ensure that orders of the court are obeyed. It comes in many forms, both statutory and under the common law.

Anyone who is disruptive or threatening in a courtroom or its precincts can be punished immediately for contempt by being sent by the magistrates or judge to the court's cells, and in some cases subsequently to jail, as such contempt is an offence.

Case law indicates that the greatest risk of the media committing contempt is by publishing material which could jeopardise the fairness of a criminal trial by:

- giving the impression to jurors that a defendant is likely to have committed the crime—for example, jurors may remember information about the defendant's background that the media published months ago when the defendant was arrested—which could *prejudice* the jury against the defendant, or by
- vilifying a suspect or defendant or a witness, which by denigrating the person's character creates the risk that suspect is a bad person or might make witnesses decide against coming forward to help the defence, which would *impede* the administration of justice.

As this chapter will explain, there are other ways in which prejudice or impediment (types of interference with justice) can be caused.

Also, contempt law protects proceedings in all courts, including civil courts and tribunals, not just those dealing with criminal cases.

19.2 Types of contempt

Journalists must be particularly aware of:

- contempt in common law, which occurs when how someone misbehaves inside or outside court, or when what is published, *interferes with or creates a real risk of interference with the administration of justice*, either in a particular case or generally as regards future cases, and there was intent to interfere or create that risk; in practice common law contempt is rarely used against publishers;
- strict liability contempt under the Contempt of Court Act 1981, which occurs when publication of material creates a substantial risk that the course of justice in a particular court case, or a particular criminal investigation, which is 'active' will be seriously prejudiced or impeded, irrespective of whether there was intent to create that risk.

This chapter will explain 'strict liability' and what types of material if published could create such 'substantial risk'. In contempt law, 'real risk' means much the same as 'substantial risk'. 'Substantial' means 'not merely minimal' (*Attorney General v English* [1983] 1 AC 116).

*** Remember**

The punishment for committing contempt—whether in common law or under the 1981 Act—is up to two years' jail and/or a fine unlimited by statute.

19.2.1 Other contempts are explained in other chapters

Other chapters explain that it is also a contempt of court to:

- audio-record a court's hearing without its permission—see 12.1.
- seek to discover or to publish information from the jury's confidential discussions about a verdict—see 12.3.

- publish an account of the proceedings of a court hearing held in private, if the case falls within certain categories, or publish improperly material from case documents—see 12.6 and 12.7.
- publish information in breach of an order made under the 1981 Act—for example, by naming a blackmail victim in reports of a court case—see 12.5.
- publish information in breach of a court order (injunction) made in common law—see 12.9, 12.10, 14.10, 26.4 and 27.11.2.

NB: The punishment for publishing material in breach of an order made under a statute other than the 1981 Act—for example, under the Youth Justice and Criminal Evidence Act 1999, explained in ch. 10—should be that specified by that statute, rather than as a contempt (*R v Tyne Tees Television* [1997] EWCA Crim 2395, *The Times*, 20 October 1997).

19.3 How the media might commit a contempt in common law

This is a rather arcane and rarely used species of contempt, which is derived from case law. There are various ways in which journalists, or a media organisation, might commit a contempt in common law.

For example, one way in which a common law contempt is committed is by publication of material which creates a *real risk of interference with legal proceedings which are imminent or pending*, but it must be proved that there was intent to create such a risk. In this context, the term 'intent' could mean either deliberate intention to create the risk by publishing material, or publishing material which the person responsible should have foreseen would create the risk.

In a case in 1988, Dr B was questioned by police regarding a rape allegation by an eight-year-old girl but, due to insufficient evidence, the DPP declined to prosecute him. *The Sun* obtained the story and decided that it would offer the mother financial support to fund a private prosecution. Before this started, *The Sun* published several highly critical articles about Dr B under headlines such as 'Rape Case Doc: Sun acts' and 'Beast must be named'. As he had not been arrested, there was no statutory active period under the 1981 Act but the court still found *The Sun* guilty of common law contempt and fined it £75,000.

The overlap here with 'strict liability' statutory contempt means there are very few cases of common law contempt, but it does cover a period when a case may not yet be 'active' under the 1981 Act, (see 19.4.2), so care still needs to be taken.

19.3.1 Imminent

There is no clear categorisation in case law of when criminal proceedings are 'imminent'. But proceedings are definitely imminent 'if it must be obvious that a suspect is about to be arrested'—for example, because police have surrounded a house (*R v Horsham Justices, ex parte Farquharson and another* [1982] 2 All ER 269). A media organisation should be cautious for example in that situation about reporting that the

for 'presumption of innocence', see 5.1

suspect already has a criminal record. There is a presumption of innocence in criminal trials which means that juries are not always told about past offences.

As it could be foreseen that a jury could be prejudiced against the defendant if any juror remembered such a report about previous offending, which might make a 'guilty' verdict more likely, the Court might rule that the media organisation—because of that report—committed a common law contempt. For the same reason, when an arrest is known to be 'imminent', care must be taken not to publish anything suggesting the person has definitely committed the alleged offence being investigated.

19.3.2 Pending

The Contempt of Court Act 1981 largely superseded the common law by creating what is known as the 'strict liability' rule in respect of cases which are 'active' under the Act—for example, as this chapter will explain, a criminal case becomes 'active' if there has been an arrest, or an arrest warrant has been issued. If someone has been arrested, this is one situation in which proceedings are 'pending' (*R v Horsham Justices*, cited earlier), and so the common law of contempt could apply here, but it is generally simpler to prosecute the publisher under the 1981 Act (see below) because the 'intent' element does not have to be proved.

The **additional material** on **www.mcnaes.com** for this chapter has case studies about common law contempt in the 'pre-active' period, concerning media organisations.

19.3.3 Interviewing a witness or offering a witness payment

In many instances before anyone is arrested, or before an arrest is imminent, and when the identity of the perpetrator is perhaps not known, journalists may have interviewed eye-witnesses to or victims of a crime about what happened, and published those reports.

But caution may still be needed. A reporter who interviews a person about any type of case in which they are due to testify in court, or when it could be reasonably foreseen that the person would be called to testify in a pending case, might be ruled to have committed a common law contempt, even if the reporter does not intend to publish a report of the interview until *after* the case concludes. This is because there might be a risk that the reporter in conducting the interview will contaminate the witness's memory, or create a real risk of contamination—for example, by telling them what other witnesses said, and so influencing what the witness remembers or thinks they remember, or otherwise affecting their testimony. If the witness does not testify solely from their own memory, that could prejudice (improperly influence) the outcome of the trial.

Even if no interview has been conducted, if a media organisation offers such a witness (perhaps the alleged victim of a crime) money to buy their story, or pays the witness for that story while they are still involved in the court case, that conduct could be a common law contempt if the interaction was ruled to have influenced the witness's evidence, or created a real risk of such influence. A primary concern is that the witness will embellish evidence given in court, to be sure of getting money for their story, or in the hope of other such deals. This sort of behaviour is also covered by the editorial codes.

> For context, see 2.4.7, Payments to witnesses, about clause 15 of the Editors' Code. There is similar provision in the Broadcasting Code—see 3.4.9—and the Impress Code, to help deter such contempt from being committed.

19.3.4 Molestation

It could be a common law contempt of 'molestation' if before a trial a journalist pesters a witness so much for an interview that they decide against testifying, or become agitated about testifying, which could affect how the witness gives evidence. Either circumstance could affect the verdict.

This type of contempt could also be ruled to have occurred if a journalist—for example, a photographer—harasses a defendant, witness or juror as they arrive at or leave a courthouse. For context, see 12.1.3, and the *Yaxley-Lennon* case study in 19.5.2.

19.3.5 Vilification

A media organisation which, after a case ceases to be 'active', publishes vilification of a witness could have committed a contempt in common law if the vilification is ruled to have created a real risk that other people will be deterred from being witnesses in future cases.

19.4 The Contempt of Court Act 1981—strict liability

The Contempt of Court Act 1981 was intended to replace some aspects of common law contempt and give greater certainty about what constitutes contempt by publication. Section 1 of the 1981 Act creates what is known as 'the strict liability rule'. The strict liability rule applies only (section 2) to publications 'which create a substantial risk that the course of justice in the proceedings in question will be seriously impeded or prejudiced' and then only if the proceedings in question are 'active' (Sch 1).

This law is known as 'the strict liability rule'. It applies to both civil and criminal proceedings. In this context, 'strict liability' means that intent is irrelevant. The court simply considers the actual or potential prejudicial or impedimental *effect* of what was published.

Prosecutions for alleged contempt by the mainstream media are usually of the relevant publishing company. But it is possible that the editor or another staff journalist involved in publishing the material will be prosecuted. Anyone who publishes such material, such as a blogger or 'tweeter/X poster', can be prosecuted.

- The Act defines publication as any writing, speech, broadcast or other communication—which includes material on websites—addressed to any section of the public.
- The strict liability rule applies only to what is published when proceedings are 'active'

19.4.1 Who can initiate proceedings for contempt of court under the Act?

1.7 explains the Attorney General's role

If a court considers what was published about its proceedings may have breached the Act, legal action to pursue this can be initiated only by a Crown court or higher court, or by or with the consent of the Attorney General. Crown court judges usually refer such matters to the Attorney General to decide if the case should be referred to the High Court. Magistrates cannot instigate such proceedings—the matter would have to be dealt with by the High Court.

19.4.2 When are civil proceedings active?

The Contempt of Court Act says that a civil or tribunal case is active from the time when arrangements for the hearing are made or, if no such arrangements have been made, from the time the hearing begins, until the proceedings are disposed of or discontinued or withdrawn.

19.4.3 When are criminal proceedings active?

The Act says a criminal case becomes active when:

- a person is arrested;
- an arrest warrant is issued;
- a summons is issued;
- a person is charged orally; or
- a document specifying the charge is served on the accused.

ch. 5 gives more detail about these early stages of a criminal case

These steps all mean that there is a prospect in law of that individual facing trial.

A potential problem for the media is that the police may not make clear, after a crime is committed, if a person is under arrest or voluntarily 'helping police with their inquiries'. Journalists must seek clarification to establish if the case is active.

Criminal proceedings cease to be active when any of these events occurs:

- the arrested person is released without being charged (except when released on police bail or 'released under investigation');
- no arrest is made within 12 months of the issue of an arrest warrant;

- the case is discontinued, either through the prosecution being dropped or through the police telling a person who was 'released under investigation' that they will not be prosecuted;
- the defendant is acquitted or sentenced (but see 19.4.4); or
- the defendant is found unfit to be tried or unfit to plead, or the court orders the charge to lie on file.

ch. 5 explains police bail

19.4.3.1 What does 'released under investigation' mean?

In 2017 a change in the law stopped police from keeping people on bail for weeks, months or even years. But if police need more time to investigate an alleged crime, they can categorise a suspect released after arrest as 'released under investigation'. An associated change to the Contempt of Court Act 1981 means that although these suspects are not on police bail or charged, their cases remain 'active' until police tell the individual, in writing, that they will not be prosecuted.

19.4.3.2 What do 'unfit' and 'lie on file' mean?

A defendant suffering acute physical or mental illness can be ruled to be unfit to stand trial, or to plead, and such a ruling halts the case.

An order that a charge should 'lie on file' means that the defendant has not been acquitted or convicted, but the court agrees that the charge is no longer worth pursuing. For example, if after a lengthy trial a defendant is convicted of four charges but the jury cannot agree on the fifth, the judge may order that charge to 'lie on file'. This would probably be because the expense of a re-trial involving that single charge would be excessive, and/or a conviction on that charge would not lead to the defendant getting a longer prison sentence.

But in all these circumstances, the proceedings become active again if they are recommenced.

19.4.4 Period between verdict and sentence at Crown court

If a defendant is found guilty at Crown court, the case remains active until the defendant is sentenced. This means it is technically possible for a media organisation to publish material during this period which breaches the 1981 Act even though the jury's involvement in the case has ended. But Crown court judges are regarded as too experienced, including in their sentencing decisions, to be influenced by media coverage. Therefore, it is thought unlikely that there can be any substantial risk of serious prejudice, whatever is published, after all verdicts are delivered but before an adjourned sentencing. Media organisations are therefore generally safe in publishing background features about such a case, including material which did not feature in the trial, as soon as the last verdict in the case is given—although judges have been known to order the postponement of publication of such material until after sentencing.

19.4.5 Proceedings become active again when an appeal is lodged

The 1981 Act says that:

- when an appeal is lodged, the case becomes active again, so the strict liability rule takes effect again;
- the case ceases to be active when the hearing of any appeal is completed—unless the appeal court's decision is that there should be a re-trial of the case, or the case is remitted to a lower court.

Lawyers often announce at the end of a criminal (or civil) case that their clients will appeal, but it usually takes some weeks for an appeal to be prepared and lodged, so there is a time when the case is not active between, in a criminal case, the sentence and the lodging of an appeal.

for context, see 9.8, The Court of Appeal

- Even if an appeal is lodged against a Crown court conviction, the media still have considerable freedom on what can be published about such a case, even though it has become active again, because the appeal will be heard by the judges of the Court of Appeal.

It can generally be assumed that nothing the media publishes will create a substantial risk of serious prejudice to the way experienced judges deal with appeals, (and it is very unlikely that any witness will give evidence in person at the Court of Appeal). But if the Court of Appeal decides to order a re-trial—that is, another jury trial—the media must be wary of publishing anything which creates a risk of serious prejudice or impediment as regards the re-trial, as witnesses and potential jurors will be considered susceptible to publicity about the case before and during the re-trial.

for context, see 16.7.4, The possibility of re-trial does not mean it is 'pending or imminent'

19.4.5.1 Where to check if an appeal has been lodged

Appeals to the Court of Appeal from Crown courts may be lodged at the Crown court office. Appeals on a point of law to the King's Bench Divisional Court (the High Court) from a Crown court appeal hearing must be lodged at the Royal Courts of Justice in London. Appeals from magistrates' court summary trials may be lodged at a local Crown court office. Criminal court staff must tell enquirers whether a verdict has been appealed—see 15.15.3.

19.4.6 Police appeals for assistance

Sometimes police seek the public's help to trace a suspect after an arrest warrant is issued or because the suspect disappeared after being 'released under investigation'; or to trace a defendant who has escaped custody or failed to turn up at court at the case's next hearing. Police appeal to the public for information.

Police may give the media a photograph and/or physical description of the person for publication with such an appeal. Police may warn the public that the person could be dangerous—for example, by warning that the person should not be approached. Technically, a media organisation publishing such a photograph, description or warning about the person could be accused of creating a substantial risk of serious prejudice or impediment as regards an active case—see explanations in 19.5 about visual identification evidence and the contempt risk in publishing that a person has a bad character. But the then Attorney General said in the House of Commons during the debate on the Contempt of Court Bill in 1981:

> “The press has nothing whatever to fear from publishing in reasoned terms anything which may assist in the apprehension of a wanted man and I hope that it will continue to perform this public service.”

There is no known case of a media organisation being ruled to have committed a contempt by publishing such a police appeal. But there is no defence in the 1981 Act for thus assisting police. The Attorney General's 1981 assurance would not apply if the information supplied by police for the appeal was published after (or remained online after) the person is apprehended.

* Remember

The Attorney General may decide what was published was not 'in reasoned terms' if it suggests, by tone or content, by adding to what the police have said officially in a measured statement, that the person being sought is definitely guilty of the alleged offence suspected or with which they have been charged.

* Remember

Police may also issue a warrant for someone's arrest, for example, to facilitate an extradition request. Even if the 1981 Act's strict liability rule does not apply at the time of the publication of a police appeal for information (because no warrant has been issued, so the case is not 'active'), there remains risk that what is published about the suspect could be ruled to be a common law contempt (see 19.3) if not couched 'in reasoned terms' and if published when their arrest is apparently 'imminent'.

19.5 What type of material can cause serious prejudice or impediment of criminal proceedings?

The 1981 Act does not define what creates a substantial risk of serious prejudice or impediment. But cases in which editors and media organisations were convicted under the Act's strict liability rule involved publication of material concerning criminal proceedings which:

- mentioned a suspect or defendant's previous conviction(s);
- suggested that they are dishonest or of bad character in other ways;
- referred to what is suggested to be evidence linking them to the crime of which they are suspected or accused;
- suggested in other ways that they are guilty of that crime.

✱ Remember

If the person is tried, the magistrates or jury will probably not be told of their previous convictions, while 'bad character' evidence may be admissible only in certain circumstances—see 5.1 and 7.5.1.

Clearly, a pre-trial report referring to the defendant's previous conviction(s) could influence the trial verdict because, for example, if one juror remembers that report, that person may tell the whole jury.

Also, publishing other material which suggests a suspect or defendant is of bad character, such as by vilifying the person, could stop a witness coming forward in their defence, which would be an impediment to a fair trial.

Publishing material which vilifies a defendant could so agitate that person that they could not focus on the trial, which would also be an impediment.

As this chapter explains, there are other ways the 1981 Act can be breached by what is published about an active case.

✱ Remember

Contempt law is enforced more strictly in Scotland. This means particular care must be taken in cross-border publication, including on the internet. See the chapter on Other UK Jurisdictions on www.mcnaes.com.

19.5.1 Mentioning a defendant's previous conviction(s)

In 2008 the High Court fined ITV Central £25,000 for breach of the 1981 Act because on the morning on which the trial of five men was due to start, it broadcast a report about that trial which said that one of the defendants, who in that trial faced a murder charge, was in jail serving a sentence for another murder. As a consequence, the trial was postponed. ITV Central said in mitigation that it had not anticipated that a trained journalist would make such an error (*PA Mediapoint*, 16 July 2008).

19.5.2 Other information suggesting a suspect or defendant is dishonest or of bad character

The *Daily Mirror* was fined £50,000 and *The Sun* £18,000 in July 2011 for contempt under the Act, because their coverage vilified former teacher Christopher Jefferies, the landlord of landscape architect Joanna Yeates, after he was arrested by police investigating her murder. He was later released without charge. The High Court heard that one *Daily Mirror* front page carried the headline 'Jo Suspect is Peeping Tom' beneath a photograph of Mr Jefferies, and another front-page headline read 'Was killer waiting in Jo's flat?', with subheadings below reading 'Police seize bedding for tests' and 'Landlord held until Tuesday'. *The Sun*'s front-page headline read

'Obsessed by Death' next to a photograph of Mr Jefferies and below the words 'Jo suspect "scared kids"'. Attorney General Dominic Grieve QC said material in the articles gave an 'overall impression' that Mr Jefferies had a 'propensity' to commit the kind of offences for which he had been arrested. The Lord Chief Justice, Lord Judge, said 'impeding the course of justice and prejudicing the course of justice are not synonymous concepts.' Vilification of a suspect under arrest was a potential impediment to the course of justice, he said, adding:

> "At the simplest level publication of such material may deter or discourage witnesses from coming forward and providing information helpful to the suspect, which may, (depending on the circumstances) help immediately to clear him of suspicion or enable his defence to be fully developed at trial."

It was not an answer, Lord Judge said, to argue that the combination of the trial judge's directions and the integrity of the jury would ensure a fair trial—the evidence at trial might be incomplete 'because its existence may never be known, or indeed may only come to light after conviction' (*Attorney-General v MGN Ltd and another* [2011] EWHC 2074 (Admin); [2012] 1 Cr App R 1, [2012] EMLR 9, [2012] ACD 13; [2012] 1 WLR 2408). Another man was later convicted of murdering Ms Yeates.

> Mr Jefferies also won damages from newspapers for libel because of the falsehoods published about him—see 5.11.1, Defamation risk in reporting a suspect's identity.

Case study

In 2019 Stephen Yaxley-Lennon, who uses the name Tommy Robinson and was the founder of the English Defence League, was jailed for nine months after being found by the High Court to have committed contempt of court in three ways. Yaxley-Lennon turned up outside Leeds Crown Court courthouse to 'report' on a trial at Leeds Crown Court of a number of men of Asian heritage charged with grooming and sexually exploiting young women. He had a video camera and aggressively confronted and filmed defendants as they arrived at court. The High Court ruled these actions amounted to common law contempt, including because the filming was within the precincts of the court. He had created a real risk that the defendants would be in an upset and agitated state in court, unsuitable for participation in their trial. So, he had created a real risk that their participation would be seriously impeded. Yaxley-Lennon also live-streamed the footage on the internet, and in it referred in derogatory terms to the defendants' religious and ethnic backgrounds, and left no doubt that he believed they ought to be convicted. He therefore breached the 1981 Act by creating a substantial risk of serious prejudice in respect of the trial, because in the footage he incited people to harass the defendants, and because of the 'significant adverse effect' the footage could have had on the defendants if any had seen it. The High Court also ruled that Yaxley-Lennon committed a contempt by breaching a reporting restriction order made by a judge under section 4(2) of 1981 Act, which had banned publication of reports of the trial until after the conclusion of that trial and of other trials linked to the case. It rejected his claim that he believed that a reporting restriction order on the case had come to an end, saying he clearly had not bothered to check. It also rejected his claim that the section 4(2) order was improperly made and thus did not bind him, emphasising that reporting restriction orders must be obeyed, even if it subsequently turned out that they were incorrect or should not have been made (*Attorney General v Yaxley-Lennon* [2019] EWHC 1791 (Admin); *Media Lawyer*, 11 July 2019).

section 4(2) orders are explained later in this chapter

Case study

In 2011 the *Daily Mail* and *The Sun* were found guilty of breaching the 1981 Act after both published on their websites a photograph, copied from a social networking website page, in reports of a trial at Sheffield Crown court in which Ryan Ward was accused of murder. The photo showed him posing with an automatic pistol. The murder he was accused of did not involve a gun. The Crown court judge established that no juror had seen the reports which contained the photo, so the trial continued. But the High Court said later that the image of Ward brandishing the pistol, and apparently doing so in a brazen manner, created an adverse impression of a young man who enjoyed demonstrating a propensity for violence. The High Court ruled that by publishing it the *Daily Mail* and *The Sun* had created a substantial risk of serious prejudice, because had any juror had seen it, the jury would have had to have been discharged, which would have meant the trial (in which Ward was convicted of the murder) would have had to be abandoned (which would have necessitated a re-trial). The case was the first time website operators in the UK had been found guilty of contempt. The High Court fined each paper £15,000 and ordered them to pay the Attorney General's costs of £28,117 (*Attorney General v Associated Newspapers Ltd and another* [2011] EWHC 418 (Admin), *Media Lawyer*, 19 July 2011).

Remember

Publishing material when a case is active which vilifies a witness could be ruled to have created a substantial risk of serious prejudice or impediment, because the jury could be influenced against the witness, or the witness be deterred from testifying, or be agitated by what was published and so be unable to focus when testifying.

19.5.3 Publishing a witness's detailed account

When a case is active, publishing a witness's detailed account of a relevant event may be deemed a contempt under strict liability rule because of the risk that:

- the witness might, because such a detailed account has been published, feel obliged to stick to it as regards their evidence, and so be less able honestly to retract or vary some detail after further reflection; or
- what the witness says happened might not figure in the case at all—it might be ruled inadmissible as evidence or have been retracted—but if such an account has already been published, other witnesses or jurors in the case might have read or heard it or been told about it, and been influenced by it.

what a witness says in court can be published—see 19.10

19.5.4 Visual identification evidence

Publishing any image of a suspect or defendant when the relevant criminal case is active could be a contempt if visual identification evidence could be in issue and might be disputed in a trial.

For example, police investigating a crime, such as a robbery or rape, when the identity of the perpetrator is initially unknown may ask the media to publish a sketch or computer-generated image of the perpetrator's face as described by a witness such as the victim, or to publish a verbal description of the perpetrator, obtained from a witness—for example, that the perpetrator has fair hair and a dragon tattoo. The police aim is to get members of the public to say or suggest who the perpetrator is, or say whether they saw such a person at or near the crime scene, which could be useful evidence. For the same reason, police may provide for publication an image of a suspect from CCTV footage. Also, a reporter may track down such footage, or later someone may offer a photo or footage of the person charged in the case (the defendant); for example, a wedding photo or showing the defendant standing outside the courthouse.

The need to avoid breaching the 1981 Act—that is, to avoid creating a substantial risk of serious prejudice—means that as regards a case in which visual identification evidence could feature, the media should not publish such an image or description or any such photo or footage after the case becomes active, to protect the validity of such evidence until that risk can no longer occur (for example, there can be no such risk after all verdicts in the case have been delivered).

Publishing such material soon after an arrest could influence or confuse an eye-witness, and consequently later the jury might not be sure whether that witness's evidence—for example, given to police during an 'identity parade'—is based on what they saw of someone's appearance at the crime scene, or on recollection of what was published. Also, any such witness may also be asked in the trial to describe who they saw.

If the computer-generated image initially released by police or CCTV footage is shown to the jury, the media may be allowed to publish it in coverage of the trial—see 15.21.

Case study

In 1994 *The Sun* was fined £80,000 and its editor, Kelvin MacKenzie, £20,000, for contempt, because the newspaper published a photograph of a man charged with murder. The picture was published before an identity parade in which witnesses picked the suspect out (*The Independent*, 6 July 1994).

Remember

The examples of prejudicial material in this chapter relate mainly to the contempt risk of saying or suggesting in what is published that a suspect or defendant is guilty. But it is possible that the 1981 Act could be breached by publishing material suggesting or asserting before a trial that a suspect or defendant is innocent, because that too could improperly affect a jury's verdict, including by discouraging people to provide evidence which may be helpful for prosecutors. Also, remember that the Act applies to all types of court cases, including to protect the authenticity of witness testimony.

19.6 What can be published after a criminal case becomes active?

Contempt law does not mean that the media cannot publish anything about a crime after a case becomes active.

Non-prejudicial basic information about the crime can be published—for example, that there was a robbery, where it took place and that later someone was arrested. Media organisations should not report that 'the robber was later arrested' as this says the arrested person is guilty of the offence.

In most cases, it will not be contempt to publish the name of the arrested person, because they will be named at the trial. But to publish the identity of a suspect or arrested person before they are charged incurs risks as regards defamation, privacy and data protection law. Ch. 5 explains those risks, and outlines other law which gives pre-charge anonymity to a teacher accused of an offence against a pupil.

In contempt law it is safe to identify the alleged victim(s) of crime before a prosecution begins. But a reporting restriction may apply to media reports of the court case, as chs. 10 and 12 explain. Also, victims/alleged victims of sexual offences, trafficking, forced marriage and female genital mutilation offences have automatic, lifetime anonymity from the time the offence is alleged—see ch. 11.

19.6.1 Common ground

It is not prejudicial when a case is active to publish material which will be common ground between the defence and prosecution at the trial. This will include neutral, background material about a defendant or victim, such as their age and job. Also, in a murder case, there is rarely a dispute about where the body was found. Similarly, the nature and extent of any victim's injuries will probably be common ground because much of the forensic or medical evidence will be beyond dispute—the trial issue will be how the injuries were caused or who caused them.

19.7 What might give rise to a substantial risk?

In *Attorney General v MGN Ltd* ([1997] 1 All ER 456) Lord Justice Schiemann set out the principles a court should follow when deciding whether published material created a substantial risk of serious prejudice as regards a case which became or had a potential to be jury trial. The court, he said, should consider what risk occurred at the time the material was published. He warned that the mere fact that by reason of earlier publications there was already some risk of prejudice did not in itself prevent a court finding that the later publication had created a further risk. He also said the court should consider:

- the likelihood of the publication coming to a potential juror's attention;
- its likely impact on an ordinary reader; and
- crucially, the residual impact on a notional juror at the time of the trial.

The court will also consider whether what was published would have given rise to a seriously arguable ground of appeal if the trial had been allowed to continue and ended with a conviction.

19.7.1 Juries are told to put pre-trial publicity out of their minds

At the start of Crown court trials, judges tell juries to reach verdicts only on the evidence presented to them and to put pre-trial publicity about the case, or media coverage of the trial, out of their minds, and not to research the internet for material.

Judges have made clear that juries must be trusted and that jurors given directions by a judge are capable of looking at the evidence fairly. In *Re B* ([2006] EWCA Crim 2692; [2007] EMLR 145; [2007] HRLR 1; [2007] UKHRR 577) Sir Igor Judge, presiding at the Court of Appeal, stressed the robustness and independence of juries in a case in which the Court lifted an order postponing reporting of a hearing at which Dhiren Barot, self-confessed terrorist, was to be sentenced.

Sir Igor said that 'juries up and down the country have a passionate and profound belief in and a commitment to' the defendant's right to a fair trial and went on:

> “They know that it is integral to their responsibility. It is, when all is said and done, their birthright; it is shared by each one of them with the defendant. They guard it faithfully. The integrity of the jury is an essential feature of our trial process. Juries follow the directions which the judge will give them to focus exclusively on the evidence and to ignore anything they may have heard or read out of court.”

The judge at the trial would give the jury appropriate directions, he said, adding:

> "We cannot too strongly emphasise that the jury will follow them, not only because they will loyally abide by the directions of law which they will be given by the judge, but also because the directions themselves will appeal directly to their own instinctive and fundamental belief in the need for the trial process to be fair."

There were, he added, at least two safeguards against the risk of prejudice—the media's responsibility to avoid publishing inappropriate comment, which might interfere with the administration of justice, and the trial process, including the integrity of the jury. For more context on the *Barot* case, see 16.7.2.

19.7.2 The 'fade factor'

Judges and lawyers sometimes refer to the 'fade factor'. The term recognises that by the time a jury is selected the public will probably have forgotten detail in reports published in the early stages of a criminal case—for example, soon after the crime about someone being arrested or charged. Other factors a court takes into account include the extent of the area where the material was published, and other indicators of the potential 'reach' it had with audiences.

for context, see 19.6 about previous convictions

Some material may be so striking, even when published some time before a trial, that it will be ruled to have created a substantial risk of serious prejudice or impediment as regards the trial. Such material has been said to include, especially, disclosure of a defendant's criminal record.

Case study

The lapse of time was a factor when the High Court assessed the degree of risk of serious prejudice in a contempt case in 1997. The *Daily Mail* and *Manchester Evening News* reported that a home help had been caught twice on video film stealing cash from an 82-year-old widow's fridge. The reports included images of the home help taking the cash, filmed by a camera hidden by the widow's son, and what seemed to be her confession to stealing it, in what she said when confronted by two journalists. At the time of publication, the case was active because she had been charged with both thefts, and the video was evidence in the case. Two months later she admitted both charges in a magistrates' court and was jailed. Later the High Court ruled that neither newspaper had committed contempt of court by publishing its report. Lord Justice Simon Brown, who delivered the Court's judgment, said his initial view was that the reports were a plain contempt of court as they carried the clearest statements that the home help was guilty. But had there been a jury trial, the reports would by then have been several months old, he said. The High Court ruled that the contempt allegation was not proved against either paper. But Lord Justice Brown warned the media against thinking that when someone was apparently caught red-handed, and had 'confessed', there was no possibility of a 'not guilty' plea at trial. He said the video evidence was not in itself proof that the home help took the cash dishonestly (*Attorney General v Unger* [1998] 1 Cr App R 308).

✱ Remember

The 'fade factor' will not protect a publisher if the Attorney General argues that the published material created a substantial risk of serious impediment as regards witnesses not coming forward, because the issue then is not what a juror may remember but the risk that such witnesses' evidence will never come to light—see the Jefferies case in 19.5.2.

19.7.3 Publishing material shortly before or during a trial

The 'fade factor' offers no protection for material published shortly before a trial, such as in the ITV Central case referred to in 19.5.1, or after the trial has started.

Case study

In 2002 the *Sunday Mirror* was fined £75,000 for contempt over articles which led to the collapse of the first trial of two Leeds United footballers on assault charges. The two-page spread—published while the jury was deliberating and had been sent home for the weekend—contained an interview in which the victim's father said his son was the victim of a racial attack, although the jury had been told that there was no evidence of a racial motive. The spread also contained a story commenting on the credibility of a major witness in the case. In the contempt proceedings, counsel for the Attorney General estimated the cost of the aborted trial at £1,113,000 and the cost of the subsequent retrial at £1,125,000 (*Attorney General v Mirror Group Newspapers Ltd* [2002] EWHC 907 (Admin)).

19.7.4 Archive material on news websites

'Fade factor' protection does not apply to material which, although when it was first published was not in contempt, remains accessible to the public in a media organisation's online archives. Although jurors are told not to do their own research, they might see stories in news archives referring to a defendant's previous convictions, or misleading accounts of the alleged crime which is being considered in that trial. Also, if a witness finds an archived account of the alleged crime, the discovery might affect their testimony in ways described earlier—see 19.5.3.

If the police, or defence or prosecution lawyers draw a media organisation's attention to material in its accessible archives which they believe creates a substantial risk of serious prejudice or impediment as regards an active case, the safest course to avoid a contempt problem is to remove the material or block access to it until it can no longer create that risk. It can be made accessible again, for example, if the defendant pleads guilty or when the jury has delivered its verdict(s).

* Remember

Crown courts, using section 45 of the Senior Courts Act 1981, and higher courts can issue injunctions to stop the media publishing material deemed capable of being a contempt of court.

19.7.5 Readers' postings

Media organisations must be wary of allowing readers to post material online about an 'active' criminal case, as the material might contain facts or comments or allegations—for example, about a suspect's character or appearance, or a defendant's criminal history—which could create a substantial risk of serious prejudice or impediment, because of the risk of witnesses or jurors reading or being told of them.

Best practice is not to provide any place for readers' postings under a report of any arrest or any case potentially heading for, or which has become, a jury trial. If a reader posts matter potentially creating such risk elsewhere on the site, the media organisation should, as soon as it becomes aware of the posting, remove it to avoid any liability for its publication.

Case study

In 2016 the Court of Appeal ordered several media organisations not to allow readers to post comments under reports of a forthcoming trial and not to place reports of it on their organisations' Facebook pages. At that time they had no control over the Facebook facility which allows readers to post comments. The trial was of two teenagers accused of murdering vulnerable adult Angela Wrightson. Previously, defence lawyers had successfully applied for the original trial, at Teesside Crown court, to be abandoned because of a torrent of hostile comments posted by readers about the defendants on those Facebook pages (*Ex parte British Broadcasting Corporation and others, R v F and another*, [2016] EWCA Crim 12).

For more on this murder case, see the **additional material** for ch. 12 on **www.mcnaes.com**.

19.8 Civil proceedings

While it is possible to be in contempt of active (see 19.4.2) civil or tribunal proceedings, for example an employment tribunal, in practice because in most cases these cases are heard by judges alone and unlike many criminal cases, do not involve a jury, it is generally less risky to include background material about those who are involved in such cases. As with appeals, judges are thought to be experienced enough to rise above and ignore anything potentially prejudicial that might be published. It is still possible that what is published pre-trial about an active, civil case, or during its trial, could be ruled to have breached the strict liability rule if the article or programme delves so deeply into the case's circumstances that a witness's testimony could be improperly influenced or a witness is deterred from coming forward. This could happen if a high level of detail is published as an account of a relevant event, as supplied for the article or programme by a witness due to testify. For how contempt problems might occur, see 19.5.3.

ch. 13 explains civil courts and which cases could involve juries

But when a jury is or is due to be involved in a civil trial, (false imprisonment, malicious prosecution or fraud and, albeit very rarely, defamation) particular care must still be taken not to breach the strict liability rule, and the same caution that applies with a criminal trial should be adopted.

See 13.7.5, Formal offers to settle, for an explanation of the contempt danger of reporting that such an offer has been made in a civil case.

✱ Remember

When media organisations research or cover a civil case, they should take care to avoid committing contempt in common law, which is described earlier in this chapter mainly in the context of criminal cases but, for example, 'molestation' could occur in respect of parties or witnesses in a civil case.

19.9 Defences

19.9.1 Section 3 defence of not knowing proceedings were active

Section 3 of the 1981 Act provides two defences for an alleged breach of the strict liability rule.

Under section 3(1) a defence will apply if:

- the person responsible for the publication, having taken all reasonable care, did not know and had no reason to suspect when the material was published that relevant proceedings were active.

The section says that 'the burden' of proving any fact 'tending to establish' the defence lies on the publisher. Therefore, media organisations must be able to prove that all reasonable care was taken. So, to be sure of this section 3 defence, a journalist reporting a crime story must check regularly with police (or whichever law enforcement agency is investigating the alleged crime), especially before a publication deadline, about whether someone has been arrested or charged. Or the journalist might need to check whether a suspect has been 'released under investigation'; or check with a magistrates' court whether an arrest warrant or summons has been issued, if circumstances necessitate that check.

The checking has to be done, because any such event would make the case active, and if it is, what was planned for publication (including broadcast) may need to be re-edited to remove details or an image or images which could breach the Act if published—see 19.5.

If the police force, enforcement agency or court spokesperson says the case is not active, the journalist should keep a note of what was said, by which individual and when, to be able to prove that all reasonable care was taken to establish if the case was active.

See 19.12 for detail of when a civil case is active. See 17.9 for when an inquest is active, and 18.6 for detail of when cases before certain types of tribunal are active.

19.9.2 The defence in section 3(2) of the 1981 Act

Section 3(2) of the Contempt of Court Act 1981 says that a person [or organisation] is not guilty of contempt of court under the strict liability rule as the distributor of a publication containing matter breaching the rule if at the time of distribution, having taken all reasonable care, he [it] did not know that the publication contained such matter and had no reason to suspect that it did.

In the 2016 case just cited (see 19.7.5), the Court of Appeal said that as regards postings by readers, a media organisation would be regarded under section 3(2) as being a 'distributor' of them. It directed that other media organisations nationally be alerted to its order that the specified organisations must not allow readers to post comments under reports of the teenagers' trial, and must not place those reports on Facebook. The Court warned that those alerted organisations too should take 'appropriate steps' to avoid such risk of the Act's strict liability rule being breached in respect of that trial. The Court said that the alert would mean they had foreknowledge that readers would seek to post such comments, and therefore the defence of having taken 'reasonable care' provided by section 3(2) would not be available to those organisations.

see 19.9, Court reporting—the section 4 defence

Note that section 4(1) of the Contempt of Court protects fair and accurate contemporary reports of proceedings held in public, published in good faith from amounting to a contempt.

* Remember

The Independent Press Standards Organisation (Ipso) has published guidance to its member organisations that when linking a social media platform to a report on active criminal proceedings, they should warn readers against posting comments on the platform that may prejudice the investigation or a fair trial, and consider removing readers' ability to post comments there about the report, if that is possible. The guidance says: 'A failure to provide a warning could be cited as evidence of a lack of reasonable care should prejudicial comments by readers subsequently be posted on your story.' For this guidance, see Useful Websites at the end of this chapter. Ipso is introduced in ch. 2.

19.9.3 Court reporting—the section 4 defence

In some circumstances, a media report of a court hearing might create a substantial risk of prejudice to a later stage of the same case or to another due to be tried.

But section 4(1) of the 1981 Act gives the media a defence. It says (in essence) that a person [or organisation] cannot be found guilty of breaching the Act's strict liability rule in respect of a report of a court hearing, if the report is:

see 22.5.1.4 for the definition of 'contemporaneous'

- of a hearing held in public;
- a fair and accurate report of that hearing;
- published contemporaneously; and
- published in good faith.

The Act does not define 'good faith'. But the overall effect of section 4 is that a court is expected to make a specific order restricting the media if the court does not want all or part of any hearing in public to be reported contemporaneously.

The section 4 defence does not protect a report of a court hearing held in private, even if the report is fair and accurate, etc., if its publication creates a substantial risk of serious prejudice or impediment. For other contempt law about private hearings, see 12.6.

19.9.3.1 Inaccurate reporting of a jury trial which is ongoing

The section 4 defence does not protect an unfair or inaccurate court report.

In May 2024, the trial of a woman accused of illegally aborting her baby collapsed after BBC Points West reported she had taken an abortion pill. The defendant accepted purchasing abortion pills online but denied taking them. Her barrister applied for the jury to be discharged due to the reporting, saying it would go to the issue of his client's credibility. The judge said it was 'appalling and sloppy' reporting from the BBC and dismissed the jury. (https://www.bbc.co.uk/news/articles/c5yd9j8j62go)

19.10 Section 4(2) orders

In some circumstances, it might be argued that fair, accurate and contemporaneous reporting of a trial could prejudice a later stage of that case or other proceedings linked to it.

5.1, Standard of proof in criminal law, explains this principle

For example, if several defendants are to be dealt with in two trials, reports of the first trial could arguably influence people who read or see them and are then selected as jurors for the second trial, concerning different allegations against the same defendants. Jurors in the second trial, because of the principle of the presumption of innocence for defendants, might be told nothing in court about the earlier trial.

But a juror in the second trial who remembers reading media reports of the first trial, or who is told about such reports by acquaintances, might be more likely to find the defendants guilty, especially if the juror knows from those reports that the defendants were convicted in the first trial.

To avoid this danger when a case involves a series of trials, section 4(2) of the 1981 Act gives a court power to postpone publication of reports of its proceedings. In the example just given, a judge could order that no report of the first trial should be published until the second has finished.

Section 4(2) says a court may order the postponement of the reporting of its proceedings or any part of them:

- where this appears to be necessary for avoiding a substantial risk of prejudice to the administration of justice in those proceedings; or
- in any other proceedings, pending or imminent.

see 19.3 for definitions of 'pending' and 'imminent'

It says that the period of postponement may be as long as the court thinks necessary for this purpose. Note that a court may make a section 4(2) order if there is a substantial risk of any prejudice, not necessarily 'serious' prejudice.

Publishing material which breaches a section 4(2) order is punishable as contempt, with a fine unlimited by statute and/or up to two years in jail.

Normally all charges against a defendant can be reported before a trial, even under the automatic reporting restrictions of other statutes as described in chs. 7–9. But in cases involving a defendant facing more than one trial, a Crown court judge may at a stage prior to trial—for example, at the **arraignment**—make a section 4(2) order postponing publication of the charge(s) the defendant is due to face at a subsequent trial until after the end of the first, to stop people who could become jurors in the first trial knowing that the same defendant faces another trial.

→glossary

16.7 explains the grounds on which the media may challenge the imposition of a section 4(2) order

19.10.1 What if a section 4(2) order is not made?

Arraignments are public proceedings when pleas are taken from defendants in a Crown court. Sometimes a defendant facing a number of charges will, when arraigned, plead guilty to some but deny the others. They will be tried on the denied charges.

Suppose that a media organisation publishes a report shortly before that trial, or during it, which includes that the defendant has admitted the other charges in the case. If the jury has not been or is not due to be told of those charges, or those guilty pleas, the judge might feel obliged—to ensure fairness to the defendant—to order that the trial be abandoned, because there is now a risk that jurors will know from that report that the defendant has previous convictions, and that this would make it more likely they will find him guilty of the charges in that trial. The judge could order there to be a new trial later, with a fresh jury, elsewhere.

Had the judge made a section 4(2) order during arraignment, to postpone reporting of the other charges and guilty pleas, the media's position would have been clear, and they should have obeyed the order. But if the judge did not make such an order, the legal position would be less clear on whether reporting the other charges or guilty pleas before or during the trial was a contempt.

Some experts say the section 4 defence should protect the media in these circumstances, arguing that the defence should apply unless the court made a section 4(2) order.

But the section 4 defence is subject to 'good faith' in publishing. This means the defence would fail if it could be proved that the person responsible for publication of the admitted charges did that intentionally in a plan to prejudice the trial. Arguably, even if the publisher did not have that plan, they could face contempt proceedings in common law. As was explained earlier in this chapter, the term 'intent' in common law can mean that a publisher should have foreseen that publishing the information in question would create a real risk of interference with the administration of justice.

19.10.2 Proceedings in court in the absence of the jury

During trials, judges often have to rule on the admissibility of evidence or other matters after hearing argument from defence and prosecution lawyers in the absence of the jury (which is kept out of the courtroom). The process of making such a ruling is nevertheless normally done in public, because normally people stay in the public gallery and reporters stay on the press bench.

But the judge may have kept the jury out of the courtroom because they might be prejudiced in their verdict(s) if they get knowledge of the matter discussed in their absence, which might be evidence which the judge decides is inadmissible in the trial because, for example, new facts have come to light suggesting it was gathered improperly or casting grave doubt on the reliability of the witness due to give it.

Publishing a report during the trial of such a ruling, and the discussion between judge and lawyers which led to it, creates a risk that the jury gains that knowledge from seeing the report or being told if it. But judges do not always make section 4(2) postponement orders covering such discussions or rulings in the jury's absence, because the expectation is that the media will realise that these should not be published until after all verdicts are given.

19.10.3 The law is not clear

The application of the law of contempt in both the circumstances outlined above—publication before or during a trial of any guilty plea(s)/other charge(s) in the case, or contemporaneous reporting of a discussion held or a ruling made in a jury's absence—is unclear if no section 4(2) order has been made.

Journalists should not, even if no section 4(2) order has been made, contemporaneously publish a report of any matter discussed or any ruling made in the absence of the jury at a Crown court trial. Even if such publication cannot be ruled to be a contempt, there is a risk—explained in 19.13—that a media organisation could be accused of 'serious misconduct' under section 93 of the Courts Act 2003 and consequently be held liable for the costs of an aborted or delayed trial. Such a report can be published after all verdicts are reached, unless the judge orders otherwise.

Similarly, a media organisation should adopt a cautious approach to publication of any other charge faced, or guilty plea entered, by a defendant who is shortly to be or is being tried on matters in the same case, unless it is clear that the jury will be or has been told, as part of the trial, of the defendant's pleas to all charges in the case.

19.11 Section 5 defence of discussion of public affairs

Section 5 of the Contempt of Court Act 1981 says:

> "A publication made as or as part of a discussion in good faith of public affairs or other matters of general public interest is not to be treated as a contempt of court under the strict liability rule if the risk of impediment or prejudice to particular legal proceedings is merely incidental to the discussion."

The defence was introduced because of complaints that freedom of expression in the UK was unnecessarily restricted by a ruling in a case in 1973 involving the *Sunday Times*, who wanted to publish an article about the way the drug thalidomide was tested and marketed—at a time when civil actions were pending against the manufacturer. More details of the case can be found in the **additional material** for this chapter. The House of Lords ruled that the proposed article would be in contempt in respect of those pending cases (*Attorney-General v Times Newspapers Ltd* [1973] 3 All ER 54 (HL)).

The European Court of Human Rights ruled that the Lords' decision violated the right to freedom of expression under Article 10 of the European Convention on Human Rights. The Government's response was to introduce the section 5 defence.

Case study

Two newspapers were prosecuted in 1981 for contempt arising from comments published during the trial of Dr Leonard Arthur, a paediatrician accused of murdering a newborn baby with Down's syndrome. It was alleged that the doctor, complying with the parents' wishes, let the infant starve. Dr Arthur was acquitted of murder. The *Sunday Express* and its editor John Junor admitted that a contempt was committed by what was published in a comment article written by Junor, which said the baby was drugged instead of being fed and died 'unloved and unwanted'. Junor was fined £1,000 and the newspaper's owners, Express Newspapers, £10,000 for breaching the 1981 Act's strict liability rule.

But the *Daily Mail* denied contempt, arguing that its article was protected by the defence in section 5 in the Act. The House of Lords ruled that while the article, which trenchantly considered whether severely disabled babies should be allowed or encouraged to survive, did create a substantial risk of serious prejudice to Dr Arthur's trial, it was written in good faith and was a discussion of public affairs because it was written in support of a 'pro-life' candidate at a by-election. Lord Diplock said the article made no express mention of Dr Arthur's case and the risk of prejudice would be properly described as merely incidental (*The Times*, 16 and 19 December 1981; *Attorney General v English* [1983] 1 AC 116).

19.11.1 Safest course

To be sure of section 5 protection, a media organisation should not, when publishing a general feature or discussion about a societal issue, refer in it to any active case in which the issue figures, and in particular should not suggest that the defendant in such a case is or is not guilty.

✱ Remember

The section 5 defence is only needed if what was published is ruled to have created a substantial risk of serious prejudice or impediment.

19.12 Media could face huge costs if 'serious misconduct' affects a case

Section 93 of the Courts Act 2003 enables a magistrates' court, a Crown court or the Court of Appeal to order a third party (which could be a media organisation) to pay costs incurred in a court case if these arose from 'serious misconduct' by that third party. This power is set out in detail in the Costs in Criminal Cases (General) (Amendment) Regulations 2004.

The 'serious misconduct' could be ruled to have occurred through publication of material or through a reporter's action even if there was no breach of the 1981 Act's strict liability rule.

The creation of this power in the 2003 Act was largely inspired by the costly abandonment of the trial in the Leeds footballers case following the *Sunday Mirror* articles, referred to earlier. If a trial is abandoned because of 'serious misconduct', the media organisation held responsible could become liable for huge costs (the costs of the abandoned trial) if a new trial has to be held.

19.13 The Law Commission Consultation on Contempt

In July 2024, the Law Commission, the statutory independent body which keeps the laws of England and Wales under review and recommends reform where it is needed, launched a wide-ranging consultation on contempt of court, including contempt by publication when proceedings are active. Its provisional proposals included the introduction of a specific offence of contempt by publication when proceedings are active. The murders of three young girls in Southport, near Liverpool, in July 2024 and the subsequent public disorder that arose put a renewed focus on liability for contempt of court, specifically, on what can be said after a suspect has been arrested. Given the public interest in these issues, in March 2025, the Law Commission published a short supplementary consultation paper.

The Law Commission published Part 1 of its Recommendations on liability in November 2025. (Part two will be published in 2026 and will address powers, procedure, sanctions, costs and appeals). As far as contempt by publication where proceedings are active is concerned, the Law Commission has recommended that

- the prosecution should have to show that a defendant was aware of a risk that proceedings were active
- the period during which criminal and extradition proceedings are considered active would change and would move from arrest to charge and not extend as far as sentencing: 'We recommend that criminal proceedings should be considered active from the point at which a suspect is charged until the point of verdict or guilty plea'
- the section 5 defence should be expanded to make clear that whether a publication is 'merely incidental' will depend on how closely the subject matter of the publication relates to the specific legal proceedings.

The Law Commission also recommended that the government consider reviewing section 41 of the Criminal Justice Act 1925 (see 12.1) and section 85B of the Courts Act 2003 (see 12.1.8) to ensure that photography, video recording, and transmission or live-streaming of audio or video of proceedings are captured, and that there is consistency in the application of contempt to in-court and remote proceedings. Finally, the Law Commission expressed the view that publishing details like a suspect's name, age, nationality, ethnicity, religion or immigration status will generally not create a substantial risk that the course of justice will be seriously impeded or prejudiced. (This approach is also reflected in recent draft guidance from the College of Policing and the National Police Chiefs' Council, which recommends releasing such information in 'high profile or sensitive investigations or operations' where there is, for example, 'a policing purpose' or a 'related risk or impact on public safety'). However, publishers would still have to assess whether such information risked seriously prejudicing proceedings.

Recap of major points

- For the media, the greatest danger of committing contempt of court lies in publishing material which, under the Contempt of Court Act 1981, could be ruled to have created a substantial risk of serious prejudice or impediment to an 'active' case.
- Certain types of information are more likely than others to be regarded as creating such risk—for example, details of a suspect or defendant's previous convictions.
- Journalists should know when, under the 1981 Act, a criminal or a civil case becomes active and when it ceases to be active—because the 'active' period determines what can be published.
- Juries are rarely used in civil cases, so the media have greater leeway about what can be published about active civil cases than in relation to active criminal cases.

- In prosecuting under the Act for strict liability contempt the Attorney General does not have to prove intent to cause prejudice.
- Under section 4(2) a court can order the media to postpone publishing a report of a court case, or part of it, to avoid a substantial risk of prejudice.
- Section 5 provides a defence if what is published is a discussion in good faith of public affairs where the risk of prejudice is merely incidental to the discussion.
- The media should not report legal discussions held, or rulings made, in the jury's absence during a trial until all the verdicts are reached.
- It is possible for a journalist or media organisation to commit a contempt in common law.
- Under the Courts Act 2003, any party, including a media organisation, ruled to have committed 'serious misconduct' affecting a court case could be liable for huge costs.

Useful Websites

IPSO, www.ipso.co.uk

- Court reporting guidance
- Sexual offences guidance

Law Commission consultations on Contempt of Court, https://lawcom.gov.uk/project/contempt-of-court

February 2026 Guidance published by the College of Policing: Media and communications (APP), https://www.college.police.uk/app/media-and-communications

Online resources

Visit the online resources at **www.mcnaes.com** to test your knowledge of this chapter with **self-test questions** and a **flashcard glossary**, and to read **updates** about law and regulatory matters affecting journalism, as well as **additional material** to further your learning.

Part 3

Defamation and related law

20

Defamation—definitions and dangers

Chapter summary

This chapter explains defamation law and why the danger of being sued for defamation is of such concern to journalists and publishers. It explains definitions of what is defamatory and warns that publication of defamatory material could lead to the publisher having to pay huge costs and damages. The following chapters explain who can sue for defamation, what the **claimant** must do to bring an action, and the defences which a publisher may be able to use if sued. Defamation is one of the greatest legal dangers for anyone who earns a living with words and images—so handling a complaint or drafting an apology about something published is not a job for an inexperienced journalist. England and Wales share the same defamation laws. There are differences in such laws in Northern Ireland and Scotland (see online ch. 36 for detail on media law in Northern Ireland and Scotland).

→glossary

20.1 Seeking legal advice

Defamation law is complex, so this book can provide nothing more than a rough guide. While journalists can sometimes safely go further than they might suppose in publishing criticism of people and organisations, they must stop and reflect before publishing allegations which could seriously harm someone's reputation.

The golden rule is that if what is planned for publication seems likely to lead to someone threatening to sue for defamation, journalists should take professional advice (which is a main reason why large media organisations have 'in-house' lawyers).

Nevertheless, media investigations into alleged wrongdoing by people or organisations—investigations which can trigger those being probed to make such a threat to deter publication—are extremely important. As Mr Justice Lawton said in a case in 1965:

> “It is one of the professional tasks of newspapers to unmask the fraudulent and the scandalous. It is in the public interest to do it. It is a job which newspapers have done time and time again in their long history.”

Of course, this remains an important task for journalists, including those working in magazine, broadcast and internet fields.

20.2 Introduction to defamation law

Defamation law protects an individual's reputation from unjustified attack. Publication of a statement making such an attack may be found to be a **tort**—a civil wrong for which a court may award damages.

→glossary

As this chapter will explain, a defamatory statement is one which lowers a person's reputation in the minds of right-thinking members of society, A defamatory statement published in written or any other permanent form—including online, for example as a tweet/X post or blog—is a libel, for which damages can be awarded, if what it says cannot be successfully defended.

A defamation action begins with the issue of a claim form, in common with procedure in other civil cases. The person or organisation suing over what was published is 'the claimant'. The person or organisation being sued is 'the defendant'. If the defendant intends to fight the case, the court must be informed within strict time limits, usually 14 days.

ch. 13 explains procedure in civil cases

A publisher sued for defamation may choose to defend the case all the way to a full trial at the High Court—for example, involving witnesses testifying that what was published was true.

However, legal costs will quickly mount as the case proceeds, because in most cases each side will be paying lawyers. If it becomes apparent that what was published cannot be defended, the publisher would be well advised to settle such a case by apologising and if necessary, paying an agreed sum in damages as soon as possible.

The current ceiling for general reputational damages awards in libel actions is around £300,000–£350,000 (see 20.3.3).

Recent settlements include:

- In February 2025, Associated Newspapers Ltd (ANL), the publisher of the *Mail on Sunday*, paid the green energy entrepreneur Dale Vince £40,000 in damages after they repeated false allegations that he supported Hamas (a proscribed terrorist organisation in the UK). (He had settled a case with ANL over identical allegations published in 2024 by the *Daily Mail* and online, when ANL had given an undertaking not to repeat the allegations). Under the terms of the settlement, ANL agreed to pay £30,000 of Mr Vince's legal costs and to publish an apology online and in the *Mail on Sunday*, Vince said he donated his damages to charity.
- In October 2025, Steve Coogan and the producers of the film *The Lost King* settled a libel case with academic Richard Taylor for 'substantial damages' and legal costs due to his defamatory portrayal in the film, about the discovery of Richard III's remains. Mr Taylor launched High Court action claiming the film had made him appear 'misogynistic' and 'weasel-like'. As a result of the settlement, the film will carry a message at the beginning, and the defamatory comments will not be repeated.

- In November 2025, musician Pascal Robinson (Bob Vylan) secured an apology and 'substantial damages' of £16,000 from Reach PLC following a false accusation of performing Nazi salutes.

A defamatory statement which is spoken is slander, which may incur damages unless a defence applies. But a defamatory statement spoken in a radio, television, or cable broadcast, or in an internet webcast, or in the public performance of a play, will be classed as libel by the Broadcasting Act 1990 and Theatres Act 1968, respectively, if the statement cannot be successfully defended. Libel and slander have different requirements in terms of what a claimant must prove. Ch. 21 and ch. 25, which has a focus on slander, explain this.

The Defamation Act 2013, which reformed defamation law in various ways, abolished the presumption of jury trial for defamation cases, so they are heard by a judge alone unless the judge orders otherwise. The judge decides the key issues of what the words mean and whether they have caused or are likely to cause 'serious harm' and, if there is no jury, the judge will decide the level of damages if the publisher loses the case at trial. There have been no jury trials in defamation cases since the 2013 Act took effect.

As explained in Ch 21, to bring a claim for defamation in E&W, a claimant must satisfy four elements: there must be:

- a defamatory statement
- published
- about them
- which causes or is likely to cause serious harm to their reputation within E&W (s 1 Defamation Act 2013).

The first of these elements will be looked at in more detail below. The remainder are considered in Ch 21.

20.2.1 A defamatory statement

There are a number of definitions in common law of what is a defamatory statement. For example, a statement is defamatory if it seriously harms a person's reputation by:

- exposing them to hatred, ridicule or contempt, or causing them to be shunned or avoided;
- lowering them in the estimation of right-thinking members of society generally; or
- disparaging them in their business, trade, office or profession.

✻ Remember

It is almost always defamatory to say of a person that they are a liar or a cheat, are insolvent or in financial difficulties, or have committed a violent crime; whether the statement is a libel will depend on whether the publisher has a defence.

20.2.2 Meaning of words

If there is a dispute in a defamation case about what the words published mean, the test in law is what an 'ordinary reasonable reader' would think they mean. In defamation law, it is ultimately down to the judge, if a case goes to court, to decide what the statement complained of means. The judge must find that the statement has just one meaning. Meaning is generally assessed according to three 'levels' (known as the '*Chase*' levels) after a case, ranging from Level 1 'guilt' (i.e. XX is corrupt), through to Level 3 'grounds for an investigation' (there are questions to be asked about XX's conduct).

see 22.2.3 on levels of meaning when reporting wrongdoing

If there is an argument over what an article means, the decision on meaning is usually dealt with early in the court process, before a defence has been filed. The meaning will not necessarily be the meaning intended by the author or publisher, nor the meaning suggested by the claimant. The outcome of that ruling on meaning may mean the case will not proceed. This could be because the publisher had not intended the meaning found by the judge and realises it is unable to defend that meaning, or because the claimant cannot, as a consequence of the ruling, prove what was published caused or was likely to cause 'serious harm'. In the *Banks v Cadwalladr* case (see Ch 21), investigative journalist Carole Cadwalladr had to abandon her defence of truth and rely solely on the statutory defence of publication on a matter of public interest, because she had not intended to say what the judge found her 2019 TED Talk meant, and knew she could not produce the evidence to defend that meaning on the basis of truth. (*Banks v Cadwalldr* [2019] EWHC 3451 QB)

In *Koutsogiannis v The Random House Group Ltd* [2019] EWHC 48 QB Mr Justice Nicklin set out the principles which a court will consider when ruling on meaning. He said:

> "(1) The governing principle is reasonableness. (2) The intention of the publisher is irrelevant. (3) The hypothetical reasonable reader is not naïve but he is not unduly suspicious. He can read between the lines. He can read in an implication more readily than a lawyer and may indulge in a certain amount of loose thinking but he must be treated as being a man who is not avid for scandal and someone who does not, and should not, select one bad meaning where other non-defamatory meanings are available. A reader who always adopts a bad meaning where a less serious or non-defamatory meaning is available is not reasonable: s/he is avid for scandal. But always to adopt the less derogatory meaning would also be unreasonable: it would be naïve. (4) Over-elaborate analysis should be avoided and the court should certainly not take a too literal approach to the task. (5) Consequently, a judge providing written reasons for conclusions on meaning should not fall into the trap of conducting too detailed an analysis of the various passages relied on by the respective parties. (6) Any meaning that emerges as the produce of some strained, or forced, or utterly unreasonable interpretation should be rejected. (7) It follows that it is not enough to say that by some person or another the words might be understood in a defamatory sense. (8) The publication must be read as

a whole, and any 'bane and antidote' taken together. Sometimes, the context will clothe the words in a more serious defamatory meaning (for example the classic 'rogues' gallery' case). In other cases, the context will weaken (even extinguish altogether) the defamatory meaning that the words would bear if they were read in isolation (e.g. bane and antidote cases). (9) In order to determine the natural and ordinary meaning of the statement of which the claimant complains, it is necessary to take into account the context in which it appeared and the mode of publication. (10) No evidence, beyond publication complained of, is admissible in determining the natural and ordinary meaning. (11) The hypothetical reader is taken to be representative of those who would read the publication in question. The court can take judicial notice of facts which are common knowledge, but should beware of reliance on impressionistic assessments of the characteristics of a publication's readership. (12) Judges should have regard to the impression the article has made upon them themselves in considering what impact it would have made on the hypothetical reasonable reader. (13) In determining the single meaning, the court is free to choose the correct meaning; it is not bound by the meanings advanced by the parties (save that it cannot find a meaning that is more injurious than the claimant's pleaded meaning). ”

see 20.2.5, Bane and antidote

In rulings on meaning, the words must be read in full and in context, because a statement which is innocuous when standing alone can acquire defamatory meaning when juxtaposed with other material. Juxtaposition is a constant danger for journalists, particularly subeditors and production staff. Those editing footage must take care how pictures interact with each other and with any commentary—what meanings are being created?

see also 21.2.2.5, Juxtaposition

20.2.3 Inferences

- An inference is a statement with a secondary meaning which can be understood by someone without special knowledge who 'reads between the lines in the light of his general knowledge and experience of worldly affairs'.

For example, an inference is created if someone says: 'I saw the editor leave the pub, and he was swaying and his speech was slurred.' The inference is that the editor was drunk, though the term 'drunk' is not used. But for some statements there may be dispute about whether a defamatory inference was created. Some recent court rulings on meaning are listed in the additional materials for this chapter.

20.2.4 Innuendoes

- An innuendo in the law of defamation is a statement which seems to be innocuous to some people but is defamatory to people with special knowledge.

For example, saying 'I saw our editor go into that house on the corner of Sleep Street' would not in itself be defamatory, unless it was said to someone who knows the house was a brothel.

A claimant who says they have been defamed by an innuendo must show not only that the special facts or circumstances giving rise to the innuendo exist but also that they are known to some of the people to whom the statement was published.

In *Vince v Associated Newspapers* [2024] EWHC 1806 (KB), the High Court held that the rule in *Charleston* (see below) applies not just when ascertaining the 'natural and ordinary meaning' but equally where an innuendo meaning is pleaded. The Claimant accepted that if the entire article he complained about was read by the hypothetical reader, the article bore no defamatory meaning, and the claim would fail. However, he tried to argue that there was a class of 'innuendo reader', who would only have looked at the article's headline and the pictures of the Claimant beneath it, and would have concluded (wrongly) that he was a '"sex harassment" donor'. The court held that *Charleston* required the court to consider what meaning the words complained of would be understood to bear by the hypothetical reader reading the whole piece. On that basis, the article bore no defamatory meaning of the Claimant and was struck out. Mr Vince subsequently issued a new claim based on data protection against Associated, on the basis that his personal data had not been processed fairly. He tried to argue that the approach in *Charleston* should not apply when assessing fairness in a data protection claim. The judge rejected this argument, holding that to determine whether personal data was processed fairly, an approach that, like the rule in *Charleston*, takes account of the entirety of the publication, was appropriate. On that basis, the data protection claim was also struck out. (*Vince v Associated Newspapers* [2025] EWHC 1411 (KB). He has been given permission to appeal against this judgment.)

Case study

In 1986 Lord Gowrie, a former Cabinet Minister, received 'substantial' damages because an article in the *Daily Star* newspaper created the innuendo that he took drugs. He had recently resigned as Minister for the Arts and the *Daily Star* article said: 'What expensive habits can he not support on an income of £33,000? I'm sure Gowrie himself would snort at suggestions that he was born with a silver spoon round his neck'. His **counsel** said the reference to expensive habits, the suggestion he could not support those habits on his ministerial salary, the use of the word 'snort' and the reference to a 'silver spoon around his neck' all bore the plain implication to those familiar with the terminology that Lord Gowrie took illegal drugs, particularly cocaine, and that he had resigned as a Minister because his salary was not enough to finance the habit. →glossary

---

A journalist would be mistaken to believe that using inference or innuendo is any safer in defamation law than making a direct allegation.

20.2.5 Bane and antidote

A defamatory meaning may be conveyed by a particular sentence, but might be removed by the context which follows in the article. A judge said in 1835 that if in one part of what was published, something disreputable to the claimant was stated, but that was removed by the conclusion, 'the bane and the antidote must be taken together'.

The House of Lords applied this rule in 1995 (*Charleston v News Group Newspapers Ltd* [1995] 2 AC 65), when it dismissed a case in which two actors from the television serial *Neighbours*, sued the *News of the World* over headlines and photographs in which their faces were superimposed on models in sexual poses. In *Neighbours* the actors played the roles of a respectable married couple called Harold and Madge Bishop.

The *News of the World* article, which had a main headline stating 'Strewth! What's Harold up to with our Madge?', said as its first paragraph: 'What would the Neighbours say . . . strait-laced Harold Bishop starring in a bondage session with screen wife Madge.'

It said in the next paragraphs: 'The famous faces from the television soap are the unwitting stars of a sordid computer game that is available to their child fans. The game superimposes stars' heads on near-naked bodies of real porn models. The stars knew nothing about it'.

In court, it was argued for the actors that readers would have drawn the defamatory inference from the headlines and photos that the actors had been willing participants in the production of pornographic photos, either by posing for them personally or by agreeing that their faces should be superimposed on the bodies of others.

The actors' barrister said that many readers were unlikely to go beyond the photographs and headlines.

In the House of Lords judgment, Lord Bridge said that often in defamation cases the debatable question which had to be resolved was whether the antidote was effective to neutralise the bane. The answer depended not only on the nature of the libel conveyed by a headline and the language of the text which was relied on to neutralise it but also on the manner in which the whole of the material was set out and presented, he added. He said that no person who read beyond the first paragraph of the *News of the World* article could possibly have drawn any such defamatory inference about the two actors, and that any people who had not taken the trouble to read beyond the first paragraph, and went away with the impression that the two well-known actors in legitimate television had also been involved making pornographic films, could hardly be described as ordinary, reasonable, fair-minded readers.

Lord Nicholls warned in the judgment that: 'It all depends on the context, one element in which is the layout of the article. Those who print defamatory headlines are playing with fire.' The ordinary reader might not notice 'curative' words tucked away low down in an article, he said.

In *Hemming v Poulton & Ors* [2025] EWCA Civ 1494, the Court of Appeal handed down a judgment on meaning. It is rare for the Court of Appeal to intervene in the determination of meaning in a libel claim, because it is a very fact specific exercise that is ultimately in the discretion of the judge. The claim related to two publications made by a journalist Sonia Poulter in 2019: a YouTube video of an interview and a written statement. On appeal, the Court substituted clarified determinations of meaning for each publication. Warby LJ restated that the natural and ordinary meaning of a publication is that which the ordinary reasonable reader would take from the publication as a whole, emphasising that the repetition rule and 'bane and antidote principle' are 'subsidiary' to this overarching principle and are simply 'tools' to help the court decide the meaning.

20.2.6 **Meaning in social media publications**

The courts see social media as a fairly 'casual' medium, which people scroll through quickly and where their reactions are often impressionistic and fleeting. Context is important when deciding the meaning of social media posts (see *Hopkins v Monroe* [2017] EWHC 433). In *Stocker v Stocker* [2019] UK SC 17, the Supreme Court ruled in favour of Mrs Stocker, in a defamation lawsuit filed by her ex-husband, over her use of the phrase 'he tried to strangle me,' which she had posted on Facebook. The court said this was not defamatory because, within the context of a social media exchange, a reasonable reader would not understand it to mean that he had tried to kill her: the context and the conversational nature of social media must be considered when interpreting the meaning of online statements. Contrast this with the High Court's finding in *Vardy v Rooney* [2020] EWHC 3156, where the High Court accepted that sometimes a post will have been composed with care, and it would be clear to readers that it was meant to be taken seriously.

20.2.7 **Changing standards**

Imputations which were defamatory 100 years ago might not be defamatory today.

During the First World War a UK court ruled that it was a libel to publish falsely of a man that he was a German. Nowadays it is not defamatory to state that someone is a German.

It used to be defamatory to call someone homosexual, but now no 'right-thinking member of society' would think less of someone because they are gay (see *Ahmadi v GNM* [2025] EWHC 1191). So wrongly stating that someone is gay would not usually be defamatory—although it could be if it were to imply that they had lied about their sexual orientation.

> See the **additional material** for this chapter on **www.mcnaes.com** for a case study about singer Robbie Williams receiving an apology and damages for a publication alleging he had concealed his sexuality in an autobiography.

20.3 **Why media organisations may be reluctant to fight defamation actions**

Defamation law tries to strike a balance between the individual's right to a reputation and the right to freedom of speech, and so there are defences in that law for those who make defamatory statements about others for acceptable reasons—see subsequent chapters. But media organisations can be reluctant to fight defamation actions, for a variety of reasons.

20.3.1 Uncertainty of how a judge will interpret meaning

- The first is the uncertainty about how a judge will decide the meaning of what was published—for example, a statement which seems innocuous to one person may be clearly defamatory to another. As this chapter has indicated, a media organisation can be successfully sued because of a meaning its journalist did not intend to create.

20.3.2 Difficulty of proving the truth

Even if a journalist and their editor are convinced of a story's truth, they may be unable to prove it in court.

The truth defence is explained in 22.2

- People needed as witnesses to an event may not wish to become involved in a defamation case; witnesses' memories may prove unreliable; they may forget detail by the time the trial begins; by the time the case gets to trial they may have moved and cannot be traced.

20.3.3 Huge damages could be awarded if trial lost

Media organisations considering contesting a defamation action may also find it difficult to estimate the amount of damages which, if they lose the case after a trial, they would have to pay to the claimant. A court which rules that the claimant's case is proved in a trial must award an amount of damages which (1) compensates the claimant for the damage to their reputation, taking into account the extent to which the libellous material was published and how grave the attack on the claimant's character was; (2) vindicates their good name; and (3) (for any claimant who is a person, not an organisation) takes account of the distress, hurt and humiliation which the defamatory publication has caused (*John v MGN Ltd* [1997] QB 586). Also, the level of damages awarded by the judge can take into account any 'impact on the claimant's feelings' caused by the proceedings (*Lachaux v Independent Print Ltd and Evening Standard Ltd* [2021] EWHC 1797 (QB)). For example, the claimant might have found the cross-examination in a trial by the defendant's lawyer to have been a harrowing ordeal.

In the past, when juries were still involved in libel trials, they sometimes awarded huge sums in damages. In 2000 the magazine *LM* (formerly *Living Marxism*) shut down after a jury awarded a total of £375,000 damages to two television reporters and ITN because *LM* published an article falsely accusing them of having sensationalised the image of an emaciated Muslim pictured through barbed wire at a Serb-run detention camp in Bosnia (*The Guardian*, 21 March 2000).

The current ceiling is likely to be around £350,000 (this was said by Mr Justice Nicklin in 2021 in *Lachaux*, cited earlier). This highest level of damages awards is reserved for the gravest of allegations, such as imputations of terrorism or murder. Mr Justice Warby made that general point when ruling on damages to be awarded in a defamation action brought by three Labour MPs against Jane Collins, a former UKIP

Member of the European Parliament, who falsely alleged in a conference speech that for political purposes they had for years ignored the fact that gangs of men were sexually abusing children in Rotherham. The speech was webcast on the UKIP website. She made 'an offer of amends' (see 22.9), so there was no trial. The judge ruled that Ms Collins should pay each MP £54,000 damages (*Barron & Ors v Collins* [2015] EWHC 1125 (QB), [2017] EWHC 162 (QB)).

The **additional material** for this chapter on **www.mcnaes.com** explains why in law there is a 'ceiling' to the amount of compensatory damages, and the circumstances in which 'aggravated' or 'exemplary' damages can also be awarded. It also explains controversy about section 40 of the Crime and Courts Act 2013—law created to make press organisations more vulnerable to awards of costs being made against them in civil cases if they are not part of the Royal Charter system of press regulation explained in ch. 2. Section 40 has now been repealed.

20.3.4 Huge costs

Damages might be high, but they are usually much lower than legal costs in the case. In defamation cases, as in all civil cases, if there is a trial the losing side—as well as having to pay all or most of its own legal costs—must usually pay most of the winning side's legal costs.

In September 2025, the actor Noel Clarke was told to pay £3m on account of costs to *The Guardian*'s publisher after losing a libel trial with the newspaper. He had sued Guardian News and Media over seven articles and a podcast, including an article in April 2021 that said 20 women had come forward with allegations of misconduct, including harassment and sexually inappropriate behaviour. In a trial which lasted 6 weeks, *The Guardian* had put forward defences of truth and public interest, both of which succeeded. The judge ruled that Clarke had to pay £3m ahead of a detailed assessment into the total costs to be recovered, estimated to be above £6m. (*Daily Telegraph*, 24 September 2025, p 2)

20.3.5 It may be better to settle

It is not surprising that, faced with these kinds of figures and risks over costs and damages, even ardent campaigning editors may decide either not to carry a story or, having carried it, to avoid a trial by apologising and paying damages, a decision which saves on costs.

As most defamation cases are settled out of court, with the sums involved rarely disclosed, the ongoing cost of defamation actions to media organisations is often underestimated. A settlement usually involves paying some or all of the other side's costs.

20.3.5.1 'No win, no fee' legal representation

Legal aid was never available for defamation actions, so historically the courts were beyond the reach of people on modest incomes who felt or claimed they had been →glossary

→glossary

defamed. But the use of **Conditional fee agreements (CFAs)**, known as 'no win, no fee', was introduced for defamation cases in 1998. CFAs meant litigants without the means to sue could do so, represented by lawyers who received nothing if they lost a case but could claim a 'success fee' of up to a 100 per cent increase on their fees from the other side if they won. However, in January 2010 the European Court of Human Rights held that a 100 per cent success fee claimed by Naomi Campbell's lawyers after she won a privacy claim against Mirror Group Newspapers was a breach of the publisher's right to freedom of expression.

see ch. 27, Privacy

The media argued the CFA system allowed claimants without enough money to fund legal action to hold publishers to ransom. If the claimant lost, the media defendant was unlikely to recover its costs, while if they won, the media defendant had to pay damages *and* the claimant's lawyers' 'success fees', as well as associated insurance premiums. There was little incentive for a claimant on a CFA to control their costs. The pressure on media defendants to settle such cases rather than go to court was therefore considerable.

In 2019 the Government announced that from 6 April that year lawyers working on CFAs would no longer be able to recover success fees from defendants—such as media organisations—which lose defamation or privacy cases. Claimants would, however, still be able to recover premiums for so-called after-the-event (ATE) insurance to protect them from adverse costs orders should they lose.

20.4 Errors and apologies

Sometimes an innocent error leads to publication of a libel. The arrival of a solicitor's letter from a potential claimant which could start the journey to the High Court is the moment to take legal advice. Defamation law is not a matter for an inexperienced person, because of the dangers of aggravating a problem by mishandling it. A reporter who receives a complaint about something which has been published should refer the issue to the relevant executive or editor. Publishing an apology or an inadequate correction can itself, in certain circumstances, create a further libel problem. For the danger of publishing ill-considered apologies, see 22.8.

Taking the correct legal steps, including, if necessary, publishing a prompt apology or correction, can remove the heat from a threat to sue, and save thousands of pounds even if the claim is settled. A prompt apology can play a significant part in a court's consideration of whether a statement caused 'serious harm' to reputation, and could prevent a claim from being viable in the first place. Also, as ch. 25 explains, failure to correct an article which is known to be wrong, especially if it remains visible online, could leave the publisher liable to pay damages for malicious falsehood.

* Remember

The most common cause of defamation actions against media organisations is a journalist's failure to apply professional standards of accuracy and fairness. The best protection against becoming involved in an expensive action is to make every effort to get the story right.

20.5 Summary disposal

Sections 8 and 9 of the Defamation Act 1996 enable a court to 'dispose summarily' of a case in some circumstances, which means there is not a full trial of that defamation action.

The circumstances are that:

- the court may dismiss the action if it appears to the court that the claim of defamation has no realistic prospect of success and there is no reason why it should be tried.
- the court may give judgment for the claimant if it appears to the court that there is no defence to the claim which has a realistic prospect of success, that there is no other reason why the claim should be tried, and that adequate compensation for the claimant will be a declaration that the published statement was false and defamatory, an order that the defendant publish or cause to be published a suitable correction and apology, and an award of damages not exceeding £10,000.

20.6 Data protection law and defamation actions

A claimant can bring a claim under the Data Protection Act 2018 alongside a defamation action and may choose to do so in order to have an alternative remedy if their defamation claim fails. For example, a claimant who is unable to establish that they have been caused 'serious harm' as a result of an article published online may be able to prove that it contains personal information about them which is inaccurate. Consequently, the claimant can require the publisher to correct or delete that information to comply with the Act, and may be able to win damages for distress they suffered because of the inaccuracy.

In 2017, the Court of Appeal observed, in a case in which the claimant was Prince Moulay Hicham of Morocco, that there was 'no good reason of principle' why a Data Protection Act claim could not be brought together with a defamation claim. The prince sued *Elaph*, a UK-based Arabic news website, over an article which wrongly alleged he plotted to undermine his cousin, King Mohammed VI. Lord Justice Simon said that, if *Elaph*'s defence succeeded, the prince's data protection claim 'may found an appropriate alternative means of redress'. A settlement was later agreed and *Elaph* offered redress under the Data Protection Act by correcting and erasing the inaccurate personal data, agreeing not to republish the article and paying damages and costs (*Prince Moulay Hicham v Elaph Publishing* [2017] EWCA Civ 29; *Press Gazette*, 13 November 2018). In *Pacini v Dow Jones* [2024] EWHC 1709, despite repeated threats, no defamation proceedings had been issued but, in March 2023, 6 years after the publication of the article, the claimants issued a UK GDPR claim against the defendants for failing to process their personal data fairly and failing to ensure the data was accurate. The Judge declined to strike out the case as an abuse of process. For more detail on data protection law, see ch. 28.

Recap of major points

- A defamatory statement made in permanent form is generally libel, and if in transient form, it is generally slander—if it cannot be defended.
- In a defamation action, the test of what the words actually mean is what a reasonable person would take them to mean.
- Words may carry an innuendo, a 'hidden' meaning clear to people with special knowledge, or create an inference, obvious to most people.
- The financial implications of losing a defamation action in terms of damages and costs are so punitive that journalists must always consider whether what they are writing or plan to broadcast will be defensible if a defamation action results.

Useful Websites

Defamation Act 2013 and accompanying explanatory notes, https://www.legislation.gov.uk/ukpga/2013/26/contents

The International Forum for Responsible Media Blog, inforrm.org

Inform blog site, which publishes analysis of defamation and other law

Online resources

Visit the online resources at **www.mcnaes.com** to test your knowledge of this chapter with **self-test questions** and a **flashcard glossary**, and to read **updates** about law and regulatory matters affecting journalism, as well as **additional material** to further your learning.

21

Who can sue for defamation and what they must prove

Chapter summary

This chapter details who can sue for defamation. It sets out the four elements that a claimant must show to bring a legal claim for defamation. A **claimant** must prove that the material was published to a third party—a formality in a case against the media—that bears a defamatory meaning that they have been identified in it and that their reputation has suffered, or is likely to suffer, serious harm. However, the defamation claimant does not have the burden of proving the material is false. A claimant can sue anyone who 'publishes' the defamatory statement, including individual reporters.

→glossary

21.1 Who might sue?

All citizens as individuals have the right to sue for defamation—that is, to be a claimant.

The availability of 'no win, no fee' arrangements, described in ch. 20, has meant that more people can afford to sue. This reinforces the need for journalists to be accurate and approach stories thus:

- Is what I am writing or preparing to broadcast potentially defamatory?
- If so, do I have a defence?

21.1.1 Corporations, including companies

A corporation can sue for a publication injurious to its trading reputation. But section 1 of the Defamation Act 2013 requires a claimant to show that the publication caused or was likely to cause 'serious harm' to reputation (see 21.2.4). To meet this requirement a body that 'trades for profit' must show that the publication 'has caused or is likely to cause the body serious financial loss'. Previously the threat of being sued by a company was significant. Although some companies are likely to find it difficult to prove that they have suffered or are likely to suffer serious see also 21.1.4, Disparaging goods

financial loss, for a smaller company even the loss of one prospective client may help to establish such loss. The mere fact that a company's share price has fallen is insufficient (*Collins Stewart Ltd and another v The Financial Times* [2004] EWHC 2337 (QB)). But individual directors and managers may be able to sue, if 'identified'—see later.

21.1.2 Local and central government

→glossary

ch. 25 explains malicious falsehood

The House of Lords ruled in *Derbyshire County Council v Times Newspapers* [1993] AC 534 that institutions of local or central government cannot sue for defamation in respect of their 'governmental and administrative functions' as this would place an undesirable fetter on freedom of speech. But they can sue as institutions if the publication of defamatory material affects their property, and for malicious falsehood if they can prove there was **malice**. Political parties are also unable to sue for defamation for the same reason, although their individual members and officials can do so (*Goldsmith and another v Bhoyrul and others* [1989] QB 459).

Individual councillors or officials *can* sue if what is published is seen as referring to them personally. Lord Keith said in the *Derbyshire County Council* case:

> "A publication attacking the activities of the authority will necessarily be an attack on the body of councillors which represents the controlling party, or on the executives who carry on the day-to-day management of its affairs. If the individual reputation of any of these is wrongly impaired by the publication any of these can himself bring proceedings for defamation."

An individual can sue for defamation if what is published 'identifies' them, which can happen even if they are not named. The legal test for identification in defamation cases is explained later in the chapter.

As a general rule, an association, such as a club, cannot sue unless it is an incorporated body, but words disparaging an association will almost invariably reflect upon the reputations of one or more of the officials who, as individuals, can sue if 'identified' in what is published.

21.1.3 Trade unions

The 2024 decision in the case of *Prospect v Evans* [2025] EWHC 499 confirmed that trade unions have the legal standing and a distinct reputation, separate from their individual members, to bring defamation claims. This ruling overturned previous legal interpretations that questioned a union's ability to possess a reputation capable of being defamed. A union's officers can also sue.

21.1.4 Disparaging goods

Can a publication defame a person or a firm by disparaging goods? This is an important question as product testing is commonplace on websites and in newspapers, magazines and other media.

The answer is yes. But it is not enough for the statement to simply affect the person adversely in their business—it must also infer discreditable conduct in that business, or tend to show that they are ill-suited or ill-qualified to do it (*Griffiths v Benn* [1911] 927 TLR 26, CA, applied in *James Morford and others v Nic Rigby and the East Anglian Daily Times Co Ltd* [1998] EWCA Civ 263).

For example, it will be defamatory to write falsely of a businessman that he has been condemned by his trade association, or of a bricklayer that she does not know how to lay bricks properly, if either can show that their reputation suffered, or was likely to suffer, serious harm as a result of the publication.

Not all words criticising a person's goods are defamatory—for example, a motoring correspondent could criticise a car's performance without reflecting on the character of the manufacturer or dealer. But the statement might prompt an action for malicious falsehood—see ch. 25.

Imputations of dishonesty, carelessness and incompetence give publishers the most problems in this context. In 1994 a jury awarded £1.485 million damages to the manufacturer of a yacht, Walker Wingsail Systems plc, over an article in *Yachting World* which contrasted the manufacturer's striking claims for the yacht's performance with its drastically poorer performance when tested by the journalist.

21.2 What the claimant must prove

A claimant suing for defamation has to prove that:

- the publication is defamatory (see Ch 20);
- it may be reasonably understood to refer to them—that is, 'identification'; and
- it has been published to a third person.
- it has caused or is likely to cause 'serious harm'.

21.2.1 Defamatory statement

see 20.2.1, Definitions of a defamatory statement

Legal definitions of defamatory statements are given in ch. 20.

The claimant does *not* have to prove that the statement is false. If a statement is defamatory, the court's starting point is to assume it is false. If the journalist can prove it is true, then there is a defence, or another defence may apply, as the next chapter explains.

21.2.2 Identification

The claimant must prove that the published material identifies them.

Some journalists believe they can play safe by not naming an individual in what is published—but omitting the name may prove no defence.

- If identification is in dispute, the general test in defamation law of whether the published statement identified the claimant is whether it would reasonably lead people acquainted with them to believe that they were the person referred to.

A judge said in 1826: 'It is not necessary that all the world should understand the libel; it is sufficient if those who know the claimant can make out that he is the person meant' (*Bourke v Warren* (1826) 2 C&P 307). That is still the law.

Identification can be done either through the words themselves (intrinsic reference) or by reference to particular facts known to the hypothetical reasonable reader or viewer acquainted with the claimant(s) (extrinsic reference or reference innuendo). A claimant must usually identify one or more individuals who read the statement complained of and who knew special facts from which reasonable people would reasonably understand the statement to refer to the claimant.

Derogatory comments published about an institution, business or company can affect the reputation of the person who heads or manages it—newspapers have had to pay damages to head teachers, who were not named in the articles, for reports criticising schools which were identified.

21.2.2.1 **Wrong photos or wrong caption**

People are identified by what they look like, so publishing the wrong photo in a defamatory context, even if the person's name is not included, can be very costly.

In 2003 *The Sun* carried a report of how Norwich Crown court had given a paedophile, who the report named, a lifetime ban on meeting or talking to anyone under the age of 16 after he admitted indecently assaulting two young girls. The report included a photo of a man's face beside the headline: 'Face of kid ban pervert'. But the photo was of the wrong man. *The Sun* took out adverts in the local press in Great Yarmouth, where he lived, to apologise to him for the mistake, and paid him £50,000 compensation for the libel, and £32,633 to his lawyers for their fees (*Press Gazette*, 17 April 2003 and 18 March 2004).

Using file or 'stock' photographs or film to illustrate news stories or features is fraught with libel risks. For example, publishing a photo of an event, with people holding drinks, is perfectly acceptable to report it. But if that photo is later published as a stock shot to illustrate the perils of drinking alcohol, those pictured, particularly any teetotallers, may sue—because the inference is that they have an alcohol problem.

21.2.2.2 **Importance of ages, addresses and occupations**

It can be dangerous to make a half-hearted effort at identification, particularly in reports of court cases.

Case study

In *Newstead v London Express Newspapers Ltd* [1940] 1 KB 377, the *Daily Express* reported that 'Harold Newstead, a 30-year-old Camberwell man', was jailed for nine months for bigamy. Another Harold Newstead, who worked in Camberwell, sued, claiming the report was understood to refer to him—and won. He argued that if the words were true of another person, which they were, it was the paper's duty to give a precise and detailed description of that person, but the paper had 'recklessly struck out' the offender's occupation and address.

✱ Remember

To avoid defamation problems, a defendant's age, address and occupation, if mentioned in court, or provided by the court, should be included with their name in reports of the case unless the court directs otherwise. Ch. 15 explains that courts should give reporters such details.

21.2.2.3 Blurring identity can increase risk

The problem with not fully identifying the subject of a story is not only that the person may argue in a defamation case that they were the person referred to but also that someone else might claim that the words were also taken to refer to them. A newspaper quoted from a district auditor's report to a local council, criticising the authority's deputy housing manager. The paper did not name him. But a new deputy manager had taken over. He sued, saying what was published by the paper made people think he was the official criticised.

21.2.2.4 Defaming a group

If a defamatory statement refers to someone as being a member of a group and includes no other identifying detail of that person, all members of the group, if it is sufficiently small, may be able to sue for defamation, even though the publisher intended to refer to only one of them.

For example, publishing that 'One of the detectives at Blanktown police station is corrupt' without naming that individual will allow all the detectives there to sue because the statement 'identifies' them to their acquaintances and colleagues. Even if the publisher has evidence that one is corrupt, the rest will win damages. But if the group referred to is large, no one in it will be able reasonably to claim to have been identified merely by a reference to the group.

Case law does not set a clear figure for when a group is too large for those in it to claim that reference to the group identifies them as individuals. In one case, reference to a group of 35 police dog-handlers in one area of London was ruled by a court to be enough to identify them as individuals (*Aiken and others v Police Review Publishing Ltd*, 12 April 1995, unreported [1995] CA Transcript 576-T). See too *Kneafsey and others v ITN and others* [2013] EWHC 4046 (a libel claim by six officers from the Enfield Crime squad).

Case study

A case in 1986 concerned a reference published by a newspaper to an allegation that detectives at Banbury CID had raped a woman. The newspaper did not name those allegedly involved. It was successfully sued by members of the group, which comprised only 12 detectives (*Riches and others v News Group Newspapers Ltd* [1985] 2 All ER 845).

Referring to a group may also identify those with particular responsibility for it. Publishing that 'The supermarket in Blanktown Road is run badly' refers to a small group of managers, each of whom could sue.

21.2.2.5 Juxtaposition

Placing a photograph incorrectly, or using the wrong picture, can cause expensive problems if it wrongly suggests by juxtaposition that someone shown is a person 'identified' in the accompanying story.

In 2002 motivational therapist and part-time nightclub doorman Shabazz Nelson won 'substantial' damages from *The Sun* after it used his picture with an article in which Oasis star Liam Gallagher alleged he and his girlfriend were assaulted by door attendants at the Met Bar in London. The piece was illustrated by a picture of Mr Nelson, who was working there that night as a doorman. Mr Nelson had not assaulted Mr Gallagher or his girlfriend, had 'conducted himself in a perfectly proper and responsible manner', and was 'understandably concerned' that *Sun* readers who saw the article 'would have understood that he was the subject of Mr Gallagher's claims', Mr Justice Eady was told at the High Court.

Lack of care in the editing and 'voice-over' of footage can also cause trouble if the commentary is 'juxtaposed' with an unconnected image.

Case study

In 1983 a Metropolitan Police detective constable won £20,000 damages from Granada TV after being shown walking out of West End Central police station during a *World in Action* programme on Operation Countryman, an anti-corruption investigation into the force. As he was shown emerging from the station the voice-over said: 'Since 1969 repeated investigations show that some CID officers take bribes.' The officer was not identified by name and there was no suggestion that he was guilty of such behaviour—he was merely a figure in a background shot. But this was enough to earn him damages, because it wrongly 'identified' him as corrupt.

21.2.3 Publication

The claimant must prove that the statement was published. There is no defamation if the words complained of, however offensive or untrue, are addressed, in speech or writing, only to the person to whom they refer. To substantiate defamation, they must have been communicated to at least one other person. In the case of the news media, there is no difficulty in proving this—publication is widespread.

21.2.3.1 If very few readers see online material

There is an exception to this rule about publication for claimants suing over items published on the internet.

Case study

In 2005 the Court of Appeal rejected a Saudi Arabian businessman's claim for defamation by ruling that it would be an abuse of process for any claimant to bring an action over material on the internet unless 'substantial publication' in England could be shown. In that case, the complained-of material was downloaded by only five people in England—three, including the claimant's lawyers, were in his 'camp' and the other two were unknown. There was no 'real or substantial' **tort** (*Dow Jones and Co Inc. v Yousef Abdul Latif Jameel* [2005] EWCA Civ 75).

→glossary

But a tweet published to 65 people can justify a substantial five-figure award of damages (*Cairns v Modi* [2013] 1 WLR 1015, CA), as can internet publication to 550 people (*Times Newspapers Ltd v Flood* [2014] EWCA Civ 1574).

The court will not assume that internet publication is necessarily substantial publication (*Amoudi v Brisard* [2006] 3 All ER 294).

21.2.3.2 Who are the 'publishers'?

A person who has been defamed by a media publication may sue the reporter, sub-editor, editor and publisher (for example, the company which owns the relevant website, newspaper, magazine or radio or TV station). All have participated in publishing the defamatory statement and are regarded as 'publishers' at common law. Individuals can be sued for what they blog or tweet. Others, such as the printer and distributor, may be protected from an action by section 1 of the Defamation Act 1996 or section 10 of the Defamation Act 2013 or other law—see 22.11, 'Live' broadcasts and readers' online postings.

21.2.3.3 Repeating statements of others

- Every repetition of a libel is a fresh publication and creates a fresh cause of action. This is called the 'repetition rule'. It is no defence to say that you, the publisher, are not liable because you only repeated the words of others.

The person who originated the statement may be liable, but anyone who repeats the allegation—for example, by publishing material from a defamatory press release or retweeting a defamatory tweet—may also be sued. A common cause of defamation actions is repeating statements made by interviewees without being able to prove the truth of the words. Also, a publisher who 'lifts' (copies and publishes) material published elsewhere is liable.

In 1993 and 1994 newspapers paid damages to defendants in the Birmingham Six case, who were jailed for terrorism but later cleared on appeal. Former West Midlands police officers were accused of fabricating evidence in the case, but prosecution of the officers was abandoned. The *Sunday Telegraph* subsequently reported one of the three officers as referring to the Birmingham Six and saying: 'In our eyes, their guilt is beyond doubt.' *The Sun* newspaper published an article based on the *Sunday Telegraph*'s interviews. It later carried an apology and reportedly paid £1 million in damages to the six.

21.2.3.4 Repeating by republishing

Journalists must also be alert when republishing material. A doctor received damages for statements published afresh in 1981 in the 'Looking Back' column of the *Evening Star*, Ipswich. The statements, repeated from an article published 25 years previously, went unchallenged when first published.

The repetition rule dates from the 1849 case involving the Duke of Brunswick—see the **additional material** for this chapter on **www.mcnaes.com** for details of this case.

21.2.3.5 Online archives and repetition

As ch. 22 explains, the limitation period for a defamation action can be expressed generally as being 12 months from the date of publication—the defamation action must be launched in the limitation period, or else it will fail.

Under the repetition rule, each time an article or footage or sound recording in an internet archive is accessed by someone it is deemed to amount to a new publication. However, this does not necessarily create a further period of another year in which a defamation action can be launched—because the online publisher could have protection under 'the single publication rule'.

21.2.3.6 The 'single publication rule' and online archives

Section 8 of the Defamation Act 2013 introduced the 'single publication rule'. This means that in England and Wales the 12-month limitation period for bringing a defamation action runs from the date of the first publication of the complained-of statement 'to the public'. This means that if the article is only online, the first publication is the first time any member of the public accessed it. Note that, in exceptional circumstances, courts can extend the 12-month limitation period.

Also, the 2013 Act says that the 'single publication rule' will not apply if the manner of the subsequent publication by the same publisher is 'materially different' from the manner of the first and that, when a court is deciding if there is a material difference, factors it can consider include 'the level of prominence that a statement is given' and 'the extent of the subsequent publication'. The Act's Explanatory Notes, referring to what may be 'materially different', say:

> “A possible example of this could be where a story has first appeared relatively obscurely in a section of a website where several clicks need to be gone through to access it, but has subsequently been promoted to a position where it can be directly accessed from the home page of the site, thereby increasing considerably the number of hits it receives.”

Publication by a *different* publisher of the same allegation will trigger a new limitation period for that specific publication, giving anyone who claims to have been defamed by the allegation the opportunity to sue that different publisher for defamation.

✻ Remember

It can still be important to remove from an archive any material which has been ruled to be libellous.

Case study

In 2006 a businessman, Jim Carr, won two libel damages payouts from the *Sunday Telegraph* over one story. In April that year he won £12,000 and an apology over an article published in November 2005. The newspaper later paid him a further £5,000 in damages over the same defamatory story, which, by an oversight, it had left on its website (*Media Lawyer*, 26 June 2006).

21.2.3.7 Hyperlinking to defamatory material

In what circumstances can a media organisation or journalist who publishes a hyperlink to material put online by another party be successfully sued by a person defamed by that material? In the case of *Caine v Advertiser and Times Ltd & Ors* [2019] EWHC 2278, a court held that in certain situations hyperlinking might attract liability, and in a case in 2010 involving *The Spectator*, the court considered whether the web pages a *Spectator* article had linked to, could inform the meaning of their article. The judge found, on the facts, that the material made no difference to the article's meaning but did not rule out the possibility that they could have had an impact on the meaning (*Islam Expo Ltd v The Spectator (1828) Ltd* [2010] EWHC 2011). The test applied by the courts, asks would the reasonable reader have followed the link. In *Banks v Cadwalladr*, above, (Tweet linking to TED Talk), the court said yes, the reasonable reader would; in *Mueen-Uddin v Home Secretary* [2023] UKSC 21 (footnote in online report), the court said they would not.

See also the ECtHR case of *Magyar Jeti Zrt. v Hungary* (Application no. 11257/16) in the online additional materials.

21.2.4 Serious harm

A statement may be defamatory on its face, it might identify the claimant, and it may have been published, but unless it causes or is likely to cause serious harm, it will not be actionable. Section 1 of the 2013 Defamation Act says a statement is not to be considered as defamatory unless it has caused, or is likely to cause, serious harm to a claimant's reputation. The Supreme Court in *Lachaux v Independent Print Ltd and another* ([2019] UKSC 27; [2019] 3 WLR 18; [2019] EMLR 22) ruled on what factors a judge should take into account when deciding whether such serious harm was caused or likely to be caused. In the *Lachaux* case, aerospace engineer Bruno Lachaux sued two media organisations over articles which aired allegations that he had mistreated his ex-wife, including that he was violent to her during their marriage.

For more details of *Lachaux*, see ch. 23

In its decision on the 'serious harm' issue, the Supreme Court agreed with Mr Justice Warby, who had ruled in the High Court that Mr Lachaux's reputation *had* suffered serious harm, based on a combination of factors—including the meaning of the words published, the circumstances and scale of publication, and the likely adverse consequences for him because of what was published. After further High Court hearings, Mr Lachaux won the case.

Case study

Arron Banks, a businessman and Brexit supporter, issued proceedings for defamation against investigative journalist Carole Cadwalladr in relation to a TED Talk entitled 'Facebook's role in Brexit—and the threat to democracy', which she gave in April 2019. The TED Talk was published online to a substantial audience in the UK. During the time the case took to come to court, official investigations had found no evidence that Mr Banks had broken the law. Ms Cadwalladr had also abandoned her defence of truth and at trial relied solely on the statutory defence of publication on a matter of public interest.

The trial judge held that although the initial publication of the TED Talk had caused serious harm to Mr Banks's reputation, it was protected by the public interest defence in section 4 of the Defamation Act 2013 (see ch. 23). However, the judge also found that from the date of the official investigation concluding that Mr Banks had not breached the law, the ongoing publication of the TED Talk was *not* protected by the public interest defence. But the judge said this ongoing publication had not caused serious harm to Mr Banks and was therefore not actionable. Mr Banks appealed a number of the judge's findings about the interpretation and application of the serious harm requirement. The Court of Appeal looked at whether, where a defendant has a public interest defence which 'falls away', the fact that the first, lawful phase of publication caused serious harm to the claimant's reputation continues to apply thereafter. The Court of Appeal agreed with the judge on this point, namely that serious harm *had to be re-evaluated at each phase of publication*, so where for example a public interest defence stopped, serious harm had to be looked at afresh at that point.

The Court of Appeal disagreed with the judge that the ongoing publication of the TED Talk had not caused serious harm to Mr Banks. Ms Cadwalladr was therefore found to be liable for defamation in respect of the TED Talk *after* the publication of the findings of the official investigation. The case emphasises the need for journalists and publishers to continually reassess whether a defamatory statement that remains published (e.g. online) continues to be in the public interest. Failure to do so could result in the collapse of any public interest defence previously relied upon. (*Aaron Banks v Carole Cadwalladr* [2023] EWCA Civ 219).

Where there is widespread publication and a serious allegation, serious harm will generally be inferred without the need for actual evidence (see *Banks v Cadwalladr*). However, where there is publication to a limited number of people, a claimant will not be able to rely on an inference, and evidence will be needed (see *Amersi v Leslie*

[2023] EWHC 1368). In *Fox v Blake* [2025] EWCA Civ 1321, the Court of Appeal, taking account of the social media mechanics of X, concluded that tweets accusing Laurence Fox of being a racist, had caused him serious reputational harm.

The practical difficulty with serious harm, is that it is often only capable of being assessed at the full trial of a defamation claim. This means that while it creates a threshold test for a claimant, it may be costly for a media defendant to be able to prove it.

Under the 2013 Act a body that trades for profit, such as a company, which wishes to pursue a defamation action must prove that the published statement has caused it, or is likely to cause it, serious financial loss, in order to meet the serious harm test.

See the **additional material** for this chapter on **www.mcnaes.com** for case studies on 'serious harm'.

Recap of major points

- A claimant suing for defamation must prove four things: (1) a statement is defamatory; (2) it may be reasonably understood to refer to them; (3) it has been published to a third person; and (4) that it has caused serious harm.
- The test of 'identification' is whether the words would reasonably lead people who know the claimant to believe they are the person referred to.
- Whether publication has caused serious harm may be proven, or the court may infer it from evidence and the seriousness of the defamatory meaning it carries.
- Publication is assumed to have occurred in the case of traditional media. But this is not always the case with online publication.
- Every repetition is a fresh publication. The journalist is liable for repeating a defamatory statement made by an interviewee or source.
- The single publication rule gives some protection from the repetition rule.
- The serious harm requirement means that trivial or low-level defamatory statements may not be actionable.

Online resources

Visit the online resources at **www.mcnaes.com** to test your knowledge of this chapter with **self-test questions** and a **flashcard glossary**, and to read **updates** about law and regulatory matters affecting journalism, as well as **additional material** to further your learning.

22

Defamation defences

Chapter summary

Media organisations sued for defamation may be able to win the case by using one or more of the defences in law—without them many of the stories published and broadcast each day would be suppressed for fear of a libel action. This chapter explains the main defences and gives practical advice on what a journalist must do when preparing a story to ensure it meets their requirements.

22.1 Introduction—the main defences

Journalists need to know about how defamation defences work, as the steps they take in researching and writing, broadcasting or webcasting a story will often determine whether a defence is available to avoid a costly defamation action. Some defences are in the Defamation Act 2013.

The main defences are:

- **truth**—section 2 of the 2013 Act, replacing the common law defence of justification;
- **honest opinion**—section 3 of the 2013 Act, replacing the common law defence of honest comment or fair comment;
- **public interest**—section 4 of the 2013 Act, replacing the common law defence which was known as the 'Reynolds' defence (see ch. 23 for more detail on this defence).
- absolute privilege;
- qualified privilege;
- accord and satisfaction;
- offer of amends.

As this list shows, statutory defences introduced in the 2013 Act replaced the common law defences of justification, honest comment and public interest. Rulings concerning those common law defences, made before the statute came into force, which include some rulings referred to in this chapter, may be a guide to the correct approach, but only after the court has considered the statutory requirements.

22.2 Truth—its requirement

The defence requires that the published material complained of can be proved in court to be 'substantially true'. Meeting this requirement gives the publisher complete protection against a defamation action (the only limited exception arises under the Rehabilitation of Offenders Act 1974—see ch. 24).

The defence applies to statements of fact. If the words complained of are an expression of opinion, they may be defended as honest opinion. Media organisations sued for defamation over an article or programme often rely on both truth and honest opinion as defences, applying each as appropriate to different elements of what was published.

- The standard of proof needed for a truth defence to succeed is that used in civil cases generally—the material must be proved true 'on the balance of probabilities'.

This means that, when presented with different accounts, the court decides which version of events is most likely to be true.

Although this is a lower standard of proof than 'beyond reasonable doubt', which is the standard of proof required in criminal cases for the accused person to be convicted of the charge, a media organisation relying on a truth defence in a defamation case must have enough evidence to persuade a judge at the trial that its version of the event(s) is correct.

There is an intrinsic relationship between meaning and the defence of truth. The defence of truth applies to whatever meaning(s) the statement complained of is found to bear by the court. As explained in 20.2.2, it is ultimately a decision for a judge as to what a statement means—and that may not be the meaning that the journalist thought or intended the piece to convey. This can sometimes mean that the journalist does not have the evidence to sustain a truth defence. The libel battle between the now disgraced cyclist Lance Armstrong and the *Sunday Times* shows how difficult it can be to pursue investigations when the burden of proof is on the publisher to prove the truth of what it published. The Lance Armstrong story landed the *Sunday Times* in court in 2004, when Armstrong sued over allegations he was a drug cheat. Armstrong's lawyers argued the article meant 'he had taken drugs in order to enhance his performance in cycling competitions and by doing so and denying that he had done so, he was a fraud, a cheat and a liar'. The *Sunday Times* argued that the article had a much 'lower' meaning (see 22.2.3), namely that there were 'reasonable grounds to suspect' he was a drug cheat. After several court hearings, it was determined that 'once the article was read in conjunction with its headline, photographs and their captions', the meaning—which was what the *Sunday Times* would have to prove the truth of—was that Armstrong was a 'cheat and a liar'. This was a very high level of meaning and the *Sunday Times* decided it could not risk going to trial (which in those days would have been before a jury) as it did not believe the evidence it had, while strong, was enough to satisfy a jury that Armstrong was a cheat, and so it settled the case. (Later Armstrong admitted, in an interview with Oprah Winfrey in 2013, that he had used banned performance-enhancing drugs throughout much of his cycling career; he later had to repay the Sunday Times the damages and costs they had agreed to pay him).

22.2.1 The most damaging imputation must be proved true

→glossary

Section 2(3) of the 2013 Act says that, in a defamation case involving publication of two or more imputations involving the **claimant**, 'the defence under this section does not fail if, having regard to the imputations which are shown to be substantially true, the imputations which are not shown to be substantially true do not seriously harm the claimant's reputation'.

This means a defendant does not have to prove the truth of every statement in what was published. But the most damaging imputation must be proved and the reputational damage it has caused or is likely to have caused must outweigh any damage caused or likely to have been caused by unproved allegations.

22.2.2 Examples of the 'truth' defence succeeding

Case study

In 2025, actor Noel Clarke lost a libel action against Guardian News and Media, the publisher of *The Guardian*, over a series of articles published in April 2021 that accused him of misconduct, including harassment and sexually inappropriate behaviour. At a six-week trial at the High Court in London in 2025, *The Guardian* put forward defences of truth and public interest. For its truth defence, *The Guardian* relied on testimony from 26 different people, including some of the women who had made the accusations against Clarke. Many of the women who gave their testimony in court, some of whose identities were protected, were faced with intimidating tactics both before and during the trial. For example, it was alleged that some of them were engaged in a 'conspiracy to lie', which the judge rejected. She found that, in the absence of a conspiracy, 'Clarke's case that more than 20 witnesses - none of whom are parties or have a stake in this case, as he does - have come to court to lie is inherently implausible.' In August 2025, the judge found that the paper's allegations were substantially true and that Clarke had behaved in a sexually inappropriate way including unwanted sexual contact At a subsequent costs hearing, the judge said that Clarke had 'maintained a far-fetched and indeed a false case that the articles were not substantially true, by pursuing allegations of dishonesty and bad faith against almost all of the defendant's truth witnesses.' (*Noel Clarke v GNM*, [2025] EWHC 2193 (KB))

Hollywood actor Johnny Depp lost a libel action against News Group Newspapers (NGN), publisher of *The Sun*, over a 2018 column which labelled him a 'wife beater'. NGN, with his ex-wife Amber Heard as key witness, defended the claim, putting forward a defence of truth. The publisher relied on allegations of violence made by Ms Heard against Mr Depp over 14 separate incidents. During a trial at the High Court in London which lasted more than three weeks in July 2020, Mr Justice Nicol heard evidence from Mr Depp and Ms Heard as well as around 24 other witnesses. In his ruling in November 2020, the judge concluded the article was 'substantially true', having found that Mr Depp assaulted Ms Heard on a dozen occasions and caused her to fear for her life three times. The Court of Appeal rejected a bid by Mr Depp to challenge the ruling in March 2021, with Lord Justice Underhill observing both Mr Depp and NGN had 'put in evidence a wealth of more or less contemporaneous material'. The case is believed to have cost the actor around £5 million in legal fees. This high-profile case demonstrates how much evidence a media organisation sued for defamation may be required to produce in order to satisfy the burden of proof (*Depp v News Group Newspapers and another* [2020] EWHC 2911 (QB)).

See the **additional material** for this chapter on **www.mcnaes.com** for a further case study of the truth defence succeeding after Andrew Mitchell MP sued *The Sun* over an article which said he had called police officers 'fucking plebs'.

22.2.3 Levels of meaning and reporting on police investigations

As explained at 20.2.2, when considering reports linking a claimant with criminal or wrongful conduct, the courts recognise three levels of meaning. Called *Chase* level 1, 2 and 3 meanings—because they were detailed by Lord Justice Brooke in *Chase v News Group Newspapers* [2002] EWCA Civ 1772, [2003] EMLR 2180—they are that the person:

- is guilty of the criminal offence or misconduct (a level 1 meaning)—if the court decides this meaning applies, a publisher using the truth defence has to prove that the offence or misconduct occurred; or
- is reasonably suspected of the offence or misconduct (level 2); or that
- there are grounds for an investigation—for example, by police (level 3).

22.2.3.1 Proving reasonable suspicion or that there were grounds for an investigation

It may be defamatory to say someone is reasonably suspected of an offence or that there are grounds for investigating their conduct, because it implies there was conduct on the person's part which warrants the suspicion. So a successful plea of truth must prove conduct by the individual which gives rise to the suspicion or the grounds. It is no use saying other people told you about their suspicions (*Shah v Standard Chartered Bank* [1999] QB 241).

Case study

In *Chase v News Group Newspapers*, *The Sun* newspaper paid £100,000 damages to children's nurse Elaine Chase for a story headlined 'Nurse is probed over 18 deaths'. Police were investigating the deaths of a number of terminally ill children she had treated but concluded—after the newspaper's story appeared—that there were no grounds to suspect her of an offence. *The Sun* tried to show there were reasonable grounds for suspicion, but the Court of Appeal said it was relying almost entirely on the fact that a number of allegations against Ms Chase had been made to the hospital trust and police. The only respect in which the newspaper's case focused upon the nurse's conduct concerned an allegation made after publication, which the court said could not be taken into consideration.

22.2.4 Avoid implying habitual conduct

The statement that someone 'is a thief' may be true—but if the basis for the statement is just one minor conviction, for example, for stealing a packet of bacon from a shop, a defence of truth would almost certainly fail, as the individual would argue that the words meant they were a persistent thief, whereas they were essentially an honest person who had had a single lapse.

22.2.5 Inferences and innuendoes must be proved

see also ch. 20 on meanings of words

The truth defence involves proving not only the truth of each defamatory statement but also any reasonable interpretation of the words and any innuendoes lying behind them.

Also see 20.3, Why media organisations may be reluctant to fight defamation actions.

22.2.6 Persisting with a truth defence can be financially risky

Persisting in a defence of truth has financial risks. If it fails, the court may view critically a defendant's persistence in sticking to a story which it has decided was not true, and may award greater damages—in *Cairns v Modi* [2012] EWHC 756 (QB) Mr Justice Bean awarded cricketer Chris Cairns £75,000 in damages over match-fixing allegations, adding a further £15,000 in aggravated damages because of the defendant's 'sustained and aggressive assertion of the plea of justification'.

22.3 Honest opinion

The defence of honest opinion protects published opinion, not any statement put forward as factual. Section 3 of the Defamation Act 2013, which created the honest opinion defence, abolished the common law defence of 'honest comment', formerly known as 'fair comment'.

22.3.1 The requirements of honest opinion

The requirements of the honest opinion defence, all of which must be met, are that the published comment *must*:

- be the honestly held opinion of the person making it (even though it may have been published by another party);
- be recognisable to the reader/viewer/listener as opinion rather than as a factual allegation;
- be based on a provably true fact or privileged material—so media organisations relying on the honest opinion defence should be prepared to run another defence, such as truth, absolute privilege or qualified privilege in tandem;
- explicitly or implicitly indicate, at least in general terms, the fact or information on which it is based.

privilege is covered later in this chapter

22.3.1.1 Opinion must be 'honestly held', not 'fair'

The law does not require the 'truth' of the comment to be proved—comment may be responsible or irresponsible, informed or misinformed, but cannot be true or false. Defendants pleading honest opinion do not need to persuade the court to share their views. But they do need to satisfy it that the opinion on an established fact represents a view an honest person could hold. Mr Justice Diplock said in his summing up to the jury in *Silkin v Beaverbrook Newspapers* [1958] 1 WLR 743 (QB):

> “The basis of our public life is that the crank and the enthusiast can say what he honestly believes just as much as a reasonable man or woman. It would be a sad day for freedom of speech in this country if a jury were to apply the test of whether it agrees with a comment, instead of applying the true test of whether this opinion, however exaggerated, obstinate, or prejudiced, was honestly held.”

The defence will fail if a claimant can show that the person expressing the opinion did not genuinely hold that opinion. It will also fail if, for example, the editor of a newspaper which published the comment—for example, in a column—did so when they knew, or should have known, that the author did not hold the opinion being expressed.

22.3.1.2 Only recognisable comment, not facts

A judge gave an example of an opinion protected by the fair comment defence, saying that if one accurately reports what some public man had done, and then says 'such conduct is disgraceful', that is merely an expression of one's opinion—a comment on the person's conduct. But if one asserts that the man is guilty of disgraceful conduct without saying what that conduct was, one is making an allegation of fact for which the only defences are truth or privilege.

Case study

Subeditors must take special care if they introduce comment into headlines. In 2003 the *Daily Telegraph* published articles making allegations about left-wing MP George Galloway based on documents said to refer to him which a reporter found in a ruined Government building in Baghdad soon after the invasion of Iraq. One story was headlined 'Telegraph reveals damning new evidence on Labour MP'. When sued, the paper did not claim the allegations were true but said the headline was an expression of opinion. But the judge said 'damning' had a plain meaning—'that is to say, that the evidence goes beyond a prima facie case and points to guilt'. The MP won the libel case (*Galloway v Telegraph Group Ltd* [2004] EWHC 2786 (QB)).

For more detail of this case, see the **additional material** for ch. 23, The public interest defence, on **www.mcnaes.com**.

22.3.1.3 The basis on fact or privileged material must be indicated

→glossary

The requirements of section 3 of the 2013 Act reflect the decision of the **Supreme Court** in *Spiller and another v Joseph and others* [2010] UKSC 53 that the comment 'must explicitly or implicitly indicate, at least in general terms, the facts on which it was based'. The new statutory defence provides that an honest person must be able to hold the opinion on the basis of 'any fact' which existed when the statement complained of was published.

The exception to the rule that comment must be based on a true fact is when the comment is based on privileged material, such as a report of judicial proceedings or proceedings in Parliament. This means that a media organisation can safely make scathing comments about a defendant convicted of a crime, if based on privileged reports of the trial's evidence, and can safely publish criticism of judges, magistrates and coroners, based on privileged reports of their actions in court. Similarly, it can make scathing criticism of someone based on what was reported to have been said about them or by them in a Parliamentary debate, provided that the report is protected by the qualified privilege defence. Privilege defences are explained later in this chapter (and require reports to be accurate, for example).

22.3.2 Imputing improper motives

The suggestion that someone has acted from improper motives has in the past been hard to defend as honest comment. However, the Court of Appeal took a more helpful view when entrepreneur Richard Branson sued biographer Tom Bower for libel (*Branson v Bower* [2001] EWCA Civ 791, [2001] EMLR 800). Bower wrote of Branson's attempt to run the National Lottery: 'Sceptics will inevitably whisper that Branson's motive is self-glorification.' Bower said this was fair comment (which at that time was the name of the honest comment defence) but Branson said it was a factual allegation (that he had a questionable intention in bidding for the National Lottery) and was untrue.

Lord Justice Latham said in the Court of Appeal that comment was 'something which is or can reasonably be inferred to be a deduction, inference, conclusion, criticism, remark, observation', and that the judge in the lower court was fully entitled to conclude that Bower was expressing a series of opinions about Branson's motives.

22.3.3 Reviews

The honest opinion defence protects expressions of opinion—including strong criticism—in reviews of, among other things, performances, books, holidays and restaurants. But, again, all the defence's requirements must be met.

Case study

In 2001 the actor and singer David Soul accepted £20,000 damages from *The Mirror* newspaper in a settlement after it published a critical review of a West End show he was in. The newspaper also had to pay legal costs estimated at £150,000. The High Court was told that the review was written as if the newspaper's showbiz correspondent Matthew Wright had seen the show but in fact it had sent a freelance to do the review. This meant that the review of the performance was not Mr Wright's opinion. Mr Soul said of the case: 'You have to see the play, you have to be there' (*The Guardian*, 11 December 2001).

22.3.4 Humour, satire and irony

In 2008 Sir Elton John sued *The Guardian*, claiming he was libelled in a spoof article written by Marina Hyde under the headline 'A peek at the diary of . . . Sir Elton John'—a regular feature in the paper's Weekend section satirising the activities of celebrities and others. Sir Elton claimed the article meant his commitment to the Elton John Aids Foundation was insincere and that, once the costs of his White Tie and Tiara fund-raising ball were met, only a small proportion of the funds raised would go to good causes. *The Guardian*'s defence was that the words were clearly comment and could not have the meaning claimed by the claimant.

Mr Justice Tugendhat struck out Sir Elton's claim, accepting *The Guardian*'s argument that the words were a form of teasing, and that had it actually unearthed a story about a charity ball's costs leaving nothing for good causes, it would have treated it as a serious story and written it without any attempt at humour (*Sir Elton John v Guardian News and Media Ltd* [2008] EWHC 3066 (QB)).

22.4 Privilege

The public interest sometimes demands that there should be complete freedom of speech without any risk of proceedings for defamation, even if the statements are defamatory and even if they turn out to be untrue. These occasions are referred to as 'privileged'. Privilege exists under **common law** and **statute**. More details about the ambit of the honest opinion defence can be found in the additional material for this chapter.

→glossary

22.5 Absolute privilege

The defence of absolute privilege, where it is applicable, is a complete answer and bar to an action for defamation. It does not matter if the words are true or false, or if they were spoken or written maliciously.

But while someone may speak on an occasion which is protected by absolute privilege, it does not follow that a journalist's report of those comments will also be protected by absolute privilege. Members of Parliament may say whatever they wish in a House of Commons debate without fear of being sued for defamation, because what they say there is protected by absolute privilege. The reports of parliamentary proceedings published on Parliament's behalf in *Hansard*, its official record, are protected by absolute privilege, as are reports published by order of Parliament, such as White Papers. But media reports of what MPs say in parliamentary debates or of the contents of such parliamentary publications are protected by qualified privilege (if that defence's requirements are met), not absolute privilege. The qualified privilege defence, as this chapter explains, depends on there being a proper motive in publication.

22.5.1 The requirements of absolute privilege

ch. 18 explains tribunals

The only time journalists can have absolute privilege is in contemporaneous reporting of court cases, including the cases of tribunals which are courts.

The requirements of absolute privilege, a defence set out in section the Defamation Act 1996, are that what was published was:

- a fair and accurate report of judicial proceedings held in public in a court anywhere in the world, published contemporaneously.

The court can be one established under the law of a country or territory outside the UK, and any international court or tribunal established by the Security Council of the United Nations or by an international agreement, such as the European Court of Human Rights. A 'court' includes 'any tribunal or body exercising the judicial power of the State'.

Privilege for court reports is vital for the media because what is said in court is often highly defamatory (for example, people being accused of murder, or sexual offences, or of lying in their evidence), and reporting it would be impossible without this protection.

The law thus recognises that the media help sustain open justice, a principle examined in ch. 15. Privilege does not apply if the court hearing was held in private.

22.5.1.1 Reports must be fair and accurate

For absolute privilege to apply, a report of a court case must be 'fair and accurate'. This does not mean that the proceedings must be reported verbatim—a report will be 'fair and accurate' if:

- it presents a summary of what is said by both sides in the case;
- it contains no substantial inaccuracies;
- it avoids giving disproportionate weight to one side or the other.

In *Bennett v Newsquest* [2006] EWCA Civ 1149, Mr Justice Eady pointed out that a newspaper report of a criminal case, which was the subject of a defamation action, contained inaccuracies, then said:

> "The report must be fair overall and not give a misleading impression. Inaccuracies in themselves will not defeat privilege. Omissions will deprive a report of privilege if they create a false impression of what took place or if they result in the suppression of the case or part of the case of one side, while giving the other."

A court report does not have the protection of absolute privilege if its contents are ruled to be unfair or inaccurate in any important respect.

- To be fair, a report of a criminal trial must make clear that the defendant denies the charge(s) and, while it proceeds, that no verdict has been reached—for example, the report can conclude by stating: 'The case continues.'

22.5.1.2 How much of a court case must be reported to be fair?

In 1993 the *Daily Sport* paid substantial damages to a police officer acquitted of indecent assault. It had reported the opening of the prosecution case at his trial and the alleged victim's main evidence, but did not include her cross-examination by the defence, which began on the same day and undermined her allegation. Later the paper briefly reported the officer's acquittal. He nevertheless sued. The fact that this defamation action was settled out of court means that the issue of how much of a day's proceedings in a case must be covered for a report to be fair remains a grey area.

Criminal trials may last for days, weeks or months, and in later stages the defendant's barrister may show in court that statements made earlier by the prosecution were wrong. Reports of lengthy trials might not be published each day, but the safest practice is that if a media organisation has reported allegations that are later rebutted in the trial, it should also report the rebuttals.

22.5.1.3 Reports must attribute allegations and avoid carelessness

In a court report, any allegation which has not been proved must be attributed to whoever said it in court, whether that was a lawyer, a witness or the judge, because a report that presents what is merely an allegation as if it were a proved fact is inaccurate. Do not write 'Brown had a gun in his hand' but 'Smith said Brown had a gun in his hand'.

A media organisation has no protection at all if it carelessly identifies as the defendant someone who is only a witness or unconnected with the case. A report which gets the charge or charges a defendant faces wrong could prove expensive in libel damages.

Journalists must also avoid wrongly reporting that the defendant was convicted when they were in fact acquitted. One newspaper had to pay damages to a man because it reported his acquittal on drug charges in terms which gave the impression that he was in fact guilty.

The courts do allow some leeway to publications compressing material in reports (*Elizabeth and Peter Crossley v Newsquest (Midlands South Ltd)* [2008] EWHC 3054 (QB)).

The need for a report to fully identify a defendant is explained in 21.2.2, Identification. See, too, the **additional material** for ch. 22 on **www.mcnaes.com**, 'Case study on accuracy'. For context about the need for charges or offences to be accurately reported, see ch. 6.

22.5.1.4 **Reports must be contemporaneous**

To have the protection of absolute privilege, court reports should be published contemporaneously with the proceedings.

chs. 12 and 19 explain postponement orders

- Contemporaneous means 'as soon as practicable'—for example, in the first issue of a newspaper following the day's hearing. For a broadcaster, it can be construed that the report should be aired on the same day of the hearing or early on the next day. For a weekly paper, contemporaneous publication may mean publishing the following week.

Sometimes reports of court proceedings have to be postponed because a court order compels this. Section 14(2) of the Defamation Act 1996 says that in these circumstances a story is treated as if it were published contemporaneously if it is published 'as soon as practicable after publication is permitted'.

A report of an earlier stage of a case published with or within a report of a later stage, 'so far as it was reasonably necessary to give context', should still be regarded as having absolute privilege (the *Crossley* case, cited earlier), if it is fair and accurate.

Even if a court report is not contemporaneous, it will still be protected by qualified privilege, if the defence's requirements are met—see later.

22.5.2 **Privilege is only for reports of proceedings**

Suppose a 'court report' in the media contains background matter or comment which did not originate from the court's proceedings. In the *Bennett* case referred to earlier, the judge said this would not destroy the privilege of the court reporting: 'Extraneous comments can be included or other factual material but it must be severable, in the sense that a reasonable reader could readily appreciate that the material did not purport to be a report of what was said in court.'

However, the additional material is not covered by privilege. See too *Curistan v Times Newspapers Ltd* [2009] QB 231 and *Harcombe v Associated Newspapers Ltd* [2022] EWHC 543 (QB).

22.5.2.1 Reporting from case documents officially made available

for context on privilege and court documents, see too 15.28

Journalists have 'open justice' rights to apply to see case documents when reporting court proceedings. Reports including or based on documentary material officially made available by a court to help journalists to report the proceedings, or on documents which can be inspected or provided as copies under court rules, will be protected by privilege if the defence's requirements are met—for example, the reporting is accurate and a fair reflection of the case. But any reporting restrictions must be obeyed.

For more detail on access rights to and using such case documents, see ch. 15. Its **additional material** on **www.mcnaes.com** has a case study concerning privilege in reporting from civil case documents.

22.5.3 Outbursts from the public gallery

Privilege may not protect defamatory words shouted out in court—for example, from the public gallery by someone who is not part of the proceedings.

But if the comment is shouted by someone who has given evidence as a witness in the case, privilege would protect its inclusion in a court report, provided all the defence's requirements were met.

If the shouted comment is not defamatory, it can be reported safely, no matter who made it.

22.6 Qualified privilege

Qualified privilege is available as a defence for the publication of certain types of information. This law, in effect, categorises this information as being important to society. The defence allows these 'statements'—including media reports of certain documents and certain events—to be freely published in the public interest, with no requirement for the publisher to be able to prove them as true, though there are some preconditions.

22.7 Qualified privilege by statute

Schedule 1 of the Defamation Act 1996—now amended and expanded by the Defamation Act 2013—lists 'statements' to which the statutory form of qualified privilege applies, if the defence's requirements are met. For example, the defence applies to media reports of: press conferences; parliamentary debates held in public; public meetings; public meetings of councils, their committees and their subcommittees; and media reports of statements issued for the public by Government departments, councils, police and other governmental agencies. It also protects a non-contemporaneous report of a court case held in public, which could be a reference to a person's past convictions. The Schedule is set out in this book's Appendix 2.

ch. 24 covers reporting past convictions

22.7.1 The requirements of qualified privilege

The defence's requirements differ from those of absolute privilege. For absolute privilege, the publisher's motive is irrelevant. But a qualified privilege defence will fail if the claimant can show **malice** by the publisher or author.

→ glossary

22.7.1.1 Fair and accurate, without malice and in the public interest

The basic requirements of the qualified privilege defence relating to those 'statements' listed by Schedule 1 are that:

- the published report must be fair and accurate, and published without malice.

There is also a general requirement for qualified privilege that:

- the matter published must be a matter of public interest, the publication of which is for the public benefit.

This can be summarised as 'published in the public interest'. The question of what is in the public interest is decided objectively by a court considering whether this defence applies, and does not depend on the journalist or editor's views.

Malice in this context means ill-will or spite towards the claimant, or any indirect or improper motive in the defendant's mind.

A journalist or editor would be denied the protection of qualified privilege if the judge in a defamation case ruled that the dominant motive for publication was not a duty to inform the public but spite—for example, the publisher aired a defamatory allegation merely to settle a private score.

Also, if a journalist published a report of an allegation they knew was not true but in a way which suggested it might be or was true, that would be malicious.

For example, suppose that a journalist published that a businesswoman was convicted of theft two years ago. Normally, such a report would be protected by qualified privilege as a non-contemporaneous report of a court case. But if the journalist knew—yet did not include in the report—that the businesswoman's conviction was overturned a year ago on appeal, it would have been published maliciously (and the publication of that misleading report would not be in the public interest).

> See the **additional material** for ch. 15 on **www.mcnaes.com** for a case study of how in 2012 the *Mail on Sunday* lost a defamation action when a judge ruled that its report of a court case was not protected by qualified privilege because it was not sufficiently fair or accurate, and therefore publication was not in the public interest.

22.7.1.2 Is there a requirement to publish explanation or contradiction?

Schedule 1 to the 1996 Act sets out in Part I a list of statements having qualified privilege 'without explanation or contradiction' and in Part II a list of statements thus privileged but 'subject to explanation or contradiction'.

This difference is important.

- A publisher relying on qualified privilege under Part II to protect a report must, to retain the protection, publish a 'reasonable letter or statement by way of explanation or contradiction' if required to do so by anyone defamed in the report.

This will apply, for example, if a person wants the publisher to publish a letter or statement from them responding to a report of a council meeting which defamed them. Suppose, for example, that the defamatory matter in the report was the quoting of a councillor's claim made in that meeting that the person is corrupt. Failure to publish a letter or statement of explanation or contradiction from that person would destroy the qualified privilege defence as regards the report's publication of the allegation. The Act says such a statement must be published 'in a suitable manner', meaning 'in the same manner as the publication complained of or in a manner that is adequate and reasonable in the circumstances'.

* Remember

Get legal advice if any statement that the complainant wants published gives rise—because they make counter-allegations—to any risk of libelling another person. Publication of a statement of 'explanation or contradiction' is not protected by privilege under the 1996 Act, so the statement must be 'reasonable' in this respect, though common law privilege may apply if the statement the complainant wants published is a reply to an attack on their character.

see 22.7.3, Privilege at common law, on replies to attack

A statement listed in Part I of Schedule 1—for example, a report of what is said in public in a legislature such as the UK Parliament, or a report of material published by a legislature, including *Hansard*, or by a Government department, or a report of what is said in a public register open to inspection, discussed later in this chapter—is not subject to the requirement to publish such a letter/statement by anyone defamed by the report (though an editor may decide it is newsworthy or ethical to do this).

Part I is the means by which the 1996 and 2013 Acts greatly widened the categories of statements protected, by including reports of proceedings held in public in foreign legislatures and foreign courts, and of what is said in open sessions of all public inquiries instigated by Governments.

22.7.2 Statute only protects a report of the occasion or material specified

The protection of statutory qualified privilege applies only to reports of the actual proceedings, events or material listed in Schedule 1 to the 1996 Act, as amended by the 2013 Act.

- For example, this qualified privilege in Part II of the Schedule protects a report of speeches by councillors in a council meeting held in public, but will not protect a report of defamatory allegations a councillor makes after the meeting when asked to expand on statements made during it.

What the councillor says in the meeting—such as that a builder is corrupt—can, if the meeting was held in public, be safely reported. But if the comment is made afterwards, the publisher who airs it would have no privilege and so would need to rely on the truth defence—that is, would have to prove the builder was corrupt, which might be impossible.

22.7.2.1 **Reports of public meetings, press conferences, scientific, and academic conferences**

Reports of a public meeting on a matter of public interest held anywhere in the world are now protected by qualified privilege, by virtue of the 2013 Act, as are reports of press conferences held anywhere in the world for the discussion of a matter of public interest, and reports of scientific or academic conferences held anywhere in the world, or copies of, extracts from or summaries of material published by such conferences.

22.7.2.2 **What is a public meeting?**

Paragraph 12 of the Schedule defines a 'public meeting' as:

- a lawful meeting held anywhere in the world for the furtherance or discussion of a matter of public interest, whether admission to the meeting is general or restricted.

This definition is fairly wide, covering public meetings about and within a particular community (for example, to discuss a controversial planning proposal or the problem of local burglaries) or those held about national issues. The term 'restricted' means the definition can apply, for example, to a meeting called by residents of one village who exclude from it people from the neighbouring village. Again, the privilege is subject to the 'explanation and contradiction' requirement—see 22.7.1.2.

22.7.2.3 **The nature of press conferences**

The 2013 Act extended qualified privilege to coverage of press conferences held anywhere in the world on matters of public interest. This codified in statute a decision by the House of Lords in 2000 that reports of a press conference could be protected by qualified privilege, if the defence's requirements were met and if the conference was held after the issuing of 'a general invitation to the press', because in those circumstances it is a form of public meeting (*McCartan Turkington Breen v Times Newspapers Ltd* [2001] 2 AC 277).

In *McCartan*, the House of Lords also ruled that a written press release—handed out at the press conference by its organisers, but not read aloud, and which was reported by the media—was in effect part of the press conference. This means that fair, accurate reports of documents handed out at a press conference by the organisers also have qualified privilege in the context of coverage of the press conference.

> See this chapter's **additional material** on **www.mcnaes.com** for more detail of the *McCartan* case.

22.7.2.4 Stories from documents open to public inspection

Paragraph 5 in Part I to the Schedule gives privilege for a fair and accurate copy of or extract from a document which the law requires to be open to public inspection.

! Remember your rights

Paragraph 5 means, for example, that the media have qualified privilege for material quoted fairly and accurately, etc., from publicly available records such as those at Companies House, the Land Registry or other public registries, even if the records themselves turn out to be inaccurate. The reporting should make clear it is quoting from such records.

Paragraph 5 also gives qualified privilege to media reports of court documents which court rules say can be inspected—see 22.5.2.1. But it does not apply to reports of documents released under the Freedom of Information Act 2000, though the public interest defence in section 4 of the Defamation Act 2013 may apply to such reports. That defence is explained in ch. 23.

for context on privilege and court documents, see too 15.28

22.7.2.5 Reports of statements issued for the public by government agencies

online ch. 37 explains the FoI Act

Paragraph 9 in Part II of the Schedule gives qualified privilege, subject to explanation or contradiction, to 'a fair and accurate copy of or extract from' a notice or other matter issued for the public by governments anywhere in the world and authorities anywhere in the world which have governmental functions. This includes government departments, councils, and police forces and authorities, so would cover, for example, fair and accurate reports of official police statements, and statements made on behalf of local authorities—for example, press releases about consumer protection or environmental health matters.

- These statements could be defamatory—for example, a police press release might name a man and say that officers want to question him about a murder. But the qualified privilege allows the media to report this without fear of being sued by the man, provided, if asked, that they publish his 'reasonable letter or statement of explanation or contradiction'.

There will be many occasions when a journalist will wish to report the misdeeds of a person but may be inhibited by the fear of a defamation action. The answer is often to obtain confirmation of the information in the form of an official statement by a police or local authority spokesperson, and to base the report on that.

✱ Remember

Statutory qualified privilege does not protect reports of information unofficially 'leaked' from such authorities, or of what was said by people who are not official spokespersons.

22.7.2.6 **Not all authorities are covered**

Paragraph 9 of the Schedule does not cover reports of all statements by people in authority—it does not cover, for example, reports of statements by spokespersons for British Telecom, a gas board, a water board, the rail companies, London Regional Transport, British Airport Authority or other bodies created by statute which are involved in providing day-to-day services to the public. But it seems likely that a fair and accurate account of the official statements of such a body would be held to be covered by privilege in common law, referred to later in this chapter.

22.7.2.7 **Verbal comments by press officers**

Suppose that a reporter telephones a press officer at one of the bodies of the type specified under paragraph 9 of the Schedule. Is the report of the spokesperson's verbal comments protected by qualified privilege under the Act? The general position seems to be 'yes' if the comments were given for publication, unless the spokesperson was given no chance to make considered comments.

Case study

In *Blackshaw v Lord* [1984] QB 1, Lord Justice Stephenson, referring to the protection paragraph 9 gives the media, said: 'It may be right to include . . . the kind of answers to telephoned interrogatories which Mr Lord [a *Daily Telegraph* reporter], quite properly in the discharge of his duty to his newspaper, administered to Mr Smith [a Government press officer]. To exclude them in every case might unduly restrict the freedom of the press . . . But information which is put out on the initiative of a Government department falls more easily within the paragraph than information pulled out of the mouth of an unwilling officer of the department.'

22.7.2.8 **Disciplinary actions by private associations**

Paragraph 14 in Part II of the Schedule gives qualified privilege to media reports of the findings or decisions of a wide variety of bodies—for example, in the field of sport, business or learning—anywhere in the world which have a constitution empowering them to make disciplinary decisions about members. So, for example, the media can safely report a decision by the British Horseracing Authority disciplinary panel to ban a jockey from racing, the Football Association Independent Regulatory Commission to discipline a player or a scientific association to censure an academic, if the association is of the type listed in paragraph 14. The protection does not apply to a report of the proceedings of such bodies, and is subject to the 'explanation and contradiction' requirement referred to earlier.

For what privilege covers reports of the Court of Arbitration for Sport, see the **additional material** for this chapter on **www.mcnaes.com**.

22.7.2.9 Reports about companies

The 1996 and 2013 Acts also greatly extended qualified privilege with respect to reporting company affairs. Previously, qualified privilege only covered reports relating to proceedings at public companies' general meetings. The Acts extended Part II privilege to documents circulated among shareholders of a listed company with the authority of the board or the auditors or by any shareholder 'in pursuance of a right conferred by any statutory provision', and to fair and accurate copies of, extracts from, or summaries of, any document thus circulated to members of the company about the appointment, resignation, retirement or dismissal of directors of the company or its auditors.

22.7.3 Privilege at common law

There are some circumstances in which the media can benefit from privilege which exists in common law. This type of qualified privilege will apply, within certain limits, to a defamatory statement made by a person in response to an attack upon their character or conduct—known as 'reply to attack'. Privilege will not apply to a statement made in response to an attack which the person who made the statement knows to be justified, nor will it apply to any response wider than necessary to meet the specific allegations which prompted the reply. A media organisation publishing—for example, in a quote or a letter—a person's lawful response to an attack by another on their character or conduct would share in the privilege, as long as it is a proportionate response. Mr Justice Warby, as he then was, set out in *HRH The Duchess of Sussex v Associated Newspapers* [2021] EWHC 273 (Ch) that the same principles will apply to a third party—for example, a media organisation—which assists a person responding to an attack, as to the person themselves. It is fairly common for media organisations to publish replies to attacks, for example when covering political discourse, so care must be taken that the response is proportionate to the attack.

Common law qualified privilege also applies to fair and accurate reports of court cases and parliamentary proceedings, if held in public, in addition to statutory privilege. For more detail, see the **additional material** for ch. 22 on **www.mcnaes.com**.

22.8 'Accord and satisfaction', apologies and corrections

A media organisation can use the defence of 'accord and satisfaction' to halt a defamation case on the basis the issue has already been disposed of—for example, by publication of a correction and apology which the claimant accepted at the time as settlement of their complaint. But negotiating such an apology or correction is not a job for an inexperienced journalist.

22.8.1 'Without prejudice'

A solicitor acting for a client demanding a correction and apology will always avoid suggesting that this action by the media organisation will be enough in itself to settle the dispute, and will make it clear that the request is made 'without prejudice' to any other action that might be thought necessary.

What does this mean? The basic principle is that parties attempting to settle a dispute out of court should be encouraged to speak frankly, so anything said or written in the course of negotiations to settle and described as 'without prejudice' (that is, off the record) cannot subsequently be used against a party in court if negotiations fail. The rule applies whether or not the phrase 'without prejudice' is expressly used, but it can be good practice for the media organisation to use it too.

Journalists speaking with someone complaining about a story need to distinguish between:

- discussions over an offer to publish a follow-up story and/or a correction; and
- discussions over settling a claim.

In the former case, which often involves the journalist and the complainant themselves, the discussion need not necessarily be 'without prejudice'; the journalist may well want to refer to this discussion in court, to show fairness or lack of malice, or to mitigate damages.

In the latter case, often involving solicitors and mention of money, the discussion should be 'without prejudice'. As a general rule media organisations should notify their insurers about potential claims immediately, and, if there are solicitors 'on the other side', the publisher should also instruct its own lawyer(s).

22.8.2 Care needed in apologies and corrections

It is no defence for a media organisation to publish a correction and apology not agreed by the claimant.

Publishing such an apology can make matters worse for the publisher, because:

- a court may find that it constitutes an admission that the material which prompted the complaint was defamatory;
- a badly drafted apology or correction might also repeat the original defamatory statement, further angering the person who complained about it, or even unwittingly libel someone else.

For example: 'In our article yesterday we said Mr Red hit Mr Green. But we wish to point out that Mr Red says Mr Green struck him first'. If this is published, both Mr Red and Mr Green may sue over the wording of the apology.

On the other hand, if the claimant sues and wins, the fact that the media organisation took prompt and adequate steps to correct the error, and to express regret, will reduce the damages if their reputation was seriously harmed despite the apology.

Complainants might also be prepared to sign waivers—statements saying they waive their right to legal redress in exchange for the publication of a correction and apology—which will provide a complete defence of 'accord and satisfaction'.

A practical danger for an editor who asks a complainant to sign a waiver is that the reader may not previously have realised that they have a claim for damages and, thus alerted, may consult a lawyer. The waiver is therefore most useful when the complainant has already threatened to consult a lawyer.

See the **additional material** for ch. 22 on **www.mcnaes.com**, 'Practical advice on waivers'.

Inexperienced reporters sometimes try to avoid the consequences of errors without referring them to the editor, by trying to shrug them off or by incorporating a scarcely recognisable 'correction' (without apology) in a follow-up story—a highly dangerous course of action, which may further aggravate the damage and prompt the potential claimant to take more formal steps to secure satisfaction. Reporters should always tell the editor or another editorial executive about such a problem immediately so it can be dealt with properly.

22.9 Offer of amends

The media can defame a person unintentionally. The classic example was the case of Artemus Jones, in which a journalist introduced a fictitious character into a descriptive account of a factual event in order to provide atmosphere—referring to what he thought of as his fictional character as being at the Dieppe motor festival 'with a woman who is not his wife'. Unfortunately, the name he chose was that of a real person, a barrister—and former journalist—from North Wales. Stung by the comments of his friends about what was published, the real Artemus Jones sued and recovered substantial damages. Another example is when a story about one individual is understood to refer to another as in the case of Harold Newstead, explained in 21.2.2.2, Importance of ages, addresses and occupations.

The Defamation Act 1996 provides a defence known as 'offer to make amends'. To use it, a defendant who has allegedly published a defamatory statement must make a written offer to publish a suitable correction and apology, in a reasonable manner, and to pay the claimant suitable damages and legal costs.

If the offer of amends is rejected, and is not withdrawn, it will be a complete defence unless the claimant can show that the defendant 'knew or had reason to believe' that the published statement was false and was also defamatory of the claimant.

Editors planning to make an offer of amends must not delay. If the resulting compensation is to be assessed by a judge, they will start by deciding what would be 'suitable damages' if the editor had made no offer of amends and will then award a 'discount' of perhaps 50 per cent as a 'reward' for making the offer. The *News of the World* received only a 40 per cent discount after it was slow to respond to a complaint and published an apology six months after the original story.

Once an offer is made it is binding.

22.10 Leave and licence

The 'leave and licence' defence is that the claimant suing for libel had previously agreed that the material could be published. If it is clear the material is defamatory, a publisher intending to rely on this defence needs to be sure they can prove there was such pre-publication agreement. The person who is going to be defamed by the material should either be asked to sign a statement agreeing to its publication or be recorded agreeing. Otherwise it might be difficult to prove that consent was given if it was merely verbal.

Sometimes, even without an explicit agreement, the context may show that leave and licence was given—for example, by a pop star who chooses in an arranged interview to speak on the record about false allegations made against them, seeking to dispel them.

But in other circumstances, such as a media investigation into wrongdoing, a journalist cannot secure the leave and licence defence merely by giving the subject the opportunity to comment.

22.11 'Live' broadcasts and readers' online postings

Newsagents and booksellers have a defence of 'innocent dissemination' as they are merely the conduit for the passage of the words complained of and are not responsible for them. Section 1 of the Defamation Act 1996 and section 10 of the Defamation Act 2013 extended this defence to anyone other than the author, editor or publisher (as defined by the Act) of the statement complained of, who took reasonable care in relation to its publication, and who did not know and had no reason to believe that whatever part they had in the publication caused or contributed to the publication of a defamatory statement.

A court deciding whether a person took reasonable care, or had reason to believe that what they did caused or contributed to the publication of a defamatory statement, must have regard to:

- the extent of their responsibility for the content of the statement or the decision to publish it;
- the nature or circumstances of the publication; and
- the previous conduct or character of the author, editor or publisher.

Section 10 of the 2013 Act says a court does not have jurisdiction to hear and determine an action for defamation brought against a person who was not the author, editor or publisher of the statement complained of unless it is satisfied that it is not reasonably practicable for an action to be brought against the author, editor or publisher.

22.11.1 Live broadcasts protected by section 1 of the 1996 Act

The list of categories of people who are not authors, editors or publishers for the purposes of the defence includes broadcasters of live programmes who have no effective control over the maker of the statement complained of.

In 1999 the research firm MORI and its head, Bob Worcester, sued the BBC over defamatory remarks made by controversial politician Sir James Goldsmith during a live radio interview. The BBC said it had a defence under section 1—but could it be said it had taken 'reasonable care'? It was argued the broadcaster should have known Sir James was likely to say something defamatory and it should at least have used a 'delay button'. The case was settled before the jury reached a verdict.

Broadcasters in 'live' situations need to react quickly to halt or cut off defamatory utterances to be sure of benefiting from section 1.

22.11.2 Internet service providers and website operators

The section 1 defence is also available in defamation cases for internet service providers (ISPs) which provide a service as 'host' to enable people and companies to publish their own content on their websites. ISPs play a merely passive role in the process of transmission of any defamatory matter and are therefore not publishers under section 1. But an ISP may be successfully sued for libel if it fails to quickly take down defamatory material on a site it hosts after receiving a complaint about it. In *Godfrey v Demon Internet Ltd* [2001] QB 201 the ISP was successfully sued for material on a newsgroup it hosted which it left online for about 10 days after receiving a complaint. The claim was for damages for those 10 days.

22.11.3 Section 5 defence

Section 5 of the 2013 Act provides a defence for website operators who follow the procedures detailed in the Defamation (Operators of Websites) Regulations 2013. The defence protects a website operator from a defamation action over postings from users if it follows the steps intended to allow a would-be claimant to act directly against the individual or individuals who posted the material, and ensures that it keeps within the specified timetable for doing so.

((•)) see Useful Websites at the end of this chapter for the Regulations

See the **additional material** for ch. 22 on **www.mcnaes.com** for a detailed explanation of this defence.

As regards postings by readers which are unlawful, there is also general protection in other law for those who 'host', 'cache' or are 'mere conduits' for internet publication, if they comply with the 'notice and take down' (NTD) procedure. The source of this protection was originally an EU directive. For more information about how the host of a website, such as a media organisation, can have NTD protection from legal liability, see ch. 30, Readers' postings and online safety issues.

22.11.4 The moderation of readers' postings which are defamatory

Newspapers, magazines, TV channels and radio stations cannot use the section 1 defence in the 1996 Act in respect of content which staff place on their websites, as they are clearly publishers.

As regards defamatory material posted there by readers, the section 1 defence or that in section 5 of the 2013 Act will offer protection for a media organisation, provided that the requirements of either of these defences are met, including that any necessary procedural step is followed. Also, the media organisation might have a defence under regulation 19 of the Electronic Commerce (EC Directive) Regulations 2002.

Section 1 is less likely to provide a defence if the media organisation's staff pre-moderate readers' postings—that is, check their content before they appear online—or subsequently check a posting which is clearly defamatory or attracts complaint, but let it remain online. For example, if the checking fails to spot that a reader's posting is clearly libellous, that is not meeting the requirement in section 1 for reasonable care to be taken. If a media organisation's employee makes a decision to allow a posting to appear or remain online, it will be argued by a person suing for defamation over that posting that the organisation has become the publisher and (in effect) the editor of it. If the court agrees, the section 1 defence cannot apply in the case.

But the section 5 defence in the 2013 Act may offer some protection, as it specifies that the defence 'is not defeated by reason only of the fact that the operator of the website moderates the statements posted on it by others'.

- The safest course is to remove a reader's posting from the website quickly if there is a complaint that it is defamatory. The material can be re-posted later if, after consideration, it is deemed safe.

Case study

In 2009 Mr Justice Eady ruled that the *Croydon Guardian* was not liable as the publisher for comments posted on its website by others. A man had tried to sue for defamation about readers' comments posted about a report of a disciplinary tribunal case in which he was struck off as a solicitor. Mr Justice Eady said the newspaper was protected by the regulation 19 defence because it had not had actual knowledge of the alleged 'unlawful activity or information' until the man complained, and it had then removed the material including the comments, as soon as it became aware of the nature of his complaint (*Karim v Newsquest Media Group Ltd* [2009] EWHC 3205 (QB)).

see ch. 30 for more about regulation 19

22.12 Other defences

Defences which might be available are as follows.

The claimant has died A defamation action is a personal action. A dead person cannot be libelled. Similarly, an action begun by a claimant cannot be continued by their heirs and executors if they die.

Proceedings were not started within the limitation period If the person suing did not begin the action within 12 months of the material being published, this should be a complete defence, unless there is a new publication of offending material. A court may extend the limitation period if it thinks it is in the interests of justice to do so. Reporters should date their notebooks, recordings and research material, and store them carefully, in case this proof is needed if someone sues towards the end of the limitation period or there is a possibility of using this material again after that. Journalists must remember that every repetition is a new publication.

For context, see 21.2.3.4, Repeating by republishing, for the case of the 'Looking Back' column, and 21.2.3.6, The 'single publication rule' and online archives.

Recap of major points

- The main defences against an action for defamation are truth, honest opinion, public interest, and absolute and qualified privilege.
- It is a complete defence (with one exception arising under the Rehabilitation of Offenders Act 1974) to prove that the words complained of are substantially true.
- A defendant can plead that an article expressing comment was an honestly held opinion on a matter of public interest.
- Absolute privilege applies to court reports, but reports must be fair, accurate and contemporaneous.
- Qualified privilege is available on many occasions under statute—for example, for a report of a public meeting. The defence is qualified because it is lost if the motive in publishing is malicious.
- Other defences include 'accord and satisfaction' and 'offer of amends'.

Useful Websites

legislation.gov.uk

The Defamation (Operators of Websites) Regulations 2013

Online resources

Visit the online resources at **www.mcnaes.com** to test your knowledge of this chapter with **self-test questions** and a **flashcard glossary**, and to read **updates** about law and regulatory matters affecting journalism, as well as **additional material** to further your learning.

23

The public interest defence

Chapter summary

The public interest defence was created in section 4 of the Defamation Act 2013. Its origin was in the common law *Reynolds* defence, which it replaced. The section 4 defence exists so that journalists have greater scope to fulfil their duty to report stories in the public interest. An attempt to use the defence in a defamation case will lead to the court examining whether what was published was on a matter of public interest. Also, to decide if the defence applies, the court will scrutinise how information was researched and presented and whether the publisher reasonably believed that its publication served the public interest. This chapter details the requirements of the defence and the way courts have interpreted it, and highlights the real difficulties journalists face in using it successfully. Journalists should never consider using this defence without taking legal advice.

23.1 Introduction—the birth of the defence

The defence created by section 4 of the Defamation Act 2013 was intended to protect publication of defamatory material in reports covering matters of 'public interest', even if the publisher cannot prove the material to be true. The defence originated from the *Reynolds* defence, which evolved in common law to protect 'responsible journalism' and took its name from a 1999 case in which former Irish premier Albert Reynolds sued Times Newspapers, publisher of the *Sunday Times* (*Reynolds v Times Newspapers* [2001] 2 AC 127). This case is referred to later in this chapter. Section 4 replaced and so abolished that common law defence. The rationale for the two defences is not materially different—and the principles underlying them are the same. But the key elements of and the approach to the defences are different. As the Supreme Court said in the first case on section 4 that came before it (*Serafin v Malkiewicz and others* [2020] UKSC 23)—it is 'wrong' to consider that the elements of the defences can be 'equiparated'—that is, regarded as the same: section 4 does not codify the old defence, it creates a new one. It is no longer a question of deciding whether the publisher acted 'responsibly' in publishing what it did.

23.2 The section 4 defence

Section 4(1) of the 2013 Act says it is a defence to an action for defamation for the defendant to prove that:

> "(a) the statement complained of was, or formed part of, a statement on a matter of public interest; and
> (b) the defendant reasonably believed that publishing the statement complained of was in the public interest."

Therefore, section 4(1) requires the court to determine three issues when deciding whether the defence protects the publication of the defamatory material (*Economou v de Freitas* [2019] EMLR 7):

- (i) was the statement complained of, or did it form part of, a statement on a matter of public interest?
- if so, (ii) did the defendant believe that publishing the statement complained of was in the public interest?
- if so, (iii) was that belief reasonable?

It is for the defendant who seeks to rely on the public interest defence to satisfy the court that the answer to all three questions is 'yes'. Section 4 requires the court to 'have regard to all the circumstances of the case' when determining these issues. It also states that the court, when deciding whether it was reasonable for a defendant to believe that publication was in the public interest, 'must make such allowance for editorial judgement as it considers appropriate'. As far as meaning is concerned, the court takes a more flexible approach to meaning than it does with a truth defence. The public interest defence is not assessed simply by reference to the single meaning, but by reference to the statement complained of and the range of meanings that it bears: (*Harcombe v Associated Newspapers Ltd,* [2024] EWHC 1523 KB).

23.2.1 Was the statement complained of, or did it form part of, a statement on a matter of public interest?

This is a very simple test. Judges have, in successive rulings, stated that the question of whether what was published was 'on' a matter of public interest is an objective question for the court. This requirement is not whether the statement 'is published in the public interest' but whether it is 'on a matter of public interest'.

The 2013 Act does not define 'the public interest', and there is no single definition in law of what 'the public interest' is. But when seeking to explain that something was 'on a matter of public interest', a media organisation can, for instance, cite examples of what media regulators accept in their codes as being journalism which is 'in the public interest' (see 2.4.1, 2.5 and 3.4.11 in this book.)

In *Doyle v Smith* [2018] EWHC 2935 (QB), Mr Justice Warby said it was 'impossible' to provide a complete list of matters of public interest, but that the Court of Appeal's judgment in the *Reynolds* case contained the following 'useful' passage indicating the nature of such matters:

> "matters relating to the public life of the community and those who take part in it, including ... activities such as the conduct of government and political life, elections and public administration ... [and] more widely ... the governance of public bodies, institutions and companies which give rise to a public interest in disclosure, but excluding matters which are personal and private, such that there is no public interest in their disclosure."

In *Harcombe*, Mr Justice Nicklin said matters of public interest are of 'potentially wide compass save that they exclude purely personal or private matters'.

23.2.2 Did the defendant believe that publishing the statement complained of was in the public interest?

If the court accepts that what was published was on a matter of public interest, it must then consider the second issue under section 4(1), which concerns the defendant's actual state of mind at the time of publication, because the defendant must prove to the court that they believed that it was in the public interest to publish the defamatory material. A failure to prove this will mean the public interest defence will fail (*Doyle v Smith*, cited earlier, and the *Lachaux* case, see later). The importance of contemporaneous documents recording, and evidencing, the decision-making process prior to publication has been emphasised (see *Harcombe* and *Lachaux*). As this chapter will explain, a media organisation should therefore have internal procedures to create and retain documents which evidence that the belief was held at the relevant time by whoever took the decision to publish, and why. See too the section on having an audit trail in 2.6.

23.2.3 Was the defendant's belief that publication was in the public interest a reasonable belief?

If the defendant can prove to the court that they believed that publication of the defamatory material was in the public interest, they must also—for the defence to apply—prove that this was a reasonable belief.

> "[This] final question, which only arises if the first two questions have been answered affirmatively, is whether, judged objectively, the defendant's honest belief that publication was in the public interest was reasonable ... The focus must be on things the defendant said or knew or did, or failed to do, up to the time of publication: *Harcombe* [279]. The court should take a fact-sensitive and flexible approach, having regard to practical realities. (*Clarke v GNM* [2025] EWHC 2193 KB)"

As stated earlier, the section 4 defence can protect the publication of allegations which turn out after publication to be untrue. But when deciding whether there was 'reasonable' belief that publication was in the public interest, the court will consider what journalistic checks were made to discover whether what was alleged was true or untrue. The court will expect a media organisation attempting to use the defence to have guarded so far as practically possible against the publication of untrue defamatory material. The fact that such checks were made will help demonstrate that a reasonable belief was held that what was published could be true, and therefore that publication was in the public interest, to help establish the truth. However, court rulings show that to have the defence, the publisher should not report the material in a way which suggests it is definitely true, because that would mislead readers about the status of the information in the report, so—for example—the tone in which the material is written and its phrasing should be neutral in that respect.

In section 4(4) there is a reference to editorial judgement—this applies both as to what steps need to be taken before publication and what should be included in the publication. In the Clarke case against *The Guardian*, the judge, Mrs Justice Steyn said this meant that it was 'important to consider the process and the publication in the round, reaching an overall judgement as to the availability of the public interest defence. It is well established that the court must tolerate recourse to a degree of exaggeration or even provocation on the part of a journalist.' (*Banks v Cadwalladr* [2022] 1 WLR 5236, and *Harcombe*).

23.2.4 Lessons of the *Lachaux* case

Bruno Lachaux, a French aerospace engineer, brought defamation claims against the *Independent* and the *Evening Standard* newspapers over articles published in 2014. These aired allegations that he had mistreated his ex-wife, Asfana, including that he had been violent to her during their marriage, causing her to flee their home in Dubai, and that he gained custody of their infant son Louis through the Dubai legal system on a false basis, including by dishonestly claiming that she had abducted Louis. Mr Justice Nicklin, the judge who presided in the High Court trial of Mr Lachaux's libel actions, accepted that Asfana, a British citizen, was the ultimate source of these allegations against Mr Lachaux.

The *Independent* and the *Evening Standard* initially put forward defences of 'truth' under section 2 of the Defamation Act 2013, and public interest under section 4, but withdrew the truth defence following the publication in 2017 of a judgment in family law proceedings in England between Mr Lachaux and Asfana. Mr Justice Nicklin said in the High Court libel judgment that while Mr Lachaux did not emerge 'entirely unscathed' as regards being criticised in the family proceedings judgment, it was a 'comprehensive demolition' of Asfana's allegations.

For context on the *Lachaux* appeal issue, see 20.2.1, and on the 'truth' defence, see 22.2.

The defamation trial was delayed because of appeals about interpretation of part of the 2013 Act, which went to the Supreme Court.

But, following the trial in 2021, the first in which any major news organisation had relied entirely on the section 4 defence, Mr Lachaux won his case, because Mr Justice Nicklin ruled that neither the *Independent* nor *Evening Standard* had proved the defence. He ordered the *Independent* to pay Mr Lachaux damages of £50,000 and the *Evening Standard* to pay him damages of £70,000 (*Lachaux v Independent Print Ltd and Evening Standard Ltd* [2016] QB 402; [2018] QB 594; [2020] AC 612; [2021] EWHC 1797 (QB)).

Mr Justice Nicklin ruled that both had proved that what they published was or formed part of a statement on a matter of public interest, including because the articles contained information concerning a woman (Mrs Lachaux) alleging that she had suffered domestic violence, and that she had been mistreated by Dubai authorities and 'let down' by British authorities in their dealings with Dubai about her situation there. But he ruled that the *Independent* had failed to demonstrate that it believed publication of its article was in the public interest. This was because the staff journalist responsible for deciding that it should be published had no recollection when testifying at the 2021 trial of details of the process which led to its publication, or of 'his state of belief' at that time in 2014, and the *Independent* was unable to produce any document from that time to evidence such belief.

Mr Justice Nicklin also ruled that neither the *Independent* nor *Evening Standard* had proved it was reasonable for them to believe that publishing Mrs Lachaux's allegations against her ex-husband was in the public interest. The judge reached this conclusion for various reasons, including because (the quotes are the judge's):

- The *Independent* had received the draft of its article from a 'practically unknown freelancer' and published the article three days later without carrying out any significant checks on him and without putting its very grave allegations to Mr Lachaux to give him the chance to say something in rebuttal of them, which was 'a serious failure in basic journalist good practice', and without as a check obtaining documents from the Dubai legal proceedings; and that consequently the article was 'wholly one-sided' and—beyond some inconsistent use of terms such as 'claims' and 'allegations'—contained nothing to signal to the reader that there was any reason to doubt his ex-wife's account of events, which was therefore wrongly presented as 'credible and truthful' despite the *Independent*'s insufficient checking of it.
- Although the *Evening Standard* had employed a (different) freelance to interview Mrs Lachaux's adult son (from a previous marriage), about her allegations, the freelance's efforts to check their veracity was inadequate, and Mr Lachaux had not been contacted for his version of events, and therefore as a result the article published by the *Evening Standard* was 'almost entirely one-sided', with the newspaper 'clearly siding' with Mrs Lachaux, including by presenting Mr Lachaux as dishonest and by providing a link so that readers could sign a petition in support of his ex-wife (who at that time was facing prosecution in Dubai for abducting Louis during her dispute with Mr Lachaux, of which she was convicted).

By contrast, in the case brought by Noel Clarke against *The Guardian* in 2025, Mrs Justice Steyn, upheld their section 4 defence. *The Guardian*'s right to reply to Clarke, was said by him to be 'outrageously unreasonable and oppressive' because it sought reply 'within less than 24 hours then another 24 hours.' The judge said 'the time given to Mr Clarke to reply (more than 29 hours . . . and ultimately a period of more than three weekdays) was not unreasonable in the circumstances. While there were many allegations for Mr Clarke to address, they all concerned matters that were within his direct knowledge and *The Guardian* knew that for Mr Clarke the right to reply email would not come out of the blue. For several weeks, he had been aware, broadly, of the nature of allegations received by BAFTA'.

Commenting on presentation and tone she said, 'Everyone . . . was "*cognisant of the seriousness of publishing these sorts of allegations*" . . . and they took the responsibility very seriously. The editorial team decided to run a long article to enable them to tell the story by laying out the allegations individually, in each case, in parallel with Mr Clarke's response . . . . Mr Clarke's statement for publication was included high up in the article. The positioning of Mr Clarke's individual responses to each allegation provides balance and enables the reader to form their own view of the credibility and significance of *The Guardian*'s findings. *The Guardian* excluded from publication matters which they considered were properly matters of the private lives of Mr Clarke, his professional associates and his family.'

23.2.4.1 **Significance of media codes**

Section 4(2) of the 2013 Act says that, in determining whether the public interest defence is made out, a court must have regard to all the circumstances of the case. In his judgment in *Lachaux*, Mr Justice Nicklin made clear that the case's circumstances included that, by failing to contact Mr Lachaux about his ex-wife's allegations, the *Independent* and the *Evening Standard* staff journalists responsible for publication of the articles had failed to comply with their employer's written 'code of conduct' for journalism.

The judge said that—by failing to create a documentary record (an 'audit trail') at the time they published Mrs Lachaux's allegations, to record why they reasonably believed that publishing the highly defamatory material about her ex-husband was in the public interest—they had no such evidence to 'demonstrate' that they held such a belief.

In his judgment, Mr Justice Nicklin noted the requirement in the Human Rights Act 1998, which came into force in 2000, for a court in a privacy case involving consideration of Article 10 rights to consider too 'any relevant privacy code' (see 27.9 in this book). He said he felt this requirement should also be considered by courts in relation to use of the section 4 defence in a defamation case, 'because the law should strive to achieve a level of coherence between the publication torts'.

The judge was told in the *Lachaux* trial that neither the *Independent* nor the *Evening Standard* had, at the relevant time in 2014, a formal policy about how they could demonstrate fully that they had reasonably believed that publication of a particular article was in the public interest. He said:

> My immediate reaction on hearing that answer was that this demonstrated a lax and, frankly, amateurish approach . . . I have asked myself whether it is unrealistic for a Court to expect documents to be available that record (or at least shed some light on) decisions taken as to what was identified, at the time, as the public

> interest justification for publication? I do not think it is. In other areas, where professionals are asked to account for events that have happened and decisions they have taken, the Courts are used to seeing contemporaneous records. For example, doctors, nurses, teachers, police officers, lawyers, surveyors, dentists, accountants, opticians, and architects routinely take notes and keep records of their professional lives; information received, advice given, decisions made, and actions taken.”

Mr Justice Nicklin said that, while a court has no power to require journalists to maintain records, a defendant seeking to establish that such 'reasonable belief' had been held is 'likely to find that the prospects of success are enhanced by being able to produce contemporaneous records of the decision(s) taken'. He said: 'Defendants seeking to rely upon such a belief—whether in support of a section 4 defence or otherwise—would be well advised to ensure that they are able to demonstrate that they reasonably believed that publication would be in the public interest and how, and with whom, that was established at the time.'

See in particular sections 2.6 and 3.4.11, for the various editorial code audit trail requirements, on being able to demonstrate why it was justified 'in the public interest' to breach one of the code's normal rules.

23.3 Lord Nicholls' list

As stated earlier, the public interest defence in section 4 of the 2013 Act replaced a public interest defence which first evolved in the House of Lords judgment in 1999 in a case in which Albert Reynolds sued the *Sunday Times* for defamation. The House of Lords ruled that the newspaper could have had such a defence in common law if its article had met the standards of what they termed 'responsible journalism' (for example, the article failed to include Mr Reynolds' explanation of the relevant events).

In the House of Lords judgment, Lord Nicholls set out a non-exhaustive list of factors a court could consider when examining whether what was published was the product of responsible journalism and therefore whether it could be protected by the common law defence. The Supreme Court said in 2020 that it is 'inappropriate' for a court to consider the 10 factors detailed by Lord Nicholls as a 'checklist' (*Serafin v Malkiewicz*). In the *Noel Clarke* case, the judge said that '[a]lthough not to be regarded as a checklist, one or more of the ten illustrative factors identified by Lord Nicholls in *Reynolds* . . . may well be relevant.' Lord Nicholls' list of factors therefore remains relevant today; it is as follows (with summarised explanation added in italics):

1. The seriousness of the allegation. The more serious the charge, the more the public is misinformed and the individual harmed, if the allegation is not true. *Therefore, the more serious the allegation, the greater should be the reporter's efforts to ensure that what is published is correct if the story is to be protected by the defence.*

2. The nature of the information, and the extent to which the subject matter is a matter of public concern. *The less the matter is of public concern, the weaker the defence. The defence will fail if a judge decides the matter is not of public concern—judges often say that what interests the public and what is in the public interest are two different things.*
3. The source of the information. Some informants have no direct knowledge of the events. Some have their own axes to grind when making allegations. Some are being paid for their stories. *Note that courts are wary of unidentified informants, although a newspaper or broadcaster will not necessarily be penalised for refusing to identify a source.*
4. The steps taken to verify the information. *It is always important to check, whenever possible, to ensure that what you have been told is true or correct. Making no or insufficient checks before publication will be regarded as irresponsible journalism and the defence will fail.*
5. The status of the information. The allegation may have already been the subject of an investigation which commands respect. *For example, if a reputable agency—such as the police—has already decided the relevant allegations are not true, then the media must have sufficient reason to air them if the defence is to apply.*
6. The urgency of the matter. News is often a perishable commodity. *The courts, when deciding if the defence applies, must take into consideration that journalists need to work and publish quickly.*
7. Whether comment was sought before publication from the claimant [*the person who claims they were defamed*]. He may have information others do not possess or have not disclosed. An approach to the claimant will not always be necessary. *Generally the person who is the subject of an allegation should be approached. It is also important to make it clear in a story that, if the person about whom allegations have been made cannot be contacted, efforts have been made to reach them. Only rarely will an approach to the subject not be necessary.*
8. Whether the article contained the gist of the plaintiff's [*claimant's*] side of the story. *The journalism must be fair if it is to benefit from the defence. Leaving out the claimant's side is a recipe for disaster.*
9. The tone of the article. A newspaper can raise queries or call for an investigation. It need not adopt allegations as statements of fact. *For example, the defence is unlikely to apply to material which brashly and unfairly suggests that unproven allegations are true. It is important to mind your phrasing. Make sure that what you write is what you mean—and that your meaning is clear to anyone who reads your copy, including what courts sometimes refer to as the 'ordinary reasonable reader'. Sloppy writing will almost undoubtedly prove expensive.*
10. The circumstances of the publication, including the timing. *Was it really so urgent that the story had to be published when it was? Could it have waited an hour or two, or a day or so?*

The **additional material** for this chapter on **www.mcnaes.com** has details of other cases in which media organisations failed or succeeded in using either the section 4 or the *Reynolds* defence.

23.4 Neutral reportage

Section 4(3) of the 2013 provides a particular category of the public interest defence, which can be referred to as the 'neutral reportage' defence.

Section 4(3) says: 'If the statement complained of was, or formed part of, an accurate and impartial account of a dispute to which the claimant was a party, the court must in determining whether it was reasonable for the defendant to believe that publishing the statement was in the public interest disregard any omission of the defendant to take steps to verify the truth of the imputation conveyed by it.'

This defence can protect a defamatory report of a dispute between two parties if the reporting is even-handed, and if the criteria in section 4(1), referred to earlier in this chapter, are met (that the report was a statement on a matter of public interest, and the publisher reasonably believed that it was, etc.).

By saying that a court considering whether the defence applies can disregard any omission by the publisher 'to take steps to verify the truth of the imputation conveyed' by such a report, the Act recognises how hard it may be for journalists to discover to what extent the parties to the dispute are making truthful allegations about each other.

Again, when considering if the public interest defence applies, judges can be guided, but not bound, by case law, such as those outlined below, on a variant of the *Reynolds* defence which was an earlier version of the 'neutral reportage' defence.

23.4.1 The *Al-Fagih* case

In *Al-Fagih v HH Saudi Research & Marketing (UK) Ltd* ([2001] EWCA Civ 1634) (a case based on the *Reynolds* defence which was decided before the Defamation Act 2013) the Court of Appeal ruled that a newspaper could rely on the 'responsible journalism' defence where it reported, in an objective manner, an allegation about someone made by an opponent during a political dispute. The defence was not lost merely because the newspaper had not verified the allegation. The newspaper had argued that, where two politicians made serious allegations against each other, it was a matter of public importance to report the dispute, provided that this was done fairly and accurately and that the parties were given the opportunity to explain or contradict. This principle formed the basis of what is now section 4(3) of the 2013 Act.

23.4.2 The *Flood* case

In *Flood v Times Newspapers Ltd* [2012] 2 AC 273, Lord Phillips said in the Supreme Court that neutral reportage justified a journalist being relieved from the normal obligation to verify, because it was 'a special, and relatively rare, form' of the *Reynolds* defence, adding: 'It arises where it is not the content of a reported allegation that is of public interest, but the fact that the allegation has been made. It protects the publisher if he has taken proper steps to verify the making of the allegation and provided that he does not adopt it.'

Such a proviso against 'adoption' means the publisher must not present the allegation as being definitely true. For details of the *Flood* case and a further case study, see the **additional material** for this chapter on **www.mcnaes.com**.

23.5 Risk arising from continued publication online in changed circumstances

Media organisations aiming to rely on the section 4 defence when publishing material online should bear in mind that a change in circumstances may mean it is no longer in the public interest to publish it, or to continue to publish it without adequate amendment. For example, a person against whom an allegation was aired may subsequently be exonerated of it by an official inquiry (this happened in the *Flood* case).

In the *Lachaux* case, Mr Justice Nicklin criticised the *Independent* and the *Evening Standard* because they continued to publish online Mrs Lachaux's allegations against her ex-husband in substantially the same versions even after the 2017 judgment in the family proceedings case which, Mr Justice Nicklin said, had been a 'comprehensive demolition' of her allegations. The *Independent* and the *Evening Standard* had in 2017 added to their online articles a brief reference to that judgment and a link to a news report of it. But Mr Justice Nicklin ruled that adding the reference and link was insufficient for these media organisations to reasonably believe that continued publication of those versions until 2021 was in the public interest. Part of the damages awarded to Mr Lachaux arose from that continued publication.

see too 20.2.1 and this chapter's additional materials for the case of *Banks v Cadwalladr*

Professional advice should be taken (such as from a lawyer) before adding anything to an online article after a complaint is made by a person who claims it defames them—for context, see 22.8 on corrections.

23.6 Expect to be scrutinised

As this chapter seeks to emphasise, in a defamation case in which the section 4 defence is relied on, the judge will consider in detail the state of mind of the relevant journalists when they made decisions on what should be published, and how they researched that material.

The best hope of using the defence successfully arises from planning before publication to rely on it, so that all reasonable care is taken, including in research, in keeping records and in phrasing what is published to avoid the impression that a defamatory allegation is being presented as definitely true.

Recap of major points

- The statutory 'public interest' defence, which has its origins in the *Reynolds* defence, has two principal elements—the publication must be a statement on a matter of public interest, and the defendant must believe that publication was reasonable.
- As regards such matters, the defence can protect publication of allegations which turn out to be untrue, but the journalists involved must have complied with proper standards—for example, normally the person who is the subject of the allegations should be given the opportunity to respond to them.
- A publisher intending to rely on the defence, if that proves necessary, as regards material planned for publication should get legal advice before it is published.
- The defence can protect 'neutral reportage'—accurate and impartial reports—of a dispute in which the claimant is involved.

Useful Websites

www.legislation.gov.uk, Defamation Act 2013 and accompanying explanatory notes

Bailii, High Court's decision in *Lachaux v Independent Print Ltd & Anor*, www.bailii.org

Judicial website, High Court decision in *Noel Clarke v Guardian News and Media*

Parliament.uk, House of Lords' decision in *Reynolds v Times Newspapers Limited and Others*

Online resources

Visit the online resources at **www.mcnaes.com** to test your knowledge of this chapter with **self-test questions** and a **flashcard glossary**, and to read **updates** about law and regulatory matters affecting journalism, as well as **additional material** to further your learning.

24

The Rehabilitation of Offenders Act 1974

Chapter summary

The Rehabilitation of Offenders Act 1974 allows some criminal convictions to be ignored (i.e. 'spent') after specified 'rehabilitation periods'. Its purpose is that people do not forever have a blot on their records and can make fresh starts. It also limits the defences journalists have against a defamation claim over a published reference to a 'spent' conviction if the **claimant** can prove it was published maliciously. The Act presents no problem for journalists if disclosing someone's criminal record is in the public interest. However, the Act does not sit easily among current data protection and privacy laws and it should not be assumed that journalists are free to publish 'spent' convictions simply if they are covered by the Act.

→glossary

see 24.3, 'Right to be forgotten', and 27.13, Privacy and the 'right to be forgotten'

24.1 Rehabilitation periods

The 1974 Act created the concept of **spent convictions**. Convictions become 'spent' after a 'rehabilitation period', which varies according to the sentence imposed, and includes a so-called Buffer period which runs from the end of the sentence. Some convictions, such as murder, which carries an automatic life sentence, are never spent.

→glossary

There is no legal obligation to declare a 'spent' conviction when applying for most jobs, whatever the application form says, although there is for some occupations, such as working with children.

The length of the rehabilitation period depends on the length of an offender's sentence (it makes no difference whether the sentence was suspended or had immediate effect). Serious crimes for which convictions never become spent are those for which an offender received a jail sentence, or a term of detention in a young offender institution, of more than four years, or an extended sentence for public protection, or an extended determinate sentence used for 'dangerous' offenders. For detail about extended sentences, see the Nacro guide in Useful websites at the end of this chapter.

for types of sentence, see 7.6, Sentencing by magistrates and 9.7, Sentencing at Crown court

see Useful Websites at the end of this chapter for the rehabilitation periods

The rehabilitation periods determining when less serious convictions become spent vary from two years, for a prison sentence of six months or less, to seven years for a jail sentence of between 30 months and four years. But a further conviction during the rehabilitation period can extend it. Cautions and **absolute discharges** become spent immediately. Rehabilitation periods for many convictions are halved for those under 18, and in some cases are even shorter for those aged 12–14.

→glossary

24.2 The Act's effect on the media

The 1974 Act limits the defences available for a media organisation sued for defamation for publishing any reference to a person's spent conviction.

→glossary

(1) A defence of **truth**—that the report of the previous conviction was true—will fail if the claimant can prove that the conviction was spent *and* the publication was malicious. This breaches the principle that truth is a complete defence to a defamation action, because the Act aims to deter the media from referring to a spent conviction without good reason.

(2) The defences of absolute or qualified privilege are not available for reporting a spent conviction which is mentioned in court proceedings but is then ruled inadmissible by the court.

see ch. 22 for explanations of all these defences

Example A man sues a newspaper for defamation after it publishes an accurate reference to his previous criminal conviction. Three defences may be available even if the conviction referred to is 'spent', as long as the publication was not malicious:

- *Truth*—because there was a conviction, defamation law accepts that the conviction is proof that the person committed that crime (if the conviction was in a UK court or service court—section 13 of the Civil Evidence Act 1968). So a media organisation, once it proves the conviction—for example, from a UK court record—is not required to re-prove that the claimant committed the offence.
- *Qualified privilege* protects non-contemporaneous reports of court cases if the defence's requirements are met. Mention of a conviction is, in effect, a report of the court case in which the conviction occurred when the defendant pleaded guilty, or when magistrates or a jury announced the guilty verdict. The defence also protects quotations from the case, such as the judge calling the convicted defendant 'a scoundrel'.
- *Honest opinion* protects opinion based on a fact provable as true, or on a privileged report, if the defence's requirements are met. For example, if a council election candidate has a criminal conviction, an editorial comment column could safely publish the author's honestly held opinion that the conviction made the person unfit for public office. Similar comments from others could also be safely published if these were their honestly held opinions. Even if no such comment is made explicitly, a media organisation publishing the conviction in this context creates an inference that the person could be regarded as unfit for public office. The honest opinion defence would normally protect the media organisation over that inference.

see 20.2.3, Inferences, which explains this term

The above defences apply unless the publication was malicious. There will be **malice** if a journalist or editor publishes a reference to a spent conviction merely to further some interest of their own or out of spite, and that is the dominant motive. The 1974 Act means proof of malice negates the truth defence, so that cannot protect such reference to the spent conviction. Malice negates qualified privilege too, and without a basis of 'truth' or privilege, the honest opinion defence would fail too. →glossary

* Remember

Usually the media can refer to and comment on spent convictions—such as the criminal record of a dodgy businessperson—with no fear of defamation consequences because the disclosures are in the public interest and no malice is involved, but they may still be vulnerable to other legal complaints under data protection and privacy laws.

24.2.1 Spent convictions revealed in court proceedings

A person giving evidence in any civil proceedings should not, generally, be asked about spent convictions.

But rehabilitated people who appear before criminal courts again, after their convictions have become spent, can still be asked about them.

Absolute or qualified privilege applies to media reports of a spent conviction mentioned in a court case unless the court ruled that the fact the conviction exists was inadmissible.

Judges have been directed that spent convictions should never be referred to in criminal courts, unless this is unavoidable, and that no one should refer in open court to a spent conviction without the judge's authority.

24.2.2 Other legal considerations

It may be an offence in data protection law for a public servant to disclose unofficially to a journalist that a person has a criminal conviction, irrespective of whether it is spent. Journalists should be aware of their rights and obligations under that law.

A journalist who gets information about a conviction from official records by fraud, dishonesty or bribery could be prosecuted under data protection or other law.

Journalists can request a court to supply detail of a criminal conviction—see 15.15.3 and 15.18. Ch. 28 explains data protection law, and ch. 34 explains 'misconduct' law and bribery law.

24.3 Privacy and the 'Right to be forgotten'

Privacy and data protection principles have led to the creation of what has become known as 'a right to be forgotten', which is often used by people to try and get 'old' references to previous convictions removed. For example, data protection has been used to require Google to prevent its search engine from finding a report of a past conviction if the person's name is the search term. Although the 'right to be forgotten' was originally conceived by the Court of Justice of the European Union in 2014, in what has become known as the *Google Spain* case, it has now also become part of the jurisprudence of the European Court of Human Rights (ECtHR).

Although the ECtHR, in 2018, in *M.L. and W.W. v Germany*, distinguished between the roles of primary publishers and search engines, noting that the work of the primary publisher 'is generally at the heart of what freedom of expression is intended to protect', and contrasting this with the role of search engines, which it described as facilitating public access to information about individuals, it has subsequently enforced the 'right to be forgotten' against newspaper archives. In 2021, in *Biancardi v Italy*, the ECtHR decided that an editor could be held liable for failing or refusing to de-index information published on a newspaper website. Most recently, in July 2023, in the case of *Hurbain v Belgium*, the ECtHR held that an order of a Belgian court that Belgian newspaper *Le Soir* had to anonymise a 30-year-old archived article (about a series of fatal road-traffic accidents, which referenced the name of the driver ('G') responsible for one of them) on its website did not violate *Le Soir*'s freedom of expression.

see 27.13, Privacy and the 'right to be forgotten'

The ECtHR found that the archived piece had the effect of creating a 'virtual criminal record' of G, especially considering the length of time that had passed since the incident. In those circumstances, the Court concluded that anonymisation would not impose an excessive burden on Mr Hurbain as publisher of *Le Soir*, while being the most effective way to protect G's privacy.

For Ipso adjudications on whether articles should have referred to previous convictions, see the **additional material** for ch. 4 on **www.mcnaes.com**.

Recap of major points

- Convictions become spent at the end of the rehabilitation period.
- A conviction leading to a jail term of more than four years is never spent.
- The rehabilitation period varies between seven years (in respect of a jail sentence of between 30 months and four years) and three months, although some convictions become spent immediately.
- The Rehabilitation of Offenders Act 1974 restricts the defamation defences available to journalists who maliciously refer to spent convictions.

Useful Websites

Nacro, 'Rehabilitation of Offenders Act 1974: A Nacro Guide', www.nacro.org.uk

Nacro guide to the Rehabilitation of Offenders Act 1974, with charts showing rehabilitation periods

Online resources

Visit the online resources at **www.mcnaes.com** to test your knowledge of this chapter with **self-test questions** and a **flashcard glossary**, and to read **updates** about law and regulatory matters affecting journalism, as well as **additional material** to further your learning.

25

Slander and malicious falsehood

Chapter summary

Defamation in its spoken form is slander unless it can be defended in law, and so what a journalist says could lead to them being successfully sued for damages. This chapter examines how that could happen, and covers malicious falsehood—which is the publication of a statement which, while false, is not defamatory but can be shown to have caused financial loss.

25.1 Slander

→glossary

The most obvious difference between the **torts** of libel and slander is, as ch. 20 explains, that a defamatory statement in permanent form (for example, written words, a drawing or a photograph) is actionable as a libel, while a defamatory statement that is spoken or in some other transient form is actionable as a slander. But:

- defamatory statements broadcast on radio or television, or in a cable programme are actionable as libel—Broadcasting Act 1990;
- as are defamatory statements in a public performance of a play—Theatres Act 1968.

For there to be slander, as with libel, the statement must be published to a third person (for slander, 'publication' is that someone other than the claimant heard what was said), must refer to (that is, 'identify') the **claimant**, and must cause their reputation serious harm, and cannot be successfully defended in defamation law (for example, it is not true).

→glossary

A claimant in a slander case must prove the financial damage suffered, except in the case of:

ch. 21 explains what a claimant must prove to win libel damages

- an imputation that they have committed a crime punishable by imprisonment; or
- a statement calculated to disparage them in their office, profession, calling, trade or business.

Journalists are less likely to be sued in an action alleging slander than in one alleging libel, but must be aware of the dangers.

Suppose that someone tells a reporter that a borough councillor used his position to secure building contracts—an allegation actionable because it disparages the councillor in his public office. A reporter checking the allegation will have to interview people to reach the truth and must be wary of being sued for slander by the councillor over questions asked during those interviews in which the allegation might be repeated. There is a risk too that a message left by the reporter on a phone system, referring to the allegation, could prompt the councillor to sue for slander if the message is heard or re-played by someone other than the councillor. There is also a risk when broadcasters shout, in public, questions referring to allegations at people who have refused to be interviewed about them. Broadcasting the encounter live or later could spark an action for libel, while the fact that such a shouted question was heard by members of the public at the scene might tempt the subject to sue for slander as well.

The limitation period for bringing a slander action is one year—the same as for a libel claim (see 22.12).

25.2 Malicious falsehood

Publication of a false statement may cause a person financial damage even though it does not cast aspersions on their character or fitness to hold an office or follow a calling. For example, a false statement that a solicitor has retired from practice could cause financial loss as their clients might seek other solicitors to do their work. But it is clearly not defamatory to be considered retired.

The wronged person cannot sue for libel or slander if a published statement is not defamatory—but might be able to sue for malicious falsehood. The tort of malicious falsehood is governed by a mixture of statute and case law. The relevant statutory law is contained in the Defamation Act 1952. Malicious (or injurious) falsehood (sometimes referred to as 'trade libel') is not concerned with reputation, and it is not necessary to show that any statement complained of is defamatory. The claimant in a malicious falsehood action must prove the statement is untrue—in contrast with a libel action, where the court assumes that a defamatory statement is false unless the defendant can prove it to be true. The claimant must also prove that the statement was published maliciously.

As with the defence of qualified privilege in defamation law, **malice** would be ruled to have occurred if a person publishes a statement they knew was false, and there can also be proof of malice if the person who published the statement was reckless because they were uncaring whether it was true or not.

→glossary

ch. 22 explains qualified privilege

Also, a person who believes a false statement is true but publishes it with the aim of injuring the claimant will also be viewed as motivated by malice (*Spring v Guardian Assurance plc* [1993] 2 All ER 273, CA). Negligence—that is, wrongly believing a statement to be true, and so failing to check it, when there is no aim to injure—is not malice.

The claimant in a malicious falsehood case does not have to prove that they have suffered actual damage if the words are in permanent form, such as printed words, and are likely to cause financial damage, or they are spoken or written and likely to cause them financial damage in their office, profession, calling, trade or business. The UK Supreme Court's decision in *George v Cannell* [2024] UKSC 19 addressed the interpretation of section 3(1) of 1952 Act and established that, while section 3(1) eases the burden of proving financial loss by creating a presumption of some loss, it does not automatically entitle claimants to more than nominal damages without substantial evidence of financial harm. This distinction ensures that it will be necessary to prove significant loss for more sizeable damages.

If a claimant has proved financial damage, they can also claim damages for emotional distress, hurt feelings and so on—and these damages could be substantial because the defendant will be shown to have acted maliciously.

The limitation for bringing a malicious falsehood action is one year.

for context, see 20.2.2 about rulings in defamation cases and the meaning of words

25.2.1 Meaning

Claims for malicious falsehood also differ from those for defamation because they are not based on the notion that a statement has only one meaning (*Ajinomoto Sweeteners Europe SAS v Asda Stores Ltd (No 2)* [2010] EWCA Civ 609, [2011] 1 QB 497).

Journalists must be aware of the need for clear and concise writing, and the risk that, in a malicious falsehood claim, a court will take account of a range of meanings for a statement, one or more of which could leave them liable to pay damages.

25.2.2 Malice

for context, see 20.5, Errors and apologies

An editor may realise that the facts of a story are wrong, but they were not defamatory and it was an honest mistake. If so, they should act quickly to publish an adequate correction. A failure to correct a story which is known to be wrong, especially if it remains visible online, could be held to be malicious.

25.2.3 Slander of goods and title

Two types of malicious falsehood are known as 'slander of goods' (false and malicious statements disparaging the claimant's goods) and 'slander of title' (false and malicious denial of the claimant's title to property). The word 'slander' is misleading in both cases because the damaging statement can be in spoken or permanent form.

Recap of major points

- Slander, a civil wrong (like libel), concerns defamatory words which (unlike libel) are spoken or in some other transient form.
- In slander (unlike libel), financial damage may need to be proved.
- Malicious falsehoods are false statements that, though not defamatory, may still be damaging. The claimant must prove that the statement is untrue and was published maliciously.

Useful Websites

Bailii, Court of Appeal judgment in *Cruddas v Calvert & Ors*, www.bailii.org

Supreme Court website, Judgment in *George v Cannell*

Online resources

Visit the online resources at **www.mcnaes.com** to test your knowledge of this chapter with **self-test questions** and a **flashcard glossary**, and to read **updates** about law and regulatory matters affecting journalism, as well as **additional material** to further your learning.

Part 4

Confidentiality, privacy and copyright

26

Breach of confidence

Chapter summary

The law of breach of confidence is based upon the principle that a person who is given information in confidence should not take unfair advantage of it. This chapter explains the kind of information and relationships considered confidential. Governments, businesses and individuals use this law to protect information they regard as officially or commercially secret, or private. A media organisation which publishes this type of information needs a legal defence—for example, that publication exposed information which the public had a right to know—to avoid having to pay damages. The main
→glossary means of preventing a breach of confidence is an **injunction** banning publication of confidential information. This area of law was also the foundation of the law of privacy, the focus of the next chapter.

26.1 Development of the law

The law on breach of confidence is at its most straightforward in protecting commercial secrets. An employee has a duty to protect commercially sensitive information they create or gain in the course of employment—such as market research data or plans for new products. That duty arises from the employment relationship. If an employee disloyally passes that information to the employer's commercial rival, that is a breach of confidence. In most instances the betrayed employer could, apart from sacking the employee, successfully sue them and the rival in the civil courts for damages to compensate for any financial loss suffered, because breach of confidence
→glossary is a **tort**, a civil wrong. The duty to preserve confidentiality can automatically pass to anyone else who receives the material and realises its confidential nature. So, a media organisation to which a business's commercial secrets are leaked may also be successfully sued if it publishes these, unless it has a defence.

The law of breach of confidence can also protect material which is personally private. Queen Victoria's husband Prince Albert used it in 1848 to prevent commercial publication of private family etchings depicting their children and pets after copies were purloined from the printers to which they were sent by the Royal household to be printed merely as a personal collection (*Prince Albert v Strange* (1848) 1 Mac. & G. 25).

But what is now the wide scope of this law—including the way in which high-profile figures have sought to use it to protect their reputations—is a comparatively recent development.

26.1.1 Development of privacy law

Until 2000 UK law recognised no general right to privacy. So in previous decades people who believed their privacy was about to be infringed had to use the law of breach of confidence to prevent intrusions. Their main difficulty lay in the different nature of the two kinds of right. An obligation of confidence, by definition, arises, first, from the circumstances in which the information is given—a relationship which gives rise to one party owing a duty of confidence to another.

In contrast, a right of privacy relating to information arises from the nature of the information itself and from the principle that certain kinds of information are private and for that reason alone should not be disclosed. Many cases involving invasions of privacy did not result from breaches of confidence.

Privacy law evolved as judges began abandoning their strict view on the circumstances in which an obligation of confidence could occur. In the *Spycatcher* case in the House of Lords in 1988 (*Attorney General v Times Newspapers* (1992) 1 AC 191) Lord Goff of Chieveley said:

for context on *Spycatcher*, see 26.3

> A duty of confidence arises when confidential information comes to the knowledge of a person (the confidant) in circumstances where he has notice, or is ruled to have agreed, that the information is confidential, with the effect that it would be just in all the circumstances that he should be precluded from disclosing the information to others.

Lord Goff said he had expressed the duty in wide terms to include the situation where 'an obviously confidential document was wafted by an electric fan out of a window into a crowded street, or when an obviously confidential document such as a diary was dropped in a public place and then picked up by a passer-by'.

In this scenario the passer-by has no relationship with the person whose information they have picked up—but, because it is obviously confidential (for example, a patient's medical records), the law says the passer-by should not, for example, give or sell it to a media organisation for publication, unless there is a legal defence.

In 2000 the Human Rights Act 1998 came into force, directly incorporating into UK law the European Convention on Human Rights. Article 8 of the Convention sets out the right to respect for private and family life, as chs. 1 and 27 explain. In cases involving alleged breach of personal privacy, the courts started abandoning the legal contrivance of implying a confidential relationship where none existed, and so a separate type of tort—misuse of private information—developed. That is the focus of the next chapter.

26.2 Elements of a breach of confidence

There are three elements in a breach of confidence. The information:

- must have 'the necessary quality of confidence';
- must have been imparted in circumstances imposing an obligation of confidence; and
- there must be an unauthorised use of that information to the detriment of the party communicating it (*Coco v AN Clark (Engineers) Ltd* [1969] RPC 41).

The phrase 'the party communicating it' means the person who originally communicates the information—that is, the person to whom the confidence is owed. For example, a company allows its employees to access commercially sensitive information about its products and finances—in effect (practice?), it communicates such information to them, so they owe it a duty of confidence. A patient who tells a doctor about an ailment, or allows them to take blood tests or conduct a pregnancy test, is communicating information. The doctor and any other staff at the surgery or hospital owe the patient a duty of confidence in respect of that information.

Remember that a court enforcing the law of confidentiality does not require a direct relationship to exist between the person who wishes to protect the information and the person who wishes to publish it, having somehow received it. This is because the law of equity operates on the consciences of the parties, so the legal criterion is whether a reasonable person would understand from the nature and circumstances of a disclosure that they were receiving information or material in confidence. Thus, a journalist who receives a leak of a company's commercially sensitive data or someone's medical records usually has a duty not to reveal it to others, just as an employee of that company or the patient's doctor has.

26.2.1 The quality of confidence

The law of breach of confidence safeguards ideas and information imparted or obtained in confidential circumstances. Generally, information is not confidential if it is trivial—for example, a company's canteen menu—or is already in the public domain. The mere fact that a document is marked as 'confidential' or similar does not mean that it automatically has this quality or is private. For example, in the case of *Axon v Ministry of Defence* [2016] EWHC 787 (QB), Mr Justice Nicol ruled that the claimant, the Commanding Officer of a Royal Navy warship who was relieved of his duties following bullying allegations, did not have a reasonable expectation of privacy when *The Sun* published information from leaked Ministry of Defence documents—despite the documents being marked 'restricted'.

26.2.2 Obligation of confidence

An obligation of confidence can arise in a variety of ways.

Contractual relationship Employees might have signed agreements not to disclose an employer's secrets or other information. This applies as much to a celebrity's chauffeur who wants to sell to the media tales of what he saw and heard in his employment as it does to scientists employed in commercial research. Even if the written contract does not make this clear, there is an implied term in every employment relationship that an employee will not do anything detrimental to an employer's interests.

Personal relationship In 1967 the Duchess of Argyll prevented the *People* newspaper, and her former husband, from publishing marital secrets (*Argyll v Argyll* [1967] Ch. 302). This was an early example of the courts accepting that a couple in a relationship owe a duty of confidence to each other about intimate matters, which still applies after they split up. By the 1980s the courts had extended the protection to prevent the publication of kiss-and-tell stories originating from less formal relationships. Disputes about whether such stories can be or should have been published are now generally dealt with under privacy law.

see 27.3.4, Relationships, which gives context

Unethical behaviour It now seems to be established by case law (such as *Niema Ash and another v Loreena McKennitt and others* [2006] EWCA Civ 1714) that someone who obtains confidential information by unethical means such as trespass, theft, listening devices or long-range cameras is usually in breach of an obligation of confidence owed to the targets of this activity—an obligation created and breached by the tactics used.

If not, the case will probably be covered in privacy law. Electronic snooping is covered too by criminal law.

See 27.5.1 on information obtained covertly, and ch. 34 on 'hacking' (snooping) offences.

26.2.3 Detriment

The confiding party must suffer, or be at risk of suffering, a detriment of some sort to be able to claim a breach of confidence, such as financial loss from exposure of commercially sensitive information to rivals. Another example: if a media organisation published a company's designs for new products without its consent, the detriment could also be that the company was consequently unable to benefit fully from preparing and coordinating—to maximise impact on the public—an advertising launch for these products. In the *Spycatcher* case in the House of Lords, Lord Keith of Kinkel said it would be a sufficient detriment to an individual that information they gave in confidence was to be disclosed to people they would prefer not to know it. The detriment could be the adverse effect on someone's mental well-being or physical health, caused by unauthorised publication of their confidential, personal information.

Case study

In October 2017 there were reports in the United States that dozens of women had accused film mogul Harvey Weinstein of rape, sexual assault and sexual abuse over a period of 30 years. The accusations sparked the emergence on social media of the *#metoo* movement, in which others told of similar experiences at the hands of employers and others in positions of authority. In October 2018 the *Daily Telegraph* reported that it had been gagged from identifying a high-profile

British businessman who, it said, was the subject of allegations of sexual misconduct and racism, which he denied. These allegations were made by people employed by his business, who had subsequently been paid large sums of money and had signed confidential non-disclosure agreements (NDAs) under which they would keep silent about the treatment they had allegedly suffered. But attempts by Sir Philip Green, head of the Arcadia retail empire, which owned several well-known chains of clothes shops, to keep the story under wraps ended when Labour peer Lord Hain named him in the House of Lords, under the protection of parliamentary privilege, as the person who had 'gagged' the *Daily Telegraph*. The 'gag' was that Sir Philip and two of Arcadia's companies had applied to the High Court for an interim injunction to stop the newspaper identifying Sir Philip as the man at the centre of the allegations. He had anonymity in the injunction proceedings. Mr Justice Haddon-Cave rejected the application, saying he was satisfied that the public interest in publication of the allegations outweighed any confidentiality attaching to the information, and that if the case proceeded to trial, that would be the trial judge's likely conclusion.

The Court of Appeal overruled Mr Justice Haddon-Cave and issued the interim injunction, saying the weight to be attached to an obligation of confidence could be enhanced if it was contained in an express contractual agreement (such as an NDA). The Court referred to the general, public interest in confidentiality agreements being honoured. It said there was a real prospect that publication of the allegations would cause immediate, substantial and possibly irreversible harm (detriment) to the companies which had applied for the injunction, because there could be 'adverse customer reaction'. The Court said the companies were likely to be able to demonstrate at the trial of the case that a substantial part of the information the newspaper sought to publish was obtained through breach of a duty of confidentiality. The Court of Appeal also ordered that the trial (which would have decided whether the law of confidence permitted the *Telegraph* to publish the allegations in the public interest) should be expedited. But he dropped the attempt to stop publication in February 2019—just a week before the trial was due to begin. He was left facing legal bills estimated to be up to £3 million. In 2025, the European Court of Human Rights dismissed Sir Philip's complaint that Hain's use of parliamentary privilege rendered his claim futile and thereby breached his right to a fair trial. (*ABC and others v Telegraph Media Group* Ltd [2018] EWHC 2177 (QB), [2018] EWCA Civ 2329; *Arcadia Group Ltd, Topshop/Topman Ltd and Sir Philip Green v Telegraph Media Group Ltd* [2019] EWHC 223 (QB), *Green v United Kingdom* [2025] ECHR 91; *The Guardian*, 8 February 2019).

26.3 Breach of confidence and official secrets

In 1985 the UK Government used the law of breach of confidence when attempting to stop publication of information acquired by Peter Wright during his former job as a senior officer of its internal security service, MI5. He planned to make money by selling his memoirs—a book called *Spycatcher*. The Attorney General, for the UK Government, sought an injunction to stop the book's publication, arguing that former members of the security services had an absolute and lifelong duty not to reveal any details of their employment. This began a lengthy series of legal actions by the Government, including against newspapers which had reported brief details of some allegations Wright, who had retired to Australia, planned to publish.

The Government was unsuccessful in preventing the book's publication. But the saga established that the Government was prepared to use the law of breach of confidence to protect official secrets.

It also established the legal principle that an interim injunction against one newspaper could apply to all the media (and everyone in England and Wales) to stop material being published.

See the **additional material** for this chapter online for a case study involving the Attorney General securing an injunction against the BBC over a planned expose on an intelligence source alleged to have been abusive to his partners.

((•)) See Useful Websites at the end of this chapter for a BBC report of the House of Lords' judgment on the *Spycatcher* legal saga.

26.4 Injunctions

As already indicated, a person or an organisation who discovers that the media intends to publish confidential information without their/its consent can apply to the High Court for a temporary (interim) injunction to stop it.

Such an order is intended to 'hold the ring' until the case is fully heard. As a condition for obtaining an interim injunction the party seeking it must undertake to pay the other side damages if, at the trial, it is ruled that the injunction should not have been made.

But a media organisation, having been injuncted, may decide that it will cost too much to fight the case in a full trial. Injunctions may give anonymity to a claimant (and sometimes a defendant) and court hearings may be held in private so that the proceedings themselves do not inadvertently reveal the information.

Anyone disobeying an injunction can face proceedings for contempt of court, which could lead to them being fined an amount unlimited by statute and/or being jailed for up to two years.

Section 12 of the Human Rights Act 1998 is intended to provide some protection against injunctions in matters involving freedom of expression. Claimants applying to the High Court for injunctions should only obtain them if they persuade the judge that they are 'likely' to establish at the trial that publication should not be allowed. Before the 1998 Act, the application might be without notice, which meant that only one party—the claimant—was represented and a defendant media organisation would only learn of the proceedings when it was served with the injunction. That can and still does happen—for example, injunctions have sometimes been granted when a newspaper has been printed and ready to go on sale. Section 12 says that if the defendant is not present when the application is made, the court must not grant an injunction unless satisfied either that the claimant has taken all practicable steps to notify the defendant or that there are compelling reasons for not giving notice.

26.4.1 The journalist's dilemma

The law of confidentiality regularly presents journalists with dilemmas. Suppose a reporter learns about some newsworthy misconduct from a source who received the information confidentially. The journalist should, as a matter of ethical conduct and because of the law of libel, approach the person alleged to have misbehaved to get their side of the story and to check facts.

For example, the BBC Editorial Guidelines tells broadcasters:

> "When our output makes allegations of wrongdoing, iniquity or incompetence or lays out a strong and damaging critique of an individual or institution the presumption is that those criticised should be given a 'right of reply', that is, given a fair opportunity to respond to the allegations."

A journalist who does make such an approach runs the risk that, as explained, the subject will immediately obtain an injunction banning use of the information, killing the story before it can be published.

See Useful Websites at the end of this chapter for the BBC Guidelines, and for context see 2.4.2 and 3.4.10.3 on getting facts right and airing the other side of the story.

Remember

You should certainly check a story which might be defamatory—but try to do so without revealing that you have confidential material, to avoid laying yourself open to the risk of an injunction.

26.4.2 Injunction against one is against all

In 1987 the Court of Appeal ruled that when an interim injunction is in force preventing a media organisation from publishing confidential information, other media organisations in England and Wales which know of it can be guilty of contempt of court if they publish that information, even if they are not named in the injunction.

In 1989 two papers were each fined £50,000 for publishing extracts from *Spycatcher* because at the time of publication they knew that interim injunctions banned *The Observer* and *The Guardian* from publishing the material. The fines were later discharged, but the findings of contempt of court were upheld and in 1991 the House of Lords confirmed the ruling on the law. Injunctions are discussed, with further detail, in the next chapter.

An injunction issued by an English or Welsh court does not prevent publication in another country. In particular, it does not prevent publication in Scotland—though Scottish judges may be asked to impose their own injunction, known as an '**interdict**' (see 27.3.1 for a case study where publication occurred in Scotland, despite an injunction being in place in England and Wales). →glossary

For laws in Scotland which particularly affect journalists, see online ch. 36, Other UK Jurisdictions, on **www.mcnaes.com**.

26.5 Remedies for breach of confidence

People or organisations claiming in a legal action that their confidential information has been unlawfully published can:

- ask a judge to issue an injunction to stop it being published again by that publisher or by others;
- seek an order for the confidential material, such as documents or pictures, to be 'delivered up'—that is, returned to the claimant and/or destroyed;
- sue the publisher for damages or 'an account of profits';
- ask a judge to order the publisher to reveal the source of the information, if this is not known, so that the source can be sued for damages and/or to stop disclosure of more confidential information.

26.5.1 Damages

These are likely to be higher in a case where the breach of confidence causes commercial loss—for example, the £1 million damages which *Hello!* magazine had to pay to *OK!* magazine in the *Douglas* case—rather than loss of personal privacy.

In the *Douglas* case it was ruled that the law of confidence protected what should have been the value of the exclusive, commercial deal which *OK!* had struck with Hollywood couple Michael Douglas and Catherine Zeta-Jones to take and publish photographs of their 'private' wedding reception, an arrangement which *Hello!* had undermined by publishing 'spoiler' photos of the occasion, secretly taken by an undercover paparazzo—see the **additional material** for ch. 26 on **www.mcnaes.com** for details of the case.

In 2008 Max Mosley, then president of the organisation which runs Formula 1 grand prix racing, was awarded £60,000 against the *News of the World* in an action alleging breach of confidence and unauthorised disclosure of personal information for its exposure of his participation in a sado-masochistic orgy with prostitutes. One of the prostitutes had breached the confidence of her arrangement with Mosley by telling the newspaper about and filming the orgy, and the newspaper was ruled to be liable for the damages (see also 27.3.4.1).

26.5.2 Account of profits

A person misusing confidential information to make money may be asked to account for the profits to the person or organisation whose confidence was betrayed. A court may rule that the person who misused the information should pay some or all of these ill-gotten profits to the party betrayed. But for a media organisation, the order is more likely to be for damages, because of the difficulty a judge would face in deciding which story in its output at that time led to what profit.

26.5.3 Order to reveal source

A court can order a journalist to disclose the source of the confidential information. A journalist who has promised the source anonymity has an ethical obligation to keep that promise—and face the consequences of disobeying the court's order. The defiance could be deemed a contempt of court which could lead to a fine or, conceivably, to the journalist being jailed, though they may have some protection from Article 10 of the European Convention on Human Rights and the 'shield law' in section 10 of the Contempt of Court Act 1981.

Case study

In 1989 an engineering company, Tetra Ltd, obtained injunctions against *The Engineer* magazine and trainee reporter Bill Goodwin. The company, which was in financial difficulties, had prepared a business plan to help negotiate a substantial bank loan. A copy of the draft plan 'disappeared' from its offices, and the next day a source telephoned Mr Goodwin and gave him information about the company, including the amount of the projected loan and Tetra's forecast results. Mr Goodwin phoned the company and its bankers to check the information. Tetra obtained a **without notice** injunction banning publication of information derived from the draft plan, and later obtained an order that Mr Goodwin and *The Engineer* should hand over notes which would disclose the source. Mr Goodwin refused, and was fined £5,000. In 1996 the European Court of Human Rights ruled that the court order and the fine violated his right Article 10 right to receive and impart information. Mr Goodwin was supported by the National Union of Journalists (*Goodwin v United Kingdom,* Application no. 17488/90 (1996) 22 EHRR 123).

→glossary

See ch. 33 for journalists' ethical obligation to protect identities of sources, including 33.8 on Goodwin.

26.6 What can the media argue as a defendant in a breach of confidence case?

There are several grounds on which a media organisation facing a claim of breach of confidence to stop it publishing information, or for damages if it has been published, can justify publication.

26.6.1 The information is trivial or already in the public domain

The media organisation can argue that the information never had 'the necessary quality of confidence' because it is trivial and/or its disclosure is not likely to cause or have caused any or much detriment.

Also, if a media organisation publishes commercially sensitive information leaked from a business, or information leaked from a public institution, a court is unlikely to grant an injunction or award damages for breach of confidence if the material was already widely in the public domain, because that means the quality of confidence no longer exists or is much reduced—for example, it had already been published by other media outlets, or by members of the public on internet sites and other social media.

But, as ch. 27 sets out, the scope for the public domain defence is more limited if personal privacy is infringed—for example, a judge might ban the media from publishing embarrassing private footage improperly copied from a celebrity's computer, to spare the celebrity further distress, even if thousands of copies are already on the internet.

> The issue of what was already in the public domain was a feature of the *Watford Observer* case, which is outlined in the **additional material** for this chapter on **www.mcnaes.com**.

26.6.2 The public interest in exposure of iniquity

Case law makes clear that if a document has been created for an 'iniquitous' purpose, such as the furtherance of a crime, it cannot be regarded as confidential. The term 'iniquity' covers more than criminal purposes. It 'extends to fraud or equivalent underhand conduct which is in breach of a duty of good faith or contrary to public policy or the interests of justice' (*R v Norman* [2016] EWCA Crim 1564).

Therefore, if a media organisation wants to publish or has published a leaked copy of a communication (such as an email, memo or letter) created for such a purpose—for example, the contents show there was underhand conduct to improperly deceive or exploit someone or the public—those who created the communication should not be able to argue successfully in a court that such contents are confidential information. It is in the public interest that the contents should be revealed.

Section 12 of the Human Rights Act 1998 says a court considering imposing an injunction in a matter affecting freedom of expression in which journalistic material is involved must have particular regard to the extent to which it is, or would be, in the public interest for the material to be published.

26.6.3 There does not have to be iniquity to justify publication

Even before the 1998 Act, journalists had successfully used the defence in common law which permits publication of confidential information when this is in the public interest, even when the disclosure was not of iniquity.

Case study

The Court of Appeal ruled in 1984 that it was in the public interest for the *Daily Express* to publish information from an internal memo, leaked from a company making breathalyser equipment, which cast doubt on the accuracy of the device at a time when police were using it to clamp down on drink-driving (*Lion Laboratories v Evans* [1985] QB 526).

26.6.4 The public interest in correcting 'a false image'

In both privacy and confidentiality cases, judges have accepted that there can be a public interest in information being published to correct a false image that the public has about a person or organisation. For example, in 2011 a judge dismissed a claim for breach of confidence and misuse of private information brought by footballer Rio Ferdinand against the publisher of the *Sunday Mirror* over an article about an affair he had. Ruling in favour of the newspaper, the judge found there was a public interest in the article because he had projected an image of himself as a reformed character who given up his past wild ways, including cheating on his long-term partner, and the article demonstrated this was false (*Ferdinand v MGN* [2011] EWHC 2454 (QB)).

26.7 Relevance of ethical codes

see 27.9, Relevance of ethical codes

As the next chapter explains, in a case involving a claim of breach of privacy, which may include a claim of breach of confidence, the judge will—if the defendant is a media organisation—take into account what the relevant regulatory code says and whether the organisation conformed to it. This could be the Editors' Code, the Broadcasting Code or the Impress Standards Code.

Recap of major points

- The law says that a person who has obtained information in confidence must not take unfair advantage of it.
- A person who believes their confidence is to be breached can get an injunction preventing this.
- Disobeying an injunction is a contempt of court.
- If confidential matter is published, the person whose confidences were breached may be able to claim damages.
- Companies can use this law to stop commercially sensitive information from being published, and to gain damages if it is published.

Useful Websites

BBC News archive, '1988: Government loses Spycatcher battle', news.bbc.co.uk

BBC News archive story in the *Spycatcher* saga

BBC Editorial Guidelines, Section 6: Fairness to Contributors and Consent, 'Right of Reply' (6.3.38), www.bbc.com

Online resources

Visit the online resources at **www.mcnaes.com** to test your knowledge of this chapter with **self-test questions** and a **flashcard glossary**, and to read **updates** about law and regulatory matters affecting journalism, as well as **additional material** to further your learning.

27

Privacy

Chapter summary

People can use the civil law of privacy to prevent publication of information about their lives and activities, including about their relationships. Judges will award damages for 'misuse of private information' and can grant injunctions to ban publication of such information. This chapter explains how UK privacy law, which has its origins in the European Convention on Human Rights, affects the media. People have won large sums in damages for media intrusion into their privacy, including for intrusion by 'phone-hacking'. But a judge may rule that a media organisation was justified in intruding into someone's private life, because what was published was in the **public interest**. Privacy law continues to evolve as courts make decisions on cases and has become one of the primary concerns for media organisations, in part because of the inherent uncertainty in defending a privacy claim. As the law has developed, media organisations have largely stopped publishing 'kiss and tell' stories, a staple of 1990s tabloid journalism, because a number of injunctions were issued by courts to prevent such reports. It has also to some extent produced 'a right to be forgotten'. In contrast to defamation law, where a media organisation can defend themselves on the basis that a defamatory statement is true, privacy law has no such 'truth' defence.

→glossary

27.1 Introduction

As ch. 1 explains, in 2000 the Human Rights Act 1998 came into force and incorporated the European Convention on Human Rights directly into UK law, giving it the specific law of privacy it had previously lacked—Article 8 of the Convention guarantees the right to respect for private and family life.

An individual will assert that their Article 8 rights have been infringed by the media when something that has been published, or something journalists have done, is alleged to have intruded into that person's privacy. As this chapter explains, a person may ask the High Court to grant an **injunction** to ban a media organisation from

→glossary

publishing information about their private life or ask the court to order removal of an article and/or award damages because such information has already been published. Damages can be awarded because UK law has evolved since 2000 to create a Convention-based **tort** of 'misuse of private information'. The court will weigh the individual's Article 8 privacy rights against the media's Article 10 right to freedom of expression, which encompasses both the media's right to receive and impart information, and the public's right to receive it.

→glossary

When hearing a legal dispute over an alleged breach of privacy, a court will firstly determine whether the claimant had a 'reasonable expectation of privacy' in the particular circumstances in which the alleged intrusion occurred. If the decision is that they did, the court will then carry out a 'balancing exercise', considering which of the competing rights should prevail, based on the particular facts of that case.

A media organisation being sued for alleged 'misuse of private information' in respect of what was published may have a defence if it can demonstrate to the court that there was a strong 'public interest' in disclosing an individual's private information. In this context, use of the term 'public interest' denotes information which has a high value to society. Article 10 protects 'public interest' journalism in particular, but the courts must also take into account that there is also a general 'public interest' (high value to society) in protecting personal privacy.

Recent examples of legal actions in privacy cases include:

- A businessman, ZXC, successfully suing financial news organisation Bloomberg for misuse of private information because it revealed he was under investigation by a UK law enforcement agency. The High Court ruled in his favour, finding that he had a reasonable expectation of privacy because the information which identified him was in a confidential letter of request sent by the agency to a foreign state where ZXC resides, which was obtained by Bloomberg. The judge ordered that his identity as a suspect could not be revealed and awarded him £25,000 in damages. The High Court's decision was upheld by the Court of Appeal and the Supreme Court (*ZXC v Bloomberg LP* [2020] EWCA Civ 611; *Bloomberg LP v ZXC* [2022] UKSC 5)—see too 5.11.3.
- The Duke of Sussex being awarded £140,600 in damages in December 2023 after suing Mirror Group Newspapers (MGN), publisher of the *Daily Mirror*, *Sunday Mirror* and *Sunday People* for misuse of private information in relation to unlawful information gathering (including phone-hacking) at its titles. The High Court ruled that 15 out of 33 articles complained of by Harry, published between 2003 and 2009, were the product of unlawful information gathering. Actor Michael Turner (whose professional name is Michael Le Vell) was awarded £31,650 in relation to four out of 27 articles complained of (*The Duke of Sussex and ors v MGN Ltd* [2023] EWHC 3217 (Ch)).
- The Duchess of Sussex successfully suing Associated Newspapers, publisher of the *Mail on Sunday* and *MailOnline*, in 2021 over five articles which quoted extensively from a letter she wrote to her estranged father Thomas Markle, see 27.3.3.

this chapter is about the civil law of privacy. For the criminal law of privacy, see ch. 34

For fuller details on these cases, see the **additional material** for this chapter on **www.mcnaes.com.**

27.2 What Article 8 says

Article 8 of the Convention begins:

> “Everyone has the right to respect for his private and family life, his home, and his correspondence.”

The fundamental importance of Article 8 was emphasised by Lord Nicholls in a House of Lords decision involving supermodel Naomi Campbell (see 27.6), in which he said: ‘A proper degree of privacy is essential for the well-being and development of an individual.’ Article 8 protects a person’s private life against unjustified interfering actions by a ‘public authority’, the media or anyone else. However, as Article 8(2) makes clear, this protection of privacy is subject to a number of ‘derogations’ or exceptions, including to protect ‘the rights and freedoms of others’, and so the Article implicitly acknowledges that the right to freedom of expression means that in exceptional circumstances someone’s private information should be made public.

For the full text of Article 8 and context on ‘public authority’, which includes courts, see 1.3.2.

27.3 The scope of Article 8

Article 8 makes specific reference to certain aspects of a person’s life which are private and so normally deserving of protection. Judges have made clear in their rulings that other aspects of an individual’s life are also to be regarded as private under Article 8.

27.3.1 Family life

Article 8 specifically protects the privacy of family life. Courts may consider, as well as the claimant’s Article 8 rights, those of people linked to the claimant such as family members, especially children.

Case study

The case of *PJS v News Group Newspapers* shows how complex a privacy case can become, and how the privacy rights of a claimant’s family can be a determining factor in a court’s ruling. PJS, a celebrity, sought a High Court injunction to stop the *Sun on Sunday* newspaper publishing a story about his ‘three-way’ sexual encounters with a couple, outside his marriage (PJS was how he was referred in the court proceedings). The couple told the newspaper about these encounters. PJS’s lawyers argued that for it to publish this account would be a misuse of private information about him. But the High Court judge refused to grant an interim (temporary) injunction to stop publication. This was because the judge agreed with the argument put forward by News Group Newspapers (NGN), the newspaper's publishers, that PJS had been portraying an image to the world of being in a committed relationship as regards his marriage (his partner too is well-known in the entertainment business), and that there was a public interest in the newspaper correcting that image by disclosing that PJS had engaged in casual, extra-marital sex. However, the judge also ruled that PJS's anonymity in respect of the case must be kept in place pending an appeal, and the Court of Appeal subsequently ruled that the injunction should be granted. It was effective for 11 weeks. But after articles revealing the identity of PJS as being the celebrity in the case were published overseas and in Scotland, where the injunction had no legal status, and then discussed widely on social media, news organisations in England and Wales complained that the injunction meant they were unable to report details which were now in the UK public domain. The Court of Appeal, following an application by NGN for the injunction to be revoked, agreed to revoke it, but left it in force to preserve PJS's anonymity pending his appeal to the Supreme Court. In a majority ruling, the Supreme Court decided the injunction should remain in force. The Supreme Court concluded that PJS would be likely to secure a permanent injunction should there be a trial of the privacy issue and that the interim injunction was necessary to prevent 'clearly unjustified proposed further invasion of the relevant privacy interests'. It said there was no public interest in further publication. The Supreme Court's decision was based on the privacy rights of PJS's partner and their children, as well as on his privacy rights.

In the Supreme Court judgment, Lady Hale observed: 'First, not only are the children's interests likely to be affected by a breach of the privacy interests of their parents, but the children have independent privacy interests of their own. They also have a right to respect for their family life with their parents.'

The case did not proceed to a trial, so the interim injunction remains in place, making it illegal to publish anything in England and Wales identifying PJS in connection with the case or the sexual encounters (*PJS v News Group Newspapers* [2016] UKSC 26).

For more details about injunctions in privacy cases, see 27.11.2.

Anyone applying for a privacy injunction to ban publication of reports of their own questionable behaviour will probably assert that the privacy rights of their immediate family should be included in the 'balancing exercise' conducted by the court.

27.3.1.1 Children

Children have their own rights to enjoy a private family life. They can be more vulnerable than adults to the effects of media intrusion. Publication of paparazzi pictures of the children of high-profile parents, taken in the street, has led to privacy lawsuits.

Case study

Musician Paul Weller and his wife Hannah won £10,000 in damages for their children whose faces were 'plastered' over the *MailOnline* website in October 2012. Weller sued the website's publisher, Associated Newspapers, on behalf of his daughter Dylan, who was 16 when the seven unpixellated pictures appeared, and twin sons John Paul and Bowie, who were then 10 months old. A paparazzo had followed Weller and the children on a shopping trip in Santa Monica, California, taking photos despite being asked to stop. Associated Newspapers argued the pictures were innocuous and inoffensive images taken in public places and that the Wellers had previously chosen to open up their private family life to public gaze to a significant degree. But Mr Justice Dingemans said when ruling on the case: 'In my judgment, the photographs were published in circumstances where Dylan, Bowie and John Paul had a reasonable expectation of privacy. This was because the photographs showed their faces, one of the chief attributes of their personalities, as they were on a family trip out with their father going shopping and to a cafe and they were identified by surname.' The Court of Appeal upheld the decision in November 2015, with Lord Dyson, the Master of the Rolls, saying Mr Justice Dingemans was 'plainly entitled to find that the publication of the photographs did not contribute to a current debate of general interest' and adding that the youngsters 'were only of interest to the Mail Online because they are children of a successful musician' (*Weller & others v Associated Newspapers Ltd* [2015] EWCA Civ 1176; *Media Lawyer*, 16 April 2014; 20 November 2015).

27.3.2 Home

Intrusion within someone's home needs a strong public interest justification to be legal.

Case study

The High Court ruled in 2018 that broadcaster Channel 5 breached a couple's privacy rights by filming them for the documentary series *Can't Pay? We'll Take It Away!* while they were being evicted from their home—a decision upheld by the Court of Appeal. The couple said that the broadcasting of the footage of their home's interior, including a bedroom, in the state it was in when the eviction and film crew took them by surprise, and that showing them in shock and distress was a misuse of private information. Mr Justice Arnold awarded them £10,000 each in damages. The judge said the programme contributed to a debate of general interest—about the consequences of an increasing level of personal debt—but that inclusion of 'private information' in the footage went beyond what was justified for that purpose (*Ali and Aslam v Channel 5 Broadcast Limited* [2018] EWHC 298 (Ch) and [2019] EWCA Civ 677). Channel 5 has subsequently settled several cases brought over episodes of the same programme, most recently in 2023.

27.3.3 Correspondence/private communications

People usually have a reasonable expectation that letters, texts, emails and phone calls they send or make are private. A media organisation publishing personal and private material from such communications without the sender's consent needs a public interest justification or some other defence (such as that the information was already in the public domain) to avoid having to pay damages if sued for misuse of private information.

Case study

The Duchess of Sussex sued Associated Newspapers, publishers of the *Mail on Sunday* and the *MailOnline* website, for misuse of private information and breach of data protection rights after they published parts of a five-page letter she sent to her estranged father, Thomas Markle.

The five articles, published in February 2019, showed that in the letter she asked him to stop talking to the press about her and her husband, Prince Harry. The articles quoted extensively from it, with the main article headlined 'Revealed: the letter showing true tragedy of Meghan's rift with a father she says has "broken her heart into a million pieces"'. The duchess said in evidence presented to the High Court that the contents of the letter were private and disclosed her intimate thoughts and feelings. She argued that she had a reasonable expectation that the contents would remain private. Associated argued that the duchess had no such expectation because she was aware her father might publish the letter, because of his propensity to speak to the media. It also argued that any privacy rights the duchess had in relation to the letter were outweighed by the Article 10 rights of her father and the public at large. It claimed her Article 8 rights were 'weakened' because, it alleged, she had authorised five of her friends to discuss the letter in an interview with US magazine *People*—which Associated said gave a 'misleading' account of the letter and her relationship with her father. The duchess denied authorising her friends to discuss the letter. Mr Justice Warby ruled in her favour. He said the contents of the letter were 'inherently private and personal'. He ruled that Associated's interference with her privacy rights was 'unlawful', because publishing the extracts to such an extent was not a 'necessary or proportionate' means of correcting some inaccuracies in the *People* magazine article. The duchess also sued Associated on the basis that the articles infringed her copyright in the letter. Mr Justice Warby upheld that claim too (*Duchess of Sussex v Associated Newspapers Ltd* [2021] EWHC 273 (Ch)). The Court of Appeal dismissed Associated's appeal ([2021] EWCA Civ 1810). Associated agreed to pay the duchess nominal damages of £1 for her privacy claim, as well as a confidential sum for the copyright infringement and was also expected to cover much of her legal costs. See 29.14.1 for detail of what Mr Justice Warby ruled about her copyright claim.

see 27.10 about the overlap between privacy and data protection law

27.3.4 Relationships

The courts recognise that people have a reasonable expectation that what they say and do intimately within a personal relationship is private—whether the relationship is a marriage, cohabitation, love affair or friendship. If, after the relationship ends, one person wants to reveal private information about the other which was gained in the relationship (for example, by giving a media interview) the courts may grant an injunction stopping publication, to protect the other person's Article 8 rights, or—if the information is already published—award them damages for the infringement of privacy. Judges accept that there can be a reasonable expectation of privacy not only in relation to what happened within the relationship but also over the fact that there was a relationship.

See the **additional material** for this chapter on **www.mcnaes.com** for examples of some celebrities who sought injunctions over relationships.

27.3.4.1 The privacy of sexual relationships

Courts have become more willing to rule that adulterous or casual sexual affairs are matters in which one or both of the people involved have a reasonable expectation of privacy and may grant an injunction unless the party from the relationship who wishes to reveal the intimate matters succeeds in asserting Article 10 rights to do this, or a media organisation can persuade the judge that there is a strong public interest in publishing the information (this will generally be a stronger argument if the individuals occupy a position of power or trust, rather than simply being famous). Lord Mance said in the Supreme Court's ruling in the *PJS* case, referred to earlier, that there was no public interest justification for publication of details of PJS's extra-marital encounters, 'however absorbing it might be to members of the public interested in stories about others' private sexual encounters'.

In 2008 a High Court judge awarded Max Mosley, then president of the organisation which runs Formula 1 grand prix racing (and the son of wartime fascist leader Oswald Mosley), £60,000 in damages after he won a case against the *News of the World*. He had sued the newspaper for breach of privacy and—as ch. 26 explains—for breach of confidence over stories, photos and video footage it published about his participation in sado-masochistic activities with prostitutes (*Mosley v News Group Newspapers Ltd* [2008] EWHC 1777). The judge rejected the publisher's argument—for which it was unable to provide any evidence—that the article was in the public interest because the orgy was 'Nazi-themed', concluding that it was not (nor was it intended to be).

*** Remember**

In privacy law, the term 'private information' can refer to an image or images of a person, such as a photo or film, as well as to sensitive facts or confidential conversations.

27.3.5 Health

Information about health is normally treated as being of the highest confidentiality.

In 2002 the Court of Appeal banned the *Mail on Sunday* from naming a local health authority where a healthcare worker, referred to in court as H, had quit his job after being diagnosed HIV positive. Lord Phillips, then Master of the Rolls, said there was a public interest in preserving the confidentiality of healthcare workers who might otherwise be discouraged from reporting they were HIV positive. The *Mail on Sunday* argued that H's patients were entitled to know they had been treated by someone who was HIV positive. But the Court ruled that a report of the matter which named the authority would inevitably lead to the disclosure of H's identity, as only his patients would be offered HIV tests and counselling, the judge said. The newspaper was allowed to disclose that the healthcare worker was a dentist (*H (A Healthcare Worker) v Associated Newspapers Ltd & Ors* [2002] EWCA Civ 195).

Health—therapy for drug addiction—is featured in the *Campbell* case: see 27.6.

27.4 Article 10 rights

Article 10 of the Convention begins:

> "Everyone has the right to freedom of expression. This right shall include freedom to hold opinions and to receive and impart information and ideas without interference by public authority and regardless of frontiers."

This Article 10 right, which underpins 'public interest' journalism, means that it can be legal for journalists to breach someone's privacy—for example, by revealing that a Government Minister has had a secret and adulterous affair, if that relationship led him to neglect his work or improperly grant favours, or if what was published contributes to public debate about an important matter. Section 12 of the Human Rights Act 1998 requires courts considering granting any order or injunction banning publication of information to have 'particular regard' to the importance of the right to freedom of expression.

Part 2 of Article 10 recognises that this right sometimes has to be curtailed to protect people's other human rights and to prevent disclosure of information received in confidence—see 1.3.2 in this book for the full text of Article 10.

27.5 Stage one—'Reasonable expectation of privacy'

Where a claimant in a case asserts their Article 8 privacy rights—for example, to try to stop a media organisation publishing an article, or to be paid damages because of what has been published—the judge must carry out a two-stage process and, in stage one, will decide if those rights are 'engaged'. If the decision is that they are not engaged, the claimant cannot win the case.

Case law has evolved to create a 'test' (a legal criterion) to decide whether Article 8 rights are engaged. This test is whether the claimant had 'a reasonable expectation of privacy' in respect of information which has been published, or which someone plans to publish.

To decide this issue, courts will take account of the circumstances of the particular case, including:

- the 'attributes' of the claimant (for example, their status, such as whether they hold a high office, or a high public profile, so that criticism may be more justified than for a private individual);
- the nature of the activity in which the claimant was engaged at the time of the alleged intrusion;
- the place at which the activity was happening;
- the nature and purpose of the alleged intrusion;
- the absence of consent for intrusion, and whether that absence of consent was known or could be inferred;
- the effect of the alleged intrusion on the claimant;
- the circumstances in which, and the purposes for which, the information came into the hands of the publisher or would-be publisher.

This list of circumstances to be considered is called the 'Murray factors' because it was set out in the case of *Murray v Express Newspapers plc and another* ([2007] EWHC 1908 (Ch)). It was referred to and applied in recent major cases such as *Duchess of Sussex v Associated Newspapers* and *Bloomberg LP v ZXC* [2022] UKSC 5, cited earlier.

An example: normally a claimant who is photographed or filmed doing something in a public place will not have a reasonable expectation of privacy if any onlooker or passer-by could have seen them and what they were doing. But if a person falls ill or has an accident in a public place, they are more likely to have a reasonable expectation of privacy—because the act of photographing or filming them while they are vulnerable may be an intrusion, especially if it caused them further distress, and publication of such images may be a worse intrusion because they would then be seen by a large number of people.

Case study

In 2003 the European Court of Human Rights (ECtHR) ruled there was an unjustifiable intrusion into a UK man's privacy because the media broadcast footage of his suicide attempt in the centre of Brentwood in 1994 which identified him. The council released the footage to show that its installation of CCTV cameras helped save his life because police, alerted by the camera operators, took a knife from him and arrested him. But the man, who was suffering mental illness at the time, was recognisable in images broadcast, despite the council's request that he should not be (*Peck v United Kingdom*, Application no. 44647/98 (2003) 36 EHRR 41). His complaints about this were upheld in 1996 by the broadcast regulators but he took a case to the ECtHR, because in 1996 the UK courts did not recognise a specific right of privacy.

Chapter 4 gives examples of how media regulators have interpreted 'reasonable expectation' when adjudicating on complaints that a media organisation breached a person's privacy, 4.6 explains the criminal law of 'stalking' (harassment).

27.5.1 Information obtained covertly

If a person is unaware of cameras or microphones, they may assume the situation is private and act or speak accordingly. This is one reason why case law such as *Murray*, cited earlier, requires the court to consider the nature of the alleged intrusion when deciding if the claimant had or has a reasonable expectation of privacy.

In 2006 the Court of Appeal made clear it regarded the taking of long-distance photographs as being 'an exercise generally considered to raise privacy issues' (*Niema Ash and another v Loreena McKennitt and others* [2006] EWCA Civ 1714, [2007] 3 WLR 194).

a journalist using an electronic bug could be committing a criminal offence—see ch. 34

In the *Douglas* case the wedding pictures ruled to have breached the privacy of the married couple were taken covertly by an uninvited freelance photographer—see 27.8.1. The photographs of Naomi Campbell leaving a Narcotics Anonymous therapy session—publication of which was ruled to have breached her privacy—were taken without her being aware of the photographer—see 27.6.

27.6 Stage two—the balancing exercise

If a claimant can demonstrate that they have, or had at the relevant time, a 'reasonable expectation of privacy' in respect of the information, the judge proceeds to stage two. In that stage, the judge balances the claimant's Article 8 rights to privacy against the defendant's Article 10 rights, to decide whose rights should prevail and—if the decision is not wholly in favour of one of the parties—to what extent (**proportionality**). This is known as the 'balancing exercise', and how judges should conduct it is set out in *Re S (FC) (A Child) (Identification: Restrictions on Publication)* [2004] UKHL 47.

→glossary

In that House of Lords judgment, Lord Steyn said:

> "First, neither article has as such precedence over the other. Secondly, where the values under the two articles are in conflict, an intense focus on the comparative importance of the specific rights being claimed in the individual case is necessary. Thirdly, the justifications for interfering with or restricting each right must be taken into account. Finally, the proportionality test must be applied to each. For convenience I will call this the ultimate balancing test."

Lord Steyn was emphasising that the particular facts and circumstances of each case must be intensely considered to decide which Convention right—and therefore which party to the argument—prevails in each matter to be decided. *Re S* concerned whether media reports could name a particular defendant—see 16.9.

Unless the judge's decision is wholly for the claimant or wholly for the defendant, it will involve the judge deciding how much of the information should have been or for more context on proportionality rulings, see 4.1.2

should be published. For example, did the published photograph need to show an injured person's face to help convey 'public interest' information about how serious and traumatic a motorway accident was? Did all of a personal letter need to be published to reveal something important which the public should know?

Case study

The proportionality principle was demonstrated in a House of Lords ruling in 2004, in a privacy claim brought by supermodel Naomi Campbell. In 2001 the *Daily Mirror* revealed she was attending Narcotics Anonymous therapy sessions for drug addiction. She conceded that it was in the public interest for the newspaper to expose that she had been taking drugs, because she had previously denied drug-taking and so had misled the public by promoting a false image of herself. But she sued the newspaper on the basis that its coverage had infringed her Article 8 privacy rights by revealing detail of where she had the therapy. It had published photos of her emerging onto a public street from the therapy venue. The House of Lords ruled there were five distinct 'elements' of private information: the fact of her drug addiction; the fact that she was receiving therapy for it; the fact that she was having therapy at Narcotics Anonymous (NA); details of the NA therapy and her reaction to it; and surreptitiously obtained photographs of her emerging from an NA session. It ruled that, as the model had previously publicly denied using drugs, the first and second facts could be published in the public interest, but that the rest should not have been published, because of the intrusiveness of the disclosure and the likelihood it would disrupt her treatment. She was only awarded a total of £3,500 damages, for distress and injury to her feelings, but the newspaper's publisher was left with a costs bill of £1 million (later reduced following an appeal to the European Court of Human Rights—see 20.3.5.1) and her victory demonstrated how Article 8 had changed the UK's legal landscape (*Campbell v Mirror Group Newspapers* [2004] UKHL 22).

The House of Lords appellate committee was the UK's highest court until 2009—see 9.10.

27.7 Relevant factors for the courts to consider when striking the balance

The European Court of Human Rights set out factors to be considered by judges when striking the balance between Article 8 and Article 10 rights in a ruling in 2012. The case involved a German actor well known for playing the role of a police chief in a television series. He sued a newspaper after it reported that he had been arrested for possession of cocaine at the Munich beer festival in 2004. The ECtHR overturned a decision by a German court which banned any further publication of almost the entire report. The ECtHR ruled that the decision had violated the newspaper's

Article 10 right to freedom of expression (*Axel Springer AG v Germany*, Application no. 39954/08 (2012) 55 EHRR 66).

The factors which the ECtHR said judges should consider include:

- the degree to which the relevant material contributes to a debate of general interest to society—the definition of debate here is broader than debate about politics, because there can be 'general interest' debate about wider, societal issues.
- how well-known the person concerned is, and what the subject of the report is—the ECtHR said that in 'certain special circumstances' the public's right to be informed can even extend to 'aspects of the private life of public figures', particularly where politicians are concerned, but it warned that 'this will not be the case—even where the persons concerned are quite well known to the public—where the published photos and accompanying commentaries relate exclusively to details of the person's private life and have the sole aim of satisfying the curiosity of a particular readership in that respect'. Judges in England and Wales have on many occasions drawn the distinction between the 'public interest' and matters which are of interest to the public.
- the prior conduct of the person concerned—for example, has the person themself previously published, or allowed to be published, information about their private life?—the ECtHR said as regards someone who had 'actively sought the limelight', that, having regard to the degree to which he was known to the public, his 'legitimate expectation' that his private life would be effectively protected was henceforth reduced. But the ECtHR also said that the 'mere fact' that the person had cooperated with the press on previous occasions 'cannot serve as an argument for depriving the party concerned of all protection against publication of the report or photo at issue'.
- the method of obtaining the information (for example, was it covertly obtained, see 27.5.1) and its truth—the ECtHR stressed that to be protected by Article 10, the media report concerned must provide 'reliable and precise' information in accordance with the ethics of journalism. NB: Covert methods of getting information may be ethical if a media organisation has a reasonable belief that it should be published in the public interest. Such methods may help ensure the information is accurate—see chs. 2 and 3 on what regulatory codes say about covert methods, and 27.9 for context.
- the content, form and consequences of the publication—for example, what level of significant harm or distress would publication cause to the person objecting to it?

27.7.1 The extent to which the information contributes to a 'debate of general interest to society'

The first factor a court will have to consider in 'stage 2' is to what extent material which a media organisation publishes, or seeks to publish, will contribute to a 'debate of general interest to society'. Decisions made by the ECtHR indicate that freedom of expression is viewed as having various levels of value to society, with political expression about the conduct of politicians in public office being of the highest importance. This means an elected politician who conceals their improper behaviour from the electorate is unlikely to persuade a court that the media should be banned from exposing it, because, for example, there needs to be debate about it for the public to decide whether they will vote for the politician again, or if the improper behaviour means they should resign from public office.

But in the *Axel Springer* case the ECtHR acknowledged that society has a 'general interest' in debating matters other than politics. The court quoted a Resolution of the Parliamentary Assembly of the Council of Europe which said 'public figures' must recognise that the position they occupy entails increased pressure on their privacy:

> "Public figures are persons holding public office and/or using public resources and, more broadly speaking, all those who play a role in public life, whether in politics, the economy, the arts, the social sphere, sport or in any other domain."

27.7.2 The role of the press as 'watchdog'

The ECtHR and UK judges have repeatedly emphasised the essential role played by journalists in a democratic society. The ECtHR said in the *Axel Springer* case:

> "Although the press must not overstep certain bounds, regarding in particular protection of the reputation and rights of others, its duty is nevertheless to impart—in a manner consistent with its obligations and responsibilities—information and ideas on all matters of public interest. Not only does the press have the task of imparting such information and ideas; the public also has a right to receive them. Were it otherwise, the press would be unable to play its vital role of 'public watchdog'."

27.8 Can information be private if it is in the public domain?

A judge may refuse to ban publication of material, or award damages for media publication of it, if it has already been widely published by others—for example, on many sites on the internet—or is otherwise easily available to anyone. But each case is different. In the *PJS* case, see 27.3.1, once material about the married man's extra-marital sexual activity became widespread on the internet, the Court of Appeal was persuaded to lift the injunction. But the Supreme Court restored it to protect any further intrusions into the privacy of PJS and his family. As Lord Neuberger observed:

> "There are claims that between 20% and 25% of the population know who PJS is, which, it is fair to say, suggests that at least 75% of the population do not know the identity of PJS."

The Court of Appeal confirmed in *PMC and A Local Health Board* [2024] EWHC 2969 (KB) that previous publicity which identifies an individual is not an 'automatic bar' to reporting restrictions to anonymise them being applied for and imposed at a later stage. The Court emphasised that such decisions will depend on the circumstances of each case.

The issue of what information was already in the public domain featured in the case of Alaedeen Sicri, who was awarded £83,000 in damages after being identified by *MailOnline* as one of a number of people arrested in the wake of the Manchester Arena bombing. He was soon released without charge because he had no connection with the bombing (*Sicri v Associated Newspapers Ltd* [2020] EWHC 3541 (QB)—see 5.11.2 for a detailed case study).

MailOnline argued that Mr Sicri's privacy rights had already been 'substantially curtailed' by the time it published the article which identified him, because—it argued—his arrest had already been referred to in reports by local and national media organisations, reports which had either identified him to the wider public or were capable of doing so. But Mr Justice Warby said that, while other publicity 'made inroads' into Mr Sicri's privacy, that did not mean his identity was 'universally known' nor that it was 'open season for anyone else who cared to repeat what had been said'. He added:

> "On the contrary, the claimant retained a reasonable expectation that others, including the defendant, would not make things worse."

The judge said *MailOnline*'s argument that Mr Sicri's identity was already known by people locally and had featured in local publicity was 'not borne out by the evidence' and that such matters would 'count for little anyway, when compared with the vast reach of MailOnline'.

27.8.1 Widely published photographs

Individuals may also retain a legitimate expectation of privacy in relation to photographs or footage despite such images already having been widely published.

In a case involving the actor Michael Douglas and his wife Catherine Zeta-Jones, who successfully sued *Hello!* magazine for damages after it published photographs of their wedding when the couple had exclusively sold the rights to rival magazine *OK!*, the Court of Appeal said in 2000:

> "Once intimate personal information about a celebrity's private life has been widely published it may serve no useful purpose to prohibit further publication. The same will not necessarily be true of photographs. Insofar as a photograph does more than convey information and intrudes on privacy by enabling the viewer to focus on intimate personal detail, there will be a fresh intrusion of privacy when each additional viewer sees the photograph and even when one who has seen a previous publication of the photograph is confronted by a fresh publication of it."

See the **additional material** for ch. 26 on **www.mcnaes.com** for details of the Douglas case.

Remember

Copyright law enables commissioners of photographs or footage created for 'private and domestic' purposes to be awarded damages if there is unauthorised publication—see 29.6.

27.9 Relevance of ethical codes

Section 12 of the Human Rights Act 1998 refers to cases (such as privacy cases) in which a court is considering whether to grant 'any relief' (such as damages or an injunction) which, if granted, might affect the exercise of the Article 10 right to freedom of expression. The section requires the court to have particular regard to the importance of the Article 10 right but also—if the case concerns journalistic material—to 'any relevant privacy code'. In such a privacy case, the judge will consider, depending on the media organisation involved, whether the journalistic activity conformed to the Editors' Code of Practice, or the Impress Standards Code, or Ofcom Broadcasting Code, or the BBC's Editorial Guidelines. If that activity—whether to gather information or its publication—does conform, the judge may be more likely to rule that any intrusion into privacy which has already occurred was justified by the public interest, and less likely to injunct against publication. The wording of the parts of each code relating to public interest justifications are influenced by law, so compliance with the code helps ensure compliance with privacy law.

As discussed in chs. 2 and 3, which cover the codes, the best practice for journalists who intend to rely on a public interest justification for publication of information, or for an intrusive method to get information, is to keep an 'audit trail' of documents, created at the time the relevant editorial decisions were made, to evidence a 'reasonable belief' that this justification applied, so that this documentation can be shown to a regulator or court if necessary.

In *Sicri*, Mr Justice Warby criticised *MailOnline* because staff journalists involved in publishing the report which identified Mr Sicri had not created contemporaneous records to demonstrate why they reasonably believed this was in the public interest. The judge said this meant that *MailOnline* had not complied with the requirement in the Editors' Code for 'proof that the public interest was actually considered'.

For best practice for 'audit trails' see 2.6, which also refers to *Sicri*. See ch. 4 for the codes.

27.10 Data protection law overlap

→glossary A **claimant** may argue that a media organisation's gathering or publication of information breached data protection law as well as privacy law. In cases where damages have been awarded, judges who ruled there was breach of both laws have not generally specified what portion of the damages was for each breach—a recognition of overlap in the protection these laws provide for privacy. The next chapter explains data protection law.

27.11 Remedies for breach of privacy

As indicated earlier, the remedies which a court will provide for an infringement of privacy include an order for the infringers to pay damages as financial compensation, and an injunction to prevent material being published or to stop publication continuing.

27.11.1 Damages

In December 2023, Mr Justice Fancourt awarded £140,600 in damages to the Duke of Sussex after he sued Mirror Group Newspapers (MGN), publisher of the *Daily Mirror*, *Sunday Mirror* and *Sunday People*, for using unlawful methods, including phone hacking, to gather personal information for stories. The case followed the earlier ruling of Mr Justice Mann, in May 2015, which saw damages of more than £1.2 million awarded to eight **claimants** who were also targeted by MGN. The highest sum—£260,250—went to actress and businesswoman Sadie Frost, who was the subject of a number of articles which included references to her marital troubles with actor Jude Law, her premature labour and her treatment for depression. The earlier case set a new high for damages for invasions of privacy. Some claims in which 'historic' phone-hacking and other unlawful information gathering is alleged are ongoing, but in reduced numbers.

→glossary

✻ Remember

Journalists who use electronic equipment to spy on other people could be committing a crime as well as running the risk of being sued for infringing privacy. Ch. 34 explains the risks of being charged with hacking into computers, telephone messages, email systems or otherwise 'intercepting communications'. It also outlines the phone-hacking scandal.

27.11.2 'Super-injunctions'

A person who learns that a media organisation intends to publish information they consider private can seek an **injunction** to ban its publication—see 26.4. Additionally, a claimant can seek a 'super-injunction', so called because it includes a clause which bans publication of any information about a case, including even the existence of the proceedings and the fact an injunction has been made, for a short period of time to avoid the order being rendered pointless—for example, if knowledge of proceedings might 'tip off' a proposed defendant so that they can leak information or destroy evidence before being served with a claim. Super-injunctions, which rarely need to

→glossary

be made, are often confused with regular injunctions in which the person seeking it is anonymised (see, for example, the *PJS* case earlier).

In July 2025, it was revealed a super-injunction had been in place for nearly two years to prevent the media from reporting on a data breach by the Ministry of Defence, which saw personal information of individuals who sought relocation to the UK from Afghanistan following the Taliban coup of 2021. It also prohibited disclosing the existence of the injunction itself. It was lifted by Mr Justice Chamberlain after the media opposed its renewal *Ministry of Defence v Global Media and Entertainment Ltd and others* [2025] EWHC 1806 (KB). See the **additional material** for this chapter for more detail on this case and past controversy over injunctions.

for more context, see 26.4, Injunctions

27.11.3 The permanent injunction *contra mundum*

An interim injunction which prevents a party from disclosing private and/or confidential information also prevents others who are either served with the order or otherwise aware of it, in accordance with the principle established in the *Spycatcher* case (see ch. 26). But an injunction made permanent after a full hearing (trial), binds only the particular parties—for example, media organisation(s)—against whom it was obtained. This means that another media organisation could then (in theory) publish the information covered. The response of the courts in these circumstances has been to issue so-called *contra mundum* ('against the world') orders—orders of general effect which bind anyone who knows about them, including all media organisations made aware of them.

> See 12.10 and the **additional material** for ch. 12 on **www.mcnaes.com** for detail on how a *contra mundum* injunction was used to protect the new identities of the killers of two-year-old James Bulger.

27.12 Suspects' and crime victims' right to privacy

As the *Sicri* case shows, privacy law has evolved to recognise that a person under police or other official investigation, including anyone arrested, may well have 'a reasonable expectation of privacy' in respect of that situation, and so—if they are not charged with an offence—they could successfully sue a media organisation for breach of privacy if it published a report identifying them as being such a suspect. For more detail of this development in privacy law, see 5.11.2. As explained in ch. 5, such a report could also be a defamation risk.

27.12.1 Privacy rights of people with statutory anonymity and of crime victims

Chapters 10, 11 and 12 explain that a range of statutory laws, either automatically or because a court has made an order, ban publications from identifying some categories of people as being victims/alleged victims of a crime, depending on the type of crime or the age of the person or other circumstances. A media organisation which publishes a report breaching any type of statutory anonymity, including any bestowed on a defendant or witness under 18, could consequently be fined under criminal law and/or sued by the person for damages under the civil law of privacy.

Even if the person does not have anonymity arising from UK statute, the development of the civil law of privacy is such that foreseeably a court could in some circumstances decide—for example, if the person is a victim of a traumatic crime—they have a reasonable expectation that they should not be identified as such in the media unless they have consented to this or been identified in relevant court proceedings held in public, or by an official statement from police.

Case study

In 2021 *MailOnline* paid 'substantial' damages to Dutch-Belgian actor Sand Van Roy because it reported in the UK, without her consent, that she had complained to French police that a film director had raped her in Paris. The damages were also paid because *MailOnline* published false information about her complaint. Under French law, she was entitled to anonymity in that nation as an alleged victim of rape, but at the time *MailOnline* published its coverage she had been identified widely in the French media in respect of her rape complaint, against her wishes. In a statement read out at the High Court in London, *MailOnline* agreed that by identifying her in the UK in respect of her rape complaint it breached her privacy and data protection rights in UK law. By the time the statement was made she had waived her right to anonymity (*MailOnline*, 26 August 2021; Carter-Ruck law firm press release, 21 May 2021).

27.13 Privacy and the 'right to be forgotten'

The European Court of Human Rights (ECtHR) has ruled that the right to respect for privacy and family life involves the right to reputation. This has led to the development in law of the 'right to be forgotten'. Under this right, people—so they are not dogged by the prospect of continuing adverse publicity about an event in bygone years—can cite data protection and privacy law to demand that online material about them which they consider to be 'inadequate, irrelevant or . . . excessive' is removed from search engine results and archived news pages on websites.

Case study

In 2021 the ECtHR ruled that a doctor should be anonymised in a story about his involvement in a fatal car crash in 1994 on the online archive of French-language Belgian newspaper *Le Soir*. The article was originally published the same year, but was only published online in 2008 when *Le Soir* created an online version of its archive dating back to 1989. The newspaper's publisher went to the ECtHR, arguing that a Belgian court's order to remove the doctor's name infringed *Le Soir*'s Article 10 right. But the court ruled the doctor was entitled to have his identity removed from the story. That decision was upheld in a July 2023 ruling by the Court's Grand Chamber, despite an intervention from UK publishers and media freedom organisations which argued that forcing news websites to remove archive material—which they described as 'an essential component of modern-day newsgathering and reporting'—was not a proportionate restriction on freedom of expression. The Grand Chamber's decision said the online archive had created a 'virtual criminal record' which had caused the doctor, who was not well known, 'serious harm' and had no 'topical, historical or scientific interest'. The Court rejected the contention that the ruling sacrificed press freedom and said its findings only related to this case, with one judge saying: 'It would therefore be erroneous to infer from the present judgment any obligation for news publishers to systematically anonymise all the material in their online archives' (*Hurbain v Belgium*, App (No 57292) 2023).

For more about 'the right to be forgotten', including details of this case and the first such case in the UK involving Google, see the **additional material** for this chapter on **www.mcnaes.com**. For regulators' adjudications on media references to previous convictions, see the **additional material** for ch. 4 on **www.mcnaes.com**. Ch. 24 explains when convictions are 'spent' in rehabilitation law. Ch. 28 covers data protection law.

Recap of major points

- The right to privacy is guaranteed by Article 8 of the European Convention on Human Rights.
- Courts will weigh an individual's Article 8 rights against the rights of the press and public to freedom of expression enshrined in Article 10 of the Convention.
- The test in a privacy claim is whether the claimant has 'a reasonable expectation of privacy'.
- The right to privacy is not necessarily lost because the activity happened in public.
- There is a defence that publication was in the public interest.

Useful Websites

Courts and Tribunals Judiciary, 'Practice Guidance: Interim Non-Disclosure Orders', www.judiciary.gov.uk

Master of the Rolls' Practice Guidance on privacy injunctions

Online resources

Visit the online resources at **www.mcnaes.com** to test your knowledge of this chapter with **self-test questions** and a **flashcard glossary**, and to read **updates** about law and regulatory matters affecting journalism, as well as **additional material** to further your learning.

28

Data protection

Chapter summary

Data protection law protects the privacy of personal information kept, for example, on computers and in filing systems. It covers data we give about ourselves to organisations including Government departments, councils, public institutions and commercial companies, and data they generate about us. The law affects journalists in three ways. First, because journalists generate and store data about people—for example in research, news stories, recordings, pictures and footage—media organisations and freelance journalists must act lawfully in how they keep and publish 'personal data', to avoid paying damages for breaching data protection or privacy law, or being fined by the Information Commissioner. Secondly, a journalist may be prosecuted for using underhand methods to gain access to people's 'personal data' unless they have a **'public interest'** or other defence. Thirdly, companies and public bodies sometimes misunderstand or hide behind data protection law when claiming that it prevents them from releasing information to the media.

→glossary

28.1 Introduction

Data protection law is complex and has become a major challenge for journalists. One reason for this is that a person who sues a media organisation for misuse of private information or defamation may as part of that action also sue for breach of data protection law, because it overlaps with privacy law, and can be used to seek financial redress if inaccurate information was published (this is explained in 20.6 and 27.10).

Another reason is that data protection law is of such wide scope that companies and institutions fear they will break it by passing any information to a journalist who is making inquiries relating to a particular person, or a company or institution may cite this law merely as an excuse not to provide information which might embarrass it.

However, data protection law is needed to help protect the security of the vast amounts of personal information about each of us held in computer and manual records—whether by tech giants such as Facebook and Google or by local authorities and small businesses. It has been estimated that public and commercial institutions hold in total about 700 databases on each working adult.

Rights relating to personal data have been in force since the late 1980s. Current law is in the Data Protection Act 2018 and the UK General Data Protection Regulation (GDPR), which replaced the European Union's GDPR in January 2021 following the UK's departure from the EU. The 2018 Act operates in tandem with the UK GDPR and supplements it, for example by providing exemptions—including for 'journalistic purposes', as this chapter explains. The UK GDPR contains some amendments to the previous EU regime, but is not substantially different. Organisations may need to comply with the current EU GDPR if, for example, offering goods or services in the EU, and in respect of any overseas data collected before 1 January 2021. In addition, the Data Use and Access Act 2025 is coming into force in stages up to June 2026 and, though its provisions largely do not affect journalists and media organisations, it does introduce provisions around complaints and subject access requests (see 28.2.5). For example, data controllers will be required to provide an electronic complaint form for data subjects. Complaints will need to be acknowledged within 30 days and responded to 'without undue delay'.

28.1.1 The Information Commissioner and code for journalists

The Information Commissioner has powers to enforce data protection law, including by investigating and prosecuting those who breach it.

The 2018 Act requires the Commissioner to issue a code containing practical guidance about the processing of personal data for the purposes of journalism. The Commissioner issued a finalised code in July 2023 and it came into force in February 2024. In any court case in which a media organisation or journalist is alleged to have breached data protection law, the court must take into account whether the code was complied with.

For the code and supporting reference notes, see Useful Websites at the end of this chapter.

28.2 Data protection principles

Under this law, 'personal data' is information that relates to an identified or identifiable individual. A general guide published by the Information Commissioner's Office (ICO) says that what identifies an individual could be as simple as a name and: 'If it is possible to identify an individual directly from the information you are processing, then that information may be personal data.' The code's reference notes say information is not personal data if it is a paper record (such as handwritten notes) about a person who has died or is anonymous (although it will be if someone is not named but can still be identified from the details combined with other information).

((•)) for this ICO guide, see Useful Websites at the end of this chapter

A data 'controller' is an organisation or person who determines why and how any personal data is held and used—that is, 'processed'—in what it or they do. Data controllers include local authorities, health trusts, Government departments, commercial organisations, magistrates' courts and the police—in fact, any organisation or individual keeping personal data about people, including its own staff, in computerised or other structured filing systems. Therefore, a media company which employs journalists is a controller, including because its journalists 'process'—obtain, create, keep and publish—personal data. Journalists are also controllers as they create personal data from interviews or other research, or collation. Also, photos or footage of people, showing them identifiably, are 'personal data'. A 'data subject' is a person about whom the information is held.

Article 5 of the GDPR details six principles for legal handling of personal data. It must be:

(a) processed lawfully, fairly and in a transparent manner;

(b) collected for specified, explicit and legitimate purposes only, and not further processed in a manner incompatible with those purposes;

(c) adequate, relevant and limited to what is necessary for those purposes;

(d) accurate and, where necessary, kept up to date; every reasonable step must be taken to ensure that personal data that are inaccurate are erased or rectified without delay;

(e) kept in a form which permits identification of data subjects for no longer than necessary for the purposes of the processing;

(f) processed in a manner that ensures appropriate security, including protection against unauthorised or unlawful processing and against accidental loss, destruction or damage.

Data controllers are responsible for complying with these principles but, as this chapter outlines, an exemption frees media organisations and freelance journalists from most of these obligations when the processing is for the purposes of journalism.

28.2.1 Personal data must be securely kept

The law requires personal data to be kept securely. Many news stories have highlighted data protection failures by public bodies or companies—such as when huge amounts of official or commercial data about individuals, including lists of clients or customers, their dates of birth, addresses and bank account details, have been found on unencrypted laptops or memory sticks without passwords which were left in pubs or taxis. Journalists have the same legal obligation to keep personal data secure, so must have adequate procedures and secure devices to do that.

28.2.2 Personal data must be kept 'no longer than necessary'

Data protection law does not impose a specific time limit on how long personal data can be kept by journalists and it will be reasonable to keep information, including as background, indefinitely if it relates to an ultimate aim of publishing journalism or updating it. However, the data controller should be prepared to justify why the information is kept.

28.2.3 Exemptions for journalistic purposes

Schedule 2 of the 2018 Act contains a 'special purposes exemption' which is specially designed to protect freedom of expression and information in journalism, as well as in academic activities, art and literature. The exemption is broad to reflect the importance of freedom of expression in society, but is not total. In essence, it means that media organisations and freelance journalists do not have to comply with certain provisions of the GDPR when processing personal data for 'the purposes of journalism', when acting 'with a view to publication'. However, it does not exempt them from the obligation to ensure data is processed lawfully. There is also no exemption from the obligation to keep data securely, or from the obligation to be accountable in how personal data is processed, or (the code says) from 'impact assessment' obligations related to publishing it when there is 'high risk' to a person it identifies (see later).

The special purposes exemption for journalism requires the data controller (in effect, the person who took the editorial decisions about what should be published) to have a 'reasonable belief' that publication of the relevant material would be 'in the public interest'. The code says that, for the purposes of the journalism exemption, a controller must also consider whether complying with part of data protection law is incompatible with their journalistic purpose. So if the data controller has a 'reasonable belief' that compliance with the requirement for 'fair' processing is incompatible with journalism, the special purpose exemption will apply (which, for example, means that gathering personal data by deception or 'undercover' journalism is permitted if the data controller held this 'reasonable belief'). The code says it is not the role of the ICO or a judge to 'disregard' a controller's decision lightly, and a controller does not have to prove that publication is in the public interest, or that complying with a specific part of data protection law would be incompatible with journalism.

28.2.4 'In the public interest'

The 2018 Act does not define what is 'in the public interest' to publish. The ICO journalism code gives the following examples of the general public interest in freedom of expression and in information being provided: upholding standards of integrity; ensuring justice and fair treatment for all; promoting transparency and accountability; encouraging public understanding and involvement in the democratic process; and securing the best use of public resources. It also says there may be a public interest in the general subject matter, in examples such as protecting public health and safety or exposing or detecting crime or anti-social behaviour. It says the examples are not an exhaustive list and there is a public interest in other types of journalism, such as lifestyle or entertainment journalism.

for context on these parts of the codes, see 2.4.1, 2.5 and 3.4.11

Illustrative definitions in the Editors' Code of Practice, Impress Code and Broadcasting Code of what serves the public interest are also relevant as regards publication of particular reports.

There is particular law in the 2018 Act, referring to 'substantial public interest', governing when it is legal to publish 'special category' personal data and 'criminal offence data'—see later for explanation of those terms.

28.2.5 Subject access requests

In general, the GDPR strengthens the rights of individuals ('data subjects') to see the information held about them by making a 'subject access request' (SAR), and to have the information corrected, amended or even removed.

If an individual makes such a subject access request, most data controllers are generally required to comply with it without undue delay within one month. However, media organisations and freelance journalists who are data controllers holding the information for journalistic purposes can refuse a SAR if they reasonably believe that complying with it is incompatible with journalism.

For example, they can refuse to provide information which may undermine a story by tipping someone off to forthcoming publication, or which would or may identify a confidential source. The code says that information which does not undermine journalistic activities should be given to the requestor, and that when a request is refused, it should be explained to the data subject (the requester) why, and they should be told they have a right to complain (for example to the Commissioner), as well as a right to seek court enforcement. ICO guidance states that where a request is refused on the basis of an exemption, the reasons given for not complying may depend upon the particular case—for example, if telling an individual, a particular exemption has been applied would prejudice the purpose of that exemption, the response may be more general. However, the guidance says data controllers should be transparent about reasons for withholding information where possible.

The Data Use and Access Act 2025 does not change the pre-existing time required to respond to a SAR, but codifies data controllers' right to 'stop the clock' in order to, for example, ask data subjects to clarify their request or provide more information. The Act also, helpfully, makes clear that data subjects are only entitled to data which a controller can provide 'based on a reasonable and proportionate search'.

for ICO guidance to the public about such requests, see Useful Websites at the end of the chapter

This access right under the GDPR can be of benefit to journalists. For example, journalists have a right to make a SAR for information held about themselves. Also, in investigative journalism they may be able, with the express consent of an individual, to base what is published on information secured by that individual from such a request made to a company or institution.

28.2.6 Special category personal data and criminal offence data

Article 9 of the GDPR provides particular privacy protection for what it calls 'special categories of personal data'—and bans processing of this sensitive information except in particular circumstances.

Special category personal data covers information about a person's:

- racial or ethnic origin;
- political opinions;
- religious or philosophical beliefs;
- trade union membership;
- physical and mental health;

- sexual orientation;
- sex life.

'Criminal offence data' is similarly categorised as sensitive. What it covers includes a person's criminal record, unproven allegations that a person has committed a crime, and data relating to people being victims or witnesses of crime.

Because exemptions for journalism apply, material about such matters can be published without the person's consent, but because of the sensitivity of such information, there must be a justification recognised by data protection law. These include that the person themself has already 'manifestly made public' the information. But the code says particular care must be taken when using online material, especially social media, as it may be mistakenly or deliberately inaccurate and is easily spread.

Another justification (see para. 13 of Part 2 of Schedule 1 of the 2018 Act) is if publication is 'necessary for reasons of substantial public interest' in connection with the (alleged or established):

- commission of an unlawful act; or
- dishonesty, malpractice or other seriously improper conduct, unfitness or incompetence; or
- mismanagement in the administration of or failure in services by a body or association.

But the data controller must have a 'reasonable belief' that publication would be in the public interest.

✱ Remember

Data protection law does not prevent court cases from being reported, does not prevent publication of official statements issued for publication by police about criminals, and does not prevent journalists from investigating crime and publishing articles about crime. However, if a criminal conviction is 'spent' the person may claim 'the right to be forgotten', which is a developing area of law—for context, see ch. 24, and 27.13.

28.2.7 Data protection impact assessments in 'high risk' processing

The ICO code says that controllers need to carry out a data protection impact assessment (DPIA)—a type of risk assessment—for any type of processing that is likely to result in a high risk to individuals being featured in the journalism. It says this is more likely, for example, if using special category or criminal offence data, or if using intrusive methods such as covert surveillance. The code says journalists do not necessarily have to do a DPIA for individual stories, rather an assessment can generally cover the high-risk ways personal information is used. What the code says about an obligation to conduct a DPIA reflects how publishing information about vulnerable people, or special category information about anyone, or (for example) a person's criminal record without their consent, could cause them mental harm, or expose them to physical attack. The rationale for DPIAs is partly to ensure that what is published is proportionate. For example, in the Naomi Campbell privacy case (see 27.6), in which she made an associated claim that data protection law had been breached, the House of Lords, while accepting that the newspaper had a public interest justification to publish that she had used drugs, ruled there was no justification for its disclosure of the details that her therapy was at Narcotics Anonymous meetings, details of the therapy and her reaction to it and a photograph of her leaving an NA meeting. Publication of these details meant she could no longer attend those therapy sessions, putting her rehabilitation from drug use at risk.

The code recognises that journalists can consider whether a high risk exists by using existing editorial processes to plan and discuss what may be published. For more detail, see the code (Useful Websites at the end of this chapter).

28.2.8 Evidencing compliance including 'reasonable belief'

Controllers must keep records to prove compliance with data protection law. The code says this includes records of DPIAs.

Whenever the journalistic activity ('processing') concerns sensitive information, such as those in the special categories, or involves deception or undercover journalism, there is a particular need to be able to demonstrate, from records created at the time, that the controller (in effect, the editor or another journalist who decided what was done, including what was published) had a 'reasonable belief' that the activity would serve the public interest.

Such records (an 'audit trail') are also needed to meet the requirements of media regulators as regards journalistic activity for which a public interest justification is needed under their codes. The 2018 Act requires controllers in the journalism field to take the Editors' Code of Practice, Broadcasting Code, or BBC Editorial guidelines into account, as appropriate, when determining whether it is reasonable to believe that publication would be in the public interest (and the code says the Impress members should take the Impress Standards Code into account). Creating such records is also best practice to be able to use a 'public interest' defence should any person sue alleging intrusion into privacy, or defamation. For context, see 2.4.1, 2.6, and 3.4.11 as regards relevant content in the regulatory codes, and 23.2.4.1 and 27.9.

28.3 Crimes of procuring, gaining or disclosing personal data

Section 170 of the Data Protection Act 2018 makes it an offence for anyone knowingly or recklessly, and without the consent of the controller, to obtain or disclose personal data; procure the disclosure of personal data to another person; or retain unlawfully obtained personal data. A conviction is punishable by a fine unlimited by statute.

'Blagging' by a journalist to gain someone else's personal data—for example, phoning a bank and posing as someone else to get information about their account—could be prosecuted as a criminal offence. A journalist who asks someone to leak personal data from a controller's records could be prosecuted alongside the leaker. If a journalist considers either such tactic would be justified because the story being pursued is of a high 'public interest value', the best practice is that they should seek legal advice before attempting the tactic.

It is a defence under section 170 to show that obtaining or disclosing the data was necessary for preventing or detecting crime—which may be of benefit to investigative journalists—or that it was done for journalistic purposes, with a view to publication, and in the reasonable belief that what was done was justified as being in the public interest.

Section 170 also gives a defence if the person who obtained or disclosed the data can show that they acted in the reasonable belief that the controller would have consented (that is, the controller of the organisation from which the data came).

Section 173 also makes it an offence to alter, deface, block, erase, destroy or conceal information in order to prevent disclosure under a data access request.

28.4 Dealing with other data controllers to get information

When journalists ask for information, organisations sometimes cite data protection to justify refusing to give it. But the Act covers personal data, not all data, and even personal data can be lawfully released in some circumstances—for example, if the 'data subject' agrees. For example, if a journalist is asking about a complaint a person has made against it, the institution may claim it cannot go into detail because of the person's data protection rights, despite the person wanting the journalist to follow up the complaint (and so the person should contact the institution to give it full consent to release relevant information to the journalist, and can submit a subject access request—see 28.2.5).

Data is only personal if it can lead to a living individual being identified, so the 2013 Act does not prevent release of information about dead people.

28.4.1 Justifications for disclosure

Paragraphs 10 and 11 of Schedule 1 to the Data Protection Act 2018 allow the disclosure of personal data when 'necessary for reasons of substantial public interest' for the purposes of preventing or detecting unlawful acts, or protecting the public against dishonesty, malpractice or other improper conduct, incompetence, mismanagement and failures in services provided by a body or association. Inquiring journalists may need to remind official agencies of this disclosure law.

Chapter 15 covers getting information from courts. The **additional material** for this chapter on **www.mcnaes.com** refers to ICO guidance on getting information from and covering events at schools.

Recap of major points

- Journalists seeking information should realise that it is a criminal offence to procure the disclosure of personal data, unless there is a legal defence or the 'data subject' consents.
- Sometimes data law is mistakenly used as a reason to deny journalists information.
- The law has exemptions protecting journalism which is in the public interest, but journalists should take steps to be able to demonstrate from records that they held a 'reasonable belief' at the relevant time that the 'substantial public interest' justification existed as regards publication of sensitive personal data.

Useful Websites

Information Commissioner's Office, www.ico.org.uk

- 'Data protection and journalism code of practice'
- UK GDPR (General Data Protection Regulation) guidance and resources
- 'For the public: Your right of access'—ICO guide for the public on 'subject access requests'

Online resources

Visit the online resources at **www.mcnaes.com** to test your knowledge of this chapter with **self-test questions** and a **flashcard glossary**, and to read **updates** about law and regulatory matters affecting journalism, as well as **additional material** to further your learning.

29

Copyright

Chapter summary

Copyright is a property right controlling who can copy work created by artistic and other intellectual endeavour. Copyright protects journalism articles, website content, books, photographs, films, sound recordings and music, and TV and radio broadcasts. This chapter explains how copyright law, by deterring and punishing unauthorised copying and plagiarism, protects the ability of journalists and media employers to profit from their output. Copyright lasts for decades. Copyright also protects work created by others which journalists may wish to copy—for example, by quoting from or showing it or by using photographs. The law allows very limited copying of text and footage for news journalism.

29.1 What material does copyright protect?

The source of most UK law on copyright is the Copyright, Designs and Patents Act 1988, as amended by subsequent law.

Section 1 says copyright subsists in:

- 'original literary, dramatic, musical or artistic works'—which includes all kinds of text whether handwritten, printed or online, such as journalistic and scientific articles, poems, lyrics, books, plays, scripts, shorthand or longhand records of speeches and interviews; musical manuscripts; photographs; design documents, templates; graphic works, maps, plans, sketches, paintings, sculptures; computer programs; and some databases;
- 'sound recordings, films or broadcasts', including those which are journalism, files and CDs of music, home and cinema movies, TV and radio output, and some types of internet transmissions;
- 'the typographical arrangement of published editions'—for example, how text and photos are 'laid out' in page design.

The copyright owner has the legal right to decide who can copy such works, and to what extent, and who can 'communicate' them to the public. Unauthorised copying

glossary of all or 'any substantial part' of any work in these categories is a civil **tort** unless justified by a defence or exception, and in some circumstances is a criminal offence. More than one type of copyright, with different owners, may coexist in a product. For example, the script, music and the editing of the footage in a documentary film will have separate copyrights (and there are 'signal rights', explained later). In a website there will be copyrights in, for example, its text, any hosted videos and its visual design. In a newspaper or magazine, the text, photos and page design have separate copyrights.

'substantial' is explained in 29.13.1

29.2 Who owns copyright under the 1988 Act?

The 'first owner' of copyright in an original literary, dramatic, musical or artistic work is the author as creator. This definition includes the journalist as an article's writer, the photographer as author of a photo, the artist who makes a painting or sculpture, etc. If authorship is joint, each author is a 'first owner' and permission is needed from each to copy the work. The 'first owner' has the copyright unless they agree—for example, for payment—to assign to another party the right to control who makes copies.

the 'originality' criterion is explained in 29.7.1

The Act says an employer owns the copyright in an original literary, dramatic, musical or artistic work—including a journalistic article or photo—created by an employee in the course of their employment. This is usually stated in the employment contract. This means that a staff journalist only has the copyright in an article or photo if the employer specifically agrees to this, for example, in the contract of employment (1988 Act, section 11).

Self-employed journalists, including freelances and commercial photographers, are the 'first owners' of copyright in their works.

see 29.8, Assignment and licensing

The terms, including payment, under which freelances assign copyright or licence use of their work to media publishers, so they can legally publish it, may be specific to each deal, or governed by custom and practice.

- The 'first owner' of copyright in a sound recording is the producer ('producer' is defined in the Act as the person/organisation who undertook 'the arrangements necessary' for the making of the work).
- The 'first owners' of copyright in a film made on or after 1 July 1994, whether made for journalism or entertainment, are jointly the producer and principal director. The producer owns the copyright in films made earlier which are covered by the Act.
- The 'first owner' of copyright in a broadcast is the person or organisation 'making the broadcast'—that is, transmitting it, if responsible for content, or providing that content and arranging transmission. This is usually a broadcast company.
- The 'first owner' of copyright in 'the typographical arrangement of a published edition' is the publisher.
- The 'first owner' of copyright in 'computer-generated work', a category which the Act limits to circumstances of 'no human author', is the person or organisation undertaking 'the arrangements necessary' for the work's creation.

29.3 Copying from the internet, including social networking sites

There is no such thing as an 'in the public domain' defence to using copyright material. The fact that material, including a photo, can be seen by all on the internet—for example, via Google Images—does not mean that anyone has the right to copy and re-publish it. Unless they are confident that they have a valid '**fair dealing**' or other defence, journalists should not use content from third-party sources—whether pictures, text or other media—without getting the necessary permissions. A lot of infringing material, particularly photographs and pictures, are published on the social media and other websites. Publishing material such as a photo or footage or an extract of 'original' text copied from the internet infringes existing copyright in the work, unless the copied element is not 'a substantial part', or the copyright owner consents, or a defence or exception applies. →glossary

- Publishing photos copied from a social networking site—such as Facebook, Instagram, or Twitter—may infringe the copyright held by the person who created ('took') the photo, who might not even be aware that someone else has uploaded a copy onto the site. If copyright has been transferred, then the site might also have enforceable rights.

for context, see 29.18, 'Open content' licences

See the **additional material** for this chapter on **www.mcnaes.com** for the case study of a photographer suing a dance venue after it used one of his photos of a popstar, which it sourced from the internet, in its posters.

If research discovers material—text, footage or photo—on someone's personal social media pages, a media organisation might also need to consider whether, apart from copyright law, ethical considerations mean it should not be used in news coverage.

see 4.15, Material from social media sites

29.4 Photos of TV images and photos shown on TV

Publishing a photo—for example, a 'screengrab'—of a television or film image without permission can infringe copyright under section 17 of the 1988 Act. Showing a photo on a TV programme without the copyright owner's permission is also an infringement, unless a defence applies—this chapter explains the defences.

29.5 Commissioner's copyright in older photos

Section 4 of the Copyright Act 1956 governs who owns copyright in literary, dramatic and artistic work, including photos, created before 1 August 1989—that is, before the 1988 Act came into force.

As explained earlier, the default position under the 1988 Act for work created by a freelance is that they own the copyright. But the position for freelance work created before 1 August 1989—that is, under the 1956 Act—is different if it was a commissioned photo, or commissioned painted or drawn portrait, because the 1956 Act says that, in the absence of any other agreement, the copyright is owned by the commissioner—for example, a newspaper or magazine which hired the freelance to take the photo. A commission is an agreement that the work will be created in return for payment.

This difference between the two Acts decides who, as copyright owner, can successfully object to the use of an archived photo or demand payment for its use. In summary, the default positions in law (but see 29.6 below regarding private and domestic photographs) are:

- Copyright in a commissioned photograph taken before 1 August 1989 is owned by the commissioner, even though the freelance or commercial photographer who took the photo may own the negatives or have digital copies. For example, a family wedding photo taken by a commercial photographer before 1 August 1989 will almost certainly have been commissioned by someone in the family, who therefore probably owns the copyright.
- The photographer or their employer owns the copyright in a photo taken before 1 August 1989 which was not commissioned.
- Copyright in a photograph taken on or after 1 August 1989 is owned by the photographer's employer, or by the photographer if they are self-employed. This position is not changed by the mere fact that there was a commission for it to be taken, but can be changed if the commissioner insists as part of the deal that the copyright is assigned to them.

A celebrity who commissions a photographer to take pictures of a family occasion may well insist on the copyright being assigned to them, to control their use.

29.6 'Private and domestic' photographs and films

ch. 27 explains general privacy rights

Section 85 of the 1988 Act gives a 'moral right', which in this section is a called a privacy right, to people who commission photographs or films for 'private and domestic purposes'. This would include, for example, someone commissioned to take photos at a wedding or private event.

legal remedies for infringement of copyright are explained in 29.12

- The right is that no copies of a photo or film commissioned for private and domestic purposes should be published, issued to or exhibited to the public *without* the commissioner's agreement.
- Commissioners have this right even if they do not own the copyright of that work. This moral right means they can sue and recover damages from anyone who publishes such a photo or film—for example, one that records a family occasion—without their permission.
- A publisher who uses the photo or film in breach of copyright could also be sued by whoever owns the copyright—for example, by the photographer.

Consider this hypothetical case: a woman is hurt in a train crash. A journalist traces a relative, who emails the journalist a copy of a picture of the woman, taken some years previously at her wedding. If the relative took the picture and agrees to its publication, there is no infringement of copyright. If the wedding picture was taken by a commercial photographer commissioned by the bridegroom (that is, the injured woman's husband), the photographer will probably own the copyright and may be glad to accept a fee for media publication of the picture. But the husband may not want it published. If it is published, he may sue for the infringement of his moral right and win damages, even if he is not in the photo.

This 'moral right' can be waived. But otherwise it lasts as long as the copyright—see later in this chapter.

> The term 'commissioned' means there was an obligation in a financial deal for the photographer to create the photos—see the Carina Trimingham case study in the **additional material** for this chapter on **www.mcnaes.com**, where there is also detail of other types of 'moral rights', which are held by authors.

When a big story breaks about someone, the media tend to rush to get copies of photos of the person from relatives or friends, or family-held footage, or may copy photos from social media and adopt a 'publish first, worry later' approach. Many people do not know about copyright, or the moral right arising from the commissioning of a photo or film for private and domestic purposes. But some do, and if they own either right, and did not consent to the publication, they might demand payment or damages, and/or that the photo or footage is no longer published.

29.7 The scope of copyright protection

Copyright is automatically in force as soon as a work is created in any permanent form. In the UK, copyright does not have to be registered. Copyright protects an 'original literary, dramatic, musical or artistic work', as described earlier. 'Literary' in this context includes any work, written or spoken, which exists in some permanent form—it has no reference to a work's literary or artistic merits.

29.7.1 What is 'original'?

The work is not original if it is a copy of another work. The legal definition of an 'original' work is that it is 'original in the sense that it is the author's own intellectual creation' (*Infopaq International A/S v Danske Dagblades Forening* [2009] ECR I-6569); in essence, that the person 'has exercised expressive and creative choices in producing the work' (*SAS Institute Inc v World Programme Ltd* [2013] EWCA Civ 1482).

In 2021 a High Court judge said that statements about undisputed historic events may lack the necessary originality 'if cast in their most abbreviated and abstract form', such as: 'The First World War began in 1914'. But he said that a work does not have to be 'novel' or 'ingenious' to be 'original' (*Duchess of Sussex v Associated Newspapers Ltd* [2021] EWHC 273 (Ch)). So, the 'originality' threshold is low. For example, any letter, unless very brief, is likely to have sufficient 'originality'. Judges cite the rough guideline that 'anything worth copying is usually worth protecting'.

- If the authoring involved 'free and creative choices', a bus or rail timetable, or tide table will be protected by copyright, vested in the 'first owner' or, if employed, their employer.
- Copyright could also subsist in even a fairly basic form of map, diagram, drawing or sketch, so journalists should also beware of reproducing these without permission.

But a commonplace expression such as 'love is blind'—for example, if used in a book title—will not be protected by copyright, because of lack of originality.

The European Court of Justice ruled in 2012 that no copyright subsisted in databases set up according to technical considerations, rules or constraints which left no room for creative freedom.

Additional material for this chapter on **www.mcnaes.com** outlines this 2012 ruling (which was that copyright did not exist in lists of Premier League football fixtures), and also covers copyright in TV and radio programme listings.

29.7.2 Signal rights

Copyrights in what the Act terms 'films' (which is the 'first fixation of films') and in broadcasts are 'signal rights' which a judge has described as 'entrepreneurial rights which protect the investment' of the producer and broadcaster, respectively (*England and Wales Cricket Board Ltd and Sky UK Ltd v Tixdaq Ltd and Fanatix Ltd* [2016] EWHC 575 (Ch)). Copyright in a sound recording is also a 'signal right'. The 'signal right' means such works—which include raw footage, unedited audio and 'live transmissions'—are not required to be 'original', in the sense of being intellectual creations, to be protected by copyright. This meant in the *England and Wales Cricket Board* case there was no need for the judge to rule on whether the creative input of the director and others in broadcast coverage of cricket—for example, selection of camera angles, use of 'close ups' and slow motion—should be categorised under the 1988 Act as 'original, dramatic work', although it could be (and such input into TV dramas and cinema films would be). The word content of a script or 'live' commentary in broadcasts and films is protected by its own copyright as 'literary work', if it passes the low 'originality' threshold.

See 29.13.1.3 and the **additional material** for this chapter on **www.mcnaes.com** for more details of the *England and Wales Cricket Board* case.

29.7.3 No copyright in news or in unrecorded ideas

In general, copyright does not protect ideas—it controls the right to copy the form or manner in which ideas are expressed or executed. The law of breach of confidence, explained in ch. 26, would apply in some circumstances if a considered 'idea' with commercial value were exploited in breach of 'confidential' discussions about it.

- There is also no copyright in facts, news or information. Copyright exists in the form—for example, sentences, a photo, footage—in which these things are expressed, and in the selection and arrangement of the material for publication.

29.7.4 'Lifting' stories

News organisations often include in their stories facts—such as political initiatives or a famous person's death—which are 'broken' by rivals. This is known as 'lifting' a story. There is no copyright infringement in reporting—in a *rewritten* version—the facts uncovered or published by others (*Springfield v Thame* (1903) 89 LT 242). But there may be infringement if verbatim phrases and quotes are copied from the original report and published by the news organisation doing the 'lifting', depending on the extent of the copying—as explained in 29.13.1, What is 'substantial'?, which covers paraphrasing.

the defamation danger in lifting stories is explained in 21.2.3.3

Case study

High Court judge Sir Nicolas Browne-Wilkinson said in 1990: 'For myself, I would hesitate a long time before deciding that there is copyright in a news story which would be infringed by another newspaper picking up that story and reproducing the same story in different words.' He said that ruling against such 'picking up', when the story was reproduced in different words, would not be in the public interest. He also observed that, as the practice among UK national newspapers of copying quotes from each other was so widespread and rarely led to copyright disputes, it could be argued that the newspapers gave each other implied licence for the practice by 'acquiescence' (*Express Newspapers plc v News (UK) Ltd* [1990] 3 All ER 376).

'acquiescence' is explained in 29.16

Changing the odd word or two when writing a news report by 'lifting' facts from a rival report will not be enough to avoid copyright infringement. But the 1988 Act's defence of 'fair dealing for the purpose of reporting current events' protects some (limited) copying of quotes and other sentences from a rival's report, and the broadcasting of short extracts of footage or audio already broadcast by a rival—see later in this chapter.

29.8 Assignment and licensing

Copyright owners can 'assign' copyright, wholly or in part, to another person or organisation, either temporarily or for the copyright's duration. This transfers, to that other party, control over who can copy the work and to what extent. Or the owner can 'license' another party to exploit the work in a particular deal or territory. An owner who licenses retains the copyright and so the overall control of copying.

Section 90 of the 1988 Act says an assignment of copyright is not effective unless it is in writing and is signed by or on behalf of the person assigning it—for example, the 'first owner'.

((•)) see Useful Websites at the end of this chapter for NUJ freelance guide

A licence need not be in writing. In journalism, licences are often agreed verbally, or implied by what has become custom and practice. For example, freelance journalists who regularly send articles or photos to newspapers know their fee rates, and whether they also want the right to use the work in magazine supplements and on websites, or possibly in overseas editions and for syndication.

The licence could be for the work to be published on only one occasion. Any doubts on either side about licence terms should be discussed, and the best practice then is for the terms to be agreed in writing before the work is published.

29.8.1 Readers' letters for publication

- A reader sending a letter for publication has by implication licensed the media organisation to publish it once but retains the copyright.

If the organisation subsequently wants to publish a compilation of readers' letters as a book, it will need to contact each letter-writer to seek a licence to republish the letters.

29.9 Copyright in speeches and interviews, and in notes or recordings of them

Copyright exists in spoken words such as a public speech as soon as the speaker's words are recorded in some form, with or without permission. The copyright arises even if the speech is not delivered from a script, but is, for example, uttered in an improvised comedy show or in an interview with a journalist. The speaker, as the author of a 'literary work'—that is, their words as recorded—owns the copyright in that work, unless they are speaking in the course of their employment, in which case the employer owns the copyright, or is reciting words in which someone else holds copyright (e.g. from a play script).

As copyright protects an 'original' work, in the sense of it being an 'intellectual creation', there is no copyright in casual conversational or trite remarks, in short jokes already in circulation, or in commonplace or ill-judged sayings.

29.9.1 Section 58 defence for use of notes or recordings of spoken words

Section 58 of the 1988 Act—a specific defence for journalism—says it is not infringement of copyright to use a record of all or part of a speaker's words for the purpose of reporting current events, or for the purpose of communicating to the public the whole or part of the work (that is, what the speaker says), provided the following conditions are met:

(1) the record of the words—that is, as recorded on tape or digitally, or in shorthand or longhand—is a direct record of their utterance and is not taken from a previous record or broadcast (as taking the record from such sources could infringe the copyright in those sources);

(2) the speaker did not forbid any note or recording being made of their words, and making the record of them did not infringe any pre-existing copyright (it might, if the speaker were quoting someone else's words);

(3) the use made of the record of the words, or extracts from it, is not of a kind prohibited by the speaker (or anyone else who owns copyright in words used by the speaker) before the record was made;

(4) the record is used with the authority of the person who is lawfully in possession of it—who would usually be the journalist who took notes or made a recording of the speaker's words, or their employer.

A journalist should not be overly concerned about infringing a speaker's copyright when reporting verbatim a speech from a note or recording made of it or of an interview, as usually a speaker who knows a journalist is making that record has consented to publication, expressly or by implication. Even if a speaker withholds consent, one or more of the fair dealing defences can apply as regards some quotation—see later in this chapter.

The first and fourth conditions listed earlier reflect the fact that, apart from the speaker's copyright in the recorded words, a separate copyright exists in the actual record—such as the shorthand or longhand note, because of the skill, labour and judgement involved in making it (*Walter v Lane* [1900] AC 539) or in the sound recording. The journalist who made the record will, if a freelance, be 'first owner' of that copyright. If the record was made in the course of their employment, the employer owns it.

29.10 Copying to report Parliament and the courts

Section 45 of the 1988 Act says copyright is not infringed by anything done for the purposes of reporting parliamentary and judicial proceedings. Section 45 means there is no copyright infringement in reporting proceedings of the UK, Welsh and Scottish Parliaments, and of the Northern Ireland Assembly, or in reporting the proceedings of courts or—see ch. 18—of tribunals (and a broad definition in the 1988 Act means section 45 covers reports of proceedings of any official tribunal not classed as a court).

See ch. 15 for how journalists can officially get copies of case material.

! Remember your rights

Section 45 means that the media does not infringe copyright if, when it covers court cases, it publishes copies of documents, photographs or footage supplied officially from case material to aid reporting. See the **additional material** for this chapter on www.mcnaes.com for a section 45 case study.

29.11 How long does copyright last?

Durations of copyright, set out in sections 12–15 of the 1988 Act, can be summarised as follows.

- Copyright in an 'original literary, dramatic, musical or artistic work'—including a journalism article or a photo—lasts for the author's (that is, creator's) lifetime, then a further 70 years from the end of the calendar year in which they die. The copyright can be bequeathed to the author's heirs. The duration is the same if the copyright is owned by an employer or has been assigned to a company. NB: author is the term used whatever such type of such work.
- Copyright in a sound recording published or communicated to the public lasts 70 years from the end of the year in which that first happened.
- Copyright in a broadcast lasts 50 years from the end of the year in which it was made.
- Copyright in a work of computer-generated music or graphics lasts for 50 years from the end of the year in which it was made.

There are different (but still lengthy) periods of copyright for various other works, such as films, works of unknown authorship and for some particular circumstances.

See the **additional material** for this chapter on **www.mcnaes.com** for copyright in 'orphan works'—that is, copied when the owner of the copyright could not be traced to gain permission.

29.11.1 Crown copyright

Work produced by civil servants in the course of their employment is protected by Crown copyright, which can last up to 125 years.

29.12 Legal remedies for infringement of copyright

Deliberate breach of copyright can be a criminal offence—for example, if a work is communicated to the public for gain by a person who does this in deliberate breach of copyright. However, the civil law of copyright is more relevant to journalism. The criminal law tends to be deployed only for cases of large-scale piracy (such as unauthorised, mass production of CDs).

29.12.1 Civil law

- A copyright holder who discovers that someone plans to infringe that right can get an **injunction** to stop the infringement. →glossary
- If the infringement has happened, an injunction can ban any repetition. The copyright owner can also sue the infringer for damages; or for 'an account of profits', to claim any profit made from the infringement.

- The court can also order that all infringing copies of the work must be handed to the copyright owner or destroyed.

The damages awarded by a court may be higher if there has been a flagrant breach of copyright.

29.13 Defences to alleged infringement of copyright

A question regularly asked by journalists is: 'How much can we copy or quote without infringing copyright?' One consideration is whether the copyright owner, in the case of copied text or quotes, will think it worth the effort to sue for damages—but copyright can reside in a single sentence, and the primary motive for suing may be to protect private material and not be financial.

29.13.1 What is 'substantial'?

Section 16 of the 1988 Act says it is an infringement of copyright to copy the whole or 'any substantial part' of a work. In a copyright lawsuit concerning an 'original literary, dramatic, musical or artistic work', the issue of what is a 'substantial' part may be decided by the court considering 'the quality of originality' of the copied extract (*Newspaper Licensing Agency Ltd v Meltwater Holding BV* [2010] EWHC 3009 (Ch)). In the *Meltwater* case, High Court judge Mrs Justice Proudman said of a newspaper article that 'even a very small part of the original may be protected by copyright if it demonstrates the stamp of individuality reflective of the creation of the author or authors of the article'.

A court dealing with disputed copying of a 'literary work' will also consider to what degree unauthorised verbatim publication—which might be of the most interesting or sensational part, but only of a few sentences—might devalue the commercial value in the whole work's copyright. Similarly, a face may be a small part of a photograph but is probably more important, as regards its commercial value, than the rest of the picture.

29.13.1.1 'Literary' works

In a case involving the author Rudyard Kipling's poem, 'If', four lines of the 32-line poem used without permission in a vitamin advert were held to be an infringement. In *Sillitoe v McGraw-Hill Books*, a book publisher who produced study notes on a novel, reproduced 5 per cent of the original novel. The owner of the copyright in the novel successfully sued for infringement. In the *Meltwater* case, Mrs Justice Proudman drew on the 2009 judgment in which the Court of Justice of the European Union (CJEU) ruled that a single extract of 11 consecutive words from a newspaper article could be protected by copyright as being a 'substantial' part if that work had sufficient originality. She said: 'The [CJEU] makes it clear that originality rather than substantiality is the test to be applied to the part extracted. As a matter of principle this is the only real test.'

> See the **additional material** for this chapter on **www.mcnaes.com** for the *Meltwater* judgment. It upheld copyright protection for headlines and short text extracts electronically 'scraped' from newspapers' websites by a company monitoring various news subjects for its subscribers.

29.13.1.2 Paraphrasing

The issue of what is a 'substantial part' is not always relevant for the news media when it wants to report factual revelations from a literary work (for example, a document), because its contents can be paraphrased or summarised in news coverage to avoid quoting verbatim, which means it will not have been copied.

If the copying of any work by a news media organisation, for its news output, might be ruled to be of a 'substantial' part, its editor can—unless the work is a still photo, see later—aim to rely on the defence of 'fair dealing for the purpose of reporting current events', because then the issue of how much can legally be copied must be assessed in terms of 'fairness', which gives more leeway than the substantiality criterion.

29.13.1.3 Broadcasts, sound recordings, films

As explained earlier, the 1988 Act does not require films, broadcasts or sound recordings to be 'original' to be protected by copyright. In 2016 a judge ruled that an eight-second 'clip' of footage of a key moment in a cricket match was a 'substantial part' of TV coverage of the match that day (*England and Wales Cricket Board*, cited earlier).

29.14 Fair dealing defences

The four 'fair dealing' defences in section 30 of the 1988 Act recognise the public interest in news coverage and some other types of publication being free of some copyright restraints.

29.14.1 Defence of fair dealing for the purpose of reporting current events

- Section 30 of the Act allows some publication (therefore some copying) of work protected by copyright, if the publication is 'for the purpose of reporting current events', irrespective of whether the copyright owner consents to this.
- But there must be 'fair dealing' by those publishing extracts of the work for this purpose and an accompanying 'sufficient acknowledgement' of the work copied.
- 'Fair dealing' means fair practice—for example, the publisher should not take unfair commercial advantage of the copyright owner by copying more of the work than is necessary to report the relevant current event(s).
- 'Sufficient acknowledgement' means that such a report, in a newspaper, magazine, website or other textual medium, must:
  - cite the copied work's title, or include some identifying description of it; and
  - identify its author, unless it is an anonymous work (section 178).

- Photographs are specifically excluded from this fair dealing defence for 'reporting current events', because otherwise no news photographers could earn their living by selling their pictures.

Case law suggests that a court will be less likely to uphold the fair dealing defence if the work copied has been 'leaked' to the media organisation. But the defence will probably not be undermined if the leak—for example, of an internal company memo—reveals wrongdoing or a threat to public safety. If the copyright in a text or document has a legitimate commercial value, judges will expect the media to make only limited use of verbatim extracts, so that the copyright owner's ability to exploit that value is not compromised unfairly. See, for example, the *Ashdown* case discussed in the **additional material** for this chapter on **www.mcnaes.com**. In that case, the Court of Appeal ruled that the *Sunday Telegraph*, by quoting verbatim or nearly verbatim some 20 per cent of a nine-page document, was unfair, and that 'one or two short extracts from it would have sufficed' to satisfy readers than the reporting was authoritative.

In *Ashdown* the judgment suggested that the term 'current events' could cover events which occurred two years before the disputed copying—or possibly, in some circumstances, events from 30 years ago—if the copied work helped them be re-examined in new revelations in media coverage.

Case study

In February 2019 the *Mail on Sunday* newspaper and the *MailOnline* website published five articles showing verbatim extracts from a 1250-word letter which the Duchess of Sussex, Meghan Markle sent in August 2018 to her father Thomas Markle. The extracts, amounting to 585 words, showed that she had begged him to stop talking to the UK tabloid press. The articles said that the letter revealed the 'true tragedy of Meghan's rift with her father' and that she had 'poured out her heart' in it. She sued Associated Newspapers, owners of the *Mail on Sunday* and *MailOnline,* arguing that its publication of the extracts infringed her copyright in the letter. (She also successfully sued for misuse of her private information, although Associated was only ordered to pay a nominal sum of £1 in damages for her privacy claim.)

One of Associated's arguments at the High Court was that its publication of the extracts was protected by the defence of fair dealing for the purpose of reporting current events. But Mr Justice Warby ruled that it had illegally infringed the duchess's copyright. He ruled that only one paragraph of the extracts was relevant to reporting a 'current event' (the event being Mr Markle's objection to a summary of the letter published by the US magazine *People* which he said was misleading. The judge said that the publication of such extensive extracts was not necessary and was 'wholly disproportionate' as regards correcting that inaccuracy which, he said, Mr Markle and Associated had 'considerably overstated'. He also ruled that Associated's purpose had been, essentially, to publish detailed contents of the letter, which was not itself 'a current event' (he noted that the *Mail on Sunday* had 'trumpeted' to readers that its revelation of these contents was a 'world exclusive'). The judge said the fair dealing defence did not apply. He also said that the case was not one of the 'very rare' instances when the 'public interest' defence applied to justify copying beyond what the fair dealing defence permitted. (*Duchess of Sussex v Associated Newspapers Ltd* [2021] EWHC 273 (Ch)).

The Court of Appeal upheld the judgment ([2021] EWCA Civ 1810). *MailOnline* later reported that Associated would pay the duchess a 'confidential amount' in damages for the copyright infringement and was also expected to cover much of her legal costs. *MailOnline* said these could be more than £1 million (*MailOnline*, 5 January 2022). For explanation of the public interest defence in copyright law, see 29.15.

for the privacy aspects of the *Sussex* case, see 27.3.3

29.14.1.1 The defence can cover use of copied footage and sound recordings

Although the defence of fair dealing for the purpose of reporting current events does not cover still photographs, it does cover media use—that is, if 'fair'—of copied film footage and sound recordings, including in digital forms.

The Act says sound recording, film or broadcast reports of current events do not need to acknowledge the copied work's title, or include other description of it, or the identity of its author 'where this would be impossible for reasons of practicality or otherwise'. This reflects the difficulty of including all such detail in a broadcast of a short piece of copied footage or audio. But acknowledgements—for example, by announcement or by showing in copied footage the logo of the channel from which it was copied—help prove fairness, and such use of a logo is 'sufficient acknowledgement'.

Case study

In 1991 the High Court dismissed a copyright action by the BBC against British Satellite Broadcasting (BSB) over the use in the satellite company's sports news programming of highlights from BBC coverage of the World Cup football finals, to which the BBC had bought exclusive rights. The court said BSB's use of short clips showing goals scored, 14–37 seconds in length and shown up to four times in 24 hours, with a BBC credit line included as acknowledgement, was protected by the defence of fair dealing for reporting current events (*BBC v British Satellite Broadcasting* [1991] 3 All ER 833 (Ch D)).

After this 1991 case, major UK broadcast organisations reached a formal agreement permitting limited copying in news content of each other's sports footage.

29.14.2 Defence of fair dealing for the purpose of criticism or review

Section 30 of the Act allows some copying of a work, irrespective of whether the copyright owner consents, 'for the purpose of criticism or review'.

- But the work must previously have been 'made available to the public' *with* the copyright owner's consent—for example, published or exhibited. The defence does not protect use of leaked or stolen material.
- There must also be 'fair dealing' by those publishing it for criticism or review and an accompanying 'sufficient acknowledgement' of the work.

The 'fair dealing' and 'sufficient acknowledgement' requirements are in essence the same as those required for the defence of fair dealing for the purpose of reporting current events.

Authors who have released works to the public (such as poems or novels) may well be happy for extracts from them to appear in critiques or reviews published by the media, as the works will thereby receive wider publicity. But the defence applies irrespective of whether they object.

The requirement of fairness means that in a dispute about the extent of the use of copied material a court would consider if the media organisation had genuinely sought to critique the copied work(s) or had the baser motive of taking commercial advantage by such reproduction.

Case law is that the defence can protect some copying (for example, the brief showing on TV of copies of several photos) for the purpose of criticism or review of the 'ideas or philosophy' manifest in the copied work, so in that respect, the focus need not be on the work's artistic or literary quality. NB: this fair dealing defence can protect some copying of photos.

Case studies of media organisations relying on these fair dealing defences are in the **additional material** for this chapter on **www.mcnaes.com**. It also outlines the *England and Wales Cricket Board* case, in which the judge made clear that the fair dealing defence for the purpose of reporting current events can cover the work of 'citizen journalists'.

29.14.3 Defence of fair dealing for use of quotation

In 2014, section 30 of the 1988 Act was amended to create a general defence for use of quotation. The requirements, all of which must be met, are that the work being quoted has been made available for the public (it is not—for example—a leaked or stolen document/recording), that the use is 'fair dealing' (see earlier), that the extent of the quotation is no more than is required 'by the specific purpose for which it is used' and that the quotation is accompanied by 'sufficient acknowledgement' (see earlier), 'unless this would be impossible for reasons of practicality or otherwise'. The 'quotation' could be by use of part of a recording otherwise protected by copyright (see Schedule 2 to the Act).

see Useful Websites at the end of this chapter for IPO guidance

This defence can protect quotation in journalism of short extracts when this is not covered by the other fair dealing defences—because it is not to report 'current events' or to review. This defence also protects, for example, theatres and record companies when they use in promotional material quotes from newspaper reviews.

The Intellectual Property Office (IPO) guidance is that the quotation defence can cover copying of a photograph but only in 'exceptional' circumstances.

29.14.4 Defence of fair dealing for the purpose of caricature, parody or pastiche

The 2014 amendment to section 30 also created a defence of copying for the purposes of caricature, parody and pastiche. Again, the copying must be limited so that it does not take 'unfair' commercial advantage of the copyright owner by excessive publication of the copied work. In the case brought by Icelandic fishing and processing company Samherji against performance and conceptual artist Oddur Fridriksson over a false website he created in Samherji's name, in which they appeared to apologise for their role in a fishing quota scandal (known as the Fishrot scandal) in Namibia, one of his defences was parody. The Judge ruled that because Samherji's logo and corporate design had not been altered in any significant way, defending the work as a caricature, parody or pastiche would be unlikely to succeed in a full trial: 'Parody must evoke an existing work but be noticeably different from the original and constitute an expression of humour or mockery,' 'Pastiche imitates the style of an existing work whilst being noticeably different from the original.' (*Samherji v Fridriksson* [2024] EWHC 2892).

29.15 Public interest defence

→glossary

The public interest defence—which exists in **common law**, not statute (see the 2001 case of *Ashdown v Telegraph Group Ltd* in the additional materials for this chapter) as regards copyright infringement—is narrow, and rarely used reflecting the fact that the statutory 'fair dealing' defences effectively have an inherent, public interest element and permit some copying.

But whereas the defence of fair dealing for the purpose of reporting current events cannot protect the unauthorised copying (publication) of a still photo, the 'public interest' defence might be available to protect publication of a copyrighted work, including a still photo, and all of a document, if the purpose was, for example, to expose it as an immoral work, or one damaging to public life, health, safety or the administration of justice, or as a work which incites immoral behaviour, and in some other circumstances—for example, if police ask the media to publish a photo (for which the police do not own the copyright) of a person whom they wish to trace.

Case study

In 2010 the *Reading Post* succeeded with the public interest defence in the small claims court after being sued by the owner of copyright in several photos which the *Post* had copied from a website. Police had directed the *Post* to the site, which showed the apparent exploits of 'urban explorers' inside abandoned buildings. The *Post* said it published the pictures to highlight police concerns that these activities involved criminal damage, including graffiti, and to help identify those involved. The judge said he felt the pictures were posted on the website to encourage the activities, which he said could cause an accident, and the public to suffer, and were a serious social problem (*Newspaper Society website*, 28 January 2010).

For other examples of journalistic use of the 'public interest' defence, and for detail of the 'incidental infringement' and 'innocent infringement' defences, see the **additional material** for this chapter on **www.mcnaes.com**.

29.16 Acquiescence

A copyright owner who does not complain for an extended period of time after becoming aware that a person or organisation has copied the work may be deemed by a judge to have implicitly agreed—acquiesced—to the copying.

29.17 Do hyperlinks breach the copyright in the material linked to?

Hyperlinking or framing content on a webpage is a 'communication to the public' under copyright law. A number of CJEU rulings have held that using linking or framing (a linking technique where the content from one webpage is displayed on a third-party page within a frame so that the content is viewed on the third party webpage via a deep link to the original webpage where the content is located) to embed copyright content in a website, to direct a reader or viewer to another website does not infringe copyright in the material displayed there if it can be seen there by any internet user, and has been displayed there by, or with the consent of, the owner of the copyright in that material, or otherwise lawfully. While these CJEU decisions are not binding authority in the UK after Brexit, in 2021 the UK Court of Appeal in a case called *Tunein*, described them as 'highly persuasive'. For more detail on this complex law, see the **additional material** for this chapter on **www.mcnaes.com**.

29.18 'Open content' licences

Some authors—including some who post their photographs on social media sites—give a general, 'open content' licence, free of charge, for people to copy their work and distribute copies, provided that attribution to the author is included in the copies and specified conditions are honoured. The licence may be in the Creative Commons

see Useful Websites at the end of this chapter for Creative Commons site

format. One condition may be that the use of the copied work is not commercial, which would exclude use in journalism for which consumers pay. A different licence would have to be agreed with the copyright owner to permit such journalistic use, unless a defence applied.

29.19 Moral rights

Moral rights are personal rights that protect the integrity and non-economic interests of a creator of copyright work. They include the right to be identified as the author (attribution), the right to object to derogatory treatment of a work (integrity), and the right not to be falsely credited as the author of a work. These rights are non-transferable but can sometimes be waived by the author.

For more detail on 'moral rights' held by authors, and for an outline of the law on 'passing off' and trademarks, see the **additional material** for this chapter on **www.mcnaes.com**.

29.20 Copyright and AI

There are many challenges posed by generative AI, the artificial intelligence technology that can produce content, including text, imagery, audio and synthetic data. According to a survey by the World Association of News Publishers (WAN-IFRA), reported by the *Press Gazette* in May 2023, sixty-seven per cent of those who answered the survey said they were worried about plagiarism and copyright infringement.

The case of *Getty Images v Stability AI* [2025] EWHC 2863 (Ch), which was heard by the High Court in November 2025, illustrates how uncertain the future is in this area. Getty argued that Stability AI committed copyright infringement by making its AI model available in the UK, which it claimed was an 'infringing copy' of Getty's works. Getty had dropped its primary copyright and database right infringement claims at the trial. The High Court ruled that AI models like Stable Diffusion—which train on copyright works but do not store or reproduce them—are not infringing copyright. The court found that the model learned from statistical representations of images, not by storing copies. The ruling, by declaring such training as non-infringing, was seen as a blow to content creators, effectively allowing AI models to exploit copyrighted works without consequences. It appears to leave artists and photographers with little control or right to compensation for AI-generated content derived from their work. The court did find a limited, historic trademark infringement in cases where watermark text from Getty images appeared in the AI's generated outputs from older versions of the mode.

There are a number of similar cases being pursued in the US, (for example *New York Times Co v OpenAI and Microsoft*) which have not yet been ruled on. The case of *Disney v AI content companies Midjourney Inc. and Minimax* focuses not so much on the use of data for training as on the audiovisual outputs: namely the production of allegedly infringing image and video by users.

In March 2026, the Government published a Report on Copyright and Artificial Intelligence, with an accompanying Impact Assessment. This followed on from an AI and copyright **consultation** launched in December 2024. These were required to be published under the Data (Use and Access) Act 2025. →glossary

Recap of major points

- Copyright law controls who can commercially exploit literary, musical, dramatic and artistic works, including journalism articles and photos, as well as sound recordings, film, broadcasts and typographical arrangements.
- There is no copyright in news in itself, only in the form in which it is expressed.
- Defences of fair dealing are available for publication of copyrighted work if the copying is not excessive and if the publisher honours requirement for attribution to the author(s) as the creator(s).
- But photographs are excluded from the fair dealing defence which covers reporting news and current events.
- A copyright owner whose rights are infringed can seek an injunction and/or damages.

Useful Websites

Gov.uk

Intellectual Property Office, a government agency—see its guides to copyright and trade marks

Intellectual Property Enterprise Court

London Freelance (NUJ), 'Advice & tuition', www.londonfreelance.org

London freelance branch of the National Union of Journalists—advice on copyright

EPUK, Resources: FAQ, www.epuk.org

Copyright advice provided by Editorial Photographers group

Creative Commons, 'Licenses List', www.creativecommons.org

Guide to Creative Commons copyright licences

Government Report on Copyright and Artificial Intelligence, https://assets.publishing.service.gov.uk/media/69ba692226909a14239612e4/CP2602959_-_Report_on_Copyright_and_Artificial_Intelligence_web.pdf

Online resources

Visit the online resources at **www.mcnaes.com** to test your knowledge of this chapter with **self-test questions** and a **flashcard glossary**, and to read **updates** about law and regulatory matters affecting journalism, as well as **additional material** to further your learning.

Part 5

Other laws affecting publishers, journalists and their sources

30

Readers' postings and online safety issues

Chapter summary

Some media organisations provide space under online articles for readers to post comments. It is possible that a reader will post unlawful material—for example, a posting which names a person whose identity should be protected by a reporting restriction arising from a court case, or which commits a contempt of court, or which is a **tort** in civil law—for example, breach of copyright, privacy or which is defamatory. This chapter examines the law governing whether a media organisation could be prosecuted or held liable for what was published in a reader's posting. Some such law is explained in other chapters and this chapter cross-refers to that explanation. It also refers to online safety issues and guidance produced for journalists suffering abuse and harassment posted online by readers.

→glossary

30.1 Introduction—online harms

The rapid increase in journalism published online over the last two decades has created huge opportunity for readers to post comments and factual assertions underneath articles. Arguably, this has helped 'democratise' the news media, in that postings can express readers' views on current events and how these are reported. This type of 'user-generated content' can be a check on biased or erroneous journalism and stimulate important debate.

However, some readers' postings are toxic in tone or harmful in content—for example, abusive or seeking to spread disinformation. While the individual posters—if they can be identified and located—will remain liable for what they post, the media websites that host their comment may also be liable. In the case of the larger social media platforms, which are mainly based in the US and do not generally have liability for these 'below the line comments' under US law, it may sometimes be easier to pursue the individual poster, either for civil liability or to prosecute them (see 30.3).

What to do about toxic postings creates a management issue for the media. Most organisations that allow below-the-line comments will have a set of rules or terms that posters are supposed to abide by. To prevent toxic or unpleasant postings, which may deter readers in general from visiting journalism websites, or deter them from posting constructive comments, some media organisations deploy staff and software to pre-moderate (i.e. check before publication) postings submitted by readers, so that toxic and harmful ones do not appear. But this is very labour intensive, and to pre-moderate may also create a legal risk for a media organisation if a posting which has unlawful content slips through that checking, as this chapter explains. Some media organisations use a mix of methods—for example, using software to allow postings to appear without pre-moderation if they are from readers who have a track record of constructive postings, and using staff to pre-moderate other postings, Also, software can automatically block postings from appearing if racist or other harmful terms are recognised.

The issue of how to 'police' harmful content and also how to distinguish between potentially harmful but legal content—for example, around methods of suicide, self-harm or eating disorders—and unlawful content (there are four types of expression or information which countries are required to prohibit under international law: child pornography; incitement to genocide; advocacy of national, racial or religious hatred that constitutes incitement to discrimination, hostility or violence; and incitement to terrorism) has caused concern to many governments over recent years, especially around content that appears on social media platforms. The legal and ethical issues around this are beyond the scope of this book, but in the UK, the Government has now introduced a new set of laws to protect children and adults online, by trying to make social media companies more responsible for their users' safety on their platforms. The Online Safety Act was passed in October 2023. It puts the media regulator Ofcom in charge of checking whether platforms are protecting users. Ofcom has been given power to issue notices requiring service providers to identify and remove terrorism content and child sexual exploitation as well as to remove abusive content communicated publicly or privately or risk a large fine.

More details about the ambit of the Online Safety Act as far as news publishers are concerned can be found in the **additional material** for this chapter.

30.2 'Notice and take down' procedure in regulation 19

The general principle in relevant UK law is that if a website operator did not moderate (did not check) a reader's posting before it became visible, the operator will *not* be liable in law for any illegal material published in it, provided that the operator had no prior knowledge that the material would be posted, and deleted it or disabled public access to it quickly after being given notice of or otherwise becoming aware of its unlawful nature. By reacting in this way, in those circumstances, the website operator complies with what is known as the 'notice and take down' (NTD) procedure, gaining the legal protection that confers.

The source of much NTD protection is regulation 19 of the Electronic Commerce (EC Directive) Regulations 2002. This **statutory instrument** originally implemented a directive of the European Union. In most respects, including as regards the NTD protection, it has been retained post-Brexit. →glossary

Regulation 19 applies in respect of the 'hosting' ('storage') of online material by a provider of 'an information society service'—terms which include media organisations facilitating publication of postings by readers (who fall under the category of 'recipients of the service'). The regulation says:

> "Where an information society service is provided which consists of the storage of information provided by a recipient of the service, the service provider (if he otherwise would) shall not be liable for damages or for any other pecuniary remedy or for any criminal sanction as a result of that storage where—
>
> (a) the service provider—
>
> (i) does not have actual knowledge of unlawful activity or information and, where a claim for damages is made, is not aware of facts or circumstances from which it would have been apparent to the service provider that the activity or information was unlawful; or
>
> (ii) upon obtaining such knowledge or awareness, acts expeditiously to remove or to disable access to the information, and
>
> (b) the recipient of the service was not acting under the authority or the control of the service provider."

In January 2021 the UK Government said that post-Brexit it is committed to upholding such liability protections, adding: 'For companies that host user-generated content on their online services, there will continue to be a "notice and take down" regime where the platform must remove illegal content that they become aware of or risk incurring liability.'

For example, a reader's posting underneath or referring elsewhere on the same site to a legitimate report of a youth court case could contain a comment which breaches section 49 of the Children and Young Persons Act 1933, for example by stating the name of a teenage defendant who had anonymity in the report—for this 'automatic' anonymity requirement in the 1933 Act, see ch. 10 in this book. Another example: a reader's posting underneath a feature about sexual offenders could, by stating a name or referring to some other identifying detail, illegally identify a victim of a sexual offence, and so breach section 1 of the Sexual Offences (Amendment) Act 1992—see ch. 11.

Provided that such a posting was not pre-moderated and, in compliance with the NTD procedure, the posting is deleted expeditiously as soon as the website operator becomes aware of its unlawful content (for example, if a complaint was received), regulation 19 would normally protect the operator from criminal liability as regards facilitating publication of the posting. This protection applies whether the posting's content breached an automatic reporting restriction, or any restriction imposed by any type of court to bestow anonymity for a person, or to ban publication of some other information in connection with a case. However, the reader responsible for the posting could be successfully prosecuted (NB: the occasions when the NTD protection for website operators arises from regulation 19 is limited by when the 2002 Regulations took effect, and instead the protection may well arise from other law—see later).

There is little case law about how the NTD provision in regulation 19 or in other UK statutory law should be interpreted. But if, for example, a court decided that a website operator deliberately encouraged readers to post material breaching a reporting restriction, the NTD protection would not apply.

If a posting was submitted containing unlawful material, and was pre-moderated, yet was allowed to become visible, complying with NTD procedure in response to a complaint would protect the website operator in law if, in the event of any legal action over the posting, the court accepted that the nature of that material was such that it was not obviously unlawful to the moderator, and that the operator was not aware of any facts or circumstances which made it unlawful. However, a judge may expect a media organisation to train moderators about types of postings which could be unlawful in foreseeable circumstances (such as any posting which identifies a rape victim).

If a pre-moderated posting is published and does turn out to be unlawful, deleting it expeditiously will, at the very least, help reduce any fine imposed on the operator, or (see later) damages awarded in civil law for harm that publication caused to a person or business.

Small media organisations may decide the cheapest, safest course is not to pre-moderate any readers' postings, because then the NTD protection is at its fullest, or not to 'host' such postings at all.

> The Independent Press Standards Organisation has produced guidance for journalists about measures to minimise the risk of readers' postings identifying victims/alleged victims of sexual offences—see 11.7.1.4.

30.2.1 Other NTD protection as regards breach of statutory reporting restrictions

Regulation 19 only provides NTD protection in respect of material which was categorised as unlawful under law which already existed when the 2002 Regulations came into force. This meant that Parliament has had to create other law providing NTD protection for website operators in respect of any reporting restriction created by statute since then, or if the scope of a pre-existing reporting restriction has since then been extended by statute.

So, for example, in 2015 the Criminal Justice and Courts Act created section 45A in the Youth Justice and Criminal Evidence Act 1999, to enable a criminal court to make an order providing lifetime anonymity for a person aged under 18 in respect of them being a witness in a criminal trial—see ch. 10. Simultaneously, the 2015 Act also created Schedule 2A in the 1999 Act to provide NTD protection for website operators as regards a reader's posting which breaches an anonymity order made under section 45A.

It is not necessary for other journalists to know all this patchwork of NTD law, because in each instance its wording as regards the circumstances which confer exception from legal liability replicates that of regulation 19, being based on the wording of the same EU directive.

Statutory reporting restrictions bestowing anonymity are explained or referred to in chs. 5, 10, 11, 12, 14, 17, and 18. For how the Contempt of Court Act 1981 deals with legal liability for readers' postings in respect of its 'strict liability rule', and the risk of allowing readers to post comments under reports of legal proceedings which are 'active' under that Act, see 19.7.5.

30.2.2 Liability for civil torts in readers' postings

As the wording of regulation 19 indicates, observing its NTD procedure can legally protect a website operator if there is publication of a reader's posting containing material for which damages could be awarded in civil law. Again, to what extent the protection exists, if at all, will be affected by the relevant circumstances—including whether the posting was pre-moderated. For a case study about regulation 19 protection in a defamation case, in which a High Court judge accepted that a newspaper in respect of its website is an 'information society service', see 22.11.2 and 22.11.4 in this book. However, the 2002 Regulations do not apply in respect of data protection cases and 'the protection of privacy' (this is stated in regulation 3), and therefore do not offer protection in respect of such claims. For privacy and data protection law, see chs. 27 and 28.

30.3 Online safety issues

see ch. 33, Journalists' sources

The challenges that journalists encounter in undertaking their professional work are manifold. In addition to the legal threats that have been discussed, journalists face physical threats as well as risks such as state monitoring and attempts to force them to reveal their sources.

Increasingly, journalists in the course of their work suffer from abuse and other types of threatening behaviour or harassment meted out online. Such posts are usually posted anonymously and tend to disproportionately target women and ethnic minority journalists. See 1.1 for resources which are available to support journalists concerning their safety and resilience.

Individuals may be personally liable both under civil and criminal law for what they post, if they can be identified and located. For example, a reader who posts something that is defamatory will be liable under the civil law of defamation. In some cases, it may be easier to sue them than to try and go after the website that hosted the comment, especially if it is one of the large social media platforms. In July 2023, a man from Warwickshire apologised and agreed to pay £1,000 to a charity after he defamed BBC presenter Jeremy Vine on Twitter/X. The man wrongly claimed on Twitter/X that Mr Vine was the unnamed BBC presenter who *The Sun* had alleged had paid a teenager thousands of pounds in exchange for sexual pictures. A reader who posts something indecent or grossly offensive, or which amounts to a threat and causes distress or anxiety, can be committing a criminal offence, depending on the circumstances, and words used.

The content of such postings may be offences under, for example, section 1 of the Malicious Communications Act 1988, the Protection from Harassment Act 1997 or section 127 of the Communications Act 2003. For example, in July 2023 *The*

Sun published accusations against a then-unnamed BBC presenter, which resulted in a number of BBC presenters being wrongly identified and attacked online. BBC Radio's Nicky Campbell made a crime report to the Metropolitan police after being falsely accused of being the presenter. He said he had had a 'distressing weekend' after being falsely named on Twitter/X.

Journalists tend to find police slow or unwilling to act on complaints about such postings, and only a handful of such offenders have been traced and prosecuted.

Note this section has discussed these online offences in the context of their being used by journalists to protect themselves, however it is worth noting that these offences can be used against people who post material that is considered to be threatening, offensive or indecent, online, for example on social media. (see 34.14 for more details of these offences).

Recap of major points

- Complying with 'notice and take down' (NTD) procedure can protect media organisations from being held legally responsible for unlawful material posted on their sites by readers.
- However, whether the NTD protection applies depends on circumstances, and it is less likely to apply if the posting was pre-moderated.
- Journalists subjected to online abuse and harassment can consult guidance published by the Media Lawyers' Association.

Useful Website

Media Lawyers Association, 'Combatting online harassment and abuse: A legal guide for journalists in England and Wales' (second edition), https://medialawyersassociation.org/second-edition-of-combatting-online-harassment-and-abuse-a-legal-guide-for-journalists-in-england-and-wales/

Written by Beth Grossman and Cian Murphy, and published by the Media Lawyers' Association

Online resources

Visit the online resources at **www.mcnaes.com** to test your knowledge of this chapter with **self-test questions** and a **flashcard glossary**, and to read **updates** about law and regulatory matters affecting journalism, as well as **additional material** to further your learning.

31

Reporting elections

Chapter summary

The Representation of the People Act 1983 makes it a criminal offence to make or publish false statements about election candidates. There are restrictions on publishing 'exit polls'. Broadcast journalists must be impartial when covering elections and referendums.

31.1 False statements about candidates

Section 106(1) of the Representation of the People Act 1983 makes it an offence to:

- make or publish a false statement of fact about the personal character or conduct of an election candidate in order to affect how many votes they get.

This provision is wider than the law of defamation as it merely needs to be shown that the statement was false and was calculated to influence the elections. The statement must relate to the personal—as opposed to the political—character or conduct of the candidate. A statement that the candidate supports a political splinter group, for example, would not come within the section (although it could still be potentially defamatory if it was wrong).

To constitute the offence, the falsity must be expressed as a fact, as distinct from a statement which is clearly merely comment or an opinion about the candidate. It is a defence for someone accused of publishing such a false statement to show that they had reasonable grounds for believing when it was published that it was true and did at that time believe it was true (even if it turns out to be untrue).

Section 106(5) makes it an offence:

- to publish a false claim that a candidate has withdrawn from the election, if the publisher knows it to be false and published it to promote or procure the election of another candidate.

Either offence is punishable by a fine unlimited by statute. If the publisher is a company, its directors can be convicted. The law is not aimed specifically at the media, but is meant to deter 'dirty tricks' by those campaigning in elections and their supporters. In *Pirbhai v DPP* [1995] C.O.D. 259 QBD, it was held that writing in a pamphlet that Jack Straw 'hates Muslims' was a false statement of fact (and not opinion) and thus section 106 applied. In 2010, Labour MP Phil Woolas lost his seat when he was convicted of illegal practices under section 106(1) by making false statements about his opponent—Liberal Democrat candidate Robert Elwyn Watkins—in his election materials – including his attitude to Muslim extremists and his election expenses—which Woolas had no reasonable grounds for believing were true and did not believe were true (*Robert Elwyn James Watkins v Philip James Woolas* [2010] EWHC 2702 (QB) and see too *R (Woolas) v Parliamentary Election Court* [2012] Q.B. 1 In *Buchan v Elliott* [2022] EWHC 255 (QB) a local election candidate who had been unsuccessful by 10 votes in the 2021 local elections challenged the return of the winner on the grounds that she had distributed, some days before the election, a leaflet that included a statement that he, the runner-up, had supported and voted in favour of a controversial planning application. In fact, he had been ill on the day of the meeting and had sent a substitute in his place who had voted for the application. The petition was dismissed on the grounds that the statement related to *political* conduct and character rather than *personal* conduct and character. The ban on false statements applies from when formal notice is given that an election is to take place until the election ends. For local government elections, this period is about five weeks. For national Parliamentary elections, the period begins with the date of the dissolution of Parliament or any earlier time at which His Majesty's intention to dissolve Parliament is announced.

The publisher of a false statement could also be sued for defamation in civil law. But the criminal sanction in the 1983 Act gives a quicker remedy, as a candidate who can prove a **prima facie** case that they have been traduced by such a false statement can obtain an **injunction** preventing its repetition, whereas the legal rule against **prior restraint** means it is harder to get an injunction in a defamation action, which could take months to be settled or resolved at trial. The 1983 Act prohibits all such false statements, including those which are defamatory. A journalist who in 1997 published false allegations on the internet that an election candidate was a homosexual was fined £250 under the Act. An inaccurate statement that someone is homosexual is not, in itself, defamatory. But it could cost an election candidate votes, for example by persuading voters with anti-gay religious beliefs not to support them.

→glossary
→glossary
→glossary

for context in defamation law, see 20.2.6

31.2 Defamation dangers during elections

Election candidates and their supporters might make defamatory allegations about rivals, using terms such as 'racist', 'fascist' and 'liar'. A media organisation which publishes them could be successfully sued for libel if it has no defence.

There is no statutory privilege for media publications of candidates' election material or of what they say. But qualified privilege protects fair and accurate reports of public meetings and press conferences, if the requirements of that defence are met.

It is therefore important that journalists take care to be accurate in their descriptions of candidates, and likewise statements about a candidate's voting records or past speeches should always be verified.

ch. 20 has definitions of defamatory statements and ch. 22 explains qualified privilege

Remember

Journalists reporting speeches by extremist candidates should remember that speakers, and reports of their speeches, are subject to the laws against stirring up hatred, including on racial and religious grounds. The online chapter 39, 'Boundaries to expression—hate and obscenity', on **www.mcnaes.com** explains that law.

31.3 Election advertisements

Section 75 of the 1983 Act says that only an election candidate or their agent may incur any expenses relating to their campaign, including for publishing an advertisement. It is an offence for anyone else to pay for such advertising unless authorised to do so, in writing, by the election agent. This stops well-wishers from placing advertisements on behalf of candidates without their express authority.

31.4 Broadcasters' duty to be impartial

Section 6 of the Broadcasting Code has detailed rules on how broadcast output must be impartial in election and referendum periods. These rules only apply to broadcasters. Ofcom has fined several radio stations after presenters or others breached the code by making on air partial declarations supporting political candidates or parties.

See Useful Websites at the end of this chapter for section 6 and Ofcom's rules for party political and referendum broadcasts.

Case study

In 2008 Ofcom fined Talksport radio £20,000 for breach of the impartiality requirement, after presenter James Whale directly encouraged listeners to vote for Conservative candidate Boris Johnson in the London mayoral elections and criticised Labour candidate Ken Livingstone (*Ofcom Broadcast Bulletin*, issue 123, 8 December 2008).

Ch. 3 covers the Code's general impartiality requirements, including for matters of political controversy—see 3.4.9, Due impartiality and due accuracy.

31.5 Exit polls

An 'exit poll' is any survey in which people who have voted are asked which candidate and/or party they voted for. Such surveys can often produce data accurately predicting an election result hours before it is officially declared. Many democratic nations, including the UK, restrict when such data/predictions can be published on the grounds that publishing the information, or predictions based on it, before the voting period ends could skew the election result. The concern is that telling people who have yet to vote which candidate/party appears likely to win, with information apparently soundly based on votes already cast, could make people change their original voting intentions. The exit polls might undermine the democratic process because (a) the later group of voters will have made choices on data not available to those who voted earlier; and (b) those data, and any prediction apparently based on them, might be inaccurate or even falsified to influence voting.

Section 66A of the Representation of the People Act 1983 makes it a criminal offence to:

- publish—i.e. to make available to the public at large, or any section of the public, in whatever form and by whatever means—before a poll is closed, any statement about the way in which voters have voted in that election which is, or might reasonably be taken to be, based on information given by voters after they have voted; and to
- publish, before a poll is closed, any forecast—including any estimate—of that election result, if the forecast is, or might reasonably be taken to be, based on exit poll information from voters.

So, for example, it would be illegal to broadcast, or post on a website, before polling stations closed, the statement: 'Fifty-five per cent of the people we asked say they voted Conservative today.'

This law applies to Parliamentary elections and by-elections, council elections, Northern Ireland Assembly and Welsh and Scottish Parliamentary elections. It applies in respect of exit polls conducted to focus on an individual constituency or ward, or on voting nationally. Publishing material in breach of section 66A leaves the publisher liable to a fine unlimited by statute or a jail term of up to six months.

It is legal to publish, at any time, opinion poll data on voting intentions which was gathered before voting began, as the information was not based on how people say they actually voted. It is also legal to report the results of exit polls, and any forecast based on them, as soon as polling has finally closed, as TV programmes frequently do. But it is not always accurate now to talk of 'an election day'. For example, experiments to encourage more people to vote have meant that in some places voting took place over several days. It is an offence to publish an exit poll, or forecast apparently based on it, during any of the polling days, until the polls close on the final day.

31.5.1 The Broadcasting Code rules on exit polls, discussion and analysis

Rule 6.5 of the Broadcasting Code has a similar control on publishing exit polls, but goes further. It says: 'Broadcasters may not publish the results of any opinion poll on polling day itself until the election or referendum poll closes.' Rule 6.4 bans broadcasting of discussion and analysis of election and referendum issues during polling, a period which begins when polling stations open. This rule does not apply to any poll conducted entirely by post. BBC Editorial Guidelines take the same approach. Some rules do not apply for parish or community council elections.

31.6 Election counts

Journalists, including photographers and TV crews, attend election counts so declarations of the result can be quickly aired. There is no statutory right to attend a count—admission is at the discretion of the Returning Officer, who has legal responsibility for security and procedures at the count. The Electoral Commission's media handbooks say that members of the media wishing to attend a count have to apply to the Returning Officer. Rule 31 of the Parliamentary Election Rules expressly provides for a declaration of secrecy to be made by every person permitted by the returning officer to attend at the counting of the votes.

Case study

In the 2010 General Election, journalists were initially banned from the count at Staffordshire Moorlands and told by council officials running it they had to stay in a separate room, apparently because of fears that their presence in the counting hall would be disruptive. The ban was lifted after lawyers for the *Staffordshire Sentinel*, *Leek Post and Times* and the BBC wrote to the acting Returning Officer protesting that it was undemocratic and breached the right to freedom of expression under Article 10 of the European Convention on Human Rights. The *Sentinel* also planned to get round the ban by having three staff members accredited as 'observers' at the count (*Media Lawyer*, 6 May 2010).

Registering as an observer takes 10 days, and accredited observers must be allowed into the count—see Useful Websites at the end of this chapter. See also under Useful Websites, the Electoral Commission's 'Tips for Returning Officers: Working with National TV News Broadcasters at Count Events'. The Commission updates its guidance for Returning Officers for every election.

Recap of major points

- Once an election is called it is a criminal offence to publish a false statement about the personal character or conduct of a candidate with the intention of affecting the number of votes they get.
- It is an offence to publish before the end of polling any data obtained in exit polls on how people have voted, or any prediction of the election result based on such data.
- The Broadcasting Code requires broadcasters to follow certain practices to ensure impartiality in coverage of elections and referendums, and restricts use of opinion (including exit) polls.

Useful Websites

Ofcom, www.ofcom.org.uk

- Section 6 of the Broadcasting Code, on elections and referendums
- Ofcom's guidance on section 6 of the Code
- Ofcom rules on Party Political and Referendum Broadcasts

BBC, Editorial Guidelines, www.bbc.com

- Guidance on opinion polls, surveys, questionnaires, votes and straw polls

The Electoral Commission, www.electoralcommission.org.uk

- 'Guidance for (Acting) Returning Officers administering a UK Parliamentary election in Great Britain'

Online resources

Visit the online resources at **www.mcnaes.com** to test your knowledge of this chapter with **self-test questions** and a **flashcard glossary**, and to read **updates** about law and regulatory matters affecting journalism, as well as **additional material** to further your learning.

32

National security and official secrets

Chapter summary

Certain categories of official information are protected from unauthorised disclosure by the criminal law. This includes information relating to national security and intelligence, defence, and international relations. Unauthorised disclosure of these types of 'official information' that might harm national security or other important state interests is covered by the Official Secrets Act 1989. The Official Secrets Acts of 1911, 1920 and 1939 which used to provide the principal legal protection in the United Kingdom against espionage have now been replaced by the National Security Act 2023 (see Schedule 18). The relevant provisions were put into force on 20 December 2023.

The 1989 Act, which is not affected by the National Security Act, has not been used in recent years to prosecute journalists, but it has been used to jail civil servants and others because they have given journalists sensitive information. Police could search the home and newsroom of a journalist who is thought to have breached this law, seize their records, and try to identify their source. There is no public interest defence for anyone facing prosecution.

32.1 Introduction

The Official Secrets Act of 1989 and the National Security Act 2023 protect national security, and can be used to enforce the duty of confidentiality owed to the UK state by Crown servants or employees of companies doing military and other sensitive work. Crown servants include civil servants, members of the armed services, the police and civilians working for them. The Acts impose a similar duty on members of the security and intelligence services. The National Security Act 2023 has now replaced the Official Secrets Acts of 1911, 1920 and 1939, which previously covered espionage and spying offences.

Official secrets legislation can also punish those who leak sensitive information to journalists or members of the public. Publishing such material makes it available to hostile powers, terrorists and criminals, and can embarrass the UK's allies—for example, by disclosing diplomatic correspondence.

Using the law to punish leaks is controversial. Attorneys General have approved prosecutions of Crown servants and others who, on grounds of conscience, leaked information to the media to throw light on controversial Government policies. In such cases the media and others have questioned whether the prosecution was intended to protect vital state secrets or to stifle debate about matters embarrassing to the Government. A journalist seen as being an accomplice to a leak could be prosecuted. Journalists and their editors could also be prosecuted for circulating or publishing such information. The law is complex. The **additional material** for this chapter on **www.mcnaes.com** needs to be read.

see 1.7 for the Attorney General's role

32.2 The law's consequences for journalists

As this book went to press no journalist had been successfully prosecuted, let alone jailed, under official secrets legislation for many years. But there have been recent cases in which journalists were investigated for alleged breaches of this law, and periods of high tension between media organisations and UK Governments over what was or might be published.

Case study

In July 2022, as part of what was described as an 'Official Secrets Act' investigation into the 'disclosure of information relating to national security and intelligence, and information relating to defence', the Metropolitan Police seized electronic devices and documents from the home and workplace of an unnamed journalist, identified only as LXP, who claimed some of the contents were 'journalistic' materials. The Met said it was seeking 'material stolen by two crown servants and evidence of its theft' and that this was not journalistic material. In October 2023, the High Court held that the Met should not be allowed to examine the electronic devices until an assessment had been carried out by an independent barrister, and LXP should be able to identify which materials he claimed were journalistic and should not be disclosed to the force. Officers will then have to return to court to argue for permission to inspect such material. The High Court judges commented that 'If the stable door is opened by the police conducting the search, the horse named "journalistic protection" has already bolted, before the judge has considered where the balance of public interest lies.' (*R (on the application of LXP)* [2023] EWHC 2824)

See 33.6.2.1 for more detail on this case.

Although officialdom is reluctant to use official secrets law to prosecute journalists, journalists must know about the law in order to be ready to protect confidential sources of information, because this—as ch. 33 emphasises—is a moral obligation. A journalist might not be jailed for a story—but the source might. Police seeking to identify the source of leaked information could raid a journalist's newsroom, office or home, and they might be arrested and threatened with prosecution.

Sources are generally dealt with more severely than journalists. In 2007 former civil servant David Keogh and Leo O'Connor, who had worked as an MP's researcher, were jailed for six months and three months, respectively, for leaking to the *Daily Mirror* an officially secret memo about a conversation between US President George Bush and UK Prime Minister Tony Blair about the Iraq war.

> The **additional material** for this chapter on **www.mcnaes.com** provides detail of the above case, and others in which sources were jailed for breach of official secrets law, or journalists investigated for alleged breach of it, including cases in which the homes of journalists were raided by police. For police powers to search property, see 33.6.1 and 33.6.2.1.

32.2.1 Reluctance to prosecute journalists

The reluctance of officialdom to use official secrets law against UK journalists is partly an effect of the legislation. The 1989 Act contains defences which journalists can use, but some sources cannot—for example, a journalist has a defence that disclosure of the information was not 'damaging' to state interests. Damaging is defined as likely to or endangering 'the interests of the United Kingdom abroad, seriously obstructing the promotion or protection by the United Kingdom of those interests or endangering the safety of British citizens abroad'.

This defence is not available to a member of the security and intelligence services or anyone who has been notified that they are subject to the relevant provisions of the 1989 OSA but is available to a crown servant or government contractor.

John Wadham, a former director of the civil rights organisation Liberty, has said of the lack of prosecutions of journalists:

> “It is partly because governments don't like to be seen to be trying to put journalists in prison and partly because juries are less sympathetic to civil servants—who are employed to keep their mouths shut, who are aware of the rules but break them, and who breach the trust with employers and colleagues—compared with journalists, who are paid to find things out and publish them.”

> UK Governments have used injunctions to stop publication of leaked 'official secrets'. See the **additional material** for this chapter on **www.mcnaes.com**, and 26.3 in this book about the *Spycatcher* case.

32.3 The 1989 Act—what it covers and the journalist's position

The Official Secrets Act 1989 defines disclosure offences by categorising various classes of information as secret, including information:

- about the work of the UK's security and intelligence agencies, or information they hold, which if disclosed without lawful authority would or be likely to damage that work;
- about defence, such as deployment of the UK's armed forces, military planning for conflicts, and development of weapons, which if disclosed without lawful authority would or be likely to damage the capability of the armed forces to carry out tasks, or lead to loss of life or injury of members of those forces;
- about international relations, which if disclosed without lawful authority would or be likely to create damage by endangering the interests of the United Kingdom abroad or the safety of UK citizens abroad;
- concerning crime—for example, about operations by police or other agencies which if disclosed without authority would or be likely to impede the prevention or detection of crimes, or about custody or prison facilities which if disclosed without authority could make escapes more likely;
- about or from official interception of communications, including 'phone-tapping' and interception of emails and letters, by police or other agencies;
- about matters relating to security or intelligence, defence or international relations communicated in confidence by the UK state to another state or international organisation.

for more on such official 'interception', see 33.3.1

Some offences in the Act can only be committed by members of the security and intelligence services, Crown servants, Government contractors or people officially notified that they are subject to the Act's provisions, who disclose without authority information categorised by the Act as an official secret. But there are also 'onward' disclosure offences which can be committed by anyone. For example, section 5 of the 1989 Act (here summarised) says a person—for our purposes, a journalist—commits an offence by making

- a damaging disclosure (for example, in a published article) without lawful authority of information about the work of security or intelligence agencies, or about defence or international relations,
- or a disclosure without lawful authority of information about official phone-tapping or police operations against a criminal.

If the journalist knew or had reasonable cause to believe that the information is protected against disclosure by the Act, and if they received that information from a Crown servant or Government contractor either without lawful authority or in confidence or received it from someone else who received it in confidence from such a person.

32.3.1 Damage test but no public interest defence

Under the Act, the nature of the 'damage' or likely damage, caused by the disclosure, which is necessary for a conviction, or whether any specified 'damage' or likelihood of damage *is* necessary, varies according to the class of information, and the category of person accused.

There is no public interest defence in official secrets cases—and information can be classed as secret even if it has previously been published.

Breaching the 1989 Act is punishable by a jail term of up to two years and/or a fine.

See the **additional material** for this chapter on **www.mcnaes.com** for more detail of what the 1989 Act bans, and what must be proved for someone to be convicted of a disclosure offence.

32.4 The public and media may be excluded from a secrets trial

Section 38 of the National Security Act 2023 is aimed at controlling access to a secrets trial.

Section 38 allows the public to be excluded from a secrets trial if 'it is necessary in the interests of national security' (except for the passing of sentence). While section 38 does not expressly mention the media, neither did its predecessor section 8 in the 1920 Official Secrets Act and it has always been assumed this includes the press.

32.5 Background to the National Security Act 2023

New communication methods and data technology have changed the nature of espionage and leaks—for example, hostile states can conduct cyber-attacks. At the same time, as demonstrated by the Edward Snowden NSA leaks, the potential impact of leaks of official information has increased: a single disclosure could contain terabytes of data. In 2015, the Government asked the Law Commission for England and Wales to review the effectiveness of the laws that protect Government information from unauthorised disclosure. The Commission published a final report on the Protection of Official Data in 2020, which made a number of recommendations. One of those recommendations was that the 'archaic' language of the old Official Secrets Acts be updated to ensure the legislation was 'fit for purpose'. For example, they recommended replacing the word 'enemy' with 'foreign power'. The National Security Act, which became law on 11 July 2023 built upon the Law Commission's recommendations and replaced the Official Secrets Acts of 1911, 1920 and 1939. It came into force on 20 December 2023.

32.6 National Security Act 2023

The National Security Act, described by the government at the time as 'the most significant reform of espionage law in a century', builds upon the Law Commission's recommendations and replaces the Official Secrets Acts of 1911, 1920 and 1939.

The 2023 Act does not target leaks or whistleblowing activity, and it does not replace the Official Secrets Act of 1989. In response to increasing concerns from the media during the passage of the Bill, on 28 March 2023, the government published a 'factsheet on journalistic freedoms' under the Act. This factsheet was updated in June 2025. The aim of the factsheet was to offer reassurance that the government did not consider that 'legitimate journalistic activity' would meet the thresholds of the new offences introduced in the Act. There is a link to this factsheet at the end of this chapter.

In a press release issued at the time of the Act entering into law, the government stated that 'the new powers will help ensure that the UK remains the hardest operating environment for malign activity undertaken by foreign actors', and quoted the Director of MI5 as saying 'the National Security Act is a game changing update to our powers. We now have a modern set of laws to tackle today's threats.'

The core measures put in place by the Act came into force on 20 December 2023. The Act introduces new offences relating to espionage, prohibited places, foreign interference, sabotage, and new powers of arrest and detention and search and seizure.

The key takeaways of the 2023 Act as far as journalists are concerned are:

- it introduces three new espionage offences (section 1: obtaining or disclosing protected information; section 2: obtaining or disclosing trade secrets; section 3: assisting a foreign intelligence service; as well as a new sabotage offence (section 12) for which the threshold of knowledge that their conduct is prejudicial to national security is actual and constructive knowledge): '*knows, or having regard to other matters known to them ought reasonably to know*'; the government says this will '*put it beyond doubt that individuals would not be caught if they acted unwittingly or where they did not have information from which it could be concluded that they should have known*'.
- protected information is defined under section 1(2) as any '*information, document or other article where – for the purpose of protecting the UK's safety or interests – access to it is restricted or it is reasonable to expect that access would be restricted*'; the government considers that it will be clear where information is restricted, such as through classification markings or password protected information in a government building. The government also considers it will be clear where information is not formally restricted, but it would reasonably be expected that information be restricted. For example, this would cover the theft of the identity documents of an intelligence officer from within their place of work because the context of the theft would mean it would be reasonable for the person to expect that information to be protected.
- when originally introduced, the Bill did not include places owned, controlled or used for the functions of any of the Security Services or GCHQ in the list of prohibited places. These were added when the Bill was amended in the Public Bill Committee.
- the Secretary of State has the power to designate additional sites as prohibited places through secondary legislation. This power has already been used to designate places connected to the civil nuclear industry (including ships used to carry nuclear material) as additional prohibited places.

- the maximum sentence for the offence of obtaining or disclosing protected information is increased to life imprisonment from 14 years previously.
- in relation to the new section 3 offence of assisting a foreign intelligence service, which criminalises a person engaging in conduct intended to materially assist a foreign intelligence service in UK-related activities, the Act says '*likely to materially assist*'; the government feels this will take legitimate journalistic activity out of scope of the Act. According to the government's July 2023 National Security Act fact sheet, this offence was created to reduce the ability of foreign intelligence agencies to carry out hostile activities against the UK, extending beyond traditional espionage activity.
- sections 4 and 5 criminalise harmful activity in and around sensitive sites—'prohibited places' (which are defined in section 7). This now includes accessing, inspecting and passing over, whether in person or via electronic or remote means, as well as the taking of photographs of the prohibited place. Activity must either be undertaken with a purpose prejudicial to the safety or interests of the UK, or be unauthorised where the individual knows, or having regard to other matters known to them ought reasonably to know that that is the case. This means that journalists conducting activity on or near prohibited sites—for example a journalist taking photos from outside a prohibited place—where they do not have a purpose prejudicial to the safety or interests of the UK and there is nothing to suggest taking photographs is not permitted, such as signage or other distinguishing marker, would not commit an offence. However, coverage of events such as peace protests could be held to be a breach of the Act if, for example, material published could be said to jeopardise security at a defence base.
- section 7 gives a wide-ranging definition of 'prohibited places', which includes Crown land in the United Kingdom which is used for (i) UK defence purposes; (ii) extracting any metals, oil or minerals for use for UK defence purposes; or for (iii) the purposes of the defence of a foreign country or territory.

Only time will tell how this new Act will impact journalists.

32.7 Defence and Security Media Advisory Notice system

((•)) see Useful Websites at the end of this chapter to read the DSMA-Notices

The Defence and Security Media Advisory (DSMA) Committee is the head of a joint government/media system through which the media can get specific guidance on how to avoid inadvertent public disclosure of information which could compromise the UK's national security and defence. It has published five standing 'notices' giving general guidance. These are widely called 'D-Notices' (defence notices) but are now officially known as 'DSMA-Notices'.

These five standing DSMA-Notices cover:

(1) military operations, plans and capabilities;

(2) nuclear and non-nuclear weapons and defence equipment;

(3) military counter-terrorist forces, special forces and intelligence agency operations, activities and communication methods, and techniques;

(4) identification of sensitive installations;

(5) personnel who work in sensitive positions, and their families.

The system is based on voluntary self-censorship by the media. Editors who consult the DSMA-Notice secretary sometimes decide to limit what is published and sometimes publish information that they might otherwise have left out. The DSMA Committee has no statutory enforcement powers.

See the **additional material** for this chapter on **www.mcnaes.com** for further details about the DSMA-Notice system.

Recap of major points

- Official secrets law is complex and frequently controversial. There is **additional material** for this chapter on **www.mcnaes.com**.
- This law protects national security and the safety of citizens, and can be used against foreign spies.
- But journalists say it is sometimes used to punish those who leak information which is politically embarrassing for the Government, and to deter the media from revealing such information.

Useful Websites

Defence and Security Media Advisory Notice System, www.dsma.uk

UK Parliament, House of Lords Library, Research Briefing, Official Secrets Acts 1989: Disclosure of Official Information, www.lordslibrary.parliament.uk

Law Commission, Protection of Official Data: A Consultation Paper (2025), www.lawcom.gov.uk

Gov.uk, Home Office Policy Paper Journalistic Freedoms: National Security Bill Factsheet on journalistic freedoms

Online resources

Visit the online resources at **www.mcnaes.com** to test your knowledge of this chapter with **self-test questions** and a **flashcard glossary**, and to read **updates** about law and regulatory matters affecting journalism, as well as **additional material** to further your learning.

33

Journalists' sources

Chapter summary

Journalists often have to rely on information from people whose safety or careers or liberty would be at risk if they were known as the source. If their identities are not protected, journalists' jobs would be much harder—fewer people would be willing to speak to them, and many important stories would never emerge. It is an ethical principle that journalists protect confidential sources of information. In the UK, there is also some qualified legal protection for journalists who are asked to reveal their sources. However, in practice these protections are weak and journalists have needed to rely on the European Court of Human Rights to provide them with stronger legal protection.

Various bodies such as the police when investigating suspected crime have powers to demand that journalists reveal who a source is, or to obtain journalists' phone, internet and email records to identify the source. This chapter explains those powers, which can be enforced by judges, and how journalists can protect confidential sources. It warns that investigative journalists suspected of receiving leaks of sensitive official information should expect to be placed under secret surveillance. Sometimes the reason why journalists refuse to hand over material to police or give evidence is to maintain a reputation for neutrality.

33.1 Introduction—protecting your source: the ethical imperative

Journalists need to protect the identities of 'whistleblowers' and other human sources who provide information about incompetence, negligence or wrongdoing by or within organisations such as police forces, Government Ministries, councils and companies, or about other matters which the media reasonably believe it is in the public interest to disclose.

A public servant or anyone who leaks sensitive information from an organisation could—if their identity is discovered—be sacked, and be prosecuted, fined or jailed if the leaking is punishable as a criminal offence.

Chapters 28, 32 and 34, respectively, explain these laws and how under some circumstances the journalist who gets information from such a source could also be prosecuted. Because of the legal risks for sources and the recognised benefits for journalists of getting information from such confidential sources, journalists have an ethical duty to protect them. Many ethical codes specifically reflect this. Clause 14 of the Ipso Editors' Code of Practice states: 'Journalists have a moral obligation to protect confidential sources of information.' This clause is not subject to the public interest exceptions in the Code, which does not give any circumstance that justifies breaching the clause.

Chs. 2 and 3 introduce the regulators' codes.

See Useful Websites at end of this chapter for the National Union of Journalists' code.

The National Union of Journalists' code of conduct has a similar clause. It too has no exception to the principle.

The Impress Standards Code says the anonymity agreed with a source must be protected 'except where the source has been manifestly dishonest'. The Broadcasting Code says in practice 7.7: 'Guarantees given to contributors, for example relating to the content of a programme, confidentiality or anonymity, should normally be honoured.'

Journalists' codes in nations all around the world state the essence of this principle. If confidential sources were not sure that journalists would protect their identities, many stories of great public interest would never be published. This has been recognised by the UK courts: in the 1981 case of *British Steel Corporation v Granada Television Ltd* [1981] AC 1096, the court said:

> "If [newspapers] were compelled to disclose their sources, they would soon be bereft of information which they ought to have. Their sources would dry up. Wrongdoing would not be disclosed. Charlatans could not be exposed. Unfairness would go unremedied. Misdeeds in the corridors of power, in companies or in government departments would never be known."

Remember that, whether the story is local or national, if a confidential source's employer or anyone hostile discovers the source's identity this could have life-changing consequences for them. See the **additional material** on **www.mcnaes.com** for a case study.

33.2 Protecting your source: legal protections

UK law recognises to some extent that journalists need confidential sources to reveal important matters to society. Journalists facing legal consequences for refusing to identify a source and a source, if prosecuted under UK law for leaking information to a journalist, can both assert rights under Article 10 of the European Convention on Human Rights, which protects the rights to receive and impart information, and freedom of expression.

Convention rights and the ECtHR are introduced in 1.3

In section 10 of the Contempt of Court Act 1981, Parliament created what is sometimes referred to as a 'shield law' to protect journalistic activity.

Section 10 says:

> "No court may require a person to disclose, nor is any person guilty of contempt of court for refusing to disclose, the source of information contained in a publication for which he is responsible, unless it is established to the satisfaction of the court that disclosure is necessary in the interests of justice or national security, or for the prevention of disorder or crime."

The Court must only permit disclosure on one of the specified grounds—the interests of justice, national security, or for the prevention of disorder or crime. An order to disclose for other reasons—for example, to protect public health—is not allowed. Proof that disclosing the source is merely 'convenient' or 'expedient' is also insufficient. The Court must also determine whether the information is really necessary, and must conduct a balancing exercise, weighing up the importance of the specified ground against the 'journalist's undertaking of confidence'. While this may sound like it offers a fairly high level of protection, in reality it has not, because English courts have interpreted the exceptions where disclosure is said to be necessary quite broadly and have frequently ordered that sources be revealed. For example, UK courts have interpreted the phrase 'in the interests of justice' very broadly. In the Bill Goodwin case referred to below, the House of Lords said that 'interests of justice' is wide enough to include the exercise of legal rights and self-protection from legal wrongs, whether or not by court action.

Case study

In 1989 a High Court judge ordered Bill Goodwin, a trainee reporter on *The Engineer* magazine, to disclose his source of information for a story about an engineering company's financial difficulties. He refused, and was fined £5,000 for contempt of court (*X Ltd v Morgan-Grampian (Publishers) Ltd* [1991] 1 AC 1). The Court of Appeal and House of Lords upheld the decision, saying disclosure was 'necessary in the interests of justice' because the company had a right to know who was leaking information about it. Mr Goodwin went to the European Court of Human Rights, which in 1996 agreed with him that the UK courts had breached his Article 10 rights (*Goodwin v United Kingdom* (1996) EHRR 123). It said protection of journalistic sources was a basic condition for press freedom, and a court order to disclose a source could not be compatible with Article 10 unless it was justified by an overriding requirement in the public interest, and that no such requirement existed in this case.

Further, for example, history shows that UK judges tend to accept the Government's interpretation of what is needed to protect 'national security'. See the **additional material** for this chapter for a case study on the *Tisdall* case, in which the *Observer* newspaper was ordered by a judge to return to the Government a leaked photocopy of a Ministry of Defence document.

ch. 32 deals with official secrets law

Since the European Convention on Human Rights began directly influencing UK law in 2000, consideration of the effect of section 10 has been subsumed, in legal disputes over whether a journalist should be required to identify a source, in the focus on whether the journalist's Convention rights—referred to below—should prevail or if there is any 'overriding requirement in the public interest'.

33.2.1 Article 10 rights—European jurisprudence

The European Court of Human Rights (ECtHR) has ruled—for example, in 2013 in *Telegraaf Media Nederland Landelijke Media B.V. and others v The Netherlands* (Application no. 39315/06)—that:

- Article 10 protects a journalist's right—and duty—to impart information on matters of public interest provided they are acting in good faith to provide accurate and reliable information in accordance with the ethics of journalism.

This jurisprudence, to which UK judges pay heed, is that the law should only require a journalist to reveal the identity of a confidential source (for example, to the police), or surrender any material which could do that:

- if this is necessary in a democratic society because of an 'overriding requirement in the public interest'.

It could be argued in court, against the journalist, that it is in the public interest for the source to be identified to the police or another state agency because there is good reason to suspect that the source has committed a crime (whether that is the leaking of information or some other offence) or because the leaking involved sensitive information and infringed other people's right to privacy to such an extent that this becomes the overriding consideration.

for a fact-sheet on such ECtHR decisions, see Useful Websites at the end of this chapter

But the ECtHR has said, in the *Telegraaf* ruling and others, that the source's conduct—that they have committed a crime or may have some selfish motivation or has caused publication of false information—does not in itself override the journalist's Article 10 rights to refuse to reveal their identity. The crime which the state agency is investigating would have to be of sufficient gravity, not a minor one. The ECtHR has also ruled that when it is justifiable for a state agency to use the law to try to discover a journalist's source's identity, the use must be **proportionate** to a specific, legitimate aim in the particular case, and should not allow, for example, a wider trawl of records or material to discover what else the journalist has been doing. Also, to comply with the proportionality principle, the investigating state agency should have exhausted other means of identifying the source before using its powers and the law against the journalist.

→glossary

But it cannot be guaranteed, at the outset of a journalist's contact with a confidential source, that an investigating agency attempting to identify the source, or a judge asked to enforce the attempt, will agree that Article 10 rights should prevail.

Other Convention rights may apply for the journalist, as this chapter explains.

In 2020 the ECtHR ruled that the Federal Supreme Court of Switzerland had breached the Article 10 rights of journalist Nina Jecker by not upholding her challenge to a public prosecutor's order. The order was that she should disclose the identity of a man who dealt in hashish and cannabis. She had featured him with anonymity in a report on drug-dealing, including to point out he had been dealing for 10 years without being stopped. For more detail, see the **additional material** for this chapter on **www.mcnaes.com**.

33.2.2 Court orders to name or produce material which could identify a source

Police or another UK state agency investigating crime can in some circumstances apply to a judge for a court order requiring a journalist or media organisation to name a source or produce material which might identify them. Also, a state agency or a business attempting to discover who leaked information to a journalist might ask a judge for an order requiring identification of the source, to stop further leaks. A journalist or editor who decides on an ethical basis to defy either type of order must be prepared to face the legal consequences—a substantial fine, or possibly a jail sentence, for contempt of court, although in the past five decades no UK journalist has been jailed for such a contempt.

A list of practical steps journalists can take to protect sources' identities is given later in this chapter, which also outlines the law on such orders.

33.3 Be prepared for communications and records to be probed

Arguably the biggest threat to journalists' ability to protect a confidential source comes from powers which police and other state agencies have to investigate suspected crime by intercepting the content of phone and electronic communications, or analysing data these generate, or by extracting—from journalists' phones, computers or storage devices—records which could identify the source. Such powers are necessary in many crime investigations so police can, for example, monitor the phones of criminals and thwart terrorism. However, the extent of these powers is controversial.

33.3.1 Interception of communications

If serious crime is suspected, and for other specified reasons, the police and the UK's state security and intelligence agencies—MI5, MI6 and the GCHQ eavesdropping centre—can ask the Home Secretary for a warrant to intercept people's communications during their transmission in phone or internet networks or when stored as data. The warrant requires phone and internet companies to cooperate with what could include recording—tapping—phone conversations, harvesting for analysis what is said in texts, voicemail and emails, and copying posted letters. These interceptions can show who supplied what information to a journalist.

With some exceptions, material from such interceptions cannot in UK law be used as evidence in legal proceedings, because the policy of successive UK Governments has been to maintain operational secrecy about official intercepting, to preserve its effectiveness. A person whose communications are thus intercepted will almost certainly not be told it has happened (usually it will not be denied or confirmed unless a complaint to the Investigatory Powers Tribunal leads it to rule the interception was unlawful, and even then details may not be disclosed).

see Useful Websites at the end of this chapter for more on the Tribunal

If the interception identifies the journalist's source, the source could then be prosecuted with admissible evidence such as records extracted by the police from the journalist's mobile phone or laptop, or documents seized by police searching the journalist's home or office, using powers described later in this chapter.

such searches occurred in Operation Elveden—see ch. 34

The Investigatory Powers Act 2016, as amended by the Investigatory Powers (Amendment) Act 2024, was created to be the legal framework for interception, replacing earlier legislation. It had some safeguards to protect civil liberties, including that investigating agencies must alert the Home Secretary if the purpose of the proposed interception is to discover the identity of a journalist's source, so there can be particular consideration of the necessity for the warrant and that its scope is proportional. These safeguards include (secret) co-approval of each warrant by one of a team of 'Judicial Commissioners', who are current or former High Court judges, and subsequent reviews by the Investigatory Powers Commissioner. In 2019, Sir Brian Leveson, the former President of the Queen's Bench Division of the High Court, took up that role. On 14 October 2024, following a legal challenge by civil rights group Liberty, a new safeguard was introduced via the Investigatory Powers (Amendment) Act 2024, which requires investigating agencies to get independent authorisation from the Investigatory Powers Commissioner or, in urgent circumstances, a senior official representing the Home Secretary, before searching for or holding onto confidential journalistic material they obtain through 'bulk' interception of data and hacking devices. Other safeguards are explained in detail in the **additional material** for this chapter on **www.mcnaes.com**.

But official secrecy about interception means a journalist is unlikely ever to discover if their communications were intercepted, or if the safeguards protected them and therefore protected the identity of the confidential source.

The best protection for such a source is for the journalist to assume interception could happen—see 33.9, Practical steps to protect sources.

Under the Official Secrets Act 1989, it is almost always illegal for anyone to reveal operational information about interception by state agencies—see 32.4.

33.3.2 Probing of communications data

In law 'communications data' is not the content of a communication but records kept in phone or internet systems, including the name of the account holder, phone numbers used in calls and texting, dates/times a call began and ended, or when a text was sent, email addresses used by sender and recipient, date and time of sending, and a person's internet browsing history. The data will generally give some information about the locations of those involved in a communication when it occurred—for example, from the geolocation facility of smart phones or from the landline or Wi-Fi connection.

Communications data can be used by officialdom as evidence to identify, confront and prosecute, or justify sacking, someone who has leaked information to the media.

The 2016 Act gives the UK's security and intelligence services, police and a wide range of other public authorities, including local authorities, legal powers to access communications data for a wide range of purposes, including investigating suspected crime, if authorised by the designated senior official within that body.

A journalist whose communications data has been examined by such an official agency to trace their confidential source may only find out about that from a source who has been confronted with the data by, for example, the police investigating a leak.

The ease and secrecy with which police could use earlier legislation to obtain such data made a mockery of journalists' rights to protect confidential sources. For example, in the three years to early October 2014, 19 police forces accessed communications data in a total of 33 investigations into what officialdom deemed to be suspected illicit relationships between 233 public officials (sources) and 82 national, regional and local journalists.

> For more detail about those police investigations, and on how in 2017 the Investigatory Powers Tribunal ruled that Cleveland police's accessing of three journalists' communications data was unlawful—see the **additional material** for this chapter on **www.mcnaes.com**.

33.3.3 Reduced protection for journalists' communication data

The Government insisted the 2016 Act has adequate safeguards for journalists' Article 10 rights, because the Act's section 77—reflecting ECtHR jurisprudence—says that:

- if the authorisation is to get the data for the purpose of identifying or confirming a source of journalistic information, and the authorisation is not to help avert an imminent threat to life, it must be approved by a Judicial Commissioner;
- the Commissioner, when deciding whether to approve, must 'in particular' have regard to the public interest in protecting a source of journalistic information and to the need for there to be an 'overriding public interest' to justify the public authority's attempt to identify or confirm such a source.

As amended, the 2016 Act's section 195 now says the Investigatory Powers Commissioner or a senior official may only approve the searching for or holding onto of confidential journalistic material through 'bulk' interception of data and hacking devices if:

- the public interest in obtaining the material outweighs the public interest in the confidentiality of confidential journalistic material or sources of journalistic information, and
- there are no less intrusive means by which the information may reasonably be obtained.

for context, see 33.2.1, on the 'overriding' requirement

33.3.4 Information stored in networks or equipment

Police, security and intelligence agencies have powers of 'equipment interference' to extract material from computer networks, computers and mobile phones. The 2016 Act contains some safeguards about using these powers to identify a journalist's source or to gain journalistic material, explained in the **additional material** for this chapter on **www.mcnaes.com**. If the relevant device has been seized, the owner may be told extraction will follow and be required to provide an encryption key (for example, a password), and could be jailed for a refusal—for up to two years, or up to five years if the issue is national security. A journalist should not bank on a password or encryption being unbreakable. Also, if the extraction can be done remotely, they may not know of it.

33.4 Be prepared to be watched or bugged

Various **statutes** give the police and other high-level state investigation agencies powers, subject to approval procedures, to carry out surveillance to investigate serious crime. Surveillance can include following people to see who they meet, or placing secret cameras and listening bugs in cars, homes or other property. Such tactics could be deployed to attempt to identify a journalist's source.

→glossary

Case study

In 2008 *Milton Keynes Citizen* reporter Sally Murrer and Mark Kearney, a former detective accused of leaking information to her, walked free after a judge ruled that prosecution evidence gathered by police bugging Mr Kearney's car was inadmissible. Mr Kearney faced charges of misconduct in public office (the alleged leaking) and Ms Murrer was charged with aiding and abetting the misconduct. Judge Richard Southwell's ruling at Kingston Crown court meant the charges were dropped. The judge said that gathering evidence by using the listening device was an unjustifiable violation of the Article 10 freedom of expression rights of both, and of Ms Murrer's Article 10 rights to protect her sources. The judge said the information allegedly leaked was not sensitive, let alone 'highly sensitive' and the police action could not be justified (*R v Kearney and Murrer, Media Lawyer*, 28 November 2008). For detail on why journalists should know about the 'misconduct' and the 'aiding and abetting' offences, see 34.3.1.

Anyone who discovers they have been subject to surveillance can ask the Investigatory Powers Tribunal to rule on whether the infringement of privacy rights and—in the case of a journalist—of Article 10 rights was justified by an overriding requirement in the public interest and whether, if it was, the surveillance was proportionate. If the surveillance does not meet these criteria, it will be unlawful. If it leads to the journalist being prosecuted over information leaked from an organisation, the journalist should ask the court to rule on whether it was legal.

In December 2024, the Investigatory Powers Tribunal ruled that surveillance by the Police Service of Northern Ireland targeting investigative journalists Barry McCaffrey and Trevor Birney was unlawful. The PSNI suspected an individual of supplying material to journalists and requested surveillance for one week in 2018 to see whether they met with McCaffrey or Birney. The PSNI was ordered to pay £4,000 to each journalist, the first time the IPT ordered a police force to pay damages to journalists for unlawful intrusion. An independent review by Angus McCullough KC published in September 2025 revealed 21 instances of unlawful uses of covert powers by PSNI, all prior to 2015, to attempt to uncover eight reporters' sources.

Laws that enable such surveillance are outlined in the **additional material** for this chapter on **www.mcnaes.com**.

for context, see 1.3 about Convention rights, including the wording of Article 8

33.5 Article 8 rights to privacy and family life

Police or an investigating agency wanting to intercept anyone's communications or access their communications data, or—using powers outlined in this chapter—to search their home, must consider the individual's rights in Article 8 of the European Convention on Human Rights to respect for privacy and family life.

In 2013 the ECtHR ruled that a warrant for a police search of a newspaper's office issued by a Luxembourg court infringed Article 8 and Article 10 rights. For more detail of this case, see the **additional material** for this chapter on **www.mcnaes.com**.

33.6 Expect a 'production' order or a search for material

Statutes empower police and other official investigators, when investigating crime, to obtain a court order requiring a person to surrender material, and in some circumstances a court warrant to enable a search of premises without warning to seize material. If the investigation is to discover the identity of a journalist's confidential source, the order could be for surrender of documents or notes of interview. When police search, such material or objects suspected of containing it—computers, phones and memory sticks—could be seized from a home or workplace, and then material could be extracted from the devices—see 33.3.4.

33.6.1 The Police and Criminal Evidence Act 1984 (PACE)

In most circumstances, police who want access to documents or other material need a court order or a search warrant. The Police and Criminal Evidence Act 1984 (commonly referred to as PACE) is the legislation they use most when applying for these.

33.6.1.1 Special procedure material and the first set of access conditions

Sections 13 and 14 of PACE give special protection to 'journalistic material', defined as 'material acquired or created for the purposes of journalism'. This can include journalists' pre-publication research and interview material. When investigating alleged crime, police seeking to compel a journalist to surrender ('produce') such material must use PACE's 'special procedure', set out in the Act's Schedule 1. This means the police must apply to a **circuit judge** or district judge for a production order (rather than merely to a lay magistrate, who can issue production orders but not for 'special procedure' material). →glossary

If the application succeeds the judge makes the order, which requires the person or organisation holding the material to produce it to the police. Disobeying the order is a contempt of court, punishable by a jail term of up to two years and/or a fine unlimited by statute.

Under PACE, the holder of the material must be given notice that the application will be heard at court, and so can argue there that the order should not be made. After service of the notice, the holder is banned by PACE from hiding or destroying the material, and disobeying the ban could be punished by a fine or jail term as a contempt of court.

Schedule 1 says that before making the production order a judge must be satisfied that the following 'access conditions' (the 'first set') apply:

- there are reasonable grounds for believing that an **indictable** offence has been committed; →glossary
- the material the police want is likely to be both of substantial value to their investigation and evidence which is admissible in court;
- other methods of obtaining it have been tried without success, or have not been tried because they seem bound to fail;
- and producing the material to the police or giving them access to it would be in the public interest, having regard to
  - the benefit likely to accrue to the investigation if the material is obtained; and
  - the circumstances under which the person in possession of the material holds it.

If a journalist or media organisation refuses to comply with a production order, the judge can issue a search warrant for it to be seized from any property occupied or controlled by the journalist or media organisation—see later.

> PACE 'special procedure' appears to give journalistic material useful protection. But some judges have interpreted the access conditions in a way which makes the protection less valuable than was hoped—for example, see 33.11.1, Photos and footage of disorder.

33.6.1.2 **Journalistic material held in confidence is 'excluded material'**

Under section 11 of PACE, 'journalistic material which a person holds in confidence' is categorised as 'excluded material'. This means that under PACE it cannot be made subject to a production order under the first set of access conditions. So, PACE offers some specific protection for material from a source explicitly or implicitly promised confidentiality by a journalist and, therefore, protects to some extent the source's identity.

In PACE, journalistic material is 'excluded material' if it has been *continuously* held (by one or more persons) subject to such an obligation (the promise of confidentiality) since it was first acquired or created for the purposes of journalism.

33.6.1.3 **The 'iniquity exception'**

A ruling by the Court of Appeal in 2016, which is *R v Norman* [2016] EWCA Crim 1564, appears to have considerably weakened the protection given in PACE for confidential material (that is, material which a journalist 'holds in confidence').

→glossary

for context on the *Norman* case, see 34.3

The Court ruled that the **common law** means that any journalistic material created, acquired or held 'in furtherance of a crime' or for another 'iniquitous' purpose cannot be regarded as confidential, and so cannot be regarded as 'excluded material'. The Court of Appeal said the position might be otherwise if the material was from 'a genuine whistleblower acting in the public interest'.

This 'iniquity exception' was not previously thought to apply to PACE. According to the Law Commission, the Court's ruling means that:

- when a law enforcement agency wants to obtain material held by a journalist, if a judge is persuaded that the material could have been supplied to the journalist by a source who committed a crime by doing that—such as misconduct in public office—and/or that the journalist retains it criminally or has published information from it criminally, the material cannot have confidential status under PACE, and so a production order can be successfully made under the first set of access conditions to compel the journalist to surrender it, because it can only be categorised as 'special procedure' material.

The News Media Association (NMA), calling for better protection in such law for journalists, said that they and whistleblowers are 'particularly vulnerable to unwarranted and unscrupulous accusations' that they have committed crime in their disclosures, including alleged breach of wide-ranging data protection law covered in ch. 28 of this book. The NMA said the continued failure by police and courts to ensure rigorous compliance with the law's requirements concerning production orders and search warrants could lead to 'rubber stamping' of 'iniquity exception' applications for them, and so the exception would 'fatally' undermine Article 10 rights, including the protection of the identities of confidential sources.

For when the 'iniquity' exception in the law of confidentiality can help journalism, see 26.6.2.

For the Law Commission and NMA views on what the *Norman* ruling means, see Useful Websites at the end of this chapter.

33.6.1.4 The second set of access conditions

Under a second set of access conditions in Schedule 1 of PACE, a circuit or district judge can make a production order in respect of 'special procedure' or 'excluded material' (continuously held confidential material) if under legislation, a search warrant could have been appropriately authorised for police to seize the material in the case's circumstances—for example, authorised under section 23 and schedule 2 of the National Security Act 2023, or authorised because there is reasonable cause to believe the material is stolen property.

For this official secrets law, see 33.6.2.1.

So, in that respect this second set offers less protection to journalistic material than the first set does, because the first set has more restrictive access conditions and cannot be used for confidential material.

33.6.1.5 Search warrants under PACE

Instead of asking for a production order, police can under PACE apply to a circuit or district judge for a search warrant to obtain either non-confidential material, or confidential material which could have been seized under a search warrant issued under pre-existing law. A journalist or media organisation does not have to be told of the police application to search their premises and has no right to be heard by the judge before the warrant is executed.

Before granting a search warrant, a judge must be satisfied that either the first or second set of access conditions are satisfied (see earlier), and that at least one of the following circumstances applies:

- it is not practicable to communicate with anyone entitled to grant entry to the premises;
- it is not practicable to communicate with anyone entitled to grant access to the material;
- the material contains information which is subject to an obligation of secrecy or a restriction on disclosure imposed by statute (for example, material subject to the Official Secrets Act), and is likely to be disclosed in breach of that obligation or restriction if a warrant is not issued; or
- giving notice of an application for a production order may seriously prejudice the investigation.

See the case study at 33.6.2.1 below, regarding LXP, for an example of the police using a search warrant to access a journalist's material.

See the **additional material** for this chapter, for a case study on the investigative journalists Barry McCaffrey and Trevor Birney (mentioned at 33.4), who were served with search warrants and had their confidential, journalistic material seized by the Police Service of Northern Ireland in 2018.

33.6.2 Other statutory powers which could reveal the identity of journalists' sources

Various other statutory powers, including others in PACE, could affect journalists, because in specified circumstances they enable the police or another law enforcement agency to search a person's home or work premises, or to place a person under a legal obligation to disclose the source of information they hold, and for them to be punished by a fine or jail term if they disobey. For example, the Information Commissioner has such powers to investigate alleged breach of data protection law—see 34.6.

The National Crime Agency has such powers under the Serious Organised Crime and Police Act 2005. The Financial Conduct Authority has such powers under other law—for example, during an investigation into fraud or financial market 'abuse' in share-dealings.

* Remember

Whatever the laws being used against them, a journalist arguing against such a power being used, or that seized material should be returned unexamined, should cite Article 10 rights.

See the **additional material** for this chapter on **www.mcnaes.com** for more detail of such statutes.

33.6.2.1 National Security Act

Section 23 and Schedule 2 of the National Security Act 2023 (repealing Section 9 of the Official Secrets Act 1911) gives police power to search a person and premises when an offence in that Act or in the Official Secrets Act 1989 (in respect of most of that Act's offences) is reasonably suspected.

In the recent case of *R (on the application of LXP)*, the Metropolitan Police (MPS) were granted, after a 'without notice' application to a judge, warrants pursuant to section 9(1) of the Official Secrets Act 1911 (which remained in force until 20 December 2023). The MPS submitted that there were reasonable grounds to suspect that offences had been committed by LXP (under section 5 of the Official Secrets Act 1989) and by two other individuals,(referred to only as 'X' and 'Y'), under sections 1 and 2 of the 1989 Act, respectively. The hearing was conducted in private, in open and closed session. The MPS application indicated that '[t]he police are aware of their obligations in respect of journalistic source material' but said that '[n]one of the material sought falls within that protection as [LXP], [X] and [Y] are not journalists'. The warrants were executed at LXP's residential address and his work premises and a large quantity of electronic devices and documents belonging to LXP were seized. LXP indicated that some of the material was journalistic, and challenged the seizure of the materials on the basis that he was a journalist and access could only lawfully be sought to journalistic materials under section 9 of the Police and Criminal Evidence Act 1984, by way of a procedure which had regard to journalistic rights under Article 10 of the European Convention on Human Rights and section 10 of the Contempt of Court Act 1981. The MPS disputed that LXP was a journalist and applied for permission to examine the seized materials. Their application was heard at a private hearing. The MPS argued that the seized material could not be 'journalistic' if it was stolen, a submission that the judge agreed with. On that basis, the judge decided that he did not need to conduct any balance of the competing rights and interests under Article 10(1) and (2) and granted the MPS's application. LXP applied for a judicial review of the judge's decision. The High Court concluded that the judge's finding that stolen material was distinct from journalistic material, and therefore was not confidential journalistic material, was erroneous and such material could not be accessed or otherwise examined by the MPS until it had been independently examined by an independent barrister and LXP had had the opportunity to identify those 'materials' which he claimed were 'journalistic'. The case would then go back to the judge to apply the Article 10 balancing exercise on whether to permit inspection by the MPS of journalistic materials (Matrix Chambers website, 16 November 2023; Press Release, Bindmans (solicitors), 10 November 2023; *Press Gazette*, 27 November 2020; *R (on the application of LXP)* [2023] EWHC 2824).

see ch. 32 for this case in relation to official secrets legislation

For more detail of police powers under official secrets law, see the **additional material** for ch. 32 on **www.mcnaes.com**.

33.6.2.2 **Counter-terrorism legislation**

For an investigation into terrorism, the Terrorism Act 2000 enables a court to issue a warrant for police to search premises, or a court to issue an order for a journalist to 'produce' (surrender) research material to police, for a journalist's source to be identified. The 2000 Act's requirements for police seeking such an order are much easier to meet than the requirements imposed by PACE. On 20 December 2023, a revised code of practice, PACE Code B (2023), was introduced which states that if police obtain an order to search a premises under the 2000 Act, or the National Security Act 2023, that does not authorise a constable to retain confidential journalistic material. If confidential journalistic material is seized, a constable seeking to retain it must apply to a Circuit Judge for a warrant, which may impose conditions on its retention and use. The police sought to use the 2000 Act in Suzanne Breen's case—see 33.7. It was also used by West Midlands police in 2022 when they sought a production order against the journalist Chris Mullin, requiring him to disclose material from his investigations into the Birmingham pub bombings in 1974, which featured in his 1986 book, *Error of*

Judgment: The Truth about the Birmingham Bombings. A judge ultimately ruled that while he was satisfied there were 'reasonable grounds for believing' that Mullin's material was 'likely to be of substantial value' to the police, he did not 'find an overriding public interest to displace the journalistic source protection right' (Ruling on TACT production order 22 March 2022).

The **online chapter 40**, 'Terrorism and the effect of counter-terrorism law', on **www.mcnaes.com** includes content on protection of sources.

33.6.2.3 Other routes used to try and access journalistic material

The sole proper procedure for acquiring unpublished journalistic material (e.g. interview notes or undercover footage) for use in criminal proceedings should be an application using the PACE process described above, which has safeguards built into it for journalists. However, journalists may sometimes find themselves contacted by the police in a criminal prosecution referring to their 'third party disclosure obligations' under the Criminal Procedure & Investigations Act 1996 (CPIA) and asking the journalist to produce any relevant material that they may have. However, third parties such as media organisations are not under any duty to provide any such material voluntarily (see *Director of Public Prosecutions v Wood; Director of Public Prosecutions v McGillicuddy* [2006] EWHC 32 (QB)) and the PACE route should always be used.

See also in the **additional material** for this chapter, the reference to the 2018 application made on behalf of the BBC and *The Guardian* resisting a PACE order sought against them by Cheshire Police at the trial of ex-football coach Barry Bennell (*R v Richard Jones (aka Bennell), Liverpool Crown Court* (unreported)).

Journalists may also find themselves summonsed to give evidence in a criminal court and to produce their documents and material, through the service of a witness summons under section 2 of the Criminal Procedure (Attendance of Witnesses) Act 1965 (CPAWA). However, using CPAWA or other similar routes rather than PACE against journalists is inappropriate: a witness summons cannot be used to obtain material for the purposes of disclosure or cross-examination (*R (B) v Derby Mags* [1996] AC 487 (HL), *R v Basra (Wasted Costs)* [1998] P.N.L.R. 535). Note however that the position is different in civil proceedings (see CPR r. 34.4 and the case of *Assistant Deputy Coroner v Channel 4 Television Corporation* [2007] EWHC 2513 (QB); in the **additional material** for this chapter).

Note too that if a journalist is a party to a civil action—for example, they have been sued for defamation or privacy—separate and different disclosure obligations are imposed on them in terms of what material they have to produce.

33.7 Article 2 'right to life' may also be engaged

In some circumstances a journalist resisting a police application for a production order might need to cite their rights in Article 2 of the European Convention on Human Rights, as well as citing Article 10 rights. Article 2 protects the right to life.

Case study

In 2009 a judge accepted that the Article 2 rights of Suzanne Breen, the then Northern Editor of Ireland's *Sunday Tribune* newspaper, meant that she should not be compelled to give police notes and records of a phone call she received from a spokesperson for the Real IRA terrorist group claiming responsibility for two murders. The judge ruled that her life would be at 'real and immediate' risk from the Real IRA were she to be forced to produce the information. She has condemned terrorist violence (*In the matter of an application by D/Inspector Justyn Galloway, PSNI, under paragraph 5 Schedule 5 of the Terrorism Act 2000 and Suzanne Breen* [2009] NICty 4).

33.8 Article 10 in breach of confidence cases

Common law gives judges the power to order disclosure of the identities of wrongdoers (*Norwich Pharmacal Co v Customs and Excise Comrs* [1974] AC 133). The term 'wrongdoer' can include a person who breaches a duty of confidence—for example, owed by an employee to a Government department or a company—by leaking sensitive information gained in that employment to the media.

ch. 26 explains breach of confidence; see 26.5.3 for more detail of the *Goodwin* case

Breach of confidence was the legal basis used against Bill Goodwin of *The Engineer* in the case study referred to in 33.2. In these cases, courts will need to balance the competing rights against each other. Generally, a court order to disclose a source would not be compatible with Article 10 unless it was justified by an overriding requirement in the public interest.

33.9 Practical steps to protect sources

When a source who wants to remain confidential offers information for publication, the journalist should consider the following points:

for context, see 34.2, Guidance for prosecutors on whether a journalist should be prosecuted

- The journalist should only promise the source confidentiality if the nature of the information means publishing the story will be defensible ethically as being in the public interest, as this is the best defence for the journalist to resist an investigation by a law enforcement agency, or a court order, which aims to discover the source's identity; and the best defence to prevent the journalist from being prosecuted for an offence related to leaking of information—for definitions in ethics codes of 'public interest' stories, see chs. 2 and 3.

- Such stories include journalists exposing injustice, crime and politicians or others who mislead the public.
- Staff journalists should generally obtain authority from their editor to promise confidentiality to a source, whenever legal consequences may follow for the media organisation.
- The journalist should alert the source to steps they should take to avoid being identified and warn of the risk of that happening which might already exist, particularly if the method of initial contact—such as a phone call to a newspaper—has created such a risk.
- To avert such risk, journalists should consider providing and publicising an online, secure file-sharing service for sources who want confidentiality to make contact.
- The journalist should double check with the source whether they are fully disguised in any footage or photo to be used in the story, if publication of any such image(s) is agreed, so that it does not betray their identity, and double-check too how the source wants to be described in what is published—see the BBC guidance in Useful Websites at the end of this chapter.
- The journalist should ensure by double-checking with the source that none of the supplied information due to be published will in itself identify them as the source.

If the story being pursued is likely to be sensitive for police, other state agencies or other public bodies, who have the investigatory powers are described in this chapter, or may provoke a claim for breach of confidence or of data protection law, or of intrusion into privacy, these steps should be among the security measures adopted:

- The journalist and source should not email each other.
- If phones have to be used for contact, the journalist and source should each have a pay-as-you-go mobile bought anonymously with no GPS facility.
- These phones should not be used to go online or for anything else apart from calls related to the story, as they might otherwise come to the attention of potential investigators.
- The journalist and source should not carry or take any phone with them when they meet, because all phones produce some geolocation in communications data.
- The journalist and source should keep their pay-as-you-go phones a distance apart from the devices they routinely use, as communications data tracking the movement of their usual devices might match that of the pay-as-you-go phones, which could reveal who is using them.
- The journalist and source should not meet where there are CCTV cameras.
- The journalist should avoid keeping any material which might help identify the source, including any material the source has supplied, on any device or in any place where it may be found.
- If such information has to be stored, it should be kept secure.

- A document or computer file supplied as a leak from within an organisation should be copied by being typed out to create a fresh document or file, and the original then destroyed—otherwise some markings in the original document (see the *Tisdall* case study in the **additional material** for this chapter) or metadata in the original file could lead to the source being identified.
- If the material has to be kept digitally, it should be in an encrypted device—such as a memory stick or external hard drive—which should only be opened using a computer which is not linked to any physical or Wi-Fi network.
- The journalist and the source should consider using a virtual private network in communications or other internet activity, and consider using the Tor browser—see Useful Websites at the end of the chapter.
- Payments to the source should be untraceable.

((•)) see Useful Websites at the end of this chapter for other steps

✱ Remember

If a journalist pays a UK public servant for 'leaked' information, or offers payment, the source is much more likely thereby to have committed the offence of misconduct in public office, and the journalist could be charged with an associated offence—see 34.3. However, payments have led to 'public interest' revelations—for examples, see 34.5.

33.10 Tribunals of inquiry

A journalist who, by refusing to name a source, refuses to cooperate with an inquiry held under the Inquiries Act 2005 could be punished by the High Court for contempt. For more detail, see the **additional material** for ch. 18 on **www.mcnaes.com**.

33.11 Maintaining a reputation for neutrality

Reporters who cover events which lead to prosecutions of those involved or to civil lawsuits may be asked—for example, by the prosecution or defence—to give evidence of what they have seen. Most journalists in this situation will wish to retain their reputation for neutrality and will agree to be a witness only after receiving a **subpoena** (in civil cases) or witness summons (in criminal cases).

→glossary

33.11.1 Photos and footage of disorder

Some police applications to judges for production orders under PACE (see earlier) have been to obtain all photographs taken and all footage shot by the media in coverage of riots or other disorder, much of which may not have been published. Such material could help police make arrests. Although this type of material does not reveal the identity of any sources promised anonymity, there is the principle of the media maintaining neutrality. Most editors and journalists take the view that they should hand over such material only after careful consideration, and generally only after a court order. They argue that if it becomes routine for police to obtain such unpublished material, journalists, photographers and camera operators will be seen as an arm of state surveillance, which could increase the danger that they will be attacked when covering such events. Judges tend to grant such police applications. But a case study of when a judge did not grant one and a separate case of a photojournalist who faced down potential legal action from police to hand over photos of riots in August 2024, are in the **additional material** for this chapter on **www.mcnaes.com**.

In the **additional material** on **www.mcnaes.com** there is a case study of how in 2019 UK media organisations, to avoid journalists being seen as police agents, refused to surrender to the Metropolitan police records of interviews with Shamima Begum who went to Syria to join the ISIS terrorist group.

Recap of major points

- It is an ethical imperative that a journalist does not reveal the identity of a source who has been promised confidentiality.
- The European Court of Human Rights has ruled that a court order compelling a journalist to disclose a source's identity cannot be compatible with Article 10 of the Convention unless the order is justified by an overriding requirement in the public interest.
- This safeguard for journalism in European jurisprudence also applies to use of powers deployed by police and other state agencies when trying to discover who a source is.
- But various laws can allow such agencies to conduct such investigations including by putting journalists and others under surveillance, so journalists should presume that might happen and act accordingly.

Useful Websites

National Union of Journalists, Code of Conduct, www.nuj.org.uk

European Court of Human Rights, 'Factsheet—Protection of journalistic sources', www.echr.coe.int

Investigatory Powers Commissioner's Office, www.ipco.org.uk

Investigatory Powers Tribunal, www.investigatorypowerstribunal.org.uk

Law Commission, Search Warrants project, www.lawcom.gov.uk

2020 report on search warrants, including News Media Association views on the 'iniquity exception' as regards PACE and other laws

Crown Prosecution Service, 'Prosecuting Cases Where Public Servants Have Disclosed Confidential Information to Journalists', www.cps.gov.uk

CEU Democracy Institute, 'Best Practices and Tips for Using Confidential Sources' by Gill Phillips, cmds.ceu.edu

BBC, Editorial Guidelines, Guidance: Anonymity, www.bbc.com

BBC guidance on anonymity for sources and contributors

journalism.co.uk, 'Protecting journalist sources: Lessons in communicating securely' by Sarah Marshall from interview with James Ball

Global Investigative Journalism Network, 'Digital Security', gijn.org

International News Safety Institute, Safety Advisory: 'Staying safe online', newssafety.org

Online resources

Visit the online resources at **www.mcnaes.com** to test your knowledge of this chapter with **self-test questions** and a **flashcard glossary**, and to read **updates** about law and regulatory matters affecting journalism, as well as **additional material** to further your learning.

34

The risks of being charged with other criminal offences

Chapter summary

The way journalists gather information for the purposes of reporting may leave them and their sources at risk of prosecution. A journalist offering or paying money to a source for information may be accused of bribery, or of conspiring with or encouraging that person to commit 'misconduct in public office'. Unauthorised access ('hacking') into a computer, phone voicemail or email system, including to intercept communications, is a criminal offence too. Most of these offences do not contain a public interest defence for anyone using such a method, or encouraging someone else to use it, to gain information. But the Crown Prosecution Service has said in guidance to prosecutors that the public interest should always be considered when deciding whether to prosecute journalists in cases arising from their work. Journalists need to think carefully, when they embark upon 'newsgathering' activities, about whether these might infringe the criminal law. In some cases, journalists and their editors may need to consider whether there is a sufficient public interest to justify the method they are planning on using and get legal advice. Using such methods may also leave them open to being sued in the civil courts for damages for intrusion into someone's privacy.

Additionally, journalists need to think about the language they use when they publish. Making or publishing statements that might be considered to be threatening or incitement could be a crime.

This chapter details a range of risks in criminal law that journalists need to be aware of (see also ch. 32).

34.1 Introduction

In 2011, as part of their reopened investigation into the 'phone-hacking' scandal at the now-defunct *News of the World*, the Metropolitan Police investigated a number of alleged offences against journalists. In 2015, *Press Gazette* reported that at least 67 journalists who had worked or were working for London-based national newspapers had been arrested or charged in connection with alleged offences including hacking into mobile phone messages, hacking into emails and making corrupt payments to police officers and other public servants for information.

The police investigation into allegedly corrupt payments, Operation Elveden, led to 34 journalists being arrested or charged, according to *Press Gazette*. Only three of these journalists were convicted, and all three convictions were overturned on appeal. But 34 non-journalists, including public servants—police officers, prison officers and civil servants—were convicted of offences arising from selling/leaking information to journalists. In the light of the Leveson Inquiry, which followed on from the phone-hacking scandal, the Crown Prosecution Service (CPS) issued guidance on the circumstances when a journalist should be prosecuted. That guidance contains a list of offences 'most likely to be committed' in cases involving journalists. Those offences included bribery, computer misuse, data protection, fraud, misconduct in a public office, official secrets, harassment and theft. The consent of the Director of Public Prosecutions (DPP) or Attorney General is needed before proceedings can be launched for some of these offences. This chapter outlines some of them.

34.2 Guidance for prosecutors on whether a journalist should be prosecuted

The Crown Prosecution Service has published guidance for prosecutors on the factors they should consider when deciding whether journalists—or their sources—should be charged with criminal offences alleged to have been committed in the course of the journalists' work. The guidance, which is titled 'Assessing the Public Interest in Cases Affecting the Media' (see Useful Websites at the end of this chapter), acknowledges that prosecuting journalists might have an impact on the rights of the media and public to freedom of expression and to receive and impart information, both in common law and under Article 10 of the European Convention on Human Rights.

ch. 1 explains Article 10 rights

The guidance points out that it is important at the outset to distinguish between the public interest served by these rights and the separate question of whether a prosecution is in the public interest—for example, the public interest in punishing criminality. The guidance says too that 'neither journalists nor those who interact with them are afforded special status under the criminal law'.

It says that if prosecutors decide that there is sufficient evidence to prosecute, they must—when considering a case affecting the media in which freedom of expression and the rights to receive and impart information are in issue—ask themselves this question: Does the public interest served by the conduct in question outweigh the overall criminality? The guidance says that if the answer is 'yes', it is less likely that a prosecution will be required in the public interest.

Here, 'the conduct in question' is what the journalist did to seek or gain the information and/or what the person who was the source of the information did (if there was such a source) in the dealings with the journalist.

The guidance says this decision on whether to prosecute involves various considerations. The nature of the information gained or sought by the journalist would be

for an example of such a CPS decision, see 34.5 on the *Tubb* case

one. For example, was the 'conduct in question' capable of disclosing information that a crime has been or is likely to be committed by someone?; or that someone has failed or is likely to fail to comply with a legal obligation?; or that a miscarriage of justice has occurred?; or of disclosing information raising or contributing to an important matter of public debate?

The guidance indicates that if the journalist gained or sought information in these categories, the manifest public interest in such information coming to light can outweigh the public interest in a prosecution for alleged criminality in their method(s) to get it, and in any source's role in supplying it.

But the guidance says too that prosecutors also have to consider the overall criminality of that activity—including its effects, the vulnerability of any of its victims and whether the journalist's or source's behaviour was repeated or involved corruption. For example, someone whose private information was leaked to a journalist could be considered a victim.

A journalist considering doing anything which could risk them being prosecuted under law referred to in this chapter should first take legal advice, which for a staff journalist involves also consulting with an editorial executive.

34.2.1 'Audit trails'

For more on the relevance of the codes, see 27.9. For more on audit trails, see 2.6.

The CPS guidance does not mention the codes of media regulators. However, a journalist using a method likely to attract the attention of a law enforcement agency should regard compliance with the relevant code as essential, as it is for all journalism. Evidence of compliance could make it less likely that the CPS will decide the journalist should be prosecuted. Also, compliance makes it less likely that a civil claim for damages—for example, a claim alleging misuse of private information—will be successful.

> See Useful Websites at the end of this chapter for the DPP guidance to prosecutors, which includes the list of offences 'most likely to be committed' in cases involving journalists.

34.3 Misconduct in public office

This is a common law offence dating from the thirteenth century. In recent decades, it has been used to charge public officials accused of disclosing to the media (or others) information which is not specifically protected in legislation such as the data protection law or Official Secrets Acts. Journalists can be prosecuted as an 'accessory' for 'helping' public officials disclose information (see below). The key element of the offence involves the public officer abusing the public's trust in them without reasonable excuse or justification (*Attorney General's Reference No. 3 of 2003* [2004] EWCA Crim 868). Public officials include police and prison officers, civil servants, magistrates, judges, registrars, and council and court officials. The offence can be committed even if no money changes hands.

Case study

In June 2015 at the Old Bailey, Robert Norman, aged 54, a prison officer at top-security Belmarsh prison, was jailed for 20 months after being convicted of misconduct in public office. For five years he had been the paid 'mole' of a reporter who worked for the *Daily Mirror* and *News of the World*. Norman supplied him with information about prison matters including incidents concerning prisoners—some of whom were identified in the newspapers' articles about the incidents. Prison rules forbade Norman from such unauthorised communication with the media. He was secretly paid more than £10,000 by these newspapers for the 40 'tips' of information supplied. The prosecution argued that most of this information was not 'in the public interest' to be disclosed. Norman appealed unsuccessfully to the Court of Appeal against his conviction. It said that what Norman had done caused 'significant public harm' because the corruption of a prison officer on this scale undermined public confidence in the prison service, and his leaks of information were capable of damaging the efficient and effective running of the prison (*R v Norman* [2016] EWCA Crim 1564).

For more on the significance of the *Norman* case, see 33.6.1.3.

See the **additional material** for this chapter on **www.mcnaes.com** for another case study.

The penalties for misconduct in a public office, which is an indictable-only offence, are up to life imprisonment and/or a fine. In practice, this offence has mainly successfully been used against public officials, rather than against journalists, but journalists have been arrested and charged with aiding and abetting or conspiracy.

34.3.1 Plotting or encouraging the misconduct

The associated charge for a journalist would be conspiring to commit the misconduct—for example, an agreement involving the public official and the journalist for information to be supplied, or encouraging or assisting or aiding and abetting the misconduct. There is no public interest defence for media organisations and those working for them. The 'aiding and abetting' offence was the basis for the controversial and discredited prosecution of journalist Sally Murrer in 2008—see 33.4.

The convictions of former *News of the World* crime editor Lucy Panton for conspiring to commit misconduct in public office, and of former *News of the World* and *Sun* journalist Ryan Sabey for aiding and abetting misconduct in public office, were overturned by the Court of Appeal in 2015, on the grounds that the judges at their trials should have told the juries that, in order to convict, they had to be satisfied that the alleged misconduct had sufficiently harmed the public interest (see *R v Chapman and others* [2015] EWCA Crim 539). This Court of Appeal ruling, including about the nature of the 'misconduct' offence, led to cases against another nine journalists being dropped, including the reporter whose 'mole' was Robert Norman (*Press Gazette*, 27 April 2015).

34.4 The Bribery Act 2010

A journalist who pays a source for information might in some circumstances be charged under the Bribery Act 2010. A source could also be charged under the Act if they were accused by another party—for example, an employer—of acting improperly by giving the journalist information. Offences under this Act can be committed by anyone, not just public officials.

By the end of 2025 no journalist had been charged under the Act. But this legislation, and the 'misconduct' cases, have caused media organisations to review procedures about paying or otherwise rewarding sources of information, to avoid breaching these laws. The CPS guidance notes that the Act's offences do not include 'the high threshold that is required for the offence of misconduct in public office'.

34.4.1 The bribery offences

The 2010 Act creates four main offences—bribing someone, accepting a bribe, bribing a foreign public official and failing, as a commercial organisation, to prevent bribery. The Act does not include a public interest defence. The descriptions given here of the offences are summaries.

It is an offence to offer, promise or give a financial or other advantage to induce someone 'improperly to perform a relevant function or activity' or to reward someone for such improper performance, or to do so knowing or believing that accepting the inducement would itself be improper performance.

It is irrelevant whether the person to whom the advantage is offered, promised or given is the same person who performs the function or activity concerned, and it does not matter whether the offer is made directly or through a third party.

Under the Act, the offence of being bribed can occur in each of the following four sets of circumstances, where someone:

- requests, agrees to receive or accepts a financial or other advantage—a bribe—intending that as a result they or someone else will improperly perform a relevant function or activity;
- seeks or accepts a bribe when doing so constitutes improper performance of a relevant function or activity;
- seeks or accepts a bribe as a reward for their own or someone else's improper performance of an activity;
- improperly performs an activity in anticipation of or as a consequence of either themself or someone else having sought or accepted a bribe.

The Act says that it does not matter whether the bribe is accepted directly or through a third party, or whether it is, or is to be, for the benefit of that person or another person.

The Act covers:

- any function of a public nature,
- any activity connected with a business, trade or profession,

- any activity done in the course of employment,
- any activity performed by or on behalf of a body, whether corporate or unincorporated,

as long as a person performing the function or activity is expected to do so in good faith, or impartially, or is in a position of trust by virtue of what they are doing. They are covered by the Act even if they have no connection with the UK or the function or activity is performed outside the UK.

The Act also contains the offence of bribing a foreign public official, committed if the person paying intends to influence the official in their capacity as a public official and also intends to obtain or retain business or an advantage in the conduct of business.

34.4.2 Penalties

The penalties under the Bribery Act are up to six months in prison and/or a fine unlimited by statute for a **summary offence**, and up to 10 years in jail and/or an unlimited fine for an **indictable offence**. →glossary →glossary

34.4.3 Companies failing to prevent bribery

Under the Act, a company—such as a media organisation—is guilty of the offence of failing to prevent bribery if someone associated with it bribes someone with the intention of obtaining or keeping business for the company, or getting or keeping an advantage in the conduct of the company's business.

This is a **strict liability** offence—meaning the prosecution does not have to prove any intention to commit it—but it is a defence for a company to prove that it had adequate procedures in place intended to stop people associated with it from bribing others. The offence is punishable by an unlimited fine. →glossary

The first conviction under the Bribery Act arose because *The Sun*, in the public interest, paid Redbridge magistrates' court office worker Munir Yakub Patel a £500 bribe—which it secretly filmed him accepting. This was done to stand up a story that he was taking bribes to keep details of traffic offences off a court database. This led to Patel, 22, of Green Lane, Dagenham, being jailed (*BBC Online*, 18 November 2011).

See the **additional material** for this chapter on **www.mcnaes.com** for hypothetical case studies on whether a journalist paying for information could be deemed to breach the Bribery Act 2010.

34.5 The Computer Misuse Act 1990

The Computer Misuse Act 1990 created offences to punish unauthorised access to a computer (including to a mobile phone), including offences committed with the intention of getting to any program or information it holds; and the offence of facilitating the commission of a further unauthorised access offence.

Penalties range from six months in prison and/or an unlimited fine on summary conviction, to up to 10 years in prison and/or an unlimited fine if convicted on indictment.

The offences in the Act clearly cover hacking activities, such as hacking or trying to hack into someone's email account. These unauthorised access offences require that the defendant must have known that the intended access was unauthorised—which will generally be the case if a journalist has accessed someone else's emails or phone without their consent. However, the offence may also include getting access without permission to, say a Google document, located on a third party's computer. Journalists should always exercise care before clicking on links to documents they may have been sent by a source.

The Act itself does not contain a public interest defence. Acting in the public interest may help protect journalists from prosecution or conviction under the Act, but not if the probing activity is disproportionate to the 'public interest' aim.

Case study

The Crown Prosecution Service announced in March 2013 that Sky News reporter Gerald Tubb would not be prosecuted for hacking into the email accounts of canoeist John Darwin and his wife Anne in 2008. At that time the couple were under police investigation for making a fraudulent life insurance claim after staging Mr Darwin's 'death by drowning' in 2002. By guessing passwords and security question answers, Mr Tubb accessed (hacked) their email accounts after Sky approved him doing this in his investigations into the case. Sky later handed copies of relevant emails to police. They were used as evidence in the successful prosecutions of the Darwins, who were jailed for the fraud. The CPS said that a prosecution of Mr Tubb for the hacking would not be in the public interest, because the evidence indicated that the public interest served by his conduct outweighed the potential overall criminality, should an offence be proved. Ofcom subsequently cleared Sky of having breached the Broadcasting Code by the hacking. Ofcom said it had concluded that the 'exceptional circumstances of this case outweighed Mr and Mrs Darwin's expectation of privacy', and that Sky's conduct was 'warranted' because the emails were accessed 'with a view to detecting or revealing a serious crime [the Darwins' fraud] in circumstances where there appears to have been a real prospect that the relevant evidence would go unnoticed by investigating authorities'. However, Ofcom criticised Sky for not having formal procedures in place at that time to authorise the hacking (*Ofcom Broadcast Bulletin*, issue 233, 13 July 2013).

ch. 3 explains Ofcom's role, and ch. 4 explains the Code's privacy section

---

34.6 The Data Protection Act 2018

The Data Protection Act 2018, and the associated General Data Protection Regulation created a number of general offences relating to the unauthorised obtaining, procuring or disclosing of personal data. Hacking, and use of hidden cameras, hidden microphones or electronic 'bugs', could breach this criminal law in the Act, and its civil law. Some of the general offences, and defences which could apply to journalists, are mentioned in ch. 28.

The Information Commissioner's Office (ICO)) has wide powers to investigate what personal data is being held, or leaked. To obstruct such an investigation would be another offence. For example, section 148 of the 2018 Act makes it an offence to destroy or otherwise dispose of, or conceal or falsify information when the ICO has given a notice requiring access to it, if the intention is to prevent that access. The ICO can get warrants to search properties.

Case study

As ch. 33 points out, the Commission's powers to investigate data law breaches could be used to try to identify a journalist's source. In July 2021, two days after *The Sun* published footage of then health secretary Matt Hancock kissing an aide in his Westminster office (in breach of social distancing Covid rules), the ICO authorised raids on two premises, saying it was carrying out an investigation into an alleged data breach arising from *The Sun*'s use of leaked CCTV footage. Electronic devices were seized. 'Forensic analysis revealed that the leaked images were most likely obtained by someone recording the CCTV footage screens with a mobile phone,' the statement said. 'Six phones retrieved during the execution of search warrants did not contain the relevant CCTV footage. After taking legal advice, the ICO concluded that there was insufficient evidence to charge anyone with criminal offences under the Data Protection Act 2018.'

(https://www.itv.com/news/2021-07-15/matt-hancock-electronic-devices-seized-following-searches-of-homes-in-relation-to-cctv-footage-leak)

34.7 Law banning 'interception' such as phone-hacking

Those prosecuted because of the police investigation into the *News of the World* phone-hacking scandal faced charges under the Regulation of Investigatory Powers Act 2000, which was then the law banning unauthorised 'interception' of communications. The phone-hacking involved accessing, without consent, private voicemail messages left by and for celebrities and other people in the news. In law, messages stored for later retrieval are classified as still being 'in the course of transmission', thus making hacking into voicemails a type of 'interception'.

see Useful Websites at the end of this chapter for more about that hacking

Private investigator Glenn Mulcaire, who hacked (intercepted) phone messages on behalf of *News of the World* royal correspondent Clive Goodman, admitted five offences under the 2000 Act when the two men were jailed in January 2007. Mulcaire was given a six-month sentence and Goodman received four months. He admitted the Criminal Law Act 1977 offence of conspiracy, relating to the interception of communications without lawful authority. Mulcaire also admitted this.

The scandal erupted again in 2011 when *The Guardian* revealed the huge scale of phone-hacking at the *News of the World* and that it had hacked voicemails on a murdered schoolgirl's phone—which led to the *News of the World*'s closure in June 2011.

In July 2014 former *News of the World* editor Andy Coulson was given an 18-month jail term after being convicted of conspiring to intercept voicemail messages when at the newspaper. He was also former director of communications for Prime Minister David Cameron. Six other former *News of the World* journalists were convicted of phone-hacking.

As this book went to press, there continue to be cases of people suing for civil law breach of privacy claims in 'historical' claims alleging hacking of voicemails or other unlawful gathering of information involving journalists. It has been estimated that News Group Newspapers (NGN), which owned the *News of the World*, has paid out over £1 billion to settle more than 1,300 civil claims since the phone hacking scandal broke. This includes substantial, but undisclosed, settlements with high-profile individuals like Prince Harry and Hugh Grant. NGN gave a 'full and unequivocal apology' to the Duke of Sussex for 'serious intrusion' into his private life from 1996 to 2011 and agreed to pay him 'substantial damages' after admitting private investigators used 'unlawful activities' to obtain 'private information'. In Prince Harry's case against Mirror Group Newspapers in 2023, the court awarded him £140,600 in general and aggravated damages. People who sued have said how devastating it was to suffer newspaper articles airing private matters, and to have wrongly suspected those close to them of leaking to journalists. For an example, see the statement made in 2021 by actress Sienna Miller, in Useful Websites at the end of this chapter. (In agreeing to settle her case NGN made no admission of liability).

In March 2023, seven prominent public figures, including Elton John, Prince Harry and Doreen Lawrence, issued civil legal claims against Associated Newspapers, alleging widespread illegal behaviour by individuals working for the *Daily Mail* and the *Mail on Sunday* between 1993 and 2018. The alleged unlawful acts are said to include:

- hiring private investigators to secretly place listening devices inside cars and homes;
- paying police officials for inside information;
- commissioning individuals to surreptitiously listen into and record people's live, private telephone calls while they were taking place;
- impersonating individuals to obtain medical information from private hospitals, clinics, and treatment centres by deception.

Associated Newspapers have strongly denied all the allegations. The trial lasted 10 weeks and ended in March 2026. No judgment had been delivered by the time of this book's publication.

34.8 The Investigatory Powers Act 2016

The Investigatory Powers Act 2016, as amended by the Investigatory Powers (Amendment) Act 2024, replaced much of the Regulation of Investigatory Powers Act 2000 and is primarily concerned with regulating how public authorities such as the security services, GCHQ, the police and other agencies carry out investigations.

But section 3 of the Act contains the offence of unlawfully intercepting any communication 'in the course of its transmission' through a public or private telecommunication system or public postal service. It therefore bans, for example, phone-hacking or obtaining through interception copies of text or email messages (unless there is 'lawful authority' as defined in the Act). The maximum sentence for the offence is a two-year jail sentence and/or an unlimited fine.

See Chapter 33 for more information on this Act.

34.9 General relevance of regulatory codes

As chs. 2, 3 and 4 explain, the codes used by media regulators aim to protect the privacy of people's communications, and so normally ban interception of them, and the use of covert cameras and covert microphones, including 'bugs', and subterfuge, unless a public interest justification applies.

Case study

In 2020 the *Financial Times* (*FT*) published an apology to *The Independent* news website after it complained that an *FT* reporter had 'without authorisation' joined a Zoom conference meeting held for *Independent* staff and had revealed in an *FT* article 'confidential' information from the meeting. The *FT* said that 'access details had been shared with him', but that he had 'now resigned' from the *FT*. It also apologised to the *Evening Standard* (now *The London Standard*) *The Independent*'s sister publication, which said that the same reporter had accessed a Zoom staff meeting it held. Both meetings were about the financial impact of the coronavirus pandemic on staff employment. *The Independent*'s report of the incidents did not allege breach of the law, but suggested that the *FT* reporter breached the Editors' Code of Practice by using subterfuge to access the 'private' meetings, to 'intercept' and 'eavesdrop' what was said there (*The Independent* and *FT* online, 1 May 2020).

For the relevance of the codes in civil law cases concerning alleged breach of confidence, intrusion into privacy and breach of data protection law, see 26.7, 27.9 and 28.2.8.

34.10 Unauthorised access into online meetings

After the incident involving the *FT* reporter, lawyers said that a person who accesses a private meeting held 'virtually' online—such as in Zoom or Microsoft Teams software—and does this without the permission of its organiser, may be committing an offence under the Computer Misuse Act 1990, or Data Protection Act 2018, or the Investigatory Powers Act 2016 (as regards interception of communications), and that such an access is likely to constitute a breach of the civil law as regards data protection, misuse of private information and breach of confidence. However, it was said that whether any law was broken would depend on the terms on which the meeting was set up, the means by which people accessed the log-ins, and whether any public interest justification applied (*Byline Investigates* website, 28 April 2020; *The Guardian* website, 1 May 2020; *Press Gazette*, 1 May 2020).

34.11 Recording phone calls

Journalists frequently record the calls they themselves make or receive. In law, interception occurs in the course of transmission, so recording a conversation by using a device at either end of the communication is not interception. Therefore, in the UK there is not a breach of the criminal law if, for example, the recording of a telephone call is done by the person making or receiving the call, even if the other person talking in it is unaware of the recording (but check the law of the relevant nation before doing this abroad). For content in regulatory codes which pertains to recording phone calls, see 2.4.4.2, Recording interviews and phone calls, and 3.4.13, Secret filming and recording—deception and privacy.

34.12 The Wireless Telegraphy Act 2006

Under section 48 of the Wireless Telegraphy Act 2006 a person commits an offence if without lawful authority they use wireless (radio) apparatus with intent to obtain information about the contents, sender or addressee of any message (whether sent by wireless telegraphy or not), or disclose such information. This law, which covers such illegal use of 'bugs' (hidden, radio devices which eavesdrop on people unaware of them), could be used if the Investigatory Powers Act does not apply.

34.13 The Serious Crime Act 2007

Sections 44–46 of the Serious Crime Act 2007 make it an offence intentionally to encourage or assist an offence, or to do so believing the offence will be committed, or to do so believing that offence or another will be committed.

The penalty for each offence is any penalty the offender would be liable to face if they were convicted of the anticipated offence. These 2007 Act offences would cover, for example, the position of a journalist or editor who commissions a private investigator or someone else to hack into someone's emails.

34.14 Incitement and other criminal speech offences journalists need to be aware of

UK law imposes some criminal liability limiting freedom of expression on the publication of certain 'extreme' material by people. This is mainly around what is generically known as 'hate speech'. The CPS states that the term 'hate crime' may be used to describe a range of criminal behaviour where the perpetrator is 'motivated by hostility or demonstrates hostility towards the victim's disability, race, religion, sexual orientation or transgender identity'. Ofcom defines it as: 'All forms of expression which spread, incite, promote or justify hatred based on intolerance on the grounds of disability, ethnicity, social origin, gender, sex, gender reassignment, nationality, race, religion or belief, sexual orientation, colour, genetic features, language, political or any other opinion, membership of a national minority, property, birth or age.' As the CPS explains, a hate crime can include threats, verbal abuse and harassment. It is important to note here that expressing opinions that may offend or shock will generally not amount to 'hate speech'. When looking at when expression may amount to a criminal offence, it is important to look at the context, the speaker, the intent, the content and tone, the extent of the speech, and the likelihood/imminence of harm. See the **Additional Material** for this chapter about the case of *Paul Chambers*.

The key offences in this area include a number of offences created by the Online Safety Act 2023, which repealed some provisions of the Malicious Communications Act 1988 and the Communications Act 2003, dealing with false messages, and threatening communications. The MCA 1988 and CA 2003 continue to encompass 'grossly offensive' and 'indecent' messages. The CA 2003 also encompasses messages which are obscene or menacing.

The OSA 2023 introduced a series of new communications offences which came into force from 31 January 2024, including:

- a false communications offence (Section 179 OSA 2023);
- a threatening communications offence (Section 181 OSA 2023);
- an offence of sending/showing flashing images electronically (sometimes known as epilepsy trolling) (Section 183 OSA 2023); and
- an offence of encouraging or assisting serious self-harm (Section 184 OSA 2023).

While these laws are mainly used against social media posters, they can also apply to journalists, so journalists need to think about the language they use when they publish. That may include, for example, when reporting on the statements made by others. (see for example the reporting in August 2025 of the mass protests against the proscription of Palestine Action). This is an area where all the main UK regulatory codes (see chs., 2 and 3) reinforce, and in some instances go further than, the general law—for example, all contain provisions to the effect that the media should avoid the use of 'prejudicial, pejorative or derogatory' references to anybody based on the sort of characteristics that could put the person at risk of discrimination.

Part 3 of the Public Order Act 1986 as amended contains a series of criminal offences involving acts—including words or behaviour, or the display of written material—intended or likely 'having regard to the circumstances' to stir up hatred against people because of their race or religious beliefs or their sexual orientation. Such offences can be committed in speech, or in printed, broadcast or online material. In October 2024, a woman, Lucy Connolly, was given a 31-month prison sentence after pleading guilty to a charge under Section 19 of the Public Order Act 1986, of stirring up racial hatred. She had posted a message on X, on the day three girls were stabbed to death in Southport, which called for 'mass deportation now' and urged her followers on X to 'set fire' to hotels housing asylum seekers. Connolly added: 'If that makes me racist, so be it.' At the time she had about 9,000 followers on X. Her message was reposted 940 times and viewed 310,000 times, before she deleted it three and a half hours later. Generally, it will be necessary to prove intent, which will provide a defence to journalists republishing extremist views. Other legislation covers 'credible' threats of violence to a person or damage to property and threats to kill (see online ch. 39 for fuller details).

Trespass is usually a private civil matter, but in certain situations can give rise to criminal liability (see 35.3).

Terrorism and counter-terrorism offences and other laws that protect national security are not especially aimed at journalists, but the wide terms in which some offences are framed and applied may catch out journalists. Journalists can be associated with terrorist groups that they report on, and sometimes counter- terrorism offences are so vague and broadly drafted that they encompass legitimate reporting activities. (see online ch. 40).

✱ Remember

If a journalist is under official investigation for any alleged offence, they or anyone else who attempts to thwart the investigation—for example, by falsifying, concealing or destroying evidence or potential evidence, such as emails, records or files—could be jailed for the common law offence of perverting the course of justice. Police who reopened inquiries into allegations of widespread phone-hacking by *News of the World* journalists arrested a number of people in connection with allegations of perverting the course of justice in relation to that investigation.

For defences in the Digital Economy Act 2017 for journalists who receive leaked information from Government departments, see the **additional material** for this chapter on **www.mcnaes.com**. Ch. 4 deals with the risk of journalists being charged with harassment. The risk of journalists being charged under counter-terrorism law is discussed in the **www.mcnaes.com** online ch. 40, 'Terrorism and the effect of counter-terrorism law'.

Recap of major points

- News-gathering activities may leave journalists at risk of being charged with criminal offences such as conspiracy to commit misconduct in public office or with bribery.
- Public officials—police, prison officers and others—who sell information to the media may face criminal prosecution for misconduct in public office.
- Hacking into computers, emails and voicemail messages is normally a criminal offence.
- The Director of Public Prosecutions has issued guidance saying that public interest factors must be considered before journalists are prosecuted in connection with news-gathering activities.

Useful Websites

Crown Prosecution Service (CPS), www.cps.gov.uk

- Guidelines for prosecutors assessing whether journalists should be charged: 'Assessing the Public Interest in Cases Affecting the Media'. The list of offences most likely to be concerned in such cases appears in Annex A to the document
- CPS guidance: 'Prosecuting cases where public servants have disclosed confidential information to journalists'
- 'Bribery Act 2010: Joint Prosecution Guidance of The Director of the Serious Fraud Office and The Director of Public Prosecutions'

The Guardian, 'News of the World: 10 years since phone-hacking scandal brought down tabloid', www.theguardian.com

The Guardian article on the phone-hacking scandal, including about how the hacking was done

BBC News, 'Sienna Miller says Sun illegally sought medical records of pregnancy', www.bbc.co.uk

BBC report of Sienna Miller's statement after her case was settled

Online resources

Visit the online resources at **www.mcnaes.com** to test your knowledge of this chapter with **self-test questions** and a **flashcard glossary**, and to read **updates** about law and regulatory matters affecting journalism, as well as **additional material** to further your learning.

35

The right to take photographs, film and record

Chapter summary

Journalists should know their rights when gathering visual images or making recordings in the streets or countryside. Generally speaking, there is no specific criminal law restricting photography, filming or recording in public places (but journalists need to be aware of what the ethical codes say, as well as of the impact of civil laws such as privacy and data protection). Further, 'public' property may not always be as public as it seems—most land in the UK is owned by someone, even if it appears to be publicly accessible. Highways are usually land which the public at large have the absolute right to use to 'pass and repass' without hindrance, where the relevant highway or local authority will have obligations to maintain at the public's expense. Some public places have by-laws which impact on commercial and professional photography in those spaces—for example, Parliament Square and Trafalgar Square.

Over-zealous police officers, security guards and members of the public often try and raise objections to journalists using cameras or recording devices. There are some aspects of the criminal law that may, however, be deployed against journalists in public spaces—such as obstructing the police or the highway and public nuisance offences. This chapter covers laws which are sometimes officiously cited or used against journalists in public spaces. Separately, some apparently public spaces have been designated as restricted access areas—for example, areas around the royal palaces and parliament, and it can be an offence to access such spaces without permission. Further, the civil law of trespass applies to private land and events.

see too ch. 32 on National Security and official secrets

35.1 Introduction

Many police officers and members of the public help the media. But some do not and become officious or hostile to journalists going about their lawful business. In tense situations, journalists may find laws being invalidly used or cited against them. Official guidance for police reflects the law—that officers have no power to prohibit the taking of photographs, film or digital images in a public place, whether the shots are of crowds, bystanders or buildings.

Controversially, urban development has meant some apparently 'public' spaces—for example, shopping mall thoroughfares—are now private property, not public highways. Security staff may intervene unless journalists get permission to take pictures, film, or record there. The civil law of trespass will be deployed here to prevent access.

35.2 Trouble with the police in public places

A photographer, radio reporter, video-journalist or film crew must get in close for their pictures and/or sound. They may be attacked by disorderly people and—even during a small-scale event—be arrested by police as tension rises. This can be particularly tricky when journalists and photographers are covering public protests.

Case study

In November 2022, Rich Felgate, a documentary maker, Tom Bowles and Ben Cawthra, both photographers, and Charlotte Lynch, a reporter for LBC, were arrested by Hertfordshire police as they covered Just Stop Oil protests on the M25. All were on a public footpath on a bridge overlooking the motorway. Bowles later said on Twitter that officers turned up at his home at 11pm before he had returned home, waking his wife and daughter and searching the property. Writing on Twitter, Felgate said the police had 'no interest in seeing press ID and handcuffed us instantly'. Felgate said he and Bowles were held in custody for 13 hours and questioned by police who tried to get him to 'reveal my journalistic sources and give them the pin to my phone'. Cawthra was arrested and detained for 16 hours on suspicion of conspiracy to cause a public nuisance. Lynch was also arrested on suspicion of conspiracy to commit public nuisance and was handcuffed and placed in a cell. All were ultimately released without further action and all later received public apologies from the police. A review by Cambridgeshire police of Lynch's arrest concluded that her arrest 'was not justified and that changes in training and command need to be made'. After Cawthra began legal action, Hertfordshire constabulary admitted their officers acted unlawfully by arresting him and violated his right to free speech, and the force accepted liability for false imprisonment over his detention.

In July 2023, police were given more powers to police protests. The changes, contained in the Public Order Act 2023, do however include some protections for journalists who are 'observing or reporting on a protest', or on the 'exercise of police power' in relation to a protest. In October 2023, it was announced that, as part of the UK Government's National Action Plan for the Safety of Journalists, police were to receive specific training to teach them how journalists are allowed to operate.

In October 2025, the government announced that every police force in the UK should have a Journalist Safety Liaison Officer as a direct point of contact if issues arise while they are doing their jobs.

Remember that individuals may still object to having their photo taken even if it is in a public space and that children and vulnerable adults may be entitled to expect a higher level of protection (See ch. 4 on unjustified intrusion and chs. 27 and 28 on privacy and data protection.)

((•)) see Useful Websites at the end of this chapter for this guidance

35.2.1 Police guidelines on media photography and filming

Journalists having problems at an incident or crime scene should refer police to guidance issued by the College of Policing. Its section on 'Engagement and communication—media relations' includes the following:

- Reporting or filming from the scene of an incident is part of the media's role and they should not be prevented from doing so from a public place.
- Police have no power or moral responsibility to stop the filming or photographing of incidents or police personnel. It is for the media to determine what is published or broadcast, not the police.
- Once an image has been recorded, police have no power to seize equipment, or delete or confiscate images or footage without a court order.
- Where police have designated a cordoned area, the media must respect it in the same way as the public, unless officers have authorised a media facility within a cordoned area.
- The best possible vantage point for media should be considered, providing it does not compromise operational needs.

The College's guidance to police on 'Public order—communication' includes these points:

((•)) for the UK Press Card accreditation scheme, see Useful Websites at the end of this chapter

- Production of a UK Press Card should allow the holder release from any area subject to containment, unless the holder's behaviour is cause for concern.
- Police cannot give or deny the media permission to enter private premises, regardless of whether the premises are directly involved in a police operation—the person who owns or controls the property makes that decision.
- If someone who is distressed or bereaved asks police to intervene to prevent members of the media filming or photographing them, officers may pass on their request, but have no power to prevent or restrict media activity.

! Remember your rights

Police who want to view or seize journalistic material such as photographs or notes must first get a court order under the Police and Criminal Evidence Act 1984, as explained in ch. 33. If a person is searched by police because of a reasonable suspicion of a terrorism offence, they can seize a camera for its images to be inspected—see 35.2.5, 'Stop and search' under the Terrorism Act 2000.

35.2.2 Designated and protected sites

It is a criminal offence to trespass on a protected site designated under the Serious Organised Crime and Police Act 2005. A protected site means either a licensed nuclear site or a designated site. See the **additional material** for this chapter, for a more detailed list of protected and designated sites, which will include Crown land, a number of the royal palaces, as well as some Government offices and nuclear sites.

35.2.3 False imprisonment

for context, see 5.3.2, False imprisonment

A journalist who is subject to unlawful physical restraint—such as being locked in the cells or physically restrained by a police officer—might be able to sue for false imprisonment.

Movement must be completely restricted; barring a photographer from going in one particular direction—for example, towards the scene of a crash—is not false imprisonment.

35.2.4 Public order and 'obstruction' offences

Police officers sometimes warn media photographers or video-journalists that they may be arrested.

The arrest might be for a **common law** breach of the peace or under section 5 of the Public Order Act 1986. Arrest for breach of the peace is only justified if harm has been done or is likely to be done to a person or their property in their presence, or when a person is put in fear of being harmed. Section 5 allows arrest if anyone uses threatening or abusive words or behaviour, or disorderly behaviour, likely to cause 'harassment, alarm or distress' to another person. Though the journalist is not intending to cause distress, etc., in some situations the mere fact that they are taking pictures or shooting footage, perhaps of someone or a group who object to this, may prompt an arrest.

→glossary

see Useful Websites at the end of this chapter for further guidance on public order offences

Section 137 of the Highways Act 1980 makes it an offence for someone 'without lawful authority or excuse' to obstruct free passage along a highway in any way. This power allows police to arrest journalists in a public place who fail to move on when asked to do so.

Section 89 of the Police Act 1996 says that a person commits an offence if they 'resist or wilfully obstruct a constable in the execution of his duty, or a person assisting a constable in the execution of his duty'. The obstruction does not have to be a physical act—it may occur, for example, if someone makes it more difficult for the constable to perform their duty. A journalist who persists in taking photographs or shooting footage, and engages in argument with a police officer, therefore runs the risk of arrest.

> For case studies of photographers being paid compensation or acquitted after arrest, see the **additional material** for this chapter on **www.mcnaes.com**. For the police's general powers of arrest, see 5.2.

35.2.5 'Stop and search' under the Terrorism Act 2000

Complaints by photographers of excessive use by police of 'stop and search' powers under the Terrorism Act 2000—for example, stopping and searching a journalist who was taking a picture of a building—have decreased since the Government amended the law to produce a more tightly defined 'stop and search' power in the Act's section 47A. This change was primarily concerned with the criteria which police can use to designate areas as being at risk of terrorist attack. Police in such areas are still permitted to stop and search an individual, and seize equipment, without 'reasonable suspicion'. Outside such areas police must, under section 43 of the Act, 'reasonably suspect' someone is a terrorist before as a counter-terrorism measure they can lawfully stop and search, and seize equipment from, that person. Section 43 does allow officers to view digital images contained in mobile phones or cameras but there is no power, for example, to delete such images. Deletion or destruction may only take place following seizure if there is a lawful power (such as a court order) that permits such deletion or destruction.

A revised code of practice issued to police makes clear that:

- they have no power under the 2000 Act to stop anyone filming or photographing incidents or police officers;
- it is not an offence to film/photograph a public building or in public places;
- a permit is not needed to film/photograph in public places.

Case study

In 2017 freelance photographer Eddie Mitchell was arrested outside Hove Town Hall council offices and searched by police, including by inspecting images in his camera. The police told him they were using powers in section 43 of the Terrorism Act 2000. He was allowed to leave after they accepted he was not doing anything illegal. A Sussex police spokesperson said the action was appropriate in that the 'threat level' of terrorist attacks was high (*MailOnline* and *The Guardian*, 4 May 2017).

See Useful Websites at the end of this chapter for the code of practice in full. See the **www.mcnaes.com** online ch. 40, 'Terrorism and the effect of counter-terrorism law', for other counter-terrorism laws which could affect journalists.

35.3 Trespass and bye-laws

If you are on private land and the owner asks you to leave, failure to do so will be classed as trespass. Property owners who object to photography or filming or recording on their sites may decide to enforce objections by using the civil law of trespass, which forbids unlawful entry to land or buildings. Because trespass is a **tort**, the

→glossary

remedy is an action in the civil courts which could result in an injunction to prevent further trespass, and/or an award of damages. Also, the occupier of property or land may use reasonable force to eject the trespasser. Police may lawfully assist, though they have no duty to do so.

for context see ch. 4 on news-gathering avoiding intrusion and ch. 27 on privacy

There is no trespass if, as regards an event on private land, a journalist photographs, films or records it from an adjoining site where they have permission or a right to be—for example, a public highway. But such media activity might lead to a subject suing for intrusion into privacy, or complaining to Ipso, Impress or Ofcom.

Trespass can also include 'trespass to the person'—for example, compelling a person to be filmed by stopping them from entering their home or workplace. 'Trespass to goods' means, for instance, picking up a document without permission and photographing it.

Trespass is not usually a criminal offence, so a police officer threatening an arrest for civil trespass is wrong in law. However, there is a specific offence of aggravated trespass.

ch. 32 explains law which could punish photography or filming of 'prohibited places'

There are trespass offences for certain sites—for example, Ministry of Defence (MoD) land, rail tracks and railway property. A journalist who wants to take photos or footage in a tube or rail station or on a bus generally needs permission—see Useful Websites at the end of this chapter. Also, bye-laws ban photography in and around MoD establishments.

> For details of the criminal offence of aggravated trespass, which has been used to prosecute protesters in 'occupations' and could be used against photographers there, see the **additional material** for this chapter on **www.mcnaes.com**.

Chapter 4 covers what regulatory codes say about intrusive photography, filming and recording, including when a child is the subject, and about intrusion into grief and harassment. The chapter warns that paparazzi who stalk people could be sued or prosecuted for harassment. Ch. 12 explains the ban on photography and filming in courts and their precincts.

Recap of major points

- There is no law against photography, filming or recording in public places.
- But journalists need to be familiar with the law on trespass and the general powers police have to arrest those 'obstructing' them or the highway.
- Police have been issued with guidelines saying they should help the media take photos and gain footage, but individual officers may need reminding of these.

Useful Websites

College of Policing, Media Relations[1], www.app.college.police.uk/app-content/engagement-and-communication/media-relations

Metropolitan Police, 'Photography advice', www.met.police.uk

Liberty, Explainer: Monitoring & reporting on protests, www.libertyhumanrights.org.uk

The UK Press Card Authority, presscards.co.uk

UK Press Card accreditation scheme

Gov.uk, Policy paper, Police stop and search powers: code of practice

Revised code of practice for police 'stop and search' powers under the Terrorism Act 2000 and Police, Crime, Sentencing and Courts Act 2022

Crown Prosecution Service, www.cps.gov.uk

- Guidance on 'Trespass and Nuisance on Land'
- Guidance on 'Transport Offences'

Greater London Authority, 'Pre-Authorisation Scheme for filming and photography undertaken on Trafalgar Square and Parliament Square Garden by the Professional News Media', www.london.gov.uk

Network Rail, 'Guidelines for taking photos at stations', www.networkrail.co.uk

National Union of Journalists London Freelance, 'Advice for photographers covering demonstrations', www.londonfreelance.org

Editorial Photographers of United Kingdom and Ireland, Resources section, www.epuk.org

Online resources

Visit the online resources at **www.mcnaes.com** to test your knowledge of this chapter with **self-test questions** and a **flashcard glossary**, and to read **updates** about law and regulatory matters affecting journalism, as well as **additional material** to further your learning.

[1] At the time of publication, the College of Policing were consulting on updating this guidance

Part 6

Online chapters

36

Other UK jurisdictions

Chapter summary

Media law in Northern Ireland and Scotland is, including in defamation law, broadly the same as that in England and Wales but care needs to be taken as there are some specific individual differences, especially around reporting restrictions in both jurisdictions. For example, media organisations based in other parts of the UK may need to pay special consideration to what they publish in Scotland, because contempt laws there are often interpreted differently. The Scottish legal system also operates and uses quite different terminology from England and Wales. This chapter will outline the key differences.

Chapter 36 is available online at **www.mcnaes.com**.

37

The Freedom of Information Act 2000

Chapter summary

The Freedom of Information (FoI) Act 2000 created the UK's first general right of access to information held by Government departments and public authorities. Use of this right has produced many exclusive stories, some about the highest reaches of Government. But FoI is bedevilled by bureaucratic delay and wide-ranging exemptions. This chapter deals with FoI law as it applies in England, Wales and Northern Ireland, and information access rights in the Environmental Information Regulations 2004.

Chapter 37 is available online at **www.mcnaes.com**.

38

Other information rights and access to meetings

Chapter summary

The public and journalists have rights to information under various laws, most notably about the workings of local government. These rights can be used to obtain policy documents from public bodies and ensure journalists can report important meetings. For some types of material the laws are better than the Freedom of Information Act 2000 (see online ch. 37), as they offer quicker rights to obtain copies of or inspect documents.

Chapter 38 is available online at **www.mcnaes.com**.

39

Boundaries to expression—hate and obscenity

Chapter summary

Freedom of expression has boundaries. One boundary is that making or publishing some kinds of threatening statement is a crime. As this chapter explains, it is illegal to stir up hatred against people because of their race, religious beliefs or sexual orientation. Such offences can be committed in speech, or in printed, broadcast or online material. This chapter also briefly examines law banning publication of obscene material.

Chapter 39 is available online at **www.mcnaes.com**.

40

Terrorism and the effect of counter-terrorism law

Chapter summary

The heightened threat of terrorism in recent years has led to more counter-terrorism laws in the UK, some controversial because of their actual or potential interference with journalists' work. These laws ban the gathering of certain information and restrict what can be published. As this chapter shows, the wide scope of counter-terrorism law has the potential to deter journalistic investigation of the causes and control of terrorism. Journalists who interview people who have joined terrorist groups—for example, the so-called Islamic State—should be aware that a court may order that the interview records and these sources' identities must be disclosed to the police.

Chapter 40 is available online at **www.mcnaes.com**.

41

Strategic lawsuits against public participation

Chapter summary

Strategic lawsuits against public participation (SLAPPs) are legal actions typically brought by corporations or individuals with the intention of harassing, intimidating and financially or psychologically exhausting opponents and so silencing criticism, via the improper use of the legal system. SLAPPs often target financially weak defendants such as individual investigative journalists and writers. They are typically brought by wealthy individuals or corporations. According to the UK Government, 'at their heart, SLAPPs fundamentally undermine freedom of speech and the rule of law'.

SLAPPs present a growing problem in both the UK and more widely as claimants explore new ways to suppress legitimate reporting. While SLAPPs are often framed as defamation cases, they can occur across a broad spectrum of legal actions, including actions for privacy, data protection and copyright. In 2023, the UK Government passed the Economic Crime and Corporate Transparency Act which contains for the first time, anti-SLAPP legislation, albeit only in the specific context of economic crime. Section 195 contains a definition of what amounts to a SLAPP. This chapter examines the issues around SLAPPs.

Chapter 41 is available online at **www.mcnaes.com**.

Appendix 1
The Editors' Code of Practice

The Independent Press Standards Organisation (IPSO), as regulator, is charged with enforcing the following Code of Practice, which was framed by the Editors' Code of Practice Committee and is enshrined in the contractual agreement between IPSO and newspaper, magazine and electronic news publishers. This version of the Editors' Code came into effect on 1 January 2025.

The Code

The Code—including this preamble and the public interest exceptions below—sets the framework for the highest professional standards that members of the press subscribing to the Independent Press Standards Organisation have undertaken to maintain. It is the cornerstone of the system of voluntary self-regulation to which they have made a binding contractual commitment. It balances both the rights of the individual and the public's right to know.

To achieve that balance, it is essential that an agreed Code be honoured not only to the letter but in the full spirit. It should be interpreted neither so narrowly as to compromise its commitment to respect the rights of the individual nor so broadly that it infringes the fundamental right to freedom of expression—such as to inform, to be partisan, to challenge, shock, be satirical and to entertain—or prevents publication in the public interest.

It is the responsibility of editors and publishers to apply the Code to editorial material in both printed and online versions of their publications. They should take care to ensure it is observed rigorously by all editorial staff and external contributors, including non-journalists.

Editors must maintain in-house procedures to resolve complaints swiftly and, where required to do so, co-operate with IPSO. A publication subject to an adverse adjudication must publish it in full and with due prominence, as required by IPSO.

1. Accuracy

i) The Press must take care not to publish inaccurate, misleading or distorted information or images, including headlines not supported by the text.

ii) A significant inaccuracy, misleading statement or distortion must be corrected, promptly and with due prominence, and—where appropriate—an apology published. In cases involving IPSO, due prominence should be as required by the regulator.

iii) A fair opportunity to reply to significant inaccuracies should be given, when reasonably called for.

iv) The Press, while free to editorialise and campaign, must distinguish clearly between comment, conjecture and fact.

v) A publication must report fairly and accurately the outcome of an action for defamation to which it has been a party, unless an agreed settlement states otherwise, or an agreed statement is published.

2. *Privacy

i) Everyone is entitled to respect for their private and family life, home, physical and mental health, and correspondence, including digital communications.

ii) Editors will be expected to justify intrusions into any individual's private life without consent. In considering an individual's reasonable expectation of privacy, account will be taken of the complainant's own public disclosures of information and the extent to which the material complained about is already in the public domain or will become so.

iii) It is unacceptable to photograph individuals, without their consent, in public or private places where there is a reasonable expectation of privacy.

3. *Harassment

i) Journalists must not engage in intimidation, harassment or persistent pursuit.

ii) They must not persist in questioning, telephoning, pursuing or photographing individuals once asked to desist; nor remain on property when asked to leave and must not follow them. If requested, they must identify themselves and whom they represent.

iii) Editors must ensure these principles are observed by those working for them and take care not to use non-compliant material from other sources.

4. Intrusion into grief or shock

In cases involving personal grief or shock, enquiries and approaches must be made with sympathy and discretion and publication handled sensitively. These provisions should not restrict the right to report legal proceedings.

5. *Reporting suicide

When reporting suicide, to prevent simulative acts care should be taken to avoid excessive detail of the method used, while taking into account the media's right to report legal proceedings.

6. *Children

i) All pupils should be free to complete their time at school without unnecessary intrusion.

ii) They must not be approached or photographed at school without permission of the school authorities.

iii) Children under 16 must not be interviewed or photographed on issues involving their own or another child's welfare unless an adult with legal parental responsibility or similarly responsible adult consents.

iv) Children under 16 must not be paid for material involving their welfare, nor parents or guardians for material about their children or wards, unless it is clearly in the child's interest.

v) Editors must not use the fame, notoriety or position of a parent or guardian as sole justification for publishing details of a child's private life.

7. *Children in sex cases

1. The press must not, even if legally free to do so, identify children under 16 who are victims or witnesses in cases involving sex offences.
2. In any press report of a case involving a sexual offence against a child—
   i) The child must not be identified.
   ii) The adult may be identified.
   iii) The word 'incest' must not be used where a child victim might be identified.
   iv) Care must be taken that nothing in the report implies the relationship between the accused and the child.

8. *Hospitals

i) Journalists must identify themselves and obtain permission from a responsible executive before entering non-public areas of hospitals or similar institutions to pursue enquiries.

ii) The restrictions on intruding into privacy are particularly relevant to enquiries about individuals in hospitals or similar institutions.

9. *Reporting of Crime

i) Relatives or friends of persons convicted or accused of crime should not generally be identified without their consent, unless they are genuinely relevant to the story.

ii) Particular regard should be paid to the potentially vulnerable position of children under the age of 18 who witness, or are victims of, crime. This should not restrict the right to report legal proceedings.

iii) Editors should generally avoid naming children under the age of 18 after arrest for a criminal offence but before they appear in a youth court unless they can show that the individual's name is already in the public domain, or that the individual (or, if they are under 16, a custodial parent or similarly responsible adult) has given their consent. This does not restrict the right to name juveniles who appear in a crown court, or whose anonymity is lifted.

10. *Clandestine devices and subterfuge

i) The press must not seek to obtain or publish material acquired by using hidden cameras or clandestine listening devices; or by intercepting private or mobile telephone calls, messages or emails; or by the unauthorised removal of documents or photographs; or by accessing digitally held information without consent.

ii) Engaging in misrepresentation or subterfuge, including by agents or intermediaries, can generally be justified only in the public interest and then only when the material cannot be obtained by other means.

11. Victims of sexual assault

The press must not identify or publish material likely to lead to the identification of a victim of sexual assault unless there is adequate justification and they are legally free to do so. Journalists are entitled to make enquiries but must take care and exercise discretion to avoid the unjustified disclosure of the identity of a victim of sexual assault.

12. Discrimination

i) The press must avoid prejudicial or pejorative reference to an individual's race, colour, religion, sex, gender identity, sexual orientation or to any physical or mental illness or disability.

ii) Details of an individual's race, colour, religion, gender identity, sexual orientation, physical or mental illness or disability must be avoided unless genuinely relevant to the story.

13. Financial journalism

i) Even where the law does not prohibit it, journalists must not use for their own profit financial information they receive in advance of its general publication, nor should they pass such information to others.

ii) They must not write about shares or securities in whose performance they know that they or their close families have a significant financial interest without disclosing the interest to the editor or financial editor.

iii) They must not buy or sell, either directly or through nominees or agents, shares or securities about which they have written recently or about which they intend to write in the near future.

14. Confidential sources

Journalists have a moral obligation to protect confidential sources of information.

15. Witness payments in criminal trials

i) No payment or offer of payment to a witness—or any person who may reasonably be expected to be called as a witness—should be made in any case once proceedings are active as defined by the Contempt of Court Act 1981. This prohibition lasts until the suspect has been freed unconditionally by police without charge or bail or the proceedings are otherwise discontinued; or has entered a guilty plea to the court; or, in the event of a not guilty plea, the court has announced its verdict.

ii) *Where proceedings are not yet active but are likely and foreseeable, editors must not make or offer payment to any person who may reasonably be expected to be called as a witness, unless the information concerned ought demonstrably to be published in the public interest and there is an over-riding need to make or promise payment for this to be done; and all reasonable steps have been taken to ensure no financial dealings influence the evidence those witnesses give. In no circumstances should such payment be conditional on the outcome of a trial.

iii) *Any payment or offer of payment made to a person later cited to give evidence in proceedings must be disclosed to the prosecution and defence. The witness must be advised of this requirement.

16. *Payment to criminals

i) Payment or offers of payment for stories, pictures or information, which seek to exploit a particular crime or to glorify or glamorise crime in general, must not be made directly or via agents to convicted or confessed criminals or to their associates—who may include family, friends and colleagues.

ii) Editors invoking the public interest to justify payment or offers would need to demonstrate that there was good reason to believe the public interest would be served. If, despite payment, no public interest emerged, then the material should not be published.

The public interest

There may be exceptions to the clauses marked * where they can be demonstrated to be in the public interest.

1. The public interest includes, but is not confined to:

    i) Detecting or exposing crime, or the threat of crime, or serious impropriety.

    ii) Protecting public health or safety.

  iii) Protecting the public from being misled by an action or statement of an individual or organisation.
  iv) Disclosing a person or organisation's failure or likely failure to comply with any obligation to which they are subject.
  v) Disclosing a miscarriage of justice.
  vi) Raising or contributing to a matter of public debate, including serious cases of impropriety, unethical conduct or incompetence concerning the public.
  vii) Disclosing concealment, or likely concealment, of any of the above.

2. There is a public interest in freedom of expression itself.
3. The regulator will consider the extent to which material is already in the public domain or will become so.
4. Editors invoking the public interest will need to demonstrate that they reasonably believed publication—or journalistic activity taken with a view to publication—would both serve, and be proportionate to, the public interest and explain how they reached that decision at the time.
5. An exceptional public interest would need to be demonstrated to over-ride the normally paramount interests of children under 16.

Appendix 2
Schedule 1 to the Defamation Act 1996

Statements having qualified privilege

This is the text of Parts 1 and 2 of Schedule 1 to the 1996 Act, paras 1–16, as amended by the Defamation Act 2013. (See 22.7 in this book.)

Part 1: Statements privileged without explanation or contradiction

1. A fair and accurate report of proceedings in public of a legislature anywhere in the world.
2. A fair and accurate report of proceedings in public before a court anywhere in the world. [*para. 17 makes clear that this includes the European Court of Justice, the European Court of Human Rights, and any international criminal tribunal established by the United Nations or by an international agreement to which the UK is a party*]
3. A fair and accurate report of proceedings in public of a person appointed to hold a public inquiry by a government or legislature anywhere in the world.
4. A fair and accurate report of proceedings in public anywhere in the world of an international organisation or an international conference. [*para. 17 limits these definitions to a conference attended by representatives of two or more governments or an organisation of which two or more governments are members, including any committee or other subordinate body of such an organisation*]
5. A fair and accurate copy of or extract from any register or other document required by law to be open to public inspection.
6. A notice or advertisement published by or on the authority of a court, or of a judge or officer of a court, anywhere in the world.
7. A fair and accurate copy of or extract from matter published by or on the authority of a government or legislature anywhere in the world.

'court' is defined later in the Schedule

8. A fair and accurate copy of or extract from matter published anywhere in the world by an international organisation or an international conference. [*same definitions as for para. 4*]

Part 2: Statements privileged subject to explanation or contradiction

9. (1) A fair and accurate copy of, extract from or summary of a notice or other matter issued for the information of the public by or on behalf of—

   (a) a legislature or government anywhere in the world;

   (b) an authority anywhere in the world performing governmental functions;

   (c) an international organisation or international conference.

   (2) In this paragraph 'governmental functions' includes police functions.

10. A fair and accurate copy of, extract from or summary of a document made available by a court anywhere in the world, or by a judge or officer of such a court.

11. (1) A fair and accurate report of proceedings at any public meeting or sitting in the United Kingdom of –

   (d) a local authority or local authority committee;

   (e) in the case of a local authority which are operating executive arrangements, the executive of that authority or a committee of that executive;

   (f) a justice or justices of the peace acting otherwise than as a court exercising judicial authority;

   (g) a commission, tribunal, committee or person appointed for the purposes of any inquiry by any statutory provision, by Her Majesty or by a Minister of the Crown, a member of the Scottish Executive, the Welsh Ministers or the Counsel General to the Welsh Assembly Government, or a Northern Ireland Department;

   (h) a person appointed by a local authority to hold a local inquiry in pursuance of any statutory provision;

   (i) any other tribunal, board, committee or body constituted by or under, and exercising functions under, any statutory provision.

   (2) In the case of a local authority which are operating executive arrangements, a fair and accurate record of any decision made by any member of the executive where that record is required to be made and available for public inspection by virtue of section 22 of the Local Government Act 2000 or of any provision in regulations made under that section.

   (3) In sub-paragraphs (1)(a), (1)(aa) and (1A)'local authority' means—

   (j) in relation to England and Wales, a principal council within the meaning of the Local Government Act 1972, any body falling within any paragraph of section 100J(1) of that Act or an authority or body to which the Public Bodies (Admission to Meetings) Act 1960 applies,

   (k) in relation to Scotland, a council constituted under section 2 of the Local Government etc (Scotland) Act 1994 or an authority or body to which the Public Bodies (Admission to Meetings) Act 1960 applies,

(l) in relation to Northern Ireland, any authority or body to which sections 23 to 27 of the Local Government Act (Northern Ireland) 1972 apply; and

'local authority committee' means any committee of a local authority or of local authorities, and includes –

(m) any committee or sub-committee in relation to which sections 100A to 100D of the Local Government Act 1972 apply by virtue of section 100E of that Act (whether or not also by virtue of section 100J of that Act), and

(n) any committee or sub-committee in relation to which sections 50A to 50D of the Local Government (Scotland) Act 1973 apply by virtue of section 50E of that Act.

(4) In sub-paragraphs (1) and (1A) 'executive' and 'executive arrangements' have the same meaning as in Part II of the Local Government Act 2000.

(5) A fair and accurate report of any corresponding proceedings in any of the Channel Islands or the Isle of Man or in another member state [*that is, a European Union member nation*]

11A. A fair and accurate report of proceedings at a press conference held anywhere in the world for the discussion of a matter of public interest.

12. (1) A fair and accurate report of proceedings at any public meeting held anywhere in the world.

(2) In this paragraph a 'public meeting' means a meeting bona fide and lawfully held for a lawful purpose and for the furtherance or discussion of a matter of public interest, whether admission to the meeting is general or restricted.

13. (1) A fair and accurate report of proceedings at a general meeting of a listed company.

(2) A fair and accurate copy of, extract from or summary of any document circulated to members of a listed company—

(o) by or with the authority of the board of directors of the company,

(p) by the auditors of the company, or

(q) by any member of the company in pursuance of a right conferred by any statutory provision.

(3) A fair and accurate copy of, extract from or summary of any document circulated to members of a listed company which relates to the appointment, resignation, retirement or dismissal of directors of the company or its auditors.

(4) In this paragraph 'listed company' has the same meaning as in Part 12 of the Corporation Tax Act 2009 (see section 1005 of that Act). [*'listed company' means a company (a) whose shares are listed on a 'recognised stock exchange'—that is, recognised by the UK tax authorities,—and (b) which is neither a close company nor a company that would be a close company if it were UK resident. So, the 'listed company' definition means—according to the Explanatory Notes of the Defamation Act 2013—UK public companies and 'public companies elsewhere in the world'*]

14. A fair and accurate report of any finding or decision of any of the following descriptions of association formed anywhere in the world or of any committee or governing body of such an association –

(a) formed for the purpose of promoting or encouraging the exercise of or interest in any art, science, religion or learning, and empowered by its constitution to exercise control over or adjudicate on matters of interest or concern to the association, or the actions or conduct of any persons subject to such control or adjudication;

(b) formed for the purpose of promoting or safeguarding the interests of any trade, business, industry or profession, or of the persons carrying on or engaged in any trade, business, industry or profession, and empowered by its constitution to exercise control over or adjudicate upon matters connected with the trade, business, industry or profession, or the actions or conduct of those persons;

(c) formed for the purpose of promoting or safeguarding the interests of a game, sport or pastime to the playing or exercise of which members of the public are invited or admitted, and empowered by its constitution to exercise control over or adjudicate upon persons connected with or taking part in the game, sport or pastime;

(d) formed for the purpose of promoting charitable objects or other objects beneficial to the community and empowered by its constitution to exercise control over or to adjudicate on matters of interest or concern to the association, or the actions or conduct of any person subject to such control or adjudication.

14A. A fair and accurate—

(a) report of proceedings of a scientific or academic conference held anywhere in the world, or

(b) copy of, extract from, or summary of matter published by such a conference.

15. (1) A fair and accurate report or summary of, copy of or extract from, any adjudication, report, statement or notice issued by a body, officer or other person designated for the purposes of this paragraph by order of the Lord Chancellor.

(2) An order under this paragraph shall be made by statutory instrument which shall be subject to annulment in pursuance of a resolution of either House of Parliament.

Part 3: Supplementary provisions

16. In this Schedule—'court' includes—

(a) any tribunal or body established under the law of any country or territory exercising the judicial power of the State;

(b) any international tribunal established by the Security Council of the United Nations or by an international agreement;

(c) any international tribunal deciding matters in dispute between States;

'international conference' means a conference attended by representatives of two or more governments;

'international organisation' means an organisation of which two or more governments are members, and includes any committee or other subordinate body of such an organisation; 'legislature' includes a local legislature; and 'member State' includes any European dependent territory of a member State.

Glossary

Absolute discharge A decision by a court after conviction that the offender should not be punished for the crime.

Affidavit A statement given on oath to be used in court proceedings.

Alibi A claim by an accused that they can show they were not at the scene when a crime was committed and is therefore innocent.

Allocation The procedure at magistrates' courts to determine whether an either-way criminal case is dealt with by magistrates or by a Crown court. Also known as the **mode of trial hearing**.

Arraignment The procedure at Crown courts when charges are put to defendants for them to plead guilty or not guilty.

Automatic, automatically Terms used for reporting restrictions (which ban publication of certain information) if no court order is needed to put them into effect in respect of a particular case or individual. Statutes specify the circumstances in which they operate.

Bail The system by which a person awaiting trial, or appeal, may be freed by a court pending the next hearing. See also **Police bail**.

Bailiff A court official who enforces its orders.

Case law The system by which reports of previous cases and judges' interpretations of the common law are used as precedents where the legally material facts are similar.

Circuit judge A judge appointed to sit at a Crown court or the County Court within a circuit—one of the regions of England and Wales into which court administration is divided. Unlike High Court judges, circuit judges do not go on circuit—that is, travel to various large centres dispensing justice.

Claim form The document which begins many types of civil action.

Claimant The person who brings an action in the civil court.

Committal for sentence, committed for sentence When a defendant at a magistrates' court who has admitted an offence or been convicted at trial is sent to Crown court to be sentenced because the magistrates decide their powers of punishment are insufficient. (There are no reporting restrictions on committals for sentence.)

Common law Law based on the custom of the realm and the decisions of judges through the centuries rather than on Acts of Parliament.

Community punishment An order that an offender must do unpaid work in the community under a probation officer's supervision.

Concurrent sentences Two or more sentences of imprisonment imposed for different offences but served together; the longest one is the sentence actually served.

Conditional discharge A decision by a court that a convicted defendant should not be punished unless they reoffend—the condition of the discharge being that if they commit another crime within a specified period (e.g. a year) they can be punished for both the new and the original offences.

Conditional fee agreements (CFAs) 'No win, no fee' agreements under which lawyers do not charge clients unless their legal action succeeds.

Contra mundum An injunction or order which binds all those who are aware that it has been made. Although the Latin means 'against the world', such orders only have effect within the jurisdiction in which they are made.

Copyright The law which protects the rights of the creators of original literary, dramatic, musical and artistic works, including photographs.

Counsel Barrister (singular or plural), not solicitor.

Disclosure and inspection The process whereby each side in a court action serves relevant documents on the other, which has the right to inspect them.

District judge A County Court judge who also decides smaller cases, family law cases, presides at public examinations in bankruptcy and deals with cases under the informal arbitration procedure.

District judge (magistrates' courts) A full-time legally qualified magistrate.

Editors' Code of Practice Code of ethics enforced by the Independent Press Standards Organisation (Ipso) as regulator for newspapers, magazines and their websites.

Either-way offence One triable either summarily at magistrates' court or by a jury at Crown court. In an either-way case a defendant who has indicated a plea of not guilty has the right to opt for jury trial at Crown court. But if they opt for summary trial, the magistrates may decide that the case is too serious for them to handle and must be dealt with at Crown court. See also **Allocation; Mode of trial hearing**.

Evidence-in-chief The main evidence a witness gives before being cross-examined.

Ex parte See **Without notice**.

Fair dealing The limited use of copyright material for reporting news or current affairs, or for criticism or review or quotation, under which the work is properly identified and attributed to its author.

Honest opinion A defence to a libel action, formerly known as 'honest comment' or 'fair comment'; the defendant does not have to show the words were fair, but must show they were an honestly held opinion.

Hybrid hearing A court hearing in which some participants are in a physical courtroom but some are attending remotely by phone or electronic link.

Impress Standards Code The code of ethics overseen by Impress, the regulator recognised by the Press Recognition Panel.

In camera Proceedings in a courtroom which are heard in secret, with the media and public excluded (for example, in Official Secrets Acts or terrorism cases).

In chambers Used to describe the hearing of an application which takes place in the judge's room. If there is no legal reason for such a hearing to be held in private, journalists who want to report it should be admitted if 'practicable'.

In private A term used of a court hearing in camera or one in chambers which the press and public are not entitled to attend.

Indictable offence A charge which may be tried by a jury at Crown court, which will therefore be either an indictable-only offence or an either-way offence.

Indictable-only offence One which can only be tried by a jury at Crown court.

Indictment A written statement of the charge(s) put to the defendant at the arraignment at Crown court.

Inherent jurisdiction The powers of a court deriving from common law rather than statute. The inherent jurisdiction of lower courts (e.g. magistrates' courts) is more limited than that of the higher courts (e.g. the High Court).

Injunction A court order requiring someone, or an organisation, to do something specified by the court, or forbidding a specific activity or act.

Interdict The Scottish term for an injunction.

Judicial review A review by the King's Bench Divisional Court, part of the High Court, of decisions taken by a lower court, tribunal, public body or public official.

Legal aid Public money provided to pay for legal advice and representation in court for a party in a civil case or a defendant in a criminal case, if their income is low enough to qualify.

Malice In law not only spite or ill-will but also a dishonest or improper motive. Proof of malice can be used by a claimant in a libel action to defeat a defence of qualified privilege.

Mitigation A plea for leniency in the sentence due to be imposed, citing extenuating circumstances, which is made in court by or on behalf of a convicted offender.

Mode of trial hearing The hearing at a magistrates' court to decide whether an either-way offence case is dealt with by that court or proceeds to a Crown court. Also known as the **allocation** procedure.

Narrative verdict/narrative conclusion A brief statement by a coroner or inquest jury detailing the circumstances and manner of a person's death which takes the place of the traditional 'short-form' verdicts.

Newton hearing A hearing involving a defendant who has pleaded guilty but offers a substantially different version of events to that alleged by the prosecution, at which the court hears evidence so it can decide which version it accepts as forming the basis for the sentence. Newton was the defendant's name in the relevant precedent case.

Ofcom Broadcasting Code Code of ethics used by Ofcom to adjudicate on complaints against broadcasters.

Physical hearing A court hearing in which all participants are present in a courtroom, not a hybrid or virtual hearing.

Police bail The system whereby police can release a person under ongoing investigation on conditions, including that they return to a police station on a later date, when they may be questioned again, charged or told there will be no charge. They can be arrested if they breach the conditions. After being charged, they can be bailed by police to attend court or may be taken there in custody.

Preliminary hearing A hearing, before any trial, at a magistrates' or Crown court.

Prima facie Literally, 'at first sight'. In criminal law a 'prima facie case' is one in which a preliminary examination by a court has established that there is sufficient prosecution evidence for it to proceed to trial. In journalism ethics the term 'prima facie grounds' means that preliminary inquiries have established there is sufficient evidence or sufficient ground of suspicion to justify use of deception or undercover tactics in an investigation.

Prior restraint The power which courts have to stop material being published. In defamation law there is a general rule against prior restraint. Judges are extremely reluctant to ban publication of material which the media argue can be successfully defended in any future trial.

Privilege A defence, absolute or qualified, against an action for libel which attaches to reports produced from certain events, documents or statements.

Proportionate/Proportionality The principle that an action must not exceed what is reasonable or necessary to achieve the desired objective; and that competing rights must wherever possible be kept in balance. So, for example, a judge may rule that some private information about a person can be published in the public interest by the media but not the most private. Another example: A newspaper's undercover investigation into wrongdoing is proportionate if it does not intrude into people's privacy or use deception to an extent more than necessary for the investigation's aim.

Public interest The phrase 'in the public interest' is used by judges to define when an individual's rights, for example to privacy, can legally be infringed if this produces a sufficiently major benefit to society—for example, from investigative journalism into a scandal or contributing to a general debate about a societal issue. But judges may also decide that a general 'public interest' (e.g. in the confidentiality of medical records) needs to be upheld against media activity. Codes of ethics use the phrase too, to indicate when journalists may be justified in infringing people's rights.

Recorder An assistant judge at Crown court who is usually appointed to sit part-time (e.g. for spells of a fortnight). Barristers and solicitors are eligible for appointment as recorders.

Released under investigation The system under which police release suspects in investigations but without giving them bail. Cases remain 'active' for the purposes of strict liability contempt while someone is 'released under investigation'—a period which can last months or years. See also **Bail** and **Police Bail**.

Remand An individual awaiting trial can be remanded on bail or in custody.

Remote or wholly remote hearing See **Virtual hearing**.

Robbery Theft by force or the threat of force. The word 'robbery' is often wrongly used to describe simple theft.

Skeleton arguments The documents in which each side in court proceedings sets out the bases of their cases. Journalists should normally be allowed to see them to help them report the proceedings.

Spent conviction A conviction that is no longer recognised after the time (varying according to sentence) specified in the Rehabilitation of Offenders Act 1974. After this time, a media organisation referring to the conviction might not have available some of the normal defences in the law of libel.

Statements of case Documents including the claim form, particulars of claim, defence, counterclaims, reply to the defence and 'further information documents' in a civil action—reports of which are normally protected by privilege.

Statute An Act of Parliament (i.e. primary legislation created by Parliament).

Statutory instrument Secondary legislation which can be enacted without parliamentary debate by a Minister to make detailed law (e.g. rules and regulations) or amendment to the law, under powers given earlier by a statute. Statutory instruments are also used to phase in gradually, for administrative convenience, legal changes brought about by Acts.

Strict liability A strict liability offence does not require the prosecution to show intent on the part of the accused. Statutory contempt of court is a strict liability offence.

Sub judice Literally 'under law'. Often applied to the risk which may arise in reporting forthcoming legal proceedings. Frequently used by authority as a reason for not disclosing information. But the case may not be 'active' under the Contempt of Court Act 1981.

Subpoena A court order compelling a person to attend court to give evidence.

Summary offence A comparatively minor offence which can usually only be dealt with by magistrates.

Summary trial Trial at a magistrates' court.

Supreme Court The name originally given to the Court of Appeal, the High Court and the Crown courts as a combined system. From October 2009 the House of Lords appellate committee (the court commonly referred to as 'the House of Lords' or 'Law Lords') became the UK Supreme Court.

Surety A person, usually a friend or relative of the defendant, to whom a court entrusts the responsibility to ensure that the individual, having been released on bail, returns to court on the due date. The surety may pledge a sum of money as the guarantee that the defendant will answer bail and risks losing it if the defendant fails to do so.

Taken into consideration The system under which a defendant admits having committed offences with which they have not been charged, thus clearing the slate and avoiding risk of subsequent prosecution for those offences.

Theft Appropriation of another's property with the intention of permanently depriving the other of it.

Tort A civil wrong, such as defamation or medical negligence, for which monetary damages may be awarded.

Truth The defence in defamation actions that the words complained of are substantially true.

Virtual hearing A court hearing in which all participants are in different locations communicating by telephone or by electronic link in software, and none is in the same place as the judge or magistrates, and so the hearing is not in a physical courtroom.

Warranted Term used in the Ofcom Broadcasting Code to indicate that an ethical norm can be breached if there is a public interest justification or some other exceptional justification.

Without notice Previously known as ex parte, meaning 'of the one part'. An injunction without notice is one granted after a court has heard only one side of the case. An order granted inter partes is one made after a hearing at which all sides involved were represented.

Table of Cases

Table of Legislation

Statutes

Note: The European Convention on Human Rights (ECHR) is tabled under Schedule 1 to the Human Rights Act 1998

Statutory Instruments

European Materials

International Instruments

INDEX

B

D

E

F

I

J

N

P

Q

S

W